T0113509

Who's Who in Modern History

The Routledge Who's Who series

Accessible, authoritative and enlightening, these are the definitive biographical guides to a diverse range of subjects drawn from literature and the arts, history and politics, religion and mythology.

Who's Who in Ancient Egypt
Michael Rice

Who's Who in the Ancient Near East
Gwendolyn Leick

Who's Who in Christianity
Lavinia Cohn-Sherbok

Who's Who in Classical Mythology
Michael Grant and John Hazel

Who's Who in Contemporary Gay and Lesbian History
Edited by Robert Aldrich and Garry Wotherspoon

Who's Who in Contemporary Women's Writing
Edited by Jane Eldridge Miller

Who's Who in Contemporary World Theatre
Edited by Daniel Meyer-Dinkegräfe

Who's Who in Dickens
Donald Hawes

Who's Who in Europe 1450–1750
Henry Kamen

Who's Who in Gay and Lesbian History
Edited by Robert Aldrich and Garry Wotherspoon

Who's Who in the Greek World
John Hazel

Who's Who in Jewish History
Joan Comay, revised by Lavinia Cohn-Sherbok

Who's Who in Military History
John Keegan and Andrew Wheatcroft

Who's Who in Modern History
Alan Palmer

Who's Who in Nazi Germany
Robert S. Wistrich

Who's Who in the New Testament
Ronald Brownrigg

Who's Who in Non-Classical Mythology
Egerton Sykes, revised by Alan Kendall

Who's Who in the Old Testament
Joan Comay

Who's Who in the Roman World
John Hazel

Who's Who in Russia since 1900
Martin McCauley

Who's Who in Shakespeare
Peter Quennell and Hamish Johnson

Who's Who of Twentieth-Century Novelists
Tim Woods

Who's Who in Twentieth-Century World Poetry
Edited by Mark Willhardt and Alan Michael Parker

Who's Who in Twentieth Century Warfare
Spencer Tucker

Who's Who in World War One
John Bourne

Who's Who in World War Two
Edited by John Keegan

Who's Who in Modern History

From 1860 to the present day

Alan Palmer

LONDON AND NEW YORK

First published 1980 by Weidenfeld and Nicolson as
Who's Who in Modern History 1860–1980

Second edition published 1996 as *Who's Who in World Politics from 1860 to the present day*
by Routledge

Published 2019 by Routledge
2 Park Square, Milton Park, Abingdon, Oxon OX14 4RN
52 Vanderbilt Avenue, New York, NY 10017

This edition first published 2002 as
Who's Who in Modern History

Routledge is an imprint of the Taylor & Francis Group, an informa business

British Library Cataloguing in Publication Data
A catalogue record for this book is available from the British Library

Library of Congress Cataloging in Publication Data
A catalogue record for this book has been requested

ISBN 13: 978-0-415-11885-9 (pbk)

Contents

To John, Claire, Lucy and Cressida McLaughlin

Preface to the 1996 Edition

Who's Who in Modern History is a reference guide to the lives of men and women who have shaped or determined the process of government over the last six or seven generations. I have included not simply rulers, their chief ministers or insurgent leaders but the great stategists, soldiers and seamen as well. Also included are many theorists, from Marx and Mill to Marcuse, and a few neglected 'originals', such as Hyndman and William Morris or more recently Haya de la Torre and Petra Kelly. The greatest worldwide social revolution in the period covered by this book has been the gradual emancipation of women, and I have therefore given more attention than in many other books to the pioneer champions of women's rights, particularly in Britain, the United States and Japan.

The starting point of 1860 was chosen because it was in itself a historic year and also the eve of a decade of great significance in world affairs. It was in 1860 that Abraham Lincoln won America's presidential election, a victory which swept away the mastery of the slave-owning gentry from the South, who had dominated the political life of the USA since its inception. In 1860, again, two European powers – Britain and France – intervened jointly for the first time in China. It was also in 1860 that the Italians became the first European people to create a new nation-state. These events were a presage of even greater change over the next few years. What Cavour achieved for Piedmont and Italy, Bismarck was soon to surpass for Prussia and a unified Germany. At the same time the spread of the telegraph and speedier communications over land and sea brought the five continents closer together, imposing a Europeanized pattern on ancient cultures, especially across Asia. Conversely, the appeal of distant places – the Orient; central America; 'darkest Africa' – excited upper- and middle-class society in London and Paris. With the abolition of serfdom in Russia and slavery in the States, there can be no doubt that, by the end of the 1860s, the world picture is more recognizably 'modern' than at their start.

The terminal date for this book is 'the present day': I therefore include most names that have dominated news reports throughout the past year. But it is always hard to assess the significance of contemporary events, and some apparent lead actors may soon prove to have played no more than walk-on roles on the world stage. Events and biographical details are updated to March 1996.

Some material in the book first appeared in my *Who's Who in Modern History, 1860–1980*, published in 1980 by Weidenfeld & Nicolson in London and St Martins Press in New York. The style of the new biographies follows the earlier pattern: so far as possible, entries stress the social and educational background of their subjects, as well as their achievements and ultimate fate. But *Who's Who in Modern History* differs from this predecessor in one respect: it has a bibliographical guide included below most entries. These are not, of course, full bibliographies; I have listed only books in English that are known to me. Unless otherwise indicated, the books are published in London. The titles are placed, not in alphabetical order of authors, but with memoirs or autobiography first, followed by what seems to me to be the most useful follow-up reading for a particular entry. I hope this arrangement will prove useful; most of these 'follow-ups' contain fuller bibliographies which would enable readers who know other languages to further extend their search for information.

I am grateful to Kieron Corless, at Routledge, for having sought advice for me on Far Eastern and Latin American topics and sources and for collating the information he received; and I would like, also, to thank Catherine Turnbull and Ann Grindrod for their editorial work. I much appreciate the skills of Soleyman and Dawn Naddafy of Caspian Print, Turl Street, Oxford, in speedily producing a complete photocopied manuscript of old and new material. Among several patient book finders who have helped me, I remain especially grateful to Helen Rogers, Vera Ryhaljo and Tina King of the Upper Reading Room staff in the Bodleian Library and, at an earlier stage in the Radcliffe Camera, to Dorothy Beaumont. John McLaughlin has served as a literary agent for myself and for my wife, Veronica, for over twenty years; in appreciation of his help and guidance, and for our friendship with his family, I am dedicating this book to him, to Claire, and to their daughters, Lucy and Cressida.

Alan Palmer
Woodstock, March 1996

A

Abd El-Krim (1882–1963), Moroccan nationalist: born in Ajdir, became a tribal chief (*Kaid*) in north-eastern Morocco. As a young man he visited Germany and was encouraged to raise the Rif tribes against Spanish and French infiltration into Morocco during the First World War. On 21 July 1921 at Annual he led Rif tribesmen in an assault on a Spanish punitive expedition and gained an astonishing victory, in which the Spanish were routed with heavy casualties. For five years Abd El-Krim was military dictator of a Rif Republic, which successfully defied the Spanish. In 1925 Rif troops also penetrated French Morocco. MARSHAL PÉTAIN was thereupon given command of a joint French–Spanish army which attacked the Rif Republic on two fronts, forcing Abd El-Krim to surrender to the French in May 1926. He was imprisoned in the French colony of Réunion, but in 1947 was given permission to return to Europe. During the journey he evaded his escort and found refuge in Egypt, where he was accorded privileged treatment as the first North African Arab nationalist to win victories against imperialism. He died in Cairo in May 1963. D. S. Woolman: *Rebels in the Rif: Abd el Krim and the Rif Rebellion* (Stanford, 1969); W. B. Harris: *France, Spain and the Riff* (1927); A. Barea: *The Track* (1958); Lord Kinross and D. Hales-Gary: *Morocco* (1971).

Abdul Aziz (1830–76), Sultan of the Ottoman Empire, 1861–76: succeeded to the throne when his half-brother Abdul Mejid died from tuberculosis in June 1861. Abdul Aziz, a bearded giant weighing almost 150 kilos, was personally extravagant, spending huge sums on his Bosphorus palaces. The first ten years of his reign saw the completion of reforms in the banking system, higher education and provincial administration and the publication in 1869 of the *Mecelle*, a civil code of law. In 1867 Abdul Aziz became the first Sultan to visit western Europe; he was received in state in Paris, London and Vienna, and he returned home eager for his empire to acquire a railway system (begun in 1872–3) and an ironclad fleet. From 1871 onwards his absolutism became capricious, with lavish spending of personal funds, frequent paroxysms of fury, rapid changes of ministers, as well as problems caused by pan Slav unrest in his Balkan provinces. In October 1875 the payment of interest on the Ottoman Debt was suspended, a virtual admission of state bankruptcy. On 30 May 1876 he was deposed by a military *coup* in favour of his nephew, who acceded (briefly) as Murad V. On 4 June Abdul Aziz was found dead in the Ciragan Palace, officially having slashed his wrists; it is more probable he was murdered. R. H. Davison: *Reform in the Ottoman Empire, 1856–1876* (Princeton, 1963); A. Palmer: *The Decline and Fall of the Ottoman Empire* (1992).

Abdul Hamid II (1842–1918), Sultan of Turkey from 1876 to 1909: a younger son of Sultan Abdul Mejid (reigned 1839–61). His mother, suspected of infidelity, died mysteriously when the boy was 7, and he was neglected both in the reign of his father and of his successor, the boy's uncle, ABDUL AZIZ. On 30

May 1876 Abdul Aziz was deposed and died five days later. Abdul Hamid's elder brother, Murad v, had reigned for only twelve weeks when Turkey's military and political leaders declared him to be insane and offered Abdul Hamid the throne on condition he granted his empire a constitution. First reports from ambassadors in Constantinople were favourable: the new Sultan was 'conscientious', 'well-intentioned' and 'disposed to make economies'. Soon, however, he rescinded the constitution and ruled as an absolute monarch for over thirty years, having his opponents strangled or banished and living in daily expectation of finding his food poisoned or his palace seized by dissident young army officers. To counter the rapid decline of Turkish power in the Balkans, Abdul Hamid reasserted the Sultan's claim to lead the Muslim world as 'Caliph', or 'Defender of the Faith'. His failure to check the massacre of Christian Armenians by irregular bands of Kurdish cavalry in 1895–6 aroused the hostility of the British, Americans, French and Russians, and he achieved notoriety as 'Sultan Abdul the Damned'. He retained a certain personal charm which he exercised on foreign diplomats and on the Kaiser, WILLIAM II, who befriended him from 1898 onwards. In 1900 Abdul Hamid announced his intention to construct a pilgrim's railway from Damascus to Medina and Mecca, financed by voluntary contributions from pious Muslims. Such displays of Pan-Islamic sentiment made no impression on the 'Young Turks', a group of army officers who wished to modernize the State and who from 1902 onwards had links with influential Turks in exile. Mutiny in Salonika on 4 July 1908 was followed by the establishment of a 'Committee of Union and Progress' in Constantinople later in the month. Abdul Hamid agreed to restore the constitution of 1876 and summoned a parliament. When in April 1909 he attempted a counter-revolution, he was deposed by the Young Turks (led by ENVER) and exiled to Salonika. His 64-year-old brother succeeded him as Sultan Mohammed v (reigned 1909–20). Abdul Hamid was allowed to return to Constantinople in 1912, living there under house restraint until he died, of natural causes, on the eve of Turkey's military defeat in 1918. E. Pears: *The Life of Abdul Hamid* (1917); J. Haslip: *The Sultan* (1958); A. Palmer: *The Decline and Fall of the Ottoman Empire* (1992).

Abdullah (1880–1951), ruler of Jordan as Emir or King from 1921 to 1951: born in Mecca, the son of Sherif Hussein ibn Ali, who ruled the Hijaz as Emir from 1909 and as King from 1916 to 1924. Abdullah spent most of the years 1891–1908 in Constantinople, returning there as parliamentary deputy for Mecca from 1912 to 1914. He assisted his father and his brother FAISAL in the Arab Revolt of 1915–18 against Turkish rule, collaborating with T. E. LAWRENCE in guerrilla raids against garrisons holding the railway from Damascus to Medina. After the collapse of the Turkish Empire, Emir Abdullah became *de facto* ruler of 'Transjordan' in 1920, his position being regularized by the British in 1921 when he was accorded nominal sovereignty over the area of mandated territory east of the river Jordan and west of his brother's kingdom of Iraq. Abdullah maintained cordial and tactful relations with the British colonial authorities, notably during the Second World War. On the expiration of the British mandate in May 1946 he became King of Transjordan, and in December 1948 a Pan-Arab Congress meeting in Jerusalem proclaimed him King of Palestine. No great power accorded him recognition and in June 1949 he contented himself, as an alternative, with sovereignty over the 'Hashemite Kingdom of Jordan', an area larger than inter-war Transjordan since it included a segment of Palestinian territory west of the river. Abdullah, a man of long experience and skill in negotiations, hoped to reach a settlement with the new Israel and in 1949–50 he held secret talks with MOSHE DAYAN at Shuneh. In Cairo, however, his independent traditionalism and his prestige among the Bedouin Arabs aroused resentment. On 20 July 1951 he was assassinated by a 'modern' Arab nationalist outside one of the Muslim holy places in Jerusalem. With him, and uninjured, was his 15-year-old grandson HUSSEIN, who was himself to become King of Jordan thirteen months later. N. H. Aruri: *Jordan* (The Hague, 1972); M. E. Wilson: *King Abdullah, Britain and the Making of Jordan* (1988).

Abdullah, Sheikh Mohammed (1905–82), Kashmiri Muslim leader: emerged, at the age of 25, as the determined leader of those Muslims in his native Kashmir who sought a constitutional government from the ruling Hindu Maharajah. His persistence in pressing for both the British and the Hindu Prince to 'quit Kashmir' led to the Sheikh's imprisonment by the British Indian government in 1931 and 1946; he was also imprisoned for alleged treason by the government of the Indian Republic from 1953 to 1968. From his Islamic compatriots, however, Sheikh Abdullah won lasting respect as 'the Lion of Kashmir'. He always insisted on the right of the Kashmiri people 'to decide the future of the State' and was recognized as chief minister in Kashmir from 1947 until his arrest in 1953 and again from 1975 until his death. He was succeeded as minister in Kashmir by his son, Dr Farooq Abdullah (1937–). M. Abdullah: *Flames of the Chinar, an Autobiography* (New Delhi, 1993); R. C. Wirsings: *India, Pakistan and the Kashmir Dispute* (1994).

Abdul Rahman Putra, Tunku (1903–90), Malaysian statesman: born in Alor Star, a son of the Sultan of Kedah. He was educated in Bangkok and at St Catharine's College, Cambridge, and was later called to the bar of the Inner Temple. He was a district officer in the Kedah Civil Service during the 1930s and official 'Director of Passive Defence' during the Japanese occupation, 1942–5. He opposed the British Labour government's proposed fusion of states and colonies into a Malayan Union and entered politics in the Federation of Malaya in 1949, working for independence as leader of the Malayan Nationalist Party (UMNO), which absorbed other groups to form the Alliance Party a few years later. In December 1955 the Tunku led the delegation to London which negotiated independence, and on 31 August 1957 he became Malaya's first Prime Minister. His political objectives extended beyond the peninsula to include North Borneo and Sarawak (and, originally, Singapore) in a federation of Malaysia, which was created in September 1963. As virtual founding-father of Malaysia, it was natural for the Tunku to serve as chief minister, especially as Malaysia was threatened by Indonesia's policy of 'confrontation', a three-year guerilla campaign encouraged by President SUKARNO. With Commonwealth backing, the Tunku countered this threat but he was disappointed over Singapore. The island joined the federation at its inception but its people, overwhelmingly Chinese in origin, soon complained of Malay discrimination; under the leadership of LEE Kuan Yew, Singapore seceded from Malaysia on 9 August 1965. Increasingly, the Tunku allowed his strict Muslim code of conduct to influence his judgement, and he accepted office as Secretary-General of the Islamic Conference of Foreign Ministers from 1969 until 1973. He recognized that anti-Chinese riots in Kuala Lumpur in May 1969 threatened the unity of the federation, and accordingly he retired from active politics in January 1970, though remaining a powerful influence on his successors. H. Miller: *Prince and Premier*

(1959); M. N. Sopiee: *From Malayan Union to Singapore Separation* (Kuala Lumpur, 1974).

Acheson, Dean Gooderham (1893–1971), US Secretary of State from 1949 to 1953: born in Connecticut, his mother being Canadian. He was educated at Groton, Yale and Harvard Law School and became a lawyer in New York City. At age 39 he was made Under-Secretary of the Treasury by Franklin ROOSEVELT but he resigned later in 1933 because the New Deal financial policies offended his innate conservatism. In August 1940 his public avowal of the President's right to sell US destroyers to Britain without specific congressional approval pleased Roosevelt and he returned to government service as assistant to the Secretary of State, Cordell HULL, from 1941 to 1945. TRUMAN appointed Acheson Under-Secretary of State in his first administration and from 1947 onwards he was a powerful policy-maker. Thus it was Acheson who on 27 February 1947 outlined, in the State Department, the principles of what became known a month later as the 'Truman Doctrine', a policy seeking containment of Soviet influence by military and economic assistance to 'free peoples' threatened by a Communist takeover; and on 8 May 1947 Acheson made the first speech advocating the European aid programme associated in name with Secretary of State George MARSHALL. As the principal sponsor of America's new role in defending western and southern Europe against the Soviet Union, it was natural that Acheson should succeed Marshall as Secretary of State, in January 1949. Yet although Acheson continued to build up NATO, he was criticized for neglecting the Chinese threat in the Far East until after war came to Korea in June 1950. In style, appearance and background Dean Acheson seemed an atypical American. His forthright impatience with demagogic politics made him a butt for Senator MCCARTHY who alleged that the State Department under Acheson was full of 'Reds' and 'liberal do-gooders'. After the Republican electoral triumph in 1952 Acheson withdrew from public life, but John KENNEDY treated him as a respected elder statesman and Acheson drafted important papers giving advice on foreign affairs in 1961, 1962 and 1963. Dean Acheson: *Present at the Creation, My Years in the State Department* (1969); D. Brinkley: *Dean Acheson, The Cold War Years, 1953–71* (1992); D. Brinkley (ed.): *Dean Acheson and the Making of US Foreign Policy* (1993).

Acton, Lord (John Emerich Edward Dalberg Acton) (1834–1902), British historian: born in Naples, a member of a wealthy English Roman Catholic family. He was educated privately and travelled widely in Russia, America and Italy as well as spending many years at German universities, where he was influenced by the scientific scrutiny of archives introduced to historical studies by the great Leopold von Ranke, Professor of History in Berlin from 1825 to 1872. Acton, a close friend of GLADSTONE, sat as a Liberal in Parliament from 1859 to 1865 and was created Baron Acton in 1869. His erudition staggered the earnest-minded mid-Victorians, none of whom doubted he had read and assessed all 59,000 volumes in his private library. Respect for freedom of conscience impelled Acton to criticize the narrowly doctrinaire Catholicism of the Vatican Decrees in 1870 and the dogma of papal infallibility, although he never formally broke with his Church. In 1886 he helped found the *English Historical Review*, a scholarly periodical which served as a model for similar journals on both sides of the Atlantic. From 1895 to 1902 he was Regius Professor of Modern History at Cambridge. He planned the original *Cambridge Modern History* and yet wrote little himself: three volumes of lectures and essays were published posthumously. His importance lies in his work as teacher and exemplar: against materialistic theories of historical struggle, he offered the claim that history was the unfolding of human freedom, asserting that its study should be treated as a quest for truth and insisting the historian has a moral duty to judge as well as to narrate. These imperatives were questioned by his successors in Britain and America, many of whom argued that selectivity of facts precludes impartial judgement. Yet Acton restored the prestigious dignity of historical thought in an increasingly scientific age while also widening the range of historical studies in the English-speaking community. G. P. Gooch: *History and Historians of the Nineteenth Century* (1952); D. Matthews: *Lord Acton and his Times* (1968).

Adams, Gerard (Gerry) (1948–), Irish nationalist: born in Belfast, where he grew up in the Falls Road region and became active in the civil rights movement in the late 1960s. As a suspect member of the IRA he was interned at Long Kesh by the British authorities from 1972 to 1976 and from 1978 to 1983. In 1979 he became Vice-President of Sinn Féin, succeeding in 1983 as President of the movement. His popularity among Roman Catholics in his native city remained high: he was elected a Northen Ireland assembly member in 1982; and from 1983 until 1992 he was the elected Member of Parliament for Belfast West. But, in accordance with Sinn Féin policy, he declined to take his seat either at Stormont or at Westminster. Under the Prevention of Terrorism Act he was banned from coming to the United Kingdom in October 1993. In the following year he gave cautious support to the peace initiative of the British and Irish governments, and he influenced the IRA to offer 'a complete cessation of military operations' on 31 August 1994, after twenty-five years of violence in Northern Ireland. Gerry Adams received an enthusiastic reception in New York as a guest for the St Patrick's Day celebrations in March 1995 and met President CLINTON in Washington. Eleven months later, the IRA's sudden return to a bombing campaign, while Adams was in America, raised doubts over his political influence. Gerry Adams: *Falls Memories* (Dingle, Co. Kerry, 1982) and *Free Ireland, Towards A Lasting Peace* (Dingle, Co. Kerry, rev. edn 1993); T. P. Coogan: *The IRA* (rev. edn 1985); P. Arthur and K. Jeffery: *Northern Ireland since 1968* (Oxford, 1988).

Addams Jane (1860–1935), American social worker and first woman awarded a Nobel Peace Prize: born into a deeply religious family from the Midwest (Cedarville, northern Illinois). She graduated from Rockford College, Illinois in 1881 and began the study of medicine in Philadelphia, when her health failed her. Subsequently she travelled widely in Europe and was deeply impressed by the work of the Toynbee Hall Settlement in Whitechapel, London. Her conscience was troubled by having to live prosperously and comfortably 'shut off from the common labor' and she began to work in the slums of Chicago, helping immigrant and coloured families. In 1889 she established Hull House in Chicago which became a model settlement for social rescue activities throughout America. She collaborated with John ALTGELD, the reforming Governor of Illinois, from 1893 to 1897, sponsoring child labour laws, educational schemes for foreign-born adults, protection for immigrant girls and improved sanitary conditions. In 1899 she secured the establishment of separate juvenile courts in Illinois, a reform soon followed in other countries. Her tract *The Spirit of Youth in the City Streets* encouraged civic bodies to plan parks and playgrounds in their overcrowded towns. Politically she considered herself a progressive Republican but, from 1898 onwards, she was an active pacifist campaigner and an anti-imperialist. She was a founder-member, in 1909, of the National Association for the Advancement of Colored People (NAACP) and, in her late sixties, led the Women's International League for Peace and Freedom. It was for this activity, rather than for her world-famous social settlements, that she was awarded the Nobel Peace Prize for 1931, sharing the award with the President of the Carnegie Endowment for International Peace, Dr Nicholas M. Butler, the head of Columbia University. J. Addams: *Twenty Years of Hull House* (New York, rev. edn 1960); J. C. Farrell: *Beloved Lady* (Baltimore, 1967); D. Levine: *Jane Addams and the Liberal Tradition* (Madison, 1971); J. W. Linn: *Jane Addams* (New York, 1935).

Adenauer, Konrad (1876–1967), Chancellor of the Federal German Republic from 1949 to 1963: born in Cologne, where he practised law from the turn of the century and where he was *Oberbürgermeister* (Lord Mayor) from 1917 to 1933 and in 1945. He entered German national politics towards the end of the First World War as a member of the Centre Party, the strictly disciplined Roman Catholic political movement, and he presided over meetings of the Prussian State Council from 1920 until dismissed by the Nazis. In 1922 and 1926 he was a strong contender for the chancellorship but his candidacy was opposed by the influential STRESEMANN, who thought Adenauer had been too favourably disposed towards French plans for an autonomous Rhineland in 1919. On two occasions, in 1934 and 1944, Adenauer was imprisoned by the Nazis. Although the British occupation authorities dismissed him as Mayor for alleged 'inefficiency', he remained in public life and was principal founder of a new Catholic party, the Christian Democratic Union (CDU), in 1947. His hostility towards communism ensured him substantial support in his native Rhineland; but the CDU was never so blatantly denominational as the old Centre Party and it offered a programme of free enterprise, secure employment and moderate conservatism to middle-class voters who were not always Catholics. After the CDU's narrow victory in West Germany's first election, Adenauer became Federal Chancellor by a single vote in September 1949. He rapidly strengthened both his personal prestige and his party-following and held office continuously until October 1963, a longer period of time than any German chancellor except BISMARCK. From 1951 to 1955 he was also Foreign Minister. He set himself two main objectives: economic recovery, and recognition from the British, Americans and French that his Germany was a partner in western Europe rather than a former enemy. He therefore supported every move towards European integration, notably the setting up of a Coal and Steel Community in April 1951 and of the Common Market in 1957. In May 1955 he secured formal acceptance by his European partners of the Federal Republic's sovereign status, and West Germany was duly admitted to NATO. Four months later he visited Moscow and surprised his opponents within Germany by securing diplomatic recognition from the Soviet Union. In his later years he lost some support through disputes with his economic specialist and party rival, Ludwig ERHARD, and some CDU voters felt he accepted too readily the division of Germany as emphasized by the crisis over the Berlin Wall in 1961. Adenauer personally regarded his final success as the conclusion of a Franco-German Treaty of Friendship, signed by DE GAULLE and himself on 22 January 1963, and marking – as he hoped – the end of a century of hostility and suspicion between the two nations. Even after his resignation as Chancellor, Adenauer continued as leader of the CDU for two and a half years, a source of political embarrassment to his successor as Chancellor, Erhard. T. Prittie: *Konrad Adenauer* (1972); R. Hiscocks: *Germany Revived, an Appraisal of the Adenauer Era* (1966); A. Grosser: *Germany in Our Time* (1974).

Aga Khan III (Aga Sultan Sir Mohammed Shah), (1877–1957), Indian statesman and Muslim religious leader: born in Karachi. He succeeded his father as Aga Khan at the age of 8 but could not be accepted as (forty-eighth) Imam of the Ismaili sect of Muslims until 1893, thereafter remaining until his death effective leader of over twelve million Muslims, living in widely separated regions of three continents. He urged his followers to integrate socially and politically within the communities where they lived. In England the Aga Khan was best known for his stable of racehorses, five of whom won the Derby; but from the turn of the century until the Second World War he played an active role in British Indian affairs: he served on the Viceroy's Legislative Council from 1902 to 1904, became Founder-President of the All-India Muslim League in 1906, and led the British India delegation to the Round Table Conferences on the future of India in London, both in 1930 and in 1932; he also went to Geneva as chief Indian delegate to the League of Nations Assembly in 1932 and from 1935 to 1937. During the First World War he used his standing as a spiritual leader to counter Ottoman attempts to raise the Muslims in a holy war against the British and their allies; he was especially influential in Egypt, where there was a large Ismaili community. Among the philanthropic enterprises which the Aga Khan sponsored was the Aligarh Muslim University in Uttar Pradesh, of which he was the virtual founder. His spiritual authority was never in question, but his political influence in the Indian subcontinent declined with the rise of JINNAH and with Partition. He spent most of his later years in Egypt or in Europe, and died in Switzerland. He was buried in an impressive tomb at Aswan, in Upper Egypt. *The Memories of the Aga Khan* (1954); M. Bose: *The Aga Khans* (Kingswood, 1984); A. Edwards: *Throne of Gold, the Lives of the Aga Khans* (1995).

Aguinaldo, Emilio (1869–1964), Filipino revolutionary: born on Luzon Island when the Philippines were still a Spanish colony. He became a militant nationalist in his twenties and for twelve months led an armed rebellion against the Spanish authorities until, in 1896, he accepted from them a substantial sum of money (which he used on building up a more effective movement) and went into exile in Hong Kong. When war broke out between Spain and the United States in April 1898, an American vessel secretly landed 'General' Aguinaldo on Luzon and he organized guerrilla resistance around Manila, seeking to establish a 'Visayan Republic' as a first step to independence in the Philippines. Admiral DEWEY, however, found collaboration with Aguinaldo difficult and a war began between Aguinaldo's followers and American troops in February 1899 which dragged on for two years, costing the lives of over 4,000 Americans and more than twice as many Filipinos. Aguinaldo accepted American rule in July 1901 and, with his followers, received an amnesty from the Governor-General, the later President TAFT. For forty years Aguinaldo continued to press for total independence, unsuccessfully standing for the presidency of the Philippines when the islands became an autonomous commonwealth in 1935. He collaborated with the Japanese on Luzon during the Second World War and was imprisoned by the Americans when they reoccupied Manila in February 1945 but released six months later. He spent his last years in private life, respected as a legendary rebel leader, the Filipino Garibaldi. F. H. Golay (ed.): *The United States and the*

Philippines (1966); E. Wildman: *Aguinaldo* (Boston, 1903).

Aitken, William Maxwell: see *Beaverbrook*.

Alanbrooke, Lord (Alan Francis Brooke) (1883–1963), British Chief of the Imperial General Staff from 1941 to 1946: born at Bagnères-de-Bigorre in southern France. He was educated at French lycées and at the Royal Military Academy, Woolwich, being commissioned in the artillery in 1902 and serving for most of the First World War with Indian or Canadian forces in France. He was in command of the Second Corps of the British Expeditionary Force in 1939–40 before becoming Commander-in-Chief of home forces when invasion threatened in 1940. He became Chief of the Imperial General Staff on 1 December 1941 and throughout the remainder of the war was largely responsible for shaping British strategy in Europe and Africa, modifying, amplifying or curbing the broad projects of the Prime Minister, Winston CHURCHILL. His work, hidden from the public, was recognized by a Field Marshal's baton on 1 January 1944, by the barony which made him Lord Alanbrooke in 1945, and by the award of the Order of Merit, a knighthood of the Garter, and a viscountcy when he retired as CIGS in 1946. Lord Alanbrooke was widely respected as an ornithologist. His younger brother, Basil (1888–1973) was Prime Minister of Northern Ireland from 1943 to 1963 and was created Viscount Brookeborough in 1952. A. Bryant (ed.): *The Turn of the Tide* (1957), *Triumph in the West* (1959); D. Fraser: *Alanbrooke* (1982).

Alexander (1888–1934). King of Yugoslavia from 1921 to 1934: born in Cetinje, Montenegro, a great-grandson of Karadjordje Petrović (*c.* 1765–1817), leader in 1804 of the first successful Serbian national revolt. Alexander's father, Peter Karadjordjević (1844–1921), spent most of his life in exile and much of it in poverty, and Alexander began his education at an elementary school in Geneva. It was completed, however, by several years of predominantly military studies at court in St Petersburg where he remained until he was 21. In 1903 the Karadjordjević dynasty was restored to the Serbian throne after a lapse of forty-five years, Alexander's father ruling as King Peter I. Six years later Alexander became heir-apparent when in March 1909 his elder brother, George (1887–1972), renounced his claims after several unfortunate episodes, including the mysterious death of his valet. King Peter's ailing health forced Alexander to take a prominent role in Serbian politics from 1911 onwards while he also commanded the army which defeated the Turks at Kumanovo in the First Balkan War (1912). On 24 June 1914 Alexander was appointed Regent and Commander-in-Chief of Serbia. For most of the First World War he was at the Serbian headquarters, accompanying the army in its epic retreat over the Albanian mountains in 1915 and regrouping his forces at Salonika, 1916–18. During the war he destroyed the powerful secret society of officers, the so-called 'Black Hand', and authorized the Serbian Prime Minister, PAŠIĆ, to reach agreement with spokesmen for the other south Slav nationalities (Croats and Slovenes) for establishment of a unified southern Slav kingdom after the war. This 'Kingdom of the Serbs, Croats and Slovenes' was formally created on 4 December 1918, with Alexander as Regent for his father until Peter I's death on 16 August 1921.

Alexander's reign was hampered by the impossibility of reconciling the weternized the Catholic Croats and Slovenes to the political and military predominance of the traditionally Balkan and Orthodox Serbs. Political outrages, even in parliament, induced him to assume dictatorial powers in January 1929 and rule autocratically for the remainder of his life. Nine months later he changed the name of the state to 'Yugoslavia', hoping that it might be possible to create a common Yugoslav patriotism by suppressing the old concepts of loyalty to Serbia, Croatia, Slovenia, Montenegro or Macedonia. This policy met with little success. He was threatened by Communist dissidents, by Macedonian terrorists and by the extreme right-wing Croatian nationalists (the Uštaše group).

In foreign policy his role as 'Strong Man of the Balkans' induced him to seek collaboration between Yugoslàvia, Greece, Romania and their former enemies Bulgaria and Turkey. The cornerstone of his foreign policy was, however, a close alliance with France. Suspicion of Hitler's Germany prompted the King to undertake a state visit to France in October 1934, but soon after he landed at Marseilles he was assassinated by a Macedonian in the pay of the Uštaše. The French Foreign Minister, Louis Barthou, died with him. Alexander was succeeded as King by his 11-year-old son, Peter II (1923–70), for whom Alexander's cousin, Prince Paul (1893–1976) acted as Regent until 27 March 1941, the young King being forced into exile by German invaders a fortnight later. S. Graham: *Alexander of Yugoslavia* (1938); R. West: *Black Lamb and Grey Falcon* (2 vols) (1942); J. B. Hoptner: Yugoslavia in Crisis, 1934–41 (New York, 1962); A. N. Dragnich: *The First Yugoslavia* (Stanford, 1983).

Alexander II (1818–81), Tsar of Russia from 1855 to 1881: born in Moscow, the eldest son of Nicholas I (reigned 1825–55). His mother was Princess Charlotte of Prussia and Alexander admired his mother's homeland throughout his reign, King Frederick William IV of Prussia and his successor, WILLIAM I, being the Tsar's uncles. Alexander belived that Russia's defeat in the Crimean War of 1853–6 showed a need to modernize and, within limits, liberalize his empire. The first nine years of his reign saw the achievement of reforms long contemplated but postponed for reasons of internal security. Greatest of these was the emancipation of the serfs, a measure improving the status of over twenty million of the Tsar's most wretched subjects (March 1861). Other reforms modernized the legal code, created new administrative units in local government, encouraged secondary and university education, and made the burden of conscripted army service more equitable. A nationalist uprising in Russian Poland (1863–4) was followed by years of increasing repression and revolutionary unrest. The Tsar narrowly escaped assassination in St Petersburg in April 1866 and in Paris in June 1867. Russia's economy improved slowly, largely through the development of credit institutions and the growth of a railway system. Alexander's Foreign Minister, GORCHAKOV, raised Russia's influence in European affairs until the crisis years of 1876 to 1878 when the Tsar allowed free rein to pan-Slavism, especially in the army, and war against Turkey carried his troops to the outskirts of Constantinople. This success was offset by a diplomatic defeat at the Congress of Berlin (June–July 1878), and Russia's chief territorial gains in Alexander's reign were limited to central Asia, the absorption of Bokhara and Samarkand in 1868 being followed by increased influence in Afghanistan. By 1879 the Tsar's reluctance to countenance further political reforms in European Russia led to the formation of secret terrorist societies, notably 'The People's Will'. After several unsuccessful attempts on the Tsar's life, he was eventually killed by a Polish student who hurled a bomb at Alexander's sledge as he was returning to the Winter Palace in St Petersburg on 13 March 1881. He had that morning, in private, accepted the need for a modernized constitution. In 1841 Alexander married Princess Marie of Hesse, who became the mother of seven sons and daughters. Soon after her death in June 1880 Alexander married Catherine Dolgoruky (1847–1922), once his ward, and from 1865 onwards his mistress, who bore him several children. As Princess Yurievskaya she outlived the Tsar by more than forty years, most of them spent in Nice. W. E. Mosse: *Alexander II and the Modernization of Russia* (1958); E. M. Almedingen: *The Emperor Alexander II* (1962); H. Seton-Watson: *The Russian Empire, 1801–1917* (Oxford, 1967).

Alexander III (1845–94), Tsar of Russia from 1881 to 1894: the second son of ALEXANDER II, becoming Tsarevich in 1865 when his elder brother, Nicholas, died of consumption. Alexander was trained as a soldier rather than educated for the responsibilities of government. His tutor was the arch-reactionary POBEDONOSTSEV, who succeeded in making his pupil a dutiful Orthodox believer, strict in personal morals. Alexander's massive physique won for him the nickname 'young bull' within his family; he became a man of great physical strength but limited intelligence, a conscientious worker who hated any social gathering more sophisticated than a beer evening. His first act as Tsar was to tear up plans for a constitution agreed by his father on the eve of his assassination in St Petersburg (13 March 1881). Alexander maintained firm autocratic rule, tightening the censorship, intensifying secret police activity, seeking 'to root out the horrible sedition now dishonouring our Russian land'. Hangings and exile to Siberia drove political discontent underground. The Tsar also authorized the first systematic anti-Semitic campaign, marked by the imposition of savage restrictions on Jewish believers from May 1882 onwards. In foreign affairs he showed considerable mistrust of BISMARCK and even more of Kaiser WILLIAM II, after his accession in 1888. Despite his hatred of revolutionary ideas, the Tsar deliberately cultivated closer relations with the French Republic from 1891 onwards, secretly accepting a Franco-Russian military alliance in January 1894. He supported expansionist plans for Russian penetration into Asia, also approving the proposals of WITTE for a Trans-Siberian Railway (1891). He died from nephritis at Livadia in the Crimea (November 1894) and was succeeded by his 26-year-old son, NICHOLAS II. Alexander's widow, the Empress Marie Feodorovna (by birth a Danish princess and sister to the English Queen Alexandra) survived the Russian Revolution, dying in Copenhagen in 1928. H. Seton-Watson: *The Russian Empire, 1801–1917* (Oxford, 1967); E. Crankshaw: *The Shadow of the Winter Palace* (1976).

Alexander of Battenberg (1857–93), Prince of Bulgaria from 1879 to 1886: born in northern Italy, the second son of Prince Alexander of Hesse (1823–88) and his morganatic wife, Julie Hauke (1825–95), for whom the extinct title Countess of Battenberg was revived upon her marriage in 1851, her rank being raised to Princess in 1858. As his father's sister was married to Tsar ALEXANDER II, the young Battenberg Prince was commissioned in the Russian army and fought bravely in the war which liberated Bulgaria from Turkish rule in 1877–8. He accepted the throne of an autonomous Bulgarian principality offered to him in April 1879 by a Bulgarian national assembly, acting under Russian pressure. As ruling prince he showed himself too autocratic for Bulgaria's liberals and too independent to please his Russian sponsors. He was a strong personality who, by encouraging the incorporation in his principality of a Bulgarian province still under Turkish sovereignty, disturbed the diplomatic balance imposed in the Balkans by the Great Powers. After a Russian-backed palace revolution in Sofia, Prince Alexander was induced to abdicate (September 1886) and go into exile. Marriage links between two of his brothers and the English royal dynasty helped Alexander become a favourite with Queen VICTORIA, who welcomed his expressed desire to marry her granddaughter, Princess Victoria of Prussia (1866–1929). BISMARCK distrusted Battenberg influence and opposed the marriage which was finally prohibited by the young Kaiser, WILLIAM II, soon after his accession (1888). Alexander found consolation for this frustrated romance a year later by marrying the opera singer, Johanna Loisinger. In November 1893 Alexander died suddenly from peritonitis, in Graz, Austria. His body was interred in Sofia, where he was belatedly honoured as the 'Liberator Prince'. His elder brother was father of Earl MOUNTBATTEN of Burma and Alexander was therefore a great-uncle of Prince Philip, Duke of Edinburgh. E. C. Corti: *Alexander of Battenberg* (1954).

Alexander, Harold Robert Leofric George (1891–1969), British soldier distinguished for his campaigns in North Africa and Italy from 1942 to 1945: born in Tyrone, a younger son of the fourth Earl of Caledon. At Harrow he was best remembered as a subtle spin-bowler in the school cricket eleven of 1910. From Sandhurst he was commissioned in the Irish Guards. Throughout most of the First World War he served in France where he won several decorations, including the Military Cross, and was a Major at the age of 25. He was wounded three times. In 1919 he commanded an auxiliary force (many members of which were German) which fought against the Bolsheviks in the former Baltic provinces of Russia. He served in the Northern Command in England. 1932–4, and on the North-Western Frontier of India in 1935.

When war broke out in 1939 Alexander crossed to France as Major-General commanding the First Corps of the British Expeditionary Force and he was Commander of the final stages of the Dunkirk evacuation in 1940. After eighteen months with the Southern Command, preparing for a possible German invasion, he was hurriedly flown to Burma in March 1942 and successfully evacuated British troops from Rangoon through thick jungle to Imphal in northern Assam, a remarkably difficult operation. He was appointed Commander-in-Chief, Middle East, in August 1942 with MONTGOMERY as subordinate field commander of the Eighth Army, and thus directed the advance from El Alamein to Tunisia, capturing the city of Tunis on 7 May 1943. He was Deputy Allied Commander under EISENHOWER during the pincer movement which ended the war in Africa and brought Allied armies to Sicily in July 1943; and he was subsequently Commander-in-Chief of the multinational Allied army which landed in Calabria to advance on Rome in the winter of 1943–4. Here his plans were checked by three disappointments: loss of men and material to prepare for the cross-Channel invasion of France; inability to crack the German mountain defences around Cassino until the spring of 1944; and failure of field commanders to exploit rapidly his strategically imaginative landing at Anzio, sixty miles behind the German lines and only thirty-five miles from Rome. Nevertheless German defences south of Rome were overrun in the spring of 1944 and Alexander entered the city on 4 June.

In December 1944 he was promoted to the rank of Field Marshal and appointed Supreme Allied Commander in the Mediterranean. Although his armies overwhelmed the Gothic Line defences in the Apennines and enforced the surrender of nearly a million German troops north of the Po on 1 May 1945, his broader strategic plans were frustrated by the need to subordinate his theatre of war to the Allied policy for Europe as a whole. Hopes of advancing into central Europe and on to Vienna and the Danube before the arrival of the Russians came to nothing. In 1946 he was created Viscount and, for six years, served as Governor-General of Canada.

In 1952 Winston CHURCHILL brought him into the government as Minister of Defence – the first Field Marshal since the Duke of Wellington to hold Cabinet rank in time of peace. He gave valuable advice over Korea and the running-down of British bases in the Middle East before his final retirement in 1954. Honours included the Garter in 1946, an earldom – Earl Alexander of Tunis – in 1952 and the Order of Merit in 1959. Among his qualities as a General were the ability, quietly and methodically, to use to advantage the skills of subordinate commanders, British or foreign, and to remain imperturbably confident of ultimate success. Alexander of Tunis: *Memoirs* (1962); N. Nicolson: *Alex* (1973).

Alfonso XIII (1886–1941), King of Spain from 1902 to 1931: the son of Alfonso XII (reigned 1874–85), who died before his birth. Until his sixteenth birthday royal authority was vested in the Regency of his mother, Queen Maria Christina (1858–1929). Her influence remained considerable even after the formal end of the Regency, and her unpopularity helped the growth of republican ideas, which owed much, too, to the abuse of Spain's parliamentary system by corrupt political bosses. Anarchist outrages reached a climax with the throwing of a bomb at Alfonso's wedding coach in Madrid in May 1906. A succession of strikes, notably in Bilbao and Catalonia, was followed by the 'Tragic Week' of 26 July to 1 August 1909 when over a hundred civilians were killed and many buildings destroyed in rioting in Barcelona. Alfonso tried to combat these outrages by repressive measures but was never able to win public confidence. There were, in all, five attempts to assassinate him between 1906 and 1932. Military reversals in the war with the Riff tribes in Spanish Morocco weakened the prestige of the army, the chief pillar of the monarchy. In September 1923 Alfonso invited General PRIMO DE RIVERA to 'be my Mussolini', and for two years the General tried to set up a fascist system in Spain. Mounting disorder forced Primo to end the dictatorship in December 1925 although the King induced him to remain Prime Minister until January 1930, thereby identifying the monarchy closely with authoritarian government. Republican successes in the municipal elections in 1931 seemed to Alfonso to threaten bloodshed and revolution, and on 14 April 1931 he left the country to settle in Rome, where he died ten years later without ever formally abdicating his throne. C. Petrie: *King Alfonso XIII* (1963); R. Carr: *Spain, 1808–1939* (Oxford, 1966).

Allenby, Edmund Henry Hynman (1861–1936), British soldier noted for his campaign in Palestine in 1917–18: born in London, educated at Haileybury (where he was a good classical scholar), and commissioned in the Inniskilling Dragoons in 1882. He served in the Sudan in 1884–5 and was leader of a mobile column of cavalry during the Boer War of 1899–1902. In 1914 he commanded the cavalry division in the British Expeditionary Force, his men seeing action on the Franco-Belgian frontier as early as 21 August. He remained in France until the summer of 1917 and was for two years Commander of the Third Army, his most striking success being the battle of Arras (April 1917), in which the Canadians captured the vital ridge above Vimy. Allenby was appointed Commander-in-Chief of the Egyptian Expeditionary Force two months later. A meticulously planned offensive against the Turks and Germans in Palestine enabled him to advance in October 1917 from Gaza into Judaea and on 9 December 1917 he accepted the surrender of Jerusalem (which had been in Turkish hands since its capture from the Crusaders in 1244). Allenby's second offensive, beginning on 18–19 September 1918 with the victory of Megiddo, cleared Palestine, captured Damascus and on 30 October forced Turkey to accept an armistice. From 1919 to 1925 Field Marshal Viscount Allenby (as he became) was High Commissioner for Egypt and the Sudan, showing the tact and firmness of a great proconsul in restraining nationalist rioting. As a General he was the last commander to make imaginative use of cavalry, both around Arras and to destroy the Turkish army along the Jordan. A. P. Wavell: *The Palestine Campaigns* (1928); L. James: *Imperial Warrior: The Life and Times of F.M. Lord Allenby* (1993).

Allende, Salvator (1908–73), President of Chile from 1970 to 1973: born in Valparaiso and qualified as a doctor of medicine. From 1937 to 1970 he sat in the Chilean National Congress, either as a Deputy or a Senator and was leader of the Chilean Socialist Party, a left-wing group distinct from the narrowly doctrinaire Communist Party. He was an unsuccessful presidential candidate in 1952, 1958 and 1964, but won the election of September 1970, the first victory of a Marxist in any democratic presidential election. Allende set himself to create a socialist Chile while retaining the parliamentary system, but the task was beyond him. He was hampered by strikes and violence from extremists on the Left and by opposition from foreign business enterprises, which were supported by the American Central Intelligence Agency (CIA). On 11 September 1973 his government was overthrown by a military junta, headed by General PINOCHET. Allende perished in the assault on his presidential palace in Santiago. In the ensuing period of repression the National Congress was dissolved and all political organizations banned, a development familiar elsewhere in Latin America but rare in Chile, where for over a century there had been a tradition of basically liberal parliamentary government. A. Horne: *Small Earthquake in Chile* (1972; rev. edn 1990); N. Davis: *The Last Two Years of Salvador Allende* (1985).

Altgeld, John Peter (1847–1902), American progressive reformer: born in Germany, emigrated as a child to Ohio but settled in Chicago, where he practised as a lawyer. His book *Our Penal Machinery and its Victims* (1884) exposed the difficulties facing the poor in their search for justice from the courts. He was elected Governor of Illinois in 1892 and for four years carried out a series of state reforms, often drafted in collaboration with the social worker, Jane ADDAMS. Penal conditions were improved, new laws regulated child labour, and the monopolistic hold of business bosses over such urban utilities as tramways and railways was loosened. But Altgeld made powerful enemies who sought to discredit him nationally. Soon after taking office he pardoned three alleged anarchists imprisoned since 1886; and in July 1894 he condemned President CLEVELAND for his decision to send federal troops into Illinois to protect railway services disrupted by the Chicago Pullman Strike. For both these actions the American Press vilified Altgeld as a defender of anarchy, an 'Illinois Jacobin', and he was defeated when he sought reelection in 1896. He was a pioneer reformer, at least two generations ahead of public opinion. H. Barnard: *Eagle Forgotten* (New York, 1938); A. Lindsey: *The Pullman Strike* (Chicago, 1942).

Amin, Idi (1926–   ), President of Uganda from 1971 to 1979: born into a Muslim community in northern Uganda, enlisted in the King's African Rifles and rose to the rank of Sergeant, becoming an officer when Uganda attained independence within the Commonwealth in 1962. On

25 January 1971 Amin, as Commanding General of the army, seized power in Kampala while President Milton OBOTE was attending the Commonwealth Prime Ministers' Conference in Singapore. Amin declared himself Head of State and for eight years ruled Uganda through a Defence Council, of which he was the dictatorial Chairman. Most Ugandan Asians were expelled in 1972, many British nationals leaving soon afterwards. Systematic repression in the interests of a small group of Muslims from his own tribe was denounced by other Commonwealth leaders, and diplomatic relations between Britain and Amin's Uganda were broken off in the summer of 1976. Amin's support for the Palestine Liberation Organization prompted a raid by Israeli commandos on Entebbe airport in July 1976 in order to release hostages held on an Air France airliner, many of them Jewish. Early in the following year Amin was accused of causing the sudden death of the Archbishop of Uganda. Armed clashes between Ugandan and Tanzanian troops culminated in a Tanzanian invasion, which was supported by anti-Amin forces. In April 1979 he was forced to flee from the country, seeking refuge in Libya. His rule had ruined the Ugandan economy. G. Ivan Smith: *Ghosts of Kampala* (1980); J. J. Jorgenson: *Uganda, A Modern History* (1981).

Andreotti, Giulio (1919–), Italian Prime Minister: born in Rome, where he studied law at the university and carried out historical research on papal naval power in the Middle Ages. He was a Christian Democrat delegate to the constituent assembly of the Italian Republic in 1946–7, subsequently representing the party in parliament from 1948 until 1994. After serving in DE GASPERI's inner council as an under-secretary, he became Minister of the Interior in Scelba's administration in February 1954 and remained a member of every government until 1992, holding thirty-three portfolios, including every major department, serving as Foreign Minister from 1983 to 1987 and forming seven coalition governments (1972–3, 1976–9 and July 1989 to May 1992). He was thus the outstanding Italian political figure of the 1970s and 1980s, even if his governments survived only because of the inability of the four main parties of the Left to work together. Andreotti was a personal friend of Savo Lima, a long-term mayor of Palermo, who was murdered in March 1992. Exactly a year later Andreotti was among many leading figures placed under investigation for association with Cosa Nostra, the Mafia crime syndicate in Sicily, and the Camorra, the equivalent organization in Naples. Three months later his parliamentary immunity from arrest was removed in connection with investigation into the murder of the journalist, Mino Pecorelli, and allegations were made that he had sought to suppress information damaging to himself in connection with the death of his colleague, Aldo MORO. In July 1994 Andreotti was formally charged with membership of the Mafia, which he was said to have 'protected' while in office 'from at least 1978'. Many prominent Italian politicians were implicated in similar scandals, further weakening public respect for a democratic system in which the average length of governments since the founding of the republic had been no more than eleven months. C. Richards: *The New Italians* (1994); D. Hine: *Governing Italy, the Politics of Bargained Pluralism* (Oxford, 1993); F. Spotts and T. Wieser: *Italy, a Difficult Democracy* (1986).

Anderson, Elizabeth Garrett (*née* **Garrett**) 1836–1917), British pioneer of women's rights in the medical profession: born in London, the elder sister of Millicent FAWCETT and brought up, like her, at Aldeburgh, Suffolk. From 1860 to 1870 she trained as a doctor but found great opposition to the idea of women progressing within the medical profession. She took her doctor of medicine degree at the University of Paris, and was permitted to serve as a visiting physician at the East London Hospital in 1870, subsequently practising as a doctor for women and children. A year after her husband's death she became the first woman mayor in England, elected at Aldeburgh in May 1908. J. Manton: *Elizabeth Garrett Anderson* (1965).

Andrassy, Gyula (1823–90), Hungarian nationalist leader and Austro-Hungarian Foreign Minister: born into one of the great Magyar aristocratic families at Kassa (Kosice). He fought for the Hungarians seeking independence from Austrian rule in 1848–9 and was forced to live in exile until pardoned eight years later. When he returned to political life Count Andrassy showed more moderation than in his youth and was prominent in negotiating the 'Compromise' (*Ausgleich*) which created the dual monarchy of Austria-Hungary in 1867. He was Hungary's first Prime Minister, serving from 1867 until 1871 when he accepted office as Foreign Minister to the Emperor-King, FRANCIS JOSEPH. Andrassy remained at the Foreign Ministry in Vienna for eight years, improving relations with Bismarck's Germany, strengthening the influence of the monarchy in the western Balkans, and attending the Congress of Berlin in 1878 as one of the leading statesmen in Europe. His final achievement was the conclusion of a secret Austro-German alliance (October 1879), which remained valid until 1918. He spent his last ten years of life managing the vast Andrassy estates. I Dioszegi: *Hungarians in the Ballhausplatz* (Budapest, 1983); F. R. Bridge: *The Habsburg Monarchy among the Great Powers, 1815–1918* (New York, Oxford, Munich, 1990); A. Palmer: *Twilight of the Habsburgs* (1994).

Andropov, Yuri (1914–84), Soviet communist leader: born at Nagutskaya, a village in Stavropol province, northern Caucasus. He was trained as a river transport engineer and began work at the age of 16 in the Rybinsk shipyards, on the Volga, soon becoming a Communist Party official. When Karelia was ceded by Finland in March 1940 Andropov was appointed to help 'sovietize' the new region, remaining to direct partisan resistance during the war and becoming second secretary of the Karelian Party in 1945. After a short term in Moscow working for the Central Committee he was appointed ambassador in Budapest in 1954 and played a key role in crushing the Hungarian Revolution of 1956. A year later he was brought back to Moscow as a KGB official; he was made KGB Chief in 1967 and admitted to the central Politburo in 1973. As head of the KGB he personally investigated party corruption and inefficiency. When BREZHNEV died in November 1982 Andropov succeeded him as Party Secretary; he caused some surprise by favouring reforms in both party and state, using as a spokesman GORBACHEV, who came from his region of Russia and was his protégé. Andropov sacked lazy and inefficient party bosses and officials, arresting the more blatantly corrupt. But Andropov's health soon gave way; he died from a kidney disease in February 1984, with CHERNENKO succeeding him. Z. A. Medvedev: *Andropov* (Oxford, 1983); V. Solovyov and E. Klepikova: *Andropov* (1984); D. Remnick: *Lenin's Tomb* (1993).

Anthony, Susan Brownell (1820–1906), American suffragette: born in Adams, Massachusetts, into a Quaker family. During the 1850s and 1860s she was a vigorous campaigner against slavery and in favour of temperance and women's rights, courting arrest in the presidential election of 1872 by seeking to cast a vote. In 1869 she became leader of the National American Woman Suffrage Association and by 1880 she had acquired an international reputation. In 1888 she organized a Council of Women which was to further the feminist cause throughout the western world. Two years before her death she established the International Woman Suffrage Alliance. During her lifetime four American states gave the vote to women: Wyoming as soon as it achieved statehood in 1889; Colorado in 1893, and Idaho and Utah in 1896. Her example as a militant campaigner was followed in America by Carrie CATT and in Britain by Mrs PANKHURST and her daughters. I. H. Harper: *The Life and Work of Susan B. Anthony* (2 vols) (Indianapolis and Kansas City, 1899); K. S. Anthony: *Susan B. Anthony, her Personal History and her Era* (New York, 1954); A. Kraditor: *The Ideas of the Woman Suffrage Movement, 1890–1920* (New York, 1965).

Antonescu, Ion (1882–1946), dictator of Romania from 1940 to 1944: born in Piteşti and commissioned in a crack regiment of the Romanian Army in 1904, ending the First World War as a Colonel. During the 1920s he was military attaché in London and in Rome, where he admired Italian fascism. He was appointed Chief of General Staff in 1937 but was suspected by King CAROL II of plotting to overthrow the pro-French Government in Bucharest and was briefly imprisoned. German influence grew in the Balkan capitals after the rapid victory of Hitler's army in Poland in 1939, and Antonescu's fortunes swiftly changed. He was appointed Minister of War and, after Carol's surrender of Romanian territory to Russia, Bulgaria and Hungary, Antonescu emerged as the strong man of the country. He forced Carol into exile in September 1940 and four months later was proclaimed *Conducator* ('Leader'), much as Hitler and Mussolini were known respectively as *Führer* and *Duce*. When Germany invaded Russia in June 1941 Antonescu allied Romania with the Axis Powers and sent an army of thirty divisions into the Ukraine. The Romanians cut off the seaport of Odessa within six weeks, although it took another ten weeks for them to capture the city, with German tank support. Antonescu (raised to the rank of Marshal on 21 August 1941) declared the south-western Ukraine annexed to Romania, with Odessa henceforth to be known as 'Antonescu'. But these triumphs did not last. The Romanian army suffered heavily in the winter of 1942–3, especially on the Volga. Soviet victories in the spring of 1944 brought the Russians back to the Romanian frontier and on 23 August 1944 Carol II's 23-year-old son, King Michael, had Antonescu arrested in a palace revolution, subsequently bringing Romania into the war as an ally of Britain, America and Russia against Germany. In May 1946 Antonescu was charged with war crimes, condemned to death after a brief trial, and shot on 1 June. A. Polonsky: *The Little Dictators* (1975); A. Palmer: *The Lands Between; East-Central Europe since the Congress of Vienna* (1970); K. Hitchins: *Rumania, 1866–1947* (Oxford, 1994).

Aquino, Cory (1933–), President of the Philippines from 1986 to 1992: born Maria Curazon Cojuangco, the daughter of a wealthy sugar merchant. She received convent schooling in Manila before graduating in mathematics in New York and undertaking further studies at the Far Eastern University, Manila. At the age of 21 she married Benigno Aquino Jnr. and was the mother of four daughters and a son. Her husband became a political opponent of President MARCOS, who imprisoned him for alleged subversion in 1972. The sentence of death imposed on him in 1977 aroused such protest that it was commuted, and in May 1980 he was allowed to go into exile in the USA for heart surgery. On his return in August 1983 he was assassinated by a military guard at Manila airport. This action united Opposition parties against Marcos and, with full backing from the Church, Cory Aquino stood as Liberal candidate in the presidential elections of February 1986. Their fraudulent character induced Cory Aquino to support a non-violent campaign of civil disobedience which forced the Marcos family to flee the country at the end of the month: Mrs Aquino was sworn in as President on the same day. She supervised the preparation of a new, democratic constitution, effective from July 1987. As President, she was faced by Communist insurgency in the outer islands and by the discontent of wealthy political factions, who used time-wasting procedures in the legislature to obstruct reforms. Remarkably, Cory Aquino survived seven attempted military *coups* before retiring into private life in June 1992, after giving her backing to her successor, President Fidel Ramos. J. Bresnan: *Crisis in the Philippines, the Marcos Era and Beyond* (Princeton, 1986); I. Criosostomo: *Cory, Profile of a President* (Quezon City, 1986); C. A. Buss: *Cory Aquino and the People of the Philippines* (Stanford, 1987).

Arabi Pasha (Ahmed Orabi/'Urabi) (1841–1911), Egyptian soldier and protonationalist leader: born the son of a village sheikh from near Zaqaziq, in Sharqiyya province, and educated at al-Azhar, the historic Islamic university in Cairo. He entered the army in 1854 and was a Lieutenant-Colonel by the age of 20. Thereafter Arabi received no promotion, either because higher rank was reserved for Turco-Circassians or because, while his campaigning record in the Sudan was good, he became a skilled and intelligent spokesman for the non-Turkish officer class. He led a mutiny in favour of better conditions of service in January 1881. When Khedive Tewfik's government prevaricated there was a second mutiny, on 9 September 1881, with the officers receiving popular backing in a call for a constituent assembly, a demand conceded by Tewfik. Arabi accepted office as Minister of War at the end of the year and, for the first time, popularized the demagogic slogan 'Egypt for the Egyptians'. This concept alarmed British and French investors, whose governments backed intervention after riots in Alexandria led to more than fifty European deaths. British troops landed in force in late August under WOLSELEY, who defeated Arabi's army at Tel-el-Kebir (13 September 1882). Arabi and his colleagues were put on trial by the occupying authorities. Sentences of death were commuted to exile; Arabi remained in Ceylon until pardoned in 1909. His programme of radical nationalism and constitutionalism set a precedent for the Egyptian officer corps during the NASSER era. A. Scholch: *Egypt for the Egyptians* (1981); M. Rowlatt: *Founders of Modern Egypt* (1952); P. J. Vatikiotis: *The History of Modern Egypt* (4th edn 1991).

Arafat, Yasir (Muhammad Abed Ar'ou Arafat) (1929–), President of the Palestinian National Authority: born in Cairo but, after his mother's death in 1933, spent his early boyhood in Jerusalem. In 1946 he began gunrunning for Palestinian guerillas, whom he assisted in the 1948 war against Israel. As an engineering student at Cairo University in the early 1950s he established contact with the Free Officers' Movement, before becoming an engineer in Kuwait, where in September 1957 he was co-founder of Al-Fatah, a resistance group recruited from Palestinian refugees. In May 1964 Al-Fatah, then based in Syria, merged with other factions in Jordan to form the Palestine Liberation Organization (PLO), and Arafat was accepted as Chairman in 1969. He could not always hold in check the more militant terrorists within the PLO who were defeated in Jordan's civil war of September 1970. The regrouping of the PLO in Syria and Lebanon enhanced Arafat's personal standing and when the PLO gained UN recognition in 1974, he became a familiar figure at international meetings, his head always symbolically covered by a traditional *kaffiyeh*. Arafat was forced to leave Lebanon in 1983, eventually establishing headquarters in Tunisia. He failed to retain support from Arab hardliners because of his diplomatic willingness to modify PLO aims so as to accept coexistence with a Jewish state, provided the Israelis withdrew from certain regions of Palestine. Despite the *intifada* guerrilla warfare, which in 1987 began in areas occupied by Israeli troops, Arafat persisted in supporting peace attempts from 1991 onwards and, on 13 September 1993, signed a declaration on interim self-government arrangements with the Israeli Prime Minister, YITZHAK RABIN, for which both men were nominated for the Nobel Peace Prize. An administrative centre was established at Gaza City, where Arafat assumed office as President, pending a proposed eventual return to East Jerusalem. A. Hart: *Arafat* (1994); H. Cobban: *The Palestinian Liberation Organisation* (Cambridge, 1984).

Aristide, Jean-Bertrand (1953–), President of Haiti: born at Port Salut but educated by the Salesian Fathers in Port-au-Prince, where his family moved when he was a child. In 1966 he entered a Salesian seminary, subsequently studying in Palestine and Quebec before being ordained priest in 1982. He returned to Haiti in January 1985, after nearly six years abroad, to find his homeland under the brutal dictatorship of the younger DUVALIER. As parish priest at the Church of St John Bosco in Port-au-Prince, Fr Aristide courageously spoke out in favour of human rights. He survived several assassination attempts and in September 1987 his church was burned down and many worshippers murdered while at mass. Despite disapproval from the Church hierarchy, Fr Aristide entered politics as leader of a National Front for Change and Democracy which, on 16 December 1990, won a presidential election forced on the ruling junta by foreign pressure. He was sworn in as President on 7 February 1991 and launched an anti-corruption campaign which provoked a military *coup* six months later. President Aristide found sanctuary in the United States. Trade sanctions and financial pressure on the military regime failed to secure the President's return. After reports that at least 3000 pro-democracy activists had been murdered, on 31 July 1994 the UN Security Council approved the use of force to overthrow the regime. The imminent threat of invasion by US forces led the junta on 18 September to agree to a restoration of Haiti's constitutional President. By mid-October 1994 President Aristide was able to resume the reforming programme for which he had received a mandate four years before. He accepted the constitutional ruling that no President should stand for a second consecutive term and duly stepped down from office in January 1996. J-B. Aristide (with C. Warigny): *An Autobiography* (1993); A. Wilentz: *The Rainy Season, Haiti since Duvalier* (New York, 1989).

Armstrong, Neil (1930–), American astronaut and first man on the moon: born near Wapokoneta, Ohio, the son of an itinerant auditor. He saved his pocket-money to take flying lessons at the local airfield and flew solo before his sixteenth birthday. In 1948 he joined the US Navy to train as a fighter pilot, remaining in the service until 1952, winning three decorations for skill and bravery in the Korean War and flying on seventy-eight combat missions. After ten years as a civilian test pilot, he was accepted, in September 1962, for astronaut training at Houston, Texas. On 16 March 1966 he was co-pilot of the Gemini 8 spacecraft which made the first docking in outer space. In January 1969 he was selected for intensive preparations for a flight to the moon, with Edwin Aldrin (1930–) and Michael Collins (1930–) sharing the training programme with him. After blast-off from Cape Kennedy on 16 July 1969, Armstrong landed the lunar module 'Eagle' in the Sea of Tranquillity on the moon on 20 July 1969, commenting as he went down a ladder to the moon's surface, 'That's one small step for a man, one great leap for mankind.' After fifteen hours' scientific study on the moon, Armstrong and Aldrin rejoined Collins in the 'Eagle', splashing down in the Pacific three days later. The returned astronauts were accorded a welcome as national heroes. Armstrong was sent on what were, in effect, US propaganda missions to several countries and during the Christmas season of 1969 he travelled to Vietnam on a trip intended to boost morale among American troops engaged in their fifth year of war. He accepted a professorship in aerospace engineering at the University of Cincinnati in 1971. Tim Furniss: *One Small Step* (Sparkford, 1989); US Government: *Astronauts and Cosmonauts* (Washington, 1985).

Arnold, Henry Harley (1886–1950), Chief of the US Army Air Force in the Second World War: born in Pennsylvania and graduated from the Military Academy at West Point in 1907. He was a pioneer airman among army officers, learning to fly from Orville Wright himself. In 1938 he became Chief of the Army Air Corps, immediately initiating an accelerated programme of aircraft manufacture and schemes for training civilian pilots as cadets. He believed in the power of massive bomber formations to influence strategy as effectively as the threat of an invading army. Throughout the war he was a member of the Joint Chiefs of Staff team and was promoted to full General in 1944. Three years later his long advocacy of independence for the Air Corps from the US army was successful and he was given the rare 'five-star General' rank, equivalent to a Marshal in other armies. More than any other individual, General Arnold was responsible for making the US Army Air Force of 1945 the most powerful military striking force in the world. H.H. Arnold: *Global Missions* (New York, 1951); F.O. Dupre: *Hap Arnold, Architect of American Air Power* (New York, 1972).

Arthur, Chester Alan (1830–86), President of the United States from 1881 to 1885: born at Fairfield, Vermont, the son of a Baptist minister from Ulster. He practised law in New York City where he was active in the Republican Party and was rewarded with the remunerative post of customs collector for the port of New York. His use of this position for political corruption led President Hayes and the Senate to demand his removal in July 1878. But the New York Republicans insisted Arthur was a martyr to the party cause and he was selected as running-mate to GARFIELD for the election of 1880. When President Garfield died within six months of his inauguration, Arthur succeeded him and held office from September 1881 to March 1885. As President he behaved circumspectly, raising the social tone of the White House, showing independence of the party bosses, exposing frauds in the Post Office Department, and in 1883 securing enactment of the first reform intended to clean up the Civil Service. Resentment at his reforming zeal made the Republicans look elsewhere for their candidate for the 1884 campaign, which was won by the Democrat, GROVER CLEVELAND. Chester Arthur died eighteen months after the end of his presidency. G.F. Howe: *Chester A. Arthur; a Quarter Century of Machine* (New York, 1957); T.C. Reeves: *Gentleman Boss* (New York, 1957).

Asquith, Herbert Henry (1852–1928), British Prime Minister from 1908 to 1916: born in Morley, Yorkshire, the son of a cloth manufacturer. He was educated at the City of London School and

Balliol College, Oxford, and was called to the bar when he was 24. In 1886 he was elected Liberal MP for East Fife, a constituency he represented for thirty-two years. GLADSTONE brought him into the Cabinet as Home Secretary and he inherited the traditions of Gladstonian liberalism, basing his conduct of policy on what he regarded as moral imperatives. But, unlike other Liberal politicians, Asquith married into 'smart' society, in 1894 taking as his second wife Margot Tennant (1864–1945), an extrovert hostess with strong prejudices, a sharp mind and a ready tongue. From the summer of 1895 until December 1905 Asquith was out of office, differing from many members of the party in being strongly anti-Boer during the South African War of 1899–1902. From December 1905 until the spring of 1908 he was Chancellor of the Exchequer under CAMPBELL-BANNERMAN, whose ill-health left Asquith with many opportunities for dominating debates in the Commons. He was a natural successor as Prime Minister when 'C-B' finally resigned (3 April 1908). The social reforms of Asquith's premiership were overshadowed by bitter parliamentary disputes with the House of Lords, which began with the 'People's Budget' of LLOYD GEORGE in 1909. They culminated in the Parliament Act of 1911, which deprived the Lords of all power over money bills and restricted the right of the upper house to veto legislation passed in the Commons. The militant suffragette movement, led by Mrs PANKHURST, challenged Asquith's fundamental principles and was answered by harsh treatment which horrified public opinion. But Asquith was also faced by syndicalist violence from some trade unions and by a virtual rebellion in Ulster against his government's proposals for Irish Home Rule (1913–14). This widespread unrest weakened the effectiveness of his administration. He was, moreover, Prime Minister through four major international crises: the Austro-Hungarian annexation of Bosnia-Herzegovina in 1908; the German naval presence at Agadir in Morocco in 1911; the Balkan Wars of 1912–13; and, finally, the assassination of Francis FERDINAND at Sarajevo in 1914, the event which precipitated the First World War. Asquith remained Prime Minister for the first twenty-eight months of the war (in which one of his sons was killed and another gravely injured). He was not a dynamic wartime leader. In May 1915 he headed a coalition government, but the Conservatives thought him indiscreet and he was ousted in December 1916 in favour of Lloyd George. The subsequent feud between the supporters of Asquith and Lloyd George weakened the Liberal Party in the immediate post-war period. Asquith lost his seat at East Fife in 1918 and was out of Parliament until 1920, when he was elected for Paisley. In 1923 he was again accepted as leader of the Liberal Party, but he was defeated at Paisley in October 1924, when he accepted a peerage (Earl of Oxford and Asquith). He retired from party politics in October 1926, and died sixteen months later. H.H. Asquith: *Memories and Reflections* (2 vols) (1938); R. Jenkins: *Asquith* (1964).

Assad, Hafez al- (Hafiz al-Wahsh) (1930–), President of Syria: was born into a peasant family of the minority Shi'ite sect of 'Alawi at Qardaha, in northwestern Syria. After secondary schooling in Latakia, he joined the Ba'ath socialist party in 1947, entered Homs military academy in 1952 and trained as an airman. From 1958 to 1961 he commanded a night fighter squadron defending Cairo, where he developed a great admiration for NASSER. With the Ba'ath military *coup* in Damascus in February 1966, Assad entered poltics, serving as Minister of Defence until 1970; when he became Prime Minister and, in March 1971, President. A new constitution in 1973 strengthened presidential authority on the model of Nasser's Egypt. His foreign policy favoured a Greater Syria, with Damascus co-ordinating Arab policies towards Israel. American and western European assumptions that he supported terrorism lessened from 1987 onwards; his suspicion of Saddam Hussein's Iraq modified his hostility towards Israel in 1991, a year in which he also helped secure the release of hostages seized in Lebanon. He was re-elected President in 1978 and, despite a heart attack in 1983, he gained further electoral victories in 1985 and December 1991. P. Seale: *Asad of Syria* (1988); M. Ma'oz: *Asad: The Sphinx of Damascus* (1988); M.E. Yapp: *The Near East Since the First World War* (1991).

Atatürk: see *Kemal, Mustafa*.

Attlee, Clement Richard (1883–1967), British Prime Minister from 1945 to 1951: born in Putney, Surrey, the son of a London solicitor who sent him to Haileybury and to University College, Oxford. In 1905, while reading for the bar, Attlee helped to run a boys' club for the poor of Stepney in London's East End. This experience induced him to become a socialist and join the Independent Labour Party in 1907. From 1914 to 1919 he served in the South Lancashire Regiment, seeing action on Gallipoli, in Mesopotamia and on the Western Front, and attaining the rank of Major. In 1919 and 1920 he served as the first Labour Mayor of Stepney, and in 1922 was elected as Labour MP for neighbouring Limehouse, a constituency he represented until the seat was abolished in 1950. Under MACDONALD Attlee was Under-Secretary of State for War in 1924, Chancellor of the Duchy of Lancaster in 1930 and Postmaster-General in 1931, but he never sat in MacDonald's Cabinet. He refused to join the National Government of 1931, serving LANSBURY as deputy leader of the rump of the Labour Party in opposition. On Lansbury's retirement in 1935 Attlee was elected party leader, narrowly defeating Herbert MORRISON on the second ballot. Attlee's parliamentary stature increased considerably in the following five years: he was a shrewd and decisive chairman, who could keep moderates and Leftists in partnership; he was an able parliamentary manager; and he soon acquired standing in European affairs, notably by his backing for the Spanish government in its fight against the fascism of FRANCO (Attlee visited the International Brigade fighting on the Guadalquivir at the height of the Spanish Civil War, December 1937).

In May 1940 Attlee led the Labour Party into coalition, serving as Lord Privy Seal in the War Cabinet under Winston CHURCHILL and becoming Deputy Prime Minister and Dominions Secretary in February 1942. As soon as the war in Europe ended Churchill proposed to Attlee that the coalition should continue until final victory over Japan was achieved, a task taking, perhaps, eighteen months. Attlee was prepared to support a coalition until the autumn of 1945, but insisted that there should be a General Election before the end of the year. Churchill favoured an early election: the coalition formally ended on 23 May; the election was held on 5 July and gave Labour a huge parliamentary majority. Attlee became Prime Minister on 27 July 1945. He had already attended the first sessions of the Potsdam Conference as an observer: he returned there as principal British spokesman. Japan surrendered less than three weeks after Attlee became Prime Minister.

In home affairs Attlee presided over changes long advocated by the Labour Party, such as the nationalization of the principal public services (gas, coal, steel, electricity and the railways) and the introduction by BEVAN of a National Health Service. In foreign affairs he supported the efforts of BEVIN to retain an

American interest in Europe through the creation of NATO and he accepted British obligations to fight in Korea. Attlee personally speeded up negotiations over the independence of India and Pakistan. His dry manner and his dislike of rhetorical flamboyance cost him popularity among the electorate, and his parliamentary majority was cut to five after he called a General Election in May 1950. Ill-health was by now weakening his hold on his Cabinet, where the Left sought a more specifically socialist programme – something only possible with a larger majority. Attlee's attempt to improve his position by holding a General Election in October 1951 rebounded: Labour was narrowly defeated, and Attlee became Leader of the Opposition until December 1955 when he retired from the Commons (he had represented West Walthamstow since 1950) and accepted a peerage. Earl Attlee was succeeded as leader of the Labour Party by Hugh GAITSKELL. In 1951 King GEORGE VI bestowed on Attlee the Order of Merit, an honour accorded at that time to only one previous British Prime Minister, Churchill. C. Attlee: *As It Happened* (1954); K. Harris: *Attlee* (1982).

Aung San Suu Kyi (1945–), Burmese democratic leader: born in Rangoon, the daughter of General Aung San, who, after supporting the Japanese in 1942, led a guerrilla army against them and co-operated closely with ATTLEE and MOUNTBATTEN to secure Burma's independence; he became Burma's Prime Minister but was assassinated at a Cabinet meeting in Rangoon in July 1947. His daughter was educated at English schools in Rangoon, at Delhi and at St Hugh's College, Oxford; she married a fellow Oxonian, Michael Aris, in 1972, after working for two years for the UN Secretariat. She then taught at Bhutan and at Kyoto and Simla Universities and completed a biography of her father, not returning to Burma until 1988. Soon afterwards the leader of the armed forces, General Saw Maung, assumed power (offically changing Burma's name to Myanmar in June 1989). Aung San Suu Kyi's family prestige and personal qualities made her a natural leader of the National League for Democracy (NLD), but in July 1989 the dictatorial regime placed her under house arrest. Even so, the NLD won multiparty elections held in May 1990. The Myanmar authorities, however, refused to transfer power to the elected government and continued to hold Aung San Suu Kyi in detention, ignoring international condemnation of such conduct. Even when she was awarded the Nobel Peace Prize for 1991, Aung San Suu Kyi remained under house arrest until 10 July 1995. Aung San Suu Kyi: *Freedom for Peace and Other Writings (1991)*; B. Lintner: *Aung San Suu Kyi and Burma's Unfinished Renaissance* (Clayton, Victoria, Australia, 1991).

Avon, Earl of: see *Eden, Anthony*.

Awolowo, Obafemi (1909–84), Chief, Nigerian political leader: born at Ikenne, in the Ogun region, the son of a Yoruba farmer. While working as a teacher and (later) a journalist, he studied for a bachelor's degree in commerce and in 1943 helped establish the Nigerian Trade Union Congress before coming to England to study law. As founder of the Action Group he emerged as leader of the Yoruba people of western Nigeria, becoming premier of the region in 1951 and introducing comprehensive educational reforms. As leader of the opposition in the federal assembly 1959–62 he criticized policies which favoured the Ibo and Hausa peoples at the expense of the Yoruba. In 1962 Prime Minister BALEWA (a Hausa) alleged that Chief Awolowo was implicated in a treasonable conspiracy and he was sentenced to ten years' imprisonment. He was released by GOWON in 1966 after Balewa's assassination and served as Commissioner for

Finance in the Gowon administration, but stood aside from political life from 1971 until 1978, when he founded the Unity Party of Nigeria. Chief Awolowo unsuccessfully contested the presidential elections of 1979 and 1983. He continued to work for improved education in Nigeria; he was appointed Grand Commander of the Federal Republic in 1980 and, after his death, the University of Ife was renamed in his honour. O. Awolowo: *Thoughts on the Nigerian Constitution* (Oxford, 1968); M. Crowder and G. Abdullahi: *Nigeria, an Introduction to its History* (1979).

Ayub Khan, Mohammad (1907–74); Pakistani soldier and President: born at Abbotabad, the son of an NCO in the (British) Indian Army. He completed his schooling at the Muslim university of Aligarh and became a cadet at the Royal Military Academy, Sandhurst, receiving a commission in 1928. Distinguished service against the Japanese in Burma won him high regard from MOUNTBATTEN and he became Pakistan's second senior General when the dominion as created. Promotion continued: he was Pakistan's first Commander-in-Chief in 1951, combining the post with Minister of Defence in October 1954 and receiving his Field Marshal's baton. Four years later President Mirza imposed martial law on Pakistan, appointed the Field Marshal as martial law administrator and, on 28 October 1958, handed executive powers over to him. President Ayub Khan's authority received retrospective electoral backing in February 1960 and he remained President until 25 March 1969, a longer term than any other head of state in Pakistan's first half-century. Ayub Khan carried through limited land reforms and imposed what he called 'basic democracies', a form of devolved responsibility which became unpopular, especially in East Pakistan, because of its militaristic, repressive character. He rapidly lost prestige in 1965 when the Pakistan Army was checked in fighting against India, both in the Ran of Kutch area and in Kashmir. Student protests became so riotous in the winter of 1968–9 that the army leaders induced him to hand over the presidency to General Yahaya Khan (1907–80, President 1969–71) and retire into private life. M. Ayub Khan: *Friends, not Masters* (1967); L. Ziring: *The Ayub Khan Era in Pakistan* (Syracuse, New York, 1971).

Azaña, Manuel (1880–1940), President of Spain throughout the Civil War of 1936–9: born in Alcala de Henares, twenty miles north of Madrid, became a civil servant and a literary journalist. When he was 44 the secret police arrested him as a founder-member of the Spanish Republican Party, but he was soon released. He became Minister of War in May 1931, after the flight of ALFONSO XIII, and head of the Republican Government from December 1931 to September 1933. In the spring of 1936 he was the principal Popular Front candidate for the presidency of the Republic, and was sworn in as head of state ten weeks before FRANCO and other dissident generals plunged Spain into civil war. It was difficult for President Azaña to keep the anti-Franco Republicans united, for they included liberals, democratic socialists, communists and anarchists. When, in the winter of 1938–9, Franco's military success seemed assured, Azaña vainly sought foreign mediation to check the bloodshed in Spain. He fled to France in February 1939, dying there a year later. F. Sedwick: *Tragedy of Manuel Azaña and the Fate of the Spanish Republic* (Columbus, Ohio, 1963); R. Carr: *Spain, 1808–1939* (Oxford, 1966).

Azikiwe, Nnamdi (1904–), first President of independent Nigeria: born a member of the Ibo tribe, at Zungeri in northern Nigeria and educated at American universities. From 1937 he conducted a propaganda campaign in favour of Nigerian nationalism, using his wealth as a banker to finance a newspaper chain. He was principal director of the African Continental Bank and his standing ensured that when Nigeria became independent in 1960 he should be a natural choice as Governor-General, succeeding to the presidency of the Republic when it was proclaimed in October 1963. The central authority within Nigeria was weakened by tribal divisions, some tribes looking down contemptuously on the Ibo, and civilian government was overthrown by a military *coup* in January 1966. The officers, most of whom were Ibo, did not harm Azikiwe but forced his retirement into private life. He returned to federal politics in 1978 as leader of the Nigerian People's Party and stood in the presidential elections of 1979, 1983 and 1986 before retiring again to his home at Nsukka. N. Azikiwe: *My Odyssey, an Autobiography* (1970); A. Igwe: *Azikiwe, the Philosopher of Our Time* (Enugu, 1992).

B

Baader, Andreas (1943–77), West German anarchist: born in Munich, drifted from normal state schooling through a phase of adolescent revolt into violent anarchism. With Ulrike MEINHOF he led the *Rote Armee Fraktion* ('Red Army Group'), a band of urban guerrillas responsible for a series of terrorist outrages in the Federal German Republic from 1970 to 1972. The Baader–Meinhof group was the most notorious product of the student protest movement, which was especially militant in France and Germany in 1968. Baader rejected the capitalist affluence of West Germany's economic miracle and sought the withdrawal of American forces from Europe as a first step towards the radical reconstruction of society. Before Baader became associated with Meinhof he had been imprisoned for setting fire to a department store in Frankfurt in April 1968. He was rescued in May 1970, while working under police guard in a library, in an action directed by Meinhof, but re-arrested in June 1972. With two assistants Baader was convicted of murder, bombings and bank raids and he was sentenced to life imprisonment in April 1977. An attempt to secure his release by holding airline hostages at Mogadishu was thwarted by German long-range police commandos who freed the hostages in a dramatic descent on Mogadishu airport (18 October 1977). The West German authorities announced that, on hearing news of what had happened at Mogadishu, Andreas Baader and his two associates killed themselves while held in Stammheim Jail, Stuttgart. J. Bicker: *Hitler's Children, the Story of the Baader–Meinhof Gang* (1977); E. Kolinsky: *Parties, Opposition and Society in West Germany* (1984).

Baden-Powell, Robert Stephenson Smyth (1857–1941), British soldier and founder of the scouting movement: born in London, the son of a mathematics professor at Oxford University. He was educated at Charterhouse, subsequently entering the army and serving in India and Afghanistan. Colonel Baden-Powell first attracted attention by the skill with which he organized the policing of the countryside around Bulawayo after a rising of the Matabele in 1896. In October 1899 he was in command of a small force garrisoning the town of Mafeking when it was surrounded by 10,000 Boers under General Cronje. Baden-Powell improvised the defence of Mafeking so effectively that the town withstood a siege of 217 days. News of the relief of Mafeking (17 May 1900) unleashed wild celebrations in London: Baden-Powell was promoted to Major-General and, later, knighted. His prestige helped spread his enthusiasm for 'scouting', a belief that boys should be trained to use their initiative in worthwhile leisure-time activities. Sir Robert Baden-Powell produced his book *Scouting for Boys* in 1906 and the first scout troops were started a year later. By 1909 he was able to inspect 11,000 Boy Scouts at a jamboree at the Crystal Palace, London. A parallel movement, the Girl Guides, was set up by Sir Robert and his sister in 1909–10. The scouting movement spread rapidly overseas: it was established in America by Daniel C. Beard (1850–1941) in 1910.

Probably the movement was at its peak of influence in the 1920s and 1930s, Sir Robert continuing to take a wide interest in its spread throughout the world. His part in its development was recognized by conferment of a peerage in 1929. Seventy years after its foundation the scout movement could claim a membership of thirteen-and-a-half million in over a hundred countries of the world. E. E. Reynolds: *Baden-Powell* (Oxford, 1957); M. Rosenthal: *The Character Factory; Baden-Powell and the Origins of the Boy Scout Movement* (1986).

Badoglio, Pietro (1871–1956), Italian soldier, Prime Minister from 1943 to 1944: born in Piedmont, at Grassano Monferrato. He served in the artillery, seeing action in the Adowa campaign against the Ethiopians in 1896 and against the Turks in Tripoli in 1911. As a General he helped restore order after Italy's rout at Caporetto in 1917. After the war he received his Marshal's baton and was Governor-General of Libya from 1929 to 1933. He returned to Abyssinia in 1936, completing the conquest of the country and entering Addis Ababa in triumph on 5 May. In 1940 he was Chief of the General Staff. He opposed Italy's entry into the Second World War and strongly advised MUSSOLINI not to attempt the invasion of Greece. He resigned in disgust in December 1940 and thereafter became a cautious anti-fascist. By the winter of 1942–3 he had established contact with the Italian royal family and arranged with King VICTOR EMMANUEL III to take over power from Mussolini if it were possible for him to be arrested. Badoglio was duly appointed Prime Minister on 26 July 1943. Two months later in Malta he signed a formal document of surrender to the Allies and on 13 October 1943 he brought Italy into the war against Germany. He remained Prime Minister until the liberation of Rome in June 1944, retiring into private life when the anti-fascist politicians made it clear that they were not prepared to collaborate with the Marshal because of his earlier role in building up Italy's African empire. P. Badoglio: *Italy and the Second World War, Memoirs and Documents* (Greenwood, Conn., 1976); F. W. Deakin: *The Brutal Friendship* (1962).

Bakunin, Mikhail (1814–76), Russian aristocratic anarchist: born on family estates near Tver, commissioned in an Imperial Guard regiment but resigned from the army in disgust at his countrymen's treatment of Polish radical nationalists. By February 1848 he was in Paris and over the following eighteen months he helped encourage revolts in Prague and in Saxony. After many years spent in Prussian and Austrian prisons, he was handed over to the Russians who exiled him to Siberia in 1855. Six years later he escaped to western Europe where his rebellious and emotional temperament exasperated MARX and ENGELS. They complained that his negative anarchism disrupted the First International Workingmen's Association, especially between 1869 and 1872. Although he took part in anarchist revolts at Lyons (1870) and inspired anarchist disturbances in Spain soon afterwards, Bakunin was, above all, a Russian revolutionary. His claim that 'the passion for destruction is also a constructive passion' epitomized the muddled thinking of committed 'nihilists' in pre-Leninist Russia. E. H. Carr: *Michael Bakunin* (1937); J. Joll: *The Anarchists* (1964).

Balch, Emily Greene (1867–1961), American pacifist and internationalist: born in Massachusetts, she was one of the first graduates from Bryn Mawr, the college established in 1885 by Quakers in Pennsylvania to provide a liberal higher education for women. Emily Balch spent several years in social work at Boston before becoming in 1913 Professor of Economics and Social Science at the women's college of Wellesley in Massachusetts. By 1913 she was already well known as a pacifist leader. Her vigorous denunciation of war induced the trustees of Wellesley to insist on her resignation in 1918. A year later she founded the Women's League for Peace and Freedom and for the next quarter of a century devoted her efforts to encouraging mothers and wives of the various nations to put pressure on their governments to seek a peaceful solution to problems between the nations. Her work for international understanding was recognized when in 1946 she shared the Nobel Peace Prize with her fellow-countryman, the missionary pacifist John Raleigh Mott (1865–1955). M. M. Randall: *Improper Bostonian* (New York, 1964).

Baldwin, Stanley (1867–1947), British Prime Minister in 1923, from 1924 to 1929 and 1935 to 1937: born at Bewdley in Worcestershire and educated at Harrow and Trinity College, Cambridge. His father was an ironmaster and Conservative MP for Bewdley; the son succeeded him in the seat, representing Bewdley from 1908 until his retirement in 1937. Although Baldwin remained for eight years an undistinguished backbencher in the Commons, his subsequent rise to eminence was rapid. He held the influential post of Financial Secretary to the Treasury in the LLOYD GEORGE Coalition, coming into the Cabinet in April 1921 as President of the Board of Trade. His dislike of Lloyd George's warlike attitude towards Turkey in October 1922 induced him to resign from the Cabinet, precipitating the breakup of the Coalition. Baldwin's moderation and financial common sense appealed to important business circles. Under Bonar LAW, Baldwin showed himself, in six months of office, a competent Chancellor of the Exchequer and, when Law's health gave way, King GEORGE V sent for Baldwin rather than Lord CURZON to form the next Conservative government. When he failed to gain a clear majority in the General Election of 1923 Baldwin resigned, after a mere seven months of office. He was back in power in November 1924 forming a cautious Conservative government which moved slowly, for Baldwin liked to prepare public opinion, inclining the electorate to think as he did before taking actions which appeared to be in response to the will of the community. Conflict with the miners culminated in a General Strike in the spring of 1926, but his policy drove a wedge between the miners' leaders and other trade unionists. Rising unemployment, a recession in his own family business, personal worries, a tendency to spend long holidays abroad while seeking to appeal to the electorate as the most English of country squires – all these factors contributed to the defeat of Baldwin's Conservatism in the General Election of May 1929. Unexpectedly the grave economic crisis of 1931 brought Baldwin back into the government as Lord President of the Council in the National Coalition, headed by MACDONALD, from August 1931 to June 1935. During these years Baldwin particularly concerned himself (as an elder statesman without departmental responsibility) with imperial questions, notably the preparation of the Indian subcontinent for eventual independence. He was Prime Minister for two years from June 1935 to June 1937, tending to leave foreign affairs to EDEN and concentrating on the problems of the monarchy, especially the potentially dangerous constitutional crisis provoked by the obduracy of EDWARD VIII. He retired soon after the coronation of GEORGE VI and was succeeded by his Chancellor of the Exchequer, Neville CHAMBERLAIN. Baldwin accepted a peerage, sitting in the Lords as Earl Baldwin of Bewdley, saying little when he became a scapegoat for Britain's unpreparedness for war in 1939 and, in his last years, gaining satisfaction only from the honorific chancellorship of his old university. R. K. Middlemas and A. J. Barnes: *Baldwin, a Political Biography*

(1969); H. Montgomery Hyde: *Baldwin, the Unexpected Prime Minister* (1973).

Balewa, Alhaji Abubakar Tafawa (1912–66), Nigerian federal Prime Minister: born, a Hausa butcher's son, at Bauchi in Muslim north-central Nigeria. He was educated at Bauchi Middle School and Katsina Training College, becoming a teacher in 1932. Twelve years later he was appointed headmaster of his old school, but was awarded a scholarship to the London Institute of Education and, while in England in 1945, came into contact with pan-African students. On returning home as a school inspector, he entered politics as co-founder of Nigeria's Northern People's Congress, a party respected by the colonial authorities for its apparent efficiency and moderation. Tafawa Balewa joined the legislative assembly at Lagos in 1952 (the year in which he received an OBE), becoming Minister of Works and, later, Minister of Transport in the Federal Council of Ministers. In 1955 he was the first Nigerian minister to make an official visit to the United States. He went on pilgrimage to Mecca in 1957 and, in August that year, was appointed Prime Minister, with responsibility for establishing a democratic federal government in Lagos and, in partnership with AZIKIWE, guiding Nigeria to dominion status (October 1960) and independence within the Commonwealth (October 1963). His task was made harder by the discovery in 1958 of oilfields in southern (non-Muslim) Nigeria and resentment in the potentially wealthy south of alleged exploitation in favour of the Muslim north. The authorities in London continued to respect and honour Tafawa Balewa: a CBE in 1955 and a knighthood in 1960 were followed by admission to the Privy Council in 1961. Liberal critics, however, deplored his treatment of the Yoruba chief, AWOLOWO, and of the Hausa's old enemies, the Ibo people of western Nigeria. The task of promoting federal unity among such disparate peoples was beyond him. Adminstrative corruption, violent strikes and the spread of urban anarchy led to Tafawa Balewa's assassination on 14 January 1966 in the course of a military *coup*, of which Colonel GOWON became the eventual beneficiary. T. Clark: *A Right Honourable Gentleman, Abubakar from the Black Rock* (1991); M. Crowder and G. Abdullahi: *Nigeria, an Introduction to its History* (1979).

Balfour, Arthur James (1848–1930), British Prime Minister from 1902 to 1905 and thereafter an elder statesman: born at Whittingehame in East Lothian and educated at Eton and Trinity College, Cambridge. His mother was a sister of Lord SALISBURY. Balfour was a Conservative MP for forty-eight years, representing Hertford (1874–85), East Manchester (1885–1905) and after a three-week gap the City of London (1906–22). He served in the British delegation to the Congress of Berlin in 1878 as secretary to his uncle, then Foreign Secretary. Balfour entered the Cabinet in November 1886 as Secretary for Scotland, but made his reputation by the firmness with which he served as Irish Secretary from March 1887 to October 1891. For the last ten months of his uncle's second ministry, Balfour was First Lord of the Treasury, the post normally held by the Prime Minister but used in this instance to enable Balfour to act as chief government spokesman in the Commons. Balfour was again First Lord of the Treasury for Salisbury from June 1895 to July 1902, when he seemed the natural successor to his uncle as Prime Minister. The Balfour government of 1902–5 achieved little, apart from an education act and the successes of LANSDOWNE as Foreign Secretary. Internal disputes over tariff reform with Joseph CHAMBERLAIN weakened the party considerably and it was decisively defeated by the Liberals in the election of January 1906. Balfour remained leader of the Opposition until November 1911, when his apparent casualness in the conduct of business prompted the Conservatives to choose Bonar LAW as party leader. He came back to office as First Lord of the Admiralty in the ASQUITH coalition of 1915 and was Foreign Secretary under LLOYD GEORGE from 1916 to 1919. In this capacity he sent the formal open letter to Lord Rothschild of 2 November 1917 which is known as the 'Balfour Declaration', pledging British support for a Jewish national home in Palestine, provided safeguards were reached for the non-Jewish communities living there. At the Paris Peace Conference of 1919 he was second British plenipotentiary, and he represented Britain at the assembly of the League of Nations in 1920 and the Washington Conference over problems of the Pacific and of naval rivalry in 1921–2. In February 1922 he was created a Knight of the Garter, receiving an earldom (Earl Balfour) two months later. He served in the Cabinet under BALDWIN from April 1925 to June 1929, showing great interest in imperial affairs and the future of Palestine, but he was a sick man for the last two years of his life. Balfour, a bachelor, was one of the most intellectual of British statesmen. His apology for Christian faith, *A Defence of Philosophic Doubt*, was published when he was 31 and not yet a Member of Parliament. His *Foundations of Belief* (1895), aroused wide interest, and he also delivered the Gifford Lectures on 'Theism and Humanism' in 1914 and on 'Theism and Thought' in 1922–3. B. E. Dugdale: *A. J. Balfour* (2 vols) (1936); K. Young: *Arthur James Balfour* (1963).

Banda, Hastings Kamuzu (1907–), founding President of Malawi: born in the British Protectorate of Nyasaland and worked in the goldfields of the Rand before going to America. There he received a grounding in medical studies which were completed at the University of Edinburgh. For ten years Dr Banda was a general practitioner in north London. When he returned to Nyasaland shortly after his fiftieth birthday he organized the Malawi National Congress in opposition to the Central African Federation, a political entity created in 1953 which gave the white Rhodesians political and economic dominance of the later Zambia and Malawi as well as Zimbabwe-Rhodesia. Dr Banda was imprisoned as a dangerous agitator for twelve months (1959–60), but when the Federation broke up in 1963 he became Prime Minister of the self-governing colony of Nyasaland, presiding over the transformation of his country into the independent state of Malawi, established on 6 July 1964. Two years later Malawi became a republic within the Commonwealth and Dr Banda was elected President. He proved himself to be politically cautious in his relations with South Africa. Within Malawi he established a one-party state. He was sworn in as President for life on 6 July 1971, and in a sixteen-man government he retained personal control of the Ministries of Justice, Foreign Affairs, Agriculture and Natural Resources, and Works and Supplies. Financial pressure from abroad forced Banda to accept reforms in 1992–3 which led to his electoral defeat in May 1994 by Bakili Maluzi of the United Democratic Front. In January 1995 ex-President Banda was placed under house arrest for having allegedly ordered the murder of four political rivals in 1983; a jury acquitted him of this charge in December 1995. K. K. Virmani: *Dr Banda in the Making of Malawi* (Delhi, 1992); J. L. Lwanda: *Kamuzu Banda of Malawi* (Bothwell, 1993).

Bandaranaike, Mrs Sirimavo (*née* **Ratwatee**) (1916–), Sri Lankan Prime Minister: born, the daughter of a wealthy landowner, at Ratnapura, Ceylon. At the age of 24 she married the president of the Ceylon National Congress movement,

Solomon BANDARANAIKE. On his assassination in September 1959 she succeeded him as head of the Sri Lanka Freedom Party and parliamentary deputy for Attanagalla. The Party gained an overwhelming electoral victory in July 1960 and she became the world's first woman Prime Minister. Her attempts to promote Sinhalese cultural and linguistic predominance in the island and her policies of socialist nationalization of basic industries led to threats of a military *coup* and, in 1965, to electoral defeat. But in May 1970 she was returned to power, with a more radical programme, pledged to 'advance socialist democracy'. A new constitution in 1972 replaced the Dominion of Ceylon by the Republic of Sri Lanka, though remaining in the Commonwealth. Mounting discontent at the narrow power base of Mrs Bandaranaike's administration led to grave rioting and arson during the election campaign of July 1977, in which she was defeated by Julius Jaywardene's United National Party. Allegations of unconstitutional procedure by a parliamentary commission led to her disfranchisement in October 1980. She never recovered from this setback, although she stood as a presidential candidate in the 1988 Sri Lankan election. J. Manor: *Sri Lanka, in Change and Crisis* (1984); and see following entry.

Bandaranaike, Solomon West Ridgeway Dias (1899–1959), Sinhalese socialist leader: born in Colombo and educated locally and at Christ Church, Oxford, being called to the bar in 1925. Throughout the 1930s and 1940s he led the Ceylon National Congress movement favouring the political rights of the Sinhalese, which he saw denied to them both by the British and by the Hindu Tamils (who formed about a quarter of the total population). When Ceylon gained independence in 1948 Solomon Bandaranaike became Minister of Health, showing such effective authority that within three years his ministry had virtually stamped out malaria in the island. In 1951 he founded the Sri Lanka Freedom Party, a movement which was narrowly Sinhalese in composition and socialist in inspiration. Five years later (10 April 1956) he became Prime Minister of a United Front Government which ended the British military and naval presence in Ceylon but which provoked riots from the Tamils by attempting to insist that Sinhalese should be the only official language. In September 1959 Solomon Bandaranaike was assassinated. He was succeeded as leader of the Sri Lanka Freedom Party by his widow, Mrs Sirimavo BANDARANAIKE. S. W. R. D. Bandaranaike: *The Spinning Wheel and the Paddy Field* (1958); A. J. Wilson: *Politics in Sri Lanka 1947–71* (1974); J. Manor: *The Expedient Utopia: Bandaranaike in Ceylon* (1989).

Baruch, Bernard Mannes (1870–1965), American financier and presidential adviser: born in South Carolina into a New York Jewish family, and educated at the City College of New York. Shrewd investments enabled him to make a fortune on Wall Street before he was 30. His business energy induced President Woodrow WILSON to seek his help with manpower problems in the First World War and from 1917 to 1919 he enjoyed unprecedented economic powers as Director of the War Industries Board. He advised Wilson on economic matters at the Paris Peace Conference of 1919, presided over an agricultural commission established by President HARDING in 1922, returned to advise Franklin ROOSEVELT on manpower problems in the Second World War, and was appointed US spokesman on the UN Atomic Energy Commission by President TRUMAN in 1946. The 'Baruch Plan' of December 1946 amplified proposals made by Dean ACHESON for international control of fissionable material and for inspection of atomic plants in other countries. The plan was welcomed by most members of the United Nations but rejected by the Soviet Union, to whom Baruch was a suspect big-business man. It was Baruch who, in a speech to the legislature of South Carolina on 16 April 1947, coined the phrase 'cold war' ('Let us not be deceived – we are today in the midst of a cold war'). For more than thirty years he was a close friend of Winston CHURCHILL. B. M. Baruch: *Baruch* (2 vols) (New York, 1959, 1962); M. Rosenbloom: *Peace Through Strength* (New York, 1953).

Batista, Fulgencio (1901–73), President of Cuba from 1939 to 1944 and from 1952 to 1958: born in eastern Cuba and enrolled in the army. He had risen to the rank of Sergeant when, in September 1933, he led a military *coup* which installed Ramon San Martin as President. Batista, rapidly promoted to Colonel, was effective ruler of the country from 1933 onwards. At first he sought to establish a fascist-style corporative state but in 1937, possibly as a concession to American opinion, he permitted the foundation of alternative political parties and won an 'open' presidential election in 1939. After five years of office General Batista went into voluntary exile in the Dominican Republic, but on 10 March 1952 he returned to power by yet another military *coup*. His corrupt and oppressive dictatorship provoked armed resistance, led from 1956 by Fidel CASTRO. Batista's backing in the towns of Cuba fell away rapidly in the closing months of 1958 and on the last day of the year he fled to Santo Domingo. His reputation for ruthlessly inefficient government ensured that, once in exile, he faded from the political scene, too discredited even to receive encouragement from the anti-Castro lobby in Washington. E. A. Chester: *A Sergeant Named Batista* (New York, 1954); H. Thomas: *Cuba, or the Pursuit of Freedom* (1971), *The Cuban Revolution* (1977).

Bazaine, François-Achille (1811–88), Marshal of France under the Second Empire: born at Versailles, enlisted as a Private in 1831, transferring as a Sergeant to the Foreign Legion in 1832, being commissioned a year later. After active service in Algeria and Spain he reached the rank of Brigadier-General in the Crimea (1855) and commanded a division at the battle of Solferino in 1859. When, four years later, NAPOLEON III sent an expedition to Mexico so as to safeguard French bondholders against the radical government of JUAREZ, General Bazaine was in command. He sought to establish orderly rule on behalf of Napoleon's protégé, Emperor MAXIMILIAN but the French could not pacify the country and suffered more casualties from disease than from battle. Bazaine was ordered to bring his troops back to France in March 1867 when Napoleon feared intervention by the United States. During the Franco-Prussian War, Bazaine – created a Marshal in 1864 – commanded an army of some 180,000 men who were besieged in Metz and forced to surrender on 27 October 1870. After the war he was accused of treachery, court-martialled at Versailles in 1873 and sentenced to death. President MACMAHON commuted the sentence to twenty years' imprisonment. In August 1874 Bazaine made a daring escape from the island fortress of Ste Marguerite and spent his last years in Madrid. His misfortunes won Bazaine some sympathy from contemporaries and historians, much as did the fate of Marshal PÉTAIN seventy years later. Bazaine's champions maintain he was a scapegoat both for the general military inefficiency of France in 1870 and for the failure of other field commanders who came from more distinguished families. P. Guedalla: *The Two Marshals* (1941); M. Howard: *The Franco-Prussian War* (1960).

Beaconsfield, Lord: see *Disraeli*.

Beatty, David (1871–1936), British Admiral distinguished for his actions in the North Sea from 1914 to 1916: born at Nantwich, Cheshire, entered the Royal Navy in 1884, scraping wretchedly through every paper examination. He saw action with the Nile flotilla under KITCHENER from 1896 to 1898, gaining the DSO by his enterprise. After serving, mainly on land, in the relief of the Peking Legations during the Boxer Rising of 1900, he was given command of a battleship and became a Rear-Admiral at the age of 38. In 1912 he served as Naval Secretary to the First Lord of the Admiralty, Winston CHURCHILL, who was impressed by Beatty's energy and panache (and by his sociability and excellence at polo). Beatty was given command of the First Battle Cruiser Squadron in 1913, knighted in 1914, promoted to Vice-Admiral in 1915 and appointed Commander-in-Chief of the Grand Fleet in November 1916. He was created an Earl, promoted Admiral of the Fleet in 1919, and ended his naval career as First Sea Lord from 1919 to 1927. Beatty's reputation as the 'Nelson of the battle-cruisers' rests on three actions: his decisive intervention in the later phases of the battle of Heligoland Bight on 28 August 1914; his initiative in giving chase (at 29 knots) to a German squadron off the Dogger Bank on 24 January 1915, a running battle in which his flagship, *Lion*, was crippled; and the way in which he enticed the German High Seas Fleet towards the British Grand Fleet under JELLICOE at Jutland on 31 May 1916. Critics maintain that he took tactical risks and failed to keep his squadron in cohesive formation. He looked upon battle-cruisers as a heavy brigade of naval cavalry. His intrepidity at sea in *Lion* was in marked contrast to his caution as Commander-in-Chief responsible for the fleet as a whole. W. S. Chalmers: *The Life and Letters of David, Earl Beatty* (1951); C. Beatty: *Our Admiral* (1980).

Beaverbrook, Lord (William Maxwell Aitken) (1879–1964), British newspaper tycoon and member of the War Cabinet from 1940 to 1942: born in Maple, Ontario, the son of a Presbyterian minister. He accumulated a personal fortune, largely from cement mills, before emigrating to England in September 1910. Under the patronage of the Conservative leader Bonar LAW (whose family origins were similar to those of Aitken) he entered British politics, sitting as Conservative MP for Ashton-under-Lyme from December 1910 to December 1916, receiving a knighthood in June 1911. From May 1915 he was on the Western Front, as an observer of the Canadian Army, but remained in close touch with Westminster politics and helped reconcile his fellow-Conservatives to the emergence of LLOYD GEORGE as Prime Minister in 1916. In January 1917 Aitken received a baronetcy, taking the title Beaverbrook. He was Chancellor of the Duchy of Lancaster and Minister of Information in 1918. Between the wars he concentrated on the 'Beaverbrook Press', remaining a firm champion of the British Empire in the *Daily Express* (which he had purchased in the winter of 1916–17 and which he built up into the daily newspaper with the biggest circulation in the world). He also owned the *Sunday Express* (from 1921) and the London *Evening Standard* (from 1929). The newspapers reflected his strong prejudices – against anyone favouring the breakup of Britain's Indian Empire, against BALDWIN, for 'Empire Free Trade', for Winston CHURCHILL and for EDWARD VIII until, as Duke of Windsor, he visited HITLER (towards whom Beaverbrook, unlike other newspaper proprietors, was consistently hostile). Churchill, a close friend, appointed Beaverbrook Minister of Aircraft Production in May 1940. Beaverbrook's drive more than doubled the output of aircraft in three months. He was Minister of Supply (1941–2) and Lord Privy Seal

(1943–5), conducting vital talks with the Russians in Moscow in 1941 and supervising Lend-Lease administration in the United States in 1942. He remained actively concerned with the running of his newspapers until his death from cancer in June 1964. A. J. P. Taylor: *Beaverbrook* (1972); A. Chisholm and M. Davie: *Beaverbrook, a Life* (1992).

Begin, Menachem (1913–92), Israeli Prime Minister: born in Brest-Litovsk, Russian Poland, and educated at Warsaw University, playing a prominent part in the Polish Jewish Youth Movement on the eve of the Second World War. After the Soviet occupation of Brest-Litovsk in September 1939 he was arrested and spent several months in 1940–1 in a Siberian concentration camp. He reached Palestine early in 1942 and was associated with the extremist Zionist group, Irgun Zvai Leumi, of which he became nominal Commander-in-Chief. During the years 1946–8 Irgun claimed responsibility for more than 200 terrorist operations against Arabs and British, the most notorious being the blowing up of the King David Hotel in Jerusalem on 22 July 1946 with the loss of ninety-one lives. In 1948 Begin entered the Knesset as a member of the Herut (Freedom) Party and wrote some memoirs of his Irgun activities, which appeared in book form a year later. He was a member of the parliamentary opposition until 1967 when he joined Levi Eshkol's government as a minister without portfolio. Three years later he was back in opposition to Golda MEIR and in 1973 he became joint chairman of a right-wing alliance party known as Likud (Unity) which won the General Election of May 1977. On 21 June 1977 Begin was installed as Israel's sixth Prime Minister (all of whom had been born, like himself, in Russian Poland except his immediate predecessor, Yitzhak RABIN). Begin's premiership saw an intensification of Israel's struggle on her northern border with Lebanon and the easing of relations with Egypt. In November 1977 Begin received the Egyptian President, Anwar el-SADAT, in Tel Aviv and began a series of meetings aimed at the signature of an Israeli–Egyptian peace treaty. These culminated in a visit by Begin and Sadat to Camp David in Maryland, 5–17 September 1978, where under the chairmanship of President CARTER a settlement was worked out which provided for normal diplomatic and economic relations to be established between the two states. Begin shared the Nobel Peace Prize for 1978 with Sadat. After gaining a narrow electoral victory in 1981 he retired from politics in September 1983. Sasson Sofar: *Begin, an Anatomy of Leadership* (Oxford, 1988); D. Peretz: *The Government and Politics of Israel* (Boulder, Colo., 1983); I. Peleg: *Begin's Foreign Policy 1977–1983* (1987).

Ben Bella, Mohammed Ahmed (1916–), founding President of Algeria: born at Maghnia, on the Algerian–Moroccan frontier. After service in the French Army, he organized from 1947 onwards an extremist group of Algerian nationalists, the 'Special Organization', seeking an end to French colonial rule. He was arrested by the French in 1950 but in March 1952 escaped and settled in Cairo where he founded the Algerian National Liberation Front (FLN) which began a guerrilla war against the French military and administrative authorities on 1 November 1954. In October 1956 the French induced a Moroccan airliner, in which Ben Bella and five other prominent nationalists were passengers, to land at Algiers. All six were arrested and interned in metropolitan France. Their removal left the FLN under the control of extremists, and the Algerian War dragged on savagely for another five years. In March 1962 President DE GAULLE released Ben Bella to take part in discussions with the French Prime Minister, Georges POMPIDOU, at Evian. Agreements were reached on a ceasefire, followed by independence and the withdrawal of French forces. Ben Bella became Prime Minister of the provisional Algerian government set up in September 1962 and, despite the opposition of rivals who had come to the forefront while he was interned, he was duly elected as the first President of the Algerian Republic in April 1963. His government sought to follow the Arab socialist principles of NASSER in Egypt, but Ben Bella remained suspicious of Soviet interest in Algeria and was more critical of pan-Arab policies than were many leaders of the Algerian Army. On 19 June 1965 Ben Bella was overthrown in a military *coup* led by Colonel BOUMÉDIENNE, Commander of the Algerian People's Army. For fourteen years the fallen President was kept under house arrest at M'Sila, in the mountains south west of Algiers. After the death of Boumédienne in December 1978, President Chadli's Government eased the restrictions on Ben Bella and he was freed from house arrest on 3 July 1979 and was then exiled to France. The restoration of a pluralist electoral system in Algeria in 1989 prompted him to return to Algiers as leader of the Movement for a Democratic Algeria (MDA). But in the local elections of 1990 the MDA failed to meet the modern Islamic radical challenge of the Islamic Salvation Front (FIS) and Ben Bella was unable to make the political comeback for which he had hoped. A. Horne: *A Savage War of Peace, Algeria, 1954–1962* (1977); D. C. Gordon: *North Africa's French Legacy, 1954–1962* (Cambridge, Mass., 1962); W. B. Quandt: *Revolution and Political Leadership, Algeria 1954–1968* (Cambridge, Mass., 1969).

Benedict XV (Giacomo della Chiesa) (1854–1922), Pope from 1914 to 1922: born at Pegli, near Genoa, and ordained in 1876, spending most of his early years in the papal diplomatic service either in Madrid or in the Vatican. He became Archbishop of Bologna in 1907 and succeeded PIUS X as Pope in September 1914. In April 1916 and in August and September 1917 he made vigorous efforts to end the First World War by mediation, and he denounced every fresh inhumanity brought into the fighting; but he left little mark on the Church or on the form of the new Europe shaped by the Paris Peace Conference of 1919. He died in Rome on 22 January 1922. W. H. Peters: *The Life of Benedict XV* (Milwaukee, Wisc., 1959); H. E. G. Rope: *Benedict XV, the Pope of Peace* (1941).

Beneš, Eduard (1884–1948), Czechoslovak statesman: born into a peasant family at Kozlany in Bohemia. His academic brilliance enabled him to pass on from Prague University to the University of Paris where he took his doctorate in sociology. In 1915 he escaped from Austria-Hungary, joining Thomaš MASARYK in exile and assisting him to interest eminent Frenchmen in supporting the cause of Czechoslovak independence. From 1918 to 1935 Beneš served as Czechoslovak Foreign Minister, developing close links with France, the Soviet Union, Romania and Yugoslavia and taking a prominent part in League of Nations affairs. In December 1935 Beneš succeeded Masaryk as President of Czechoslovakia but he resigned after the Munich Agreement of September 1938 which, by transferring one-third of the Czechoslovak people to German, Polish or Hungarian rule, seemed to him a betrayal of the republic created, with the backing of the West, in 1918. Beneš settled in London after the outbreak of the Second World War, forming a provisional Czechoslovak government in exile which received recognition by the British on 18 July 1941. From 1943 onwards his policy was regarded with suspicion by both the British and the Americans since he sought to act as interpreter of the 'Anglo-Americans' to the Russians and of the Russians to the Anglo-Americans. In March 1945 he flew from London to Moscow and followed the Czechoslovak Corps attached to the Red Army back through Slovakia to Prague where, in May, he once more assumed presidential powers. He held office for three more years, seeking to keep the presidency free from the mounting communist control which GOTTWALD imposed on Czechoslovakia. On 6 June 1948 Beneš recognized that Gottwald wished to turn the republic into a Stalinist state; he resigned office and died, broken in spirit, twelve weeks later. E. Beneš: *My War Memoirs* (1928), *Memoirs of Dr Eduard Beneš, from Munich to New War and New Victory* (1954); M. Kaplan: *The Communist Coup in Czechoslovakia* (Princeton, N.J., 1960); A. Palmer: *The Lands Between* (1969).

Ben Gurion, David (1886–1974), Israeli Prime Minister from 1948 to 1953 and 1955 to 1963: born in Plonsk, Russian Poland, under the name of David Green. He emigrated to Palestine at the age of 20 and became a Zionist while working on farming settlements, subsequently studying law at the universities of Constantinople and Salonika. His Zionism led the Turks to expel him from all lands subject to the Sultan's rule and in 1915 he joined a Jewish battalion in the British Army fighting to free Palestine from the Turks. His socialist beliefs prompted him to serve as Secretary-General in the Jewish Labour Federation within mandated Palestine. By 1930 he was leader of the Mapai Socialist Party and from 1935 to 1948 was Chairman of the Jewish Agency, the principal representative institution of the Jewish community during the years of British mandate. Ben Gurion gained administrative experience in local self-government, promoted Jewish settlement and handled delicate relations between his community and the British High Commission. Since the Agency formed a nucleus for the future government of Israel, Ben Gurion was well suited to become Israel's first Prime Minister when the state was proclaimed in May 1948. Conflict with the Arabs prevented complete fulfilment of the ambitious industrial and agrarian programme he had prepared in the months before independence, but much was achieved in the development of mineral resources (copper, phosphates, potash and natural gas), the construction of new public works (such as the port of Eilat) and an increase in the yield of citrus fruits for export. Ben Gurion retired in 1963, but two years later he returned to active politics, joining a militant breakaway group from the Mapai Party made uneasy by the policies of Golda MEIR. He died, honoured as a founding father of the state of Israel. S. Teveth: *Ben Gurion, the Burning Ground 1886–1948* (Boston, Mass., 1987); M. Bar Zohar: *The Armed Prophet* (1967).

Benn, Tony (1925–), British Labour politician: born, in London, when his father William Wedgwood Benn (1877–1960) was a Liberal MP who later joined the Labour Party, was Indian Secretary under MACDONALD and accepted a peerage, as Viscount Stansgate, in 1942. Anthony Wedgwood Benn was educated at Westminster School and New College, Oxford, and served in both the RAF and the Royal Navy. He was elected Labour MP for Bristol South-East in 1950 and in 1957 joined the Fabian Society executive. As heir to a peerage he was automatically debarred from the Commons on his father's death, though he had tried to renounce the succession in 1955. He refused to regard himself as the second Viscount Stansgate, offered himself for re-election as an MP on 4 May 1961, and doubled his majority. Even so, he could not take his seat in the Commons, an Election Court declaring his Conservative opponent elected. Accordingly he instigated a movement which, on 31 July 1963, secured enactment of a bill allowing peers to renounce inherited titles; three weeks later, having formally disclaimed his title, he was re-elected for Bristol South-East, which he represented until 1983, when the constituency boundaries were redrawn. He was Postmaster-General 1964–6, Minister of Technology 1966–70, Secretary of State for Industry 1974–5, and Secretary of State for Energy 1975–9. His radical socialism intensified during the 1970s: he dropped his double-barrelled surname, preferring the simpler 'Tony Benn', and emerged as leader of the 'New Left', favouring constitutional reform, opposing the EEC, and seeking more influence for constituency members on the shaping of party policies and the election of the leader. He failed in contests for the deputy leadership, although he remained a constituency favourite at party conferences. He returned to the Commons as MP for Chesterfield, after a by-election in March 1984, and continued to fight Thatcherism with vigour. After making an unsuccessful bid for the party leadership at the Blackpool Conference of 1988 his national prestige seemed to decline. Though he held his seat in 1992, he ceased to be an influential member of the shadow cabinet. He never compromised the sincerity of his historic radical beliefs in order to court electoral backing. He has published several volumes of political diaries. T. Benn: *Arguments for Socialism* (1979), and *Arguments for Democracy* (1981); Jad Adams: *Tony Benn, A Biography* (1992).

Bennett, Richard Bedford (1870–1947), Canadian Prime Minister: although a New Brunswicker by birth and a barrister by profession, he represented the interests of Canada's high plains in the federal Parliament, as member for Calgary 1911–17 and 1925–38. He was Director-General of National Service in the First World War, became leader of the Conservatives in 1927 and, having defeated the Liberals in the July 1930 election, headed a 'progressive Conservative' government until October 1935. He shared with his fellow New Brunswicker, Lord BEAVERBROOK, an enthusiasm for Empire Free Trade and in 1932 was Chairman of the Ottawa Conference, convened to enable the Prime Ministers and Finance Ministers of the Empire and Commonwealth to promote reciprocal imperial preference in trade during the world recession. His hopes of guaranteeing wheat prices were not realized, and he subsequently lost support in the provinces by seeking greater powers for the Civil Service across the dominion in order to combat the Depression by federal-sponsored public works programmes. The voters turned against Bennett in the election of January 1935. Three years later he settled in England, receiving a viscountcy in 1941. J. H. Gray: *R. B. Bennett, The Calgary Years* (Toronto, 1991); L. A. Glassford: *Reaction and Reform, the Politics of the Conservative Party under R. B. Bennett* (Toronto, 1992).

Beria, Lavrenti Pavlovich (1899–1953), Soviet secret-police chief from 1938 to 1953: born in Morkheuli, Georgia. As an 18 year-old college student he organized a Bolshevik group in Baku and from 1921 to 1931 was head of the secret police in Georgia, where his work was singled out for praise by his compatriot, STALIN. Beria became Commissar for Internal Affairs in December 1938, taking charge of the NKVD, the Soviet Security Service, in succession to YEZHOV. He modelled himself closely on Stalin. Both MOLOTOV and KHRUSCHEV convinced themselves that he hastened Stalin's death in March 1953 and planned to liquidate prominent members of the Politburo, including Stalin's nominated successor, MALENKOV. Beria, prominent at Stalin's funeral, disappeared from the public eye soon afterwards. Malenkov announced on 10 July 1953 that Beria had been dismissed and on 23 December that he had been shot after being found guilty of treason. Two later statements by Khruschev suggest he was killed, without a trial, in June. S. Wolin and R. M. Slusser: *The Soviet Secret Police* (1957); R. Conquest: *The Great Terror* (1968).

Berlusconi, Silvio (1936–), Italian Prime Minister and businessman: born in Milan, where he received his university education, which he supplemented with engagements as a cruise-liner crooner. In the late 1960s, he emerged as a property magnate, developing wider interests with the purchase of the chain of La Stampa stores and by 1979 controlling a media empire, centred on the Fininvest conglomerate, which gave him control of the newspaper *Il Giornale*, 90 per cent of Italy's commercial television, the Mondadori publishing house and (from 1986) the prestigious football club AC Milan. Berlusconi did not intervene directly in politics until October 1993, when he founded Forza Italia (FI), a movement taking its name from the 'Come on Italy' call familiar on football terraces, especially during the 1990 World Cup. FI candidates were, in many cases, experienced public relations men or media personalities from the Fininvest organization. When the centre-coalition Chiampi government resigned in January 1994, the FI allied with the Northern League and a group based on the neo-fascist MSI to form a right-wing 'Freedom Alliance', which won 322 of 630 parliamentary seats in the March election, with promises of a million new jobs, tax reforms and the return of national pride; Berlusconi became Prime Minister on 20 May 1994. His government was soon in difficulties: a million jobs were not to be found. He did not share the objectives of his two allies; he tried to push his nominees into control of the Bank of Italy and the state televison; he restricted the powers of magistrates investigating corruption at a time when there was speculation over his own family interests. He was forced to resign on 21 December 1994. Although in June 1995 a national referendum supported his right to retain control of three television channels, veteran parliamentarians continued to try to discredit him. Berlusconi's meteoric career is of greatest significance in posing a different challenge to traditional parliamentary democracy: it showed the latent power available to a media tycoon with political ambition. C. Richards: *The New Italians* (rev. edn, Harmondsworth, 1995).

Bernadette (Marie Bernarde Soubirous) (1844–79), French peasant girl and Saint: born at Lourdes in the Hautes-Pyrenées. Her father was a miller and Marie Bernarde, known in the family as 'Bernadette', was the eldest of six children. Between 11 February and 16 July 1858 she witnessed eighteen apparitions of the Virgin Mary in the grotto of Massabieille, near Lourdes. Bernadette reported that the Virgin commanded the building of a church and manifested herself as the 'Immaculate Conception', a dogma formally defined by Pope PIUS IX in December 1854. A spring of water appeared in the grotto and faithful believers soon reported miraculous healings. Bernadette, who had nearly succumbed to cholera in 1854, remained shy, reticent, frail and poor. She was forced to accept endless questioning from Church dignitaries and from sceptics. From 1861 to 1866 she lived with nuns near her home but she spent her last thirteen years secluded in the mother house of the Sisters of Notre-Dame at Nevers on the Loire, more than 350 miles away. The cult of Lourdes was especially encouraged by the Assumptionists, a French religious order founded in 1843 and coming under Pius IX's patronage in 1854. When the railway reached Lourdes in 1867 it began to bring many pilgrims to the grotto, more than 100,000 in 1872 alone. A basilica above the grotto was consecrated in 1876, although Bernadette remained at

Nevers on that great occasion. In the year of her death French doctors formally established a medical authentication office at Lourdes and by the turn of the century the grotto was accepted as the holiest shrine of modern Catholicism. Intellectuals deplored the cult, notably Emile Zola in his novel, *Lourdes* (1894). Although Bernadette was not beatified until 1925 and not canonized until 1933 (a year of strong anti-clerical feeling in France) her spiritual experience helped rally popular religion to accept and support the newly defined articles of faith imposed on a questioning Church by Pius IX. A. Dansette: *Religious History of Modern France* (2 vols) abridged in translation (Edinburgh, 1961); J. McManners, *Church and State in France, 1870–1914* (1972).

Bernadotte, Count Folke (1895–1948), Swedish humanitarian: a descendant through five generations of Marshal Bernadotte, the Napoleonic commander elected to the Swedish throne and reigning as King Charles XIV in Stockholm from 1818 to 1844. Folke Bernadotte, a nephew of King Gustavus V of Sweden, began his military career on the eve of the First World War. Sweden's neutrality gave him the opportunity to assist in humanitarian work, helping with the Red Cross and arranging exchanges of prisoners from 1917 onwards. He continued to show interest in the Red Cross during the 1920s and 1930s, as well as encouraging the growth in Scandinavia of the scouting movement founded by BADEN-POWELL. In October 1943 and in September 1944 Count Bernadotte presided over exchanges of sick and disabled prisoners-of-war at Gothenburg; and in February 1945 he was an unoffical intermediary in a proposal by HIMMLER that German troops would cease fighting the British and Americans provided they could continue to resist the Russian advance – a proposal turned down by both Allied governments. In May 1948 the Count was invited by the Secretary-General of the United Nations, Trygve LIE, to go to Palestine as UN mediator between the warring Jews and Arabs. He was assassinated by Jewish extremists on 17 September 1948 while seeking to secure a truce. A. Ilan: *Bernadotte in Palestine, 1948* (Oxford, 1989); R. Higgins: *United Nations Peacekeeping 1947–68*, Vol. 1 (1973).

Bernstein, Eduard (1850–1932), German socialist critic of Marxism: born in Berlin, spent many years in Switzerland and in London, where he met MARX, ENGELS and the early Fabians including SHAW. By the 1880s, however, he was one of the younger active socialists in Berlin, criticizing the cult of the state. As editor of the *Sozialdemokrat*, a periodical founded by voluntary exiles in Zurich, he became an influential theorist. In 1896–8 he attracted attention by articles which argued (i) that Marxist theory was misleadingly rigid, (ii) that the collapse of capitalism was more distant than the conventional Marxists maintained and, (iii) that German socialists should seek reform within the existing system rather than its overthrow. Bernstein's 'revisionism' was attacked by the German Social Democrat Party in its congresses at Hanover (1899) and Dresden (1903) and denounced by many other continental socialists, including LENIN and the young STALIN. During the First World War, Bernstein collaborated with his former opponent, KAUTSKY, to organize the anti-militarist 'Independent Socialists' in Germany. He remained a theorist rather than a practical politician, but his influence was considerable in Germany and Austria because he provided a reasonably argued and convincing evolutionary socialist alternative to the revolutionary dictatorship of the proletariat envisaged by Marx and Engels. E. Bernstein: *My Years of Exile* (1920); G. D. H. Cole: *A History of Socialist Thought*,

Vols 2–4 (1954–8); L. Labetz (ed.): *Revisionism* (1962).

Besant, Annie (*née* **Wood**) (1847–1933), British secularist, feminist, theosophist: born in London of part Irish descent and educated privately, her governess being a sister of the novelist, Captain Marryatt. In 1867 she married the Reverend Frank Besant in a fit of revolt against her mother, who thought she was too flighty and good-looking for life in a country vicarage. She gave birth to three children in rapid succession before separating from her husband in 1873. A year later she joined BRADLAUGH in championing secularism and birth control. Their republication of a banned pamphlet on birth control, *The Fruits of Philosophy*, led in 1876 to a much publicized trial. Sentences of imprisonment on both Bradlaugh and Mrs Besant were quashed on appeal. Thereafter she became, for some years, a heroine to 'enlightened' opinion in London. She was a pioneer Fabian socialist in the 1880s, helping to organize a famous strike by female match workers in the East End of London in 1888. By 1889, however, an old interest in psychic phenomena had been rekindled by the tenets of Helena Blavatsky (1831–91), whose Theosophical Society – founded in New York in 1875 – was now established in India, at Adyar near Madras. Mrs Besant abandoned her secularist beliefs and in 1895 settled in India, divine wisdom being illuminated more clearly beside the Ganges than on the Chelsea Embankment. She helped found the institutions which became the Hindu University at Benares and was accepted at Adyar as leader of the Theosophical Society after Madame Blavatsky's death. At the same time Mrs Besant maintained her interest in politics, vigorously leading a 'Home Rule for India League' in 1916 and accepting the presidency of the Indian National Congress in December 1918. Her views (which led to a spell of internment in India at the time of the Russian Revolution) were too westernized to win acceptance from Mohandas GANDHI, whose civil disobedience campaign began in 1920. Mrs Besant returned to England in 1925, seeking to identify the Labour Party with Indian home rule, and she made several journeys between London and Bombay, arousing interest by sometimes travelling by air over sections of the route, despite her age. Finally in 1931 she settled at Adyar, dying there eighteen months later, the last survivor of the small group of feminists who had wholesomely shocked the Victorian mind more than half a century before. A. Besant: *An Autobiography* (1893); P. Fryer: *The Birth Controllers* (1965).

Bethmann Hollweg, Theobald von (1856–1921), German Chancellor from 1909 to 1917: born at Hohenfinow, a great estate in Brandenburg on which Bethmann's father (in 1877) arranged the first roebuck shoot for the future Kaiser WILLIAM II. Bethmann himself became a lawyer and a typically efficient Prussian civil servant who worked his way up through the provincial administration to become Prussian Minister of the Interior in 1905. He was minister responsible for the internal affairs of Germany as a whole from 1907 until July 1909 when the outgoing Chancellor, BÜLOW, recommended him as a successor. As Chancellor, Bethmann showed intelligence in seeking reform of the outdated constitutional system, but he was confronted by a succession of problems in foreign affairs about which he knew nothing and he could not avoid pressure from the navalists, led by Admiral TIRPITZ, and the officer corps in the army. By 1913 he had come to believe that war would be forced sooner or later on Germany, that a localized conflict begun at a time convenient to Germany would bring a swift victory, and that the improved relations he had sought with 'England' would keep Britain neutral in any short campaign. Belatedly, in the crisis of 1914, he realized that Germany would be faced with a continental war rather than a localized one and he tried, unsuccessfully, to restrain the militarists. The rapid German successes on the Western Front prompted him to prepare on 9 September 1914 a draft programme of war aims which included the annexation of large areas of Belgium and France, but his later policy suggests that he was on this occasion reflecting the views of pan-Germans at headquarters rather than stating his own beliefs: he wanted German economic mastery of central Europe, not a war of conquest. Throughout his three years as wartime Chancellor Bethmann tried to limit the effects of the conflict, notably by seeking to delay unrestricted submarine attacks for fear of adding the United States to Germany's enemies. Eventually Bethmann's political rearguard action was defeated by threats from the much-vaunted HINDENBURG and LUDENDORFF combination that they would resign their military commands unless Bethmann gave up office. Bethmann resigned as Chancellor on 13 July 1917. He was succeeded by a nonentity, Georg Michaelis (1857–1943), and in effect Germany came under military dictatorship for fifteen months after his fall. K. H. Jarausch: *The Enigmatic Chancellor; Bethmann Hollweg and the Hubris of Imperial Germany* (1973); V. R. Berghahn: *Germany and the Approach of War in 1914* (1973); F. Fischer: *War of Illusions, German Policy from 1911 to 1914* (1975).

Bevan, Aneurin (1897–1960), British socialist: born in Tredegar, south Wales, a miner's son. By 1911 he was working on the coal-face, at a time of great industrial unrest, and he became a militant trade unionist. During the General Strike of 1926 he was a spokesman for the south Wales miners and active in the Independent Labour Party (ILP). He was returned to Parliament as Member for Ebbw Vale in 1929 and represented this constituency until his death, although he fought later general elections for the Labour Party rather than the ILP. Bevan had a Welsh gift for radical oratory, his imagery less sustained but more trenchant than in LLOYD GEORGE'S torrent of words. Like CRIPPS, Bevan fell foul of the Labour Party Executive in the winter of 1938 for advocating a Popular Front movement against the Conservatism of Neville CHAMBERLAIN and he was expelled from the party. He opposed conscription in 1939 and throughout the war remained a critic of Winston CHURCHILL, particularly his conduct of affairs in Greece in 1944, where it seemed to Bevan he favoured the monarchist landowners. In 1945 Bevan entered the Cabinet as Minister of Health, and the National Health Service, established in 1948, was his creation. In January 1951 he became Minister of Labour but resigned three months later when GAITSKELL, as Chancellor of the Exchequer, imposed the first Health Service charges. From 1951 to 1957 he led the left wing of the Labour Party (the 'Bevanites'), which was critical of defence expenditure. In December 1955 Bevan was defeated by Gaitskell in the contest for Labour leadership. The two men shared common views in opposition to the Suez policy of EDEN, and Bevan became the chief Labour spokesman on foreign affairs. His speeches in the House of Commons on 5 December 1956 and at the Labour Party Conference on 2 October 1957 were exercises in statesmanship as well as fine examples of inspired debate. In 1959 he was recognized as deputy leader of the Labour Party, but he was already suffering from cancer and he died in July of the following year. M. Foot: *Aneurin Bevan*, 2 vols (1966, 1973); J. Campbell: *Nye Bevan and the Mirage of British Socialism* (1987).

Beveridge, William (1879–1963), British economist: born at Rangpur, Bengal, the son of an Indian civil servant. He was educated at Charterhouse and Balliol College, Oxford, became a Fellow of University College from 1902 to 1909 and Master from 1937 to 1944. In 1908 he became a senior civil servant at the Board of Trade and was responsible for the first detailed administration of unemployment exchanges. He continued at the Board of Trade until 1916, and was consulted by LLOYD GEORGE over state health insurance. After a few months in the Ministry of Munitions he was moved to the Ministry of Food, 1917–18, where he was responsible for the first butter- and meat-rationing scheme introduced into Britain. He was knighted in 1919, when he became Director of the London School of Economics, a post he held for eighteen years. Successive governments continued to consult Beveridge on economic problems, notably on the future of the coal industry, and in 1941–2 he was Chairman of an interdepartmental committee of senior civil servants which produced the famous 'Beveridge Report' on 'social insurance and allied services', written by Sir William himself and published on 1 December 1942. His proposals for social security 'from the cradle to the grave' formed a basis for much later welfare legislation, especially during the Labour government of 1945–50. Beveridge was Liberal MP for Berwick in 1944–5 and went to the House of Lords as a Baron in 1946. He was later responsible for an important report on the future of British television. W. Beveridge: *Power and Influence, an Autobiography* (1953); J. Beveridge: *Beveridge and his Plan* (1954).

Bevin, Ernest (1881–1951), British trade unionist and Foreign Secretary from 1945 to 1951: born in Somerset, receiving an elementary education at Crediton in Devon and working as a farm labourer before moving to Bristol. There he emerged as a powerful but reasonable organizer of the dockers' union. Between 1911 and 1921 he unified some fifty different unions into a single body, the Transport and General Workers' Union, the largest in the capitalist world. He remained, above all, the dockers' spokesman, showing gifts of compromise in disputes with wage tribunals and with dock owners. He was a prominent member of the council of the Trades Union Congress from 1925 to 1940 and Chairman in 1937. More than any other English trade union leader Bevin was an internationalist, undertaking an important tour of the overseas dominions shortly before the outbreak of the Second World War to see for himself the labour problems in Australia, New Zealand, Canada and South Africa. When Winston CHURCHILL formed his coalition government in May 1940 Bevin became Minister of Labour and National Service, entering the Commons as MP for Central Wandsworth. Within nine days of taking office Bevin introduced an Emergency Powers Bill which gave him directive authority over thirty-three million men and women workers. He had the ability to win and retain popular support for this vast organization of labour. From October 1940 he was a member of the War Cabinet. A masterly survey of European affairs which he delivered to the Party Conference at Blackpool on 19 May 1945 strengthened his claims to be Foreign Secretary under ATTLEE, an appointment finally decided by the new Prime Minister on the advice of King GEORGE VI. Bevin proved a tough watchdog of Britain's traditional interests: he was suspicious of the European Left and of the Israeli case against her Arab neighbours; he favoured collaboration with America through the United Nations, warmly supporting the recovery plan of Secretary of State George MARSHALL; he backed the creation of a North Atlantic Treaty Organization, and favoured restoration of the *entente* between Britain and France. His concern for the unity of the Empire and

Commonwealth made him slow to respond to schemes designed further to integrate Europe. Early in 1950 he took the initiative in summoning a conference of Commonwealth foreign ministers to discuss ways in which the richer dominions and the home country could help the backward regions of southern and south eastern Asia; and from this conference emerged the 'Colombo Plan' of aid. The strain of international problems – the Soviet blockade of west Berlin, the Korean War, the nuclear-arms race – weakened Bevin's health. He resigned as Foreign Secretary on 9 March 1951, hoping to continue serving in Attlee's government as Lord Privy Seal, but he died on 14 April. A. Bullock: *Life and Times of Ernest Bevin* (3 vols) (1960–83); H. Pelling: *A History of British Trade Unionism* (rev. edn 1970).

Bhutto, Benazir (1955–), Pakistani Prime Minister: born in Karachi, the daughter of Zulfiqar Ali BHUTTO (see next entry), during whose premiership she completed her education at Lady Margaret Hall, Oxford. She remained in exile after her father's execution but received a warm and popular welcome when she returned to Pakistan in April 1986 to lead the opposition to President ZIA. A year later she married Asif Ali Zardar but continued her political activities, building up the strength of the Pakistan People's Party (PPP) once more. Three months after Zia's death a General Election on 16 November 1988 allowed the PPP to emerge as the largest single group in the National Assembly and, on 2 December 1988, Benazir Bhutto formed a government in which she was Prime Minister, Defence Minister and Finance Minister. On 1 October 1989 she brought Pakistan back into the Commonwealth. Her westernized ideas lost her some support in rural areas, where Islamic fundamentalism was strong. Early in 1990 Benazir Bhutto became the first Prime Minister to give birth to a child while head of a government. Shifting sympathies towards old traditions led to an electoral defeat in October 1990, and she led the Opposition for three years. Further elections on 6 October 1993 confirmed the PPP's hold on the main provinces and Benazir Bhutto formed a second ministry. Within a year its stability was threatened by Shiah Muslim unrest in areas where Afghan *Mujaheddin* ('holy warriors') had gained influence during the twelve-year civil war across the Afghan frontier. B. Bhutto: *Daughter of the East* (1988); C. Lamb: *Waiting for Allah, Pakistan's Struggle for Democracy* (Harmondsworth, 1992).

Bhutto, Zulfigar Ali (1928–79), political leader of Pakistan from 1971 to 1977: born in southern India, a member of an aristocratic family and educated in the United States and at Christ Church, Oxford. He was a lawyer in Pakistan, serving in a number of government posts under President Ayub Khan from 1958 to 1963. He then became Foreign Minister, improving Pakistan's relations with China but taking a firm stand against India in the long dispute over Kashmir. The Tashkent Truce between India and Pakistan in January 1966 seemed to him a betrayal and he resigned from the government. A year later he founded the People's Party, anti-Indian and Muslim socialist in principle. His party gained an electoral victory in December 1970, and when Pakistan was defeated by India in the Bangladesh War of December 1971 popular demonstrations against President Yahya Khan brought Bhutto to power. As soon as Britain recognized the independence of Bangladesh, Bhutto took Pakistan out of the Commonwealth and on 21 April 1971 he was formally inaugurated as the first civilian President of Pakistan. During the following two years he was able to carry through some basic reforms, including measures of nationalization. A revised constitution, downgrading the presidency, was introduced in the summer of 1973. He thereupon resigned the presidency, taking office as Prime Minister and keeping personal control of defence, foreign affairs and the development of atomic energy. On 7 March 1977 the People's Party claimed an electoral victory, with 154 out of 200 seats in the National Assembly. These figures were disputed and there were several days of rioting, followed by political arrests, until on 5 July 1977 Bhutto's government was overthrown by a military *coup d'état* led by the army Chief of Staff, General ZIA, who imposed an authoritarian regime on the country. In September Bhutto was charged with conspiracy to murder a political opponent. He was put on trial and sentenced to death in March 1978, spending more than a year in the death cell at Rawalpindi before being hanged. S. Wolpert: *Zulfiqar Bhutto, his Life and Times* (Oxford, 1993); S. J. Burki: *Pakistan under Bhutto* (1980).

Bidault, Georges (1899–1976), French politician: born at Moulins in the Bourbonnais. He joined the Free French under General DE GAULLE in Algiers, serving as an important political link between the General and the non-communist resistance within France. Bidault accompanied de Gaulle when he entered Paris on 19 August 1944. Two years later Bidault helped found the Mouvement Républician Populaire (MRP), a Catholic party slightly to the left of centre, which emerged as the biggest political group after elections for the constituent assembly of the Fourth Republic in June 1946. He became head of the provisional government as well as Foreign Minister, and held office again as Prime Minister of a coalition from October 1949 to June 1950. Thereafter he moved steadily to the Right. He deplored any concessions to the Algerians and was disillusioned with de Gaulle, whose return to power in 1958 he had welcomed. For two years from April 1961 he was identified politically with the militarist terrorists of the Organisation de L'Armée Secrète (OAS) and President de Gaulle ordered his arrest on a charge of treason. Bidault, however, succeeded in escaping to Brazil in the spring of 1963 and remained in exile for five years, returning home only in the summer of 1968 when the charges against him were dropped. G. Bidault: *Resistance, The Political Autobiography* (New York, 1967); P. Williams and M. Harrison: *Political and Society in de Gaulle's France* (Harlow, 1971); D. C. Gordon: *North Africa's French Legacy, 1954–1962* (Cambridge, Mass., 1962).

Bismarck, Otto von (1815–98), German Chancellor from 1871 to 1890: born at Schönhausen, some 60 miles west of Berlin. He was educated at the universities of Göttingen and Berlin, held minor civil service posts (1836–8), and acquired a reputation for reactionary politics in the Prussian Diet of 1847. From 1851 to 1862 he was in the Prussian diplomatic service, at Frankfurt, St Petersburg and Paris. In the autumn of 1862 he became Prime Minister of Prussia, pledged to secure for WILLIAM I army reforms for which the Prussian parliament refused to vote credits. Bismarck disregarded the will of parliament, interesting the Prussians in German national causes as an alternative to domestic political advancement. In alliance with Austria, Bismarck went to war against Denmark in 1864, securing cession by the Danes of the largely German-speaking areas in Schleswig-Holstein. A quarrel with Austria over the future of these two duchies enabled Bismarck to lead Prussia into the Seven Weeks War of 1866, in which Austria and most of the smaller German states were defeated by Prussia's new army. Bismarck became Chancellor of the North German Confederation in July 1867, thus achieving in practice Prussia's mastery over Germany and central Europe. Fear that his statecraft sought a unified Germany dominant over the continent induced France to declare war on Prussia on 19 July 1870. Eight weeks later Bismarck was present on the battlefield of Sedan when NAPOLEON III surrendered to William I. The Franco-Prussian War continued until the following spring, and in the course of it a German Empire was proclaimed at occupied Versailles (18 January 1871), Bismarck thereafter serving as Imperial Chancellor until required to resign from office by WILLIAM II on 20 March 1890. Throughout his nineteen years as Imperial Chancellor, Prince Bismarck (as he became in April 1871) sought to perpetuate European peace, fearing any major war would tilt the delicate balance within Germany as well as within the continent as a whole. A system of alliances with the Russians, the Austrians and later the Italians kept defeated France from provoking a war of revenge and ensured that, so long as Bismarck was in power, the French Republic had no allies in Europe. In order to prevent Balkan unrest causing a European war Bismarck agreed to preside over an international congress at Berlin in 1878, an event which marked his eminence as a statesman but which left the Russians dissatisfied with the diplomatic pattern he was imposing on the continent. Bismarck was less successful in home affairs after 1871 than in foreign policy: he failed to check the power of two international movements which he believed weakened the structure of Prussian-dominated Germany – his conflict with Roman Catholicism (the *Kulturkampf* of the 1870s) ended in a compromise which favoured Pope LEO XIII rather than Germany; and his conflict with the socialists in the 1880s strengthened rather than weakened the working-class cause.

In later years he was a pragmatist rather than the doctrinaire conservative depicted by his opponents: the social insurance schemes he introduced in the late 1880s provided Germany with the basis of a welfare and pensions system more than twenty years earlier than other European countries. Bismarck accepted the need for colonies in Africa and Asia with some reluctance, as he thought they would be a burden for the German taxpayer and a cause of international friction. He never saw the need for the liberal German constitution favoured by Kaiser FREDERICK III or for the German navy first sought by William II and TIRPITZ in the years of Bismarck's retirement. His ideas were shaped by the political values and truths of mid-century Europe: he never understood the 'World Policy' favoured by William II and the younger generation – but he feared its implications for the Greater Prussia which he had created and called the German Empire. O. Pflanze: *Bismarck and the Development of Germany* (2 vols) (Princeton, N.J., 1963, 1988); L. Gall: *Bismarck, the White Revolutionary* (1982); A. Palmer: *Bismarck* (1976); A. J. P. Taylor: *Bismarck, the Man and the Statesman* (1955).

Black, Hugo La Fayette (1886–1971), Associate Justice of the US Supreme Court from 1937 to 1971: born in Harlan, Alabama, orphaned as a child and brought up by an elder brother. He received a law degree from Alabama University in 1906 and practised in Birmingham, Alabama, in the early 1920s. As Democrat Senator for Alabama from 1927 to 1937 Hugo Black showed himself a tenacious opponent of big business. His mastery of senatorial business (as when he pushed through a controversial thirty-hours-a-week bill to protect labourers in April 1933) won him the respect of President Franklin ROOSEVELT, who treated him as a New Deal ally. Black's 'Fair Labour Standards Bill' of July 1937 (not enacted until 1938) introduced minimum wage legislation at federal level to the United States. In August 1937 Roosevelt appointed Black to the Supreme Court, but a week later a Pittsburgh newspaper sought to discredit him by revealing that in 1923 the new Associate Justice had been a member of the Ku Klux Klan. Black defended his reputation in a broadcast to which fifty million people listened, for his appointment aroused interest and high hopes from the underprivileged. He explained that his membership of the Klan had been a temporary expediency. As an Associate Justice his record over civil rights and welfare legislation remained consistently liberal, the first ruling he delivered being a condemnation of the state of Florida for obtaining the conviction of a Negro by 'third degree' methods. He treated cases against American labour unions with fairness, but his principal task was to ensure that the provisions of the federal Bill of Rights were carried into the civil and political life of the individual states. His final ruling, delivered on 30 June 1971, concerned the freedom of the Press to print official papers dealing with the origins of the Vietnam War. He died on 25 September 1971, eight days after his retirement from the Supreme Court. T. A. Freyer: *Hugo Black and the Dilemma of American Liberalism* (1990); C. Williams: *Hugo L. Black* (New York, 1950); W. Mendelson: *Justices Black and Frankfurter: Conflict in Court* (New York, 1961).

Blaine, James Gillespie (1830–93), US Secretary of State in 1881 and from 1889 to 1892: born at West Brownsville, Pennsylvania, educated at Washington College, Pennsylvania, but settled in Maine where he practised law, built up the Republican Party in the state and was returned to Congress in 1863, serving as Speaker of the House from 1869 to 1875. He nearly won presidential nomination in 1876 but was discredited by evidence that he used his political influence to aid railway companies in which he had a financial interest. This scandal did not prevent his election to the Senate, nor deter him from vainly seeking the nomination again in 1880. He was briefly Secretary of State under GARFIELD, thereafter using his personal charm, gifts of oratory and skilled journalism to lead the Republican Party, shaping its programme throughout the 1880s. In 1884 he at last won the Republican nomination, conducted a vituperative campaign at the expense of CLEVELAND, and lost the election largely through defections in New York State, where his supporters alienated the Roman Catholic vote. The victory of HARRISON in the presidential election of 1888 finally brought Blaine back to the Department of State where he was able to improve relations with Latin America. Blaine, who was of Scottish and Irish descent, had a honeyed tongue which made him an idol with many voters but thoroughly distrusted by his fellow politicians. His policy of economic pan-Americanism was some twenty years ahead of its time, but his cynical politicking and mudslinging tactics were too familiar to win from the voters the backing they would have given to a presidential candidate with qualities of moral leadership. C. E. Russell: *Blaine of Maine* (1931); A. F. Tyler: *The Foreign Policy of J. G. Blaine* (1965).

Blair, Anthony Charles Lynton (Tony) (1953–) British Labour politician: born in Edinburgh, educated at Fettes and St John's College, Oxford. He was called to the bar, Lincoln's Inn, in 1976, specializing in labour law. In 1983 he entered the Commons as Labour MP for Sedgefield, became the principal Opposition spokesman on energy in 1988 and subsequently on employment. When Neil KINNOCK was succeeded by John Smith (1938–94), Blair became shadow Home Secretary and, on John Smith's sudden death, his popularity with the constituencies made him a strong contender for the succession. He was elected party leader on 21 July 1994, with John Prescott (1938–) as deputy leader. Over the following year Tony Blair campaigned vigorously, and with increasing success, to modify 'Clause Four' of the party objectives agreed in 1918, the commitment to common ownership. J. Sopel: *Tony Blair, the Moderniser* (1995).

Bliss, Tasker Howard (1853–1930), US Chief of Staff from 1917 to 1919: born in Lewisburg, Pennsylvania, and commissioned in the artillery in 1875. From 1885 to 1888 he was Professor of Military Science at the US Naval War College. He saw active service in Puerto Rico in 1898 and was for many years stationed as a Brigadier-General in the Philippines. From 1909 onwards he was Deputy Chief of Staff and was responsible for drafting the instructions to PERSHING both for his punitive expedition into Mexico and his general strategy in France. Bliss was promoted General and appointed Chief of Staff soon after America's entry into the war. At the end of 1917 he became the US military representative on the Supreme War Council in France, with the difficult task of reconciling his President's insistence that the United States was an 'associated power', rather than an 'ally', with the needs of joint military action. Bliss's skill in working with FOCH and CLEMENCEAU made Woodrow WILSON appoint him third US delegate to the Paris Peace Conference of 1919. He helped draft the military clauses of the Treaty of Versailles, but had little confidence in a lasting peace although he loyally supported Wilson in his attempts to induce America to join the League of Nations. His services to the 'allied and associated powers' was recognized by King GEORGE V, who conferred on General Bliss the rare distinction of an honorary knighthood. F. Palmer: *Bliss, Peacemaker; the Life and Letters of General Bliss* (New York, 1934); J. T. Shotwell: *At the Paris Peace Conference* (New York, 1937).

Blum, Léon (1872–1950), French socialist leader from 1925 until his death: born in Paris, his family being Jews from Alsace. For twenty-four years he was a member of the administrative judiciary, the Conseil d'État, but he owed his fame as a young man to his writings, for from 1893 to 1903 he contributed literary and dramatic criticism to *La Revue Blanche*, an intellectual review which first familiarized the French with the works of Tolstoy and Ibsen. The persecution of DREYFUS induced Blum to join the Dreyfusard socialists under JAURÈS, whose private secretary he became. Blum always rejected Marxism; he was an intellectual who found in socialist ideals the inspiration of a religious faith. He entered the Chamber of Deputies in 1919, becoming leader of his party six years later. In June 1936 he formed the famous 'Popular Front' government, becoming the first Jewish and the first socialist Prime Minister in France. The Popular Front was an attempt to push through basic reforms common to the parties of the Left, to check the spread in France of paramilitary fascist bodies, and to keep peace in Europe – for Blum was at heart a pacifist. The anti-socialist majority in the Senate limited Blum's programme and forced him out of office after a year. He returned briefly as Prime Minister in 1938, but was insulted as a Jew and a 'Red'. In October 1940 he was imprisoned by the Vichy French and taken into custody by the Germans in 1942, spending more than two years in the concentration camps at Buchenwald and Dachau. He was Prime Minister of the provisional government in 1946–7 and helped reorganize the reformist, non-Marxist wing of French socialists. Blum excited more exaggerated feelings of affection or hatred than any other French statesman in the interwar years, an unfashionable respect for the rights of the individual earning him abuse from the Right and the Left. J. L. Colton: *Leon Blum, Humanist in Politics* (New York, 1966); W. Logue: *Leon Blum, the Formative Years, 1872–1914* (De Kalb, Ill.,

1973); J. Joll: *Three Intellectuals in Politics* (1960).

Bokassa, Jean Badel (1921–), ruler of the Central African Republic, 1966–79: born at Bagandou, Lobaye, in Ubanghi Shari colony, within French Equatorial Africa. He was educated at missionary schols and enlisted in the French colonial army in 1939, showing such efficiency, pride in the regiment and courage that he received the Légion d'honeur and the Croix de Guerre. He was commissioned and, as Captain Bokassa, anticipated rapid promotion when Ubanghi Shari gained independence as the Central African Republic in August 1960. He helped organize the presidential bodyguard of the republic's first head of state, David Dacko, a kinsman. On 1 January 1966 Colonel Bokassa overthrew President Dacko in a military *coup* in the capital, Bangui. Bokassa monopolized all the offices of state, bolstering his power by assertions of Francophilism and of personal friendship with President GISCARD D'ESTAING. He proclaimed himself Marshal of Central Africa in 1974 and two years later published a new constitution by which guardianship of the country's professed parliamentary democracy was entrusted to himself as Emperor. In December 1977, in a rich and costly ceremony, Bokassa crowned himself at a coronation, modelled on Napoleonic precedent. Early in 1979 there were demonstrations in Bangui against his capricious tyranny and extravagance. Reports reached Paris that Bokassa had ordered and witnessed the sadistic killing of forty children, who were allegedly protesting at having to wear uniforms made in a factory owned by the Emperor's family. While Bokassa was abroad, French airborne troops overthrew his administration and reinstated President Dacko (20 September 1979). Although Bokassa remained in exile, he was tried *in absentia* in December 1980 and sentenced to death on charges of murder, cannibalism and corruption. He returned unexpectedly to Bangui in 1986, was arrested and arraigned in person, but had the death sentence commuted to life imprisonment. S. Decalo: *Psychosis of Power; African Personal Dictatorships* (1989); H. Kalck: *Historical Dictionary of the Central African Republic* (1980).

Borden, Robert Laird (1854–1937), Canadian Prime Minister: born at Grand Pre in Nova Scotia and a barrister by profession. He entered the Canadian Parliament in 1896 and was accepted as head of the Conservative Party in 1901. After ten years leading the Opposition to LAURIER, Borden was Prime Minister of a Conservative government from October 1911 until October 1917, thereafter heading a two-party coalition until July 1920; he was knighted in 1914. During the First World War, Borden ensured that the Canadian army made a valiant contribution to the battles on the Western Front. With great parliamentary dexterity he secured passage of a conscription bill, despite intense hostility from the French-Canadian community. He insisted that British dominions should have equal status in world affairs with the 'mother country'. Recognition of his statesmanship induced ASQUITH to invite Borden to a Cabinet meeting in London in July 1915 – the first occasion when a dominion Prime Minister sat in Cabinet. At the Paris Peace Conference in 1919 Borden secured recognition that delegates from self-governing dominions could sign the peace treaties on behalf of their own governments. In 1930 Sir Robert Borden emerged from retirement to represent Canada at the League of Nations in Geneva. R. Borden: *Memoirs* (Toronto, 1969); R. C. Brown and R. Cook: *Canada 1896–1921* (Toronto, 1974).

Boris III (1894–1943), King of Bulgaria from 1918 to 1943: born in Sofia, the eldest son of FERDINAND, ruler of

Bulgaria from 1887 to the end of the First World War. Boris commanded an army on the Macedonian Front from 1915 to 1918, winning widespread respect from the soldiery who served under him. He narrowly escaped death or exile in communist disturbances at the time of his accession (3 October 1918). Politically, he was astute and ruthless, freeing himself on more than one occasion from the political dominance of demagogues or army officers. For the last seven years of his life the King was a virtual dictator, following a devious foreign policy which enabled him to acquire territory from Yugoslavia and Greece, as a nominal ally of HITLER in 1941, with virtually no loss of men or equipment. Boris was prepared to declare war on distant Britain and America, with whom it seemed to him in 1942 that there was little risk of actual conflict, but he would not declare war on the Soviet Union or assist Hitler on the Eastern Front. German exasperation culminated in a peremptory demand from Hitler for Boris to come to his field headquarters in East Prussia in August 1943, but the King still declined to change his policy. Three days after his return to Bulgaria from Hitler's headquarters, King Boris suddenly died (29 August 1943). There is no evidence he was murdered (as rumour maintained at the time) but the political strain may have weakened his heart. In 1930 he had married Princess Giovanna (1907–), a daughter of King VICTOR EMMANUEL III of Italy, and their son Simeon (1937–) was titular ruler of Bulgaria until forced into exile by the establishment of a 'People's Republic' in 1946. P. Dimitroff: *King of Mercy, Boris of Bulgaria* (Lewes, 1986); B. Jelavich: *History of the Balkans*, Vol. 2 (Cambridge, 1984).

Bose, Subhas Chandra (1895–1945), Indian nationalist leader: born in Calcutta, where he received the first part of a university education, completed at Cambridge. He entered the (British) Indian Civil Service, but was imprisoned in 1924 for civil disobedience. For much of the following decade he was in prison or in exile, his political views tending towards the socialism favoured by NEHRU. Bose, always a skilled orator, gained a considerable following in Bengal, especially after the publication in 1935 of his book *The Indian Struggle*; he became President of the All-India Congress in 1938, resigning a year later to oppose participation in the Second World War. In July 1940 he was imprisoned for propaganda favourable to the Axis cause. Six months later he escaped, crossed into Afghanistan and made his way to Berlin, where he received encouragement to raise an Indian army which would fight British imperialism. With German backing he began broadcasts, relayed from Afghanistan, in which he advocated sabotage. In 1942 he went by submarine to Tokyo, where he was appointed *Netaji* (leader) of the Indian National Army (INA), a force recruited from Indian and Tamil prisoners-of-war, and reckoned by British intelligence reports to have attracted two out of every seven captured. The *Netaji* set up battle headquarters in Rangoon; in 1943–4 more than 20,000 INA troops supported a Japanese thrust across the Burmese frontier into India. But Bose was faced with large-scale desertions. He perished in an air crash in Taiwan in 1945. His courage in seeking to advance nationalism by treasonable means has won respect for his memory in modern India. S. K. Bose (ed.): *A Beacon across Asia* (Delhi, 1973); E. P. Hoyt: *Japan's War* (1986).

Botha, Louis (1862–1919), Boer General and first Prime Minister of South Africa: born in Natal at Honigfontein, a 5,000-acre farm where he learned to look after sheep, cattle, ostriches and horses. From the age of 18 he was accustomed to trekking deep into Zululand, occasionally having to defend himself from attack by Zulu tribesmen. These formative years made him a natural fighter and he enlisted in the army of the Transvaal, invading Natal, and commanding the area in which Boer raiders derailed an armoured train on 15 November 1899, taking Winston CHURCHILL prisoner. As a General, Botha organized Boer resistance within the Transvaal throughout the last two years of the war. He was eager for reconciliation with the British and became Prime Minister of the Transvaal in 1908, playing a prominent part in the conventions of 1908–9 which prepared a constitution for the Union of South Africa. His 'South African Party' won the first elections in the Union (September 1910) and Botha became Prime Minister, holding office until his death. He was faced by a pro-German Boer rebellion in October 1914 which, with the assistance of SMUTS, he suppressed with clemency. The two men then undertook a successful campaign against South West Africa, accepting the German colonial surrender on 9 July 1915. General Botha attended the Paris Peace Conference in 1919, signing the Treaty of Versailles less than nine weeks before his death. F. V. Engelenberg: *General Louis Botha* (1929); B. Williams: *Botha, Smuts and South Africa* (1946).

Botha, Pieter Willem (1916–), South African President: born at Paul Roux, Orange Free State, the son of a Boer farmer. After working for twelve years for the National Party he was returned to the Pretoria Parliament in 1948 for the George constituency (Cape Province) and gave warm support to the apartheid policies of MALAN, STRIJDOM and VERWOERD. Eventually he entered the government in 1966 as Minister of Defence under VORSTER. He succeeded Vorster as Prime Minister in September 1978 and, under new constitutional provisions which increased the executive power of the Head of State, Botha became Executive President in September 1984. Early hopes of reform, under international economic and financial pressure, were dashed after Botha returned from talks with Margaret THATCHER in England (at Chequers, June 1984). A State of Emergency was proclaimed in 1985, lifted under financial pressure a year later, but reimposed before the end of 1986: thereafter the Emergency was renewed annually during Botha's presidency. Under the Emergency powers, seventeen 'moderate' democratic organizations were banned in 1988; much brutality was shown towards demonstrators by the police. Botha suffered a stroke on 18 January 1989 and resigned as National Party leader a fortnight later. He remained titular President until succeeded on 20 September 1989 by F. W. de KLERK. D. J. Venter: *South Africa, Sanctions and Multinationals* (1989); C. R. Hill: *Change in South Africa; Blind Alleys and New Directions* (1983).

Boulanger, Georges Ernest Jean Marie (1837–91), French political General: born in Rennes, Brittany. He entered the army in the heyday of neo-Bonapartism, serving the Second Empire in Algeria and Italy before distinguishing himself by his courage in the Franco-Prussian War of 1870–1. He became a Brigadier-General in 1880, entered radical politics in 1884, originally as a protégé of CLEMENCEAU, and served as Minister of War from June 1886 to May 1887. Boulanger was a popular hero, especially with the junior officers; he was handsome, with a blond beard and a sleekly groomed horse, which he rode with elegance. Speeches against Germany, patriotic gestures – such as ordering all sentry boxes to be painted red, white and blue – and denunciation of political corruption made Boulanger a natural candidate for political advancement and intrigue. When he was placed on the retired list because of his demagogic gestures, he began to press for constitutional reform, envisaging himself as an autocratic President. His 'League of Patriots' had spectacular electoral successes in 1888 and in January 1889 it seemed as if he would attempt a *coup d'état*. But his nerve failed him: he was forced to flee to Belgium to escape arrest in the early spring of 1889, and the movement which he had encouraged rapidly lost its appeal. In 1891 he shot himself over the grave of his mistress in Brussels. His significance was, however, more enduring than the episodic absurdities of his life suggest: he represented the romantic authoritarian alternative to uninspiring parliamentary government; and, as Clemenceau warned his colleagues, there was always the danger of another political general providing the Bonapartist leadership which Boulanger, in the last resort, was found not to possess. General Boulanger's son-in-law and former aide-de-camp, Colonel Émile Driant (1855–1916), showed great heroism in the defence of Verdun, being killed while tenaciously holding the Bois des Caures against the first wave of the German assault. F. H. Seager: *The Boulanger Affair* (Ithaca, N.Y., 1969); T. Zeldin: *France 1848–1945*, Vol. 1, *Ambition, Love and Politics* (Oxford, 1973).

Boumédienne, Houari (Mohammed Bou Kharrouba) (1925–78), President of Algeria from 1965 to 1978: born at Guelma, between Bone and Constantine. He was educated at Constantine, the El Azhar University in Cairo, and briefly in Paris. When the armed insurrection against French rule (which became the Algerian War) began in November 1954, Boumédienne was a schoolmaster, teaching in Algiers. By the following spring he was Commandant of the Vilayet 5 Group of the Algerian National Liberation Front (FLN), responsible for Algerian nationalist attacks in the Oran area. In 1960 he was recognized as Chief of Staff of the FLN's 'National Liberation Forces', with his headquarters across the Tunisian frontier, and he became Minister of National Defence in September 1962, two months after Algeria gained independence. President BEN BELLA appointed him Vice-President of the Ministerial Council in 1963 but Boumédienne was politically to the left of Ben Bella, who seemed to him lukewarm in the pan-Arab cause. On 19 June 1965 Colonel Boumédienne carried through a military *coup*, deposing Ben Bella and establishing government through a Council of Revolution, of which he was President. In his thirteen years of power he built up the Algerian economy by a succession of national development plans. Abroad he envisaged an expanded North African Socialist' Arab state, openly seeking to incorporate Morocco, Tunisia, Mauritania and much of the former Spanish Sahara in his republic. His health gave way soon after his fiftieth birthday, and he was unable to attain his objectives in foreign affairs. He died in December 1978, having been incapacitated for several months, and was succeeded as President by Benjedid Chadli. M. Bennoune: *The Making of Contemporary Algeria*, 1830–1987 (1988); A. Horne: *A Savage War of Peace, Algeria 1954–62* (1977).

Bourguiba, Habib ibn Ali (1903–), Founder-President of the Tunisian Republic: born at Monastir, near Sousse, when Tunisia was a French protectorate. He studied law in Paris, settling in Tunis in 1921. At first he supported the constitutionalist Destour Party in the consultative assembly set up in 1922, but by the early 1930s he was leading a more radical group which seemed so threatening to the French authorities that he was imprisoned for subversion from 1934 to 1936, and again from 1938 to 1942. Bourguiba resolutely refused to collaborate with the Italian or German armies of occupation during the war. The French, however, still regarded him as a dangerous revolutionary and in 1945 he fled to Egypt, convinced that only the total independence of his country from French domination would enable the Tunisians to shape their nation's future development. From 1949 to 1952 he campaigned freely in Tunisia, only to serve two more years in prison for subversive propaganda, but in 1954 the French Radical-Socialist government began to encourage the more moderate Muslims in their North African colonies and protectorates so as to check the growing influence of the committed Marxists. Bourguiba was accordingly released, showing wise restraint in his dealings with successive governments in Paris. When Tunisia became independent (March 1956) Bourguiba served as Prime Minister and in July 1957 he was elected President on the abolition of the monarchical authority of the Bey of Tunis. Bourguiba followed a non-aligned policy of moderate Arab socialism, firmly opposing the use of France's naval and air bases on Tunisian soil during the Algerian War, but establishing close trading relations with the French as soon as peace returned to Algeria. He was proclaimed President for life by the Tunisian National Assembly in March 1975. In 1978 his son and namesake was brought into the Tunisian Cabinet as 'Special Counsellor to the President', whose health 'was failing'. Yet, despite mounting tension and the spread of Islamic fundamentalism, with riots in Tunis in 1983–84, the Founder-President remained titular Head of State until 7 November 1987. He was then deposed by General Zine el-Abidine Ben Ali, whose assumption of the presidential office was confirmed by elections in 1989 and 1994 at which there were no other candidates. D. Hopwood: *Habib Bourguiba of Tunisia, the Tragedy of Longevity* (1992); N. Salem: *Habib Bourguiba, Islam and the Creation of Tunisia* (1984).

Boutros-Ghali, Boutros (1922–), sixth UN Secretary-General: born in Cairo, where he studied law at the university, subsequently extending his academic interests in Paris and at Uppsala University. In 1949 he returned to Cairo as Professor of International Law, a chair he held for fourteen years. From 1977 to 1991 he was Minister of State for Foreign Affairs in the Egyptian Government and briefly deputy Prime Minister. He was elected to succeed Perez de Cuellar at the UN at the beginning of 1992. On assuming office the Secretary-General was asked, by a special session of the Security Council, to find ways of strengthening the UN's peace-keeping ability. The Boutros-Ghali Report of June 1992 reverted to proposals put forward in 1945 for a UN army of national contingents retained on permananent standby for UN service. At first, in May 1992, he opposed peace-keeping activities in Bosnia but was drawn increasingly into the conflict by force of opinion, although often criticized for failing to give a clear lead on policy. By the close of 1994 there were seventeen UN peace-keeping operations, costing more than 3,000 million US dollars a year to maintain. To a greater extent than any of his five predecessors, Boutros-Ghali was faced by a threat of financial collapse.

Bradlaugh, Charles (1833–91), British secularist: born in Hoxton, London. He enlisted in the army in 1850 but bought his discharge in 1853 and became a solicitor's clerk, subsequently becoming a freelance journalist who supported free thinking and radical causes and wrote under the name 'Iconoclast'. He was President of the London Secular Society from 1858 until shortly before his death, and from 1860 edited the *National Reformer*, a secularist periodical. He was an active supporter of parliamentary reform and of changes in the pattern of social behaviour. In 1876 he was charged, together with Mrs BESANT, for having published a banned pamphlet on birth control, *The Fruits of Philosophy*. The trial provided him with a platform for his views and, as the heavy sentences imposed were quashed on appeal, he benefited considerably from the prosecution. After three unsuccessful attempts to enter Parliament, he was returned as Radical MP for Northampton in April 1880. As an atheist he refused to take his oath on entering the Commons. Since the Speaker would not allow him to make an affirmation of allegiance instead of swearing the oath, he was forcibly escorted from the House on several occasions. Despite re-election by the voters of Northampton, Bradlaugh remained a centre of undignified scenes whenever he tried to take his seat, much of the agitation against 'radical atheism' being fomented by Lord Randolph CHURCHILL and his 'Fourth Party'. A change of Speaker after the election of July 1886 enabled Bradlaugh's willingness to affirm to be interpreted more calmly and tolerantly than in 1880; and he was able to sit in the House as Member for Northampton until his death. He helped modernize parliamentary procedure by his championship of the Parliamentary Oaths Act of 1888. The causes he championed throughout his life invariably profited from the tactical stupidity of his opponents. J. M. Robertson: *Charles Bradlaugh* (1920); W. L. Arnstein: *The Bradlaugh Case, a Study in late Victorian Opinion and Politics* (1965).

Bradley, Omar Nelson (1893–1981), commanding General of American invasion armies in 1944–5: born in Missouri, graduated from the Military Academy at West Point in 1915 (as did EISENHOWER). When America entered the Second World War he was in his second year as Commandant of the Infantry School at Fort Benning. He held a senior post on Eisenhower's staff in the invasion of North Africa (November 1942), took over from PATTON as Commander of the US Second Corps, and captured Bizerta in May 1943. Subsequently his troops landed in Sicily and, in five weeks of heavy fighting against the Germans, crossed the island, capturing Messina on 16 August. Two months later Bradley was transferred to England where he prepared the US First Army for the invasion of France in June 1944. After initial difficulties Bradley's troops broke through the German defences on 24 July. On 1 August Bradley was given command of the US Twelfth Army Group with the task of penetrating into France. Friction subsequently arose with MONTGOMERY, in command of the Twenty-first Army Group, a General of more battle experience and less reticence. Disagreements over strategy (in which Eisenhower backed Bradley) became acute when Bradley was slow to perceive that the German efforts against his division in the Ardennes in December 1944 were part of a major counter-offensive, and it was necessary for some of Bradley's troops to be placed under Montgomery's command as a temporary expedient to check the Germans. Bradley's irritation over his own role in Allied plans led him to seize the initiative in advancing on the Rhine, south of Cologne, and it was units of Bradley's First Army which unexpectedly secured a bridgehead over the river at Remagen on 7 March 1945. In the last two months of the war Eisenhower gave particular weight to Bradley's military arguments. The two commanders agreed on a thrust through southern Germany to link up with the Red Army on the Elbe, rather than making a dash for Berlin, as the British wanted. Bradley returned to Washington in the winter of 1945–6, and for two years was responsible for demobilization. He became Chief of Staff in 1948 and from August 1949 until the summer of 1953 served as Chairman of the Joint US Chiefs of Staff, a post of great responsibility during the building up of NATO and the Korean War. It was General Bradley who bluntly told a Senate committee in May 1951 that the proposal of MACARTHUR to carry the Korean conflict into China was 'the wrong war, at the wrong place, at the wrong time, and with the wrong enemy.' O. Bradley: *A Soldier's Story* (1951); J. Keegan: *Six Armies in Normandy* (1982); C. Macdonald: *The Battle of the Bulge* (1984).

Brandeis, Louis Dembitz (1856–1941), American 'people's attorney' from Boston who served as a Supreme Court Associate Justice from 1916 to 1939: born of Jewish parentage in Louisville, Kentucky. He graduated from the Harvard Law School in 1877 and practised as a lawyer in Boston for thirty-seven years from 1879, defending without fee those whom he considered victims of social injustice. He carried his passionate fight against monopolies into print in his book, *Other People's Money* (1914), which finally determined President WILSON to appoint him to the Supreme Court. There his judgments invariably favoured collective bargaining, free speech and experiments undertaken by individual states to encourage rationally equitable social and commercial legislation. Although critical of the way in which Franklin ROOSEVELT handled the Supreme Court, his ideas inspired much New Deal legislation. Brandeis was a prominent member of the American Zionist movement. P. Strum: *Brandeis; beyond Progressivism* (Lawrence, Kans., 1993).

Brandt, Willy (Karl Herbert Frahm) (1913–92), Chancellor of the Federal German Republic from 1969 to 1974: born in Lübeck, fled to Norway in 1933 when he anticipated arrest by the Nazis because of his socialist political activities. In Norway he changed the name Frahm to Brandt and became a Norwegian citizen, gaining a degree at Oslo University. He escaped from Norway ahead of the German invaders in 1940, settled in Sweden and served as a contact between the German and Norwegian resistance movements. In 1945 he crossed to Germany, settled in west Berlin, resumed his German citizenship (though not his name of birth) and began to build up a democratic socialist party, being returned to Parliament in Bonn as a Social Democrat (SPD) Deputy in 1949. From 1957 to 1966 he was Mayor of West Berlin, showing independence and courage when faced by constant hostility from the East Germans and the Soviet authorities. In 1964 he was elected Chairman of the SPD and entered the Coalition government of the Christian Democrat Chancellor, Kurt Kiesinger, in 1966. Brandt's international contacts (and good English) made him a much-respected Foreign Minister, and SPD electoral gains in the autumn of 1969 enabled him to become West Germany's first socialist Chancellor (21 October 1969). Brandt worked for improved relations with the Soviet Union and Poland and the acceptance of a *modus vivendi* by the two German governments, in Bonn and East Berlin. This *Ostpolitik* was balanced by a legal recognition of Federal Germany's obligations in NATO and the European Community. For his gestures of reconciliation he was awarded the Nobel Peace Prize in 1971. The German electorate showed confidence in his policy in November 1972, despite the hostility of large sections of the West German Press. In the spring of 1974, however, newspaper revelations that he had unwittingly employed an East German spy in his personal entourage weakened his position, and he resigned office on 6 May 1974. W. Brandt: *My Life in Politics* (1992); R. Tilford: *The Ostpolitik and Political Change in Germany* (Farnborough, 1975).

Bratianu, Ionel (1864–1927), Romanian Prime Minister: born at Florica, the son of Ion Bratianu (1831–91) who, with his brother Demeter Bratianu (1818–91), stimulated Romanian nationalism in the 1848 revolutions and led successive governments in Bucharest between 1876 and 1888. Ionel Bratianu built up the

Romanian Liberal Party, founded by his father and uncle, and was – like them – a Francophile, with great influence on foreign policy from 1904 onwards. He became Prime Minister in March 1909 but was out of office from 1911 until January 1914 when he headed the ministry which brought Romania into the First World War against Germany and Austria-Hungary in August 1916. The collapse of the Eastern Front, with the coming of the Russian Revolution, forced Romania out of the war on 9 December 1917. Over the following year, however, dexterous diplomacy brought Romania great territorial gains, despite this defeat: a peace treaty with Germany in May 1918 secured the former Russian province of Bessarabia, in return for economic concessions to Berlin. But in November the imminent collapse of Germany led Bratianu to bring Romania back into the war on the Entente side two days before the final armistice. At the Paris Peace Conference Bratianu and his colleagues were able to obtain Transylvania and the Bukovina from Austria-Hungary, while also retaining Bessarabia; these gains doubled the size of Romania between 1916 and 1920 and left Bratianu as a key figure in the French-dominated Little Entente alliance system, which shaped policies in Eastern Europe before the coming of HITLER. Ionel Bratianu also influenced Romanian internal affairs in the 1920s, introducing a centralist constitution in 1923. On his death he was succeeded as Prime Minister by his brother, Vintila Bratianu (1867–1930). From 1944 to 1946, a younger member of the family, Constantine Bratianu, sought to save the Liberal Party in the aftermath of the Second World War and was, briefly, deputy premier; but he could not check the imposition of communist control after the occupation of the country by Soviet troops. R. W. Seton-Watson: *A History of the Roumanians* (Cambridge, 1934); S. D. Spector: *Roumania at the Peace Conference* (New York, 1962); K. Hitchins: *Rumania* (Oxford, 1994).

Braun, Wernher von (1912–77), German pioneer of rocket science: born in Wirsitz, educated at the Charlottenburg Institute of Technology and the University of Zurich. From October 1932 he conducted research into rocket propulsion for the ordnance department of the German Army, becoming Director of the Rocket Research Centre established at Peenemünde on the Baltic coast at the age of 20. Even before the outbreak of war he perfected a rocket capable of carrying a warhead 11 miles. Development was hampered by the demands of the aircraft industry and it was not until 1943 that HITLER authorized him to work on the weapon which became known as the V-2 (*Vergeltungswaffe-2* – 'reprisal weapon 2'), a rocket with a range of slightly under 200 miles and carrying a ton of explosive. Some 1,050 of these rockets landed in southern and eastern England between 8 September 1944 and 27 March 1945. They were represented by the German propaganda service as avenging the destruction of German cities by mass bombing raids. Braun evacuated his staff from Peenemünde in order to escape Russian internment as the Red Army advanced along the shore of the Baltic and, with more than a hundred of his scientific workers, he surrendered to the Americans (who also captured a considerable number of unfired missiles). He was taken to the United States to work on the American space programme, becoming Director of the US Ballistic Missile Agency in Alabama which developed a rocket to launch America's earth satellite in January 1958. In 1965 Braun was naturalized as an American citizen. His Saturn rockets were used in the Apollo missions, including the famous moonflight in July 1969.

Brezhnev, Leonid Ilyich (1906–82), Soviet leader, 1964–82: born at Dneprodzerzhinsk in the Ukraine. He studied engineering, worked on land conservation and became a Communist Party official during the Stalinist purges of the late 1930s. In the 'Great Patriotic War' of 1941–5 he held the rank of Colonel, responsible for political training. In 1950 the district of Dnepropetrovsk returned him to the Supreme Soviet where his political future was advanced by his compatriot, KHRUSCHEV, who secured Brezhnev's election to the Central Committee of the party shortly before the death of STALIN and to the inner Politburo in 1957. From May 1960 to July 1964 Brezhnev was Soviet President, a post which was then largely honorific, but in July 1964 he took charge of party affairs, as Khruschev's deputy. Three months later, on 15 October 1964, Brezhnev ousted Khruschev from his post as First Secretary of the party, KOSYGIN becoming at the same time Prime Minister. Although the Soviet leadership was nominally a partnership between Brezhnev and Kosygin, it was Brezhnev alone who took important decisions over foreign policy, notably the military intervention in Czechoslovakia to check the apparent liberalism of DUBCEK in 1968. In the spring of 1977 Brezhnev secured a revision of the Soviet Constitution which enabled him once more to assume the Soviet presidency while continuing to shape policy. Despite failing health, he appeared to keep tight control on party and state, yet in reality the system was becoming increasingly corrupt and inefficient. Brezhnev himself was largely responsible for Soviet intervention in Afghanistan in December 1979, a military occupation which became a lasting strain on Soviet resources. When Brezhnev died, on 10 November 1982, he was succeeded by his chief of secret police (KGB), ANDROPOV. D. R. Kelley (ed.): *Soviet Politics in the Brezhnev Era* (1980); R. Edmonds: *Soviet Foreign Policy in the Brezhnev Years* (Oxford, 1983); N. V. Riasanovsky: *A History of Russia* (4th edn Oxford, 1984).

Briand, Aristide (1862–1932), French Prime Minister on eleven occasions between 1909 and 1929: born at Nantes, became a lawyer and a journalist, entered the Chamber of Deputies as a Socialist from the Loire in 1902 and remained a Deputy for the rest of his life (representing the Loire Inférieure from 1919 onwards). He first attracted public attention by his sponsorship, in 1905, of legislation to end the collaboration of Church and State in France. In 1906 he accepted office in the Radical–Republican Coalition of Sarrien and was expelled from the Socialist Party. After a controversial period as Minister of Justice and Public Worship under CLEMENCEAU (who later came to dislike him intensely), Briand formed his first government on 24 July 1909. He faced industrial unrest with great determination, conscripting railway strikers who were army reservists so as to keep the trains running under military discipline. As wartime Prime Minister from October 1915 to March 1917 Briand lacked decisive leadership but in the 1920s he emerged as a far-sighted champion of the League of Nations and international arbitration. With STRESEMANN he was awarded the Nobel Peace Prize of 1926 for his advocacy of a Franco-German understanding, and in 1927 he collaborated with the US Secretary of State, KELLOGG, in drafting an international agreement by which the governments of sixty-five countries formally renounced aggressive war as an instrument of policy. T. Zeldin: *France 1848–1945*, Vol. 1 (Oxford, 1973); J. Jacobson: *Locarno Diplomacy, Germany and the West 1925–1929* (Princeton, N.J., 1972).

Bright, John (1811–89), British radical politician: born in Rochdale and educated at Quaker schools in Lancashire and Yorkshire. His father owned a cotton mill and the son entered the family business. At an early age he showed an interest in public affairs, notably in the problems of maintaining peace in the eastern Mediterranean and the Balkans. Bright became famous for his collaboration with Richard COBDEN in organizing the Anti-Corn Law League. He entered the Commons as MP for Durham in 1843 and, after the repeal of the Corn Laws in 1846, represented the Liberal Free Trade city of Manchester until 1857, when he was elected for Birmingham. Bright consistently upheld pacifist causes: he vigorously denounced the Crimean War in 1854 and the military intervention of his Liberal colleagues in Egypt in 1882, but he spoke out strongly in support of Lincoln and the Union during the American Civil War. He helped organize a campaign for extension of the franchise, which culminated in the Second Parliamentary Reform Act of 1867, and earlier he had successfully asserted the right of Jewish believers to sit in the House of Commons (1858). Bright held office as President of the Board of Trade under GLADSTONE from 1868 to 1870 and he was Chancellor of the Duchy of Lancaster, with a seat in the Cabinet, from April 1880 until July 1882. Like his fellow radical Joseph CHAMBERLAIN, Bright opposed Gladstone's Irish Home Rule policy from 1886 until his death. G. M. Trevelyan: *John Bright* (1913); J. T. Mills: *John Bright and the Quakers* (1935); A. Briggs: *Victorian People* (1954); A. J. P. Taylor: *The Trouble Makers* (1957).

Brooke, Alan Francis: see *Alanbrooke, Lord*.

Bruce, Stanley Melbourne (1883–1967), Australian Prime Minister: born and educated at Melbourne before studying law at Trinity Hall, Cambridge, and gaining his rowing blue in the 1904 university boat race. He practised at the English bar and fought at Gallipoli and in France with the Royal Fusiliers before entering Australian federal politics in 1918, returning to Europe as Australian delegate to the League of Nations in 1921. He was Treasury Minister under HUGHES in 1922 and Prime Minister of a Country Party/Nationalist coalition from February 1923 to October 1929, giving Australia its most self-consciously Anglicized conservative government, relaxing federal controls in order to promote free enterprise. He favoured 'men, money and markets', i.e., white immigration, capital loans (mainly from the City of London) and protected outlets for Australian products through imperial preference. The spread to Australia of the great agricultural depression discredited his policies. From 1932, however, he was Australia's main spokesman overseas, first at the Ottawa Economic Conference and from 1933 to 1945 as High Commissioner in London. For the last three years of the Second World War he was frequently present at CHURCHILL's meetings of the War Cabinet. He never settled again in Australia, accepting a United Kingdom peerage as Viscount Bruce of Melbourne in 1947 and devoting much of his later years to encouraging rowing as a sport. S. M. Bruce: *The Imperial Economic Situation* (1931); C. Edwards: *Bruce of Melbourne, Man of Two Worlds* (1965).

Brundtland, Gro Harlem (1939–), Norwegian Prime Minister: born Gro Harlem in Oslo, the daughter of a physician who was also a government minister. She was educated at Oslo University, completing her medical training at Harvard and in 1960 married Dr Arne Brundtland, a leading Norwegian Conservative politician. Nine years later she joined the Norwegian Labour Party (DNA), while serving as a medical officer in the public health service in the capital. She was appointed Minister of the Environment in 1974 and a year later was chosen as deputy leader of DNA, but she was not elected to parliament until 1977, representing Oslo itself. Early in 1981 she became party leader and Prime Minister, but Labour lost the election later that year. Mrs Brundtland was in opposition until May 1986, when she headed a minority Labour government which remained in power for three years. She was Chairman of the World Commission on Environment and Development, giving her name to the Brundtland Report of 1987 on 'Our Common Future', which, with its warnings of ecological disasters, prepared world opinion for the UN Earth Summit conference at Rio in 1992. The report won her the Third World Foundation prize in 1988, for the leadership she had given over environmental issues. Although enjoying widespread respect abroad, within Norway Mrs Brundtland's political position was never strong. She returned to office in 1990, gave up leadership of the DNA in November 1992, but remained Prime Minister after Labour emerged as the largest single party once more in the elections of September 1993. A. C. Kiel (ed.): *Continuity and Change, Aspects of Contemporary Norway* (Oslo, 1993).

Brüning, Heinrich (1885–1970), German Chancellor from 1930 to 1932: born into a middle-class Roman Catholic family at Münster. He was educated at Bonn, where he took a doctorate of economics. In 1914 he won an Iron Cross, First Class, on the Western Front. He joined the Roman Catholic Centre Party and was returned to the Reichstag as a Deputy from Silesia in 1924. Four years later he became parliamentary head of the Centre Party, although the party leadership was in the hands of a Church dignitary, Monsignor Kaas. On 28 March 1930 President HINDENBURG appointed Brüning Chancellor of an emergency government with the triple task of countering the economic depression, satisfying demands for a reform programme and stemming the right-wing revolutionary fervour engendered by HITLER and his Nazi movement. Brüning, however, had no majority in parliament and was forced to govern by decrees issued in Hindenburg's name. These measures needed the President's approval and, since he was suspicious of a Catholic Chancellor, they depended ultimately on the goodwill of the army leaders who advised Hindenburg. Brüning's attempt to alleviate distress in central Europe by proposing an Austro-German customs union in March 1931 was abandoned when it aroused strong opposition from the French and their European allies. Hindenburg finally turned against Brüning when he proposed to split up some huge estates facing bankruptcy in East Prussia so that they might become smallholdings. He was bluntly told by the President on 29 May 1932 that he would sign no more emergency decrees and resigned next day. Brüning escaped to Holland in 1934, settled in America and lectured at Harvard, returning to Cologne in 1947 but taking no further part in German politics. Critics maintain that his willingness to govern by decree helped discredit the parliamentary system of Germany and thereby made easier the Nazi dictatorship. G. A. Craig: *Germany 1866–1945* (Oxford, 1978); A. J. Nicholls: *Weimar and the Rise of Hitler* (1968); F. L. Carsten: *The Reichswehr and Politics, 1918–33* (1966).

Brusilov, Alexei Alexyevich (1853–1926), Russian General of the First World War: a cavalry officer, who had served in the Balkans in 1877–8 and the Far East 1904–5. As Commander of the Russian Eighth Army he invaded Galicia in 1914 but was forced to make an orderly withdrawal in the following spring. At the end of March 1916 Brusilov was appointed Commander on the South-West Russian Front with authority to prepare a major summer offensive. On 4 June 1916 'Brusilov's Offensive' began with an attack on

Austrian positions between the Pripet Marshes and the Carpathian Mountains. Within four weeks Brusilov had broken through, along a corridor nearly 200 miles deep and in places over 60 miles wide, a victory which brought the Russians more than a quarter of a million captives. Failure of support, and particularly of munition supplies, halted the advance in mid-August. The Tsarist armies never again went over to the offensive. Brusilov held Supreme Command under the provisional government from May to July 1917, and after the Revolution he was adviser to the Red Army during the campaign in Poland (1920). Later he was inspector of Soviet cavalry, establishing a new stud farm for cavalry horses outside Moscow in 1924–5. A. A. Brussilov: *A Soldier's Notebook, 1914–1918* (1930); B. Pares: *The Fall of the Russian Monarchy* (1939); N. Stone: *The Eastern Front, 1914–1917* (1975).

Bryan, William Jennings (1860–1925), American political orator and Secretary of State from 1913 to 1915: born in Salem, Illinois, graduated from Illinois College in 1881 and read law at Union College of Law in Chicago, served as a lawyer in Nebraska and sat as a Democrat Congressman from 1891 to 1895. His denunciation of the Gold Standard at the Democratic Party's Chicago Convention on 8 July 1896 – 'You shall not press down upon the brow of labour this crown of thorns, you shall not crucify mankind upon a cross of gold' – brought crusading fervour to the populist and agrarian denunciation of big business. Bryan won the Democratic Party nomination in 1896, and again in 1900 and 1908. His thunderous denunciation of imperialism and his impassioned zeal for reform disturbed the party bosses in 1912 and they 'played safe' in selecting Woodrow WILSON, whom Bryan, too, backed. When Wilson was elected, he appointed Bryan Secretary of State. This partnership worked well over purely American affairs, but there was an anti-European twist to Bryan's intensive Presbyterianism, and he feared that Wilson's protests to Germany after the sinking of the British ship *Lusitania* on her voyage from New York to Liverpool in May 1915 foreshadowed American entry into the European war. Bryan resigned in June 1915. For the last ten years of his life he became increasingly concerned with the need to uphold the old-fashioned fundamentalism of America's 'Bible Belt', and in July 1925, he made his last speeches as State Prosecutor in the trial at Dayton, Tennessee, of the Darwinian schoolteacher, Scopes. The trial exhausted Bryan and he died at Dayton five days after it ended. His audacity, integrity and passion, together with a primitive poetic imagery in the spoken word, ensured that Bryan had an impact on American public life out of all proportion to the brief twenty-six months in which he held office. W. Williams: *William Jennings Bryan* (New York, 1913); P. W. Glad: *The Trumpet Soundeth* (Lincoln, Nebr., 1960); R. Hofstadter: *The Age of Reform, from Bryan to FDR* (New York, 1955).

Buchanan, James (1791–1868), President of the United States from 1857 to 1861: born at Stony Batter in Pennsylvania, of Irish descent. After graduating from Dickinson College, Pennsylvania, he practised as a lawyer in his home state and sat in Congress for ten years (1821–31). President Andrew Jackson sent him to Russia as America's diplomatic representative in St Petersburg in 1832–3 and he negotiated the first formal Russo-American Commercial Treaty. Ten years in the Senate (1835–45) were followed by four as Secretary of State (1845–9), a term marked by the annexation of Texas and the settlement of a long dispute with Britain over the Oregon boundary. From 1853 to 1856 Buchanan was American Minister in London. He was nominated as Democratic candidate in 1856, partly because of his long experience, but even more because he was uncommitted on the vexed question of slavery. After winning the presidential election comfortably, Buchanan was inaugurated on 4 March 1857. Within less than a year he was in trouble over the slavery issue, backing proposals to admit Kansas to the Union as a slave state under the so-called 'Lecompton Constitution'. Northern Democrats followed Stephen A. DOUGLAS in denouncing President Buchanan's action as an attempt to preserve the institution of slavery. This split among the Democrats remained unhealed so long as Buchanan was at the White House. It thus helped LINCOLN win the 1860 election for the Republicans. In the winter of 1860 1, during the four-month interval between election and inauguration, the outgoing President showed himself unable to check the drift away from the Union of the Southern slave-owning states. The last seven years of Buchanan's life were spent in gloomy retirement from public affairs at his home in Lancaster, Pennsylvania. P. S. Klein: *James Buchanan* (New York, 1963); G. T. Curtis: *Life of James Buchanan* (2 vols) (New York, 1883); R. F. Nicholls; *The Disruption of American Democracy* (New York, 1948).

Bukharin, Nikolai Ivanovich (1888–1938), eminent Bolshevik: a close associate of LENIN from 1912, and highly popular with the Bolshevik Party. He was a man of great intellectual precision. Originally Bukharin shared the distrust felt by STALIN for TROTSKY and from 1926 to 1929 he controlled the Communist International. Bukharin did not agree with Stalin's enforced policy of agricultural collectivization and the two men fell out in 1929. For some years Bukharin still had sufficient following to remain in opposition to Stalin, but he never seems to have had the army contacts essential if Stalin's power were to be destroyed. In March 1938 Bukharin, and twenty Bolsheviks of lesser eminence, were charged with treason and put on trial in Moscow. Bukharin and seventeen others were found guilty and shot. Attempts by the prosecutor, VYSHINSKY, to prove that the accused were Nazi agents were not successful. He was formally rehabilitated in July 1988 by GORBACHEV, after a lengthy battle to clear his name by his widow, Anna Larina (1914–). S. F. Cohen: *Bukharin and the Bolshevik Revolution* (2nd edn Oxford, 1980); N. N. Kozlov and E. D. Weitz: *N. I. Bukharin, a Centenary Appreciation* (1990); D. Remnick: *Lenin's Tomb* (1993).

Bulganin, Nikolai (1895–1975), Soviet Prime Minister from 1955 to 1958: born in Nizhni-Novgorod (Gorki), fought in the Tsarist army from 1914 to 1917, becoming a communist at the Revolution and serving in the secret police for four years. In 1931 he was appointed Chairman of the Moscow Soviet – or, as the western press called him, 'Mayor of Moscow'. Much publicized town-planning projects and new metro lines gave him a superficial importance. In 1941 he helped prepare the defences of Moscow, with the rank of Lieutenant-General, and was created a Marshal of the Soviet Union in 1945, taking over the Commissariat of Defence from STALIN himself a year later. He was vice-premier under MALENKOV from 1953 until February 1955 when he became Prime Minister, sharing authority with KHRUSCHEV as head of the party. Although Marshal Bulganin became well known in the West for his visits, with Khruschev, to London and other cities, he was of much less importance than his partner. When Khruschev was certain of his supremacy within the Soviet hierarchy, Bulganin was induced to hand over the premiership to him (27 March 1958). Within five months Bulganin faded from the public eye, ending his official career as Chairman of the Soviet Bank. S. Bialer: *Stalin's Successors; Leadership. Politics and*

Change in the Soviet Union (1980); H. R. Swearer and M. Rush: *The Politics of Succession in the USSR* (Boston, Mass., 1964).

Bülow, Bernhard von (1849–1929), German Chancellor from 1900 to 1909: born at Flottbek on the Elbe, the son of a diplomat who served BISMARCK as Foreign Minister in 1877–8. The younger Bülow was educated at the University of Lausanne and was a Hussar officer in the Franco-Prussian War of 1870–1. He became a diplomat in 1873 and, after serving in Paris, St Petersburg, Vienna and other capitals, was appointed ambassador in Rome in 1894. His rapid advancement owed much to his friendship with Eulenburg, the close companion of Kaiser WILLIAM II. In June 1897 Bülow became Foreign Minister and in October 1900 the Kaiser made him the fourth Chancellor of a united Germany. Bülow was adroit, not trusted by other statesmen, and inclined to allow the specialists in the Foreign Ministry to settle matters in his name. He had few ideas on domestic policy. Until 1908 he retained authority, largely because the Kaiser was blind to his indolence and indulgent to his vanities, even creating him a Prince in June 1905. Bülow's repeated attempts to check the Kaiser's initiatives in foreign affairs, discrediting even those which were well-intentioned, culminated in his failure to support his sovereign when William was criticized in the Reichstag for his so-called interview printed in the *Daily Telegraph* on 28 October 1908. This episode destroyed the Kaiser's confidence in his Chancellor's ability or loyalty. When Bülow in his turn clashed with the Reichstag over the budget proposals of July 1909, William took the opportunity to dismiss him from the chancellorship. For six months in 1914–15 Bülow returned to the Rome embassy, trying unsuccessfully to prevent Italy from entering the war against Germany. In retirement Bülow wrote four large volumes of self-righteous memoirs, published posthumously and so damaging to his reputation that the fallen Kaiser remarked that 'Prince Bülow was the first person to commit suicide after death'. Prince von Bülow: *Memoirs* (4 vols) (1932); K. A. Lerman: *The Character as a Courtier; Bernhard von Bülow and the Governance of Germany, 1900–9* (Cambridge, 1990).

Bunche, Ralph Johnson (1904–71), American UN mediator: born in the Negro community of Detroit, orphaned as a child and brought up by his maternal grandmother, spending some of his youth in the Watts area of Los Angeles. He graduated in 1927 from the University of California at Los Angeles and undertook advanced sociological studies, subsequently becoming Professor of Political Science at Howard University, Washington DC. He was chief research analyst for the definitive study of the American Negro by the Swedish sociologist, Gunnar Myrdal. During the war he was given high responsibilities in the Department of State, joining the American delegation to the Dumbarton Oaks Conference of 1944 to work out proposals for the United Nations Organization which it was intended to set up at the end of the war. From 1947 onwards Dr Bunche worked entirely for the United Nations, accompanying Count BERNADOTTE as principal aide on his mission to Palestine, taking over his role as mediator in 1948, and negotiating a cease-fire between the Arabs and Jews. He served as Director of the Trusteeship Division of the United Nations from 1948 to 1954 and was awarded the Nobel Peace Prize in 1950 for his work in the Middle East. Under Dag HAMMARSKJÖLD he was UN Under-Secretary for Political Affairs, trying to sort out the troubled affairs of the Congo in 1960. He helped set up the UN peace-keeping force in Cyprus in 1964 and used his skill as a mediator in both Kashmir and the Yemen. No other black American has reached such eminence in world statesmanship. B. Urquhart: *Ralph Bunche, An American Life* (1993); R. Higgins: *UN Peacekeeping, 1947–65*, Vol. 1 (1973).

Burns, John (1858–1943), British socialist: born at Vauxhall in London and apprenticed as an engineer. His great gifts as an orator were acquired at temperance meetings and his socialism sprang from experience, allied to his friendship with survivors of the Paris Commune of 1871. Burns became a leader of the new and vigorous trade unionism, and helped organize the first dock strike in London (19 August to 14 September 1889). He was elected to the London County Council on its formation (1889) and entered Parliament as an Independent Member for Battersea in 1892. The 'Man with the Red Flag' became a pioneer of 'Lib–Lab' collaboration. He was President of the Local Government Board in the Campbell-Bannerman Liberal Government of December 1905, thus becoming the first man from the working classes to be sworn of the Privy Council or to sit in Cabinet. Burns was President of the Board of Trade for six months in 1914, but his pacifist principles induced him to resign from the government when war was declared. He remained in the Commons until 1918, a silent individualist who puzzled and exasperated many later socialist MPs. Burns, who had seemed to property owners such a dangerous bogyman in 1889, lived through the inter-war period as a forgotten recluse. A. P. Grubb: *John Burns* (1908); C. Hazelhurst: *Politicians at War* (1971).

Bush, George Herbert Walker (1924–), President of the United States from 1989 to 1993: born in Milton, Massachusetts and served in the US Navy during the Second World War. From Yale, where he graduated in economics, Bush went into business and made a considerable fortune from Texan oil while in his thirties. He campaigned vigorously for the Republicans in the mid-term elections of 1962 but failed in his bid for a Senate seat in 1964. From 1964 to 1970 he was a congressman. He was briefly US ambassador to the UN and to China and was also head of the CIA. He sought presidential nomination in 1980 and, when this bid failed, stood as running-mate for REAGAN, whom he served as Vice-President, from 1981 to 1989. In 1988 Bush became the first incumbent Vice-President for 150 years to win a presidential election, easily defeating the Democrat contender, Michael Dukakis. Although Bush pursued a vigorous foreign policy, especially over Iraq, the Republicans lost support at home, partly because of increased federal self assertiveness, but also because of the natural swing of the political pendulum, which facilitated the return of CLINTON and Democrat victories in both houses of the Congress in November 1992. President Bush retired to Texas. C. Campbell, S. J. and B. A. Rockman: *The Bush Presidency, First Appraisals* (Chatham, N.J., 1991) N. King: *George Bush; a Biography* (New York, 1980); D. M. Hill and P. Williams (eds): *The Bush Presidency, Triumphs and Adversities* (Basingstoke, 1994).

Bustamente, (William) Alexander (1884 1977), Jamaican Prime Minister from 1962 to 1965: born, the son of an Irish planter, near Kingston in Jamaica. After spending many years overseas (notably in New York, Cuba and Panama), Bustamente returned to Jamaica in 1932 and aroused the politically apathetic Jamaican workers into militant trade unionism. Emergency powers enabled the Governor to intern him in 1940 but by 1943 he had founded the Jamaican Labour Party, which won the elections of the following year to the island's House of Representatives. Successive British governments recognized Bustamente as Jamaica's leader and he received a knighthood in 1955. His opposition was largely responsible for defeating proposals for federation between the principal Caribbean islands. In August 1962 Jamaica was given dominion status and Sir Alexander Bustamente was a natural choice as the first Prime Minister, but ill-health limited his term of office to two years. G. K. Lewis: *The Growth of the Modern West Indies* (1968); F Hill: *Bustamente and his Letters* (Kingston, Jamaica, 1976).

Buthelezi, Mangosuthu Gatsha (1928–), Zulu tribal chief: born at Mahlabatini, the son of Chief Mathole Buthelezi, whom he succeeded in 1953. He was educated at Adams College and Fort Hare University. From 1953 to 1968 he helped King Cyprian administer the Zulu territories within apartheid-divided South Africa. He worked in partnership with successive South African governments and, with Pretoria's backing, was elected leader of the Zululand central authority at Ulundi, in 1970. Buthelezi became Chief Minister of the Kwa Zulu district of Natal in 1976, although titular Zulu leadership was exercised by the Zulu King, Goodwill Zweletinhi. Chief Buthelezi favoured traditional cultural ways, mistrusting the militant radicalism of the African National Congress. In the early 1970s he was encouraged to revive the Inkatha Zulu cultural association, to which South African governments had been hostile for half a century; and in 1975 Buthelezi began to incorporate political objectives into the association, which by 1991 was known as the Inkatha Freedom Party. Grave violence between Inkatha and ANC supporters began in 1991, especially in Natal, and continued until the eve of the multiracial election in April 1994. As Inkatha won forty-three seats in the new parliament Chief Buthelezi was brought into President MANDELA's coalition as Minister of Home Affairs. M. Buthelezi: *South Africa, my Vision of the Future* (1990); G. Marie and G. Hamilton: *An Appetite for Power, Buthelezi, Inkhata and South Africa* (Johannesburg, 1987).

Byrnes, James Francis (1879–1972), US Secretary of State from 1945 to 1947: born in Charleston, South Carolina, educated at local schools, became a lawyer and sat in Congress as one of the more temperate 'Southern Democrats' from 1911 to 1925. From 1930 to 1940 he was a Senator, critical of some aspects of the New Deal reforms of Franklin ROOSEVELT but, nevertheless, impressed by Roosevelt's dynamic leadership. In 1940 he helped overcome Southern Democrat hostility to Roosevelt's intention to stand for a third term as President. Byrnes was appointed to the Supreme Court in June 1941 but left the judiciary early in 1942 to become Director of Economic Stabilization, being appointed Director of War Mobilization in 1943. These posts were of greater importance than their titles suggest, for Byrnes was given responsibility for checking inflation and for increasing war production. Byrnes attended the Yalta Conference (February 1945) in an advisory capacity, and this experience induced TRUMAN to appoint him Secretary of State in July 1945. Byrnes avoided direct conflict with Russia over eastern European problems and encouraged the Americans to assist the Germans to build up their devastated industrial regions. He left the State Department in January 1947, handing over to General MARSHALL, and returned to Southern politics. From 1951 to 1955 Byrnes served as Governor of his native state, carefully guarding the conservative traditions of South Carolina's interpretation of civil rights but avoiding the virulence of language so often used by Southern politicians lacking his knowledge of a wider world. J. F. Byrnes: *Speaking Frankly* (New York, 1947), *All in a Lifetime* (New York, 1958).

C

Caillaux, Joseph (1863–1944), influential French politician from 1899 to 1937: born at Le Mans, became an inspector of taxes and entered the Chamber of Deputies as a moderate Republican in 1898. His knowledge of taxation led to his appointment as Minister of Finance in 1899, an office he held until 1902. Caillaux's personal politics moved to the Left and it was as a Radical Socialist that he sat in the government of CLEMENCEAU from 1906 to 1909, again serving as Minister of Finance. In 1909 he successfully steered an income tax bill through a largely hostile Chamber, although he could not secure the passage of so 'un-French' a measure through the Senate. For the last six months of the year 1911 Caillaux was Prime Minister, seeking a colonial settlement with Germany after the Agadir crisis over French penetration of Morocco. He was again Minister of Finance in 1913 and 1914. On 16 March 1914 the second Mme Caillaux shot dead the editor of the newspaper *Figaro* for publishing private letters discreditable to her husband and supplied by the first Mme Caillaux: the assassin was acquitted at her trial. Caillaux's advocacy of a compromise peace with Germany led to his arrest by the Clemenceau government in 1917: he was imprisoned, deprived of political rights and was fortunate to escape execution on a treason charge. By 1925 he had recovered his rights, sitting in the Senate for his native *département* until 1940, and holding office briefly on three more occasions as Minister of Finance. He used his parliamentary experience to marshal opposition in the Senate to the taxation proposals of the 'Popular Front' government formed by BLUM in 1936. Caillaux was a characteristic representative of what a political critic derisively nicknamed the 'Republic of Pals'. P. Shankland: *Death of an Editor* (1981); R. M. Watt: *Dare Call It Treason* (New York, 1963); T. Zeldin: *France 1848–1945*, Vol. 1 (Oxford, 1973).

Callaghan, (Leonard) James (1912–), British Prime Minister from 1976 to 1979: born and educated at Portsmouth, worked for the Inland Revenue in the 1930s and served in the Royal Navy in the Second World War. He was elected Labour MP for South Cardiff in 1945, the constituency boundaries being changed soon afterwards and renamed Cardiff South-East. He won that seat in the ten following General Elections. From 1947 to 1951 he held minor offices at the Ministry of Transport and the Admiralty and in 1963 was an 'outsider' in the contest for party leadership, won by Harold WILSON, under whom Callaghan served as Chancellor of the Exchequer from 1964 to 1967, Home Secretary from 1967 to 1970, and Foreign Secretary when Labour returned to office in February 1974. Callaghan, a 'centre of the road' socialist, stood once more for the party leadership on the eve of Wilson's resignation, winning on the third ballot. On 5 April 1976 he became the first former naval officer to head a British government. As Prime Minister he began to gain considerable popularity, his calm avuncular manner suggesting a security which was in contrast to the gloom of political commentators. These pundits he confounded on 7 September

1978 by announcing he would not call the autumn General Election which the Press had predicted. This was a tactical error. A winter of unofficial strikes weakened the standing of his government, which was defeated on a vote of no confidence on 28 March 1979. He resigned on 4 May, after defeat in the previous day's General Election, but remained leader of the Opposition to THATCHER until 15 October 1980, when he resigned the party leadership. Callaghan remained in the Commons until he received a life peerage in June 1987. J. Callaghan: *Time and Chance* (1987); H. Pelling: *A Short History of the Labour Party* (10th edn 1993); D. Kavanagh (ed.): *The Politics of the Labour Party* (1982).

Calles, Plutarco Elias (1877–1945), Mexican President from 1924–8: born in Sonora province, took part in the overthrow of DIAZ in 1910 and was active as a left-wing revolutionary until becoming President in December 1924. His four-year term of office failed to implement promised reforms but was marked by extreme anti-clericalism. Subsequently ex-President Calles sought to shape Mexican policy indirectly, through nominees to office and by setting up a National Revolutionary Party (1929). But his ambitions were thwarted by his former protégé, General CARDENAS, who became President in 1934. Calles went into exile in the United States from 1936 to 1941 but, though he received American backing against the alleged communist Cardenas, he never recovered his old primacy in Mexico's affairs. F. Brandenburg: *The Making of Modern Mexico* (Englewood Cliffs, N.J., 1966).

Campbell-Bannerman, Henry (1836–1908), British Prime Minister from 1905 to 1908: born in Glasgow, the son of Sir James Campbell, a Lord Provost of Glasgow. He was known as Henry Campbell when at Glasgow High School, Trinity College, Cambridge, and on election as Liberal MP for Stirling Burghs in 1868, a seat he held until his death. In 1871 he inherited property from an uncle and added the additional surname Bannerman. In 1886 'C-B' entered the Cabinet of GLADSTONE as War Secretary, holding that office again from 1892 to 1895. He was knighted in the resignation honours of 1895. Sir Henry was a man of common sense, not a good speaker but respected for calmly adhering to his principles. In 1898 he became Liberal leader in the Commons, principally because he had fewer enemies than any better-known colleague. He sympathized with the more progressive members of the Liberal Party, supporting their demands for social reform and their condemnation of the 'imperialist' war against the Boers in South Africa, but he was judicial and cautious in his comments. When he became Prime Minister in December 1905 his government faithfully followed the precepts he laid down in Opposition: land reforms, trade union reforms, reconciliation with the South Africans. Ill-health forced his resignation in the first week of April 1908, and he was succeeded by ASQUITH. Campbell-Bannerman died, still living in the Prime Minister's official residence, on 22 April 1908. J. Wilson: *C. B.: a Life of Sir Henry Campbell-Bannerman* (1973); J. A. Spender: *Sir Henry Campbell Bannerman G. C. B.* (1923).

Cardenas, Lazaro (1895–1970), Mexican President from 1934 to 1940: born, a peasant's son, at Jiquilpan in Michoacan province. He supported Mexico's progressive revolutionaries as an active soldier from 1913 onwards, reaching the rank of General at the age of 28 and serving as Governor of his native province from 1928–32 under the patronage of ex-President CALLES. Cardenas was too strong a personality to remain Calles' puppet. He assumed office as President on 1 December 1934 and implemented long-promised reforms, including women's suffrage and improved church–state relations. He embarked on major projects for land redistribution, as well as nationalization of railways and the sugar industry. When foreign oil companies declined to raise the wages of their workers, General Cardenas expropriated American, British and Dutch oil properties, placing them under the co-managment of the powerful Trade Union Federation. This action led to strained relations abroad. At the same time Cardenas warmly supported republican Spain in the Civil War and in 1936 he offered TROTSKY political asylum. He survived several uprisings, encouraged by Calles from the USA. Cardenas fulfilled his full six-year term, handing over the presidency to the less radical General Manuel Camacho on 30 November 1940. F. Brandenburg: *The Making of Modern Mexico* (Englewood Cliffs, N.J., 1966).

Cardwell, Edward (1813–86), British Liberal politician who modernized the army: born in Liverpool, educated at Winchester and at Balliol College, Oxford. He entered Parliament, as a supporter of Sir Robert Peel, as Member for Clitheroe in 1842, subsequently becoming a Gladstonian Liberal and holding minor office under PALMERSTON from 1852 to 1855. Four years later Cardwell entered the Cabinet as Chief Secretary for Ireland (1859–66). In the closing weeks of 1868 GLADSTONE appointed him Secretary for War. He concentrated over the following six years on modernizing the British army. No previous British war minister had reorganized or reformed the army so drastically. Cardwell introduced short-service enlistment, abolished flogging and other savage penalties, abandoned the practice of allowing commissions to be purchased, established a linked battalion system so as to provide an equitable policy for service overseas, withdrew garrisons from self-governing colonies and equipped the infantry with new and efficient rifles. He was created a Viscount in 1874 but took little further part in public life. R. Biddulph: *Lord Cardwell at the War Office* (1904); C. Barnettt: *Britain and Her Army 1509–1970* (1970).

Carol II (1893–1953), King of Romania from 1930 to 1940: born in Sinaia, the eldest son of Ferdinand of Romania (1865–1927, King from 1914 to his death) and his consort, Marie (1875–1938), a daughter of Queen Victoria's second son, Alfred, Duke of Edinburgh. While serving as an officer in the last stages of the First World War, Crown Prince Carol's private life became so scandalous that the King threatened him with forfeiture of the succession. By 1921 he had settled down sufficiently to marry Princess Helen of Greece, a son, Michael, being born to them at the end of the same year. In 1923, however, Carol met Magda Lupescu, the wife of an army officer and daughter of a Jewish chemist from Jassy. When she became Carol's mistress, King Ferdinand carried out his threat and barred him from the succession. Carol and Magda Lupescu lived together in Switzerland from 1925 to 1930, Carol's marriage to Princess Helen being dissolved in 1928. On King Ferdinand's death, a Council of Regency was established for the 6-year-old Michael, but in June 1930 Carol suddenly flew to Bucharest and was proclaimed King, with the support of the much-respected leader of the National Party, the Prime Minister Juliu Maniu. Romania retained the parliamentary apparatus of a westernized democracy until 1937 when Carol's admiration for MUSSOLINI prompted him to set up a thinly disguised royal dictatorship, with all political parties banned from February 1938 onwards. He tried to strike diplomatic bargains with the rival Great Powers, using his country's resources in oil and wheat as counters, but he was too distant from France and Britain and too easily outwitted by the European dictators for his policy to succeed.

Between June and August 1940 he was forced to retrocede Romanian territory to Hungary, Bulgaria and the Soviet Union. This humiliation turned the Romanian Army and people against him. Effective power passed into the hands of General ANTONESCU. King Carol abdicated in his son's favour on 6 September 1940, spending his remaining years in exile with Magda Lupescu. They were married shortly before his death. A. L. Easterman: *King Carol, Hitler and Lupescu* (1942); R. L. Wolff: *The Balkans in Our Time* (1956); K. Hitchins: *Rumania, 1866–1947* (Oxford, 1994).

Carrington, Lord (Peter Alexander Rupert) (1919–), British Conservative politician: eldest son of the fifth Baron Carrington, whom he succeeded in 1938. He was educated at Eton and the Royal Military Academy, Sandhurst, serving in the Grenadier Guards in Europe during the Second World War; as Major, awarded the Military Cross in 1945. He held junior office under CHURCHILL and EDEN (1951–6), was High Commissioner in Australia for three years and then entered the MACMILLAN government in October 1959 as First Lord of the Admiralty. Under DOUGLAS-HOME Carrington was Leader of the House of Lords and he served HEATH as Defence Secretary 1970–4. In THATCHER's faltering early years (1979–82) he was Foreign and Commonwealth Secretary, helping to establish independence for Zimbabwe and strengthening NATO. He resigned in April 1982, after the surprise Argentinian assault on the Falkland Islands. From 1984 to 1988 he was Secretary-General of NATO. In early August 1991 Lord Carrington began twelve months as EC mediator in the former Yugoslav lands. His proposals sought to retain a loose Yugoslav federal cohesion, but with disputed areas safeguarded within a 'cantonal' structure. His plan was unacceptable to the main belligerents; in August 1992 Lord OWEN succeeded him as EC mediator. P. Carrington: *Reflections Upon Things Past* (1988); P. Cosgrave: *Carrington; a Life and a Policy* (1985).

Carson, Edward Henry (1854–1935), barrister and Ulster Unionist leader from 1910 to 1914: born in Dublin, entered Parliament as Unionist MP for Dublin University in 1892. His fame as an advocate sprang from his handling of a number of cases in the late 1890s, notably his cross-examination of Oscar Wilde in 1895. He became Solicitor-General (with a knighthood) under SALISBURY in 1900, holding the office until December 1905. Fears that the Liberals intended to impose Home Rule on Ireland led Carson in 1910 to begin organizing resistance to Home Rule both in England and in Ulster. By 1912 he was leader of a private army of 80,000 men, the Ulster Volunteers, threatening rebellion. He served under ASQUITH as Attorney-General from May to October 1915 but found the Prime Minister antipathetic. LLOYD GEORGE appointed Carson First Lord of the Admiralty in December 1916 but he was not an effective departmental chief, and in July 1917 he was brought into the War Cabinet as minister without portfolio. Here, however, he proved an uneasy colleague and resigned in January 1918, finding it easier to criticize the government than give full support to Lloyd George once he discovered that he was drafting an all-Ireland Home Rule Bill. He sat as MP for Belfast, Duncairn 1918–21, seeking a compromise over Ulster, but he resigned as Unionist leader and spokesman in 1921, giving his main interests once more to the lawcourts. As Baron Carson of Duncairn he was a Lord Appeal from 1921 to 1929. H. Montgomery Hyde: *Carson* (1953); A. T. Q. Stewart: *The Ulster Crisis* (1967).

Carter, James Earl (1924–), President of the United States, 1977–81: born in Archery, Georgia. From South Western

College he entered the Naval Academy, Annapolis, and was commissioned in 1947, serving six years. In 1953 he returned to Georgia, sitting as a State Senator in Atlanta from 1962 to 1966. He was elected Governor of Georgia in 1971, gained the Democratic Party's nomination for the presidency at the New York Convention in July 1976 and defeated the sitting Republican President Gerald FORD in the presidential election of 3 November 1976, Carter gaining 51 per cent of the popular vote. His lack of experience of Washington politics weakened his control of domestic affairs and he suffered from an economic recession and from an energy crisis caused by the contraction of oil supplies in 1979. At first Carter was more successful in international affairs: his long series of meetings with President SADAT and Menachem BEGIN at Camp David in Maryland, 5–17 September 1978, enabled a peace treaty to be concluded between Egypt and Israel; and in June 1979 he reached agreement with the Russians over strategic arms limitation. But the seizure of American hostages by Iranian students (4 November 1979), and the Soviet occupation of Afghanistan posed major problems for his administration in an election year and he was decisively defeated by the Republican, Ronald REAGAN, in the presidential election of November 1980. In 1994–5 Carter's reputation as an elder statesman enabled him to assist President CLINTON as an international mediator. J. Dumbrell: *The Carter Presidency* (Manchester, 1993); L. H Shoup: *The Carter Presidency and Beyond* (New York, 1980).

Casement, Roger (1864–1916), Irish patriot: born in Dun Laoghaire (then known as Kingstown), and was in the British consular service from 1892 to 1911. Reports on the atrocious treatment of native workers in the Congo and Brazil won him high commendation in London and he was knighted in 1911. Ulster resistance to Home Rule proposals stimulated his sense of Irish nationalism. He went to America in 1914, travelling from New York to Berlin shortly after the outbreak of the First World War in order to secure German aid for Irish independence. For eighteen months he tried to raise a free Irish brigade from among prisoners-of-war in Germany. On 21 April 1916 he landed from a German U-boat near Tralee, apparently hoping to prevent a rebellion from taking place two days later since he knew that the Germans could not give the 'Easter Rising' military support at that stage of the war. Casement was arrested within a few hours of coming ashore. He was convicted of high treason in a trial at the Old Bailey. The so-called 'Black Diaries', containing homosexual passages and erotic fantasies, were circulated by British agents among groups likely to press for Casement's reprieve. He was hanged on 3 August 1916. B. Inglis: *Roger Casement* (1973); R. Kee: *The Green Flag*, Vol. 2 (1972).

Castro, Fidel (1927–), Cuban revolutionary leader: born near Santiago de Cuba, the son of a sugar planter. He practised law in Havana from 1949 to 1953, but was imprisoned for two years after leading an unsuccessful armed revolt against the Moncada Barracks on 26 July 1953. In 1955 he was freed, under an amnesty, and allowed to go into exile, spending most of the following twelve months in Mexico and organizing resistance among Cuban liberals and radicals to the capricious regime of BATISTA. He landed secretly with eighty followers in eastern Cuba on 2 December 1956. Thereafter for eighteen months Castro and his '26 July Movement' waged a guerrilla war against Batista from a secret base in the Sierra Maestra. Gradually Castro won for himself the reputation of a revolutionary saviour so that when, in March 1958, he called for 'total war' against Batista he received support

from many different sources, some far less sympathetic to socialism than was Castro himself. He entered Havana triumphantly on 8 January 1959 and took office as Prime Minister a month later. Close contacts with the Soviet Union and China – encouraged by his President of the Cuban National Bank, Che GUEVARA – alarmed the United States even though the Americans had at first welcomed his elimination of Batista. In April 1961 the American-sponsored landing of émigrés in the Bay of Pigs failed so absurdly that it increased Castro's prestige, as well as confirming his suspicion of American intentions. In December 1961 Castro delivered a speech in which he claimed to have been a Marxist-Leninist since his days as a student at Havana University. The individualistic character of Castro's revolutionary socialism was shown a year later when he took the opportunity of denouncing the narrowly doctrinaire orthodoxy of the recognized Cuban communist leader, Anibale Escalante, whom Castro sent into exile. But the year 1962 saw the closest collaboration between Moscow and Havana, with Soviet military experts stationed in Cuba and with world peace in jeopardy when President KENNEDY reacted firmly to the threatened installation of Soviet missiles. Castro's backing for urban guerrillas in Central and South America and his encouragement of liberation movements in Africa showed, at times, an independence in world policy which alarmed his Soviet allies. On the other hand, Castro's Cuba became in 1972 the first state in the western hemisphere to join the Soviet-sponsored economic community, Comecon, and Cuban troops collaborated closely with Soviet advisers in Angola and Ethiopia during 1977–8. Castro strengthened his position within Cuba by the revised constitution of February 1976, which enabled him to become on 2 November 1976 both President of the Council of State and head of government, the Vice-President being his younger brother, Raoul. The collapse of the Soviet Union led to the recall of Cuban 'volunteers' from Africa and to minor changes in Castro's style of government, but the (all-communist) National Assembly duly re-elected him as head of state and government for a further five-year term in March 1993. The last Russian combat troops left Cuba four months later, after thirty-one years of Soviet military presence on the island.
H. Thomas: *The Cuban Revolution* (1977), *The Cuban Revolution 25 Years Later* (Epping, 1984); S. Balfour: *Castro* (2nd edn 1995); J. O'Connor: *The Origins of Socialism in Cuba* (1970); J. I. Dominguez: *Cuba, Order and Revolution* (Cambridge, Mass., 1978).

Catt, Carrie Chapman (1859–1947), American suffragette: born in Ripon, Wisconsin, educated at Iowa State College and became a superintendent of schools. She succeeded Susan ANTHONY as champion of women's suffrage, although she was by nature more conservative and less militant than her predecessor. Carrie Catt was President of the National American Woman Suffrage Association from 1900 to 1904 and from 1915 until her death. Her constant pressure on members of Congress and on the Executive secured passage of the Nineteenth Amendment to the Constitution (proposed May 1919, ratified August 1920) declaring that 'the right of citizens of the United States to vote shall not be denied . . . on account of sex'. Thereafter she organized the League of Women Voters so as to ensure that American women were prepared to use responsibly the suffrage they had won.
R. B. Fowler: *Carrie Catt, Feminist Politician* (Boston, 1986).

Cavour, Camillo (1810–61), first Prime Minister of a united Italy: born in Turin, his family belonging to the Piedmontese aristocracy. At the age of 21 he resigned his commission in the army because of his liberal views, disapproving of the repressive policies imposed by the Piedmontese government, of which his father was a member. He then concentrated on improving the yield of the family estates by scientific farming and visited both Britain and France, also studying their political systems. He championed the idea of Italian unity in a newspaper, *Il Risorgimento*, which he established in 1847, and he entered the Piedmontese parliament in June 1848, holding several ministerial posts from 1850 to November 1852 when he was invited by King Victor EMMANUEL II to form a government. At first, Count Cavour concentrated on modernizing the finances and commercial system of Piedmont but he then began to enlarge the army and construct roads, railways and canals which would be of strategic value in any war. His government also sought to curb clerical influence and secure for the state some of the Church's wealth. Cavour believed in a unified Italian kingdom ruled by the Piedmontese dynasty, the House of Savoy, but he was convinced Italy could only be 'made' through outside help. In order to raise the Italian Question at the subsequent peace conference Cavour encouraged Victor Emmanuel to enter the Crimean War as France's ally in 1855. Three years later (July 1858) Cavour met NAPOLEON III at Plombières and concluded with him a secret agreement: France would receive Savoy and Nice from Piedmont in return for military help against Austria in a war to create a unified north Italian kingdom which would include Lombardy-Venetia, liberated from Austrian rule. Cavour provoked the Austrians to attack Piedmont in April 1859 but the heavy casualties of the subsequent battles at Magenta and Solferino induced Napoleon to conclude a premature peace, the Armistice of Villafranca, on 11 July 1859. He secured Lombardy for Piedmont but Venetia remained under Austrian rule.

This apparent treachery by Napoleon led Cavour to resign, but he returned as Prime Minister six months later in order to negotiate the union of the central Italian duchies (Tuscany, Parma and Modena), and also the Romagna, with Piedmont. He was thus again in office when, in May 1860, the radical patriot GARIBALDI sailed from Genoa with his 'Thousand' to aid rebel Italian nationalists in Sicily and Naples. Cavour, fearing the radical character of Garibaldi's redshirts and uncertain of international repercussions, gave no help to the Thousand, but shrewdly let Italian patriots believe he might do so if necessary. In September Cavour risked the dispatch of Piedmontese troops southwards through the papal states (although avoiding the 'Patrimony of St Peter', around Rome) and Victor Emmanuel was able to meet Garibaldi's victorious expedition on the river Volturno (26 October 1860), receiving from Garibaldi his conquests. A unified Italian kingdom, achieved by a combination of Cavour's diplomacy and Garibaldi's generalship, was proclaimed on 17 March 1861. Cavour became the first Prime Minister of this kingdom, but within six weeks he died in Turin from a heart attack. He had no illusions concerning the ruthless realism of his policy: 'If we were to do for ourselves what we have done for our country, we should be great rogues indeed', he remarked to his colleague, Massimo d'Azeglio (1798–1866) in September 1860. D. Mack Smith: *Cavour* (1985), *Cavour and Garibaldi, 1860* (Cambridge, (1954); D. Beales: *The Risorgimento and the Unification of Italy* (1981).

Ceauşescu, Nicolae (1918–89), Romanian communist and President: born near Piteşti, became a member of the banned Communist Party of Romania in 1936 and was for many years in charge of its youth movement. Ceauşescu remained a loyal supporter of Gheorge Gheorghiu-Dej, who was head of the Romanian Communist Party from 1945 until his death in 1965. From April 1954, Ceauşescu was a member of the party's inner secretariat, being in effect deputy to Gheorghiu-Dej from 1957 to 1965, when he succeeded him as General Secretary of the party. Ceauşescu consistently showed an independence of Soviet policy: he overcame a threat from the Russophile head of the security services in 1967, becoming head of state at the end of the year; and he denounced the occupation of Prague by troops from the other Warsaw Pact countries in 1968. He defied Soviet criticism of China, receiving HUA in Bucharest in 1978, and permitted Romanian patriotism at times to express a more intensive nationalism than was customary among the 'socialist republics'. In June 1978 President Ceauşescu and his wife were welcomed to Britain on a four-day state visit. By then, however, the harsh and repressive character of his policies was becoming increasingly apparent, especialy in the treatment of Romania's ethnic minorities, notably the Magyars in Transylvania. He promoted his own family, lived extravagantly and authorized grandiose public works projects, including the sweeping away of historic parts of Bucharest in order to enhance the grandeur of a new presidential palace. While he was in China on an official visit in December 1989 the regime was destroyed in ten days of violent revolution. On his return home the President and his wife were seized by revolutionaries and, after a summary trial, were executed together by firing squad on Christmas Day. M. Almond: *The Rise and Fall of Nicolae and Elena Ceauşescu* (1992); I. Pacepa: *Red Horizons* (1988).

Cetewayo (Cetshwayo) (*c.* 1840–84), King of the Zulus 1873–83: In his early thirties he succeeded to the kingdom established half a century earlier by his uncle Shaka (*c.* 1787–1829). Cetewayo was faced by British colonial plans to acquire territory north of Cape Colony and spread British influence into central Africa, a task which required passage through Zululand. His warrior people, armed with assegai and skilled in swift movement through familiar terrain, surprised a British column of 1,200 men and auxiliaries at Isandhlwana (22 January 1879) and slaughtered almost all the invaders. A second Zulu assault later that day on a fortified mission station at Rorke's Drift was beaten off. More than 17,000 British troops were rushed to Natal to overcome the Zulus and, in the following July, Cetewayo was defeated at Ulundi and taken prisoner. He was held in captivity, mainly near Cape Town, until restored as a British puppet ruler in 1883. The Zulus, however, refused to accept this limited sovereignty. They drove Cetewayo into exile. Soon afterwards he died, broken in spirit, at Ekowa. But the Zulu victory at Isandhlwana had so dented British imperial pride that, despite his later fate, Cetewayo remained a legendary figure, remembered with awe. J. Guy: *The Destruction of the Zulu Kingdom* (Pietermaritzburg, 1979); T. Pakenham: *The Scramble for Africa* (1991).

Chadli, Benjadid (1929–), Algerian President from 1979 to 1991: born at Sebaa, fought with the National Liberation Front (FLN) against the French from 1955 to 1958, becoming a close associate of BOUMÉDIENNE. Chadli was military commandant at Algiers in June 1965 when Boumédienne overthrew the BEN BELLA. He was at once brought into the Revolutionary Council and served as a close adviser to Boumédienne until the President's death in December 1978. Two months later Chadli was elected President. He gradually reduced the narrow power base of the Algerian socialist republic until, in 1989, he accepted a new constitution which anticipated a multiparty system. But the first local elections, held in July 1990, showed such a surge of support for the FIS, an Islamic fundamentalist movement, that Chadli postponed national elections, a decision which led to widespread unrest from June 1991 onwards. When, in December 1991, the first round of the elections were at last held, the threat to Algerian socialism from the FIS looked so formidable that President Chadli was induced to resign, passing over executive authority to a Higher Committee of State. This emergency improvisation failed to restore calm and Algeria was left in a condition of chronic political instability. M. Bennoun: *The Making of Contemporary Algeria, 1830–1987* (1988).

Chamberlain, Austen (1863–1937), British Foreign Secretary from 1924 to 1929 born in Birmingham, the eldest son of Joseph CHAMBERLAIN and half-brother to Neville CHAMBERLAIN. He was educated at Rugby and Trinity College, Cambridge. From 1892 to 1937 he sat as a Unionist/Conservative MP for East Worcestershire. He entered the BALFOUR Cabinet in July 1902 as Postmaster General, his father sitting in the same Cabinet for fourteen months as Colonial Secretary. Austen became Chancellor of the Exchequer in 1903, introducing two cautiously conventional budgets even though he was known to favour tariff reform. During the Liberal governments of CAMPBELL-BANNERMAN and ASQUITH, Austen Chamberlain increased his reputation as a good parliamentarian. When Balfour was ousted as party leader in 1911, Austen's claims were passed over, largely because he seemed too honest and too self-consciously public school for tough political contests. It was said of him that 'he always played the game and he always lost it.' In the LLOYD GEORGE Coalition of 1916–19 he was Indian Secretary (outside the Cabinet) until January 1918 when he entered the War Cabinet as minister without portfolio, becoming Chancellor again from 1919 until March 1921. His sense of loyalty made him abstain from the manoeuvres which brought down Lloyd George. By declining to serve under LAW, he ruled himself out of succession to the premiership in 1923. He agreed, however, to take the Foreign Office in the second Cabinet of BALDWIN (1924–9) and he showed great understanding of European affairs, helping to ease international tension so as to make possible the Locarno Treaties of 1925. For these services he was created a Knight of the Garter and shared the Nobel Peace Prize of 1925 with the American reparations expert, CHARLES DAWES. By 1931 his mental powers had begun to fail and he was given no posts in the MACDONALD or Baldwin national coalitions. He died on 16 March 1937, ten weeks before his half-brother became Prime Minister. A. Chamberlain: *Down The Years* (1935); C. Petrie: *The Life and Letters of the Rt Hon. Sir Austen Chamberlain* (1940); D. Dutton: *Austen Chamberlain, Gentleman in Politics* (1985).

Chamberlain, Joseph (1836–1914), British radical reformer and imperial statesman: born in London and educated at University College School. He became a Birmingham businessman, making considerable profits from Nettlefold's screw factory. In 1868 he was elected to the town council of Birmingham, serving the city as Lord Mayor from 1873 to 1876 and becoming famous nationally for his slum-clearance schemes. A by-election soon after the end of his mayoralty allowed him to enter the House of Commons as a radical Liberal. In 1877 he set up the first National Liberal Federation, a pioneer party 'machine' unfamiliar in British politics. In 1880 he entered the second Cabinet of GLADSTONE as President of the Board of Trade, passing two important commercial measures (the Bankruptcy Act and the Patents Act of 1883) as well as valuable legislation to protect merchant seamen. His radical zeal forced the government to accept the need for further extension of the franchise and parliamentary reform (1884), raising the electorate from three million to five million. During the election campaign of 1886 Chamberlain offered the voters an 'unauthorized programme' of radical reforms. This contributed considerably to the Liberal victory at the polls (November 1885) which brought Gladstone back to power in February 1886. Chamberlain, who might reasonably have expected a senior Cabinet post, accepted Gladstone's offer of the presidency of the Local Government Board, but resigned two months later as he could not support Gladstone's 'conversion' to Home Rule. From April 1886 until the summer of 1895 he led the Liberal Unionists, drawing politically closer to the Conservatives under Lord SALISBURY, who offered to make Chamberlain Chancellor of the Exchequer when he formed his third government in June 1895. Chamberlain took, by preference, the Colonial Office and for eight years was the most energetic and imperial-minded Colonial Secretary in British history. Only the Prime Minister himself had greater influence in the Cabinet; Chamberlain was allowed to speak authoritatively on foreign affairs as well as to dominate his own department. He was criticized for his personal contacts with Cecil RHODES and with the imperialist adventurer Dr JAMESON, whose disastrous raid almost cost Rhodes his political career. Chamberlain's forward policy in southern Africa goaded the Boers under KRUGER into resistance, thus precipitating the Boer War of 1899–1902. As Colonial Secretary, Chamberlain also favoured imperial federation, encouraging contacts between the home government and the Prime Ministers of Canada, New Zealand and Australia (which achieved unity as a Commonwealth, with Chamberlain's backing, in January 1901). In September 1903 Chamberlain resigned from the government of BALFOUR in order to campaign for tariff reform, an extension of ideas for 'imperial preference' in trade which he had first canvassed at the Colonial Conference of 1897. Chamberlain wished the British Empire to become a self-contained trading unit, protected against foreign competition from Germany, France and the United States by high tariffs. 'Imperial preference' involved the abandonment of Free Trade doctrines held by all leading British politicians, irrespective of party, for over half a century; and Chamberlain's campaign for tariff reform split the Unionist Party on the eve of the 1906 General Election. On 11 July 1906 he was struck down with paralysis. Although he lived on until 2 July 1914, he never again took any active part in political life. J. L. Garvin and J. Amery: *The Life of Joseph Chamberlain* (6 vols) (1932–9); C. H. D. Howard (ed.): *A Political Memoir 1880–1892 by Joseph Chamberlain* (1953); A. N. Porter: *The Origins of the South African War; Joseph Chamberlain and the Diplomacy of Imperialism* (Manchester, 1980).

Chamberlain, Neville (1869–1940), British Prime Minister from 1937 to 1940: son of Joseph CHAMBERLAIN by his second wife. He was born at Edgbaston and educated at Rugby, spending seven years in the Bahamas as manager of his father's sisal plantation before going into industry and local politics in Birmingham, where he became Lord Mayor in the spring of 1915. LLOYD GEORGE appointed him Director-General of National Service in 1916, dismissing him after seven months for the painstakingly thorough method he applied to work of urgency. Chamberlain was elected as Conservative MP for a Birmingham constituency (Ladywood) in 1918, changing to the Edgbaston constituency for the last eleven years of his life. LAW brought him into the Cabinet in March 1923 as Minister of Health, an office he held for five years under BALDWIN and in which he successfully applied the family experience of municipal affairs. In November

1931 he became Chancellor of the Exchequer in the National Government, introducing an Import Duties Bill in February 1932 and following it up with a Budget which promised 'Empire Free Trade' but, in reality, launched an era of tight Protection. Chamberlain succeeded Baldwin as Prime Minister at the end of May 1937. He was immediately faced by a series of crises in foreign affairs (about which, as his half-brother Sir Austen had told him a few months earlier, he did not 'know anything'). Chamberlain put more faith in the views of his personal adviser on finance, Sir Horace Wilson (1882–1972), than in the diplomats. He accepted the need to 'appease' what he thought were Germany's legitimate grievances: he flew twice to Germany in September 1938 to seek a settlement with HITLER in personal talks, believing that, by the Munich Agreement, he had ensured 'peace for our time', at the cost of requiring the Czechs to surrender border regions in which Germans, Poles or Hungarians lived in considerable numbers. Hitler's subsequent occupation of the Czech lands (Bohemia and Moravia) in March 1939 induced Chamberlain to abandon appeasement, offering military alliances to two countries now threatened by Germany (Poland and Romania) and to Greece, threatened by MUSSOLINI. At the same time Chamberlain authorized an abortive approach to STALIN for an Anglo-Franco-Soviet alliance. It was to honour Chamberlain's pledge to Poland that Britain went to war against Germany on 3 September 1939. Chamberlain's hesitancy made him a poor wartime premier, and mounting criticism from MPs of all parties forced him to resign on 10 May 1940. Although a sick man, racked by cancer, Chamberlain remained in the Cabinet until five weeks before his death, serving Winston CHURCHILL as Lord President of the Council. He died on 9 November 1940. K. Feiling: *The Life of Neville Chamberlain* (1946); I. Macleod: *Neville Chamberlain* (1970); I. Colvin: *The Chamberlain Cabinet* (1971).

Chang Hsueh-liang (Zhang Xueliang) (1901–), Chinese warlord generally known as the 'Young Marshal': the son of CHANG TSO-LIN, whose personal fortune and authority as virtual ruler of Manchuria he inherited, even though Chang Tso-lin had threatened to execute him in November 1925 when he thought he was in collusion with the rival warlord Feng Yu-hsiang (1882–1948). For two years after Chang Tso-lin's assassination his son stood aside from the warlord conflict, but in September 1930 the Young Marshal collaborated with CHIANG KAI-SHEK's nationalists, marching south from Manchuria to take Peking from Feng and give Chiang an opportunity to establish an anti-Japanese united front. An uneasy partnership continued until December 1936 when Chang, who was in command of the Chinese Northern Army in Sian (Xian), held Chiang Kai-shek, his guest, under close arrest for thirteen days so as to persuade him to fight Japan rather than Mao's communists. After releasing the 'kidnapped' Generalissimo, the young Marshal loyally pledged him his support but was held under arrest for the following ten years. China was thus deprived throughout the crucial phases of the Second World War of the skills of a gifted military commander, implacably hostile to Japan. Chang was reputedly still held under house arrest in Taiwan during the early 1970s. J. Gray: *Rebellions and Revolutions, China from the 1800s to the 1980s* (Oxford, 1990); L. Eastman: *The Abortive Revolution: China under Nationalist Rule, 1927–37* (Cambridge, Mass., 1974)

Chang Tso-lin (Zhang Zuolin) (1873–1928), archetypal Chinese warlord: born a shepherd's son in southern central Manchuria, took to brigandage and showed a natural aptitude for military command. He was, like Napoleon, small in stature but ruthless in character. In his late twenties he perfected his skills in guerrilla operations against the Russians along the Manchurian frontier, for which he received payment from Japan. He placed his troops at the disposal of the imperial Chinese authorities against the 1911 revolutionaries, but then used the political anarchy to create a personal satrapy in the north eastern provinces. On two occasions he made political alliances with SUN YAT-SEN and fought other warlords in efforts to hold and control Peking. His strength remained in his native province; he was *de facto* ruler of Manchuria from 1917 until his death, with Inner Mongolia under his control from 1921. The 'Old Marshal', as he was known when in his fifties, struck lucrative bargains with the Japanese, giving them important economic concessions; he gained financial backing from an American bank and secured recognition of his authority in Manchuria from Soviet Russia. He was forced on the defensive by CHIANG KAI-SHEK's nationalist revival in 1927. While seeking new political bargains with rival imperialist exploiters of Manchuria he was assassinated by exasperated Japanese military agents on 4 June 1928 who blew up his personal train as it crossed a viaduct south of Mukden. His son, CHANG HSUEH-LIANG, inherited his vast fortune. Chi Hsi-sheng: *Warlord Politics in China, 1916–1928* (New York, 1976); G. McCormack: *Chang Tso-lin in North East China, 1911–28* (Stanford, Calif., 1977).

Charles (1887–1922), Emperor of Austria and King of Hungary from 1916 to 1918: born in Persenbeug Castle, Lower Austria, fifth in line of succession to the reigning Emperor-King, FRANCIS JOSEPH, his great-uncle. The natural deaths of his grandfather and father, the suicide of Crown Prince RUDOL and the murder of Archduke Francis FERDINAND left Charles heir-apparent by July 1914. Most of his education had been conducted by tutors, but he spent two years as a day pupil at the Vienna Schottengymnasium. In October 1911 Archduke Charles, by now a Major in the Dragoons, married Princess Zita of Bourbon-Parma 1892–1989. He succeeded Francis Joseph on 21 November 1916, hoping to take Austria-Hungary out of the First World War by a negotiated peace and satisfy the many nationalities of his empire by major changes in the constitution which would have given the Habsburg Monarchy a federal character. He failed, however, to break free from contractual obligations to his German ally and he had to witness the disintegration of his empire in November 1918, when he withdrew into private life in Switzerland. On two occasions in 1921 he returned secretly to Hungary, vainly hoping to recover at least his Hungarian throne from the Regent, Admiral HORTHY. But the Regent insisted that a restoration would provoke the invasion of Hungary by the successor states around her frontier (Czechoslovakia, Romania, Yugoslavia) and he forced King Charles and Queen Zita to resume their exile. The following April the deposed Emperor-King died from pneumonia in Madeira, his eldest son, Archduke Otto (1912–), becoming claimant to his titles. As Dr Otto von Habsburg the Archduke was returned by the Bavarians as an elected member of the European Parliament in 1979. G. Brook-Shepherd: *The Last Habsburg* (1968), *The Last Empress* (1991); A. Polzer-Hoditz: *The Emperor Charles* (1930).

Chernenko, Konstantin (1911–85), Soviet political leader: born at Bolshaya Tes, Siberia, a peasant's son. He joined Komsomol (young communists' movement) in 1929 and became a party member at the early age of 20, spending his whole career as a party official. From 1940 onwards he was a protege of BREZHNEV, first in Moldavia and from 1956 in Moscow. He was admitted to the Central Committee in 1971, became a full member of the inner Politburo in December 1978 and was groomed by Brezhnev as his successor. Chernenko's limited experience outside the party machine told against him, however, and under ANDROPOV he was given ill-defined responsibilities as ideological spokesman for the party. When Andropov died, conservatives within the Party hurriedly chose Chernenko as his successor so as to keep out younger men with new ideas. The Chernenko era was limited to a few months in 1984: he became Communist Party General Secretary in February, Soviet President in April 1984, pressed for better relations with the West in May and became gravely ill with emphysema in July. The political initiative passed to GORBACHEV, who consolidated his powers when Chernenko died in March 1985. G. Hosking. *The Awakening of the Soviet Union* (Cambridge, Mass., 1990); C. Schmidt-Hauer: *Gorbachev, the Path to Power* (1986).

Chiang Chin (Jiang Qing) (1914–91), fourth wife of MAO TSE-TUNG: born Li Yun-ho, at Chucheng in Shantung, became librarian of Tsingtao University in 1933 and, for the next four years, a film actress. She joined the Chinese Communist Party in 1937 and became the fourth wife of Mao Tse-tung in 1939. After the establishment of the Chinese People's Republic she was head of film propaganda services, gradually extending her influence in the 1950s over other aspects of cultural life. In 1963 she undertook a notable Marxist reformation of the Peking Opera. From 1965 to 1968 she played a leading role in the 'cultural revolution', a reassertion of Maoist revolutionary principles in China, by criticizing and seeking to eradicate westernizing, liberal tendencies in the republic. She was elected to the Central Committee of the party in 1969 and re-elected in 1973 and 1975. On her husband's death in September 1976 she lost the struggle for power to the Prime Minister, HUA GUOFENG. Her activities were denounced by Hua in October 1976 and she was placed under arrest as leader of the so-called 'Gang of Four' – Chang Cunchiao, Wang Hung-wen, Yao Wen-yuan (all prominent communists from Shanghai) and herself. Allegations concerning the 'pernicious influence' of this 'Gang of Four' figured prominently in speeches at the Eleventh Congress of the Chinese Communist Party in August 1977; they were formally expelled from the party but not put on trial until November 1980. Chiang Chin was sentenced to death for sedition and conspiracy on 25 January 1981 but was reprieved. She died in custody in May 1991. D. Bonavia: *Verdict in Peking; The Trial of the Gang of Four* (1984); Lee Hong-yung: *The Politics of the Chinese Cultural Revolution* (New York, 1978).

Chiang Kai-shek (Jiang Jieshi) (1877–1975), Chinese nationalist leader: born at Fenghwa in Chekiang, trained at military academies. After the Chinese Revolution of 1911, he helped SUN YAT-SEN create a republican army. For six months in 1923 Chiang was in Moscow, where he studied the organization and training of the Red Army, returning home to establish the Whampoa Military Academy, near Canton. Thus General Chiang Kai-shek soon had at his disposal an army officered by men selected and trained by himself. This force helped him in 1925–6 to gain authority in China after the death of Sun, and by the summer of 1928 he was both Commander-in-Chief of the Chinese army and Chairman of the party Sun had founded, the Kuomintang. He enjoyed considerable personal prestige in Europe and America, which owed much to the personality of his sophisticated wife, Soong Mei-ling (born 1898 and educated at Wellesley College, Massachusetts). Chiang's image abroad was also helped by his willingness to accept

Christian baptism: a ceremony performed by a Chinese Methodist minister on 23 October 1930. Yet he never possessed the undisputed authority attributed to him by the western Press. From 1927 to 1931 he had constantly to face conflict with warlords and the communists; from 1931 onwards the Japanese hold on Manchuria threatened the great cities on the Yangtse Kiang; and in 1930, 1933 and 1936 there were serious army rebellions. They were followed by a strange episode in December 1936 when Chiang was kidnapped by CHANG HSUEH-LIANG in Sian Province and only released, after thirteen days, through the mediation of his Communist enemy, CHOU EN-LAI, who exacted from the General a pledge of common action against the Japanese invaders. In 1937, however, the Japanese secured control of much of the eastern seaboard, forcing Chiang to establish China's capital at Chungking in Szechwan province. With American assistance he kept the Chinese battle-front in being throughout the Second World War, but there is no doubt that Franklin ROOSEVELT exaggerated his qualities of leadership and his hold on the loyalty of the Chinese people. Both Chiang and his wife attended the Cairo Conference of 1943, the only moment of personal contact between Chiang and the great Allied statesmen. Winston CHURCHILL remained unimpressed by the Chinese leaders and Roosevelt was disappointed in them. Talks between Chiang and the Communist leader, MAO TSE-TUNG, under the auspices of the American General George C. MARSHALL, failed to prevent conflict between the rival Kuomintang and Communist armies from 1945 to 1949: the peak of the Civil War was reached in November and December 1948, culminating in the fall of Peking and the resignation of Chiang Kai-shek from the presidency in January 1949. Later in the year General Chiang supervised the evacuation of his remaining Kuomintang followers to the island of Formosa (Taiwan). There, with American backing, he lived out the last twenty-five years of his life as 'President of Nationalist China', without ever gaining a foothold on the mainland. He died on 5 April 1975, seventeen months before Mao Tse-tung. In Taiwan he was succeeded as leader of the Kuomintang by his son Chiang Ching-kuo (1910–88), who was State President in Taiwan for the last ten years of his life. B. Crozier and E. Chou: *The Man Who Lost China* (1976); P. P. Y. Loh: *The Early Chiang Kai-shek: his Personality and Politics, 1887–1924* (New York, 1971); J. Gray: *Rebellions and Revolutions, China from the 1800s to the 1980s* (Oxford, 1990); K. Foruya: *Chiang Kai-shek: his Life and Times* (New York, 1981).

Chifley, (Joseph) Benedict (1885–1951), Australian Prime Minister from 1945 to 1949: born in Bathurst, New South Wales, working on the railways for many years before entering the Australian Federal Parliament in 1928, becoming Minister of Defence a year later. From 1931 to 1940 he was out of office and out of Parliament but, on his return, he was rapidly advanced by Australia's wartime Prime Minister, his Labour Party colleague, John CURTIN. Ben Chifley, as Treasurer (Finance Minister), was given responsibility for post-war planning by Curtin and prepared Australia's first comprehensive social insurance scheme. Chifley's humour, firm principles and warm personality made him more popular with Australia's Labour voters than any previous political figure. He inherited, as of right, the Labour leadership and premiership on Curtin's sudden death (5 July 1945). His proposed nationalization of the banks alarmed the electorate and he suffered from his inability to check the apparent spread of communist influence among the dockers and miners. He was decisively defeated by MENZIES in the General Election of December 1949, failing as Prime Minister to measure up to the reputation bestowed on him by well-wishers in his party. L. F. Crisp: *Ben Chifley* (1960); P. Haslock: *The Government and the People: Official War History*, Vol. 2 (Canberra, 1970).

Chirac, Jacques René (1932–), President of France from 1995: born in Paris, the son of a banker. He graduated from the École Nationale d'Adminstration, taking a high position in the civil service before entering the National Assembly as deputy for Corrèze. His vigour as Minister for Agriculture and (later) Industry during the POMPIDOU presidency attracted attention and he was Prime Minister under GISCARD D'ESTAING from May 1974 until August 1976. Their relationship, however, was uneasy: Chirac was more traditionally Gaullist than Giscard; and, while Giscard's political style was undramatic, the forceful Chirac sought to live up to his reputation as a 'bulldozer'. In December 1976 he established a neo-Gaullist movement, Rassemblement Pour la Republique (RPR), and was elected Mayor of Paris in March 1977. In 1981 he stood for President but was defeated on the first ballot. He then led the 'coalition of the Right' in opposition to the socialist governments until March 1986 when he became Prime Minister again, working for two years in 'cohabitation' with the socialist President MITTERRAND. Chirac stood again for the presidency in May 1988, but lost to the incumbent Mitterrand. He declined to renew 'cohabitation' when the right-wing coalition again formed a government in March 1993; but, on Mitterrand's retirement, Chirac stood for the presidency for the third time and, on 14 May 1995, won the election on the second ballot. His presidential term began with plans to resume nuclear testing in the Pacific and with repeated calls for more vigorous military action in Bosnia. Proposals to cut social services led to rioting in Paris and a wave of strikes across France in November and early December 1995. J. Tuppen: *Chirac's France, 1986–88* (New York, 1991).

Chou En-lai (Zhou Enlai) (1898–1976), Prime Minister of Communist China from 1949 until his death: born at Shauhsing in Chekiang, receiving his education at a missionary school. He spent the years 1920–1 in Paris, partly studying and also working in the Renault car factory at Billancourt. In Paris Chou first picked up his communist ideas. After organizing communist groups in Shanghai and Nanchang, Chou became the chief adviser to MAO TSE-TUNG on urban revolutionary activity in 1931, but his contacts with the outside world and his knowledge of western languages made him invaluable as an envoy. It was Chou who secured the compromise bargain with the kidnapped CHIANG KAI-SHEK in 1936 and it was Chou who, by remaining as a liaison officer at Chungking, became the best known Chinese Communist to British and American diplomats and reporters. He took office as the first Prime Minister of the People's Republic in 1949 and was Foreign Minister until 1958, continuing thereafter to take charge of all important conversations with foreign diplomats and politicians. Chou won respect from the British, French and Americans at the Geneva Conference on Indo-China in 1954 and his skills dominated the first congress of Afro-Asian statesmen at Bandung in April 1955. From 1972 to 1974 Chou supervised the gradual Sino-American *détente*, gaining the confidence of both KISSINGER and NIXON. At home the Marxist puritanism of the 'cultural revolution' impeded his attempts to modernize the republic, forcing him to act warily at a time when the party machine was being purged. He presided over the Tenth Party Congress in Peking in 1973 and it seemed as if he, rather than Mao, was China's real master. Soon afterwards, however, his activity was drastically curtailed by cancer, and he died in January 1976. Han Suyin: *Eldest Son, Zhou Enlai and the Making of Modern China* (1994); D. Wilson: *Chou* (1984).

Chu Teh (Zhu De) (1886–1976), Marshal, Commander-in-Chief of the Chinese Red Army from 1931 to 1954: born in Szechwan, his father being a member of the imperial landowning class. Chu Teh served successively as an officer in the Chinese Imperial Army and in the Republican Army of SUN YAT-SEN, commanding a brigade as early as 1916. After a visit to France and Germany in 1924–5, he became interested in communism and, curing himself of addiction to the smoking of opium, presented his inherited wealth to the Chinese Communist Party in 1927. He established and trained the first Red Guard units in 1931. His greatest achievement was to organize the break-out from Kiangsi in October 1934 and the epic 'Long March' (8,000 miles) to Shensi, which was reached a year later. During this migration it was necessary to cross three mountain chains, to shake off the Nationalist forces of CHIANG KAI-SHEK, and to evade brigand warlords. From 1939 to 1945 Chu Teh commanded the Eighteenth Route Army against the Japanese. During the Chinese Civil War he determined the strategy of guerrilla operations and eventual set-piece battles against a tired army. Chu Teh became the first Marshal of the People's Republic in 1955 and enjoyed high favour until 1965 when the 'cultural revolution' deplored his old-fashioned and reactionary outlook. By 1967 it was considered he had purged his errors, and he spent his last nine years in honoured retirement. A. Smedley: *The Great Road; the Life and Times of Chu Teh* (New York, 1956); D. Wilson: *The Long March, 1935* (1971).

Chulalongkorn I, Phra Paramindr Maha (1853–1910), King of Siam from 1868 until 1910: born in Bangkok, the son of King Maha Mong Kut, best remembered outside Thailand as the ruler depicted in the film *The King and I*. Chulalongkorn had an English governess as a boy and acquired some knowledge of European ways before completing his traditional education in a Buddhist monastery. From 1873 onwards he launched a vigorous programme of westernization. Slavery was abolished; formal assurances were given of liberty of conscience; a Council of State was created in May 1874 and expanded into a Legislative Council in January 1895 to formulate laws initiated by Chulalongkorn as an enlightened ruler. American, British and French advisers were invited to Bangkok. Hospitals, roads and schools were built; telegraph and railways were introduced and a police force and a judicial system dependent on provincial courthouses was created. A penal code, on the Napoleonic model, was completed in 1908. Chulalongkorn visited western Europe in 1907 and was received by King Edward VII (who, however, rejected a Foreign Office proposal that his guest should be made a Knight of the Garter). In return for loans, help in building up a modern army, political advice and personal flattery, Chulalongkorn I was induced to cede more than 10,000 square miles of his lands to French Indo-China and further rights in the Malay peninsula to the British. He remains an outstanding figure in Thailand's history, using an efficient absolute monarchy to impose western ways as rapidly as in Japan. J. Finestone: *Royal Family of Thailand* (1989); E. Young: *The Kingdom of the Yellow Robe* (1907).

Churchill, Lord Randolph (1849–95), British politician, leader of the 'Tory Democrats' from 1880 to 1886: born in London, the third son of the seventh Duke of Marlborough, educated at Eton and Merton College, Oxford. In April 1874 he married Jennie Jerome (1854–

1921), the second daughter of Leonard Jerome, a New York financier and founder of the American Jockey Club. Lord Randolph sat as Conservative MP for Woodstock from 1874 to 1885 and thereafter for South Paddington, until his death. He brought to the Commons great debating skills and a revived interest in the Conservative social reform policy inaugurated by DISRAELI. The 'Tory Democracy' which he preached was primarily a means to attain for himself the premiership at an early age (he was a year younger than his political colleague, BALFOUR), but it ensured for him great publicity, intensified by his hounding of BRADLAUGH. His management of the embryonic party organization, the National Union of Conservatives, gave him an apparent power base in the country from which he hoped to attack the Conservative leader in the Commons (Sir Stafford Northcote 1818–87) and ultimately the party leader, Lord SALISBURY. He entered Salisbury's Cabinet as Secretary of State for India in June 1885 and in eight months of office he was largely responsible for the forward policy which culminated in the annexation of Upper Burma. By August 1886 Lord Randolph had achieved an importance second only to that of the Prime Minister: he was Leader of the Commons and Chancellor, the youngest politician to hold such high office since Pitt in 1783. Within five months he had committed a major tactical error, resigning because he opposed Salisbury's wish to spend more money on the army and navy. None of his colleagues supported him, and his fall proved as meteoric as his rise. A tragic illness caused sudden mental debility and by the spring of 1894 his public speeches embarrassed his friends by their streak of insanity. He died in London on 24 January 1895. W. S. Churchill: *Lord Randolph Churchill* (1906); R. Rhodes James: *Lord Randolph Churchill* (1959).

Churchill, Winston Leonard Spencer (1874–1965), British Prime Minister from 1940 to 1945 and 1951 to 1955: born at Blenheim Palace, Oxfordshire, the elder son of Lord Randolph CHURCHILL. He was educated at Harrow and the Royal Military Academy, Sandhurst, before being commissioned in the Fourth Hussars (February 1895), and received his baptism of fire on his twenty-first birthday while observing fighting between Spanish government forces and Cuban rebels south east of Havana. In September 1896 he accompanied the Hussars to India, where he served for nearly two years on the North-West Frontier. From August to October 1898 he was attached to the Twenty-first Lancers in the Sudan, taking part in the cavalry charge at the battle of Omdurman. During the Boer War of 1899–1902 he was a war correspondent. After capture by the Boers he escaped and, as an officer in the South African Light Horse, accompanied the column which relieved Ladysmith in January 1900. Ten months later he was elected Unionist MP for Oldham but in May 1904 he crossed to the Liberal benches as he opposed the tariff reform proposals of Joseph CHAMBERLAIN. In January 1906 Churchill was elected Liberal MP for North-West Manchester, although he represented Dundee from May 1908 to November 1922. ASQUITH appointed him President of the Board of Trade (with a seat in the Cabinet) in April 1908 and for two years he was responsible for a series of social reforms, notably the establishment of the first labour exchanges (1 February 1910). A fortnight later he became Home Secretary. His tenure of this office twice provoked controversy: in November 1910 he made troops available for use by the Chief Constable of Glamorgan in order to prevent looting at Tonypandy during a strike of miners in the Rhondda Valley; and on 3 January 1911 he authorized the despatch of a detachment of Scots Guards to support police seeking to arrest armed anarchist burglars who had barricaded themselves into a house in Sidney Street, Stepney, east London.

In October 1911 Churchill left the Home Office and became First Lord of the Admiralty, making certain that the Royal Navy was ready and at war stations before the despatch of the ultimatum to Germany in August 1914. His desire to see action induced him to cross to Belgium in October 1914 and rally the defenders of Antwerp, whom he supported with a naval division. By December 1914 he had become chief spokesman in the Cabinet for an expendition against Turkey, which would seize the Gallipoli peninsula and force the Dardanelles. When the Dardanelles campaign failed, Churchill was made a scapegoat for tactical blunders and was removed from the Admiralty in May 1915. After six months as Chancellor of the Duchy of Lancaster, he left the government, commanding a battalion of the Royal Scots Fusiliers in the trenches from January to May 1916. He returned to the government as Minister of Munitions from June 1917 to December 1918. As Secretary of State for War and Air (January 1919 to February 1921) he once again sat in the Cabinet, pressing for armed intervention to check the spread of Bolshevism in Europe. He remained in the Cabinet of LLOYD GEORGE as Colonial Secretary in 1921–2, achieving a notable settlement of problems in the Middle East. Defeat in the General Election of November 1922 kept him out of Parliament until October 1924 when, having broken with the Liberals, he was returned as 'Constitutional anti-Socialist' MP for Epping. Six days after this electoral victory BALDWIN appointed him Chancellor of the Exchequer and he rejoined the Conservative Party before introducing his first Budget in April 1925. He was Chancellor for four years, returning Britain to the Gold Standard, but attracting most attention for his handling of information services during the General Strike of 1926.

Churchill was out of office from 1929 to 1939, critical of his party's leadership for contemplating concessions to Mohandas GANDHI and the Indian nationalists and (later) for adopting a policy of appeasement towards Nazi Germany. Neville CHAMBERLAIN appointed him First Lord of the Admiralty once more on 3 September 1939; and in the spring of 1940 the Labour and Liberal parties made it known that they would serve in a coalition under Churchill and nobody else. His wartime premiership lasted from 10 May 1940 to 27 July 1945, when he resigned after the Conservative defeat in the first General Election for ten years. His personal prestige, enhanced during the war years by his dogged courage and his gift of inspiring oratory, enabled him to survive greater disasters than any Prime Minister had known for a century and a half – ejection from the mainland of Europe, the loss of Singapore, reversals in Libya after expectation of victory. His strategic vision was matched by the energy which induced him to meet Franklin ROOSEVELT on nine occasions and STALIN on five occasions during these years of strain.

From 1945 to October 1951 Churchill remained in the Commons as leader of the Opposition, despite a physical deterioration in his health. When he became Prime Minister again in 1951 he was a few weeks short of his seventy-seventh birthday, and out of touch with the problems of a new generation. Nevertheless he continued to seek personal meetings with the leading statesmen, flying the Atlantic twice for talks with Presidents TRUMAN and EISENHOWER. With some reluctance he finally resigned on 5 April 1955, being succeeded by Sir Anthony EDEN. Churchill declined offers of a dukedom both in 1945 and 1955, preferring to sit in the Commons until 1964 as MP for Woodford and Wanstead (as the southern half of his old constituency of Epping became in 1945). He was awarded the Order of Merit in 1946 and created a

Knight of the Garter in April 1953, receiving later that year the Nobel Prize for Literature in recognition of his historical studies. The US Congress conferred on him honorary American citizenship in 1963. Sir Winston died on 24 January 1965 receiving a state funeral attended for the first time by a reigning sovereign. He was buried in the country churchyard of Bladon in Oxfordshire, within sight of his birthplace. In September 1908 he had married Clementine Hozier (1885–1977), whom the Queen created a life baroness after her husband's death. R. Churchill and M. Gilbert: *Winston S. Churchill* (8 vols of narrative, 10 vols of documents) (1964–89); M. Gilbert: *Churchill, a Life* (1991); R. Rhodes James: *Churchill, a Study in Failure 1900–1939* (1970); H. Pelling: *Winston Churchill* (1976).

Ciano, Count (Galeazzo) (1903–44), Italian Foreign Minister from 1936 to 1943: born in Livorno (Leghorn), the son of a distinguished Admiral, Costanzo Ciano (1876–1939). He joined the fascists as a young man, was a journalist and a diplomat, representing his country in China for two years. In April 1930 he married Edda Mussolini (1911–95) the Duce's daughter. After piloting bombers in the opening phases of Italy's war against Abyssinia (1935), Count Ciano was brought back to Rome as Foreign Minister in January 1936. At first he favoured collaboration with Germany and expansion into the Balkans, but he distrusted the Nazi leaders and welcomed the opportunity to serve as ambassador to the Vatican from February to July 1943 because he thought it a possible means of extricating Italy from the war into which MUSSOLINI had entered hastily in June 1940. Ciano voted for the dismissal of Mussolini at the decisive meeting of the Fascist Grand Council on 25 July 1943, but he was subsequently tricked into travelling through Bavaria where he was arrested by the Nazi Gestapo. HITLER believed he was guilty, not only of betraying his father-in-law, but of seeking a separate peace through the mediation of the Pope, PIUS XII. Ciano was handed over to a neo-Fascist court in German-occupied northern Italy. Despite attempts to save his life by Countess Edda, he was sentenced to death for treason and shot outside Verona on 11 January 1944. M. Muggeridge (ed.): *Ciano's Diplomatic Papers* (1948); E. Mussolini-Ciano: *My Truth* (1977); E. Wiskemann: *The Rome–Berlin Axis* (1949).

Clemenceau, Georges (1841–1929), French Prime Minister from 1906 to 1909 and 1917 to 1920: born in Mouilleron-en-Pareds in a remote part of the Vendée. He studied medicine at Nantes and Paris, was briefly imprisoned for seeking to promote a riot (1862), and spent most of the years 1865–9 in the United States, teaching French and horse-riding at Stamford, Connecticut, and marrying one of his pupils, Mary Plummer (1850–1923, divorced 1892). He became Mayor of Montmartre as soon as the Republic was proclaimed in September 1870, holding office throughout the siege of Paris and narrowly escaping death from the Communards. He sat in the Chamber of Deputies as a Radical for one of the Paris districts from 1876 to 1893, returning to active politics in 1902 as Senator for Var. Early in his political career he was regarded as the 'toppler of ministers' because of his powerful attacks on governments of which he did not approve. Later his ruthlessness in debate earned him the sobriquet 'the Tiger'. He was also a powerful journalist: his newspaper, *L'Aurore*, was prominent in its championship of DREYFUS; and from 1913 onwards his *L'Homme Libre* (renamed *L'Homme Enchaine* after the imposition of wartime censorship in 1914) made him known for his patriotic anti-Germanism. He never held government office until he was 64, becoming Minister of the Interior in March 1906. Seven months later he became Prime Minister of a predominantly Radical coalition which remained in power for the unusually long time of thirty-two months. His government was marked by equally strong hostility to the Church and to the Socialists, and he was feared as a resolute strike-breaker. With the outbreak of war in 1914 he emerged as a fierce critic of military ineptitude and on 16 November 1917 he again became Prime Minister. His leadership held France together during the military crisis caused by the German spring offensives of 1918. By November 1918 the French peasants and soldiers respected him as 'the father of victory'. Although he presided over the plenary sessions of the Paris Peace Conference in 1919 he was far from happy with its outcome, fearing that the Treaty of Versailles was insufficiently statesmanlike to prevent German retaliation. He resigned in January 1920, when the votes of Socialist and Catholic deputies went against him in the preliminaries of a presidential election, their preference being for an amiable nonentity, Paul Deschanel (1855–1922), who was certified insane six months after becoming President. In retirement Clemenceau remained a formidable critic, personifying in his atheistic, opportunist and passionate patriotism both the merits and the limitations of political life under the French Third Republic. KEYNES, after attending the Peace Conference of 1919, wrote of Clemenceau: 'He had one illusion – France: and one disillusion – mankind, including Frenchmen and his colleagues not least.' D. R. Watson: *Georges Clemenceau, a Political Biography* (1974); D. S. Newhall: *Clemenceau, a Life at War* (New York, 1991); G. Bruun: *Clemenceau* (1943).

Cleveland (Stephen) Grover (1837–1908), President of the United States from 1888 to 1889 and 1893 to 1897: born in Caldwell, New Jersey, the son of a Presbyterian minister. He studied law privately and was admitted to the New York bar at the age of 22, served as a reforming Mayor of Buffalo in 1881, became Governor of New York in 1883, and made such a name for himself in combating corrupt political activities that he was nominated as Democratic 'clean government' candidate for the presidential election of 1884, gaining a narrow victory over BLAINE. He became the first Democratic President since before the Civil War, and he acted with authority (vetoing two-thirds of the bills presented to him) and a sense of justice. Attempts to moderate tariffs, to investigate pension claims put forward by powerful ex-servicemen's associations, and to conciliate the South all lost President Cleveland votes in the 1888 election, which was won by Benjamin HARRISON. But four years later Cleveland became the first (and, as yet, only) President to make a successful come-back, defeating Harrison in an unusual campaign, with more than a million votes going to a third candidate, the Populist James Weaver. Cleveland's second administration was plagued by monetary matters, including the Wall Street panic of June 1893. The President offended many Democrats by his use of federal troops to break a strike in Illinois (see ALTGELD). Over foreign policy Cleveland reaffirmed the Monroe doctrine by a belligerent message to Congress (December 1895), which contained a warning to the British not to put naval pressure on Venezuela (with whom the British had a long-standing boundary dispute concerning the limits of British Guiana). Cleveland's dignified and old-fashioned reformism stood in sharp contrast to the appeals of the new 'silver democrats' under BRYAN, who dominated the 1896 Convention although failing to carry the electorate with them. For the last eleven years of his life Cleveland was a respected counsellor, the first ex-President honoured as an elder statesman since Andrew Jackson more than half a century before. A. Nevins: *Grover*

Cleveland (New York, 1944); R. McElroy: *Grover Cleveland, man and Statesman* (2 vols) (New York, 1923).

Clinton, William Jefferson Blythe IV (1946–), President of the United States from 1993: born in Arkansas, educated at Georgetown University before becoming a Rhodes Scholar at University College, Oxford, and completing his law studies at Yale. From 1974 to 1976 he was a professor at Arkansas Law School, becoming Attorney Governor for the state in 1977 before serving as (Democrat) Governor of Arkansas, 1979–81 and 1983–92. Clinton won the US presidential election of 3 November 1992, with Albert Gore (1948–) as his running-mate and subsequent Vice-President, assuming office on 20 January 1993. Criticism of President Clinton's handling of foreign affairs and, from January 1994 onwards, a sustained Congressional attack on the Whitewater property dealings with which he was connected while Governor of Arkansas weakened the President's standing on the eve of the mid-term elections (November 1994), which returned Republican majorities in both houses of Congress, imposing restraints on the President's subsequent legislative programme. During 1995 he vigorously sought to promote peace settlements in Palestine, Bosnia-Herzegovina and Ireland and, at the end of November 1995, visited London, Belfast and Dublin. J. Moore and R. Inde: *Clinton, Young man in a Hurry* (New York, 1992) M. L. Oakley: *On the Make: The Rise of Bill Clinton* (Washington, D.C., 1994).

Cobden, Richard (1804–65), English radical politician: born near Midhurst, in Sussex, the son of a farmer impoverished by the Napoleonic Wars. Cobden became a calico printer in Lancashire, and was able to travel to America and to Turkey in 1835 and 1836–7. These experiences led him to emerge as a pamphleteer who favoured free trade and diplomatic arbitration in foreign affairs rather than the dangerous forward policies associated with PALMERSTON. From 1838 to 1846 he spent his small private income on the Anti-Corn Law League, which he led in collaboration with BRIGHT. He was MP for Stockport from 1841 to 1847 when he chose to represent the West Riding of Yorkshire. Cobden's disinterested zeal for free trade led the public to subscribe £80,000 as a gift of appreciation for his services, but his denunciation of the Crimean War made him unpopular and he was out of the Commons from 1857 to 1859 when he was elected at Rochdale. He used this parliamentary interlude to revisit the United States and he could understand America's political problems better than any other prominent figure in mid-Victorian Britain. Ill-health forced him to decline office under Palmerston in 1859, a decision which enabled him to continue to criticize the government's foreign policy. Nevertheless his unofficial activities were largely responsible for a free trade commercial treaty with France in 1859–60, one of the most beneficial acts of Palmerston's second government. Like Bright, Cobden actively supported the Northern cause in the American Civil War, criticizing Palmerston's sympathy for the Confederacy. Cobden died in March 1865 and was buried at Lavington, in his native Sussex. J. Morley: *Life of Cobden* (1881, rev. edn 1903); A. J. P. Taylor: *The Troublemakers* (1957).

Collins, Michael (1890–1922), first Prime Minister of the Irish Free State: born in County Cork, near Clonakilty, a farmer's son. After working for some years in London as a postal clerk and a bank cashier, he returned to southern Ireland as an ardent Sinn Féiner and assisted in organizing the Easter Rebellion in Dublin (April 1916). On release from prison he was returned as a member of the Convention, Dàil Eircann, and was one of the delegates sent to the London Conference in October 1921 which agreed on creating in southern Ireland a dominion, known as the Irish Free State'. Collins's behaviour at the Conference won widespread respect, and he became Prime Minister of the new dominion in January 1922. His willingness to accept a partitioned Ireland, even as a temporary expedient, seemed a betrayal to members of the Irish Republican Army, and he was assassinated in an ambush between Bandon and Macroom by an extreme terrorist faction on 22 August 1922. R. F. Foster: *Modern Ireland 1600–1972* (1988); R. Taylor: *Michael Collins* (1958).

Conrad von Hoetzendorf, Franz (1852–1925), Chief of the Imperial and Royal General Staff in Vienna, 1906 to 1911 and 1912 to 1917: born at Penzing, west Vienna, trained at the Military Academy at Wiener Neustadt and saw active service in Bosnia in 1878–9. He commanded a crack infantry regiment 1895–9, introducing 'modern' field training. His original mind made him a protégé of Archduke Francis FERDINAND, who secured his appointment as Chief of General Staff in November 1906. To the consternation of FRANCIS JOSEPH, who wished to preserve European peace, Conrad at once put forward detailed military plans for preventive wars against Serbia and Italy. When, in November 1911, he trespassed into foreign policy-making, Francis Joseph dismissed him from office, but worsening relations with Serbia led to his reinstatement in December 1912. Conrad's 'hawkish' belligerence was kept in check until after Francis Ferdinand's assassination (28 June 1914). Conrad was then largely responsible for completing war plans to defend Austria-Hungary from a Russian offensive in the Carpathians while attacking Serbia in the south. Although Conrad became a Field Marshal, he proved a poor grand strategist; on three occasions (August and October 1914 and June 1916) he failed to co-ordinate troop movements on distant battle-fronts. Soon after his accession Emperor CHARLES dismissed him (1 March 1917). Conrad ended the war as a field commander on the Southern Front, gaining limited success against the Italians in the Trentino. He was created a Baron in 1910 and became a Count in 1918, shortly before Austria-Hungary's disintegration. G. E. Rothenberg: *The Army of Francis Joseph* (West Lafayette, Ind., 1976); S. J. Williamson: *Austria-Hungary and the Origins of the First World War* (1991); I. Deak: *Beyond Nationalism* (Oxford, 1990).

Constantine I (1868–1923), King of the Hellenes 1913–17, 1920–2: born in Athens, the eldest son of King GEORGE I, educated at Heidelberg. He served in a Prussian Guards regiment before marrying Princess Sophia, sister of WILLIAM II, in October 1889. As Crown Prince, he led Greek troops against the Turks in the first Balkan War and in November 1912 captured Salonika. Constantine ascended the throne, on his father's assassination, on 18 March 1913. He sought neutrality in The First World War, in opposition to the pro-Allied policy of VENIZELOS. Misunderstandings with British and French politicians led to allied military intervention at Athens in December 1916; and in June 1917 Constantine went into exile in Switzerland, handing over royal authority to hs second son Alexander (1893–1920). But, with backing from a plebiscite, Constantine I resumed the throne after King Alexander's tragic death from a monkey bite (25 October 1920). His health, however, was failing and he was forced to abdicate on 27 September 1922, after being unjustly blamed for Greek defeats by KEMAL's Turkish nationalists in Asia Minor. He died ten weeks later at a hotel in Palermo. J. van der Kiste: *Kings of the Hellenes 1863–1974* (Stroud, 1994); Prince Michael of Greece and A. Palmer: *The Royal House of Greece* (1990).

Constantine II (1940–), King of the Hellenes, effectively 1964–73: born in Athens, son of Paul I (1901–64, reigned 1947–64) and Queen Frederika (1917–81). After spending his early years in South Africa, Constantine returned to Greece with his parents in October 1946. His father's death from cancer in march 1964 brought him to the throne shortly before his highly popular marriage to the Danish Princess, Ann-Marie (1946–). But the threat of war with Turkey over Cyprus and a conflict with the PAPANDREOU government over control of the army led to such political tension that on 21 April 1967 the King's authority was undermined by a right-wing coup, instigated by Colonel PAPADOPOULOS. A counter-coup on 13 December 1967 was unsuccessful and the royal family took refuge in Italy, and later England. In June 1973 Papadopoulos accused the exiled King of seeking to overthrow his regime and a republic was proclaimed in Athens. After Papadopoulos' fall in the following summer, a referendum was held on the future of the monarchy (December 1974) in which the Greek people voted against a royal restoration by 69.2 per cent to 30.8 per cent. King Constantine did not accept the abolition of the monarchy as final. Books: as previous entry.

Coolidge, Calvin (1872–1933), President of the United States from 1923 to 1929: born at Plymouth in Vermont, graduated from Amherst College in 1895, practised law and entered state politics in Massachusetts, serving as Governor from 1916 to 1920. His resolute action in calling out the militia to break a police strike in Boston (September 1919) ensured he became, almost overnight, a national figure. He was running-mate of HARDING in winning the 1920 presidential election for the Republicans. Vice-President Coolidge succeeded to the presidency on Harding's death in August 1923. He was fortunate to be untouched by the scandals and corruption associated with the Harding era and he won the presidential campaign of 1924. Coolidge was the archetypal inter-war Republican: he believed in allowing big business a free rein, thereby creating the illusion of 'Coolidge prosperity'; and over world affairs he was stolidly isolationist. He was a taciturn Puritan in politics, popular because of the boom conditions associated with the Coolidge years. He backed his Secretary of Commerce, Herbert HOOVER, as his successor in 1928 and retired, much respected for his personal probity. Seven months after his retirement, the Wall Street Crash of October 1929 emphasized how inadequate was the foundation of many of the projects which had appeared to flourish under his presidency. C. Fuess: *Calvin Coolidge* (Boston, Mass., 1940); (W. A. White: *A Puritan to Babylon* (New York, 1938).

Coughlin, Charles Edward (1891–1979), American priest and radio demagogue: born at Hamilton, Canada, of Irish Catholic parentage. He was ordained priest in 1916, becoming a pastor of the Shrine of the Little Flower at Royal Oak, Detroit, in 1926. In the late 1920s he achieved fame as a broadcaster, commenting on political rather than spiritual affairs. A denunciation of 'Hoover prosperity' on the eve of the Wall Street Crash in 1929 won him a listening audience throughout the States. He organized a staff of more than 100 in order to handle mailbags bringing him three million letters a year, many of them containing contributions for his crusade against 'godless capitalists, Jews, Communists, international bankers and plutocrats'. Support for Franklin ROOSEVELT in 1932–3 ('The New Deal is Christ's Deal') ended shortly before Christmas in 1934, when one of Father Coughlin's chief backers was accused of manipulating foreign exchange operations. By 1936 Father Coughlin was head of the National Union for Social Justice, which supported the right-wing radical William Lemke from North Dakota as a Union Party candidate for the presidency. Despite the 'radio priest's' shrill demagogy, his candidate polled less than 900,000 votes. Coughlin's anti-Semitism was denounced by Cardinal Mundelein of Chicago but Coughlin remained an effective isolationist speaker until 1942, when his magazine *Social Justice* was declared unacceptable by the Post Office Department for violating the Espionage Act by encouraging disloyalty to the United States. At that point, Father Coughlin was peremptorily silenced by his religious superiors. He was the outstanding political manipulator of the microphone in the New World, his only rival being President Roosevelt (whose 'fireside chats' showed a totally different mastery of the spoken word). Surviving film suggests that Coughlin's appeal was aural rather than visual; his technique would not have suited the television age. He continued to serve as a parish priest in Detroit for over forty years. C. J. Tull: *Father Coughlin and the New Deal* (Syracuse, N.Y., 1965).

Craxi, Bettino (1935–), Italian Prime Minister: born in Milan, became a journalist and entered the Italian Parliament as a socialist in 1968, becoming party leader in 1976. In July 1984 Craxi became the first Italian socialist to form a government, heading a five-party coalition in which the socialists remained in a minority, behind the Christian Democrats. His government won respect abroad for courageously bringing to trial leading terrorists of the Left ('Red Brigade') and the Right. The Craxi coalition survived, with difficulty, until April 1987. He remained a leading contender for high office until December 1992, when he was accused of corruption, particularly in financing his party in Milan. He resigned the party leadership in February 1993 and in July 1994 was convicted of corruption and sentenced to eight-and-a-half years' imprisonment. Other charges were later made of illegal party funding. The Craxi scandal, like the ANDREOTTI scandal, deeply discredited the post-fascist Italian parliamentary system. C. Richards: *The New Italians* (1994); F. Spotts and T. Wieser: *Italy, a Difficult Democracy* (1986); P. Ginsborg: *A History of Contemporary Italy* (1990).

Cripps, (Richard), Stafford (1889–1952), prominent British socialist from 1942 to 1950: born in London, educated at Winchester and at University College, London, serving in the First World War with the Red Cross and in a munitions factory. By the late 1920s he was known as a brilliant barrister who, despite socialist views, specialized in company law. He was Solicitor-General (with a knighthood) in the MACDONALD Labour government of 1930–1, retaining his seat at Bristol East when many Labour MPs were defeated in the General Election of October 1931. Sir Stafford Cripps continued to represent Bristol East until 1950, although he was technically expelled from the Labour Party in April 1939 for advocating a united Popular Front of the Left, and he was not reinstated as a party member until 1945. Cripps was sent to Moscow as ambassador in May 1940, returning to England in February 1942 to become Leader of the Commons and, for eight months, served in the War Cabinet under Winston CHURCHILL, undertaking a special mission to India in the vain hope that he would win the support of Mohandas GANDHI and NEHRU for the war by promising self-government. He remained in the government, though not in the Cabinet, as Minister of Aircraft Production from November 1942 to May 1945. After Labour's General Election victory, he entered the ATTLEE Cabinet as President of the Board of Trade, taking over as Chancellor of the Exchequer in 1947. His austerity programme (6 August 1947) kept inflation under control for two years by high taxation, economies and a voluntary wage freeze; but Cripps was forced to devalue the pound on 18 September 1949. His health gave way a year later and he retired from political life on 19 October 1950, Hugh GAITSKELL succeeding him as Chancellor. Sir Stafford Cripps, a Christian Marxist, was respected for the simplicity of his personal life and for his authoritative professionalism, especially as an economist. He died in April 1952. C. Cooke: *Life of Richard Stafford Cripps* (1957); G. D. H. Cole: *History of the Labour Party from 1914* (1948); H. Pelling: *Short History of the Labour Party* (1993).

Crispi, Francesco (1818–1901), Italian Prime Minister from 1887 to 1891 and 1893 to 1896: born at Ribera in south western Sicily. He assisted GARIBALDI when the 'Thousand' redshirts landed in Sicily in 1860 as part of the movement to unify Italy. Subsequently Crispi sat as a Member of the Italian Parliament, moving politically from the Left to the Centre. His exposure of corruption among his ministerial colleagues made him well known in the 1870s but his career suffered a set-back from unproven accusations of bigamy. Patriotic and imperialistic speeches restored him to popular favour and he became Prime Minister on 31 July 1887, holding office until January 1891. Crispi's government strengthened Italian links both with Germany and with Britain; and he encouraged a forward policy in east Africa, claiming a protectorate over Abyssinia (Treaty of Ucciali, May 1889), colonizing Eritrea and establishing a foothold in Somalia (1890). His second ministry (December 1893 to March 1896) was less successful: his attempt to annex Abyssinia led to the disastrous military defeat at Adowa (1 March 1896); and the parliamentary Opposition openly accused him of embezzlement, a charge neither proved nor disproved. In home affairs Crispi was excessively zealous in dealing with unrest among the peasants and workers, seeing even in moderate socialism the hand of a murderous anarchism, and his government dissolved nearly 300 left-wing societies, over fifty of them in Milan. His theatricality, imperial adventures and dictatorial contempt for the Left foreshadowed fascism, but he lacked the personal magnetism of MUSSOLINI. T. Palamenghi-Crispi (ed.): *Memoirs of Francesco Crispi* (3 vols) (New York, 1912–14); C. Seton-Watson: *Italy from Liberalism to Fascism* (1969).

Croker, Richard (1841–1922), notorious American political manager at the end of the nineteenth century: born in Ireland, emigrating to New York as a child. He entered New York City politics, securing control of the political machine in 1886. For sixteen years he was boss of Tammany Hall, the Democratic Party organization in the borough of Manhattan. He survived the publication in 1894 of evidence of massive corruption, especially in the police department. It was only when the reforming idealist Seth Low (1850–1916), President of Columbia University, was elected Mayor of New York in 1901 that Croker relinquished his hold on the political machine. Discretion induced him to leave America. He purchased an estate in his native Ireland, where he spent the last twenty years of his life enjoying the fruits of 'honest graft – his phrase – in the company of a Cherokee wife more than forty years his junior. Low's reforms and Croker's departure discredited Tammany Hall, but by 1914 the 'machine' had begun to function again in New York. T. L. Stoddard: *Master of Manhattan* (New York, 1931) M. R. Warner: *Tammany Hall* (New York, 1928).

Cromer, Lord (Evelyn Baring) (1841–1917), British 'agent and consul-general' in Egypt, 1883 to 1907: born into a Norfolk family of merchant bankers but chose the army as his career, receiving an artillery commission in 1858. Soon afterwards, however, while serving in British-occupied Corfu, he was seconded as personal aide to the High Commissioner and he spent his life in imperial administration. After gaining experience in Malta, Jamaica and India, he was sent to Cairo for two years in 1877 on an international commission to 'rescue' the ruling Khedive, ISMAIL, from bankruptcy. He then returned to Calcutta for three years as financial adviser to the Viceroy, receiving a knighthood in 1883, the year he was appointed 'agent and consul-general' in Cairo. His financial acumen staved off national bankruptcy in Egypt. Although Egypt was still technically a dependency of the Ottoman Empire and never became a British possession, the 'agent' asserted as personal an autocracy in Egypt as the strongest Viceroys over British India. He extended the railway network, encouraged the spread of schools, reformed the judicial administration and improved the agricultural yield by irrigation schemes and by a 'land bank' to encourage planned farming. Sir Evelyn Baring chose the name of his birthplace when he received a baronage in 1892: he became Viscount Cromer in 1899 and Earl Cromer in 1901. Although he supported KITCHENER's reconquest of the Sudan and his handling of the French during the Fashoda crisis (1898), Cromer was an early champion of the Anglo-French entente, which his diplomacy helped to achieve in 1904. As pro-consul in Cairo for almost a quarter of a century, Cromer accomplished great changes. But the Anglo-Indian form of westernization which he imposed was resented by the secularized Egyptian intelligentsia, whom no British consul-general ever understood. At the same time, Cromer appreciated the importance of protecting Egypt's dependence on the waters of the Nile. It could be argued that the Anglo-Egyptian condominium in the Sudan which he promoted in 1899 was his most enduring achievement, surviving effectively until 1955. Earl of Cromer: *Modern Egypt* (2 vols) (1908); Marquis of Zetland: *Lord Cromer* (1932); R. Tignor: *Modernization and British Colonial Rule in Egypt, 1882–1914* (Princeton, N.J., 1966); Afaf Lutfi al-Sayyid: *Egypt and Cromer* (1968).

Curtin, John Joseph (1885–1945), Australian Prime Minister: born near Ballarat, Victoria, of Irish descent. After seven years of trade union experience in Victoria he moved to Western Australia where, from 1917 onwards, he built up the Labor Party, around Fremantle and Perth. He represented Fremantle in the Canberra Parliament of 1928–31 and 1934–45, becoming Labor leader in 1935. He formed a government on 7 October 1941, only two months before Japan brought war to the Pacific. As Australia's wartime Prime Minister he clashed with CHURCHILL over the continued deployment of Australian troops in distant theatres of war. Yet, though he worked well with his American allies, he mistrusted MACARTHUR's ambitions: by late 1943 Curtin was pressing for a powerful British fleet based in Sydney, so as to lessen Australasian dependence on US grand strategy in the south west Pacific. At the Dominion Prime Ministers' conference in London in May 1944 he stressed the value of closer institutional bonds if the British commonwealth connection was to influence the post-war world. He died suddenly a month before final victory against Japan. Curtin was fortunate to have the widely respected EVATT as his Minister of External Affairs and Ben CHIFLEY as Finance Minister. The popular Chifley succeeded him. H. C. Coombs: *John Curtin, a Consensus Prime Minister?* (Canberra, 1984); C. Johnson: *the Labor Legacy: Curtin, Chifley, Whitlam, Hawke*, (1989); J. Robertson: *Australia at War 1939–45* (Melbourne, 1981).

Curzon, George Nathaniel (1859–1925), Viceroy of India from 1898 to 1905 and

British Foreign Secretary from 1919 to 1924: born at Kedleston, Derbyshire, educated at Eton and Balliol College, Oxford, and sat as Conservative MP for Southport from 1886 to 1898. Curzon's academic attainments, travels and scholarly works on Asian problems marked him out as a young politician of distinction and promise. In April 1895 he married, in Washington, Mary Leiter (1875–1906), daughter of a Chicago businessman. Curzon served SALISBURY as Under-Secretary for India in 1891–2 and as Under-Secretary for Foreign Affairs from 1895 to 1898. His passionate desire to become Viceroy of India was gratified in August 1898, still six months short of his fortieth birthday; and at the same time he accepted an Irish peerage, becoming Baron Curzon of Kedleston. He was the most active and reforming Viceroy within living memory: the North-West Frontier was strengthened and organized as a province; railways were extended; agricultural schemes introduced; irrigation projects encouraged; Bengal partitioned administratively; and the Viceroy spent many hours minutely examining suggested improvements in education and public services. Yet the combination of his dynamic energy and unwillingness to delegate authority with pride in the majesty of his office made Curzon many enemies. Major differences with the Commander-in-Chief, KITCHENER, over control of the Indian Army induced Curzon to resign. He returned to England, bitterly disappointed, in December 1905 and his sorrow was intensified by the death of his young wife a few months later. Although he entered the House of Lords in 1908 and served as Chancellor of Oxford University from 1907 onwards, he took little part in public life until the spring of 1915 when he entered the ASQUITH coalition Cabinet as Lord Privy Seal. Only Curzon and Bonar LAW were members of the LLOYD GEORGE War Cabinet throughout its existence. Earl Curzon (as he became in 1911) was concerned with the problems of manpower, the creation of an Air Ministry and major questions of foreign policy, especially in Asia. In January 1917 he remarried, again choosing an American, Mrs Grace Duggan (*née* Hinds), daughter of a US minister to Brazil. Curzon took charge of the Foreign Office in January 1919 although he did not become titular Foreign Secretary until ten months later. He was a traditionalist, doubtful of the new internationalism. His best work was as a negotiator, notably in securing a lasting peace with Turkey at the Lausanne Conference of 1922–3; but his name is associated with the proposed demarcation of the Russo-Polish frontier along the 'Curzon Line', a suggestion vainly put forward repeatedly by Curzon in the late summer of 1920, in the hope that the Line would exclude non-Polish minorities likely to endanger the stability of the new Polish Republic. To his surprise Curzon was not invited to succeed Law as Prime Minister in May 1923, GEORGE V being advised it was inappropriate to have a Prime Minister who sat in the Upper House where the new leading Opposition (the Labour Party) was not then represented. Curzon served the new Prime Minister, BALDWIN, as Foreign Secretary until January 1924, and sat in Baldwin's second Cabinet as Lord President of the Council until his death on 20 March 1925. D. Gilmour: *Curzon* (1994); K. Rose: *Curzon, a Most Superior Person* (1969); H. Nicolson: *Curzon, the Last Phase* (1934).

Custer, George Armstrong (1839–76), American cavalry commander: born in Ohio and graduated from the Military Academy at West Point in 1861, last in his class. He distinguished himself as a remarkably extrovert junior officer on the staff of MCCLELLAN early in the Civil War and by the age of 25 was an acting Brigadier-General in the Union Army. His exploits with a predominantly

'Yankee' cavalry division in Virginia and along the Shenandoah river in the later stages of the war were spectacular. Custer personally accepted the white flag of truce from the Confederates preceding the ending of the conflict at Appomattox. As a peacetime soldier he reverted to the rank of Lieutenant-Colonel and undertook a series of expeditions into the troubled Indian territories, winning several encounters against hostile Indians. His fame rests on the action fought at Little Bighorn, Montana, on 25 June 1876, when he led a frontal attack on a Sioux position, only to find his cavalry ambushed by the tactical ingenuity of the Sioux leaders, Chief Sitting Bull (1834–90) and Chief Crazy Horse (*c.* 1840–77). Custer and his force of 264 men were annihilated. 'Custer's Last Stand', depicted in a bestselling lithograph, became the most famous – and most debatable – episode in the Indian wars. E. I. Stewart: *Custer's Luck* (Norman, Okla., 1955); F. Van de Water: *Glory Hunter* (Indianapolis, Ind., 1951).

D

Daladier, Édouard (1844–1970), French Prime Minister on three occasions between 1933 and 1940: born at Carpentras, in the Vaucluse area of Provence, around Avignon. He represented Vaucluse as a Radical Deputy from 1919 to 1940 and again, under the Fourth Republic, from 1946 to 1958. He was Minister for Colonies in 1924, Prime Minister for most of the year 1933 and also for two months in 1934. Provençal political leaders encouraged the idea he was a strong man, the 'Bull of Vaucluse'; it was probably this legendary strength of personality that retained him as Minister of War and Defence from 1932 to 1934 and throughout the vital period from June 1936 to 18 May 1940. He became Prime Minister for the third time on 10 April 1938, holding office precariously until the third week of March 1940. Daladier, a competent wheeler and dealer in the parliamentary lobbies, accepted appeasement as a natural policy and readily signed the Munich Pact in September 1938. His command of the Radical Party ensured that his successor, REYNAUD, retained him in the government through the disastrous spring of 1940. Daladier, weak though he may have been, showed courage during the Occupation, contemptuously defying both the Vichy regime and the Germans. From 1943 to 1945 he was in close German custody, interned for some months in Buchenwald concentration camp. He never held ministerial office after the war. A. Horne: *To Lose a Battle; France 1940* (1969); W. L. Shirer: *The Collapse of the Third Republic* (New York, 1970); P. Larmour: *The French Radical Party in the 1930s* (Stanford, Calif., 1964).

Dalai Lama XIV (Bstan-Dzin-Rgya) (1935–), spiritual head of Tibet and exiled temporal sovereign: born Bstan-Dzin Gyatso into a peasant family at Taktser, north of the capital, Lhasa. Like his predecessors he was identified as a reincarnation of the Compassionate Buddha by the monks of Lhasa before his third birthday. He was enthroned at Lhasa in 1940 but for ten years his sovereign powers were exercised by a Chinese-dominated Regency. In 1950 the Dalai Lama broke tradition by leaving his palace, the Potala at Lhasa, and going into residence at Chumbi, in southern Tibet, where in May 1951 he negotiated a settlement with the Chinese Communist government by which Tibet was promised autonomy within the People's Republic. Although Chinese troops formally garrisoned Lhasa and other towns from September 1951, the Dalai Lama served as a nominal ruler of the country until March 1959, when an unsuccessful peasant rebellion in Tibet was brutally repressed, forcing him to join thousands of refugees in crossing the Indian frontier. He established an alternative government at Dharamsala in the Punjab. In the comparative freedom of exile the Dalai Lama was able to modify Tibet's traditional theocracy, allowing some popular representation. He championed his country's independence in visits to the United States and Europe as well as in India, but he always insisted that any liberation of Tibet must be accomplished without war. For this patient commitment to non-violence the Dalai Lama received the 1989 Nobel Peace Prize. He has indicated that, though he would never return to Lhasa as a figurehead, he was willing to co-operate with China in setting up Tibet as a self-governing province. But in 1989 and again in May 1993 peasant unrest around Lhasa effectively ruled out any further negotiations. Bstan-Dzin-Rgya, Dalai Lama XIV: *Freedom in Exile; the Autobiography of His Holiness the Dalai Lama of Tibet* (1990); M. H. Goodman: *The Last Dalai Lama* (1986); C. B. Levenson: *The Dalai Lama, a Biography* (1988); A. T. Grunfeld: *The Making of Modern Tibet* (1987).

D'Annunzio, Gabriele (1863–1938), Italian man of letters and political adventurer: born at Pescara, settled in Rome in 1881. Before he was 40, D'Annunzio was respected in literary circles throughout Europe for his sensualist novels and lyrical poetic dramas. Politically he was intensely nationalistic and in 1914–15 used all his literary gifts to arouse fervour for Italy's entry into the First World War against Austria-Hungary and Germany. For three years he served in the Italian Air Force and was awarded Italy's highest decoration for valour. Resentment at the failure of the Italian representatives at the Paris Peace Conference to gain quick rewards for the victory of 1918 led D'Annunzio to organize a private army which seized the city and port of Fiume (Rijeka) on 12 September 1919. D'Annunzio controlled Fiume for sixteen months, maintaining that the port and hinterland were Italian, even though the area had formed part of Hungary for the past half-century and was claimed by the Yugoslavs. In Fiume D'Annunzio encouraged all the patriotic postures later appropriated by fascism, including the raised-arm salute. After ejection from Fiume by an Italian naval force in January 1921, he retired to a villa on Lake Garda. He was much honoured by MUSSOLINI, who in 1924 induced King VICTOR EMMANUEL III to create him Prince of Montenevoso, the title originating from a mountain a few miles inland from Fiume. A. Rhodes: *The Poet as Superman* (1959); C. Seton-Watson: *Italy from Liberalism to Fascism* (1969).

Darlan, Jean Louis Xavier François (1881–1942), French political Admiral: born at Nérac, served in the French navy throughout the First World War and was executive Admiral from 1933 to April 1939, when he became Commander-in-Chief. He refused to order the fleet to sail for British, American or Caribbean ports (as Winston CHURCHILL requested) when France fell. After British naval action against the fleet at Oran and Mers-el-Kebir in July 1940, Admiral Darlan allowed a latent Anglophobia to come to the surface. As Vichy France's Minister of Marine he favoured collaboration with Germany. From February 1941 to April 1942 he was principal minister of the Vichy regime under Marshal PÉTAIN, and on 11 May 1941 he visited HITLER at Berchtesgaden to discuss joint Franco-German military action. The Germans, however, consistently distrusted him. A severe illness contracted by his son brought Admiral Darlan to Algiers in the first week of November 1942; and he was thus in the city when the Anglo-American forces made their surprise landings in French North Africa on 8 November. Darlan believed that, as the landings were followed by German entry into the previously unoccupied areas of France, he was freed from any obligations of service to Pétain. On 11 November 1942 General EISENHOWER accepted Darlan's claim to represent the French State in North Africa. This virtual recognition irritated the British and infuriated the 'Free French' movement of General DE GAULLE. On Christmas Eve Darlan was assassinated in Algiers apparently by a French Royalist fanatic, loyal to de Gaulle. A. de Montmorency: *The Enigma of Admiral Darlan* (New York, 1943); A. Werth: *France, 1940–55*

(1956); E. H. Jenkins: *A History of the French Navy* (1973).

Davis, Jefferson (1808–89), President of the Confederate States of America: born at Fairview, Christian County, Kentucky, but spent his boyhood in Mississippi where his father owned a profitable plantation. He graduated from the Military Academy at West Point in 1828 and served in the army for seven years, returning as a volunteer Colonel in the Mexican War of 1846–7. Mississippi elected him Senator from 1847 to 1851 and again in 1856 and during the intervening years he was Secretary of War. In the Senate he spoke out vigorously in defence of state rights and the institution of slavery. In May 1860 he carried a series of seven resolutions denying the right of Congress or any territorial legislature to prohibit slavery. When Mississippi seceded in January 1861, Davis automatically resigned his seat. He was elected provisional President of the Confederacy at a meeting of delegates from six seceding states at Montgomery, Alabama, on 9 February 1861; his appointment, for a six-year term, was confirmed nine months later and there was a formal inauguration in Richmond, the Confederate capital, in February 1862. Davis had greater political experience than other southerners and held a high opinion of his knowledge of soldiery. He was not, however, a popular figure with the Confederate commanders while the members of his improvised administration deplored his centralist tendencies. The strain of creating both a cohesive state machine and a large army taxed his ingenuity, and physically he was handicapped by chronic neuralgia. He was captured by Union cavalry in Georgia in May 1865 and imprisoned for two years in a fortress on Hampton Roads. Although indicted for treason, he was released on bail and never stood trial. A general amnesty on Christmas Day, 1868, restored his full freedom. After travelling abroad, he spent the last ten years of his life in quiet retirement on an estate bequeathed to him at Beauvoir, Mississippi. J. Davis: *The Rise and Fall of the Confederate Government* (2 vol. 1881 edn, revised by B. I. Wiley, Memphis, Tenn., 1958); B. I. Wiley: *The Road to Appomattox* (Memphis, Tenn., 1956); J. G. Randall and D. Donald: *The Civil War and Reconstruction* (Boston, Mass., 1961).

Dawes, Charles Gates (1865–1951), American financier and Vice-President: born at Marietta, Ohio, educated at Marietta College and University of Cincinnati Law School, practised law in Nebraska before entering banking corporations in Illinois. He held a high position on the administrative staff of the American Expeditionary Force in France and was then appointed head of the Reparations Committee. In this capacity he prepared a report, published in April 1924, providing for annual repayments by Germany of her reparations. This 'Dawes Plan' also recommended reorganization of the German state banking institution (Reichsbank) and foreign loans to help Germany's recovery. Dawes's farsighted and statesmanlike approach won him the Nobel Peace Prize (shared with Austen CHAMBERLAIN) in 1925. He served as Vice-President to Calvin COOLIDGE from 1925 to 1929, when he was appointed ambassador in London, a post he held until 1932. C. G. Dawes: *Journal as Ambassador* (New York, 1939); B. N. Timmons: *Portrait of an American; Charles G. Dawes* (New York, 1953).

Dayan, Moshe (1915–81), Israeli General and politician: born at Degania, near the Sea of Galilee, graduated in science from the Hebrew University in Jerusalem. Dayan was arrested by the British authorities in mandated Palestine as a suspected terrorist in 1939, but was commissioned in an auxiliary force helping the Allies clear Syria of pro-German units in June 1941. During this brief campaign he lost the sight of his left eye. In 1948 he became assistant to the Israeli chief of military operations, checking the first Arab incursions into independent Israel. He had secret talks with King ABDULLAH at Shuneh in 1949–50 but failed to find an acceptable compromise for the disputes between Israel and Jordan. His fame as a military commander rests upon his ability to command lightning operations, notably in the Sinai Campaign of 1956, when he was Chief of Staff, and in the preventive operations known as the 'Six Day War' of June 1967 (when he was Minister of Defence). He remained Minister of Defence until 1974 and was thus also responsible for the quick response to the Egyptian and Syrian attacks in the October War of 1973, a campaign in which Israeli armour crossed the Suez Canal. General Dayan became increasingly critical of Golda MEIR and was in political opposition from 1974 to 1977, when he took office again as Foreign Minister in BEGIN's government. In this capacity he began talks with the Egyptians for a peace treaty, coming to England for negotiations at Leeds Castle in Kent (18–19 July 1978). Dayan, however, found Begin intractable; on 16 October 1979 he resigned office, seeking greater flexibility in dealing with the Palestinian Arab problems. Eighteen months later Dayan launched a new Centre Party, but he died before he could organize it effectively. M. Dayan: *Diary of the Sinai Campaign* (1966); Y. Dayan: *My Father, his Daughter* (1985); R. Slater: *Warrior Statesman, the Life of Moshe Dayan* (1992).

De Gasperi, Alcide (1881–1954), Italian Prime Minister from 1945 to 1953: born at Pieve Tesino (which was then in the Austrian province of the Tyrol). He graduated from the University of Vienna and sat in the Austrian parliament from 1911 to 1914. His native district was ceded to Italy in 1919 and he entered parliament in Rome, sitting as a Deputy of the People's Party until 1925, when all non-fascist parties were banned. After a brief spell of political detention, he found sanctuary in the Vatican from 1929 to 1943. On the fall of MUSSOLINI he built up the Christian Democrat Party in Italy, becoming Prime Minister in December 1945. He was the most successful of Italy's democratic leaders, using American loans and Marshall Aid for reconstruction, championing the idea of European integration, and playing a prominent role in the foundation of the European Coal and Steel Community and the Council of Europe. His mistrust of communism, both in Italy and abroad, made him a firm supporter of NATO. P. Ginsborg: *A History of Contemporary Italy: society and Politics, 1944–1988* (1990); E. Wiskemann: *Italy since 1945* (1971).

de Gaulle, Charles André Joseph Marie (1890–1970), leader of the 'Free French' from 1940 to 1944, President in 1945 and from 1958 to 1969: born at Lille, graduated from the Military College at St Cyr in 1909, subsequently serving in the infantry regiment commanded by Colonel PÉTAIN. In February 1916 Captain de Gaulle was wounded and captured at Fort Douaumont, Verdun. He served on the French military mission to Poland in 1919. Between the wars he was a staff college lecturer, developing theories on the need for mobile armoured divisions which he publicized in a book, *Vers l'Armée de Métier*, published in 1935. His unorthodox views lost him the favour of his earlier patron, Pétain, and delayed his promotion. In May 1940 he was, belatedly, given command of the French Fourth Armoured Division and inflicted a severe check on the advancing Germans at Montcornet (17 May 1940), as well as leading sorties at Crécy-sur-Serre and towards Abbeville. He became Under-Secretary of Defence in the government of Paul REYNAUD on 9 June 1940, escaping to England eight days later and calling on his compatriots to accept his leadership in continuing to resist the Germans rather than obey the Vichy Government of Pétain. General de Gaulle's indomitable patriotism made him at times a difficult partner, frequently forced into verbal skirmishes with Winston CHURCHILL, and only reluctantly accepted as spokesman of 'Free France' by the Americans. He was recognized as head of the French Committee of National Liberation in Algiers in June 1943. A year later he returned to Normandy as a legendary hero, still personally unknown to the thousands of French people who welcomed him to a newly liberated Paris on 25 August 1944. He was, in effect, ruler of France from the autumn of 1944 to January 1946, formally recognized as provisional President of the republic during the last ten weeks of this period. His constitutional and political position was, however, imprecise: he was affronted by the failure of the British, American and Soviet leaders to treat him as an equal and invite him to the conferences at Yalta and Potsdam; but he was also increasingly alienated from his compatriots, who did not share his wish for a strong, centralized and right-wing presidency.

General de Gaulle spent the period 1946–7 building up a firm popular basis for his political ideas, formally launching the anti-communist movement known as the 'Rassemblement du Peuple Français' on 14 April 1947. For most of the following eleven years he remained at his country home of Colombey-les-deux-Églises, 140 miles east of Paris, confidently awaiting a second summons to serve France in an hour of crisis. The summons came in the last weeks of May 1958, when the revolt of French settlers in Algiers led to the fall of the Fourth Republic and the establishment of an interim 'government of national safety' under General de Gaulle. Four months later the French people, in a referendum, gave their support to a new constitution, ensuring that the Fifth Republic possessed the strong presidential executive which de Gaulle had sought in vain in 1945. On 21 December 1958 he was elected President with the support of 78 per cent of the electorate. His decision to end the Algerian War by negotiating with BEN BELLA seemed to the right-wing settlers a betrayal of the cause which had brought de Gaulle back from Colombey to Paris; and throughout 1961–2 the President was faced with armed rebellion by some senior officers and by former Gaullists, such as BIDAULT. De Gaulle narrowly escaped assassination on several occasions, notably at Petit Chamart on 22 August 1962 when his car was caught in a machine-gun ambush.

The President kept close control over his Foreign Ministers, insisting that France should show a nationalistic independence of her European partners: in 1965 he dissociated France entirely from the Common Market's agricultural policy; he withdrew French troops from NATO commands in July 1966, insisting that all NATO installations should be withdrawn from France within ten months; and he consistently vetoed British attempts to enter the European Community. At the same time he favoured bilateral understandings with ADENAUER in Germany and with the Soviet Union, favouring a Europe of 'fatherlands' which would stretch from the Atlantic to the Urals. High taxation permitted France to develop nuclear deterrents, maintain a large army, and embark on a prestigious public works programme. Gaullist centralism allowed the economy to prosper, but education and the social services were neglected. Frustration provoked industrial unrest and student demonstrations (especially in Paris) in May 1968, forcing the government to make concessions. President de Gaulle held out the prospect of decentralization, but when constitutional amendments were offered to the public in a referendum they were rejected. He immediately resigned the presidency (28 April 1969) and again withdrew into private life, dying suddenly at Colombey on 9 November 1970. C. de Gaulle: *The Army of the Future* (1940), *War Memoirs* (3 vols) (1955–60), *Memoirs of Hope* (2 vols) (1971); J. Lacoutoure: *De Gaulle* (1993); B. Ledwidge: *De Gaulle* (1962); A. Hartley: *Gaullism, the Rise and Fall of a Political Movement* (1972); S. Hoffmann: *France; Decline and Renewal* (New York, 1974).

de Valera, Eamonn (1882–1975), Irish Prime Minister for twenty-one years and President from 1959 to 1973: born in New York, his father being Spanish and his mother Irish. He was educated in Ireland and won distinction as a mathematician. During the Easter Rising of 1916 he commanded a battalion of the Irish Volunteers holding Boland's Mill, Dublin. His American birth saved him from execution by the British as a rebel and after twelve months' imprisonment in Sussex he was able to return to Ireland as President of Sinn Féin before the end of 1917. He was again arrested in 1918 but he escaped from Lincoln Prison and found refuge in the United States where he helped raise $5 million for the Irish Republican army. By 1922 he was campaigning once more in Ireland, his principal enemy now being the 'Free Staters', those who had followed Michael COLLINS in accepting dominion status for a partitioned Ireland rather than the united and independent Ireland demanded by Sinn Féin. But in 1926 de Valera, too, accepted the 'Free State' although he created a new political party, the Fianna Fáil, which he hoped would achieve by parliamentary means what Sinn Féin had sought by violence. de Valera led Fianna Fáil in opposition until the General Election of February 1932, which enabled him to form a predominantly Fianna Fáil government. Links with Britain were gradually cut during his premiership: a new constitution, applicable to southern Ireland but claiming sovereignty over the whole of Ulster as well, created Eire in June 1937; and de Valera kept the country neutral throughout the Second World War, even sending a formal message of condolence to the German minister in Dublin on the death of HITLER in 1945. The electorate rejected de Valera in 1948, but he served two further terms as Prime Minister: from June 1951 to June 1954; and from May 1957 to June 1959 when he was elected to the largely honorific dignity of President, a post he held until after his ninetieth birthday. He finally retired from public life in May 1973 and died on 29 August 1975. T. P. Cogan: *De Valera; Long Fellow, Long Shadow* (1973); J. P. O'Carrol and J. A. Murray (eds) *De Valera and His Times* (Cork, 1986); Lord Longford and T. P. O'Neill: *Eamon de Valera* (1970).

Deakin, Alfred (1857–1919), Australian statesman, of considerable influence between 1890 and 1910: born and educated in Melbourne, graduating in law from Melbourne University and serving in the Victoria State Legislature from 1879 to 1899, where he introduced progressive legislation to protect unskilled workers in sweated industries. By 1890 Deakin had emerged as an ardent champion of federation for the Australian colonies, a measure attained in January 1901 with the creation of the Commonwealth of Australia. He took office as Australian Prime Minister in September 1903. His predominantly Liberal ministry was dependent on Labour support, which he lost early in 1904 because of restrictions he wished to impose on trade union activity. He was Prime Minister again from July 1905 to December 1908, vigorously supporting the imperial preference ideas first put forward in England by Joseph CHAMBERLAIN. Deakin's government – in many respects complementary to the reforming Liberal governments of CAMPBELL-BANNERMAN and ASQUITH in England – pioneered old-age pensions and sickness benefits. Once again he was forced from office by Labour discontent. A third premiership, lasting for ten months in 1909–10, could accomplish little owing to the internal conflict of parliamentary factions. He led the Liberal Opposition from 1910 until a failing memory forced his retirement in 1913. It could be argued that his most important achievement was the patronage he gave to the earliest Australian irrigation schemes in Victoria in the 1880s. He remained a deeply spiritual person, influenced by journeys he made to India as a young man. A. Deakin: *A New Pilgrim's Progress* (Melbourne, 1877); R. Norris: *The Emergent Commonwealth; Australian Federation, Expectations and Fulfilment 1889–1910* (Melbourne, 1975); A. W. Martin (ed.): *Essays in Australian Federation* (Melbourne, 1969); A. Gabay: *The Mystic Life of Alfred Deakin* (Cambridge, 1992).

Debs, Eugene Victor (1855–1926), pioneer American socialist: born in Terre Haute, Indiana and educated there until he was 15. He began work as a fireman on the railways in 1871 and became an energetic industrial union organizer. In 1893 he was elected first President of the American Railway Union. His refusal to conform to an injunction served on him in the famous Chicago Pullman Strike of 1894 (cf. ALTGELD) resulted in six months' imprisonment but made him a national figure. In 1897 he founded the Social Democratic Party (renamed Socialist Party in 1901) and stood for the US presidency in 1900, 1904, 1908 and 1912, the Socialist vote gradually increasing in strength. Debs was a pacifist and in 1918 he was jailed for ten years for violating sedition clauses in the so-called Espionage Act of 1917. While in prison he stood for the presidency again, in the 1920 campaign, and polled 920,000 popular votes. He was released from prison on the order of President HARDING in 1921, Woodrow WILSON having declined to pardon him. Although Debs' hopes of high office were negligible – he never polled more than 6 per cent of the votes in a presidential election – he was respected for the unfashionable sincerity of his ideals and his ready acceptance of political martyrdom. H. W. Morgan: *Eugene V Debs, Socialist for President* (Syracuse, N.Y., 1962).

Delcassé, Théophile (1852–1923), French Foreign Minister from 1898 to 1905: born at Pamiers in the eastern approaches to the Pyrenees. He was a schoolteacher and journalist before being returned to the Chamber of Deputies as a Radical Republican in 1889. When he became Foreign Minister in June 1898 he was a convinced supporter of African colonialism and was thus antipathetic to British policy. He argued, however, that France could not risk conflict with Britain in Africa and with Germany in Europe, and he therefore began slowly to work for Anglo-French collaboration. This understanding he achieved in the Entente Cordiale of 1904, a settlement of all outstanding differences between Britain and France in Africa, Asia and on the high seas. In June 1905 he was forced to resign under German diplomatic pressure after he had held the French Foreign Ministry for a longer period of time than any other statesman of the Third Republic. From 1911 to 1913 he was Minister of Marine, a post which enabled him to continue his work for Anglo-French collaboration, notably in the Mediterranean. After a short spell as ambassador in St Petersburg, he returned to the French Foreign Office in August 1914 and played a crucial part in encouraging Italy to enter the war. He resigned the Foreign Ministry in October 1915. A long personal feud with CLEMENCEAU prevented him from taking office later in the war. C. Andrews: *Theophile Delcassé and the Making of the Entente Cordiale* (1968); P. J. V. Rolo: *Entente Cordiale* (1969); E. N. Anderson: *The First Moroccan Crisis 1904–1906* (Chicago, 1930).

Delors, Jacques Lucien Jean (1925–), President of the European Commission from 1985 to 1994: born in Paris, where he completed his university education before joining the Banque de France at the end of the Second World War, later working as a civil servant for fulfilment of the MONNET Plan. By the age of 44 he was special adviser on social affairs to the Prime Minister's secretariat but he remained a non-political figure until 1973, when he joined the socialists, becoming party spokesman on EEC monetary affairs; he was a member of the European Parliament, 1979–81. MITTERRAND appointed Delors Minister of the Economy and Finance in May 1981, with the unpopular task of imposing an austerity programme on France. Delors was disappointed at being passed over for the premiership in 1984, but in January 1985 he took office as President of the European Commission, with responsibility for speeding up integration and extending co-operation between members. He took the initiative in promoting the Treaty on European Union, agreed at Maastricht in December 1991, signed there by EEC members on 7 February 1992, and operative from 1 November 1993. His commitment to the European ideal was unacceptable to the THATCHER government in London; his proposals for a common currency and for an agreed social policy were denounced in the English tabloid Press with extraordinary virulence. After Thatcher's downfall the MAJOR government opted out of Delors' more far-reaching reforms and remained highly suspicious of his modified socialism. His ten-year term of office expired on 1 January 1995; he was succeeded by Jacques SANTER of Luxembourg. J. Delors: *One Europe* (1988).

Deng Xiaoping (Teng Hsiao-ping) (1902–), Chinese communist leader from 1977 to 1992: born in Sichuan (Szechwan) into a similar family background to the much older Marshal CHU TE; Deng's father owned extensive lands in the province. Deng joined the group of Chinese workers and students in France after the First World War, studying at Lyons University, where he joined the Communist Party in 1925 and first met CHOU EN-LAI. He was in Moscow in 1926, but joined the workers' demonstration against CHIANG KAI-SHEK's rule at Shanghai in April 1927. By 1934 Deng was a dedicated party member, taking part in the Long March and loyally supporting MAO in the power struggle of January 1935. He entered the central committee of the party in 1949 and became General Secretary (and Vice-Premier) in 1956, working closely with LIU SHAO-CHI, whom he accompanied to Moscow in 1960 for three weeks of acrimonious dispute over the true nature of communism. Mao's subsequent suspicion of Liu led to Deng's political eclipse, especially when his 'Later Ten Points' of September 1963 ran counter to Mao's agricultural teachings. Deng was denounced as a revisionist during the Cultural Revolution (1966) and sent, in disgrace, to Nanchang to work in a tractor factory for 'ideological re-education'. But Chou's subsequent ascendancy brought Deng rapidly back to authority in 1973; he was Vice-Premier for the Tenth Party Congress (August 1973) and made a key speech to the UN General Assembly in April 1974. In the power struggle following Chou En-lai's death, Deng was dismissed from office by HUA in April 1976. Hua, however, proved incompetent; under pressure from a people's poster campaign, Deng was reinstated as Vice-Premier in July 1977, also becoming Chief of General Staff. At the Eleventh Party Congress in August 1977, Deng made the principal speech, calling for acceptance of modern cultural ideas and technological change. Over the following ten years he advanced younger officials to the leadership and visited Japan, USA and Europe to lift China's international status. Ailing health forced him to relax his hold on policy-making in 1988–9; although Deng remained head of China's Central Military Commission, he could not control the surge of democratic feeling among students in the capital which culminated in the killing of more than 2,000 demonstrators in Tianamen Square (4 June 1989). He formally retired from office in November 1989, but he continued to shape ideas of economic reform. Remarkably, in October 1992, the Fourteenth Party Congress endorsed the veteran's call for fast and bold reforms so as to stimulate a 'socialist market economy'. D. Bonavia: *Deng* (1989); J. Gray: *Rebellions and Revolutions* (Oxford, 1990).

Denikin, Anton Ivanovich (1872–1947), anti-Bolshevik Russian General: became a military cadet in 1887, served in the Far East in 1904–5 and was a senior staff officer in the First World War, promoted to Lieutenant-General in February 1917. He served the Provisional Government as commander of the western sector of the Front against the Germans in March 1917 and commanded in the Ukraine from May to November 1917. From 1918 to 1920 he led the 'Whites' against the Bolshevik Red Army, first in the Caucasus and, more spectacularly, in the Ukraine from August to September 1919, capturing Kiev and Kharkov and leading the 'armed forces of the South' towards Moscow. His traditionalist Russian nationalism prevented him from concerting operations with the equally nationalistic anti-Bolshevik armies in the Ukraine and Poland. British assistance helped Denikin continue resistance in the Caucasus until the spring of 1920; but here, too, he wasted men and munitions in seeking to put down non-communist national independence movements in Georgia and Azerbaijan. When armed resistance finally succumbed to Red Army pressure in April 1920 Denikin escaped across the Black Sea to Istanbul, later settling in France and the USA, where he died in August 1947. A. I. Denikin: *The Russian Turmoil* (1922); D. V. Lehovich: *White Aagainst Red; the Life of General Anton Denikin* (New York, 1974); W. G. Rosenberg: *A. I. Denikin and the Anti-Bolshevik Movement in South Russia* (Amherst, Mass., 1961).

Denktash, Rauf (1924–), leader of the Turkish Cypriot community from 1974: born near Paphos, the son of a lawyer, receiving his main education at the English School in Nicosia. Denktash practised law until entering politics on the eve of Cyprus's independence in 1960. For three years he sought to work with President MAKARIOS but he went into exile in 1963, complaining of narrowly Greek dominance of the island, remaining abroad for five years. When the Turkish army invaded Cyprus in July 1974 and put one-third of the island under Turkish military 'protection', the Ankara authorities accepted Denktash as community spokesman. They recognized him as leader of the 'Turkish Federated State of Cyprus' in February 1975; in June 1985 he was elected President of the Turkish Republic of Northern Cyprus'. This newly constituted 'state' was recognized only by Turkey, and never by the UN. Denktash was re-elected President in April 1990. In 1992–3, he showed a willingness to consider UN proposals for a bizonal federal state which would unify the island once more, but the plan was rejected: zonal boundaries would allegedly have given Turkish Cypriot areas to the Greek Cypriots. R. Denktash: *The Cyprus Triangle* (1982); K. Kyle: *Cyprus* (1984).

Derby, Lord (Edward Geoffrey Smith Stanley) (1799–1869), British Prime Minister in 1852, 1858 and from 1866 to 1868: born at Knowsley Hall, Lancashire, educated at Eton and Christ Church, Oxford, entering the Commons as MP for Stockbridge in 1820. He was returned for Preston, 1826, for Windsor, 1830, and for North Lancashire from 1832 until 1844 when he went to the House of Lords as Baron Stanley of Bickerstaffe, succeeding as fourteenth Earl of Derby upon his father's death in 1851. His career defies easy party labelling. He was a member of Grey's Liberal ministry which introduced the first parliamentary Reform Act and, as Colonial Secretary with a seat in the Cabinet, he proposed the abolition of slavery in the British Empire (1833). From 1841 to 1845 he served the Conservative Peel until his protectionist views caused him to break with Peel and GLADSTONE as they moved towards free trade. By 1846 he was Tory leader in the House of Lords, working with DISRAELI who led the protectionists in the Commons. In February 1852 Lord Derby formed a minority government, but he was out of office by the end of the year. A second minority government lasted from February 1858 until June 1859, but Derby could scarcely maintain unity in his Cabinet, let alone in the Conservative Party as a whole. In June 1866 he formed his third minority government, with Disraeli showing brilliance as Chancellor of the Exchequer. Yet Derby's team, as a whole, was so lacking in talent that he had to give his own son the Foreign Office. Derby, however, in partnership with Disraeli, pushed through parliament the most remarkable of his legislative measures, a second Reform Act which made 'a leap in the dark' by enfranchising a million town labourers as well as a redistributing seats so as to acknowledge changes in the density of population. Ill-health forced Derby's resignation in February 1868 and he died in October 1869. Socially he remained the most Whiggish of Tory leaders, isolating himself from politics for weeks on end in order to shoot or to attend the great race meetings at Newmarket or Doncaster; and yet he is the only Prime Minister to have published an English blank verse translation of the *Iliad*. W. D. Jones: *Lord Derby and Victorian Conservatism* (Oxford, 1956); A. Briggs: *Victorian People* (rev. edn 1965); T. E. Kebbel: *The Life of the Earl of Derby* (1893).

Dewey, George (1837–1917), American Admiral: born at Montpelier in Vermont, educated at the Naval Academy at Annapolis, commissioned in the US navy in 1858. As Commodore in command of the Asiatic Squadron of four cruisers and two gunboats, he sailed from Hong Kong on the outbreak of the Spanish-American War, entered Manila Bay in the Philippines on 1 May 1898, and in a six-hour engagement destroyed ten Spanish vessels without damage to his own ships or American loss of life. This remarkable victory, regarded as the foundation of US naval power in the far Pacific, made Dewey a popular idol of the American people overnight. He was at once promoted to Rear-Admiral and a year later the special title of 'Admiral of the Fleet' was conferred on him, a rank borne by no other American officer (although the equivalent rank of 'Fleet Admiral' was created in 1944 for Ernest J. KING and Chester W. NIMITZ). G. Dewey: *Autobiography* (New York, 1916); L. H. Healy and L. Kutner: *The Admiral* (Chicago, 1944).

Dewey, Thomas Edmund (1902–71), American Republican politician, influential from 1942 to 1950: born at Owosso in Michigan, graduated with a degree in law from the universities of Michigan and Columbia, practised as District Attorney in New York City where he received wide publicity for his vigorous prosecution of racketeers. He was Governor of New York from 1942 to 1954 and was chosen by the Republican Party Convention to oppose Franklin ROOSEVELT in the 1944 presidential campaign. His platform abandoned the traditional isolationism of his party by accepting the need for some form of international world organization. Governor Dewey gained 22 million popular votes against Roosevelt's 25 million. In 1948 the Republicans again chose Dewey, selecting an already once-defeated candidate for the first time in the party's history. Splits in the Democratic Party and Press campaigns against the sitting President, Harry TRUMAN, made commentators rate highly the chances of Governor Dewey. But he polled almost the same popular votes as in 1944, failing to attract the electors outside the prosperous urban areas. After retiring from public life, he resumed his law career in New York City, actively supporting NIXON in 1960, but declining even to attend the Convention that nominated the right-wing GOLDWATER as Republican candidate in 1964. J. Gunther: *Inside U.S.A.* (1949).

Diaz, José Porfirio (1830–1915), President of Mexico for over thirty years: born at Oaxaca and educated for the priesthood but became an armed supporter of Benito JUÁREZ, the radical revolutionary leader of the 1860s, who came from the same district as Diaz. In 1876 Diaz seized power, his authority as President being formally recognized a year later. Except for the years 1880–4, when one of Diaz's nominees held the presidency, he was dictator and Head of State until 1911. His government favoured foreign investors, especially Americans, and he maintained an outwardly efficient administration through a team of ruthless and greedy supporters, hated by the Mexican peasantry. In 1910 a millionaire rancher, Francisco MADERO, challenged President Diaz to justify the lip-service he paid to the democratic ideal by permitting a free presidential election. Diaz's folly in seeking to imprison Madero provoked violent demonstrations in the countryside and the breakdown of civil authority in Mexico City. The threat of mob violence in the last week of May 1911 induced President Diaz to flee the country, eventually settling in France. Serious disorders continued in Mexico until 1920, emphasizing the superficial nature of the administrative system which Diaz claimed to have built up in the republic. C. Beals: *Porfirio Diaz, Dictator of Mexico* (Westport, Conn., 1971); J. Creelman: *Diaz, Master of Mexico* (New York, 1911); F. Brandenburg: *The Making of Modern Mexico* (Englewood Cliffs, N.J., 1966).

Diefenbaker, John George (1895–1979), Canadian Prime Minister from 1957 to 1963: born at Normandy Township in Ontario, educated at the University of Saskatchewan. He practised as a barrister from 1919 to 1940, when he entered parliament in Ottawa. In December 1956 he became leader of the Progressive Conservatives, forming a government in June 1957 which received increasing backing from the electorate in March 1958. Diefenbaker's Conservative government provided a six-year gap in thirty-eight years of Liberal control of the Canadian Federal Parliament. His principal objective was to strengthen economic links with Great Britain and other Commonwealth countries so as to check the dominance of America in Canada's trade. He found, however, that the interdependence of Canada and the United States over problems of defence necessitated close economic co-operation. His apparent subservience to American strategic policy lost him support in the election of April 1963. For four years he led the opposition to his Liberal successor, Lester PEARSON. He retired from politics in 1968 but continued to be treated with respect as the Conservative elder statesman in the dominion. J. G. Diefenbaker: *Memoirs; One Canada* (3 vols) (Toronto, 1976–8); R. Bothwell, I. Drummond and J. English: *Canada since 1945* (Toronto, 1981).

Dilke, Charles Wentworth (1843–1911), British radical imperialist: born in Chelsea, gaining most of his basic education from his grandfather, who had close Bonapartist friendships in Paris and Normandy, where he took the boy frequently. Charles studied law at Trinity Hall, Cambridge. Although he long professed republican principles he accepted the baronetcy which he inherited at the age of 25 and throughout his public career was always known as 'Sir Charles Dilke'. After undertaking a world tour he wrote *Greater Britain* (1868), a plea for acceptance of colonialism as a profitable outlet to ease Britain's domestic social problems. He sat as Radical MP for Chelsea from 1868 to 1886 and joined GLADSTONE's Cabinet in 1882 as President of the Local Government Board. The prospects of a brilliant parliamentary career were cut short by a divorce suit, in which he was cited as a correspondent in 1885–6. The popular Press salaciously printed full details of the scandal. It seems probable that Sir Charles was the victim of a conspiracy by political enemies. He was out of Parliament for six years, using the time to study imperial problems and make extensive journeys, notably to the Ottoman Empire and India. His two-volume study, *Problems of Greater Britain* (1890) considered the value of federation within the empire, but it also stressed the importance of safeguarding native rights in the newly established protectorates of southern Africa. He returned to parliament as Liberal MP for the Forest of Dean, 1892–1911, speaking frequently from the back-benches on colonial questions and, in his later years, vigorously opposing the spread of a social and political colour bar in South Africa. He also showed an interest in antipodean affairs, exchanging letters with the Australian statesman, Alfred DEAKIN. R. Jenkins: *Sir Charles Dilke* (1958); S. Gwynn and G. M. Tuckwell: *The Life of Sir Charles W. Dilke* (2 vols) (1917).

Dimitrievič, Dragutin (1877–1917), Serbian soldier and conspirator, alias 'Apis': born near Belgrade, receiving his schooling at the French *lycée* in the city before entering the Military Academy in 1895. He showed such clarity of mind that, on graduation, he was immediately posted to the Serbian General Staff. There he perfected the embryonic military intelligence unit, taking as an alias his nickname 'Apis' (the holy ox). He became an early supporter of a 'Greater Serbia' movement, which sought union with Montenegro and territorial expansion into Turkish-held Macedonia and Austrian-held Bosnia. Contempt for the weak rule of Serbia's King, Alexander Obrenović (1876–1903), induced Apis and six other junior officers to organize the King's assassination and his replacement by the exiled head of the rival dynasty, Peter Karadjordjević (1844–1921). Although the conspiracy was hatched in September 1901 it was not carried out until 29–30 May 1903: the King and Queen were butchered in Belgrade's royal palace and their bodies thrown from the window. When Apis sought to perpetuate his political influence, he came into conflict with Serbia's new Prince Regent, ALEXANDER Karadjordjević, but by 1910 Apis held the rank of Colonel and remained head of military intelligence. To co-ordinate war plans and harness the Serbian patriotism of young Serbs in Bosnia, he established a secret society, *Ujedinjenje ili Smrt* ('Unity or Death', commonly called the 'Black Hand') in May 1911, which trained PRINČIP and other Bosnian Serbs to assassinate Archduke FRANCIS FERDINAND at Sarajevo (28 June 1914), thus precipitating the First World War, against the wishes of

Prime Minister PAŠIĆ and Regent Alexander. Black Hand conspiracies continued throughout the war until, in December 1916, Apis and his main companions were arrested by the exiled Serbian authorities in Salonika. After a highly irregular court martial, on 26 June 1917 Apis and two other officers faced a firing-squad for allegedly plotting the Prince Regent's murder. Apis-Dimitrievič remained a legendary hero for many Serbs: the court martial verdict, obtained on perjured evidence, was quashed by the Serbian Supreme Court in 1953. Black Hand conspiratorial traditions survive. D. Mackenzie: *Apis, the Congenial Conspirator* (Boulder, Colo., 1989); V. Dedijer: *The Road to Sarajevo* (1960); W. S. Vucinich: *Serbia between East and West, the Events of 1903–1908* (Stanford, Calif. 1954).

Dimitrov, Georgi (1882–1949), leading Bulgarian communist from 1917 to 1948: born at Pernik on the upper Struma. He became a printer and trade unionist, organizing the first serious wave of strikes in 1905 while Bulgaria was still technically a principality under Turkish suzerainty. From 1917 to 1923 Dimitrov directed the underground communist movement which sought to overthrow King FERDINAND and his son BORIS. Vigorous counter-measures in the summer of 1923 forced Dimitrov to escape to Russia. He became one of the most active members of the Communist International (Comintern). While on a secret mission to Berlin in 1933 he was arrested by the Nazi authorities and placed on trial at Leipzig for alleged complicity in the burning-down of the Reichstag building (27 February 1933). His skilful defence ridiculed the evidence of the Reichstag Speaker, Hermann GOERING, and gained Dimitrov a world reputation. Upon his acquittal he was deported to the Soviet Union. He returned to Bulgaria in 1945 and, as Prime Minister from 1946 until his death, completed the 'Sovietization' of the republic. In August 1947, however, Dimitrov held conversations at Bled with Marshal TITO in which the two Balkan leaders took the first steps towards the creation of a socialist federation in south eastern Europe. Such independence was unwelcome in Moscow and Dimitrov fell out of favour with STALIN. Soon afterwards his health gave way; he left Sofia in the spring of 1949 to receive medical treatment in the Soviet Union, and died in Moscow on 3 July. R. J. Crampton: *A Short History of Modern Bulgaria* (1987) J. D. Bell: *The Bulgarian Communist Party from Blagoev to Zhivkov* (Stanford, Calif. 1985).

Disraeli, Benjamin (1804–81), British Prime Minister in 1868 and from 1874 to 1880: born in Holborn, London, of Jewish parentage, but baptized according to the rites of the Church of England when he was 12. Isaac d'Israeli, his father, was a man of letters, specializing in 'Curiosities of Literature', and he was a more formative influence on his son than the small school at Higham Hill, Essex, which Benjamin left when he was 15. After three years in a solicitor's office and a venture in journalism, he wrote a novel, *Vivian Grey* (1826), and went on a long tour of the Levant before seeking entry to Parliament. He was eventually elected MP for Maidstone in 1837, remaining in the Commons for thirty-nine years (Shrewsbury's MP, 1841–7; Buckingham's MP, 1847–76). In his early career Disraeli was a flamboyant Tory radical, leading the 'Young England' movement, whose ideas he presented in two further novels, *Coningsby* (1844) and *Sybil* (1845). Disraeli opposed Peel, GLADSTONE and the Free Traders in 1846 and was spokesman for the protectionist Conservatives in the Commons for twenty years, holding office briefly as Chancellor of the Exchequer in 1852 and 1858–9, under Lord DERBY. Disraeli was again at the Exchequer in July 1866 but his main task in Derby's third ministry was to steer a second Reform Bill through the Commons. His political acumen made him a natural successor to Derby and he took office on 28 February 1868. He remained at what he called 'the top of the greasy pole' for only nine months, his party being roundly defeated in the election of December 1868. In this short-lived ministry his greatest success was to captivate Queen VICTORIA, who was delighted by a Prime Minister 'full of poetry, romance and chivalry' (as she wrote to her eldest daughter). When Disraeli left office he asked the Queen to create his much-loved wife, who was suffering from cancer, a peeress; and Mary Anne Disraeli (1792–1872) became Viscountess Beaconsfield. Some of Disraeli's greatest speeches were made as leader of the Opposition to Gladstone from 1868 to 1874, but his fame rests on his achievements as Prime Minister between February 1874 and April 1880. His government undertook social reforms, which improved public hygiene and housing, and helped trade unions by two acts defining their status and rights. He was largely responsible for securing for Britain the principal shareholding in the Suez Canal Company and for the Royal Titles Act of April 1876 which gave the British sovereign a new status as Empress of India. Victoria created him Earl of Beaconsfield in August 1876 and it was mainly from the House of Lords that he denounced Russia's attempts to control the Balkans and Afghanistan, 1877–80. He broke with precedent in accompanying his Foreign Secretary, SALISBURY, to the Congress of Berlin in 1878. There he enjoyed a personal triumph, claiming that he had brought back 'Peace with Honour'; but the British electorate thought the Conservatives' forward policy in southern Africa and on the Afghan–Indian frontier full of danger, and in April voted back Gladstone and the Liberals. For Beaconsfield defeat was followed seven months later by publication of a final political novel, *Endymion*, but his health collapsed that winter and he died in his London house, in Curzon Street, on 19 April 1881. He was buried at Hughenden, his Buckinghamshire home. R. Blake: *Disraeli* (1966); S. Bradford: *Disraeli* (1986); W. F. Monypenny and G. E. Buckle: *The Life of Benjamin Disraeli, Earl of Beaconsfield* (6 vols) (1910–20).

Djilas Milovan (1911–), Montenegrin critic of Yugoslav communism: born at Kolasin, central Montenegro, and became a communist in his last years at Berane High School, attracting police attention while a university student at Belgrade. He was imprisoned at Sremska Mitrovica in 1933 during ALEXANDER's dictatorship and held for three years. Between 1941 and 1944 he won respect for his skill as a partisan leader in Bosnia and his native Montenegro. He was sent by TITO as an emissary to Moscow in 1944–5, returning to Belgrade to become one of the Vice-Presidents of the new Yugoslavia. By the early 1950s he was a critic of the society in which he lived: hard-hitting articles in the official journal *Borba* and in *Nova Misao* (*New Thought*, a periodical he edited) annoyed bureaucrats and prominent army officers. In 1954 Djilas was expelled from the League of Communists and deprived of all official posts; further criticism led in 1955 to a suspended prison sentence, but he still refused to be silenced. His book *The New Class*, published in the West in 1956, developed the theory that party oligarchies in communist states usurped and preserved the class distinctions enjoyed by the privileged few in pre-revolutionary days, thus producing a dictatorship which, Djilas argued, carried within it the seeds of its own destruction. Marxist theoretic revision on this scale was unacceptable in Yugoslavia, and in December 1956 Djilas was imprisoned, returning to a cell at Sremska Mitrovica in which he had been held twenty years before. He was released in 1961, arrested again in 1962, but allowed his personal freedom in 1966, his passport being restored to him in 1968. His later writings were primarily autobiographical, depicting with deep feeling the struggles of the Montenegrin and other southern Slav peoples. He was again in trouble with the authorities in Belgrade in the winter of 1979–80, shortly before Tito's death. In 1989 he was formally rehabilitated. M. Djilas: *The New Class* (1956), *Land without Justice* (1958), *Conversations with Stalin* (1962), *Memoir of a Revolutionary* (1973); S. Clissold: *Djilas, the Progress of a Revolutionary* (1983).

Doe, Samuel Kenyon (1950–90), Liberia's Head of State throughout the 1980s: born in Tuzon, Grand Gedeh, enlisted as a private in the Liberian army in 1969, acquiring some black radical progressive views which were in contrast to the placidly American principles of the 'True Whigs', the ruling party in Monrovia since 1870. Attempts by the Liberian authorities to curb the activities of the newly formed People's Progressive Party induced Master Sergeant Doe to lead a military *coup* on 12 April 1980, in which President Tolbert, the Head of State since 1971, was killed. Doe assumed authority for Liberia, as Chairman of a Military Council which controlled the republic until 1986, when Doe became President of a civilian administration of 'National Democrat' progressives, basically pro-western in sympathies. Doe, however, was no more than an improviser. His failure to build up a genuinely effective co-operative state caused mounting unrest and in September 1990 he was murdered during a National Patriotic Front uprising in the capital, Monrovia. Doe's death precipitated a civil war which dragged on for more than four years. His unfulfilled experiment, and its tragic aftermath, gravely weakened Liberia's economy: a third of the population was forced to seek refuge abroad. M. Omonijo: *Doe; The Liberian Tragedy* (Ikeja, 1990); W. A. Givens (ed.): *Liberia; policies and statements of Dr S. K. Doe* (Bourne End, 1986).

Doenitz, Karl (1891–1980), German Grand Admiral, naval Commander-in-Chief from 1943 to 1945 and Head of State in May 1945: born at Gronau, on the Dutch frontier, and entered the navy, serving in cruisers until 1916 when he became a U-boat commander. He stayed in the coastal defence service throughout the 1920s and in 1935 was entrusted by HITLER with the task of building up a new U-boat fleet. Doenitz was author of a book, published on the eve of the war, in which he emphasized the importance of U-boats hunting together, rather than attacking protected convoys singly as in 1917–18. As Flag-Officer, U-boats, from September 1939 to January 1943 he was able to put his theories into practice, developing the 'wolf pack' system by which a group of U-boats would wait for convoys to raid. Doenitz became Commander-in-Chief of the German navy on 30 January 1943, concentrating almost entirely on submarine strategy and tactics, including a 'schnorkel' apparatus which, by allowing U-boats to charge batteries under water, kept them at sea for a longer term than previously. To his surprise he was appointed President of the Reich by Hitler in his final testament. Effectively Doenitz held office only from 1 May to 8 May 1945, authorizing the German surrender. He was sentenced to ten years' imprisonment for 'crimes against peace' and for war crimes at Nuremberg in 1946; and was released from Spandau Prison, Berlin, on 30 September 1956, subsequently publishing his memoirs. K. Doenitz: *Memoirs* (1958); P. Padfield: *The Last Führer* (1984).

Dollfuss, Engelbert (1892–1934), Austrian Chancellor from 1932 to 1934: born in a farmhouse near Mank, in the Wachau valley. He was the son of an unmarried farmer's daughter (who outlived him) and was educated at the Hollabrunn Gymnasium before studying theology and law at Vienna. During the First World War he was an officer in the machine-gun section of the *Kaiserjäger* and won eight decorations for bravery, fighting mainly on the Italian Front. He took his doctorate in 1922, thereafter concentrating on agrarian problems in Lower Austria. In March 1931 he was made Minister of Agriculture, and on 10 May 1932 became leader of the Christian Socialist Party and Austrian Chancellor. He put into practice a clerical fascism, suspending parliamentary government in March 1933 and seeking, in foreign affairs, collaboration with the right-wing governments of HORTHY in Hungary and of MUSSOLINI in Italy. There was a grim civil war in Vienna for five days in February 1934 in which Dollfuss ordered artillery to shell the barrack-like workers' settlements in the inner suburbs of the capital for fear of a socialist revolt. But Dollfuss's revised constitution – which owed much to Mussolini's ideas on a corporative state – was unacceptable to the Austrian Nazis, who wanted an Austro-German union under the rule of HITLER. On 25 July 1934 Dollfuss was murdered in his chancellery in central Vienna by Austrian Nazis vainly seeking to seize power. He was succeeded by Kurt von Schuschnigg (1897–1977) who, though constantly threatened by Nazi defectors within his own party, staved off the union with Hitler's Germany until March 1938. G. Brook-Shepherd: *Dollfuss* (1961); A. Diamant: *Austrian Catholics and the First Republic 1918–1934* (Princeton, N.J., 1960); W. B. Maass: *Assassination in Vienna* (New York, 1972).

Dos Santos, José Eduardo (1942–), Angolan President: born in Luanda, educated at the Salvador Correia *lycée*, but turned against Portuguese colonial rule and joined the Popular Movement for the Liberation of Angola (MPLA) on its foundation in 1961. After an abortive rising in Luanda he went into exile in the Congo, later studying petroleum engineering at Moscow University and working briefly at Baku before being trained in military communications. He returned from the USSR in 1970 to lead MPLA guerrilla resistance to the Portuguese in northern Angola's oil-rich Cabinda region. In 1974 he was admitted to the MPLA central committee. When Portugal conceded independence in November 1975 Dos Santos became Angola's Foreign Minister and helped secure recognition for the 'People's Republic' from most countries, though not from the USA or South Africa, who supported the rival UNITA forces of SAVIMBI. Dos Santos became Deputy Prime Minister in 1978 and President a year later. His employment of Soviet and Cuban 'volunteers' against UNITA ensured hostility from Republican administrations in the USA, although he gradually abandoned the Marxist-Leninist principles of the Angolan Revolution. The MPLA ceased to be the sole legal party in February 1991, three months before a ceasefire was agreed between the MPLA and UNITA. In a presidential election in September 1992 Dos Santos won 49.5 per cent of the vote, against Savimbi's 40 per cent. Although Dos Santos was confirmed as President in November 1992, with a government which included some minor political parties, the basic conflict between MPLA and UNITA continued with fierce intensity throughout the following two years. A. J. Klinghoffer: *The Angolan War* (Boulder, Colo., 1980).

Douglas, Stephen Arnold (1813–61), American Senator: born at Brandon, Vermont but settled in Illinois in 1833. There he practised law and sat in the state legislature before being returned to

Congress in 1843. Four years later, when he moved to the comparatively new city of Chicago, he became a Senator, taking the lead in legislation which brought territorial government to Utah and New Mexico. He was again returned to the Senate in 1852, two years later introducing the Kansas–Nebraska Bill which, by accepting the idea of 'popular sovereignty', denied Congress any right to intervene in disputes concerning the 'slave' or 'free' status of new territories. The measure was passed after three months of bitter controversy which harmed Douglas's reputation as a moderate Democrat. In the 1858 senatorial election he was challenged by a nominee from the new Republican Party, Abraham LINCOLN. Douglas accepted Lincoln's proposal that the two candidates should appear on the same platform in the various Congressional districts of Illinois to debate the slavery issue. These seven debates clarified Douglas's attitude to slavery. At Freeport on 27 August 1858 he conceded that 'slavery cannot exist a day or an hour anywhere, unless it is supported by local police regulations'. Once more the Illinois electors returned Douglas to the Senate but this 'Freeport Doctrine' offended southern Democrats who believed slavery was essential to the cotton economy. The debates made both Douglas and Lincoln national figures. Douglas duly gained the Democratic nomination for the presidency in 1860 but at the cost of splitting the party, the southern Democrats running their own candidate, John Breckinridge (1821–75). In the presidential election Douglas polled some 1,300,000 popular votes but carried only the state of Missouri. After his defeat he loyally supported President Lincoln, denouncing secessionism and rallying 'war Democrats' to preserve the Union; but, after the rigours and disappointments of the presidential campaign, this task was too great a strain on Douglas's heart. He collapsed and died in Chicago on 3 June 1861. R. W. Johannsen: *Stephen A. Douglas* (New York, 1977), (ed.): *The Lincoln–Douglas Debates* (New York, 1965).

Douglas-Home, Alexander Frederick (1903–95), British Prime Minister for twelve months from 1963 to 1964: born in London, the eldest son of the thirteenth Earl of Home. He was known by the courtesy title of Lord Dunglass until 1951 when he succeeded his father as fourteenth Earl. After completing his education at Eton and Christ Church, Oxford, Lord Dunglass sat as Conservative MP for South Lanark from 1931 to 1945, gaining some experience of foreign affairs as private secretary to Neville CHAMBERLAIN from 1937 to 1939. A back injury kept him out of the war and out of parliamentary life until 1950, when he was elected MP for another Scottish constituency, Lanark. As Earl of Home he was responsible for Scottish affairs under Winston CHURCHILL from 1951 to 1955, Commonwealth Relations Secretary from 1955 to 1960 under EDEN and MACMILLAN and Foreign Secretary from 1960 to 1963, years marked by the crisis over the Berlin Wall and by the Cuban missiles crisis. His appointment as Prime Minister in succession to Macmillan (19 October 1963) was unexpected: he had no experience of tough debate in the House of Commons; and it had been assumed that, since the passing over of CURZON in favour of BALDWIN in 1923, no Prime Ministers would come from the House of Lords. However, since the Peerage Act of July 1963 enabled members of the Upper House to renounce their titles this step was duly taken by the Earl of Home on 23 October; and, as he had been created a Knight of the Thistle in the previous year, he was now styled Sir Alec Douglas-Home. The new session of Parliament was postponed from 29 October to 12 November in order to let the Prime Minister contest, and win, a by-election in Kinross and West Perthshire on 6 November. Sir Alec was an amiable and unruffled head of government, his legislative programme limited to an act abolishing retail price maintenance. His year in office was overshadowed by an imminent General Election: it was held on 15 October 1964 and won by Labour with an overall majority of five, Harold WILSON becoming Prime Minister on the following day. Sir Alec remained Conservative leader until 22 July 1965 when he was succeeded by Edward HEATH. He was Foreign Secretary again from 1970 to 1974, returning to the House of Lords as a life peer, Baron Home of the Hirsel, in 1974. Lord Home: *The Way the Wind Blows* (1976); K. Young: *Sir Alec Douglas-Home* (1970).

Dreyfus, Alfred (1859–1935), French officer accused of selling military secrets to Germany in 1894: born at Mulhouse, a member of a Jewish family long resident in Alsace where they owned a flourishing cotton-mill. From the École Polytechnique, Dreyfus passed into the artillery and was selected for staff officer's training in 1890, the year in which he married a diamond merchant's wealthy daughter, Lucie Hadamard. Secret information, contained in a memorandum (*bordereau*), was intercepted on its way to the German military attaché in September 1894: the handwriting was said to be that of Dreyfus. He was arrested on 15 October 1894, condemned by court martial, degraded and sentenced to imprisonment in the penal colony of Devil's Island. Evidence that the leakage of information was continuing led Dreyfus' family to begin an agitation for revision of the verdict in 1897, their campaign being vigorously supported by the novelist Émile Zola and by CLEMENCEAU. On 13 January 1898 Zola published his famous open letter, *J'Accuse*, in Clemenceau's newspaper, *L'Aurore*. The letter denounced the General Staff for allowing anti-Semitic prejudice to influence the original accusations against Dreyfus. Zola also named the guilty spy as Major Esterhazy, and called for Dreyfus' pardon. The deep feeling aroused by *l'Affaire* rallied socialists, liberals, radicals and Protestants in defence of Dreyfus; while most army officers, many Church leaders, conservatives and royalists refused to admit that Dreyfus was innocent, some even maintaining that it was disloyal of the Dreyfusards to conduct so public a campaign on behalf of a single individual since it discredited the army and the General Staff. Dreyfus was brought home from Devil's Island, re-tried at Rennes in September 1899, and found 'guilty with extenuating circumstances' by a five-to-two vote of the court martial. President Loubet pardoned Dreyfus a week later. In November 1903 Dreyfus petitioned the High Court for the case to be revised. On 12 July 1906 the Court at last declared the innocence of Dreyfus and the guilt of Esterhazy (who, after being tried and acquitted, had fled the country). Dreyfus was formally reinstated in the army by special legislation three days later and was awarded the Légion d'honneur on 22 July 1906. The depth of feeling over the Dreyfus Case was shown on 4 June 1908, when Dreyfus was slightly wounded by a nationalistic journalist who fired two shots at him as he left the ceremonies marking the interment of Zola's ashes in the Pantheon. Dreyfus served in the First World War, seeing action on the Marne, the Chemin des Dames and at Verdun, retiring from the army as a Lieutenant-Colonel soon after the Armistice. He died in Paris on 12 July 1935. The tension aroused by his name continued throughout the Vichy regime at the trials and accusations of former anti-Dreyfusards like the writer Charles Maurras (1868–1952) in 1945. Madame Dreyfus survived German occupation, dying in liberated Paris in December 1945. Their only son was killed in an air crash a year later; a granddaughter perished in Auschwitz. R. Kedward: *The Dreyfus Affair* (1964); G. Chapman: *The Dreyfus Case* (1955); D. Johnson: *France and the Dreyfus Affair* (1966); D. W. Brogan: *The Development of Modern France* (1940).

Duarte, José Napoleon (1925–90), President of El Salvador: born in San Salvador, became a lawyer and, after the murder of Archbishop ROMERO in 1980, emerged as leader of the Christian Democrats (PDC) who, in May 1984, won the first election under El Salvador's new democratic constitution. He was at first strongly backed by the USA, but his willingness to meet left-wing insurgents for talks to end the chronic civil war in this smallest of central American republics aroused doubts in Washington during 1985, while reports that his troops had committed atrocities swung world opinion against his government. Shortage of foreign funds prevented Duarte from fulfilling the social reform programme which the PDC had promised the electorate; and failing health made him leave decisions increasingly to a fifteen-man military junta. Terminal liver cancer forced Duarte to resign office in 1988, though he survived for a further two years. T. S. Montgomery: *Revolution in El Salvador; Origins and Evolution* (2nd edn Boulder, Colo., 1992).

Dubcek, Alexander (1921–92), Czechoslovak communist leader in 1968–9: born in Uhrovek, Slovakia, but spent his childhood in the Soviet Union, not returning to his homeland until 1938. He became a member of the illegal Slovak Communist Party in 1939, fighting with the resistance movement in 1944–5. From 1949 to 1955 he was a party official, subsequently spending three years in Moscow where he was recognized as a sound Khruschevite. In 1958 he began a ten-year term as Chief Secretary of the Slovak Communist Party in Bratislava, showing wider tolerance of liberal thought and writing than the authorities in Prague. Discontent with the economic policy and repressive political approach of Antonin NOVOTNY (who was both President and First Secretary of the Czechoslovak Communist Party) led to unrest in Prague in the closing weeks of 1967. Dubcek did not personally take part in the verbal attacks on Novotny, but when the central committee of the party met early in January 1968, he accepted nomination as First Secretary in place of Novotny. Dubcek wanted to emphasize the federal character of Czechoslovakia and ease the totalitarian structure of the party within the republic. His reforms alarmed the Soviet leaders BREZHNEV and KOSYGIN, and were eyed with suspicion by his Warsaw Pact neighbours and allies, Hungary, Poland and East Germany. At the end of July 1968 Dubcek met the Soviet leaders at the Slovak frontier town of Cierna-nad-Tisou for four days of talks in which he sought to prove that his reforms would not change the political character of the Czechoslovak republic. A few days later he gave similar assurances to his Warsaw Pact partners at a meeting in Bratislava. But Russian, Polish, Hungarian, East German and Bulgarian military units occupied Prague and other strategic cities on 20–21 August 1968, ensuring that for some weeks there was one foreign occupying soldier in Czechoslovakia for every thirteen members of the population. Dubcek was arrested, taken to Moscow, but released and allowed to remain First Secretary, although under orthodox Communist surveillance. Public order acts, a Press law and other restraints marked the abandonment of Czechoslovakia's promised reforms. Dubcek was edged out of office in April 1969, although permitted for some months to preside over the Federal Assembly as Speaker, and serving briefly as ambassador in Ankara. In 1970, however, he was formally expelled from the party and for several years worked for the Slovak forestry commission in Bratislava.

In November 1989 he returned to Prague and supported HAVEL and the Civic Forum reformers. A few months later he was again elected Speaker of the Federal Assembly. He was seriously injured in a car crash outside Prague in July 1992 and died four months later. A. Dubcek: *Hope Dies Hard* (1993); Z. A. B. Zeman: *Prague Spring* (1969); N. Stone and E. Strouhal (eds): *Czechoslovakia, Crossroads and Crises, 1918–88* (1989).

Dulles, John Foster (1888–1959), US Secretary of State from 1953 to 1959: born in Washington, DC, educated at Princeton. He practised law for the distinguished Wall Street firm of Sullivan & Cromwell, and at the age of 30 was included by President WILSON in the American delegation for the Paris Peace Conference of 1919, and spoke impressively on reparations. He served on a number of unofficial diplomatic missions both between the wars and after Pearl Harbor, making a notable visit to London in 1942 to discuss post-war security. He helped draft the UN Charter in 1945 and was an American delegate to the United Nations in 1946, 1947 and 1950. He was accorded ambassadorial rank by President TRUMAN in order to negotiate the Peace Treaty of San Francisco with Japan (September 1951). His long experience of foreign affairs and his reputation as a non-isolationist Republican made him a natural choice as Secretary of State in January 1953. He argued that Soviet aggression should not merely be 'contained' but checked in anticipation by the threat of 'massive retaliation'. 'If you are scared to go to the brink [of war] you are lost', he declared in January 1956. This 'brinkmanship', as his policy was called, led to the strengthening of NATO and of other international defence bodies. But Dulles had always been suspicious of British policy and found himself frequently in conflict with EDEN both as Foreign Secretary and Prime Minister. Dulles's insistence on seeking international collaboration after the nationalization of the Suez Canal by NASSER in 1956 exasperated the British and French. Eden, too, deeply resented Dulles' hostile reaction to the Anglo-French landings at Port Said in October 1956. It was felt, in London, that Dulles did not understand Middle Eastern problems; for the so-called 'Eisenhower Doctrine', which he formulated in January 1957, stimulated Arab nationalism by conjuring up a bogy of 'international communism' more readily perceivable in parts of the world where the United States was already accepted as an armed upholder of the balance of power. Dulles suffered from cancer for more than a year before his death, but his intensive sense of Christian vocation kept him working unceasingly until it was physically impossible for him to remain in office. He resigned on 18 April 1959, dying five weeks later (24 May). F. W. Marks: *Power and Peace; the Diplomacy of John Foster Dulles* (Westport, Conn., 1993); L. L. Gerson: *John Foster Dulles* (New York, 1968); R. Goold-Adams: *The Time of Power; a Reappraisal of John Foster Dulles* (1962); H. Finer: *Dulles over Suez* (1964).

Duvalier, François (1907–71), autocratic President of Haiti from 1957 to 1971: born in Port-au-Prince, trained as a doctor of medicine and ran Haiti's health service 1946–50. After an army-supervised election in September 1957 he became Haiti's President, beginning fourteen years of military dictatorship. 'Papa Doc', as he was called, perfected a barbaric regime dependent on a civilian militia – the Tonton Macoutes – which encouraged voodoo magic. Constitutional changes in 1964 made him President for life, with a right to nominate a successor. When he died on 21 April 1971 he was duly succeeded by his son, Jean Claude Duvalier (1951–), who continued the style of government. In

February 1986 the rise of a Christian democratic opposition movement led by Fr ARISTIDE so alarmed Haiti's senior generals that they forced 'Baby Doc' into exile in France, where he eventually settled at Mougins. J. Ferguson: *Papa Doc, Baby Doc; Haiti and the Duvaliers* (Oxford, 1987).

E

Eden, (Robert) Anthony (1897–1977), British Foreign Secretary for twelve years and Prime Minister for twenty-one months: born at Bishop Auckland, Durham, and educated at Eton and Christ Church, Oxford, where he specialized in oriental studies and was President of the University Asiatic Society. He served with the King's Royal Rifle Corps on the Western Front from 1915 to 1918, winning the Military Cross. In 1923 he was elected Conservative MP for Warwick and Leamington, his defeated Labour rival being his sister's mother-in-law, the Countess of Warwick, once an intimate friend of EDWARD VII. Eden represented the constituency continuously for thirty-four years. He had originally planned to enter the diplomatic service, and foreign affairs remained his absorbing interest. Except for the two years of Labour government (1929–31) he worked with the senior officials in the Foreign Office from July 1926 to February 1938, serving for three years as the Foreign Secretary's parliamentary private secretary, and for another three as Under-Secretary. In June 1935 he entered the BALDWIN Cabinet as Minister for League of Nations Affairs and became Foreign Secretary six months later. Differences with Neville CHAMBERLAIN over the appeasement of MUSSOLINI's Italy led Eden to resign on 20 February 1938, both the German and Italian dictators boasting that they had caused his fall. He returned to office as Dominions Secretary on the outbreak of war and was War Minister under Winston CHURCHILL from May to December 1940, making on 14 May the famous radio appeal for 'local defence volunteers' against paratroop landings, the force's name being changed to 'Home Guard' six weeks later. Eden re-entered the Cabinet when he succeeded Lord HALIFAX as Foreign Secretary in December 1940 but was soon recognized as Churchill's 'heir apparent'. He did not always agree with Churchill's attitude to world affairs, being less enthusiastic about the 'special relationship' linking Britain and the United States, and he overrated the value of the smaller European powers in any future world order. Eden headed the British delegation to the San Francisco Conference of 1945, using his long experience of the League of Nations to advantage in creating the fabric of the United Nations Organization. He was Foreign Secretary again from 1951 to 1955, but his health began to suffer, partly from his extraordinarily long hours of work and partly because of a conflict between his sense of loyalty to Churchill and his desire for the succession. When he became Prime Minister, on 6 April 1955, he continued to take the greatest interest in world affairs, sometimes making false analogies with events twenty years previously and tending to see in NASSER a new Mussolini. Eden's support for Anglo-French military intervention when Nasser nationalized the Suez Canal – although disguised as a 'police action' to keep peace in the Middle East – alienated many other governments, including the American, and was roundly condemned in the United Nations. His popularity in Britain, high ever since the early 1930s, slumped and there were 'Eden must go' demonstrations in London (4 November 1956). He had already undergone three operations and, under the strain of the Suez Crisis, his health collapsed entirely in the closing weeks of the year. He resigned on 9 January 1957, MACMILLAN succeeding him in the premiership. Eden, whose statesmanship had been recognized by conferment of the Garter in 1954, was raised to the peerage as Earl of Avon in 1961; but in the last twenty years of his life he took no part in public affairs. Avon, Lord: *Memoirs; Full Circle* (1960), *Facing the Dictators* (1962), *The Reckoning* (1965); R. Rhodes James: *Anthony Eden* (1986); V. Rothwell: *Anthony Eden, a Political Biography* (1992); D. Carlton: *Anthony Eden; a Biography* (1981).

Edward VII (1841–1910), King of Great Britain and Ireland, etc., and Emperor of India from 1901 to 1910: born in Buckingham Palace, the second child and first son of Queen VICTORIA and Prince Albert. He was created Prince of Wales twenty-eight days after his birth and educated strictly and intensively under his father's direction, spending a few largely profitless terms at Christ Church, Oxford, and Trinity College, Cambridge, as well as receiving ten weeks' military training at Dublin, during which he rose rapidly from Second Lieutenant to Colonel. Youthful indiscretions caused his widowed mother to distrust him from 1861 onwards and he was not allowed to see Cabinet papers until he was over 50. Marriage to Alexandra of Denmark (1844–1925) and his sister's marriage to the future German Emperor, FREDERICK III, gave him an interest in European affairs, accentuated by his own predilection for continental spas and the gaiety of Paris. As King he used his natural affability to encourage Anglo-French understanding, notably on a state visit to Paris in 1903; but he had less political power than continental statesmen and writers believed, and he never sought the 'encirclement' of Germany. Frequently he found his nephew, Kaiser WILLIAM II, bumptious and exasperating, but he recognized the Kaiser's desire for better Anglo-German relations on at least three occasions. Edward VII enjoyed a popularity unknown to any English king since the years immediately following Charles II's restoration in 1660. S. Lee: *King Edward VII* (2 vols) (1925, 1927); P. Magnus: *King Edward the Seventh* (1964); C. Hibbert: *King Edward VII* (1976); G. Battiscombe: *Queen Alexandra* (1969).

Edward VIII (1894–1972), uncrowned King-Emperor for 326 days in 1936: born at White Lodge, Richmond, the first child of the later King GEORGE V and Queen Mary. He was educated privately until the age of 12 when he entered the Royal Naval College at Osborne. In June 1910 he was created Prince of Wales and, at Caernarfon on 13 July 1911, he became the first Prince solemnly invested since 1616. Two years' study at Magdalen College, Oxford, were immediately followed by four years' active service in the army, close to the front line in France, Flanders, Egypt and northern Italy. From August 1919 to October 1925 the Prince of Wales undertook four official overseas tours, travelling mostly in the battle-cruiser *Renown*. He visited, in all, forty-five countries inside and outside the empire and subsequently undertook three semi-official visits to East Africa and South America. No previous member of a royal family had become known to so many people and for fifteen years he basked in the popularity of a youthful-looking bachelor prince. From 1933 the Prince was frequently in the company of Mrs Wallis Simpson, a Baltimore-born divorcée married to a former Grenadier Guards officer. Voluntary censorship kept this affair out of the British newspapers. At the same time Edward disturbed the Foreign Office by ill-considered public remarks which seemed to show sympathy with Nazi Germany and Fascist Italy. Soon after his accession (20 January 1936) he resolved to marry Mrs Simpson when she was divorced from her second husband. Concern over the King's intention first seriously troubled the Prime Minister, BALDWIN, early in October 1936. Marriage to a divorcée seemed to him inconsistent with the King's status as 'Supreme Governor' of the Church of England; and he found the dominion Prime Ministers no less strongly opposed to having Mrs Simpson as Queen than he was himself. When the affair was made public in England on 3 December 1936, most people agreed with Baldwin. Faced with a choice between giving up Mrs Simpson or the throne, Edward VIII abdicated (11 December 1936). He was succeeded by King GEORGE VI who immediately created Edward Duke of Windsor. Seven months later he married Mrs Simpson. In 1940 he became an unwitting agent of Nazi intrigue after escaping from France to Portugal. He served as Governor of the Bahamas from 1940 to 1945, spending his last years mainly in France. He died suddenly in Paris on 28 May 1972 and was buried at Frogmore, Windsor. Duke of Windsor: *A King's Story* (1951); Duchess of Windsor: *The Heart Has Its Reasons* (1956); P. Ziegler: *King Edward VIII* (1990); F. Donaldson: *Edward VIII* (1974); M. Bloch: *Wallis and Edward; Intimate Correspondence 1931–37* (1987), *The Duke of Windsor's War* (1982).

Eichmann, (Karl) Adolf (1906–62), German Austrian Nazi: born at Solingen, Bavaria, but – like HITLER before him – received his main education at Linz, in Upper Austria. Eichmann was a travelling salesman of vacuum cleaners from 1928 until 1932, when he joined the Nazi Party, soon becoming a guard at Dachau concentration camp (1933–4). He spent some months in Palestine on an assignment for the Jewish Activities Department of the German Secret Service. After the *Anschluss* (German–Austrian union) in 1938 he was sent to Vienna to control Jewish emigration: a year later he discharged similar responsibilities in Prague. By 1941 he was an SS Colonel, a departmental head in the Gestapo, supervising Jewish affairs. For three years from January 1942, Eichmann systematically organized the extinction of unwanted Jewish internees. In the summer of 1944 he controlled the deportation of Hungary's large Jewish population, organizing a special detachment of slave labourers from among them, while also attempting to strike cynical commercial bargains – 'goods for blood' – with spokesmen for Hungarian Zionists by which favoured Jews could escape to Palestine. Although interned by US troops in 1945 Eichmann escaped from custody and fled to South America, where by 1950 he was living, in some obscurity, outside Buenos Aires. But in May 1960 Eichmann was unmasked by agents of Mossad, the Israeli Secret Service, who brought him secretly from Argentina to Jerusalem. There he was accused by the Israeli government of crimes against the Jewish people and in April 1961 put on trial on fifteen specific charges of causing the death and persecution of millions of Jews. He was hanged on 31 May 1962. G. Hausner: *Justice in Jerusalem; the Eichmann Trial* (New York, 1966); P. Z. Malkin and H. Stein: *Eichmann in My Hands* (1990).

Eisenhower, Dwight David (1890–1969), American General and President from 1953 to 1961: born at Denison in Texas, spent his boyhood at Abilene, Kansas, passing out of West Point in 1915. Between the wars he was known as a competent staff officer, assistant military adviser to MACARTHUR in the Philippines from 1935 to 1940. In February 1942 he was chief of the war-plans division in Washington, and was then appointed commander of the Allied forces which landed in French North Africa in November 1942, his baptism of fire. Three months later he became

Supreme Allied Commander in North Africa, having under his orders such veterans as Harold ALEXANDER, MONTGOMERY and his compatriot, PATTON. Eisenhower's tact charmed into co-operation every commander whom he encountered except DE GAULLE. His successes in the Mediterranean led to command of the invasion of western Europe in 1944. He personally decided the timing of D-Day. His broad front advance into Germany was criticized by Montgomery, who favoured a narrow concentrated thrust eastwards, but Eisenhower was able to reach the Elbe and establish contact with his Russian allies by mid-April 1945. His greatest achievement was the maintenance of inter-Allied unity, avoiding nationalistic friction. From December 1945 to the summer of 1948 he was Chief of Staff in Washington. After three years as President of Columbia University he returned to Europe in 1951 as Supreme Commander, NATO. On 28 April 1952 he resigned from the army in order to allow his name to go forward as Republican nominee for the presidency. His personal popularity ensured his election, with more popular votes than had ever been cast for any previous presidential candidate, and he took office on 20 January 1953, the first professional-soldier President for seventy-six years. He showed firmness in implementing civil rights, in curbing Senator MCCARTHY, and in securing passage through Congress of social laws. But he tended to rely in foreign affairs on the experienced DULLES, in domestic matters on the former New Hampshire Governor Sherman Adams (his chief of White House staff until 1958), and in many matters on his Vice-President, Richard NIXON. Eisenhower was at his best in inter-Allied conferences, notably with Winston CHURCHILL and with MACMILLAN, and at the Geneva summit meeting in July 1955. He was re-elected, with an even larger popular vote (35,590,000), in November 1956. In 1960 he encouraged the nomination of Nixon, whose failure to exploit presidential backing irritated him. After the victory of John KENNEDY the ex-President retired to his farm in Pennsylvania, where he died in March 1969. D. D. Eisenhower: *Crusade in Europe* (1948), *Mandate for Change* (New York, 1963); S. E. Ambrose: *The War Years of General Dwight D. Eisenhower* (1971), *Eisenhower, 1890–1952* (1984), *Eisenhower, Soldier-President* (1990).

Elizabeth II (1926–), Queen of the United Kingdom of Great Britain and Northern Ireland, and sixteen other realms, Head of the Commonwealth: born in Bruton Street, London, the elder daughter of the Duke of York (later GEORGE VI). Princess Elizabeth served in the Auxiliary Transport Service in 1945. On 20 November 1947 she married Lieutenant Philip Mountbatten (born in 1921 a Prince of Greece, created Duke of Edinburgh on his marriage). She succeeded to the throne on 6 February 1952. The two outstanding characteristics of her concept of monarchy have been the identification of the sovereign with a multinational and multiracial Commonwealth, a process aided by frequent overseas tours mostly by air, and the reconciliation of a dignified regal tradition with the modern craving for recognizably ordinary behaviour in eminently extraordinary families. From 1963 onwards royal 'walkabouts' during official visits and the increasing use of television helped to lower social barriers separating Crown and people. But, as in Queen VICTORIA's reign, criticism of the monarchy as an expensive anachronism recurred some thirty-five years after Elizabeth II's accession. It was fed by intrusive journalism, probing the private lives of the younger members of the royal family, and by envy of apparent tax privileges. Although the sovereign is not legally bound to pay income tax, in November 1992 the Queen offered to pay tax on a voluntary basis from the following year, an arrangement settled by a parliamentary 'Memorandum of Understanding', presented in the Commons on 11 February 1993. Outside the United Kingdom, republican sentiment increased in Australia and Canada, particular attention being given to the limitations of an 'absentee' Head of State. Nevertheless the Queen's sense of inherited duty never wavered. She regularly attended biannual meetings of Commonwealth heads of government, although never as an active participant in political discussions. E. Longford: *Elizabeth R.* (1983); P Ziegler: *Crown and People* (1978).

Engels, Friedrich (1820–95), pioneer communist: born at Barmen in Germany, the son of a textile manufacturer. As a young man he was a radical poet rather than a socialist. He became Manchester agent of his father's business in 1842 and three years later compiled, largely from official commissions of inquiry, his remarkable *Condition of the Working Classes in England in 1844* (a German work, only translated into English three years before the author's death). Engels first met Karl MARX in Paris in the autumn of 1844, their collaboration lasting for thirty-nine years. Engels wrote the first draft of the *Communist Manifesto* in 1847 but it was virtually rewritten by Marx before publication in London in the last week of February 1848. He personally participated in the Badenese revolutionary movement later that year, but thereafter he settled in Manchester, enjoying a considerable private income in his later years. Most of his money was used to support Marx and his family. Engels, too, provided Marx with the precise facts on which he could build his theories of capitalism in decline. His later years were spent mainly in London, editing Marx's final volume of *Das Kapital*, a task completed a year before his own death. G. Mayer: *Friedrich Engels* (abridged translation, ed. R. H. S. Crossman, 1935); G. Carlton: *Friedrich Engels, the Shadow Prophet* (1965); G. Lichtheim: *Marxism* (rev. edn 1964).

Enver (1881–1922), Turkish soldier and dominant politician from 1910 to 1915: born at Apana, commissioned in the Ottoman Army in 1900, receiving specialized military training in Germany. While stationed in Salonika with the Third Army he joined the Ottoman Freedom Society, a revolutionary body opposed to the rule of Sultan ABDUL HAMID II. In July 1908, fearing arrest, Enver disobeyed orders to return to Constantinople for 'promotion', leading a mutiny in the hills behind Salonika. Within days the mutiny spread throughout the garrison in the city and prompted similar acts of defiance by 'Young Turk' officers in Adrianople and Damascus, threatening revolution at the heart of the empire as well. The Sultan capitulated to the 'Young Turk' demands. Enver, spokesman for the extreme nationalist and anti-liberal officers' wing of the 'Young Turk' movement, was sent to Berlin as military attaché in 1909–10. He returned to Constantinople an ardent champion of Germano-Turkish military collaboration. Active service against Italy in Libya in 1911 and in the Balkan Wars of 1912–13 emphasized to Enver Turkey's need of modern equipment. As Minister of War in 1914, he encouraged the establishment in Turkey of a powerful German military mission and headed a pro-war party. The sudden naval attack on Odessa, on 28 October 1914, appears to have been concerted between the German military and naval missions in Constantinople and Enver himself. The attack led to Russian, British and French declarations of war against Turkey, with Enver personally assuming field command for an advance into the Caucasus in the hopes of establishing a 'Pan-Turania'. Obsession with this objective, especially after the Russian Revolution of 1917, blinded Enver to Turkey's weakness on other fronts. After the Turks sued for peace in 1918, Enver continued to lead armed groups against the Bolsheviks in Turkestan. He was killed in a cavalry skirmish with Soviet forces early in 1922. F. Ahmad: *The Young Turks* (Oxford, 1969); A. Palmer: *The Decline and Fall of the Ottoman Empire* (1992).

Erhard, Ludwig (1897–1977), Chancellor of the Federal German Republic from 1963 to 1966: born at Fürth, becoming a professional economist in the 1920s and serving as Professor of Economics at Munich University from 1945 to 1949. As Dr Erhard had specialized in the study of boom and slump under the Weimar Republic, his expert advice was of considerable assistance to the Bavarians in their attempts to reconstruct the industrial system destroyed by war and the collapse of a unified Germany. In 1948 he was appointed Chairman of the Economic Executive Council which functioned throughout the British and American zones of occupation. A year later he was elected to the newly formed Bundestag as a Christian Democrat, and was made Minister of Economic Affairs by ADENAUER in his first government (September 1949). This post Dr Erhard held continuously for fourteen years, directing the 'economic miracle' which gave West Germany the soundest prosperity the region has ever known. From 1957 to 1963 he was Deputy Chancellor to Adenauer, a leader who, at times, exasperated Erhard by failing to take all his colleagues into his confidence. Erhard at last became Chancellor on Adenauer's retirement in October 1963. In his chancellorship he was hampered by his predecessor's continued influence within the party and by his own inability to maintain equable relations with President DE GAULLE. Friction within the Common Market convinced Erhard of an imminent economic recession and he therefore proposed to control the economy by tax increases in the late summer of 1966. Despite his prestige as an economist, he failed to win support from his ministers in this policy and resigned, retiring into private life (November 1966). D. L. Bark and D. R. Gress: *History of West Germany, 1945–1988* (2 vols) (Oxford, 1989); R. Hiscocks: *Germany Revived* (1966).

Evatt, Herbert Vere (1894–1965), Australian Minister of External Affairs from 1941 to 1949: born in East Maitland, South Australia, but spent all his adult life in New South Wales. He gained a doctorate from Sydney University and practised as a lawyer, specializing in trade union matters. Throughout the 1930s he was a High Court Justice but he entered the Canberra Parliament in 1940 and was appointed Minister of External Affairs by the Labour government of John Curtin (1885–1945) in October 1941. Dr Evatt acquired an international reputation for his statesmanship, partly through his representation of Australia at successive conferences in Britain in 1942–3, but even more because of his leadership of the smaller powers at the San Francisco Conference in 1945. He thus had considerable influence on the form of the United Nations, successfully proposing twenty-six detailed amendments to the UN Charter so as to counteract the dominance of the permanent members of the Security Council. His eloquent protests at the veto powers of permanent members proved unavailing. As Minister of External Affairs under CHIFLEY, Evatt strengthened Australian ties with the United States, to some extent at the expense of the old imperial connection with the 'home country'. The victory of MENZIES in December 1949 forced Evatt into opposition. He was leader of the Australian Labour Party from 1951 to 1960 but was hampered by an active pressure group of Roman Catholic party members from Victoria who thought him 'soft' on the menace of communism largely because he appeared as defending counsel for the leaders of the Communist Party when the Menzies government sought to proscribe Marxist bodies in 1950–1. After nine years in opposition Evatt retired from politics in 1960, returning to the bench as Chief Justice of New South Wales for two years. P. Crockett: *Evatt, a Life* (1993); K. Buckley, B. Dale and W. Reynolds: *Doc Evatt* (Melbourne, 1994).

Eyre, Edward John (1815–1901), British explorer and colonial governor: born in Yorkshire of Scottish descent. He settled in Australia in 1832 and explored the area around Lake Torrens in 1840, discovering another lake to which he gave his own name. With an aboriginal companion he became, a year later, the first white man to cross the Nullarbor Plain from southern to western Australia. After holding administrative posts in New Zealand and St Vincent he was appointed Governor of Jamaica in 1862. A serious revolt by squatters in the Morant Bay area was put down by Eyre with harshness, under martial law. Reports reached London that he had executed 450 Jamaicans, flogged over 600, and had 1,000 homes destroyed. A commission of inquiry blamed Eyre for hanging an influential local leader against whom there was no evidence of serious crime. Eyre, recalled to London, was unsuccessfully prosecuted by a committee of eminent Liberals, headed by MILL. Other public figures, including the historian Carlyle and the Christian socialist novelist, Charles Kingsley, rallied to Eyre's defence. The 'case of Governor Eyre' was a *cause célèbre* in London between 1867 and 1872, when the GLADSTONE government recompensed Eyre for the costs of his defence. E. J. Eyre: *Autobiographical Narrative of Residence and Exploration in Australia*, ed. J. Waterhouse (1984); S. Olivier: *The Myth of Governor Eyre* (1933); W. L. Mathieson: *The Sugar Colonies and Governor Eyre* (1936).

F

Fahd, ibn Abd-al-Aziz (1921–), fifth King of Saudi Arabia: born at Ta'if, served his full brother, FAISAL, as Minister of the Interior from 1962 to 1967 and was first deputy Chief Minister during the seven-year reign of his half-brother King Khalid (1913–82), whose deteriorating heart condition from 1979 onwards lifted Fahd's responsibility and world standing, until in August 1981 the Prince took the initiative in convening a summit conference at Fez to seek solutions of all Middle Eastern problems. His hope of serving as a mediator was frustrated by deep suspicion of Saudi motives by Syria. When Fahd finally acceded in June 1982 he had the reputation of being a relatively liberal westernizer, in the Faisal tradition. He remained his Chief Minister, conscious of the need to placate religious traditionalists, especially after fundamentalist riots within Mecca in August 1987 left 400 pilgrims dead. In November 1990 he encouraged the concentration on Saudi soil of a twenty-nine nation army to eject the Iraqis from Kuwait over the following three months. Fahd sought to counter the excessive influence of the ruling Al-Saud family by establishing in September 1993 a consultative council of sixty members, for which members of the family were ineligible. Further devolution prompted the setting up in 1993 of thirteen regional advisory councils. He suffered a stroke in November 1995 and on 2 January 1996 ordered his brother, Crown Prince Abdullah, to take over all affairs of state. K. Al-Kilani: *Progress of a Nation; a biography of King Fahd* (1985); N. Safran: *Saudi Arabia* (Cambridge, Mass., 1985).

Faisal, ibn Abd-al-Aziz (1905–75), third King of Saudi Arabia: born in Riyadh, fought alongside his father, IBN SAUD, to establish the kingdom and, in 1932, became Viceroy of the more sophisticated region, the Hejaz. He was Foreign Minister 1940–53, helping to shape policies during the first oil boom 1947–1952, years in which sudden wealth posed unexpected problems for the basically pastoral kingdom and its rulers, titular custodians of the Holy Cities of Mecca and Medina. When the conservatively inclined Saud I succeeded Ibn Saud in 1953, his half-brother Faisal argued in favour of westernization: he was Chief Minister from 1958 until 1960, when reforms which advanced the education of women aroused such hostility from traditionalists that he fell from favour. Recognition of the need to put oil revenue to good use induced Saud to reinstate Faisal in 1962, with Prince FAHD supervising internal affairs. After prolonged conflict within the palace King Saud abdicated in Faisal's favour in November 1964. Formal decrees outlawing slavery were followed by codes of work practice and a basic scheme for social insurance; in 1971 an embryonic civil service was set up. The leap in oil prices and revenue in 1973 made Faisal authorize even more ambitious public works. His reforms carefully avoided offending religious sentiment: traditional dress was maintained, as also was the basic style of living. On 25 March 1975 Faisal was assassinated in the palace at Riyadah by a mentally unstable nephew, Prince Museid, who was publicly beheaded three months later. Faisal was succeeded by his half-brother,

King Khalid (1913–82). W. Beling (ed.): *King Faisal and the Modernization of Saudi Arabia* (1980); N. Anderson (ed.): *The Kingdom of Saudi Arabia* (rev. edn 1982); D. Holden and R. Johns: *The House of Saud* (1981); R. Lacey: *The Kingdom* (1981).

Faisal I (1885–1933) (often transliterated as 'Feisal', occasionally as 'Faysal'), first King of Iraq: born at Ta'if, Arabia, son of Emir HUSSEIN and brother of ABDULLAH, of Jordan. Faisal spent much of his childhood in Constantinople, his family's loyalty being suspect to the Ottoman authorities. Faisal sat in the Ottoman parliament from 1908 to 1912. In the First World War he was, militarily, the most active Emir in the Arab Revolt, collaborating with ALLENBY in the final offensive against the Turks and entering Damascus with T. E. LAWRENCE on 1 October 1918. He attended the Paris Peace Conference in 1919, establishing himself as King of Syria and Palestine in March 1920, but was ousted by the French as the mandatory power in Syria four months later. After negotiations with the British (who had received a mandate for Mesopotamia) he was recommended as King of Iraq (the new name for Mesopotamia) and, after a referendum among his subjects, was enthroned at Baghdad on 23 August 1921. He was faced by several revolts, notably by Kurdish irregulars, and was forced to seek the assistance of Royal Air Force bombing squadrons stationed at airfields along the Euphrates. Policy was shaped by Faisal's former companion in arms, General Nuri-es-Said (1888–1958), who negotiated a military alliance with the British in 1930 and thereby secured the ending of the mandate and the formal independence of the Iraqi kingdom a year before Faisal's death. Faisal was succeeded by his son, King Ghazi, who was killed in a car crash on 4 April 1939. Faisal II, grandson of the first King of Iraq, thereupon succeeded to the throne at the age of 4 and was subject to a Regency until 1953. On 14 July 1958 Faisal II and other members of the Iraqi royal family were butchered in a military *coup* headed by Brigadier Kassem. The veteran Nuri was killed at the same time and a 'pure Iraqi' republic set up. S. H. Longrigg: *Iraq, 1900 to 1950* (1953); M. Khadduri: *Independent Iraq* (1960); J. Wilson: *Lawrence of Arabia* (1989); Lord Birdwood: *Nuri al-Said* (1959).

Farouk (1920–65), King of Egypt from 1936 to 1952: born in Cairo, the son of the first King of modern Egypt, Fuad (1868–1936, King from 1923). Farouk, educated in England, was subject to a Regency Council for two years after his succession. In 1938 he began to rule in his own right and was, at first, popular with his subjects who welcomed his promises of land reform and economic advancement. Soon, however, the corruption of the King's officials and the greed of Farouk himself destroyed royalist sentiment. At the same time Farouk fell foul of the British military authorities because of his unco-operative attitude when Italian troops invaded Egypt from Libya in 1940. From February 1941 to October 1944 the King's political activities were restricted by the British, an action which humiliated Farouk although stimulating some sympathetic reaction from his subjects. From 1944 to 1952 Farouk appointed governments pledged to end British occupation of the Canal Zone and (later) to destroy the new Israeli state; but the dismal performance of the Egyptian army in Palestine in 1948–9 intensified criticism of the monarchy as a superfluous institution. The notorious profligacy of Farouk again harmed his cause. A bloodless *coup d'état* by Brigadier-General Mohammed Neguib on 23 July 1952 brought to power a junta of army officers, the guiding spirit of whom was Colonel NASSER. Farouk abdicated three days later, taking refuge in Italy. Although his infant son was formally proclaimed King as Fuad II, Neguib soon assumed dictatorial powers and Egypt became a republic on 18 June 1953. Farouk lived in the south of France, a jumbo-size Riviera playboy and a citizen of Monaco for the last six years of his life. P. J. Vatikolis: *History of Modern Egypt* (rev. edn 1991); J. and S. Lacoutoure: *Egypt in Transition* (1958).

Farragut, David Glasgow (1801–70), first American Admiral: born, of part-Spanish descent, near Knoxville in Tennessee. In 1810 he served as a midshipman aboard the frigate *Essex*, which was commanded by his guardian, the celebrated naval Captain, David Porter (1780–1843). Farragut saw action against the British in the war of 1812–15. Eventually, at the age of 54, he reached the rank of Captain. In April 1862 he commanded a squadron of twenty-three vessels which forced their way up the Mississippi, running the gauntlet of the Confederates at Fort Jackson and Fort St Philip. Farragut's enterprise captured the South's principal seaport, New Orleans, a hundred miles upriver. He gained control of the Mississippi as far as Baton Rouge and was able to give valuable flanking support to GRANT at Vicksburg, whence he despatched vessels under his former guardian's son, David D. Porter (1813–91). After the capture of New Orleans, Farragut was created Rear-Admiral, a new rank in the US Navy. In August 1864 he destroyed Confederate gunboats in Mobile Bay, a naval action which checked southern blockade running and which led to the isolation and eventual fall of the town of Mobile, Alabama. Farragut's reported contempt for defensive minefields on this occasion increased public admiration for him as a bluff, heroic seaman; and Congress duly promoted him Vice-Admiral. In 1866 he became the first full Admiral in America's naval history. A. T. Mahan: *Admiral Farragut* (1892); C. L. Lewis: *David Glasgow Farragut* (2 vols) (New York, 1941, 1943).

Fawcett, Millicent (*née* **Millicent Garrett**) (1847–1929), pioneer British feminist: born at Aldeburgh, Suffolk, the younger sister of Elizabeth Garrett ANDERSON. In 1867 Millicent Garrett, who was already campaigning for the extension of the franchise to women, married the blind Cambridge economist and Liberal MP Henry Fawcett (1833–84) and thereafter, despite her belief in political and professional equality for women, she preferred to be known as 'Mrs Henry Fawcett' rather than by her own names at birth. In 1871 she was a founder of Newnham College, Cambridge (the first women's college established in either of the great English university cities – Girton College was founded at Hitchin, rather than at Cambridge, in 1869). Mrs Fawcett's principal task was the organization of pressure groups to campaign for votes for women. She was President of the National Union of Women's Suffrage Societies from 1897 to 1918, admiring the courage of the suffragettes led by Mrs PANKHURST but deploring their militancy. She was created a Dame of the British Empire in 1925. D. Rubinstein: *A Different World for Women* (1991).

Feisal: see *Faisal*.

Ferdinand (1861–1948), ruler of Bulgaria from 1887 to 1918: born in Vienna, a Prince of Saxe-Coburg and therefore a first cousin of both Queen VICTORIA and the Prince Consort. After serving for many years in the Austrian Army he accepted the crown of the principality of Bulgaria in August 1887, becoming King – or, as he preferred the title, 'Tsar' – of Bulgaria in October 1908, when the country finally secured total independence from the Turkish Empire. Twenty years of astute political bargaining, both with local politicians and with spokesmen of the Great Powers, earned him a reputation as the 'Fox of the Balkans'. But from 1912 onwards he made a series of miscalculations. Rivalry with Serbia and Greece after the first Balkan War in 1912 induced him to authorize his troops to begin an offensive against his Balkan neighbours in June 1913 which proved disastrously ill-timed: Bulgaria failed to secure the gains she sought in Macedonia and lost territory in the Dobrudja to Romania. In October 1915 Ferdinand entered the war on the German side in the hope of recouping his losses but, after initial successes on the Salonika Front, his army collapsed in September 1918, forcing Ferdinand to seek a separate peace. Mutiny and the threat of communist revolution induced him to abdicate on 4 October 1918 in favour of his son, BORIS III. He spent thirty years of exile mainly in France – being, indeed, through his mother, a grandson of the last King of the French, Louis Philippe (reigned 1830–48). J. Macdonald: *Czar Ferdinand and his People* (New York, 1971); S. Constant: *Foxy Ferdinand* (1979).

Ferry, Jules François Camille (1832–93), French Prime Minister from 1880 to 1881 and 1883 to 1885: born at Saint-Dié in the Vosges, became a lawyer in Paris, and headed the parliamentary opposition to the Second Empire in 1869–70. Thereafter he sat as a Deputy in the Lower House of the Third Republic until 1889 and as a Senator for the last two years of his life. He was in office as Minister of Public Instruction, Foreign Minister or Prime Minister from February 1879 to April 1885, his greatest achievement being the famous law of 28 March 1882 which made French primary education compulsory, non-clericalist and free. His attacks on Church influence in education, both primary and secondary, were accompanied by an insistence that children be taught Christian ethics without the indoctrination of a specific church's faith. He vigorously supported French colonial expansion in Tunisia, Madagascar, the Gulf of Tonkin and the Congo, and at the Berlin Conference on African frontiers in 1884–5 he showed willingness to collaborate with BISMARCK. This ability to work with the traditional enemy, together with temporary rebuffs to a costly policy of colonialism, made him a target for withering attacks by CLEMENCEAU in parliament in the spring of 1885. He never held office again, dying from gunshot wounds inflicted by a mentally deranged assassin in March 1893. T. F. Power: *Jules Ferry and the Renaissance of French Imperialism* (New York, 1944); D. W. Brogan: *The Development of Modern France* (1940).

Fish, Hamilton (1808–93), US Secretary of State from 1869 to 1877: born in New York, the son of a prominent Federalist who was a close friend of Alexander Hamilton, after whom the boy was named. Hamilton Fish graduated from Columbia University in 1827, practised law, entered politics and was Governor of New York in 1849–50, serving in the Senate from 1851 to 1857 before returning to his law practice. President Grant appointed him Secretary of State a week after his inauguration in March 1869. Fish resolved the outstanding diplomatic disputes between Great Britain and the United States, settling boundary problems, difficulties over fishing rights and the claims arising from the construction and supply to the Confederacy of commerce raiders, notably the *Alabama*. He also held in check demands for war with Spain when, in 1873, the Spanish authorities executed more than fifty Americans accused of gun-running on behalf of Cuban rebels against Spanish rule. Fish's gifts as a mediator calmed disputes within Grant's Cabinet while his statesmanlike approach to international problems lifted the level of an otherwise weak, and often corrupt, administration. The revival of the Democrats in the 1876 election induced Fish to resume his private law practice in New York City, where his family retained much influence within the Republican Party until after the Second World War. A. Nevins: *Hamilton Fish: the Inner History of the Grant Administration* (New York, 1936).

Fisher, John Arbuthnot (1841–1920), British Admiral: born at Rambodde in Ceylon, the son of a coffee planter. He went to sea as a naval cadet in 1855, first seeing action in China as an 18-year-old midshipman. He possessed drive and a natural interest in technical developments. As early as 1872 he was a torpedo specialist, constantly seeking changes in the science of naval warfare. Training and tactics were revolutionized during his three years as Commander-in-Chief in the Mediterranean, 1899–1902. Fisher returned to England, eager to promote the building of the first 'all-big-gun' battleship, the *Dreadnought*, which was laid down in October 1905, almost exactly twelve months after Fisher took office as First Sea Lord (the serving officer responsible for naval policy in general and the disposition of the fleet). Fisher's reforms modernized the Royal Navy, preparing it, for the first time, for war against Germany. He retired as First Sea Lord in 1910, was brought back by Winston CHURCHILL in October 1914 but was by then too old, too egotistic and too eccentric for such responsibilities. He resigned in May 1915. At the height of his influence, in 1909, he was raised to the peerage as Baron Fisher of Kilverstone; characteristically he chose as his armorial motto, 'Fear God and Dread Nought'. A. J. Marder (ed): *Fear God and Dread Nought* (Fisher's correspondence, 3 vols) (1952–9); R. Mackay: *Fisher of Kilverstone* (Oxford, 1973); J. Morris: *Fisher's Face* (1995).

Foch, Ferdinand (1851–1929), Marshal of France, Allied Generalissimo on the Western Front in 1918: born at Tarbes in the foothills of the Pyrenees, educated at Jesuit colleges, enlisted as a private in the infantry in September 1870 but resumed his studies in March 1871 and was eventually commissioned in the artillery in October 1873. He held staff positions and taught at the École Supérieure de Guerre from 1885 to 1901, returning as Commandant of the school from 1908 to 1912, and attended Russian and British manoeuvres with the rank of General in 1910 and 1912. He commanded the French Ninth Army at the battle of the Marne in September 1914 and was commander of the French Northern Army group in Flanders and Artois from October 1914 until the end of the battle of the Somme, November 1916. At first Foch, like most French Generals of his generation, believed in vigorous offensive operations, but by July 1915 he had come to accept the need for patient, defensive warfare until trench positions had been obliterated or there had been a collapse of enemy morale. He therefore disapproved of the Somme assaults, a strategy on which his advice was disregarded by JOFFRE and HAIG. Foch became Chief of the French General Staff in May 1917, a post which brought him into close contact with the British, Belgian and Italian war leaders as well as with General PERSHING and the first American troops, who reached France at the end of June. Foch's initiative and resolution impressed the Allied leaders and when LUDENDORFF launched his 'make-or-break' spring offensive in 1918, Foch was empowered to co-ordinate Allied resistance (26 March), becoming Commander-in-Chief of the Allied armies in France on 14 April. His calm strategic vision staved off military disaster, enabling counter-offensives to be launched on 18 July and 8 August which forced Germany to sue for peace. He conducted the armistice negotiations with a German delegation in his personal railway carriage at a siding in the forest of Compiègne between 8 and 11 November 1918. At the Paris Peace Conference of 1919 Foch was chief spokesman for a military pressure group which sought territorial acquisitions for France in the Rhineland. Together with his right-hand man, General WEYGAND, he was regarded by CLEMENCEAU as a possible originator of a *coup d'état* (April 1919), but Foch remained loyal to the Republic. He had been created a Marshal of France on 6 August 1918 and in July 1919 was appointed a British Field Marshal. Most of his last years were spent in retirement on his estate at Tréfeunteuniou, near Morlaix in Brittany, but he died in Paris on 20 March 1929, and was interred close to the tomb of Napoleon I, in the chapel of Les Invalides in Paris. F. Foch: *The Memoirs of Marshal Foch* (1931); B. H. Liddell Hart: *Foch, the Man of Orleans* (1931); C. Falls: *Marshal Foch* (1939); J. Marshall-Cornwall: *Foch as Military Commander* (1972).

Foot, Michael (1913–), English socialist: born into a famous family of West Country radical liberals, completing his education at Wadham College, Oxford. In 1937 he became assistant editor of *Tribune*, a left-wing weekly with which he was closely associated for over forty years. In 1940 he was the main contributor to the most trenchant British political pamphlet of the century: *Guilty Men*, published under the pseudonym 'Cato', attacked Neville CHAMBERLAIN and his advisers during the appeasement years. Foot was elected Labour MP for Devonport in 1945, becoming a supporter of BEVAN (whose biography he was to write) and attracting a wide following as a leader of the Campaign for Nuclear Disarmament (CND). He was out of parliament from 1955 until November 1960, when he was returned for Ebbw Vale, Bevan's old constituency, for which he sat until retiring in 1990, though it was renamed Blaenau Gwent in 1983. His *Tribune* radicalism excluded Foot from cabinet office until 1974, when WILSON appointed him Secretary for Employment. He secured passage of a Trade Union and Labour Relations Act (March 1976) and from 1976 to 1979 was Leader of the Commons and Lord President of the Council. On 10 November 1980 the parliamentary party elected him Labour leader in succession to CALLAGHAN – the first victory for a left-winger since LANSBURY in 1932. Foot was an effective leader of the Opposition to Thatcherism within the Commons, but his style did not attract the voters and he resigned in October 1983 after Labour fared badly in the General Election. Neil KINNOCK succeeded him as party leader. M. Jones: *Michael Foot* (1994); S. Hoggett and D. Leigh: *Michael Foot* (1979).

Ford, Gerald Randolph (1913–), President of the United States, 1974–7: born at Omaha in Nebraska, educated at the Universities of Michigan and Yale. Ford served as a naval officer in the Second World War, mainly aboard aircraft-carriers, and practised as a lawyer before being returned to the House of Representatives as a Republican Congressman from Michigan (Fifth District) in 1948. He sat in Congress for twenty-five years, for the most part in untarnished obscurity although he emerged as House minority leader from 1965 to 1973. In October 1973 allegations concerning money matters during Vice-President Agnew's governorship of Maryland created such a sensation in Washington that the Vice-President resigned office. Gerald Ford was chosen by President NIXON as Agnew's successor and sworn in as Vice-President on 6 December 1973, at a time when Congress was already contemplating Nixon's impeachment for his role in the Watergate scandal. When Nixon resigned on 9 August 1974 it was constitutionally proper for Vice-President Ford to become America's thirty-eighth President. His term of office was dominated by the activities of his Secretary of State, KISSINGER, although he undertook a successful visit to the Soviet Union,

Japan and South Korea in November 1974, as well as visiting China eleven months later. He was nominated as presidential candidate by the Republican Convention in 1976 but made a poor showing during the campaign and lost to the Democratic candidate Jimmy CARTER, gaining only 48 per cent of the popular vote. He had thus the unique distinction of being the only American to have held the vice-presidency and the presidency without being elected to either office. G. R. Ford: *A Time To Heal* (New York, 1979); R. Reeves: *A Ford, Not a Lincoln* (1976); A. J. Reichley: *Conservatives in an Age of Change; the Nixon and Ford Administrations* (Washington, D.C., 1981); R. T. Hartmann: *Palace Politics; an Inside Account of the Ford Years* (New York, 1980).

Franchet d'Esperey, Louis Félix (1856–1942), Marshal of France: born at Mostaganem, Algeria, and graduated from St Cyr, where in his fifties he returned as an instructor. He saw active service with the cavalry in Algeria, Tunis, Morocco, Indo-China and in Peking after the Boxer Rising (1900). In 1914 he was given command of the French Fifth Army, which he led decisively to check the Germans around Montmirail at the first battle of the Marne (9 September 1914). He remained on the Western Front until the spring of 1918 when CLEMENCEAU sent him to Salonika as Commander-in-Chief of the six-nation 'Army of the Orient', pinned down in Macedonia by Bulgarian, Austro-Hungarian, German and Turkish units. Franchet d'Esperey, like ALLENBY, was a formidable cavalry commander of great energy (nicknamed 'Desperate Frankie' by his British allies). On 15 September 1918 he spurred weary troops into an offensive which broke enemy positions on the edge of the Balkan mountains and thrust rapidly northwards through Serbia to the Hungarian plain. Bulgaria sued for peace within a fortnight, thus weakening Germany's central position and hastening the general armistice, which ended the war on 11 November 1918. By then the left flank of the Army of the Orient was on the central Danube, threatening an advance on Dresden and Berlin, while the right flank occupied Constantinople. Franchet d'Esperey was made a Marshal of France on 14 July 1922 and served for another ten years in North Africa, but his right-wing political views were mistrusted by successive governments in Paris. He was seriously injured in a car accident in Algeria in 1934. He declined to give PÉTAIN, the only other surviving Marshal of France, support at Vichy in 1940 and died two years later in unoccupied France. In 1947 he was interred, with France's greatest field commanders, at the Invalides in Paris. A. Palmer: *The Gardeners of Salonika* (1964); E. Spears: *Liaison, 1914* (1930).

Francis Ferdinand (1863–1914), Austrian Archduke, heir to the Austro-Hungarian throne from 1896 to 1914: born at Graz, the son of Archduke Charles Ludwig (1833–96), who was a brother of Emperor FRANCIS JOSEPH. From the death of Crown Prince RUDOLF at Mayerling in 1889, Francis Ferdinand was regarded as heir-apparent, since it was unlikely his father would outlive the Emperor. Francis Ferdinand, a man of temperament and strong character, was not popular at court or with his uncle's subjects. He was opposed to the Hungarian political influence in the Dual Monarchy, favouring concessions to the Slav minorities. In 1900 he married, against the Emperor's wishes, a Czech Countess, Sophie Chotek; their marriage was a morganatic union, since Francis Joseph did not rate the social status of the Countess sufficeintly high for her to be regarded as a future empress. Francis Ferdinand, an efficient and well-trained army officer, was accompanied by his wife when he attended the summer manoeuvres of 1914 in Bosnia. While visiting Sarajevo on the

Serbian National Day (28 June) both Francis Ferdinand and Sophie were killed by shots fired by Gavrilo PRINCIP, a Serbian student indignant at Austria's annexation of Bosnia, a province in which most people were of Serbian nationality. This assassination at Sarajevo precipitated the outbreak of the First World War. The murdered couple's two sons, excluded from the succession as morganatic offspring, survived the first Austrian Republic and HITLER's absorption of Austria, both being sent by the Nazis to a concentration camp. L. Cassels: *The Archduke and the Assassin* (1983); G. Brook-Shepherd: *Victims at Sarajevo* (1984).

Francis Joseph (1830–1916), Emperor of Austria from 1848 to 1916 and from 1867 also King of Hungary: born in Schönbrunn Palace, succeeded his simple-minded uncle, Ferdinand, in December 1848. For many years he was dominated by his formidable mother, Archduchess Sophie (1808–73), a Bavarian Princess by birth. She taught him a strict code of duty, subordinating his personality to the supposed needs of an autocratic dynasty. It was impossible for his family to maintain such standards: his wife, Empress Elizabeth (1837–98), was forced to spend many months of each year abroad in order to escape from the rigidity of life at the Habsburg Court, and, while on these travels, was stabbed to death by an Italian anarchist at Geneva; their son, RUDOLF, was driven to suicide at Mayerling. After defeat by Prussia in the Seven Weeks War of 1866, Francis Joseph sought stability at home and abroad. He accepted the compromise (*Ausgleich*) with Hungary of 1867, which transformed his empire into the Dual Monarchy of Austria-Hungary; thereafter he ignored all suggestion of change. Similarly he authorized the conclusion of an Austro-German alliance in 1879; it served as a key to foreign policy throughout the remainder of his reign. Reluctantly he accepted the need to 'punish' the Serbs for the assassination of Francis Ferdinand in 1914; he could not foresee that the desire of a military party in Vienna for a localized war would, within two years of his death, lead to defeat and the fall of the dynasty. When he died, at Schönbrunn on 21 November 1916, he had reigned in full sovereignty for eleven days short of sixty-eight years, a longer period than any other monarch. His great-nephew, CHARLES, succeeded him. A. Palmer: *Twilight of the Habsburgs; the Life and Times of Emperor Francis Joseph* (1994); J-P. Bled: *Franz Joseph* (Oxford, 1992); C. A. Macartney: *The Habsburg Empire, 1780–1918* (1968).

Franco y Bahamonde, Francisco (1892–1975), dictator of Spain from 1939 to 1975: born in north-western Spain at El Ferrol, Corunna. He entered the Infantry Academy at Toledo in 1907, was commissioned in 1910, and saw service against the Riff rebels of Morocco. He was promoted to full General in 1927, when he became principal of the Military Academy at Saragossa. In October 1934 he commanded troops which brutally suppressed a soviet established by the miners of the Asturias. He was briefly Chief of the Spanish General Staff in 1935–6 before becoming Governor of the Canary Islands. Resentment at the anticlerical, left-wing policies of the governments appointed by President AZAÑA induced General José Sanjurjo to lead an army revolt on 18 July 1936. Sanjurjo's move was backed by Franco, who assumed leadership of the rebels when Sanjurjo was killed in a plane crash two days later. Cadiz, Burgos, Seville and Saragossa supported Franco's rebel 'Nationalists' but Catalonia, the Basque provinces, Valencia and Madrid remained loyal to the Republican government. Civil war enveloped Spain until the end of March 1939, causing the deaths of more than half a million Spaniards. The country became an ideological battlefield for

Europe's extremists, the Left supporting Azaña while Franco was forced to seek the aid of German aircraft and of 50,000 Italian Fascist volunteers. Technically Franco was proclaimed head of the Spanish state and Generalissimo by a junta at Salamanca on 1 October 1936, the Germans and Italians recognizing his government seven weeks later. Franco never commanded in the field: his strategy was based on the need to drive a wedge through Republican Spain. This plan failed in 1937, largely through the defeat of the Italians in the battle of Guadaljara, but with modifications it succeeded by August 1938. The great cities of Barcelona, Madrid and Valencia withstood Franco's armies for another winter. Britain and France recognized Franco as Head of State in February 1939, the United States according him recognition on 1 April. Franco proceeded to build up the Spanish state on the Italian Fascist model, with himself as leader (*Caudillo*) and politics restricted to the activities of a single party, the Falange. He declined to enter the Second World War, insisting when he met HITLER at Hendaye on 23 October 1940 that Spain had been too weakened by the Civil War for effective participation in a greater conflict. Formal condemnation of Franco's government by the United Nations in 1945–6 failed to weaken his position. Revision of the constitution in July 1947 guaranteed Franco leadership of the Spanish state for life, promising thereafter a restoration of the monarchy. Yet Franco consistently declined to relax his authoritarian hold on the kingdom or to permit modernization, social or political. From 1955 onwards he received backing from the United States, DULLES recognizing him as a firm enemy of communism. Franco was criticized not only by dissident students, but by the Catholic Church which had strongly supported his cause during the Civil War. In the late summer of 1975 – at a time when Spain was feeling the first impact of Basque separatist terrorism – Franco's health gave way. Already in 1969 he had nominated as his successor Prince JUAN CARLOS, grandson of Spain's last King, ALFONSO XIII; and on 30 October 1975 the Prince assumed sovereign powers. Franco was by then too ill to realize his dictatorship had ended: he died three weeks later (20 November). P. Preston: *Franco* (1993); G. Hills: *Franco: the Man and His Nation* (New York, 1967); H. Thomas: *The Spanish Civil War* (rev. edn 1965), S. G. Payne: *The Franco Regime 1936–75* (Madison, Wisc., 1987).

Frankfurter, Felix (1882–1965), Justice of the US Supreme Court from 1939 to 1962: born of Jewish parentage in Vienna, came to America as a boy of 12 knowing not a word of English, but by 1906 had graduated with high honours from Harvard Law School. Several years as an assistant state attorney in New York brought him into contact with Franklin ROOSEVELT and with Louis BRANDEIS, whom Frankfurter much admired. From 1914 to 1939 he was a professor at Harvard Law School, stimulating an interest in social justice among a generation of lawyers and public servants. He chaired the War Labor Policies Board in 1917–18, sharing at that time the enthusiasm of Brandeis for Zionism. From 1933 onwards he became a behind-the-scenes adviser of Roosevelt and was virtually personnel manager to the New Deal executives. The President's decision to appoint him to the Supreme Court in 1939 was intended to strengthen the liberal element among the justices but, as with many similar appointments, Frankfurter showed such scrupulous impartiality that he seemed a conservative, especially where possible questions of security were concerned. Basically Frankfurter believed in harmony between legislature and judiciary, and was therefore inclined to rule against the US Congress or the state institutions only when an individual's basic rights were challenged.

Frankfurter's opinions, which were at times expressed with caustic clarity, invariably commanded respect even if they occasionally puzzled jurists who had sat at his feet in Harvard Law School. He retired in 1962. W. Mendelson: *Justices Black and Frankfurter; Conflict in Court* (New York, 1961); C. P. Curtis, Jnr.: *Lions under the Throne* (Boston, Mass., 1947).

Fraser (John) Malcolm (1930–), Australian Prime Minister from 1975 to 1983: a Melbourne man, who completed his education at Magdalen College, Oxford, entered the Australian Parliament as a Liberal in 1955, and gained wide departmental experience in coalition governments, 1966–71. He became Liberal leader in March 1975. During the constitutional crisis caused by WHITLAM's dismissal the following November, Fraser was invited to form a caretaker (minority) administration. In a General Election a month later he gained majorities in the Senate and the House, but the circumstances of his appointment aroused lasting political bitterness at Canberra, intensified by the backing his devolutionary 'new federalism' gave to state governments' initiatives. Fraser enjoyed widespread respect within the Commonwealth and among his Asian-Pacific neighbours. He resigned the Liberal leadership after electoral defeat by HAWKE in March 1983, but continued to campaign vigorously for world issues he strongly upheld, notably the ending of apartheid in South Africa. P. Ayres: *Malcolm Fraser, a Biography* (Richmond, Victoria,. 1987); T. O'Lincoln: *Years of Rage; Social Conflicts in the Fraser Era* (Melbourne, 1992).

Fraser, Peter (1884–1950), New Zealand's wartime Prime Minister: born in Scotland and did not emigrate until he was 26 years old. He played a large part in building up the New Zealand Labour Party during the First World War and represented Wellington Central in Parliament, 1918–50. Fraser won much respect as Minister of Health and Education from 1935 until April 1940, when he succeeded to the premiership on the death of SAVAGE. As a wartime leader Fraser safeguarded New Zealand's right to control the strategic employment of the dominion's army, navy and air force. He worked in harmony with CHURCHILL (notably on a visit to London in July 1941) and he collaborated closely with Australia's external affairs minister, EVATT, particularly in 1945 at the San Francisco Conference, which set up the United Nations Organization. Fraser comfortably won the 1946 General Election for Labour; his post-war government encouraged state control of New Zealand's industry and state patronage of the arts. The electorate, however, turned against Labour in 1949, forcing Fraser to resign in early December. He was, by then, a sad and weary widower and he survived defeat for barely twelve months. J. Thorn: *Peter Fraser* (1952).

Frederick III (1831–88), German Emperor for ninety-nine days in 1888: born at Potsdam, the only son of WILLIAM I. He married the Princess Royal, eldest child of Queen VICTORIA and Prince Albert in January 1858, and was the father of four sons and four daughters, the eldest boy succeeding as WILLIAM II. As Crown Prince, Frederick distinguished himself in command of the Prussian Second Army at the battle of Königgrätz-Sadowa in July 1866 (against the Austrians) and at the battles of Weissenburg and Wörth in August 1870 (against the French). In politics he was a liberal and frequently on bad terms with BISMARCK, but the two men collaborated closely at Versailles in 1871 over the establishment and proclamation of the new German Empire. In March 1887 he developed a throat ailment, later found to be cancer. Despite painful treatment and a period of rest at San Remo on the Italian Riviera to escape the rigours of a Berlin winter, his condition deteriorated. Tracheotomy was performed on 9 February 1888 at San Remo: he succeeded to the throne on 9 March and returned to Berlin as an Emperor incapable of speech. He died on 15 June, unable to carry out the liberal reforms of which he had often spoken to his wife in earlier years. Frederick III: *War Diary, 1870–71* (1927); A. Palmer: *Crowned Cousins; the Anglo-German Royal Connection* (1985); T. Aronson: *The Kaisers* (1971).

Freyberg, Bernard Cyril (1889–1963), New Zealand soldier and Governor-General: born in Surrey but, from the age of 2, lived in Wellington, New Zealand, training as a dentist. He came to England in 1914, enlisted and fought with such distinction at Gallipoli that he received the Distinguished Service Order. To this, in December 1916, was added the Victoria Cross, won through valour as a battalion commander at the battle of the Ancre in France. He became the youngest Brigadier in the British Army and was wounded six times between 1915 and 1918. Despite these disabilities, in 1923 Freyberg came within 500 yards of swimming the English Channel. In November 1939 he was given command of the New Zealand Expeditionary Force in Europe, leading the division for exactly six years – in Egypt, Greece, Crete, Libya, Tunisia and through Italy from Calabria to Trieste. He continued to show intrepid courage but was criticized for his handling of the defence of Crete (though his freedom of action was hampered by restraints imposed from London, for strategic intelligence reasons). From 1946 to 1952 he was a popular Governor-General of New Zealand, although he spent his last years in England, as Lieutenant-Governor of Windsor Castle. Sir Bernard Freyberg, VC was created a baron in June 1951 and, from his great experience, occasionally spoke on Commonwealth defence issues in the House of Lords. P. Freyberg: *Bernard Freyberg, VC* (1991); P. Singleton-Gates: *General Lord Freyberg VC* (1963).

Fulbright, J. William (1905–94), US Senator from 1945 to 1974: born at Sumner in Missouri, educated at the University of Arkansas and Pembroke College, Oxford, becoming a lawyer. He entered the House of Representatives in 1942, sponsoring the motion calling for the creation of a United Nations organization (of which, unlike the League of Nations, America would be a member) in 1943. He was returned to the Senate as a Democrat by the electors of Arkansas in 1944 and was responsible for the famous Fulbright Act of 1946 which, by providing for student and teacher scholarship exchanges between the United States and other countries, committed the federal government to a worldwide educational project for the first time. Senator Fulbright distinguished himself by his resolute hostility to Joseph MCCARTHY and in 1955 became Chairman of the Senate Banking and Currency Committee. Four years later he accepted chairmanship of the influential Senate Committee on Foreign Relations, a post which enabled him to advocate relaxation of the State Department's hostility towards Cuba and Mao's China. He was a consistent critic of the Vietnam War, questioning every decision which led to escalation and warning the American people against permitting 'war fever' to curb 'tolerance and freedom of discussion'. He declined to stand for re-election in 1974. His services to the promotion of Anglo-American understanding, going back to his days as a Rhodes Scholar at Oxford, were acknowledged in 1975 when he was made an honorary Knight of the British Empire. J. W. Fulbright: *Prospects for the West* (1965), *Arrogance of Power* (1967); E. Brown: *J. William Fulbright* (Iowa City, Ia., 1985).

G

Gaddafi (Qadhafi), Muammar al- (1942–), leader of the Libyan Revolution: born at Sirte, trained at Benghazi Military Academy from 1963, specializing in signals and electronics and completed his studies, under British Army instructors, in Wiltshire, 1966–7. While at Benghazi he formed a Free Officers Movement, in emulation of NASSER in Egypt. On 1 September 1969 Colonel Gaddafi was leader of a group of twelve junior officers who deposed King IDRIS, proclaimed a socialist republic, and governed Libya through a Revolutionary Command Council, of which Gaddafi was Chairman. From 1971 to 1974 he collaborated closely with Egypt and Syria and with the Soviet bloc. He completed nationalization of Libya's oil resources, at the expense of British and US interests. By 1977 Gaddafi had adopted internal and external policies which were markedly distinct from the traditional ways of his Arab neighbours. Although he remained Libya's virtual dictator Gaddafi held no formal post: he was, officially, 'Leader of the Revolution and Supreme Commander of the Armed Forces'. A form of direct democracy – *Jamahiriya* – was introduced, based upon a pyramidic structure of more than 2,000 consultative People's Congresses, together with regional Popular Committees, thirteen Municipality Congresses and, at national level, a General Congress. From March 1977 Gaddafi's Libya was officially styled 'The Socialist People's Libyan Arab Jamahiriya'. Gaddafi personally favoured innovation, opposing Muslim traditionalists by arguing that what mattered was not the accumulation of conservative precepts within Islamic law, but the rules of the Koran itself. This philosophy led him to support not only the Iran of the Ayatollahs, but a general concept of Islamic World revolution. By 1980 his agents were fomenting unrest in Chad, Sudan, Morocco and Tunisia: six states, including Egypt and Saudi Arabia, refused to recognize Jamahiriya Libya. His support for Arab terrorism led to exchanges of fire with US aircraft in August 1981 and March 1986. On 15 April 1986 an American air-raid on Gaddafi's Tripoli headquarters killed some of his family, but failed to topple the régime. While he began to treat his immediate neighbours with more caution (promoting a reconciliation with Egypt in November 1989) his relations with the USA and western Europe remained strained, largely because he refused to hand over terrorist suspects linked with the 1988 destruction of a Pan-Am flight over Lockerbie. The UN Security Council imposed economic sanctions on Libya in April 1992. D. Blundy and A. Lycett: *Qadhafi and the Libyan Revolution* (1987); L. C. Harris: *Libya; Qadhafi's Revolution and the Modern State* (Boulder, Colo., 1986); R. B. St John: *Qadhafi's World Design: Libyan Foreign Policy 1969–87* (1987).

Gagarin, Yuri Alexeyevich (1934–68), Soviet astronaut: born at Gzhatsk, entered the Soviet flying school at Orenburg in 1955, was seconded four years later for intensive training as an astronaut. Major Gagarin achieved world fame on 12 April 1961 when he became the first man to travel in space, orbiting the earth in a six-ton satellite of the Vostok spacecraft. This achievement appeared to confirm the Soviet lead in applied science, first noted by the West when the earth satellite, *Sputnik I*, was launched on 4 October 1957. Alarm at these Soviet space 'firsts' prompted KENNEDY to announce America's intention of landing a man on the moon by the end of the decade, thus beginning in earnest the Soviet–American space race rivalry of the 1960s. Gagarin was killed in March 1968 in an air crash, while commanding a training unit of the Soviet air force.

Gaitskell, Hugh Todd Naylor (1906–63), British Labour Party leader from 1955 to 1963: born in London and educated at Winchester and New College, Oxford. He became active in the socialist movement during the General Strike of 1926. Although he did not enter parliament until 1945 (MP for Leeds, South), he was a Cabinet minister within two years and succeeded CRIPPS as Chancellor of the Exchequer in October 1950. His decision to introduce charges for the National Health Service made him unpopular with the Left of his party. In reality he was well to the Centre, a social democrat and never a Marxist. His gifts as an economist and parliamentarian enabled him to win acceptance as Labour leader in succession to ATTLEE (December 1955), even though he was opposed by the veteran, Herbert MORRISON, and the idol of the Left, Aneurin BEVAN. Gaitskell subsequently won support from Bevan and they represented a formidable combination in opposition to the Suez policy of EDEN in 1956. Wrangles over nationalization and unilateral nuclear disarmament weakened the party nationally, and Gaitskell failed to lead it to victory in the 1959 General Election. He successfully pushed aside attempts by Harold WILSON to oust him from the leadership in 1960 and was beginning to rally the party behind him, notably at the party conferences of 1961 and 1962, when his health gave way prematurely and he died in January 1963, Wilson succeeding him as party leader. P. M. Williams: *Hugh Gaitskell* (rev. edn 1982); W. T. Rodgers (ed.): *Hugh Gaitskell, 1906–1963* (1964).

Galtieri, Leopoldo Fortunato (1926–), Argentinian political General: born at Caseta, near Buenos Aires. After completing his education at the National Military College he was commissioned in 1945 and in a conventional career had reached the rank of General when, in 1976, he joined the ruling military junta which removed PERON's widow, Maria Estela PERON, from the presidency. Galtieri became head of the junta, and effective President of Argentina, on 11 December 1981 at a time when the Republic's economy was near collapse and there was widespread condemnation of the junta's denial of human rights. To the satisfaction of the REAGAN administration, General Galtieri fiercely denounced 'communism' and sought to impose a fashionable monetarism on the economy. When his austerity measures led to riots in the capital (mid-March 1982) he encouraged patriotic feeling by a surprise assault on the Malvinas (the British colony of the Falkland Islands), long coveted by the Argentinians. The resultant Falklands War deprived him of support from Reagan and ended in military disaster: he fell from power on 17–18 June 1982. A year later he was court-martialled and sentenced to twelve years' imprisonment for having plunged Argentina recklessly into an ill-prepared conflict with Great Britain. D. Rock: *Argentina, 1516–1982* (1986); L. Bethell (ed.): *Cambridge History of Latin America*, Vol. 8, 1930–90 (Cambridge, 1991); Anon (Amnesty International): *Argentina; the Military Junta and Human Rights* (1987).

Gambetta, Léon (1838–82), founding father of the Third French Republic:

born at Cahors, practised law from 1859 onwards, becoming one of the most prominent radical liberals opposing NAPOLEON III. He gained a sensational victory in the elections for the Chamber in 1869, being chosen as Deputy for Paris largely through the appeal of 'radical democracy', whose principles he succinctly outlined in the Belleville Manifesto (December 1869). When news reached Paris of the capture of Napoleon at Sedan, Gambetta proclaimed a Republic from the Hotel de Ville in Paris (4 September 1870). He organized the 'provisional government of national defence', serving as Minister of the Interior and of War, staying in Paris after the city was besieged by the Prussians and escaping on 7 October by balloon so as to lead further resistance from Tours. He resigned office when the National Assembly, meeting at Bordeaux, favoured peace and the policies of THIERS in February 1871. Gambetta for the following eight years was leader of the moderate republican opposition, showing less radicalism than at Belleville and holding in check the extremists of the Left while denouncing the repressive policies of Thiers and the crypto-royalism of his successor in the presidency, MACMAHON. On 4 May 1877 Gambetta delivered in the Chamber of Deputies a famous speech rallying republicans against the direct and indirect power of the Catholic Church ('Clericalism – there is the enemy'). Although no republican statesman of his generation had such influence as Gambetta, he served as Prime Minister for a mere nine weeks (14 November 1881 to 27 January 1882), the leaders of other political factions fearing his dictatorial ambitions if he were allowed a long term of office. He died on 31 December 1882, apparently from a shooting accident. J. P. T. Bury: *Gambetta and the National Defence* (1936), *Gambetta and the Making of the Third Republic* (1973), *Gambetta's Final Years* (1982).

Gandhi, Indira (*née* **Nehru**), (1917–84), Indian Prime Minister: born at Allahabad, educated at Swiss and English schools and at Somerville College, Oxford. She joined the Congress Party in 1939 and spent twelve months in prison during the political crisis caused by the Japanese threat to invade India. In 1942 she married Feroze Gandhi and did not take part in national politics until after his death in 1960. Within a few weeks of the death of her father, Pandit NEHRU, in June 1964, she entered the government of his successor, Lal SHASTRI, as minister responsible for information services. When Shastri suddenly died eighteen months later, she campaigned for leadership of the Congress Party, defeated Morarji Desai in the election, and became Prime Minister of India on 24 January 1966. Her eleven years of office were marked in external affairs by frequent crises with Pakistan, the most serious ending in the thirteen-day war of December 1971 which confirmed the secession from Pakistan of Bangladesh. At home Mrs Gandhi sought to modernize Hindu social ideas, notably by encouraging birth control. In 1974 complaints were made that she was responsible for electoral malpractices by senior members of her party. On 12 June 1975 the Indian High Court found her guilty of electoral corruption and she was barred from public office for six years. She appealed against this verdict and, at the end of the month, invoked the Maintenance of Internal Security Act to have nearly 700 opponents arrested, subsequently banning many political movements and in July securing dictatorial powers from the rump of Parliament. Civil war threatened India for six months but early in 1977 the restrictions were relaxed and a General Election held on 16–18 March. Mrs Gandhi lost her seat in Rae Bareli and her followers were heavily defeated. She resigned on 22 March and was succeeded by Desai, at the head of a Congress-breakaway group, the Janata

Party. Although her career suffered a major setback, she began to restore her fortunes some eighteen months later. The Congress Party, under her leadership, won the Indian General Election of January 1980 and she again became Prime Minister. Demands for autonomy by Sikh extremists in the Punjab threatened civil war and on 5 June 1984 Mrs Gandhi ordered the army to occupy the Golden Temple complex at Amritsar and other shrines where militants had taken refuge. More than 300 Sikhs were killed. Anger at this military action induced a Sikh member of her bodyguard to assassinate Indira Gandhi on 31 October 1984 in New Delhi. She was succeeded by her son, Rajiv GANDHI. P. Jayakar: *Indira Gandhi; a Biography* (New Delhi, 1992); Tariq Ali: *An Indian Dynasty, the Story of the Nehru–Gandhi Family* (New York, 1985).

Gandhi, Mohandas Karamchand (1869–1948), Mahatma ('Great Soul') of the Indian people: born at Porbandar, studied law in London from 1889 to 1891 and practised for two years as a barrister in Bombay before settling in South Africa, where he lived from 1893 to 1914. He was leader of the Indian community from 1895, and in 1907 began the first of a series of passive resistance campaigns, protesting at discriminatory laws, especially in the Transvaal. After his return to India he was accepted as an experienced organizer by the Indian National Congress Party and in 1915 succeeded the Hindu extremist, Bal Gangadhar Tilak, as leader of the party. Gandhi's spiritually inspiring teaching, and especially his doctrine of non-violent civil disobedience, owed something to Tolstoy as well as to older Hindu traditions. Congress sought complete independence for India. Gandhi could not prevent terrorism although he curbed the incidence of outrages. A boycott of British goods was accompanied by encouragement of native village industries, and the spinning-wheel became the symbol of his movement from 1924 onwards. He was first imprisoned by the British authorities as an agitator in 1922 and again in May 1930, having 'publicly made salt in defiance of the Salt Laws'. During the eight months in which he was imprisoned the agitation became more violent and hundreds were killed in rioting. In September 1931 he came to London as Congress spokesman at 'Round Table' conferences on India's future; and his ascetic figure, in white shawl, loin cloth and sandals, made a deep impression on the English public. His demands, however, were too extreme for the MACDONALD National Government. He was arrested again after his return to India, in 1933, and interned in 1942, resorting to hunger strikes as part of his passive resistance campaign. In 1945 and 1946 he worked closely with NEHRU in seeking agreement with WAVELL and MOUNTBATTEN (the last two Viceroys) on the partition and eventual independence of the Indian Empire, which was achieved on 15 August 1947. This willingness to accept partition lost Gandhi the support of radical nationalist extremists, incapable of understanding the Mahatma's spiritual philosophy of passive self-purification. He survived one assassination plot early in 1948 but was shot dead by a young Hindu journalist in Delhi ten days later (30 January). M. K. Gandhi: *The Collected Works of Mahatma Gandhi* (82 vols) (New Delhi, 1958–80), *The Story of My Experiment with Truth* (2nd edn 1949); B. R. Nanda: *Mahatma Gandhi, a Biography* (Oxford, 1981); R. Pyarelal: *Mahatma Gandhi: the Last Phase* (Ahmedabad, 1958); G. Sharp: *The Politics of Non-Violent Action* (Boston, Mass., 1974); B. R. Tomlinson: *the Indian National Congress and the Raj, 1929–1942* (1976); D. A. Low (ed.): *Congress and the Raj; Facets of the Indian Struggle, 1917–1947* (1977).

Gandhi, Rajiv (1944–91), Indian Prime Minister: born in New Delhi, the first-born son of Indira GANDHI. He studied engineering at Cambridge but became a pilot with Indian Airlines and in 1968 married an Italian. Until the death in an air crash of his brother Sanjay Gandhi (1946–80) he shared none of the family interest in politics, but succeeded to Sanjay's parliamentary seat and became General-Secretary of his mother's wing of the Congress Party in 1983. He became head of the government on her assassination in October 1984, his authority being confirmed by victory in the ensuing election. As Prime Minister he encouraged rapid and widespread technological innovation, but continued hostility from Sikh extremists led him to order further military intervention at Amritsar in May 1988 and his government lost popularity. He was defeated in the November 1989 General Election. On 21 May 1991 Rajiv Gandhi was assassinated while campaigning to recover his lost popularity. N. Nugent: *Rajiv Gandhi, Son of a Dynasty* (1991); B. Sen Gupta: *Rajiv Gandhi: a Political Study* (New Delhi, 1987).

Garfield, James Abram (1831–81), President of the United States in 1881: born in a log cabin on the frontier in Ohio and had a hard life as a child helping to support his widowed mother. He was educated at Western Reserve Eclectic Institute (later Hiram College, Ohio) and Williams College. He became a lay preacher, teacher, a member of the Ohio bar, and in the Civil War raised his own regiment of volunteers, many of them from among his students at Hiram College. In 1863 he resigned his commission as a Major-General, and sat for seventeen years in the House of Representatives. He became Republican candidate for the 1880 Presidential Election after thirty-nine ballots at the Convention, and he chose Chester ARTHUR as his running-mate. He won the contest with a comfortable electoral vote but a narrow popular vote. On 2 July 1881, only four months after taking office, he was shot and seriously wounded by Charles Guiteau, a disappointed seeker after patronage. President Garfield died eleven weeks later, achieving posthumously some veneration through W. M. Thayer's well-known biography, *From Log Cabin to White House*. J. D. Doenecke: *The Presidencies of James A. Garfield and Chester A. Arthur* (Lawrence, Kans., 1981).

Garibaldi, Giuseppe (1807–82), Italian patriot General: born in Nice, a French possession at the time of his birth but forming part of the kingdom of Piedmont-Sardinia from 1815 to 1860. He served at sea for most of his youth but was implicated in the attempt of Mazzini's 'Young Italy' movement to seize Genoa in 1834. Under sentence of death Garibaldi escaped to South America where he gained fame as Commander of an ex-patriate Italian Legion of 'redshirts', fighting to defend Montevideo against the Argentinian forces from Buenos Aires. He returned to Italy during the revolutions of 1848 and led the defence of the Roman Republic against Neapolitan and French armies seeking to restore the temporal authority of Pope PIUS IX. After sustaining a two months' siege in Rome Garibaldi was forced to retreat across the Appennines to the Adriatic, narrowly escaping capture by Austrian counter-revolutionary soldiery. For most of the years 1850 to 1854 he continued to sail as a master mariner, trading mainly in the Pacific, but at the age of 47 he settled as a farmer on Caprera, an island off the north east coast of Sardinia. During the 1859 war between Austria and Piedmont he commanded a guerrilla force (the 'Alpine Hunters') operating around Lake Como. In May 1860 Garibaldi embarked some thousand men at Genoa on a filibustering enterprise intended to assist rebels against the King of Naples' rule in Sicily. After his 'Thousand' defeated the Neapolitan Army at the battle of Calatafimi,

Garibaldi advanced across Sicily to Palermo which was entered on 27 May, only three weeks after the Thousand's departure from Genoa. Acting in the name of a unified Italy Garibaldi now crossed to the mainland, liberated Naples and gained a further victory on the river Volturno. He then surrendered his conquests to Victor EMMANUEL II of Piedmont, whom he personally hailed as King of Italy on 26 October 1860. Garibaldi retired to Caprera although continuing to influence the politics of the newly unified kingdom. In 1862 and again in 1867 he made unsuccessful attempts to occupy Rome and in 1870–1 he fought for the French Republic against the Prussians, achieving some successes on the Upper Seine. He died and was buried at Caprera, becoming a legendary hero, outstanding among liberal nationalist patriot fighters during the closing years of Romanticism. G. M. Trevelyan: *Garibaldi's Defence of the Roman Republic* (1907), *Garibaldi and the Thousand* (1909), *Garibaldi and the Making of Italy* (1911); J. Ridley: *Garibaldi* (1974); C. Hibbert: *Garibaldi and his Enemies* (1965).

Garner, John Nance (1868–1967), Vice-President of the United States from 1933 to 1941: born in Red River County, Texas, the son of pioneers. He spent his boyhood as a cattle puncher, studying at night. Eventually he graduated from the University of the South in Tennessee, becoming a lawyer in 1890 and practising at Uvalde in southern Texas, close to the Rio Grande. He sat in the Texas legislature from 1898 to 1902 and was a Democrat Congressman from 1903 to 1933, being Speaker of the House of the Representatives for the last two of these thirty years. In 1932 'Speaker Jack', who was himself a strong candidate for nomination, accepted an offer to be running-mate to Franklin ROOSEVELT, and thus became Vice-President in March 1933. His support was invaluable to Roosevelt on two counts: he commanded a considerable following in the South; and he knew the mood of Congress intimately. Although Garner and his supporters were uneasy at the 'socialistic' implications of the New Deal, he agreed to be Roosevelt's running-mate again in 1936. Relations between the President and Vice-President deteriorated during the second term. Garner decided to run for the presidential nomination in 1940, but dropped out of the race when he proved antipathetic to the unions – 'a labour-baiting, poker-playing, whiskey-drinking, evil old man' was the uncharitable public description of him at this time by John L. LEWIS. From 1941 Garner lived in retirement in Texas, the last of the rural hickory Vice-Presidents. B. N. Timmons: *Garner of Texas* (New York, 1948); A. M. Schlesinger, Jnr.: *The Age of Roosevelt; the Coming of the New Deal* (Boston, Mass., 1958).

Gasperi, Alcide de: see *De Gasperi, Alcide.*

Gaulle, Charles de: see *de Gaulle, Charles.*

George I (1845–1913), King of the Hellenes from 1863: born in Copenhagen, second son of King Christian IX of Denmark. He was known as Prince William of Denmark until offered the vacant crown of Greece by a delegation from Athens in June 1863, formally acceding on 31 October 1863. His reign was marked by patient attempts to consolidate a democratic constitutional monarchy within an expanding kingdom. At his accession the northern frontier ran only 140 miles north of Athens: Corfu and the Ionian islands were added in 1864; Thessaly and part of Epirus in 1881, and Crete, much of Macedonia and northern Epirus in the last years of his reign. George I's tact guided Greece through twenty-one general elections (averaging one every six months between

1863 and 1881): seventeen rival Prime Ministers formed no less than seventy governments. The greatest threat to the constitutional monarchy was posed by a Military League of ambitious junior army officers from 1909 onwards; but the danger was contained by a somewhat uneasy partnership between the King and the formidable Cretan liberal, VENIZELOS. King George was assassinated by a mentally unstable Greek alcoholic on 18 March 1913 on the waterfront of Salonika, the port which Greek troops had captured from the Turks four months previously. He was succeeded by CONSTANTINE I. King George's widow, the Russian-born Queen Olga (1821–1926), survived the crises of the following eight years and was herself Queen Regent in the closing months of 1920. J. van der Kiste: *Kings of the Hellenes 1863–1974* (Stroud, 1994); Prince Michael of Greece and A. Palmer: *The Royal House of Greece* (1990); Prince Nicholas of Greece: *My Fifty Years* (1926); Prince Christopher of Greece: *Memoirs* (1938).

George V (1865–1936), King of Great Britain, etc., and Emperor of India from 1910 to 1936: born in Marlborough House, London, the second son of EDWARD VII. At the age of 11 he entered the Royal Navy, serving at sea under sail, and he retained an interest in the fleet, and a naval officer's saltiness of character, throughout his life. In January 1892 his mentally dim elder brother, the Duke of Clarence, died from pneumonia. Prince George was created Duke of York and on 6 July 1893 married the dead Clarence's fiancée, Princess Mary of Teck (1867–1953), his father's second cousin. On Edward VII's accession he and his wife undertook an eight-month voyage to Australasia, South Africa and Canada in order to emphasize the unity of the Empire. Upon his return he was created Prince of Wales (9 November 1901) and for nine years served as a close assistant to his father, with whom he was on excellent personal terms. He became King on 6 May 1910, his reign soon being overshadowed by the First World War. While visiting his troops in France he was thrown from his horse (28 October 1915) and suffered severe injuries, never fully recovering his physical strength. During the post-war period he became extremely popular, partly because of his constitutional diligence and, in later years, through his radio messages which he broadcast in an avuncular manner lacking all microphone self-consciousness. He rarely intervened in politics, accepting the guidance of his constitutional advisers over the appointment of BALDWIN as Prime Minister (1923) and over the formation of a National Government under MACDONALD in 1931. He continued, until his last hours of life, to take pride in the plentitude of Empire: in December 1911 he became the first – and only – King-Emperor to visit India and hold a ceremonial Durbar as reigning sovereign. He narrowly survived a severe illness, and two operations for septicaemia, in the winter of 1928–9. In May, 1935 he was surprised by the warmth of popular affection shown towards him during the Silver Jubilee celebrations. He died from acute bronchial trouble in the following winter at Sandringham, his son succeeding him as EDWARD VIII (20 January 1936). K. Rose: *King George V* (1983); H. Nicolson: *King George V, his Life and Reign* (1952); J. Gore: *King George V, a Personal Memoir* (1941); J. Pope-Hennessy: *Queen Mary* (1959).

George VI (1895–1952), King of Great Britain, etc., from 1936 to 1952 and Emperor of India from 1936 to 1947: born at Sandringham, the second son of GEORGE V. He served in the Royal Navy from 1909 to 1917 and was present at the battle of Jutland in HMS *Collingwood*. After spending a year in the Royal Air Force he went up to Trinity College, Cambridge for three terms. In 1920 he was created Duke of York and in April 1923 married Lady Elizabeth Bowes-Lyon (born 1900). From 1921 he was patron of an annual summer camp which sought the integration of young men from different social classes, and it was in this capacity that he was best known to the public when, unexpectedly, on 11 December 1936, he was called to the throne because of the abdication of his brother, EDWARD VIII. In the summer of 1939 he became the first reigning King-Emperor to visit the United States, achieving much personal success, especially in Washington. He remained above politics, although at times in the Second World War he had to restrain the impetuosity of his Prime Minister, Winston CHURCHILL. The burden of the war years, and of overcoming a natural shyness and a speech defect, imposed a strain on his health, and in 1951 he underwent two operations for cancer. While convalescing at Sandringham he died in his sleep in the early hours of 6 February 1952 and was succeeded by his elder daughter, ELIZABETH II. J. W. Wheeler-Bennett: *King George VI; his Life and Reign* (1958); S. Bradford: *King George VI* (1989).

George, David Lloyd: see *Lloyd George, David*.

George, Henry (1839–97), American economist: born in Philadelphia, left school at 14, becoming successively an errand boy, a sailor, a printer and a journalist. While serving as a newspaper man in northern California, he developed on his own initiative original theories of taxation. These he presented to the public in 1879 as the principal theme in his book *Progress and Poverty*, which made him a national figure overnight. He proposed the abolition of poverty by redistributing wealth through a single tax imposed on unearned increments and the rent derived from land. George made two visits to Britain, and wrote *The Irish Land Question* (1881) and three further, more orthodox, works on political economy. He failed to secure election as Mayor of New York and, in American political life, was something of a nine days' wonder. His main influence was upon British radicals and socialist intellectuals: Fabian economics owed more to George than to MARX, and his lectures in London in 1882 stimulated some of the finest minds of the younger generation, including SHAW and Beatrice Webb. C. A. Barker: *Henry George* (New York, 1955); S. B. Curd: *Henry George, Dreamer or Realist?* (New York, 1984).

Geronimo (Goyath Lay) (1829–1909), last of the warrior Apache chiefs: the principal organizer of the Indians of the south west who waged war against white settlers in Arizona after the death of the peaceful chief Cochise, in 1874. Geronimo showed himself a natural tactician of great intelligence, evading death and capture until 1883, when he was taken but escaped. In 1886 he surrendered on the understanding that his warriors would be permitted to join their families in existing reservations. This pledge was not kept. After imprisonment the survivors, including Geronimo, were settled in Oklahoma Territory. His dignity, horsemanship and qualities of leadership made him the most famous of Indian chiefs. Three years before his death he dictated some remarkable chapters of autobiography, and he was the hero of three major films between 1938 and 1962. S. M. Barrett: *Geronimo's Story of his Life* (New York, 1907); B. Davis: *The Truth About Geronimo* (Chicago, 1951); D. Brown: *Bury My Heart at Wounded Knee* (1971); O. B. Faulk: *The Geronimo Campaign* (New York, 1969).

Giap, Vo Nguyen (1912–), Vietnamese General: born near Quangbinh, gained a doctorate in economics at Hanoi University and taught history, joining the communist movement in 1933. In 1939 he was arrested for giving support to rebellions against the French authorities in Indo-China but he escaped and found temporary refuge in China. His sister was executed, and his wife died in a French colonial prison. Giap was chief assistant to HO CHI MINH in organizing communist guerrilla resistance to the Japanese in Indo-China from 1942 to 1945 and was a minister in the short-lived Vietnamese Republican Government set up by Ho in 1945. The return of the French authorities forced the Vietnamese communists into fresh guerrilla activity and Giap commanded the Viet Minh against the French from 1946 to 1954. His triumph at Dien Bien Phu in May 1954 established his reputation as a resourceful commander: he organized the siting of siege guns by 50,000 coolies in hills over the French fortified camp, thus subjecting a heroic French Army to eight weeks of constant bombardment. General Giap's victory was followed by a cease-fire within two months and the end of more than ninety years of French rule in Indo-China. He became Minister of National Defence in Ho's government established in Hanoi, and remained Commander-in-Chief of the Viet Minh throughout the Vietnam War of 1965–75. His principal campaign against the Americans – the Tet Offensive of February 1968 – was militarily a failure: it consisted of assaults on more than ninety towns and fifty villages and thereby overstretched Giap's resources; but the scale of the offensive convinced the Americans of the need to find a diplomatic solution to the Vietnam crisis rather than allow the war to absorb more and more battle units. Giap became a Vice-Premier of the new Socialist Republic of Vietnam established in July 1976, retaining his responsibility for National Defence. In 1978 he planned the successful occupation of Kampuchea (Cambodia) and the overthrow of the Khmer Rouge Government, and in the following winter he directed defensive operations against Chinese invaders along Vietnam's northern frontier. He retired from office in the spring of 1982 but gave advice on the withdrawal from Cambodia in 1988 and served as titular Vice-Chairman of the Council of Ministers until 1991. R. Stetler (ed.): *The Military Art of People's War; the Selected Writings of General Giap* (New York, 1970); P. Macdonald: *Giap, the Victor in Vietnam* (1991).

Giolitti, Giovanni (1842–1928), Italian Prime Minister on five occasions between 1892 and 1921: born at Mondovi in Piedmont, became a civil servant, entering parliament as a liberal in 1882 and forming his first government ten years later. A financial scandal abruptly cut short his career in 1893 and he was out of politics until 1900. He was Prime Minister again in 1903–5, 1906–9, 1911–14 and 1920–1, heading governments in all for 127 months, longer than any other Italian democratic politician. He supported expansion in north Africa (Libya) and the eastern Mediterranean (Dodecanese) after the Italo-Turkish War of 1911–12, and his earlier governments checked left-wing violence in the industrial cities. He was, however, forced from office in March 1914 by a general strike and his last ministry proved incapable of offering Italy alternative leadership to the extremes of Communist or Fascist. G. Giolitti: *Memoirs of My Life* (1923); C. Seton-Watson: *Italy from Liberalism to Fascism* (1967).

Giscard d'Estaing (1926–), President of France: born in Coblenz, his father holding a high administrative post there during the French occupation of the Rhineland. He won the Croix de Guerre during his years of military service, and was a civil servant attached to the Inspectorate of Finance before entering the National Assembly as a Gaullist in 1956. POMPIDOU appointed him Minister of Finance in 1962, a post he held continuously until 1974. He was elected to succeed Pompidou as third President of the Fifth Republic on 19 May 1974, his presidency being marked by an undramatic personal style which concentrated on economic problems, in contrast to the concern for national prestige shown by his two predecessors. Alleged political scandals lowered his standing during the later years of his presidency. In the election of May 1981 he was defeated by the socialist, MITTERRAND. J. Ardagh: *France in the 1980s* (1982).

Gladstone, William Ewart (1809–98), British Prime Minister from 1868 to 1874, 1880 to 1885, in 1886, and from 1892 to 1894: born in Liverpool, the son of a wealthy merchant with rich plantations in the West Indies. He was educated at Eton and Christ Church, Oxford, and was a Tory MP for Newark from 1832 to 1845, holding minor office under Sir Robert Peel in 1835 and entering Peel's Cabinet as President of the Board of Trade in May 1843. A belief in free trade and concern for basic liberal ideas on the European continent induced Gladstone gradually to discard Toryism during the eighteen years in which he was a 'Peelite' MP for Oxford University, 1847–65. As a Liberal he represented South Lancashire (1865–8), Greenwich (1868–80) and Midlothian (1880–95). He was Chancellor of the Exchequer from December 1852 to February 1855 and from 1859 to 1866, introducing a succession of meticulously planned budgets which cut tariffs and reduced expenditure. This policy of retrenchment he continued as Prime Minister from December 1868 to February 1874, adding to it an extensive programme of liberal reforms – in education, Irish affairs, the army, the legal system, and introducing secrecy of the ballot in elections. His second premiership was less productive: although it was responsible for the third parliamentary reform of 1884, it failed to keep peace in Ireland and lost credit through a hesitant imperial policy, emphasized by the death of General GORDON. Gladstone's slow conversion to the Irish Home Rule cause, championed by PARNELL, lost him the support of the radical Joseph CHAMBERLAIN and thus led to the defeat of his third ministry after only five months of government in 1886. His final ministry, from August 1892 to March 1894, was dominated by his abortive struggle to secure passage of a Home Rule Bill against the wishes of the House of Lords. Younger MPs felt that the 'Grand Old Man' was a 'survival' from earlier conflicts, out of touch with pressing questions over Africa and defence expenditure. He was succeeded as Prime Minister on 3 March 1894 by ROSEBERY. Gladstone's prestige abroad rested not so much on his record as a reformer as on his support for peaceful international arbitration rather than war, and on his consistent championship of oppressed peoples (especially Greeks, Bulgars and Armenians) and political prisoners, notably in Naples in 1850. He was a classical scholar and an intensely religious man, High Church in sympathies even though the Nonconformist tradition was strong among his Liberal supporters. He died on 19 May 1898 at his home, Hawarden Castle in Flintshire, and was buried in Westminster Abbey. J. Morley: *Life of William Ewart Gladstone* (3 vols) (1903); H. C. G. Matthew: *Gladstone* (2 vols) (Oxford, 1992, 1995); E. J. Feuchtwanger: *Gladstone, a Political Biography* (1975); R. Jenkins: *Gladstone* (1995); M. R. D. Foot and H. C. G. Matthew: *The Gladstone Diaries* (13 vols) (1968–94).

Glenn, John (1921–), American astronaut and Senator: born at Cambridge, Ohio, joined US Marines air corps in 1943 and served in the Pacific and Korea. He originally hit the headlines in 1957, when he piloted the first non-stop flight at supersonic speeds from Los Angeles to New York. Subsequently he began training with the Aeronautics and Space

Administration. On 20 February 1962, after ten postponements, Colonel Glenn became the first American to make an orbital flight in space, his *Mercury* capsule completing, in all, three orbits of the earth on a circuit of 81,000 miles in four minutes less than five hours, his maximum altitude being 160 miles. His achievement was seen as evidence of America's serious intention of pursuing space research and of overtaking the lead secured by the Soviet Union with the pioneer flight of GAGARIN ten months previously. Colonel Glenn retired from the Marines in December 1964 and turned to politics, having canvassed support as a Democratic senatorial candidate throughout the year. He was returned as Senator for Ohio in November 1974, but in 1984 he was disappointed in failing to be chosen as presidential candidate at the Democratic Convention. R. F. Fenno: *The Presidential Odyssey of John Glenn* (Washington, D.C., 1990).

Goebbels, Joseph Paul (1897–1945), German propaganda minister from 1933 to 1945: born in the Rhineland, near München-Gladbach, rejected for military service because of a club foot, and educated at Heidelberg where he received a doctorate in philosophy in 1920. He became an embittered intellectual, a shrewd mass psychologist whose cynicism saved him from falling victim to the illusions he himself encouraged. In February 1926 he was charged by HITLER with the task of building up Nazi strength in the Communist-infiltrated industrial suburbs of Berlin. He was elected to the Reichstag in May 1928 and re-elected in September 1930. By then he was already respected as a master of propaganda; it was Goebbels who posthumously turned Horst Wessel, a Berlin stormtrooper murdered by Communists in February 1930, into the best-known Nazi idealist. Hitler appointed Goebbels Minister of Enlightenment and Propaganda in February 1933. Goebbels was always totally loyal to Hitler, criticizing other Nazi figures for lacking the fanatical ruthlessness he sought in the German people after the defeat at Stalingrad in 1943. Goebbels realized, as other propagandists did not, that falsehood was less effective than partial truth, selective reporting and comment in which the prejudice was not blatantly apparent. He had, too, a shrewd sense of theatre and of the impact of visual images, while some of his most effective phrases – notably the 'iron curtain' – survived his Germany. He remained in Hitler's bunker in Berlin until 1 May 1945, when he poisoned his six children and shot his wife and himself. J. Goebbels: *My Part in Germany's Fight, 1932–3* (1938); L. P. Lochner (ed.): *The Goebbels Diaries 1942–43* (1948); H. Heiber (ed.): *The Early Goebbels Diaries, 1925–26* (1962); F. Taylor (ed.): *The Goebbels Diaries 1939–41* (1982); E. K. Bramsted: *Goebbels and National Socialist Propaganda, 1925–45* (1965); V. Reimann: *The Man Who Created Hitler: Joseph Goebbels* (1977).

Goering, Hermann (1893–1946), prominent German Nazi from 1923: born at Rosenheim in Bavaria, commissioned in the army in 1912, transferring to the air force in 1914, subsequently being credited with shooting down twenty-two aircraft. He was awarded the *Pour le Merité*, the highest German award for bravery, and was last Commander of the famous Richthofen squadron of fighters. He joined the Nazi Party in October 1922, was slightly wounded in the abortive Munich *Putsch* of 1923 and found refuge in Sweden until 1927. A year later he was elected to the Reichstag, of which he became President (Speaker) in 1932. When HITLER became Chancellor in January 1933, Goering was appointed Prime Minister of Prussia, with responsibility for internal affairs. This post, combined with his duties as Speaker, made him a prominent figure in the trials arising from the Reichstag Fire of February 1933, and in court he made a poor showing in comparison with the Communist, DIMITROV. In 1935 Hitler entrusted him with responsibility for creating a new air force (Luftwaffe) and a year later he was principal trustee for the four-year plan to build up German industry. He received a Field Marshal's baton in 1938, two years later being created *Reichsmarshal*, a unique rank. He was a poor commander of the Luftwaffe, expecting the fighter squadrons to operate as in 1918 and shifting bomber attacks away from airfields to the cities at a crucial moment of the Battle of Britain. Drugs weakened judgement and, once final victory became elusive, he was content with a hedonistic existence amid looted art treasures. In May 1945 he surrendered to the Americans in western Austria, was arraigned before international judges at Nuremberg and charged with conspiracy to wage war, crimes against peace and against humanity and with war crimes. He conducted his defence vigorously, dominating the trial of the major war criminals (November 1945 to September 1946), but he was found guilty on all counts and sentenced to death. Two hours before he was due to be hanged, his guards found he had killed himself by swallowing poison capsules (15 October 1946). R. J. Overy: *Goering: the Iron Man* (1984); W. Frischauer: *Rise and Fall of Hermann Goering* (Boston, Mass. 1951).

Gokhale, Gopal Krishna (1866–1915), pioneer of Indian self-government and social reformer: a Maratha brahmin, born at Kolhapur, who taught history at Fergusson College, Poona, and won respect as founder of the Servants of India Society. He was an early supporter of the Congress Party, of which he became President in 1905, a year after being chosen by the council as spokesman for the community on CURZON's Legislative Council. Curzon respected Gokhale's desire for Anglo-Indian collaboration. Gokhale had a considerable influence on the political philosophy and tactics of Mahatma GANDHI. For the remainder of his life, Gokhale sought to counter the appeal to the younger generation of militant nationalists within Congress. B. R. Nanda: *Gokhale, Gandhi and the Nations* (1974); S. Gopal: *British Policy in India, 1858–1905* (Cambridge, 1965).

Goldwater, Barry Morris (1909–), US Republican Senator: born in Phoenix, Arizona, the son of a Jewish father of Polish descent and a Protestant Episcopalian mother. He was educated at Stainton Military Academy and the University of Arizona. Apart from serving as a war time ferry pilot for bombers to India, he was in business from 1937 to 1953 as Chairman of 'Goldwater Stores', which marketed a brand of men's underwear known as 'Antsy Pants'. He served as Republican Senator for Arizona from 1953 to 1965. By the spring of 1957 he was recognized as a conservative leader, critical of President EISENHOWER. His right-wing views won little support at the 1960 Convention, which gave more than 1,300 votes to NIXON and only ten to Goldwater; but he was adopted as candidate at the Cow Palace, San Francisco, Convention of 1964. In his campaign he called for vigorous action against world communism and restraint of Federal rights at home, but in the election this conservatism won him only five states. He sat once more in the Senate from 1969 to 1975. Although as an elder Republican statesman he advised Nixon to resign after the Watergate scandals and personally nominated FORD in his unsuccessful bid for election in 1976, Goldwater remained outside the mainstream of political life; by 1986, however, Republican conservatism had swung much closer to his philosophy of government. B. M. Goldwater: *An Autobiography* (New York, 1988); R. H.

Rovere: *The Goldwater Caper* (New York, 1965).

Gompers, Samuel (1850–1924), American labour unionist: born in London of Dutch-Jewish parents who settled in New York while he was still a boy. He was at work by the age of 12, making cigars in New York's lower East Side. In 1863 he joined the Cigarmakers' Union, of which he became President at the age of 24. Ten years later he began to organize a powerful non-centralized trade union movement which was concerned with economic problems and not with questions of general politics. Gompers was thus virtually founder in 1886 of the American Federation of Labor (AFL), which by the turn of the century had replaced the older and highly centralized Knights of Labor (founded 1869) as the principal organization of the American workers. He was President of the AFL from its foundation until his death, except for a twelve-month gap in 1895–6. Under his leadership the movement concentrated primarily on hours and wages, although the AFL always campaigned for better education, for the abolition of child labour and for improved conditions within factories and mines. Gompers insisted that the Federation should employ salaried officials, who were skilled bargainers rather than agitators. He cautiously steered American labour away from the revolutionary ideas of DEBS and other radicals, urging workers' support for progressive Democrats like Woodrow WILSON rather than for doctrinaire socialism. G. E. Stern: *Gompers* (Englewood Cliffs, N.J., 1971); F. L. Grubbs: *The Struggle for Labor Loyalty, 1917–20* (Durham, N.C., 1963).

Gomulka, Wladyslaw (1905–82), leader of the Polish Communist Party from 1956 to 1970: born in Austrian Galicia, at Krosno. He was a trade unionist in inter-war Poland and was organizing secretary of a secret Polish Workers' Party in the resistance from 1943 to 1945. When the reinstated Polish Republic was established in 1945 he was given the important post of minister for the new territories annexed from Germany. A speech in June 1948 on the historical traditions of Polish socialism was regarded in Moscow as nationalistic, and six months later he was dismissed from office, being kept in protective custody from 1951 to 1955. A more liberal mood, which followed the de-Stalinization policy defined by KRUSCHEV at the Twentieth Soviet Party Congress of February 1956, facilitated Gomulka's return to political life. He was re-admitted to the United Workers Communist Party in August 1956, becoming party boss as First Secretary eight weeks later. Gomulka was careful to avoid the mistakes of NAGY in Hungary: he emphasized the continued defence links binding Poland to the Soviet Union; but he halted all agricultural collectivization, and from 1958 to the winter of 1962–3 he permitted greater freedom of expression in Poland. Murmurings of internal discontent made Gomulka reimpose restrictions (and in particular restore the powers of the secret police) in the mid 1960s. Riots over the rising cost of food in the last weeks of the year 1970 suggested his agrarian policy had left too much scope for the individual small farmer. He was forced out of office shortly before Christmas in 1970 and succeeded as First Secretary by Edward Gierek (1913–), from Silesia. In his ten years of office Gierek embarked on an ambitious programme of industrialization which, in its turn, ran Poland heavily into debt and prompted the rise in 1980 of the Solidarity movement under Lech WALESA. N. Bethell: *Gomulka, his Poland and his Communism* (1969); N. Davies: *God's Playground; History of Poland*, Vol. 2 (Oxford, 1981).

Gonzalez (Marquez), Felipe (1942–), Spanish democratic socialist and longest-serving Prime Minister: born in Seville, where he studied law, subsequently seeking through the courts to uphold workers' rights during the last years of FRANCO. At the age of 22 Gonzalez secretly joined the Spanish Socialist Workers Party (PSOE), a proscribed organization, though smaller and potentially less of a threat than the communists (PCE). Gonzalez was elected Secretary-General of PSOE in 1974, before the party was legalized. He built up PSOE rapidly as a non-Marxist socialist movement, winning support from PCE and making it Spain's dominant political party within eight years. Gonzalez led the parliamentary opposition when democratic government was restored in 1977. After PSOE won the General Election of October 1982, he became Spain's first left-wing Prime Minister since the Civil War. He shared the respect of King JUAN CARLOS for constitutionalism and successfully led Spain into the EEC in 1986, while carrying through moderate social reforms at home. This combination brought Gonzalez unprecedented electoral success, with victories in 1986, 1989 and 1993. His position was, however, weakened in April 1994 by a financial scandal within the Interior Ministry and in July 1995 by allegations that he connived in undercover operations against Basque separatists. He lost the General Election of March 1996. P. Preston: *The Triumph of Democracy in Spain* (1986); R. Gunther *et al.*: *Spain after Franco; the Making of a Competitive Party System* (Berkeley, Calif., 1986).

Gorbachev, Mikhail Sergeevich (1931–), last President of the USSR: born in a village near Stavropol, northern Caucasus. As a child he experienced several months of enemy occupation in 1942, thereafter alternating periods of study with work on the land. At Moscow University he graduated in law in the year of STALIN'S death, having joined the Communist Party in 1952, and returned to Stavropol to organize the communist youth movement for much of the northern Caucasus. He received backing from Yuri ANDROPOV, who also came from Stavropol. By 1978 Gorbachev was in Moscow as an expert on agriculture and he was admitted to the ruling Party Politburo a year later. Under Andropov and the ailing CHERNENKO he became the spokesman for reforms, aimed at rooting out corruption and inefficiency in both party and state. On 11 March 1985 he beame effective leader of the Soviet Union, as General Secretary of the Party. His policy was based on *glasnost* ('openness'), which gave Soviet citizens greater freedom of expression and criticism, and, from January 1987, *Perestroika*, a 'restructuring' of both the state-managed economic system and of local government, to provide some grass-roots democracy: private ownership and limited private enterprise were tolerated, and some political prisoners were released. Gorbachev was hampered by the reluctance of the West to provide him with financial backing to lift the standard of everyday life and by an increasing assertion of nationalist aspirations, first in the Baltic republics and later in Armenia and Georgia. During the second half of the year 1988 he imposed major political reforms, succeeding GROMYKO as President on 30 September and allowing liberal non-communists as well as Party members to stand for election to a Congress of (2,250) People's Deputies in December. Unilateral troops withdrawals from eastern Europe and, in December 1988, a speech at the UN in favour of 'new thinking' to end the cold war brought Gorbachev the Nobel Peace Prize, the only occasion it was awarded to a Soviet statesman. Failure to prevent a jump in the cost of living and an inability of the restructured state to ensure adequate food distribution led to mounting criticism of his policies at home by the closing months of 1990. In March 1991 six of the fifteen Soviet republics refused to vote on his revised unitary structure of the USSR. Boris YELTSIN, as President of the Russian Soviet Republic, gained increased influence which was intensified by his successful defiance of Communist hard-liners who, on 19 August 1991, staged an abortive *coup d'état* while Gorbachev was in the Crimea. Although Gorbachev remained in office after the failure of the *coup*, effective power was in Yeltsin's hands. Gorbachev refused to abandon his communist beliefs or to accept the breakup of the Soviet Union into its constituent republics. He formally resigned as Soviet President on 25 December 1991, the day before the USSR went out of existence. M. Gorbachev: *Perestroika* (1987), *The August Coup, the Truth and the Lesson* (1991); C. Schmidt-Hauer: *Gorbachev, the Path to Power* (1986); M. Walker: *The Waking Giant, Gorbachev's Russia* (New York, 1987); R. Kaiser: *Why Gorbachev Happened* (New York, 1991); D. Remnick: *Lenin's Tomb* (1993).

Gorchakov, Alexander (1798–1883), Tsarist Russian diplomat and Chancellor: born in St Petersburg, entered the diplomatic service at the age of 19 and attended the Congresses of Laibach and Verona in 1821–2. After serving briefly in London, Florence and Vienna he sank into obscurity as Russia's diplomatic envoy at Stuttgart and Frankfurt. He was, however, sent on a special mission to Vienna in 1854–5 where his statecraft so impressed the new Tsar, ALEXANDER II, that he appointed Gorchakov Foreign Minister in April 1856. For the following twenty-six years he controlled Russian foreign policy, receiving the largely honorific titles of Vice-Chancellor in 1862 and of Chancellor (a rare distinction) in June 1867. Gorchakov worked in close partnership with BISMARCK's Prussia until 1870, seizing the opportunity of the Franco-Prussian War to shake off restrictions imposed on defeated Russia by the Treaty of Paris of 1856. He collaborated with Bismarck and ANDRASSY from 1872 to 1875 but they came to distrust his personal vanity and his ability to hold in check the 'pan-Slav' agitation which sought Russian expansion in the Balkans. Gorchakov attended the Congress of Berlin in 1878, an ageing and cantankerous invalid who had become childishly jealous, not only of Bismarck's primacy in Europe, but also of able and younger diplomats in the Russian service. He remained nominally in charge of foreign affairs until April 1882, ten years too long for the good of his reputation since he left his successors a legacy of strained relations with Berlin, Vienna and London. Gorchakov died a year later, apparently after purchasing rejuvenating pills from a quack chemist while taking the spa waters of Baden-Baden. B. Jelavich: *A Century of Russian Foreign Policy, 1814–1914* (New York, 1964); A. Palmer: *The Chancelleries of Europe* (1983); B. H. Sumner: *Russia and the Balkans, 1870–1880* (1937).

Gordon, Charles George (1833–85), British General and Victorian hero: born at Woolwich, commissioned in the Royal Engineers in 1852, saw service in the siege of Sebastopol in 1855. He spent most of the years 1860–5 in China, helping to quell the Taiping Rebellion, and he became known subsequently as 'Chinese Gordon'. For six years he served the Khedive of Egypt as Governor and Military Commander in the Sudan, suppressing the slave trade and exploring the upper waters of the Nile. Ill-health forced him back to England in 1880 and he spent periods of mental recuperation in South Africa and in Palestine. In 1884 the British government asked him to return to the Sudan and rescue isolated garrisons menaced by the religious fanaticism of the Mahdi. But General Gordon, an evangelical Christian as God-fearing as his Muslim enemy, tried to check the spread of the Mahdi's revolt and, underestimating the Mahdi's power, found himself besieged in Khartoum.

After ten months of siege, the Mahdi's dervishes broke into Khartoum and murdered Gordon only two days before the arrival of a powerful relief force sent from England. Gordon's death shocked the British public, who criticized the Prime Minister, GLADSTONE, for not having fitted out a relief force earlier. J. Pollock: *Gordon, the Man behind the Legend* (1993); C. Chenevix-Trench: *Charley Gordon, an Eminent Victorian Re-assessed* (1978).

Gottwald, Klement (1896–1953), Czechoslovak Prime Minister from 1946 to 1948 and President from 1948 to 1953: born at Dedice in Moravia, served in the Austro-Hungarian army from 1914 to 1918, became a founder-member of the Czechoslovak Communist Party in 1921 and was Chief Secretary of the party from 1927 onwards. He escaped to Moscow in the winter of 1938 9, returning to his homeland with the Red Army in the spring of 1945 and serving as Vice-Premier in the first post-war government. Free elections in May 1946 returned Communist candidates to 114 of the 300 seats in the Czechoslovak parliament and Gottwald became Prime Minister of a coalition government. The public mood outside the industrial cities turned against the Communists in the following year and Gottwald, fearing electoral defeat, carried through a *coup d'état* with the help of the police and the workers' militia in February 1948. Four months later he succeeded BENEŠ as President, imposing a rigid Stalinism on Czechoslovakia. President Gottwald contracted pneumonia at STALIN's funeral on 9 March 1953 and died five days later. E. Taborsky: *Communism in Czechoslovakia 1948–1960* (Princeton, 1961); M. Kaplan: *The Communist Coup in Czechoslovakia* (Princeton, 1960).

Gowon, Yakubu Danjuma (1934–), General, federal leader of Nigeria during the Biafran Civil War: born in the Benue-Plateau region of Nigeria, the son of a Church Missionary Society evangelist from the Angas tribe. He was educated at CMS schools and the Government College at Zaria, completing his military training in England at Sandhurst and serving with Nigerian units with UN peace-keepers in the Congo, 1960–3. In January 1966 he became Battalion Commander at Ikeja, restoring order in northern Nigeria after the assassination of the Commander-in-Chief, General Ironsi, in July 1966. Gowon then made himself both Head of State and Commander of Nigeria's armed force. At a time of deep division between the Islamic north and the oil-rich south east he introduced a new federal structure, dividing Nigeria into twelve semi-autonomous states, but he was faced by the secession of the Ibo region of Biafra, under Colonel Ojuku (1933–), on 30 May 1967. Gowon sent federal troops into Biafra in July, capturing the main towns, Enugu and Port Harcourt, within ten months; but Ojuku maintained bitter resistance until overwhelmed in January 1970. Gowon's reconstruction programme of public works, dependent on anticipated revenue from future oil sales, ran into grave financial difficulties and, as an active Christian, the General himself was suspect to Nigeria's Islamic northern peoples. He was ousted as Head of State in August 1975 while attending a conference of African states at Kampala and sought exile in England, where in 1978 he enrolled as a postgraduate student at the University of Warwick. Later he settled with his family in Togo. Y. D. Gowon: *Faith in Unity* (Lagos, 1970); O. Oyediran: *Nigerian Government and Politics under Military Rule, 1966–1979* (New York, 1980).

Gramsci, Antonio (1891–1937), Italian communist: born in poverty at Ales, near Cagliari, Sardinia, but gained entry into Turin University, where he showed great intellectual brilliance and became active in the Socialist Party (PSI). In 1921 he led a left-wing faction out of the PSI and set up the Italian Communist Party, of which he became parliamentary leader until it was banned under the fascist regime in October 1926, when Gramsci was arrested. He spent the remaining eleven years of his life in prisons or penal settlements. There he developed further his intellectual interests, successfully reconciling Marxist traditions of historical materialism with Italian metaphysical philosophy. Gramsci thus evolved a more flexible attitude to the inevitability of a proletarian revolution. While in detention he filled more than thirty large notebooks with the basic tenets of a reformist Marxism. When these *Lettere del carcere* (prison letters) were published in 1947 they gave the powerful Italian communist movement principles independent of orthodox Stalinism and shaped both the polycentrism of the outstanding party leader, Pietro Togliatti (1892–1964), and the 'Eurocommunist' reformism of his successor, Enrico Berlinguer (1922–84). J. Joll: *Gramsci* (1977); J. M. Cammett: *Antonio Gramsci and the Origins of Italian Communism* (Stanford, Calif. 1967).

Grant, Ulysses Simpson (1822–85), American General and President of the United States from 1869 to 1877: born at Point Pleasant in Claremont County, Ohio. He graduated from the Military Academy at West Point in 1843 and served with credit in the Mexican War, 1846–8, but he resigned his commission in 1854, farmed for six years in Missouri and was working as a clerk in Illinois when the Civil War began. Grant was at once commissioned as a Colonel of volunteers, commanding the Twenty-first Illinois infantry regiment, and in November 1861 was promoted to Brigadier-General. Successes in the western theatre of war, notably the capture of Fort Donelson on the Cumberland River in February 1862, won for Grant support from President LINCOLN. In the savage battle of Shiloh, in Tennessee, on 6–7 April 1862 Grant's army was surprised by a larger Confederate force and suffered heavy casualties before the arrival of reinforcements allowed Grant to mount and lead a cavalry charge which forced the Confederates to withdraw. Throughout the winter of 1862–3 Grant concentrated on gaining control of the Mississippi at Vicksburg, securing the strongly fortified town at last on 4 July 1863. Success at Chattanooga in the following November enabled him to clear Tennessee and Lincoln appointed him to full command of the Union armies on 9 March 1864. Grant's strategy was based on the need to destroy his enemy as a fighting force rather than on the capture of towns and territory. He therefore divided his army into two main sections: SHERMAN was to strike into Georgia; Grant himself concentrated on defeating LEE in the Wilderness Campaign in Virginia so as to capture Richmond and eliminate the army defending the Confederate capital. Richmond fell on 3 April 1865 and Lee capitulated to Grant at Appomattox six days later. Congress honoured Grant with the rank of full General – held previously in America only by George Washington. He was chosen as Republican candidate in the presidential election of 1868, easily winning the contest, but he proved an irresolute chief executive, often incapable of understanding the matters raised in Cabinet. The successes of his Secretary of State, FISH, were offset by monetary scandals by other members of his administration. Grant was, however, re-elected in 1872, his victory owing much to the guarantee of Negro suffrage embodied in the Fifteenth Amendment which Grant had strongly supported. His second administration was plagued by monetary problems and recession, and he retired from office with relief. For most of the years 1877–8 Grant travelled in Europe, subsequently returning to

New York as a sleeping partner in a banking institution which collapsed four years later, leaving the veteran General impoverished. Only the writing of his memoirs saved Grant from bankruptcy. He died from cancer while living near Saratoga on 23 July 1885, his tomb in New York recalling the General's triumphant defence of the Union rather than the embarrassing failures of his later years. E. B. Long (ed.): *Personal Memoirs of Ulysses S. Grant* (2 vols) (1952 edition of 1885–6 original text); B. Catton: *U. S. Grant and the American Military Tradition* (New York, 1954); B. D. Simpson: *Let Us Have Peace, Ulysses S. Grant and Reconstruction* (1991); J. F. C. Fuller: *Grant and Lee, a Study in Personality and Generalship* (1933).

Grey, Edward (1862–1933), British Foreign Secretary from 1905 to 1916: born in London, a member of one of the outstanding Liberal families, being great-great nephew of Earl Grey (1764–1845), the Reform Bill Prime Minister. Edward Grey spent his infancy and boyhood at the family home, Fallodon, in Northumberland. He was educated at Winchester and Balliol College, Oxford, inheriting his grandfather's baronetcy in 1882. Sir Edward was Liberal MP for Berwick from 1885 to 1916. In private life he was an ornithologist and a keen fisherman, remaining active in politics from a sense of duty, not from choice. He was Under-Secretary at the Foreign Office from 1892 to 1895 and it was this experience that induced CAMPBELL-BANNERMAN to appoint him Foreign Secretary in December 1905. He continued the policy of collaboration with France, begun by his predecessor LANSDOWNE, and extended the entente system by concluding a convention with Russia in August 1907 which settled outstanding differences between the two empires in Tibet, Persia and Afghanistan. Grey also authorized secret military talks with the French and Belgian General Staffs, though emphasizing that Britain retained freedom of choice between peace and war should Europe be plunged in conflict. Grey, unlike his friend Winston CHURCHILL, was a firm believer in diplomatic exchanges rather than war, but he advised the House of Commons in August 1914 that Britain had treaty obligations to assist Belgium against any invader and that therefore war with Germany could not be avoided. When he ceased to be Foreign Secretary in May 1916 (after the longest ever continuous tenure of that post) he headed a special mission to the United States and helped establish the League of Nations. He was created a peer (Viscount Grey of Fallodon) in 1916 and was Chancellor of Oxford University for the last five years of his life. Grey, Viscount: *Twenty-five Years, 1891–1916* (2 vols) (1925); G. M. Trevelyan: *Grey of Fallodon* (1937); K. Robbins: *Sir Edward Grey* (1971); F. H. Hinsley (ed.): *British Foreign Policy under Sir Edward Grey* (Cambridge, 1977).

Grivas, George Theodoros (1898–1974), leader of the Greek Cypriot terrorist movement, EOKA, from 1955 to 1959 and 1971 to 1973: born in Cyprus, served in the Greek army from 1941 to 1953, retiring with the rank of Colonel. He then settled in Cyprus where he organized the EOKA terrorist guerrillas in support of union with Greece, *Enosis*. Colonel Grivas at first used the code-name 'Dighenis', a folk hero of exploits against the Arabs in the tenth century. Grivas's terrorist bomb-attacks on British bases in Cyprus were launched on 1 April 1955; bombings and murders continued for four years, and alienated British opinion, which was at first not unsympathetic to the idea of *Enosis*. When an independent Republic of Cyprus was set up within the Commonwealth in August 1960, Grivas was promoted to the rank of General and given command of the Greek Cypriot National Guard, against the wishes of President MAKARIOS. Grivas used the

Guard as an extension of EOKA, his troops raiding Turkish Cypriot villages and threatening to bring war, not only to Cyprus, but to Greece and Turkey as well. He was recalled to Athens in December 1967 but continued to regard Makarios as a traitor for having accepted Commonwealth membership rather than union with Greece. With Colonel PAPADOPOULOS in power in Athens, Grivas determined to reorganize EOKA and overthrow Makarios, believing the regime of the Greek colonels would give support denied him by earlier governments. He returned to Cyprus secretly in September 1971, but by now he was a spent force, never constituting a serious menace, although his presence in the hills weakened Makarios's standing and inhibited him from reaching agreement with the Turks. By the coming of winter in 1973 it was known the Grivas was suffering from cancer. He died at Limassol, still in hiding which the authorities did not try too hard to penetrate, in January 1974. C. Foley (ed.): *Memoirs of General Grivas* (1964); D. Alastos: *Cyprus Guerrilla; Grivas, Makarios and the British* (1960).

Gromyko, Andrei Andreyevich (1909–89), Soviet Foreign Minister for twenty-eight years: born near Gomel, studied agriculture and economics at Minsk and Moscow, working on economic problems at the Academy of Sciences from 1936 to 1939, as well as editing the journal *Voprosy Ekonomiki*. He transferred to the Foreign Ministry under MOLOTOV, serving for a time as head of the American section before going to Washington as counsellor in the embassy, where he succeeded LITVINOV as ambassador in 1943. From 1946 to 1949 he was principal Russian delegate to the United Nations, returning to Moscow as Deputy Foreign Minister in 1949. Briefly in 1952–3 he was ambassador in London. He took over the Soviet Foreign Ministry from Dmitri Shepilov in February 1957, retaining office until March 1985, the longest span for any twentieth-century Russian Foreign Minister. He appeared, however, to carry out policies rather than initiate them, as if he were a super-ambassador, and he did not even become a member of the ruling Soviet Politburo until he had been in office for sixteen years. Gromyko therefore left a lesser mark on international affairs than Litvinov or Molotov before him. In March 1985 he succeeded CHERNENKO as Soviet President, though effective power remained with GORBACHEV, in whose favour Gromyko retired from the presidency on 30 September 1988. A. Gromyko: *Memories* (1989); R. Edmonds: *Soviet Foreign Policy; the Brezhnev Years* (Oxford, 1983).

Guderian, Heinz (1888–1954), German General, pioneer of armoured warfare: born at Kulm (now Chelmno) on the Vistula, commissioned in a Hanoverian infantry regiment in 1908. He served with the infantry in Flanders and on the Aisne from 1914 to 1917, spending the last months of the war on the General Staff. After fighting with the Freikorps in the Baltic republics in 1919, he was from 1922 attached to motorized transport units, eventually as a Colonel, being appointed Chief of Staff to the Armoured Troops Command in July 1934. He was then given five years in which to develop the techniques of armoured warfare, becoming commanding General of armoured troops in November 1938. In September 1939 he led the Nineteenth Army Corps into Poland, one of his first objectives being the capture of his birthplace, in Polish territory since the Treaty of Versailles. His most famous operation was the advance through the Ardennes on Sedan in May 1940 and the subsequent rapid advance within a week to the Channel coast of France. In 1941 he commanded the Second Panzer Army in Russia but was made a scapegoat for the failure to reach Moscow and was virtually unemployed during the critical period from December 1941 to March 1943. He then became Inspector-General of Armoured Troops, vainly seeking to prevent both HITLER and individual army commanders from squandering tanks in ill-considered sparring contests rather than using them as a spearhead in concerted offensives. He became Chief of the Army General Staff in July 1944 but was unable to influence Hitler's strategy in the last months of the war, and was dismissed on 28 March 1945, being taken prisoner by the Americans in the Tyrol early in May. His influence on military thinking, and in particular on the evolution of *blitzkrieg* operations, was greater than the limited use made by Hitler of his genius would suggest. H. Guderian: *Panzer Leader* (1952); A. Horne: *To Lose a Battle* (1969); J. Erickson: *The Road to Stalingrad* (1975), *The Road to Berlin* (1985).

Guevara, Ernesto ('Che') (1928–67), Cuban revolutionary of Argentinian birth: born in Rosario, a member of a wealthy Argentinian family. He graduated as a doctor of medicine in 1953, subsequently visiting most countries in mainland Latin America. He met Fidel CASTRO in 1956 in Mexico and accompanied him back to Cuba at the end of the year, helping to organize and lead radical guerrillas in the Sierra Maestra over the next two years. Guevara's habit of addressing the young Cuban fighters by the familiar 'Che' caused them to bestow it on him as a nickname. When Castro entered Havana early in 1959, Guevara accepted high position in the administration, becoming President of the Cuban National Bank and later serving as Minister for Industries. He travelled to both China and the Soviet Union in 1960, but he was an individualist, almost as critical of the established governments in Moscow and Peking as of the bourgeois capitalism he rejected in the Americas. In a book on guerrilla warfare he argued that, in Latin America, the act of revolution should precede the propagation of doctrinaire Marxism, as a backward peasantry would respond to particular, local grievances rather than to any general theory of communism. He resigned his Cuban official posts in April 1965, travelled to Bolivia and sought to kindle a revolt among the tin miners (who lived in poverty and who were ruthlessly exploited). Support was, however, small and he received no effective assistance from the Maoist urban guerrilla movement in the more highly developed centres of Bolivia. While seeking to reassess his policy at camps in the jungle, he was wounded, captured and executed by Bolivian security forces early in October 1967. In death he became a martyr-hero for radical students, his name figuring prominently in the anarchist litany of young demonstrators in France, Germany and America in the spring of 1968. E. Che Guevara: *The Motorcycle Diaries, a Journey around South America* (1995); M. Ebon: *Che, the Making of a Legend* (New York, 1969); R. Debray: *Che's Guerrila War* (1975); G. Prado Salmon: *The Defeat of Che Guevara* (1990).

H

Haig, Douglas (1861–1928), British soldier, Commander-in-Chief of British forces in France from 1915 to 1918: born in Edinburgh, educated at Clifton College and Sandhurst, commissioned in the Seventh Hussars in 1885, serving in the Sudan, South Africa and India before helping to modernize the structure of the army in War Office appointments from 1906 to 1909. Haig, a member of the exclusive Marlborough Club, became a personal friend of the future EDWARD VII while still a comparatively junior officer, was a guest at Sandringham before the Boer War and on many later occasions, and was married to one of Queen Alexandra's maids of honour in the private chapel of Buckingham Palace (1905). He was knighted by Edward VII in 1909 and remained a valued friend of GEORGE V throughout the war years. In 1914 he commanded the First Corps of the British Expeditionary Force, at Mons, at Ypres and later at Loos. He succeeded Sir John French as Commander-in-Chief in December 1915. Haig was a professional soldier of great distinction and indomitable resolution, but with no strategic imagination. He was distrusted by the Prime Minister LLOYD GEORGE, not least because of his ready access to the King. Haig's tenacity rallied his troops after they were forced back by Ludendorff's offensive in March 1918. He served loyally under FOCH when it became essential to appoint an Allied generalissimo to co-ordinate plans for the great counter-offensive which brought final victory. He was created an Earl in 1919 and voted £100,000 by Parliament. A year later he was given Bemersyde Mansion by public subscription as evidence of the nation's gratitude for his leadership on the Western Front. He remained Commander-in-Chief of the Home Forces from 1919 to 1921, but spent the last seven years of his life as President of the British Legion, working tirelessly for ex-servicemen, especially for those maimed or blinded during the war. R. Blake (ed.): *The Private Papers of Douglas Haig, 1914–1919* (1952); J. Terraine: *Douglas Haig, the Educated Soldier* (1963); P. Warner: *Field Marshal Earl Haig* (1991).

Haile Selassie (1892–1975), effective ruler of Abyssinia (later Ethiopia) from 1916 to 1936 and 1941 to 1974: born at Harar and known as Ras Tafari Makonnen. He was educated by French mission priests and, as early as 1908, he was entrusted by his cousin, Emperor MENELEK II (1842–1913), with the administration of one of the richest provinces in the country. After a period of near-anarchy on Menelek's death, a council of notables elected Ras Tafari Regent in 1916. Modernization, notably the provision of schools and medical facilities, was accompanied during the Regency by increased influence abroad, Abyssinia becoming a member of the League of Nations in 1924. Ras Tafari succeeded to the throne in November 1930, reverting to his baptismal name Haile Selassie at his coronation. Five years of attempted modernization was followed in 1935–6 by an Italian invasion which forced Emperor Haile Selassie into exile, much of it being spent in England, at Bath. He returned to Khartoum in 1940 and followed the

Allied armies back into Abyssinia, re-entering Addis Ababa in May 1941. After the Second World War his long experience and prestige enabled him to play a prominent role in world politics and African affairs. As he became older, he lost touch with social problems in the remoter districts of Abyssinia, concentrating on spectacular improvements around his capital city. Famine in 1973–4 led to discontent, which was exploited by a group of left-wing army officers. The Emperor was deposed in September 1974 and kept under restraint, until death came to him in his former palace on 27 August 1975. Haile Selassie: *My Life and Ethiopia's Progress* (Oxford, 1976); H. W. Lokot: *The Mission: the Life, Reign and Character of Haile Selassie* (1989).

Halifax, Lord (Edward Wood), (1881–1959), Viceroy of India, British Foreign Secretary and ambassador: born at Powderham Castle, Devon, educated at Eton and Christ Church, Oxford. He represented Ripon as Conservative MP from 1910 to 1925, and was a member of the Cabinets of Bonar LAW and BALDWIN (1922–3 and 1924–5) with responsibility for education and, later, for agriculture. In November 1925 he was created Baron Irwin and early in 1926 began five years as Viceroy of India, a period of tension eased in March 1931 by an understanding with Mohandas GANDHI. In July 1932 he returned to the Cabinet as President of the Board of Education, becoming Viscount Halifax on the death of his father in 1934. He was War Minister for five undistinguished months in 1935, before being appointed Lord Privy Seal, with particular responsibility for European affairs, in November 1835. In this capacity he sought to sound out HITLER and MUSSOLINI personally and was so closely in the confidence of Neville CHAMBERLAIN that he was a natural choice as Foreign Secretary in succession to EDEN in February 1938. He was at the Foreign Office until December 1940, gradually inducing Chamberlain to abandon appeasement. A proposal that Halifax, rather than Winston CHURCHILL should succeed Chamberlain as Prime Minister in May 1940 was defeated, largely on the initiative of the Labour leaders who made it clear to GEORGE VI that they would not serve in a coalition government under Halifax. In January 1941, reluctantly, Halifax went to Washington as ambassador. There he remained for ten years, achieving greater personal success than in any other post in his public career. He was also Chancellor of Oxford University for twenty-six years, from 1933 until his death. Lord Halifax: *Fullness of Days* (1957); Lord Birkenhead: *Halifax* (1965); R. J. Moore: *The Crisis of Indian Unity* (Oxford, 1974); K. Middlemass: *Diplomacy of Illusion; the British Government and Germany, 1937–39* (1972); A. Roberts: *The Holy Fox, a Biography of Lord Halifax* (1991).

Halsey, William Frederick (1882–1959), American Admiral, Commander of the South Pacific Fleet in 1942–3 and the US Third Fleet in 1944–5: born in Elizabeth, New Jersey, graduated from the Naval Academy at Annapolis in 1904 and served in destroyers based on Queenstown, Ireland, in 1917–18. By 1941 he was an Admiral, flying his flag in the aircraft-carrier *Enterprise*. He commanded the fleet throughout the Solomon Islands campaign, gaining a decisive victory over the Japanese at Guadalcanal (12–15 November 1942). 'Bull' Halsey argued that naval battles between rival fleets of capital ships had, by 1942, become as antiquated as the tactics of Nelson's day; all Halsey's engagements were decided by air power. Planes from his carriers won the battle of Leyte Gulf in October 1944 and launched the major attacks upon the home islands of Japan in July 1945. It was appropriate that the Japanese surrender should have been signed aboard his flagship, USS *Missouri*, in Tokyo Bay on 2 September 1945. He was promoted Fleet Admiral at the end of that year. Ill-health forced him to retire from the navy in 1947. W. F. Halsey and J. Bryan: *Admiral Halsey's Story* (New York, 1946); E. B. Potter: *Bull Halsey* (Annapolis, Md., 1985).

Hammarskjöld, Dag (1905–61), Secretary-General of the United Nations from 1953 until his death: born at Jönköping in Sweden, studied at Stockholm University and held high administrative posts in the labour and finance ministries of Sweden from 1936 to 1946. From 1951 to 1953 he was Sweden's Foreign Minister, heading the Swedish delegation to the United Nations Assembly in 1952. On 7 April 1953 he succeeded Trygve LIE as Secretary-General, and was re-elected in 1957. He showed strict impartiality and dignified calm during the double crisis of 1956, caused by Soviet intervention in Hungary and by British, French and Israeli collaboration in the Suez Crisis. Nevertheless he was personally criticized by KHRUSCHEV for his attitude to the successive crises in the Congo in 1960–1. It was while on a mission to seek peace in the Congo that Hammarskjöld met his death, his plane crashing near Ndola (18 September 1961). He was posthumously awarded the Nobel Peace Prize for 1961. Sithu U THANT succeeded him as Secretary-General of the United Nations. B. Urquhart: *Hammarskjöld* (1973); W. Foote: *Dag Hammarskjöld – Servant of Peace* (1962).

Hanna, Mark (Marcus Alonzo) (1837–1904), American businessman and party boss: born in Lisbon, Ohio, entering his father's grocery business in Cleveland in 1858. As he extended his commercial interests, becoming very rich, he insisted that the wisest government for America came from its businessmen and the Republican Party was the surest guarantee of a safe, businessmen's administration. By 1890 his wealth and intelligence had made Hanna the boss of the Republican Party in Ohio, as well as gaining him extensive mining and transport interests. His chosen presidential candidate from 1890 onwards was MCKINLEY, whom he saw safely returned as Governor of Ohio in 1891 and 1893. His campaign contributions to McKinley's victory in the presidential election of 1896 were without precedent at that time. Mark Hanna himself was returned to the Senate (where he sat from 1897 until his death) and he had total control of the Republican Party machine. His only miscalculation was in compromising with the Republican Party boss in New York, Thomas Platt, in 1900, accepting Platt's nominee, Theodore ROOSEVELT as McKinley's running-mate; for when McKinley was assassinated in September 1901, Roosevelt became President, thereby depriving Hanna – and, indeed, Platt – of the power enjoyed by mastery of the party during a weak presidency. Hanna's concentration on national politics also lost him control of Cleveland where a reforming Mayor, Tom Johnson (1854–1911), was in office from 1901 to 1909, rooting out Hanna's dominance. There is no suggestion Hanna himself was blatantly dishonest, but he accepted that others in political life had their price, and he did nothing to clean up the corruption which was corroding the party machine. T. Beer: *Hanna, Crane and the Mauve Decade* (New York, 1941; a single-volume reprint of three earlier books); H. Croly: *Marcus Alonso Hanna* (New York, n.d.).

Hardie, (James) Keir (1856–1915), first British socialist Member of Parliament: born in Lanarkshire, near Holytown, the son of a ship's carpenter. He sold newspapers at the age of 7 and worked down a coalmine at the age of 10, educating himself at night-school and learning public speaking from Nonconformist chapel ministers and at temperance societies, before emerging as the miners' trade union leader. He believed that the workers' political representation suffered in Britain from too close an association with middle-class Liberals and therefore in 1888 he established a Scottish Parliamentary Labour Party. Eventually, however, he was returned to Westminster as MP for a London dockland constituency, winning West Ham, South as an Independent Socialist in 1892. A year later he became founder Chairman of the Independent Labour Party, but he lost his dockland seat in the 1895 General Election. Merthyr Tydfil returned him to Parliament in 1900 and he represented this Welsh mining constituency until his death. In February 1900 he took a major role at the meeting in Farringdon Street, London, which set up a Labour Representation Committee (LRC;) and it was Keir Hardie who proposed that Labour should form a 'distinct group' in the Commons. Only one other LRC candidate was returned in that year's election, but in 1906 the LRC put up fifty candidates, and twenty-nine of them were elected. The LRC changed its name to Labour Party later that year and accepted Keir Hardie as Chairman of the parliamentary group. His religious approach, finding socialist teachings in the New Testament and delivering political addresses which were more than once reported as 'eloquent sermons', stole much of the traditional 'chapel' vote from the Liberals and helped mark off British socialism from its so-called scientific counterpart on the European mainland. Over foreign affairs he was a pacifist and strongly anti-Tsarist, denouncing the 'secret diplomacy' which led Britain into war in 1914. K. O. Morgan: *Keir Hardie* (1975); H. Pelling: *Origins of the Labour Party, 1880–1900* (rev. edn 1965).

Harding, Warren Gamaliel (1865–1923), President of the United States from 1921 to 1923: born in Morrow County, Ohio, owned and edited a newspaper in Marion, Ohio, before entering politics in the wake of 'Boss' Mark HANNA, serving as a State Senator from 1900 to 1904 and as Senator in Washington from 1915 to 1921. Deadlock at the Republican National Convention in 1920 led to Harding's nomination as a compromise candidate. He won the presidential campaign against the Wilsonian ideal of a League of Nations. His presidency was marked by isolationism in world affairs and by large-scale corruption on the part of his cronies, the 'Ohio Gang', who were involved in the notorious Teapot Dome Scandal over the leasing of naval oil reserves. There was, however, no evidence that he had profited from the shady deals of his personal friends. President Harding died suddenly on 2 August 1923, and was succeeded by Vice-President COOLIDGE. R. K. Murray: *The Harding Era, Warren G. Harding and his Administration* (Minneapolis, Minn., 1969); K. Schriftgeisser: *This Was Normalcy* (Boston, Mass., 1948).

Harrison, Benjamin (1833–1901), President of the United States from 1889 to 1893: born at North Bend, Ohio, a grandson of the ninth President, William H. Harrison (1773–1841), who had died a month after his inauguration. Benjamin Harrison's career as lawyer at Indianapolis was interrupted by the Civil War, in which he served as a Colonel in Sherman's march through Georgia. After taking a prominent part in Indiana state politics, he was sent to Washington as Senator in 1881. In 1888 he won the presidential election for the Republicans and protection against the Democrat free-trader, President CLEVELAND. His tenure of office was honest but undistinguished: the business interests in the Republican Party effectively shaped internal policy, while public attention was accorded more readily to his honey-tongued Secretary of State, the egregious BLAINE. Harrison was defeated for re-election in 1892 by Cleveland, and retired into private life. H. E. Socolofsky and

A. B. Spetter: *The Presidency of Benjamin Harrison* (Lawrence, Kans., 1987).

Hassan II (Moulay Hassan ben Mohammed) (1929–), King of Morocco: born at Rabat, the son of Sultan Sidi Mohammed ben Youssef, who became King Mohammed V in 1956, when France and Spain acknowledged Morocco's independent sovereignty. Hassan II was educated at Bordeaux University and, as Crown Prince, led the Moroccan army before acceding in March 1961. For twenty years he ruled Morocco as a royal dictator, having suspended parliamentary government after riots in Casablanca in 1965. A new constitution was offered for approval by a referendum in March 1972, as were further amendments in May 1980: government remained a royal prerogative, with the King having a right to summon and dissolve parliaments, to veto legislation and to appoint ministers. Attempts by Hassan to absorb the western (ex-Spanish) Sahara led to a constant state of war between Morocco and the *Polisario* guerrillas, which dragged on from 1976 to 1988. The burden of the war caused unrest in Morocco's principal towns during 1984, and induced Hassan to allow a General Election and appoint a civilian 'government of national unity'. But further constitutional amendments in 1992 barely trimmed his prerogatives. When parliamentary elections indicated no clear backing, either for a single party or for a coalition, King Hassan appointed a government of chosen experts, independent of the voters' wishes (November 1992). Lord Kinross and D. Hales-Gary: *Morocco* (1971).

Havel, Vaclav (1936–), Czech political leader and dramatist: born in Prague, where he completed his education at the Academy of Dramatic Art, remaining as resident writer, and occasional stage-hand, at one of the smaller theatres from 1960 until the repression of DUBCEK's liberalism by Soviet bloc intervention in 1969. Havel gained respect for his play *The Garden Party* (*Zahradni Slavnost*), first presented in 1963, but his *Conspirators* (*Spiklenci*), in 1970, was banned as subversive. He was barred from the theatre and forced to work in a brewery, helping to found the intellectual dissident movement, Charter 77. For his liberal views Havel was arrested in 1979 and imprisoned until early 1984. On his release he completed a third major play, *Temptation*, and became spokesman for the anti-communist movement, which revived in 1988–9. Although briefly imprisoned again from February until May 1989, he was prominent in the 'Civic Forum' mass protests which swept Prague in November 1989, forcing the Communist leader, Gustav Husak, to resign after twenty years of repression. Havel was elected President of Czechoslovakia by direct vote in December 1989, accepting office with considerable reluctance, as he regarded himself as a dramatist rather than a political activist. As President, he remained a strong supporter of Czech and Slovak federation and resigned in July 1992 when it became clear that Czechoslovakia would dissolve at the end of the year. He was, however, persuaded in January 1993 to serve as the non-executive President of the newly constituted Czech Republic, for a five-year term. M. Simmons: *The Reluctant President* (1991); N. Stone and E. Strouhal (eds): *Czechoslovakia; Crossroads and Crises, 1918–88* (1989).

Hawke, Robert James Lee (1929–), Australian Prime Minister: born in South Australia, at Bordertown, but received his main schooling in Perth and studied economics at the University of Western Australia before going to Brasenose College, Oxford, as a Rhodes Scholar in 1952. On returning home he became an active trade unionist in 1958 and was President of the Australian Council of Trade Unions from 1970 to 1980, when he became Labor MP for Wills, Melbourne. He was elected leader of the Labor Party in February 1983, gaining an electoral victory a few weeks later and serving as Prime Minister from 5 March 1983 until he resigned in favour of his Treasurer (finance minister) Paul KEATING, a week before Christmas, 1990. Bob Hawke's premiership restored Labor morale after the WHITLAM crisis. It was marked by deft handling of industrial disputes, as well as by mounting respect abroad for the breadth of his statesmanship. He made a more successful appeal to the voters than any earlier Labor leader in federal elections. J. Hurst: *Hawke P. M.* (Sydney, 1983); C. Johnson: *The Labor Legacy; Curtin, Chifley, Whitlam, Hawke* (1989).

Hay, John Milton (1838–1905), US Secretary of State from 1898 until his death: born at Salem, Indiana, practised law in Springfield, Illinois, and became one of the two private secretaries of Abraham LINCOLN, whom he served from 1860 to 1865. Hay, in collaboration with the other secretary, John Nicolay, later wrote a ten-volume life of Lincoln. After Lincoln's assassination Hay became a diplomat, with minor posts in Paris, Madrid and Vienna. He was Assistant Secretary of State from 1879 to 1881 and, after a spell in journalism, became ambassador in London in 1897. A few months later MCKINLEY summoned him back to Washington as Secretary of State, Theodore ROOSEVELT later confirming him in office. Hay pursued a vigorous foreign policy, marked by the establishment of the 'Open Door' principle of 1899, designed to protect American commerce in China, and by a series of treaties with Britain, Colombia and Panama which made possible American construction of a canal across the Isthmus of Panama. Hay considerably improved Anglo-American relations. When he died, on 1 July 1905, he was preparing the way for Roosevelt's successful mediation in the Russo-Japanese War. Hay was also a writer of distinction, his works on Lincoln being supplemented by a novel, a book of travel and a collection of ballads from the Midwest. T. Dennett: *John Hay; from Poetry to Politics* (New York, 1933); W. R. Thayer: *The Life and Letters of John Hay* (2 vols) (New York, 1915).

Haya de la Torre, Victor Raul (1895–1979), Peruvian populist leader for over half a century: born in the northern provincial capital, Trujillo, and studied at the University of La Libertad, where he acquired a lasting sympathy for the *indigenistas*, the 'Indian' survivors of the pre-colonial peoples. Haya deplored the political fragmentation of Latin America and in 1924 founded a populist movement, *Alianca Popular Revolucionaria Americana* (APRA), primarily to challenge self-perpetuating junta rule in Peru, but also to spread a new radicalism in Ecuador, Colombia and Venezuela. He was forced into exile, visiting Russia and France and spending two years in both England and Germany. When he arrived back in Lima in August 1931 he challenged the incumbent ruling General in a presidential election which Haya was deemed to have lost. A protracted uprising by his followers forced him once more into exile, although his influence remained considerable. By 1944 it was recognized that his populist appeal was an antidote to orthodox communism and he was allowed openly to propagate APRA ideals. But the army leaders, fearing *indigenistas*' claims on their landed property, banned the movement again in 1948, when Haya found asylum in the Colombian Embassy. A brief interlude of civilian rule (1956–62) allowed him to reenter politics. He was a presidential candidate in 1962 and 1963, but the published results showed that, on both occasions, he narrowly failed to gain the necessary one-third of the vote to take office. The faith of his followers remained unshaken: democratic elections in 1978 gave APRA a clear parliamentary majority and Haya drafted a democratic constitution. But by then he was a sick man; he died twelve months before its provisions became effective. For the underprivileged in Peru, and its neighbours, he has remained a legendary inspiration. F. B. Pike: *Haya de la Torre* (Lincoln, Nebr., 1986); R. J. Alexander: *Aprismo, the Ideas and Doctrines of V. R. Haya de la Torre* (Kent, OH., 1973).

Hayes, Rutherford Birchard (1822–93), President of the United States from 1877 to 1881: born at Delaware, Ohio, graduated from Kenyon College and Harvard Law School and practised law in Cincinnati for twelve years before enlisting in the Union Army at the outbreak of the Civil War. He was wounded on 14 September 1862 when, as a Colonel, he led two Ohio regiments at Turner's Gap on South Mountain in the preliminaries to the battle of Antietam (Sharpsburg). Hayes recovered and finished the war as an acting Major-General. After sitting in Congress as a Republican from 1865 to 1867, he served as Governor of Ohio 1867–71 and 1875–7. He was nominated Republican candidate for the presidency in 1876, a disputed election which his Democratic opponent, TILDEN, claimed to have won. Although the subsequent Electoral Commission decided in favour of Hayes, he never received popular backing and did not consider standing for a second term. His administration carried out a measure of civil service reform and placated many Southern voters by ending 'reconstruction' through the withdrawal of Federal troops from Southern state capitals. Hayes was, however, prepared to call out the army in 1877 to deal with railway strikes and his persistence in retaining the system of rewarding political services with public appointments was widely criticized. Nevertheless in general he reasserted – sometimes stubbornly and obtusely – the authority of the chief executive against a Congress which had sought to extend its prerogatives under his predecessors, Andrew JOHNSON and GRANT. A. Hoogenboom: *The Presidency of Rutherford B. Hayes* (Lawrence, Kans., 1988); H. Barnard: *Rutherford B. Hayes and his America* (1954).

Hearst, William Randolph (1863–1951), American newspaper magnate: born in San Francisco, the son of Senator George Hearst (1820–91) who had founded a newspaper for the West Coast, *The Examiner*. After graduating from Harvard in 1885, the younger Hearst managed *The Examiner*, beginning to experiment in sensational journalism, with banner headlines and human interest stories. This trend he developed more fully when he took over the New York *Journal* in 1895, soon trebling its circulation and becoming head of a chain of newspapers and periodicals. Rivalry with Joseph Pulitzer's equally flamboyant New York *World* began with competition for the services of the cartoonist, Outcault, whose comicstrip character 'The Yellow Kid', was extremely popular with readers. The Hearst–Pulitzer conflict over this comic strip induced other newspaper owners to describe all sensationalist news coverage as 'yellow journalism'. Hearst increased the circulation of his papers by whipping up demands for war with Spain in 1898. In later years he became isolationist, and strongly opposed to seeing 'American boys being dragged into war to save England'. The Hearst Press, in general, regarded the problems of the Pacific as of greater importance to America than what happened in Europe. Hearst's irresponsible craving for sensationalism set a poor example to journalists – and in his last years to 'media men' – on both sides of the Atlantic. W. A. Swanberg: *Citizen Hearst* (1962); J. Robinson: *The Hearsts, an American Dynasty* (Newark, N.J., 1991).

Heath, Edward Richard George (1916–), British Prime Minister, 1970–4: born in Broadstairs, Kent, educated at Chatham House School, Ramsgate, and at Balliol College, Oxford. He served in the artillery from 1940 to 1946 and remained with the territorials until 1951, resigning with the rank of Lieutenant-Colonel. He was returned as Conservative MP for Bexley in 1950 and was re-elected on twelve occasions, becoming in 1992 'Father of the House', the longest serving Member. From 1955 to 1959 he was Chief Party Whip, entering the Cabinet as Minister of Labour in 1959 and serving from 1960 to 1963 as Lord Privy Seal with responsibility for conducting the negotiations which sought to secure Britain's entry into the European Community. Under DOUGLAS-HOME he was in charge of trade and industry. He was elected party leader in July 1965 and formed a government when the Conservatives won the General Election of June 1970. As Prime Minister he successfully carried Britain into the Common Market, but his government suffered from chronic disputes with the trade unions which culminated in a miners' 'work-to-rule' and a threatened miners' strike. Heath's double answer of putting industry on a three-day week and of seeking popular support by calling a General Election proved a failure. The election, held on 28 February 1974, did not give him a majority and he resigned. A second General Election the following 10 October cost his party more seats. Heath sought re-election as party leader on 11 February 1975, but was defeated by his former Minister of Education, Mrs THATCHER. When the Conservatives returned to power in May 1979 he remained outside the government and became a consistent critic of 'Thatcherism' and the anti-European prejudice of right-wing Tories. While out of office he wrote books on four of his 'joys for life': sailing (1975); music (1977); travel (1977), and carols (1977). He was winner of the Sydney to Hobart yacht race in the year before he became Prime Minister and he long continued to conduct orchestras in occasional concerts and to play the organ. During the Gulf Crisis he undertook a personal mission to Baghdad (October 1990) and secured the release of sixty-nine hostages. He became a Knight of the Garter in 1992. E. Heath: *Old World, New Horizons* (1970); J. Campbell: *Edward Heath, a Biography* (1994).

Herter, Christian Archibald (1895–1966), US Secretary of State from 1959 to 1961: born in Paris, his parents being artists and his grandfather an immigrant architect from Stuttgart who became rich on the new plutocracy's desire for ornate mansions. Christian Herter graduated from Harvard in 1915, became a diplomat, and attended the Paris Peace Conference in 1919, subsequently serving with the Hoover Relief Administration. From 1924 to 1936 he was a much respected Boston journalist. He was a Congressman from 1944 to 1953, gaining the reputation of being a liberal Republican, and was then for four years Governor of Massachusetts before becoming Under-Secretary of State to DULLES in 1957. He had known and respected Dulles since 1919, even though the two men were not always in agreement, and he was a natural successor to the ailing Dulles, taking over the State Department on 18 April 1959. In twenty-one months as Secretary of State Herter considerably improved Anglo-American relations, abandoning the brinkmanship cold war policy of his predecessor in favour of careful and cautious diplomacy by conference. G. R. Noble: *Christian Herter* (New York, 1970).

Hertzog, James Barry Munnik (1866–1942), South African Prime Minister from 1924 to 1939: born at Wellington in Cape Colony, becoming a farmer. As a Boer General in 1900 he twice commanded columns seeking to cross the

Orange River and penetrate into Cape Colony. His hostility towards Britain was more lasting than the sentiments of BOTHA and SMUTS. Although he served under Botha as Minister of Justice from 1910 to 1912, he founded the South African National Party in 1913 and opposed South African involvement in the First World War and later in the League of Nations. His National Party governed the Union from 1924 to 1929 in an uneasy coalition with the South African Labour Party, General Hertzog proving a wiser statesman than his critics had anticipated. His party never had the strength to impose the full policy of racial segregation outlined in its electoral programmes, and from 1933 to 1939 he was forced to share power with Smuts' United Party, a more liberal body. Hertzog was opposed to South Africa's entry into the Second World War, an issue that caused his downfall. Within his own party his position was undermined by his former colleague, Dr MALAN, a firm believer in apartheid. Hertzog resigned the premiership on 4 September 1939, retiring from politics a year later. L. E. Neame: *General Hertzog* (1930); T. R. H. Davenport: *South Africa, a Modern History* (rev. edn Cambridge 1986).

Herzl, Theodor (1860–1904), Hungarian founder of modern Zionism: born in Budapest, graduating with a doctorate in law at Vienna in 1884. He became a freelance writer, although employed by the Viennese newspaper *Neuen Freien Presse* from 1891 until his death, serving for four years as correspondent in Paris and, after 1895, as literary editor. Herzl was dismayed at the extent of anti-Semitism in Paris, and especially at the condemnation of DREYFUS. In 1896 he published in Leipzig and Vienna his major work, *Der Judenstaat*, subtitled 'A Modern Solution of the Jewish Question'. He proposed to develop further the ideas of 'auto-emancipation' for Europe's Jews, first suggested by Leo Pinsker in Berlin in 1882: these sought a national home in Palestine. Herzl convened the first specifically Zionist Congress at Basle in Switzerland in 1897, and secured the backing of some of the great Jewish banking-houses. A year later, when Kaiser WILLIAM II was making a much publicized visit to the Holy Land, Herzl and four other Zionists travelled from Vienna to the East seeking his support. The Kaiser received Herzl twice in audience, not unsympathetically, at Constantinople on 19 October 1898 and outside Jerusalem nine days later, but anti-Semites in his entourage effectively countered Herzl's influence. In 1901 Herzl was received by Sultan ABDUL HAMID, titular sovereign of Palestine, but failed to win his support, nor did Herzl have any success with POPE PIUS X in Rome three years later. His ideas were, however, taken up enthusiastically by the persecuted Jews of Russia when he visited Vilna in 1903. The British authorities – especially Joseph CHAMBERLAIN – responded to Herzl's vigorous campaign by a tentative plan (in July 1902) for an autonomous Jewish settlement on Egyptian territory in Sinai, but the project was opposed by the British High Commissioner in Cairo, Lord CROMER. Herzl's alternative suggestion of experimental settlements in Cyprus or Uganda came to nothing. The physical strain of Herzl's activities wore down his health: he died, exhausted at 44, on 3 July 1904 at Edlach, near Reichenau, in Lower Austria. Others took up his work, notably Chaim WEIZMANN. M. Lowenthal (ed.): *Diaries of Theodor Herzl* (1938); I. Friedman: *Germany, Turkey and Zionism* (1977); I. Cohen: *A Short History of Zionism* (1951).

Hess, Rudolf (1894–1987), deputy leader of Nazi Party from 1934 to 1941: born at Alexandria, served in the Bavarian infantry at Ypres in 1915, later being commissioned in the German air corps. In 1919 he entered Munich University, meeting the then unknown HITLER soon afterwards. From 1920 to 1931 he was Hitler's political secretary, accompanying him to prison at Landsberg after the failure of the Munich *Putsch* and assisting him to write *Mein Kampf* (in which he is the only one of the later Nazi leaders commended by name). In December 1932 he was given responsibility for co-ordinating Nazi Party activities throughout Germany; and in the last days of the following year he entered Hitler's Cabinet and was formally recognized as the party's deputy leader. On the eve of war in 1939 he became, by decree, the third-ranking figure in Germany, immediately behind Hitler and GOERING. On 10 May 1941 he flew in a Messerchmidt 110 from Augsburg to southern Scotland where he landed by parachute. This mission, undertaken on his own initiative, appears to have been intended to arrange a negotiated peace. Hitler disowned him, maintaining that he was mad, while the British interned him as a prisoner-of-war. He was sentenced to life imprisonment as a major war criminal at Nuremberg in September 1946 and remained thereafter in Spandau Prison, West Berlin, being from 1966 onwards its sole detainee. British, American and French proposals for his release were rejected by the Soviet authorities who, by treaty, possessed joint rights with their former allies to control the prison. Hess killed himself in the grounds of Spandau on 17 August 1987. P. Padfield: *Hess, the Führer's Disciple* (1993); J. Douglas-Hamilton: *Motive for a Mission; the Story Behind Hess's Flight* (1971); J. Fishman: *The Seven Men of Spandau* (New York, 1954).

Himmler, Heinrich (1900–1945), German Nazi police chief from 1934 to 1945: born in Munich, his father being a Catholic schoolmaster. He joined a Bavarian regiment in 1918 but was too young to fight at the Front. Disillusionment with the uncertainties of poultry farming induced him to join the Nazi Party in 1923. He was a fanatical believer in the superior qualities of the so-called Aryan race and found satisfaction in organizing HITLER's personal bodyguard. In April 1934 he became commander of the secret security police in Prussia, taking over responsibility for the Gestapo in the whole of Germany from 1936 onwards. The systematic genocide practised in the concentration camps originated in his orders. From 1943 to 1945 he was Minister of the Interior, loyal to Hitler until the last weeks of the war when he sought, through the mediation of Count BERNADOTTE, to secure a separate peace in the West so as to check the Russian advance into Europe. He was discovered in hiding by British troops a fortnight after Germany's surrender. A few days later (27 May 1945) he swallowed a poison capsule and thus frustrated the Allied intention to put him on trial as a major war criminal. P. Padfield: *Himmler, Reichsführer SS* (1990); R. Manvell: *Heinrich Himmler* (1965); K. D. Bracher: *The German Dictatorship* (1970); J. Noakes and G. Pridham: *Nazism, a Documentary Reader*, Vol. 3, *Foreign Policy, War and Racial Extermination* (Exeter, 1988).

Hindenburg, Paul von Beneckendorff und von (1847–1934), German Field Marshal in the First World War and President from 1925 until his death: born in Posen (Poznan), gained decorations for bravery as a junior officer in the Prussian army against Austria in 1866 and against France in 1870, being present when the German Empire was proclaimed at Versailles, 18 January 1871. He was retired from the army as a General in 1911, recalled to take over the Eighth Army in East Prussia on 22 August 1914 and, in partnership with LUDENDORFF, gained within a few weeks major victories over the Russians in the battles known as Tannenberg and the Masurian Lakes. From November 1914 until 1916 Hindenburg (promoted to the rank of Field

Marshal) and General Ludendorff controlled the Eastern Front, advancing in depth across the Polish plain. In August 1916 Hindenburg became Chief of the Greater German General Staff, again with Ludendorff as his partner. The two soldiers were the real masters of Germany until the collapse of November 1918; they imposed the peace of Brest-Litovsk on Russia, and came close to defeating the Western Allies in France. On 9 November 1918 Hindenburg was forced to recommend Kaiser WILLIAM II to abdicate and seek asylum in Holland. Hindenburg did not leave the army until July 1919, seriously considering a rejection of the peace terms which were later embodied in the Treaty of Versailles. In April 1925 he narrowly won the election for presidency of the Republic, although he insisted he was a monarchist at heart and by conviction. His influence on politics from 1925 was slight, his mind frequently becoming clouded by 1932; but ultimately he was responsible for summoning HITLER to assume the chancellorship in 1933. He died, still a revered idol of the German people, on 2 August 1934, and was buried on the battlefield of Tannenberg. P. von Hindenburg: *Out of My Life* (1920); J. W. Wheeler-Bennett: *Hindenburg, the Wooden Titan* (rev. edn 1967); A. Dorpalen: *Hindenburg and the Weimar Republic* (Princeton, N.J., 1964); G. A. Craig: *The Politics of the Prussian Army, 1640–1945* (Oxford, 1955).

Hirohito (1901–89), ruler of Japan as Regent and Emperor for sixty-eight years: born in Tokyo, eldest son of Emperor Yoshihito (1897–1926, acceded in 1921). As Crown Prince, Hirohito spent six months in 1921 in the West, becoming the first Japanese prince to visit Europe or the United States. He was appointed Regent soon after his return home, the first crisis confronting him being the devastation caused by the earthquake of 1 September 1923, which destroyed Yokohama and two-thirds of Tokyo. Fifteen months later he survived an assassination plot, finally succeeding to the throne on 25 December 1926. While technically retaining the full rights of sovereignty guaranteed to the 'Imperial Son of Heaven of Great Japan' by the 1889 Constitution, Hirohito in practice remained aloof from politics, content to indulge his interests in botany and marine biology. He accepted the expansionist policies of his generals in the 1930s and appointed General TOJO as Prime Minister in October 1941, even though he did not approve of his intention of establishing Japanese mastery over Greater Asia by war. Hirohito remained in Tokyo, despite American air raids, until in 1945 he used his imperial sovereignty to command his army and navy to accept unconditional surrender. General MACARTHUR, as Allied proconsul in Japan, rejected suggestions that Emperor Hirohito should be tried for war crimes. The new Constitution of Japan, promulgated in October 1946, retained the monarchy, the Emperor being recognized as 'symbol of state and of the unity of the people' but deprived of 'powers related to government'. Hirohito duly adapted himself to this new democratic role, shedding divinity as readily as he shed military uniform: by 1964 he was able to take a benevolent interest in the Tokyo Olympic Games; and in 1971 Emperor Hirohito and Empress Nagako were welcomed on state visits to Washington and London: uniquely, in 1971, he was reinstated as an extra Knight of the Garter. His health gave way in September 1988 and his sovereign powers were exercised by Crown Prince Akihito (1933–), who acceded on his father's death on 7 January 1989. S. S. Large: *Emperor Hirohito and Showa Japan* (1992); J. Dower: *Japan in War and Peace* (1995); E. Behr: *Hirohito, Behind the Myth* (1989); P. Manning: *Hirohito, the War Years* (New York, 1980).

Hiss, Alger (1904–93), US State Department official: born in Baltimore, graduated from Harvard Law School and practised as a lawyer before entering the State Department. He held important advisory posts during the war and was present at the Yalta Conference of 1945. Two years later he became President of the Carnegie Endowment for International Peace. A confessed former communist, Whittaker Chambers, asserted in August 1948 that Hiss had handed over to him secret documents from the State Department. Hiss denied this accusation, also asserting he had not himself been a communist. The Un-American Activities Committee of Senator MCCARTHY campaigned vigorously to 'expose' Hiss, who was a friend and former colleague of Secretary of State ACHESON. Hiss was indicted by a New York grand jury for perjury; and, after two trials, was found guilty in January 1950 and sentenced to five years' imprisonment. During the ensuing decade Hiss was a symbolic figure to intellectuals and philistines alike, a latter-day American DREYFUS, his reputation assailed by Richard NIXON and defended by the Democrat, Adlai STEVENSON. A. Hiss: *Recollections of a Life* (New York, 1983); A. Cooke: *A Generation on Trial; USA v Alger Hiss* (1950).

Hitler, Adolf (1889–1945), German Chancellor from 1933 to 1945: born at Braunau-on-the-Inn, Austria. He lived in poverty in Vienna from 1909 to 1913 and in 1914 enlisted in a Bavarian infantry regiment, subsequently fighting in France and Flanders throughout the war, receiving the Iron Cross (first and second class), suffering temporary blindness from a British gas attack and ending the war with the rank of Corporal. From September 1919 he built up a small political group in Munich, the 'National Socialist German Workers' Party', nicknamed the 'Nazis'. The movement became anti-Semitic and nationalistic, blaming Germany's ills on the Treaty of Versailles. Hitler, who had some skill in demagogic oratory, planned to seize power in Munich in October 1923 and march from Bavaria on Berlin. In this abortive *Putsch* he was assisted by the distinguished General LUDENDORFF and the air ace, Hermann GOERING. Hitler was arrested, became a national figure because of the publicity given to his trial, and served thirteen months in Landsberg Prison where he began to write his political testament, *Mein Kampf*.

Upon his release in December 1924, Hitler resumed his attempt to build up the Nazi Party and in the 1928 elections won twelve seats to the Reichstag, with 809,000 votes. The economic slump played into Hitler's hands, for in the elections of September 1930 the Nazis polled nearly six-and-a-half million votes and returned 107 deputies. Some of this success came from Hitler's remarkable ability to exploit the fears and grievances of the German people, finding scapegoats in politicians who had accepted the Versailles treaty, in the League of Nations, and in Germany's Jewish minority. Early in 1933, HINDENBURG was persuaded by PAPEN and other conservative politicians that, if he appointed the demagogic Hitler as Chancellor, they would control him, as he had no experience of government. But within a month of becoming Chancellor (on 30 January 1933) Hitler used allegations of a communist conspiracy to secure a presidential decree permitting arrest on suspicion and imprisonment without trial, and on 23 March 1933 an Enabling Act granted Hitler dictatorial powers for an initial period of four years. Hitler eliminated possible rivals within his own party and other potential opponents in what he himself called the 'night of the long knives' on 30 June 1934, when about a hundred people were summarily executed.

On President Hindenburg's death (2 August 1934) Hitler was proclaimed 'Leader of the German Reich', assuming the role of Head of State and Supreme

Commander of the armed forces, thus completing the Nazi revolution. Political repression within Germany was accompanied by economic autarky, a major public works programme and rapid rearmament. Foreign policy successes were gained by exploiting friction between possible enemies, by magnifying German resentment at national 'injustices' so as to seek appeasement, and by risking a war which Hitler assumed Germany's former enemies would be unwilling to begin. He secured the military reoccupation of the Rhineland in March 1936, the union of Austria with Germany in March 1938, and the destruction of Czechoslovakia by the Munich Agreement of September 1938 and by the entry of his army into Prague in March 1939. A temporary agreement with Stalin – the Nazi–Soviet Pact negotiated by his Foreign Minister, von RIBBENTROP, in August 1939 – enabled Hitler to partition Poland in September 1939 and then free his army to overrun north western Europe and defeat France in 1940. The German army's inability to gain a similar rapid victory against Soviet Russia in 1941 convinced Hitler of the incompetence of his Generals, and on 19 December 1941 the Corporal of the First World War became operational commander in the field. He failed to understand the need for retreat and tactical regrouping, losing his Sixth Army at Stalingrad in January 1943 because he allowed the general strategy of the war to be overshadowed in his mind by matters of political prestige until it was too late to save his troops.

Hitler survived an assassination attempt by dissident officers at his headquarters in East Prussia on 20 July 1944. In the last days of the war, cut off in the bunker shelter of his Berlin chancellery, he married his companion of many years, Eva Braun: she died by poisoning herself on the following afternoon, Hitler shooting himself a few minutes later (30 April 1945). A. Bullock: *Hitler and Stalin: Parallel Lives* (1991), *Hitler, a Study in Tyranny* (rev. edn 1964); J. Fest: *Hitler* (1974); J. Toland: *Adolf Hitler* (New York, 1976); H. Trevor-Roper (ed.): *Hitler's Table Talk, 1940–1944* (1953).

Ho Chi Minh (1890–1969), Vietnamese Communist leader from 1943 to 1969: born at Kiemlien, Assam, and known originally as Nguyen Tat Thanh, working under that name in the kitchens of the Carlton Hotel, London, during the First World War. From 1918 to 1922 he was in France, where he became a founder-member of the French Communist Party and wrote articles for publications of the Left, signing himself 'Nguyen the Patriot'. He spent the years 1922–5 in Moscow, visited China with a Bolshevik delegation, and was arrested in Hong Kong on a charge of sedition in 1930 but released on appeal to the Privy Council. After an unsuccessful conspiracy in Hanoi and Saigon in 1940, he took refuge in southern China where he was imprisoned for many months by CHIANG KAI-SHEK. In 1943 Ho returned to northern Indo-China, where he organized the Viet Minh movement of Communist guerrillas against the Japanese occupation troops. His notoriety as Nguyen now led him to assume the *nom de guerre* 'Ho Chi Minh', meaning 'Ho, the Seeker after Light'. The Japanese collapse in September 1945 left Ho's forces as temporary masters both in Hanoi and Saigon and he proclaimed the Democratic Republic of Vietnam. The French, returning to Indo-China, reasserted colonial rule and Ho called on the Vietnamese to wage a fresh war of liberation. The victory of General GIAP at Dien Bien Phu in 1954 and the subsequent international conference at Geneva recognized Ho's control of North Vietnam. From 1963 he encouraged Communist resistance in South Vietnam, sending supplies from Hanoi through jungle routes which later became famous as the 'Ho Chi Minh Trail'. While seeking to impose land reforms and a Soviet-style Five Year Plan in North Vietnam, Ho was increasingly committing his troops to large-scale operations in the South, and from August 1964 onwards North Vietnam was subjected to American bombing. His last positive act of policy was to reject American peace proposals, put forward at the end of July 1969. He died, a hero idolized by his people, on 3 September 1969. Ho Chi Minh: *Selected Writings, 1920–1969* (Hanoi, 1977); J. Lacouture: *Ho Chi Minh* (1969); T. Hodgkin: *Vietnam, the Revolutionary Path* (1981).

Holland, Sidney George (1893–1961), New Zealand Prime Minister: born in Greendale, studied and practised engineering and was a company director in Canterbury when he entered Parliament in 1935. He became leader of the Opposition in 1940, building up the strength of his conservative National Party, enabling him to succeed FRASER as Prime Minister in December 1949. The National Party government attacked trade union power, provoking a bitter twenty-three-week strike in 1951 which rallied middle-class support so strongly behind Holland that he called a snap General Election on 11 July and gained a comfortable majority. Over the following six years he ended government controls imposed by Labour and built up a free market economy. He was knighted in 1957, but retired through ill-health in September 1957, with HOLYOAKE succeeding him. G. W. Rice (ed.): *The Oxford History of New Zealand* (2nd edn Auckland, 1992); K. Sinclair: *History of New Zealand* (rev. edn 1980).

Holmes, Oliver Wendell II (1841–1935), American lawyer, Associate Justice of the US Supreme Court from 1902 to 1932: born at Boston, the son of Oliver Wendell Holmes I (1809–94), the distinguished writer and physician. He graduated from Harvard Law School, served throughout the Civil War with the Twentieth Massachusetts, and was wounded on the James River and at Antietam. Subsequently he practised law at Boston and was a professor at Harvard, as well as sitting as a judge in the Massachusetts State Supreme Court, over which he presided from 1899 to 1902. When Theodore ROOSEVELT appointed him to the US Supreme Court in 1902 he was already widely respected on both sides of the Atlantic for his philosophy of law as a constantly changing entity, shaped by experience and not bound by unalterable axioms. This pragmatism Holmes first preached in his *The Common Law* (1881) and it formed a basis for the succession of judgments which he gave in his thirty years in the Supreme Court at Washington. Originally Holmes' judgments, consistently supporting human rights, tended to be minority opinions. His most famous judgment, however, was supported by all the justices: in 1919, ruling in the case of C. T. Schenck, a socialist who had circulated seditious writings to army recruits, Holmes said that guarantees of free speech embodied in the constitution should be waived only if the community as a whole were faced by 'a clear and present danger', such as foreign war. Holmes' proud role of aloof and impartial dissenter helped mould the judicial character of later members of the Supreme Court, notably FRANKFURTER. M. de W. Howe: *Justice Oliver Wendell Holmes; the Shaping Years 1841–1870* (Cambridge, MA, 1957); F. Frankfurter: *Mr Justice Holmes and the Supreme Court* (Cambridge, Mass., 1938).

Holstein, Baron Friedrich von (1837–1909), senior counsellor at the German Foreign Ministry, 1876–1906: born, an only son to elderly parents, at Schwed, in Brandenburg. He spent a lonely childhood on the family estate of Trepenow with private tutors, his education improved by foreign travel and completed by law studies at Berlin University. In

1861 he became personal attaché in St Petersburg to BISMARCK, an occasional visitor to Trepenow. Apart from brief postings to Brazil and Paris, Holstein remained close to Bismarck throughout his chancellorship and in May 1876 began thirty years' service as policy adviser in the Foreign Ministry. After the Chancellor's fall in 1890 his successors turned to Holstein, believing that he alone knew how the Bismarckian alliance system worked. Holstein, however, never understood its subtleties: he let Russo-German links weaken, while failing to improve relations with Britain as he hoped. When confronted in 1904 by the Anglo-French entente, Holstein advocated a German forward policy in Morocco, to show the French – as he thought – that they could not rely on British backing. This disastrous advice discredited him and an offer of resignation in March 1906 was accepted. Historians once represented Holstein as the 'evil genius' of WILLIAM II: in fact, the Kaiser met him only once (in November 1904), after being long puzzled by the complexities of his memoranda. But Holstein was 'the mystery man of the Wilhelmstrasse', a consultant who for twenty years had a private room opening into the Foreign Minister's personal office. Socially he remained a recluse, completely absorbed in statecraft, and intensely suspicious of ministers or diplomats whose careers he had not personally advanced. N. Rich and M. H. Fisher (eds): *The Holstein Papers* (4 vols) (Cambridge, 1955–63); N. Rich: *Friedrich von Holstein* (2 vols) (Cambridge, 1965).

Holt, Harold (1906–67), Australian Prime Minister: born in Sydney, practised as a solicitor and in 1935 entered Parliament as a member of the United Australia Party (renamed Liberal in 1945). Holt was deputy leader to MENZIES from 1956 until 20 January 1966, when he succeeded him as head of the government. Holt's premiership was marked by enthusiastic support of American policy over Vietnam, with a rapid – and much criticized – rise in the size of the Australian contingent serving in the war zone. On 17 December 1967 Holt went swimming from a beach at Portsea, Victoria. He was never seen again and is presumed to have drowned. Z. K. Holt: *My Life and Harry: an Autobiography* (Melbourne, 1968); G. Davis and P. Weller: *Menzies to Keating: the Development of the Australian Premiership* (Carlton, Victoria, 1992).

Holyoake, Keith Jacka (1904–83), New Zealand Prime Minister and Governor-General: born, a farmer's son, at Pahiatu, North Island. Throughout his life Holyoake showed particular concern for the farming community. He was a Nationalist (conservative) MP from 1932 to 1972, Minister of Agriculture 1949–57, and succeeded HOLLAND as Prime Minister in September 1957. Twelve weeks later, however, Holyoake lost a General Election; not until December 1960 did he take office with a comfortable parliamentary majority, confirmed by further electoral victories in 1963, 1966 and 1969. In anticipation of Britain's entry into the EEC he negotiated terms by which the Community recognized the Dominion's special status as a supplier of dairy produce and frozen meat to the United Kingdom; his government also improved trade links with Australia. He vigorously championed Commonwealth multiracialism, especially in southern Africa. On retirement in February 1972 he was knighted. Five years later he became the first former premier to serve as Governor-General (1977–80). G. W. Rice (ed.): *The Oxford History of New Zealand* (2nd edn Auckland, 1992); K. Sinclair: *History of New Zealand* (rev. edn 1980).

Home, Earl of: see *Douglas-Home*.

Honecker, Erich (1912–94), last Communist leader of East Germany: born at

Neunkirchen, Saarland, became a building labourer, specializing in slating and tiling and joined the German Communist Party in 1929, organizing the anti-HITLER Youth Movement. From 1937 until 1945 he was imprisoned by the Nazis. On his release by the Russians he settled in East Germany and from 1949 to 1958 built up the Youth Movement of the German Democratic Republic (DDR). He succeeded ULBRICHT as First Secretary of the ruling party in May 1971 and as head of state of the DDR in October 1976. Honecker improved relations with the West and raised East Germany's industrial output, though it remained low compared with West Germany. At a meeting with Chancellor KOHL in September 1987 he agreed that 'war must never start again on German soil'. Honecker's health began to fail in 1989, at a time of mounting public protest across the DDR at standards of living. He resigned office in October 1989, later entering a Soviet hospital for treatment for liver cancer. In July 1992 he was extradited to Germany to face charges of manslaughter over the deaths of thirteen people who had sought escape from the DDR. His trial opened four months later but was abandoned because of his frailty. He joined his wife and daughter in Chile, where he died on 29 May 1994. E. Honecker: *Committed to Peace, Socialism and Solidarity* (Dresden, 1987); D. Childs: *Honecker's Germany* (1985).

Hoover, Herbert Clark (1874–1964), President of the United States from 1929 to 1933: born at West Branch in Iowa, brought up strictly in a Quaker family, studied engineering at Stanford University, and by the age of 40 had made a small fortune as a mining engineer in Nevada, Australia and the Far East. He was Chairman of the US Commission for Relief in Belgium, established in 1915, and later served as US Food Administrator (1917–19) before renewing his famine relief work in central Europe and Russia. President HARDING appointed him Secretary of Commerce in 1921 and he evolved a system which seemed to permit traditional capitalist competition within a planned economy, recommended rather than imposed by federal authority. This liberal Republicanism triumphed at the Party Convention in 1928 and he won a convincing electoral victory over the Democrat, Alfred E. SMITH. Soon after Hoover's inauguration the economy was weakened by a recession, which culminated in the Wall Street Crash in the last week of October 1929. Hoover declined to seek a federal remedy for what he regarded as a natural economic phenomenon, although he later agreed to a year's moratorium on inter-governmental debts so as to ease the situation in Europe. He stood for re-election in 1932 but was beaten by Franklin ROOSEVELT. Hoover was a statesman of integrity and genuine humanitarian ideals, unfortunate in the timing of his presidency. In his seventies he presided over a commission established by Congress to report on reorganization of the federal executive (1947–9); he recommended clearer definition of departmental responsibilities and greater precision of duties at the White House. Later Presidents have sometimes unwisely ignored the Hoover Commissions's recommendations. A second congressional commission, chaired by Hoover from 1953 to 1955, recommended a diminution of federal responsibility for public works, an issue which raised more controversy than the earlier report. H. Hoover: *Memoirs* (3 vols) (New York, 1951–2); G. Nash: *A Life of Herbert Hoover* (1993).

Hoover, J. Edgar (1895–1972), American lawyer, head of the Federal Bureau of Investigation for forty-eight years: born in Washington, DC, graduated in law from George Washington University in 1916 and served in the Justice Department from 1919 onwards. In 1924 he was appointed Director of the Federal Bureau of Investigation (FBI), which had been established as a minor ancillary division of the Justice Department in 1908. Within ten years Hoover created one of the three finest crime detection agencies in the world, combating in particular the gangster warfare encouraged by Prohibition. He supervised the reorganization of the FBI in 1933, when its powers were extended so as to meet the increasing threat of inter-state crime. During the Second World War Hoover was responsible for internal security, including safeguards against sabotage and treason. From 1946 onwards his methods of investigation were criticized by liberals who increasingly deplored his outspoken conservatism against the civil rights movement and publicly demonstrative forms of dissent, but he gave no indication of any wish to resign, dying in office in his seventy-seventh year. Later evidence suggests that curious sexual practices may have inclined Edgar Hoover to perpetuate personal vendettas against anyone whom a warped mind rated as dangerously liberal. A. Summers: *Official and Confidential; the Secret Life of J. Edgar Hoover* (1992); C. Gentry: *J. Edgar Hoover; the Man and the Secrets* (New York, 1991); J. R. Nash: *Citizen Hoover* (Chicago, 1972).

Hopkins, Harry Lloyd (1890–1946), American presidential adviser from 1933 to 1945: born at Sioux City, Iowa, the son of an itinerant harness-maker. He was educated at Grinnel College, Iowa, subsequently undertaking social welfare work in New York, where he met Governor Franklin ROOSEVELT in 1931. He was appointed Director of the Works Progress Administration in 1935, serving, as Secretary of Commerce from 1938 to 1940. In 1937 he underwent surgery for cancer of the stomach. His health remained poor and he showed a total lack of political ambition. This quality won him the friendship of Roosevelt. From 1940 onwards he was Roosevelt's closest aide, living in the White House when not on wartime missions to London and Moscow or spending weeks in hospital. Hopkins arranged the first meetings of the President and Winston CHURCHILL, who admired Hopkins' blunt efficiency. As well as advising Roosevelt at the Conferences of Casablanca, Teheran and Yalta, Hopkins was the administrator of Lend-Lease from 1941 onwards. He undertook one mission to Moscow for President TRUMAN, in May 1945, but was too ill to attend the Potsdam Conference and retired from public life on 2 July 1945. He died on 29 January 1946 from haemochromatosis. No other emissary showed such diplomatic skill during the war years in keeping Britain, the Soviet Union and America in partnership. R. E. Sherwood: *The White House Papers of Harry L. Hopkins* (2 vols) (1948); R. Dallek: *Franklin D. Roosevelt and American Foreign Policy 1932–1945* (New York, 1979).

Horthy de Nagybanya, Nicholas (1868–1957), Hungarian Regent from 1920 to 1944: born at Kenderes, a member of the Protestant landed gentry. He entered the Imperial-and-Royal Navy and was personal naval aide-de-camp to FRANCIS JOSEPH from 1911 to 1913, distinguishing himself in action in the Otranto Straits in 1917 and serving as last Commander-in-Chief of the Austro-Hungarian fleet in 1918. Admiral Horthy organized the counter-revolution to the first Hungarian Soviet, entering Budapest in triumph in November 1919. Hungary was thereafter considered a parliamentary monarchy with a vacant throne, the royal functions being exercised by a Regent. Horthy was elected Regent on 1 March 1920. On two occasions in 1921 the last Habsburg Emperor-King, CHARLES, secretly returned to Hungary and claimed his throne, but the Regent thought the moment politically inopportune and remained as sovereign for twenty-four years. In home affairs

Horthy was a conservative upholder of the established social order, inclined towards right-wing dictatorship and formally freeing the Regent from responsibility to parliament by a law passed in July 1937. Abroad Horthy sought the return of Hungary's lost lands, pressing for international revision of the Treaty of Trianon of 1920. With German collaboration, Horthy's Hungary recovered parts of Slovakia and districts ceded to Romania and Yugoslavia, but Horthy personally detested and distrusted HITLER. The Regent was induced to declare war on the Soviet Union in 1941 but he kept in touch secretly with Britain and the United States. On 15 October 1944 Horthy's attempt to conclude an armistice was frustrated by the Germans and by Hungarian right-wing fanatics. Horthy himself was arrested and imprisoned by the Germans. After the war the Americans declined to hand over Horthy to communist Hungary or to Yugoslavia for trial as a war criminal. He was released in 1948 and settled in Portugal, where he died on 9 February 1957. His body was returned to Hungary in 1993, for burial at Kenderes, in an official ceremony which was marked by some show of state. N. Horthy: *Memoirs* (1956); M. Szinai and L. Szucs (eds): *The Confidential Papers of Admiral Horthy* (Wellingborough, 1966); C. A. Macartney: *October Fifteenth, a History of Modern Hungary 1929–45* (2 vols) (Edinburgh, 1957).

Houmeini, Ayatollah Ruholla: see *Khomeini*.

House, Edward Mandell (1858–1938), retired American Colonel who was closest adviser to President WILSON from 1913 to 1919: born in Houston, Texas, educated in Bath, England and New Haven, Connecticut, before entering Cornell University. His education there was cut short by the death of his father, which caused him to return to Texas to manage his family's cotton plantations. He became respected in Texan state politics as 'the silent man'. He played an important part in swinging the Democratic Party Convention to support of Wilson in 1912, subsequently becoming the President's 'alter ego' (to use Wilson's own description). In 1913–14 Wilson used House as his agent in discussion with the 'captains of industry' and prominent bankers. When war came to Europe the President sent Colonel House on special missions as his personal representative to the belligerent capitals in 1914 and again in 1915 and 1916. House thus acquired far greater understanding of European politics than Wilson ever enjoyed. In the winter of 1917–18 House returned to Europe as American representative at inter-Allied conferences in Paris and Versailles. He was also the President's right-hand man at the Paris Peace Conference of 1919, a gathering which House tried to prevent Wilson from attending in person as he thought his prestige would suffer from the rough-and-tumble exchanges of peace-making. Wilson obstinately ignored House's advice on several occasions during the Conference, even though House was a member of the Mandates Commission. He helped Wilson draft the covenant of the League of Nations, but the President refused to consult him over political questions after his return from Paris to Washington. House retired into political life in Texas, where his influence helped secure nomination for Franklin ROOSEVELT in 1932. Throughout his first administration Roosevelt frequently sought the advice of House, as an elder statesman with considerable knowledge of world affairs. C. S. Seymour (ed.): *The Intimate Papers of Colonel House* (4 vols) (1926–8); A. J. Mayer: *The Policy and Diplomacy of Peacemaking* (1968); T. A. Bailey: *Woodrow Wilson and the Long Peace* (New York, 1944).

Hoxha, Enver (1908–85), leader of Communist Albania for forty years: born at Gjirokaster (Argyrokastron), near the Greek border, fled from the rule of King ZOG into exile, returning secretly from France in 1936, having joined the French Communist Party. He became a schoolmaster at Korce, in the mountains of south eastern Albania, organizing a communist resistance movement which fought pitched battles against the Germans and their puppet Albanian regime in the winter of 1943–4. In May 1944 a provisional government, headed by General Enver Hoxha, was set up in the liberated town of Permet, in a valley of the Pindus mountains. Hoxha modelled his control of the partisans and his government on the work of TITO in neighbouring Yugoslavia, until the breach between Tito and STALIN in 1948. Thereafter Hoxha closely followed Stalinist practice, content to exercise dictatorial policy as First Secretary rather than assume the impressive governmental and state titles current in Yugoslavia. Hoxha remained loyal to Stalinist principles, executed his chief rival, Koci Xoxe, in June 1949 as a Titoist, and delivered a verbal attack on KHRUSCHEV's 'revisionism' at a conference in Moscow in November 1960, subsequently receiving Chinese economic aid for Albania and breaking with the Soviet Union. He maintained Albania's independence despite constant friction with neighbouring Greece and Yugoslavia, denunciation of Moscow, a total breach in diplomatic relations with Britain and the United States, and, after the death of MAO, tension with China. His proud assertion of independence left Albania economically backward. He suffered from diabetes from 1948, but survived until 11 April 1985. Popular unrest grew rapidly after his death, with demands for social change and human rights; but not until March 1991 did Albanians have the first democratic election in seventy years. J. Halliday (ed.): *The Artful Albanian; the Memoirs of Enver Hoxha* (1986); P. R. Prifti: *Socialist Albania since 1944* (Cambridge, Mass., 1978).

Hua Guofeng (Hua Kuo-feng) (1912–87), Chinese leader who succeeded MAO: born in Hunan, where he became deputy provincial governor in 1950 after serving twelve years in the Eighth Route Army. One of his chief concerns was to increase the agricultural output in the region. Although criticized for non-Maoist ideas during the 'cultural revolution' of 1965, he subsequently strengthened his position in the Communist Party and was elected to the Central Committee in 1969. Four years later he joined the inner circle, the Politburo, and was appointed deputy Prime Minister to the ailing CHOU EN-LAI in 1975, also assuming responsibility for public security. When Chou died, Hua was appointed Prime Minister by MAO TSE-TUNG (8 February 1976). On Mao's death Hua was in the strongest position to assume control of the party, and it was announced on 8 October 1976 that he had been recognized as Chairman of the Central Committee. His immediate task within China was to counter the influence of the radicals on the Politburo, the so-called 'Gang of Four', the best-known member of whom was CHIANG CHIN. In foreign affairs Hua undertook visits to Yugoslavia, Romania and Iran (1978) and encouraged better relations with the United States. He made a protracted visit to Germany, France, Britain and Italy in the late autumn of 1979. Hua's influence was less than western observers believed. The veteran DENG edged Hua out of office as Prime Minister in September 1980 and as Chairman of the Central Committee in June 1981. D. Bonavia: *Verdict in Peking, the Trial of the Gang of Four* (1984); D. Barnett and R. Clough (eds): *Modernizing China; Post-Mao Reform and Development* (Boulder, Colo., 1986); L. Pan: *The New Chinese Revolution* (1986).

Hughes, Charles Evans (1862–1948), US Secretary of State from 1921 to 1925 and Chief Justice of the Supreme Court from 1930 to 1941: born in Glenns Falls, New

York, and graduated in law from Brown University, Rhode Island, achieving nationwide fame as a lawyer in New York City when he exposed insurance company abuses in the winter of 1905–6. He was elected Governor of New York State in 1906 and established a 'clean sweep' reforming administration. In 1910 he became an Associate Justice of the Supreme Court, resigning in 1916 so as to accept the Republican nomination in the campaign against the incumbent President, Woodrow WILSON. Hughes lost by only a narrow margin, his defeat stemming primarily from the loss of California, where there was a major schism in the Republican Party. From 1921 to 1925 Hughes served HARDING and COOLIDGE as Secretary of State, organizing the Washington Conference of 1921–2 on Far Eastern and naval affairs. For eleven years (1930–41) he presided over the Supreme Court, keeping a balance between the liberal and conservative justices and resolutely handling the difficult problems caused by the decision of Franklin ROOSEVELT to reorganize the Court in 1937. M. J. Pusey: *Charles Evans Hughes* (2 vols) (New York, 1951); S. Hendel: *Charles Evans Hughes and the Supreme Court* (New York, 1957).

Hughes, William Morris (1864–1952), Australian Prime Minister from 1915 to 1923: born in London, educated in North Wales, emigrating to Sydney in 1884. He was elected to the first Federal Parliament in 1901 and remained a Member until his death fifty-one years later. After serving as Attorney-General in the Labour government of 1910, he succeeded to the premiership in October 1915, establishing a coalition government sixteen months later, breaking with his former Labour supporters because they opposed his plans for conscription. He was much respected in London during the later stages of the First World War and at the Paris Peace Conference of 1919. His dislike of Wilsonian idealism, his strong prejudice against non-whites, and his desire to bind the white dominions of the British Empire in a closer federation marked him off as a conservatively minded statesman of fearless independence. He was out of office from February 1923 until 1934, playing a major part in the establishment of the United Australian Party. From 1937 to 1939 he was Minister for External Affairs, subsequently serving for two years as Attorney-General and accepting responsibility for naval affairs as well in 1940–1. His services in alerting Australia to the Japanese menace were considerable, but his conduct in debate was frequently vindictive and small-minded, and he was never a popular figure in Australia as a whole. F. G. Browne: *They Called Him Billy* (Sydney, 1946); L. F. Fitzhardinge: *W. M. Hughes* (2 vols) (Sydney, 1964, 1969).

Hull, Cordell (1871–1955), US Secretary of State from 1933 to 1944: born near Overton, Tennessee, and educated locally. After six years in the Tennessee legislature he entered the House of Representatives in 1907 where, apart from the years 1921–3, as Democrat Senator he remained until 1931 when he was returned for his native State. In Congress his chief interest was in economic matters, notably legislation concerning the federal income tax system in 1913. When he became Secretary of State in March 1933 he made his first objective the lowering of high tariffs by reciprocal trade treaties. His policy of 'good neighbourliness' to the Latin American states, in part a product of his trade policy, was evident at the Pan-American conferences which he attended at Montevideo (1933), Buenos Aires (1936) – an assembly opened on his initiative by President Franklin ROOSEVELT – and at Lima (1938). The mounting crises in Europe induced Congress to push through the Neutrality Acts of 1935–7 against Hull's wishes, but he stayed in office in order gradually to modify their isolationist intention. Hull's understanding of the American political mind helped him to institute 'bipartisanship' in foreign affairs. In 1941 he continued negotiations with the Japanese up to the day of Pearl Harbor, vainly hoping that conciliatory diplomacy would strengthen the more moderate Japanese politicians in their struggle against TOJO and the militarists. He was much criticized for sympathy and support shown towards PÉTAIN and the Vichy government from 1940 to 1942. Hull reached a good understanding with MOLOTOV in Moscow in October–November 1943 over basic plans for a post-war United Nations Organization. Much of his last year in office was spent in building up this new international body, a task recognized by conferment of the Nobel Peace Prize for 1945. His health gave way in the late summer of 1944; he resigned on 27 November, and was succeeded by his former Under-Secretary, Edward Stettinius, who in turn made way for the more forceful BYRNES after Roosevelt's death. Hull unexpectedly survived another ten years, living mainly in Bethesda Naval Hospital, where he completed his memoirs. C. Hull: *The Memoirs of Cordell Hull* (2 vols) (New York, 1948); R. Dallek: *Franklin D. Roosevelt and American Foreign Policy, 1932–1945* (New York, 1979); C. C. Tansill: *Backdoor to War* (Chicago, 1952).

Humphrey, Hubert Horatio (1911–78), Vice-President of the United States from 1965 to 1969: born at Wallace, South Dakota, and educated at the universities of Minnesota and Louisiana. He became Mayor of Minneapolis at the age of 33 and entered the US Senate as a 'civil rights' Democrat from Minnesota in 1948. He was respected as a liberal, interested in welfare programmes, and was a strong supporter of Adlai STEVENSON. In the closing months of 1958 he became a national figure after a much publicized visit to KRUSCHEV in Moscow. He was a candidate for the Democratic nomination in 1960, but he fared badly in the Wisconsin and West Virginia primaries and dropped out. From 1961 to 1964 he was majority Whip in the Senate, achieving notable successes in steering the Civil Rights Bill and the Nuclear Test Ban Treaty through Congress. He became running-mate to Lyndon JOHNSON in 1964, serving him loyally as Vice-President even though his public backing for the Vietnam War disappointed many earlier liberal supporters. Although he received the Democratic nomination in 1968 at the first ballot, he lost the election to NIXON. He sought the Democratic nomination again in 1972 but it went (abortively) to Senator George McGovern. Humphrey will be remembered less for his vice-presidency than for his early crusades for civil rights. H. H. Humphrey: *The Education of a Public Man* (1976); C. Solberg: *Hubert Humphrey* (1984).

Hussein ibn-Talal (1935–), King of Jordan: born in Amman, the eldest son of King Talal (reigned 1951–2, died 1972) and grandson of King ABDULLAH, who was assassinated in the 16-year-old prince's presence. Hussein was educated in Alexandria, at Harrow and at Sandhurst. He became titular King of Jordan in August 1952, when Talal was deemed mentally incapacitated; he assumed full sovereignty in May 1953. Although the King sympathized with many aspects of British life (and from 1961 to 1972 was married to an Englishwoman, Toni Gardiner) his policies cautiously avoided dependence on British advisers, notably the Commandant of the Arab Legion, Sir John Glubb (1897–1986), whom he dismissed in 1956. In February 1958 Hussein entered a federation with Iraq, a union cut short by the murder of his cousin King Faisal II in August. Hussein faced a succession of crises: the loss of the West Bank to Israel in June 1967; the rise of Arab socialism; the challenge, on Jordanian soil, of the PLO under ARAFAT. He survived, partly by dexterous statecraft, but also because he could rely on the loyalty of his Bedouin subjects, who rallied to his support in September 1970 when there was grave fighting with the PLO in Amman. On several occasions the King sought to mediate in disputes over the Middle East. He would not join in the assault on SADDAM in Iraq in 1990, although critical of the unbending character of the regime in Baghdad. From July 1988 he ceased to insist on the inclusion within Jordan of the West Bank. His emissaries agreed on an agenda for peace with Israel in September 1993, the King finally signing a treaty with Yitzak RABIN in Washington on 25 July 1994. At the same time the King tolerated the revival of multiparty politics within Jordan: in November 1993 the first election since 1956 gave his supporters fifty-nine of eighty seats in the new parliament. As the King had no son, in April 1965 he recognized his brother Hassan (1947) as Crown Prince and heir. King Hussein: *Uneasy Lies the Head* (1962), *My War with Israel* (1969); Crown Prince Hassan: *Search for Peace* (New York, 1984); U. Dann: *King Hussein and the Challenge of Arab Radicalism* (Oxford, 1989).

Hyndman, Henry Mayers (1842–1921), pioneer British communist: born in London, into a family made wealthy by the West Indian sugar trade. He was educated at Eton and Cambridge University; he was a good amateur cricketer who played thirteen first-class matches for Sussex in 1864–5, the two summers MARX was struggling to finish writing *Das Kapital*, Volume 1. Hyndman travelled widely in the United States, Europe and Asia before becoming a leader writer on the *Pall Mall Gazette* (1871–80). The Paris Commune stirred his interest in socialist radicalism. He met Marx and ENGELS several times from 1872 onwards; they regarded him as a plagiarist, when his *England for All* made Marxism almost intelligible to British readers, without acknowledging any debt to Marx by name. Hyndman joined the Democratic Federation in 1881, converting it in 1883 into a pioneer communist movement (the Social Democratic Federation), which gained a wide following in London between 1885 and 1889, partly through his skill as a speaker. The 'top-hatted socialism' of Hyndman's SDF was mistrusted both by Engels and by the Socialist League followers of William MORRIS. Hyndman remained staunchly independent of the orthodox Labour movement from 1901 onwards. He supported the Allied war effort in 1914, leading a splinter group – the National Socialist Party – for the last five years of his life. His debating skills and journalistic fluency made him an effective – and historically underrated – propagandist of early socialism. H. M. Hyndman: *England for All, the Texbook of Democracy* (1881), *Record of an Adventurous Life* (1911), *Further Reminiscenses* (1912); C. Tsuzuki: *H. M. Hyndman and British Socialism* (1961).

I

Ibarruri, Dolores (1895–1989), Spanish Communist, known as 'La Pasionaria': born near Bilbao, married a miner from Asturias, giving up the Catholic beliefs in which she had grown to womanhood and accepting his Marxism. Her natural gifts of oratory, heightened by a razor-sharp mind, won her election to the Central Committee of the Spanish Communist Party in 1930, and she was twice returned to parliament in Madrid. Her speeches in the Cortes early in 1936 were widely reported, but she became famous by her defiant 'They Shall Not Pass' call to the defenders of Madrid fighting against FRANCO in the Civil War. The fanaticism of 'the Passion Flower' was an inspiration, not only in Madrid, but in France where she sought both recruits and arms. In 1939 she settled in the Soviet Union, where STALIN accepted her as spokesman for the exiled Spanish Communists. She returned to Spain in May 1977, was allowed to speak once more at a rally in Bilbao, and was again returned to the Cortes as a Communist Deputy from Asturias. K. Low: *La Pasionaria, the Spanish Firebird* (1992); P. Preston: *The Coming of the Spanish Civil War* (1978).

Ibn Saud (Abd al-Aziz Al Saud) (1880–1953), King of Hijaz and Nejd 1926–32 and first King of Saudi Arabia: born into the Wahhabi dynasty, in Riyadh, but was forced into exile by the Turks as a child. A Bedouin revolt in 1902 enabled him to recover control of his birthplace and by 1914 he was virtual master of all the Turkish possessions along the southern shore of the Persian Gulf. The British recognized his paramountcy as Emir of Hasa and Nejd in December 1915, but he stood aside from the Arab Revolt (cf. ABDULLAH, FAISAL) because of hostility to Emir Hussein. From 1919 to 1925 Ibn Saud turned his attention to the Red Sea coast, ousting Hussein and capturing the vital cities of Jedda, Medina and Mecca, thus making him ruler of a territory four times the size of metropolitan France. His proclamation at Mecca as King of Hijaz and Nejd on 8 January 1926 was recognized by the British sixteen months later. The unification of his kingdoms under the name 'Saudi Arabia' was announced by decree on 22 September 1932. A year later he concluded an oil agreement with an American company, but it did not strike oil in commercial quantities until February 1938, thereafter exploiting a dozen wells in two years, and with considerable wealth beginning to come to the King by 1946. Ibn Saud supported the British and Americans throughout the Second World War, and was received independently by Winston CHURCHILL and Franklin ROOSEVELT in Egypt (February 1945). His personal sovereignty over his unified kingdom was maintained without concessions to popular demands up to his death, on 30 November 1953. D. Hoden and R. Johns: *The House of Saud* (1981); C. M. Helms: *The Cohesion of Saudi Arabia* (1981); M. Almana: *Arabia Unified* (1980); J. S. Habib: *Ibn Saud's Warriors of Islam* (1978).

Ichikawa, Fusaye (1893–1981), Japanese political and social feminist: born in Yokohama, settling in Tokyo as a young teacher during the First World War. Contact in the capital with American ideas encouraged her to help establish, in 1919–20, a New Women's Association – a movement whose earliest campaigning success was permission for women to be present at political meetings. Three years of study in America brought Ichikawa under the influence of Carrie CATT and the National American Woman Suffrage Association and, on returning to Tokyo in 1924, she set up a Women's Suffrage League. But Japanese women were not assured of their political and social rights until the promulgation in October 1946 of the new democratic constitution. From 1945 onwards Fusaye Ichikawa led the New Japan Women's League in a long struggle against conservative social taboos. She entered the Japanese parliament in 1952 but was defeated in the election of 1971, probably because of her campaigns to legalize prostitution, or even because of her attacks on corruption within the bureaucracy. She was returned to parliament once more in the 1975 elections and was again successful in 1980, when she was in her eighty-seventh year. H. H. Baerwald: *Japan's Parliament* (Cambridge, 1976); M. D. Kennedy: *A History of Japan* (1963).

Ickes, Harold (1874–1952), US Secretary of the Interior from 1933 to 1946: born in Blair County, Pennsylvania and educated at the University of Chicago. He practised law in Chicago and showed interest in reformist politics in Illinois. As Director of the Public Works Administration under Franklin ROOSEVELT, Ickes was honest, but aroused criticism for his slowness. His temperament was churlish, he tended to inflame petty issues, and he was an outspoken critic of some of his colleagues, notably Harry HOPKINS. Over racial discrimination he was more liberal than the President and his diary shows that he was a useful party manager. He disliked TRUMAN, possibly because he had himself hoped to be Vice-President, and resigned in disgust at the conservative character of Truman's appointments in 1946. No other American has remained so long at the Department of the Interior nor left so great a mark on its work as this least popular of the 'New Dealers'. H. L. Ickes: *The Autobiography of a Curmudgeon* (New York, 1949), *The Secret Diary of Harold L. Ickes* (3 vols) (New York, 1953–4).

Idris I (Said Mohammed Idris al-Mahdi al-Senussi) (1890–1972), King of Libya 1951–69: born at Djaraboub, a member of the Senussi family which gave its name early in the nineteenth century to a Muslim sect originating near Derna and, from 1911 onwards, long continued to resist Italian colonization of Libya. Idris was effective leader of the resistance from 1918 onwards, although he only became titular head of the Senussi in 1933, establishing his headquarters in Egypt and being accepted by the British as Emir. In September 1947 Britain recognized him as head of state in his native Cyrenaica, which was for the first time accorded a constitution. On 24 December 1951 he was proclaimed King of an independent Libya, with the historic provinces of Cyrenaica and Tripoli linked in a federal structure. Although he joined the Arab League soon after his accession, King Idris collaborated closely with the British, who maintained bases in both provinces in return for training his army. The King's decision in 1963 to abolish the federal structure was resented in Tripoli and his enfranchisement of women offended Muslim traditionalists, even among the Senussi. The rapid growth of oil exports from 1961 onwards encouraged the spread of a pan-Arab socialism opposed to the concessions which Idris granted to Anglo-American companies. In September 1969 King Idris was deposed by a military *coup* of which the young Colonel GADDAFI was principal instigator. Idris went into exile and the monarchy was abolished. J. Wright: *Libya, a Modern History* (1982); E. Evans Pritchard: *The Sanusi of Cyrenaica* (1949).

Ignatiev, Nikolai Pavlovich (1832–1908), Russian diplomat, soldier and pan-Slav: born in St Petersburg, educated in the corps of pages at the imperial court, served with a crack Hussar regiment from 1849 to 1856 and was then sent on diplomatic missions. His earliest success was at Peking, where in 1860 he secured recognition of Russian possession of the Far Eastern maritime provinces, from the River Amur northwards and including the site of Vladivostok. ALEXANDER II rewarded him with promotion to aide-de-camp General at the age of 29. From 1864 to 1877 Ignatiev was ambassador at Constantinople, advocating the extension of Russian protection to all the Slav subjects in the Balkans. He believed he had achieved this in January 1878 when, after the Ottoman Empire's military defeat by Russia, he imposed the Treaty of San Stefano, which created a big Bulgaria, extending deep into Macedonia and the western Balkans and subject to Russian domination. But Ignatiev's pan-Slav triumph was never ratified: his colleagues in St Petersburg feared that the treaty so upset the balance of power in Europe that it would lead to a general war, for which Russia was unprepared; the European Great Powers, meeting at the Congress of Berlin under BISMARCK's presidency in June and July 1878, replaced San Stefano by a settlement which accepted only a small, autonomous Bulgaria and left much of the Balkans under the Sultan's rule. Ignatiev served briefly as Russian Minister of the Interior in 1881–2, but spent the last twenty-seven years of his life in retirement. He insisted that his gravestone should carry only his name and the three words, 'Peking: San Stefano'. A. Onou (ed.): 'The memoirs of Count N. Ignatyev', *Slavonic Review*, Vol. 10 (1931–2); B. H. Sumner: *Russia and the Balkans, 1870–1880* (1937).

Inönü, Ismet (1884–1974), Turkish soldier, Prime Minister and President: born in Smyrna (now Izmir), served in the Ottoman Army from 1904 to 1918, winning distinction as Colonel Ismet in defence of Gallipoli in 1915 and being promoted to General in 1916. He was Chief of Staff to Mustafa KEMAL in 1920, defeating the Greeks in two defensive battles around the village of Inönü in August and September 1921. He headed the Turkish peace delegation which negotiated the Treaty of Lausanne in 1923, returning to Ankara where he became Kemal's Prime Minister for the following fourteen years. In 1935, when the Turks adopted surnames, he took the name of the village where he had gained his victories and was thereafter known as Ismet Inönü. From November 1938 to May 1950 he was Turkey's President, at first continuing Kemal's strict dictatorship, but gradually relaxing controls of the press and public meetings. In foreign affairs he remained neutral in the Second World War until March 1945, despite inducements offered to him by Winston CHURCHILL at a meeting in Adana on 30–31 January 1943 (the only occasion Churchill set foot on the soil of a non-belligerent during his wartime premiership). In 1945–6 Inönü permitted the formation of an opposition Democrat Party which defeated his own Republican Party in the elections of May 1950. Inönü then accepted the role of leader of the parliamentary opposition, returning to office as Prime Minister in October 1961. The Cyprus problem plagued his premiership and was partly responsible for his final fall in February 1965. Although by now an octogenarian, who had narrowly escaped assassination (21 February 1964), Inönü continued to lead the parliamentary opposition vigorously until July 1972. B. Lewis: *The Emergence of Modern Turkey* (1961); K. H. Karpat:

Turkey's Politics; the Transition to a Multiparty System (Princeton, N.J., 1959); F. G. Weber: *The Evasive Neutral* (Columbus, Mo., 1979); F. Ahamad: *The Turkish Experiment in Democracy 1950–75* (1979).

Irigoyen, Hipolito: see *Yrigoyen*.

Isabella II (1830–1904), Queen of Spain from 1833 to 1868: born in Madrid, the only child of Ferdinand VII (1784–1833) and of Maria Christina of Naples (1806–78), who was Regent for the first seven years of her daughter's reign. This period of Regency was marred by such scandal and avaricious greed at court that only an enlightened and inspiring personality could make the monarchy acceptable again. Isabella did not possess any remarkable qualities, although she enjoyed some popularity until the closing years of her reign. Her position was weakened by the alternative appeal of her uncle and cousin whose 'Carlist' claim to the throne was based on the assumption that women had no right of succession, a claim supported by much of the north of the country and by many clericalists. Isabella was unable to rally disaffected regions in support of a unified national monarchy. She was hampered by the intrigues of her devout and ineffectual husband, Francis of Cadiz, whom she married in 1846; their child, who was to reign as Alfonso XII from 1875 until 1885, was born in 1857 but proved to be consumptive. Politically the unfortunate Isabella could not check the rivalry of ambitious Generals. Newspaper revelations, feeding on rumours that the Queen was a nymphomaniac, undermined her position in the summer of 1868 and revolts in the army and navy led to the triumph of a liberal revolutionary movement controlled by General PRIM. Isabella fled to France from her summer palace at San Sebastian (29 September) and was formally deposed. From exile she remained an embarrassment – but not a threat – to her son and her daughter-in-law, Queen Maria Christina (1858–1929) who, in the curiously cyclic pattern of Spanish monarchy, was Regent during the early years of Isaballa's grandson, ALFONSO XIII. P. de Polnay: *A Queen of Spain, Isabel II* (1962); R. Carr: *Spain, 1808–1939* (Oxford, 1966).

Ismail (1830–95), Khedive of Egypt from 1863 to 1880: born in Cairo, son of Ibrahim Pasha (1789–1848) and grandson of Mehemet Ali (1769–1848), the Albanian founder of the Egyptian dynasty. Ismail was educated in France and succeeded his uncle Muhammad Said as the Ottoman Sultan's Viceroy in 1863. In return for doubling the annual tribute paid by Egypt to Turkey, he was allowed in 1867 to become hereditary Khedive. Generous bribes given by Ismail on a visit to the Sultan in 1873 gave him virtual sovereign powers in Egypt. From 1863 onwards Ismail speedily 'Europeanized' Egypt, raising foreign loans from an expanding cotton trade and warmly supporting the French construction of the Suez Canal, at the opening of which in 1869 he was host to Empress Eugenie, Emperor FRANCIS JOSEPH and other royal dignitaries. Cairo became the first Muslim city with a Parisian-style opera house. Ismail undertook internal reforms, gave the Nile delta a good railway system, and sought to expand southwards into the Sudan. But his personal and public extravagance was hit by the European recession following the Vienna stock market crash of 1873. Interest rates on his short-term loans became so high that in 1875 he sold his Suez Canal holdings to the British for £4 million. Even so, he could not stave off state bankruptcy, or Anglo-French interference in Egypt's constitutional development. Under foreign pressure the Sultan deposed Ismail in June 1879; his eldest son Tewfik (1852–92) acceded. Although Ismail died in exile in Constantinople, he imposed more lasting changes on Egypt than any other ruler in four centuries. P. Crabites: *Ismail, the Maligned Khedive* (1933); E. Fuat Tugay: *Three Centuries; Family Chronicles of Turkey and Egypt* (1963); D. Landes: *Bankers and Pashas* (New York, 1969); P. J. Vatikotis: *History of Modern Egypt* (1991).

Ito, Hiroboumi (1841–1909), Japanese westernizer: born in Choshu province of peasant stock but brought up by a modest Samurai family. Although most of his generation were 'anti-foreigner', he was selected to travel abroad, first coming to London when he was 22 to study naval science. Upon his return he was appointed Governor of Kobe province, where he introduced a modern fiscal system. He was sent abroad again on a world tour from 1871 to 1873. Ito was chief minister in Japan from 1884 to 1888, preparing the constitution which received imperial assent on 11 February 1889 and which led to the summoning of the first Imperial Diet (a bicameral parliament) a year later. As Prime Minister from 1894 to 1896 he encouraged expansion on the Asiatic mainland, acquiring mastery over Korea by the Treaty of Shimonoseki (17 April 1895) after a brief victorious war against China. He had encouraged the construction of a modern fleet and the westernization of Japan's army, but by the turn of the century he found himself deprived of influence by a group of militarists headed by Marshal Yamagata (1832–1922), his chief rival as adviser to Emperor MUTSUHITO. Ito was created a prince in 1900 and served again as Prime Minister in 1900–1 before being sent on a special embassy to St Petersburg. He voted against war with Russia at a decisive council of ministers in 1904 and fell from favour. In 1906 he was appointed Governor of Korea and was assassinated by a Korean nationalist at Harbin on 25 October 1909. His murder provided his former rivals in Tokyo with an excuse for the annexation of Korea (August 1910). R. Storry: *A History of Modern Japan* (1960); H. Borton: *Japan's Modern Century* (New York, 1955); G. Akita: *Foundations of Constitutional Government in Modern Japan, 1868–1900* (Stanford, Calif., 1967).

Izetbegović, Alija (1925–), President of Bosnia-Herzegovina: born into a Muslim family near Sarajevo and never abandoned his faith, being imprisoned as early as 1946 for 'pan-Islamic propaganda'. In 1949 he was released and qualified as a lawyer, though he became director of a building construction company. He also pursued advanced studies on the role of Islam in a multicultural world, receiving a doctorate. A secret Islamic Declaration, completed by him in 1970, was used by the Yugoslav authorities in 1983 as the basis of a show trial, for which he was sentenced to fourteen years' imprisonment, though released in 1988. In May 1990 he was elected leader of the new Democratic Action Party in Bosnia-Herzegovina, a predominantly Muslim group which won almost one-third of the seats at the ensuing General Election. Izetbegović – who favoured a multi-ethnic, multifaith republic – headed the coalition government set up in Sarajevo in December 1990, becoming President with Bosnia-Herzegovina's declaration of independence in May 1992. During the subsequent civil war his authority was challenged by the Bosnian Serb spokesman, KARADZIĆ. Despite occasional rifts within his government, Izetbegović retained official recognition from the European Community and the United Nations forces within Bosnia, and in December 1995 signed the Treaty of Paris accepting a compromise settlement of the problems of his republic. N. Malcolm: *Bosnia, A Short History* (1994); M. Glenny: *The Fall of Yugoslavia* (1992).

Izvolsky, Alexander (1856–1919), Russian Foreign Minister from 1906 to 1910:

born and educated in St Petersburg, served as a diplomat from 1875 to 1906, holding influential posts in the Balkans, Tokyo and Copenhagen. He was appointed Foreign Minister by NICHOLAS II in May 1906, his most remarkable achievement being the convention settling Asian disputes with Britain, popularly known as the Anglo-Russian Entente (August 1907). During the Bosnian crisis of 1908–9 he was placed in an invidious position by the wily Austro-Hungarian Foreign Minister, Aehrenthal. In September 1910 the Tsar sent Izvolsky as ambassador to Paris. There he strengthened Franco-Russian military links. He did not, however, have the influence attributed to him by German historians between the world wars who claimed that he was an arch-intriguer, seeking the encirclement of Germany and believing his policy had triumphed when Russia, France and Britain became allied in 1914. Izvolsky hoped his most successful work would be the negotiation, in the spring of 1915, of secret agreements providing for the Russian annexation of Constantinople and the Straits after the war. This treaty was publicly repudiated by LENIN and TROTSKY in 1918. Izvolsky remained in France after the downfall of Tsardom, dying at Biarritz while compiling his memoirs. A. Izvolsky: *Recollections of a Foreign Minister* (New York, 1921); R. P. Churchill: *The Anglo-Russian Convention of 1907* (Cedar Rapids, IA, 1939); B. Schmitt: *The Annexation of Bosnia* (Cambridge, 1937); A. J. P. Taylor: *The Struggle for Mastery in Europe* (Oxford, 1954).

J

Jackson, Thomas Jonathan (1824–63), American Confederate General, known as 'Stonewall Jackson': born at Clarksburg, West Virginia, graduated from the Military Academy at West Point in 1846 and fought in the Mexican War, 1846–8, before taking up a post as mathematics instructor at the Virginia Military Institute in the Shenandoah valley during the ten years before the Civil War. On Virginia's secession he joined the Confederate Army, together with many of his cadets, and won his soubriquet as a brigade commander when his resolute stand on Henry House Hill rallied the Confederate defenders in the first battle of Bull Run (21 July 1861). Local knowledge helped him successfully protect the South's 'granary', the Shenandoah valley, in a brilliant campaign throughout 1862. At midsummer he sustained some rebuffs in the seven-day battle to defend Richmond but he played a decisive role in the Confederate victory at Second Bull Run (29–30 August 1862). Eighteen days later he reached Antietam in Maryland in time to support LEE against an assault by a far larger army under MCCLELLAN. Jackson was Lee's principal lieutenant at Fredericksburg on 13 December 1862 and at Chancellorsville on 1–2 May 1863, but he was fired upon in mistake by Confederate troops from North Carolina in the aftermath of Chancellorsville and died from his wounds a few days later (10 May). Jackson, a strict Calvinist, was the ablest and most enterprising field commander to serve under Lee. L. Chambers: *Stonewall Jackson* (2 vols) (New York, 1959); F. Vandiver: *Mighty Stonewall* (New York, 1957).

Jameson, Leander Starr (1853–1917), anti-Boer conspirator and Prime Minister of Cape Colony from 1904 to 1908: born in Edinburgh, where he studied medicine. He emigrated to South Africa and started a medical practice at Kimberley in 1878, soon becoming an associate of Cecil RHODES. In 1891 Rhodes appointed him administrator for the British South Africa Company in Fort Salisbury, where he was a popular and respected figure. Rhodes encouraged an uprising of the non-Boer whites in the Transvaal, with Jameson leading a force of 470 mounted men from Pitsani on the Bechuanaland border to Johannesburg, 180 miles away, in order to support these 'Uitlanders' in their revolt against President KRUGER. Jameson's security was poor and, on 2 January 1896, four days after entering the Transvaal, his force was ambushed at Doornkop by General Piet Cronje (1835–1911). Dr Jameson was handed over to the British authorities, returned to England to stand trial, and in July 1896 was sentenced to fifteen months in prison, even though he was hailed as a hero by the London crowd. After serving five months in Holloway Prison he was released and returned to South Africa. He was elected to the Cape Colony Legislative Assembly in 1900 as a Progressive, taking office as Prime Minister in 1904 and working for South African union. He came to England in 1909 with eight other spokesmen for South Africa, including BOTHA, HERTZOG and SMUTS, all of whom were entertained by King EDWARD VII. Dr Jameson sat for Albany in the first Parliament of the Union of South Africa at Pretoria, and in

1911 he accepted a baronetcy from GEORGE V. After retiring from active politics in 1912 he spent the last five years of his life as President of the British South Africa Company. I. D. Colvin: *The Life of Jameson* (2 vols) (1922); E. Pakenham: *Jameson's Raid* (rev. edn 1982).

Jaruzelski, Wojciech (1923–), Polish General and political leader in the 1980s: born at Kurow into a devout Catholic family, deported to the Soviet Union when south eastern Poland was occupied by Russians in 1939. Jaruzelski was trained as a loyal communist soldier and fought with a Polish division in the Red Army 1944–5, later graduating from the Warsaw Military Academy. By 1961 he was Colonel in charge of political education in the Polish army and sat in Parliament, joining the inner politburo of the Workers' Party (PZPR) in 1964. Over the following three years he was Chief of General Staff and Defence Minister from 1968 to 1983. The threat of radical upheaval by the Solidarity movement, under WALESA, induced the PZPR to give increasing powers to Jaruzelski, as a model political General. He took office as Prime Minister in February 1981, became Chief Secretary of the PZPR in September and, in December, carried out the first military *coup* in a 'people's democracy', imposing martial law on the country for eighteen months, establishing a Military Council of National Salvation which governed Poland throughout 1982. Jaruzelski's political orthodoxy prevented Soviet intervention, while he used the Church hierarchy to counterbalance Solidarity's radicalism. In November 1985 he gave up the premiership and became Polish Head of State. As communism began to wither away in 1988–9 Jaruzelski accepted the emergence of a 'socialist pluralist' democracy. He retired from office in December 1990. In May 1993 he was formally accused of causing the deaths of forty-four workers on 16–17 December 1970 when, as Defence Minister, he ordered military intervention against strikers in Gdynia. N. Davies: *Heart of Europe* (Oxford, 1984); K. Ruane: *The Polish Challenge* (1982); M. Craig: *The Crystal Spirit* (1986).

Jaurès, Jean (1859–1914), leading French Socialist from 1898 to 1914: born at Castres in the Tarn department of south-eastern France, educated at the Ecole Normale and at the University of Toulouse, becoming a secondary school teacher and a lecturer in philosophy. He sat in the Chamber of Deputies as a moderate Republican from 1885 to 1889, returning there as a Socialist from 1893 to 1898 and from 1902 until his death. His socialism, with its great concern for the rights of the individual, owed more to French traditions than to doctrinaire Marxism. He championed DREYFUS and collaborated with the Dreyfusard radical governments of 1902–5. The Amsterdam Congress of the Socialist International in 1904 condemned this collaboration and, in order to form a united French Socialist Party (SFIO), Jaurès accepted the Congress's criticism, declining personally to hold office in any 'bourgeois coalition government'. He continued, however, to give the policies of the SFIO a reformist, rather than a revolutionary, character. From 1906 onwards he attempted to organize a common socialist policy in France and in Germany against war. The newspaper *L'Humanité*, which he had founded in 1904, emphasized the need for unity between the Socialist parties of the great European powers. Jaurès' passionate intellectual pacifism failed to prevent the workers responding to the mobilization call of the governments in the war crisis of 1914. Jaurès himself was assassinated by a fanatical French nationalist on 31 July 1914. H. Goldberg: *Life of Jean Jaurès* (Madison, Wis., 1962); J. Hampden Jackson: *Jean Jaurès* (1943); H. R. Weinstein: *Jean Jaurès, Patriotism in the French Socialist Movement* (New York, 1936); A. Noland:

The Founding of the French Socialist Party 1893–1905 (Cambridge, Mass., 1956).

Jellicoe, John Rushworth (1859–1935), British Admiral: born at Southampton, entering the Royal Navy as a cadet at the age of 13. In June 1893, as a Commander, he survived the famous collision off Beirut between the Mediterranean flagship HMS *Victoria* (in which he was serving) and another ironclad, HMS *Camperdown*. Subsequently he led a land force with distinction during the Boxer unrest in China, 1900, and was a protégé and in due course a close colleague of the energetic naval reformer, Admiral FISHER. From 1912 to 1914 he was at the Admiralty as Second Sea Lord, taking command of the Grand Fleet at Scapa Flow on the eve of war. He was victorious in the relatively minor naval engagements of Heligoland Bight (28 August 1914) and the Dogger Bank (24 January 1915), but he had difficulty in bringing the German High Seas Fleet to battle. On the evening of 31 May 1916 he successfully intercepted the Germans off Jutland after they had been enticed towards the Grand Fleet by the battle-cruiser action of Admiral BEATTY. Yet Jellicoe was much criticized, even after his victory at Jutland, and he never entirely shook off a reputation for caution. From November 1916 to Christmas 1917 he was First Sea Lord, the strain of office bearing heavily upon his health. He had been knighted in 1907 and was raised to the peerage as a Viscount in 1918. Like Fisher and Beatty, he was awarded the Order of Merit. From 1920 to 1925 he was Governor-General of New Zealand, and was created Earl on his return to England. Earl Jellicoe: *The Grand Fleet, 1914–16; its Creation, Development and Work* (1919); R. H. Bacon: *Life of Earl Jellicoe of Scapa* (1936); A. J. Marder: *From the Dreadnought to Scapa Flow* (5 vols) (1961–70); C. Barnett: *The Swordbearers* (1963).

Jinnah, Mohammed Ali (1876–1948), founder of Pakistan: born at Karachi, and from 1897 practised as a barrister in Bombay. In 1910 he became a member of the Viceroy's Legislative Council. From 1913 to 1928 he encouraged collaboration between the Indian National Congress Party of Mohandas GANDHI, of which he was a member for many years, and the Indian Muslim League, which he joined in 1913. Suspicion that Gandhi favoured narrowly Hindu interests induced Jinnah to champion the Muslim minority at the Round Table Conference on India in London (1931). Three years later he began to organize the Muslim League, which was originally a religious and cultural movement, into a powerful political force. In March 1940 a congress of Indian Muslims at Lahore backed Jinnah's call for the establishment in an independent partitioned India, of 'Pakistan'. Jinnah's support for the British war effort was in marked contrast to the refusal of the Hindu Congress to collaborate with the imperial power in halting the Japanese advance. The post-war elections gave the Muslim League majorities in all the predominantly Muslim areas of British India, both in the west and the east. These successes made Jinnah more outspoken: he favoured 'direct action' to prevent disputed regions becoming part of Hindu-dominated Congress India. Four thousand people died in rioting between Muslims and Hindus, mainly around Calcutta. The British authorities, who had earlier been not unsympathetic to Jinnah, now blamed his agitation for the bloodshed. When Pakistan was created on 15 August 1947 its extent was limited, Jinnah being denied areas he had sought in Kashmir, the Punjab, Assam and Bengal. He became the first Governor-General of what he called 'this maimed and moth-eaten' Pakistan, but his health was poor. He found the problem of refugees, the communal riots, and the statecraft shown by the new India over the

Kashmir question too much for him. The Pakistanis hailed him as *Quid-i-Azam* ('Great Leader'), but his thirteen-month tenure of the Governor-General's office was sadly ineffectual. His death on 11 September 1948 left the less experienced Liaquat Ali Khan (1895–1951) to seek solutions to the problems which had baffled Jinnah in his last years. A. Jalal: *The Sole Spokesman; Jinnah, the Muslim League and the Demand for Pakistan* (Cambridge, 1985); M. A. Chaudhuri: *The Emergence of Pakistan* (New York, 1967).

Joffre, Joseph Jacques Césaire (1852–1931), Marshal of France, commander of the French armies on the Western Front from 1914 to 1916: born at Rivesaltes, near Perpignan, and fought as an artillery cadet in defence of Paris in 1870–1. He later saw service in Indo-China and North Africa, commanding the force which, in 1894, crossed the desert to capture Timbuktu. From 1904 to 1906 he was director of the Corps of Engineers, showing gifts as an organizer and a reformer. He became Chief of the French General Staff in 1911, assuming command in the field in August 1914 and distinguishing himself by the decisive counter-offensive on the Marne in the fifth week of the war, a battle which deprived Germany of rapid victory and turned operations on the Western Front into a long war of attrition. Joffre – a patient and imperturbable General – lacked strategic imagination but was treated with affectionate respect by his troops. His policy of 'nibbling away' at the German line culminated in the staggering losses of the battle of the Somme in 1916. In December that year he was made Marshal of France (the first creation of a Marshal in over fifty years), but retired as Commander-in-Chief. In 1917 he became President of the Allied War Council. For twelve years after the war he held nominal posts at the Ministry of War. J. C. C. Joffre: *The Memoirs of Marshal Joffre* (1932); R. Recouly: *Joffre* (1931); H. Isserlin: *The Battle of the Marne* (1965); A. H. Farrar-Hockley: *The Somme* (1964); E Spears: *Liaison 1914* (1930).

John XXIII (Angelo Giuseppe Roncali) (1881–1963), Pope from 1958 to 1963: born a peasant's son near Bergamo, in northern Italy. He was ordained priest in 1904, saw service with the medical corps in the First World War, subsequently entering the papal diplomatic service. In March 1925 he was ordained a bishop, becoming apostolic delegate to Bulgaria (1925–34) and to Greece and Turkey in 1935. When Paris was liberated in 1944 he was sent as papal nuncio to France. In 1953 he was consecrated Archbishop (Patriarch) of Venice and created a cardinal. His humility and humanity made him popular in Venice. Although he was a strong contender for succession to the papacy on the death of PIUS XII, his age, and his championship of worker-priests, appear to have made some of his fellow cardinals hesitant, and he was only elected Pope on the twelfth ballot (28 October 1958). His pontificate was distinguished by five characteristics: the emphasis on reconciliation between different Christian churches; increased personal liberty within the Church's social doctrines; repeated pleas for world peace; the convening of the second Vatican Council of modern times in order to encourage progressive reforms in the Catholic Church; and acceptance of the obligation of the Pope to leave the Vatican for visits to hospitals, prisons, and special institutions within the see of Rome. He was remembered especially for his attempts to improve relations with the Orthodox Church and with Communist governments; he has sometimes been called 'the Pope of the opening to the East'. Pope John died on 3 June 1963 and was succeeded by PAUL VI. Pope John XXIII: *Letters to his Family* (1969); E. E. Y. Hales: *Pope John and his Revolution*

(1965); P. Hebblethwaite: *John XXIII, Pope of the Council* (1985).

John Paul I (Albino Luciani) (1912–78), Pope for thirty-three days in 1978: born in Canale d'Agordo near Belluno, of working-class origin. He spent most of his life in the Veneto region. In July 1935 he was ordained priest and sent to the Gregorian University at Rome for specialist studies before returning to his native parish as a curate. From 1937 to 1947 he taught in the seminary at Belluno and assumed some executive responsibilities as vicar-general within the diocese. Pope JOHN XXIII created him Bishop of Vittorio Veneto in December 1958 and he modelled his episcopate on the Pope's administration in Venice, championing liturgical reform and encouraging missionary activity in the remote mountainous villages. Outside the diocese he was a prominent member of the doctrinal commission established by the Italian bishops. In December 1969 he became Patriarch of Venice, where he sought to reduce the pomp of ecclesiastical office and wrote *Illustrissimi*, a series of letters to eminent figures of the past which he used as a means of communicating his faith and ideas. Pope PAUL VI created him Cardinal in March 1973. His judicious outspokenness made him a probable candidate at the papal conclave of 1978. There was, however, widespread surprise when he was elected on the first day of the conclave (26 August), apparently after three ballots. He broke with precedent by refusing any coronation, declining to accept any of the traditional symbols of temporal authority at the inauguration of his 'supreme pastorship' on 3 September. He died from a heart attack during the night of 28–29 September. P. Hebblethwaite: *The Year of Three Popes* (1978); D. Yallop: *In God's Name* (1984).

John Paul II (Karol Wojtyla) (1920–), first non-Italian Pope since 1522: born at Wadowice, south west of Cracow. He was educated at the local gymnasium (high school) and was studying at the Jagiellonian University of Cracow at the outbreak of the Second World War. He was forced to find work in a stone quarry and a chemical factory under German occupation, eventually continuing theological studies secretly in the Cardinal-Archbishop's palace at Cracow. After ordination in November 1946 he was sent to Rome for further study. From 1948 to 1951 he was a parish priest in Cracow and subsequently professor of moral theology at the University of Lublin. In 1958 he became auxiliary Bishop of Cracow and Archbishop six years later (January 1964). He showed greater subtlety in conciliating the Communist authorities without prejudicing the essentials of belief than his immediate predecessors or other prominent eastern European ecclesiastics. Pope PAUL VI created him Cardinal in June 1967. Subsequently the government in Warsaw allowed him to visit Canada, America and Australia as well as to participate in synodical discussions in Rome. Unexpectedly he was elected Pope by the cardinals in conclave on 16 October 1978, thus breaking the practice of choosing an Italian prelate which had endured for four-and-a-half centuries. He was able to return to his native Poland in the early summer of 1979, and in September became the first Pope to visit Ireland, where he condemned political violence. He was himself shot and wounded by a Turkish gunman in St Peter's Square, Rome, on 13 May 1981. On his recovery he continued his practice of worldwide travel, visiting seventy-five countries during the first ten years of his pontificate; in May 1982 he became the first Pope to come to England, going on to Wales and Scotland. Catholics within the Soviet bloc looked upon him as a liberal Pope, who helped undermine communism without emncouraging dangerous confrontation. But over theological questions, moral problems of family life and church discipline John Paul II showed himself staunchly conservative: he confirmed traditional teaching on marriage, divorce, homosexuality, contraception, abortion, celibacy of the clergy and the ordination of women. Progressives in Latin America, Germany and the Netherlands were disappointed by his opposition to 'liberation theology', his apparent fear that active participation by churchmen in the class struggle of the politically oppressed and socially deprived would compromise his spiritual role as 'witness of a universal love'. John Paul II's encyclical *Dives in misericordia* (December 1980) called on men and women to show a merciful understanding of each other in an endangered world; and a further encyclical – *Laboren exercens* (September 1981) – urged the introduction of a new economic order, which in rejecting both Marxism and capitalist usury, would honour the dignity of labour and assert the primacy of the individual over material things. No previous Pope exercised such direct personal influence in so many lands. Pope John Paul II: *Collected Poems* (1982); T. Szulc: *Pope John Paul II* (1995); Lord Longford: *Pope John Paul II, an Authorized Biography* (1982); M. Craig: *Man From a Far Country* (1981).

Johnson Andrew (1808–75), President of the United States from 1865 to 1869: born at Raleigh, North Carolina, worked as a tailor in South Carolina and Tennessee, advancing through local politics to the Tennessee state legislature by his twenty-eighth birthday. He was returned to Congress in 1843, was Governor of Tennessee from 1853 to 1857 when he entered the Senate. Upon the outbreak of the Civil War he was the sole Southern Senator loyal to the Union and LINCOLN appointed him military Governor of Tennessee when the eastern section of the state was cleared of rebels in 1862. Johnson's tact and local knowledge brought him such success in the recovered lands that Lincoln chose him as his running-mate in the 1864 election. As Vice-President he automatically succeeded Lincoln on 15 April 1865. Johnson sought to continue Lincoln's policy of reconciliation, vetoing congressional measures which seemed to him to perpetuate the rift between North and South. Congress passed the Reconstruction Act (1867), which disfranchised former rebels, over his veto. Congress also sought to prevent President Johnson from dismissing members of the executive from office without senatorial approval. To test the validity of this attack upon his prerogative the President dismissed his Secretary of War and defied Congress. The House of Representatives duly impeached Andrew Johnson and he was brought to trial before the Senate, which ruled by thirty-five votes to nineteen against him (26 May 1868). Since an impeachment needed a two-thirds majority to succeed, the President was saved by a single vote. He served out the remaining ten months of his term, retired into private life but was re-elected to the Senate in 1874, dying soon after taking his seat. M. Lomask: *Andrew Johnson: President on Trial* (New York 1960); E. L. McKitrick: *Andrew Johnson and Reconstruction* (New York, 1969).

Johnson, Lyndon Baines (1908–73), President of the United States from 1963 to 1969: born at Stonewall, Texas, became a teacher and was for three years secretary to a congressman before being returned to the House of Representatives as a southern Democrat in the 1936 elections. From 1942 to 1945 he was a naval officer, although still technically a congressman. Texas elected him Senator in 1948, and he was majority leader in the Senate during the Eisenhower administration. The backing of the old 'New Dealers' among the Democrats secured him the vice-presidency under John KENNEDY in 1961. Upon Kennedy's assassination at Dallas (22 November 1963), Johnson was immediately sworn in as President. In the 1964 presidential election he easily defeated his Republican opponent, GOLDWATER, to gain a bigger popular majority than any previous American President. Johnson's presidency was overshadowed by the Vietnam War, which rapidly cost him popularity at home. His domestic achievements were, however, considerable: civil rights legislation, a federal Education Act, medical benefits for the aged. Much of this programme had been planned by Kennedy, but Johnson himself claimed, in a famous speech at Ann Arbor, that he sought to 'advance the quality of American civilization . . . upward to the Great Society' (22 May 1964). Despite this high ideal, the electorate turned against the candidate whom he had backed to succeed him, Vice-President HUMPHREY, and the nation swung to NIXON and Republicanism in 1968. Johnson, whose health deteriorated under the strains of his office, retired to Texas, where he died four years later. M. Dallar: *Lone Star Rising; Lyndon Johnson and his Times* (Oxford, 1991); R. A. Caro: *The Years of Lyndon Johnson* (2 vols) (1982, 1990); V. D. Burnet: *The Presidency of Lyndon B. Johnson* (Lawrence, Kans., 1976).

Juan Carlos I (1938–), King of Spain: born in Rome, son of Don Juan, Count of Barcelona, and a grandson of ALFONSO XIII. He was educated in Switzerland and Portugal before being invited to Madrid by FRANCO for training with the Spanish army and navy. Two years of law studies at Madrid University were followed by five years of training in government administration. In May 1962 he married Princess Sophia of Greece (1938), elder sister of King CONSTANTINE II. On 22 July 1969 Franco formally recognized Juan Carlos as 'Prince of Spain', heir to a vacant throne. After the dictator's death, the Prince was proclaimed King (22 November 1975). From the summer of 1976 he took an active part in speedily dismantling the Franco system of government, allowing Spain's first democratic election in forty-one years to be held in June 1977. Juan Carlos continued to reign as a strictly constitutional monarch, though acting decisively in February 1981 to defeat a right-wing *coup* by senior dissident army officers. In August 1995 an alleged plot by Basque separatists to assassinate him was thwarted by the police. J. L. Villalonga: *The King . . .* (1993); P. Preston: *The Triumph of Democracy in Spain* (1986).

Juarez, Benito Pablo (1806–72), Mexican liberal revolutionary President: born of Indian parentage near Oaxaca. In 1854 he led a revolt against clerical, conservative dominance of the country and he was virtually Prime Minister of Mexico from August 1855 to December 1857, introducing a series of belated reforms. Laws against the Church as a property owner provoked opposition and he was forced to seek refuge in Vera Cruz where, for more than two years, his 'Liberal' army waged war with the clerico-conservative administration in Mexico City. After winning this civil war in 1860 Juarez ordered the suspension of foreign debts. NAPOLEON III responded to appeals from French investors in Mexico by mounting an expedition which sought to establish a puppet empire in Mexico at a time when America could not enforce the Monroe Doctrine against European intervention. When the French installed Archduke MAXIMILIAN as Emperor, Juarez and his followers waged guerrilla warfare from the mountains. The ending of the American Civil War brought Juarez diplomatic support from the United States: the French withdrew; Maximilian was captured and shot, on Juarez's orders and despite pleas for clemency from the administration in Washington and from other governments. Juarez was formally elected

President of Mexico on 19 December 1867 and again sought to establish a liberal administration in the country. He was re-elected in 1871 but died on 18 July 1872. B. Hamnett: *Juarez* (1994); J. Ridley: *Maximilian and Juarez* (1993).

K

Kádár, Janos (1912–89), Hungarian Communist leader, 1956–88: born at Kápoly, south western Hungary, and became an instrument maker, secretly joining the Communist movement at the age of 20. As an active member of the resistance he was admitted to the party's Central Committee in 1942 and served as Minister of the Interior from 1948 until he fell foul of the Communist boss, RÁKOSI, in 1950. He was detained and tortured by the secret police in April 1951 and not released from prison until the summer of 1954. With the removal from power of Rákosi two years later, Kádár was reinstated on the party executive and became First Secretary of what was now the Hungarian Socialist Workers Party (MSzMP) on 25 October 1956, a day after the reformer Imre NAGY took over the premiership. Kádár was soon alarmed at the tolerance shown by Nagy to representatives of the old political parties and of the old social order. On the night of 1–2 November Kádár slipped away from Budapest when the anti-Stalinist Hungarian national rising was at its peak. With Soviet backing he formed a new 'revolutionary anti-fascist government' in eastern Hungary and remained Prime Minister until 1958, accepting Russian suppression of the national rising and the eventual trial and execution of Nagy. Kádár never relaxed his hold on the party as First Secretary. Gradually and cautiously he steered Hungary towards greater freedom of expression, notably during his second premiership, from 1961 to 1965. The pace of economic reform and political liberalization quickened during the 1980s. In May 1988 he became titular Party President and was replaced as Secretary of the MSzMP by the reformer, Karoly Grosz. But, as Hungary prepared to revert to democracy in 1989, Kádár was dismissed, losing all influence in the party. He died soon afterwards. J. Kádár: *Socialism and Democracy in Hungary* (Budapest, 1984); G. H. Heinrich: *Hungary: Politics, Economics and Society* (1986); F. A. Vali: *Rift and Revolt in Hungary* (Cambridge, Mass., 1961).

Kapp, Wolfgang (1858–1922), German right-wing politician: born in New York, the son of a politician who had taken refuge in America after the 1848 revolutions. The family returned to Berlin when Kapp was 12 years old and later settled in East Prussia. Upon the outbreak of war in 1914 Kapp became Rural Governor (*Generallandschaftdirektor*) of the province and was closely associated with conservative annexationist politicians. In June 1916 he published a pamphlet urging a more vigorous conduct of the war, denouncing the Chancellor (BETHMANN HOLLWEG) and inviting him to challenge Kapp to a duel if he believed his character smeared. The circulation of Kapp's pamphlet among the troops greatly angered Kaiser WILLIAM II, while it was pointed out in the Reichstag that the Chancellor could not, by law, challenge Kapp to the duel which he sought. Kapp's behaviour, although regarded as folly by many prominent figures, gained him a following on the political Right. Early in 1920 he conspired with General von Lüttwitz (1859–1942), whose troops were about to be disbanded after service in the Baltic provinces. Lüttwitz's men seized Berlin on 13 March 1920 and set up a new nationalistic government, headed by Kapp. The lawful republican government called a general strike. Despite support from LUDENDORFF, Kapp's authority melted away in the face of opposition from the rank and file of the army, the police and the workers. He fled to Sweden on 17 March. On returning from Sweden in 1922 he was arrested and died while awaiting trial. The Kapp *Putsch*, although a fiasco, showed the dissatisfaction of the German right-wing movement with the Weimar Republic, a mood later exploited by HITLER's Bavarian-based Nazis. R. G. L. Waite: *Vanguard of Nazism; the Free Corps Movement in Germany, 1918–1923* (Cambridge, Mass., 1952); H. J. Gordon: *The Reichswehr and the German Republic, 1919–1926* (Princeton, N.J., 1957); J. W. Wheeler-Bennett: *The Nemesis of Power* (1953).

Karadzić, Radovan (1945–), Bosnian Serb political leader: a Montenegrin in origin, who spent most of his life in central Bosnia. He studied medicine at university, specializing early in psychiatry and the treatment of neuroses. He worked in the Bosnian hospital service throughout the 1980s, as well as giving counselling to the Sarajevo football club; and he has published several books of poetry. When the Serbian Democratic Party (SDS) was founded in Bosnia-Herzegovina in July 1990 he was recognized as its leader. In the election of December 1990 he won seventy-two seats in the assembly, twelve less than the Muslim followers of IZETBEGOVIĆ. On the outbreak of civil war in March 1992 Karadzić worked closely with President MILOŠEVIĆ in Belgrade, withdrawing from Sarajevo to set up 'the Serba Republic' at Pale in August 1992. Arms supplied from Belgrade gave him the nucleus of a powerful army and the opportunity to establish SDS-controlled autonomous regions within Croatia as well as Bosnia. UN observers accused him of war crimes, in authorizing 'ethnic cleansing' of towns captured by his forces. Western governments refused to recognize the Pale regime but acknowledged the need to negotiate with Karadzić to seek an end to Bosnia's protracted civil war. Under the terms of the Dayton Accord and the Treaty of Paris of December 1995 Karadzić was, however, specifically excluded from holding political office because of his alleged war crimes. N. Malcolm: *Bosnia, A Short History* (1994); M. Glenny: *The Fall of Yugoslavia* (1992).

Karamanlis, Constantine (1907–), Greek Prime Minister and President: born at Proti, eastern Macedonia. He was a lawyer in Athens when he entered Parliament in 1935 for the right-wing Populist Party. During and after the Greek Civil War (1946–9) he held a succession of government posts, finally becoming a highly efficient Minister of Public Works and, in October 1955, Greece's youngest Prime Minister. Karamanlis organized a new conservative party, the National Radical Union (ERE) which gave him parliamentary support until he resigned (over the Cyprus Question) in June 1963. During the PAPADOPOULOS 'colonels' regime' of 1967–74 Karamanlis went into voluntary exile in Paris, but political associates recalled him in July 1974 to help re-establish parliamentary government and he was again Prime Minister for a six-year term in which constitutional changes confirmed Greece's status as a democratic republic. Karamanlis created the New Democratic Party (ND) as a successor to ERE and negotiated Greece's entry into the EEC. He served as President of the Hellennic Republic from May 1980 until March 1985 and was elected for a second term in May 1990, finally retiring in March 1995. C. M. Woodhouse: *Karamanlis, Restorer of Greek Democracy* (Oxford, 1982);

J. Campbell and P. Sherrard: *Modern Greece* (1968).

Károlyi, Mihály (1875–1955), Hungarian liberal reformer: born in Budapest into one of the great Magyar magnate dynasties, whose family estates in 1914 covered 218,000 acres (one-and-a-half times as large as the English county of Middlesex). Count Károlyi entered the Budapest Parliament in 1905, with liberal views which rapidly became radical and, during the First World War, strongly in favour of Hungarian independence. King CHARLES appointed him Prime Minister on 30 October 1918. Károlyi secured an armistice with the Allied commander FRANCHET D'ESPEREY, and, on 16 November, took office as provisional President of the Hungarian Republic. As a step towards the social democracy in which he believed, Károlyi renounced his title and supervised the division of his personal estates among the peasantry. He failed, however, to secure political backing from the victorious allies, and his presidency ended abruptly in March 1919, with the short-lived communist regime of Béla KUN. Károlyi then went into exile for twenty-seven years, never reconciling his idealism with the conservative social structure upheld by Regent HORTHY. From 1946 to 1949 he served communist Hungary as a diplomat, but the doctrinaire Stalinism of RÁKOSI repelled him and he returned, 'without illusions', to voluntary exile in Switzerland. M. Károlyi: *Fighting the World* (1925), *Faith without Illusions* (1956).

Kaunda, Kenneth David (1924–), founding President of Zambia: born in Lubwa, then in Northern Rhodesia. He was trained as a teacher and for three years was headmaster of a small school. While serving as a welfare officer in the copper mines, he founded the Zambian African National Congress (1958). The movement was considered subversive and was proscribed, Kaunda being imprisoned by the government of WELENSKY in the Rhodesia-Nyasaland Federation. By 1960 he was a free man again and set up a United Nationalist Independence Party (UNIP), pledged to end the Federation, which he saw as a means for the white majority in Southern Rhodesia to exploit coloured workers in the northern copper-belt. Kaunda's electoral successes in 1963 confirmed the resolve of the government in London to break up the Federation. In January 1964 he became Prime Minister of Northern Rhodesia, assuming office as President of the Zambian Republic on 24 October 1964. As President he was faced by three main problems: a backward economy; hostility from the Rhodesia of Ian SMITH; and the difficulty of keeping unity in a republic which was larger than France and inhabited by more than seventy tribes. Kaunda's Christian humanism – which he affirmed in his book *A Humanist in Africa* (1966) – left him at variance with militant racialists, black or white. The threat of disintegration forced him to suspend the 1964 democratic constitution in December 1972, replacing it seven months later by a constitution which allowed no political party apart from his own UNIP. His standing as an elder statesman of the Commonwealth was shown by the decision to hold the 1979 Commonwealth Conference in Lusaka, despite the threat of counter-terrorist activity from Zimbabwe-Rhodesia. Increasingly, however, Kaunda's persistence in maintaining a UNIP dictatorship aroused criticism abroad. In 1991, under both internal and external pressure, he accepted the need for multiparty elections. In the ensuing presidential election Kaunda was defeated by the democratic leader, Frederick Chiluba, who succeeded him as Zambia's head of state on 31 October 1991. K. D. Kaunda: *A Humanist in Africa* (1966), *Humanism in Zambia and its Implementation* (2 vols) (Lusaka, 1967, 1974) *Letters to my Children*

(Lusaka, 1978); P. Brownrigg: *Kenneth Kaunda* (Lusaka, 1989); J. M. Mwanakatwe: *The End of the Kaunda Era* (Lusaka, 1994); M. M. Burdette: *Zambia, between Two Worlds* (Boulder, Colo., 1980).

Kautsky, Karl (1854–1938), German and central European socialist: born in Prague, visited MARX in London in 1880–1 and founded the influential German socialist newspaper *Die Neue Zeit* in 1883. The political programme adopted by the German Socialist Party (SPD) at the Erfurt Party Congress of 1891 was largely Kautsky's work and he remained an influential member of the SPD and the socialist international until 1914, opposing the revisionism of BERNSTEIN within Germany as well as countering the undoctrinaire teachings of the French leader, JAURÈS, within the international movement as a whole. Kautsky was a pacifist but he was also bitterly critical of LENIN'S Bolshevism, considering the Russian dictatatorship of the proletariat a misunderstanding of Marx's teachings. Kautsky's writings included the editing of German diplomatic documents on the origins of the First World War and a study of Sir Thomas More's alleged socialism. He lived in Vienna for most of the inter-war period, taking Czechoslovak citizenship in 1934. HITLER'S incorporation of Austria in Greater Germany (March 1938) forced him into exile, and he spent the last months of his life in Holland. C. W. Schorske: *German Social Democracy 1905–1917* (Cambridge, 1955); A. J. Berlau: *The German Social Democratic Party 1914–1921* (New York, 1949); G. Roth: *The Social Democrats in Imperial Germany* (Totowa, N.J., 1963).

Keating, Paul John (1944–), Australian Prime Minister: born at Bankstown, New South Wales into a family of Irish Catholic descent. He left school at 14, though continuing his education at evening classes. After working for a municipal employees' union he became Labor MP for Blaxland at the age of 25 and had brief ministerial experience under WHITLAM in 1975. When Labor returned to power in 1983 he became Treasurer (finance minister) to HAWKE, whom he succeeded as Prime Minister in December 1990. He was less sympathetic to the British than Hawke and in 1993 put forward plans for Australia to become a republic. He lost the election of March 1996. E. Carew: *Paul Keating, Prime Minister* (Sydney, 1992); M. Gordon: *A Question of Leadership; Paul Keating, Political Fighter* (St Lucia, 1993).

Kellogg, Frank Billings (1856–1937), US Secretary of State: born at Potsdam in New York State, his farming family moving to Minnesota in 1865. He was admitted to the bar in 1877 gaining a reputation as a corporation lawyer and as a trust-breaking counsel attached to the US Attorney-General's office before being elected as a Republican Senator in 1916. After six years on Capitol Hill he was appointed ambassador in London by President COOLIDGE in 1924, but was recalled to Washington a year later to serve as Secretary of State. His name is especially associated with the Kellogg Pact of 27 August 1928, a convention drawn up in the first instance with the French statesman BRIAND, and providing for the outlawing of war as an instrument of national policy. Eventually sixty-two governments adhered to the pact, which also provided for the peaceful settlement of disputes. Kellogg was awarded the Nobel Peace Prize of 1929 for his initiative. From 1930 to 1935 he was a judge at the Permanent Court of Justice in The Hague. D. Hunter Miller: *The Paris Pact of Peace* (1928); H. L. Stimson: *The Pact of Paris* (New York, 1928).

Kelly, Petra Karin (1947–92), leading European 'Green' campaigner: born Petra

Lehmann in Günzburg, Bavaria, changing her surname when her divorcée mother married an American colonel, J. E. Kelly. Petra Kelly received her main schooling in Virginia, completing her university education with great distinction in Washington D.C. before returning to Bavaria and settling in Würzburg in 1967. For seven years she worked as a civil servant for the European Commission in Brussels. In March 1979 she was a founder-member of *Die Grünen* (The Greens), an ecology party for which she became principal campaigner in West Germany, winning respect on both sides of the Atlantic for her sincerity and skill. She sat in parliament at Bonn 1983–90, increasingly committing the Greens to issues of civil rights and nuclear disarmament; and speaking at rallies in the USA, Britain, Ireland, Finland, Japan and Australia. The Greens, who won forty-two seats in West Germany's 1987 election, fared disastrously in the first election after reunification (December 1990). Although in April 1991 *Die Grünen* rejected her leadership, she continued to campaign widely at home and abroad, supported by her partner, Gert Bastian (1923–92), a Major-General who had resigned from the German army and become a Green parliamentary deputy. In October 1992 she was found dead in her flat in Bonn, apparently shot in her sleep by Bastian's revolver. He then shot himself; a suicide pact is unlikely. S. Parkin: *The Life and Death of Petra Kelly* (1994); M. Dittmars: *The Green Party in West Germany* (rev. edn Buckingham, 1988).

Kemal, Mustafa (1880–1938), Turkish General and President: born in Salonika, the son of a clerk in the Ottoman government service who died when he was 8. He was educated at cadet schools at Salonika and Bitolj before having a brilliant career at the staff college in Constantinople and being gazetted Captain at the age of 24. Soon afterwards, however, he was imprisoned on suspicion of revolutionary activity but his career advanced rapidly after the curbs imposed on Sultan ABDUL HAMID by the Young Turks in 1908. Kemal fought against the Italians in Libya in 1911–12 and defended the Bulair lines covering the Gallipoli peninsula in the First Balkan War, 1912–13. His reputation as a soldier was made in 1915 when he held the Sari Bair ridge on Gallipoli against the Australians and New Zealanders. He fought in the Caucasus in 1916 and in Syria in 1918. Resentment at the proposed dismemberment of the Turkish heartland led him in May 1919 to organize a nationalist revolution in Anatolia. There was severe fighting in Anatolia from 1920 to 1922, the Turks seeking to oust the Greek army from Smyrna (Izmir), where it had landed in the spring of 1919. Kemal gained a decisive victory in the last week of August 1922 and threatened to seize Constantinople which was occupied by an Allied army, predominantly British. In October 1923 he formally proclaimed a Turkish Republic, moving the capital from Istanbul (as Constantinople now became) to Ankara, where he had established a provisional administration as early as April 1920. From 1923 until his death on 10 November 1938 he was Turkey's President and dictator, forcing through measures to secularize the country, and imposing a social and political revolution which emancipated women. He introduced western styles of dress and a Latin alphabet, and encouraged Turkish nationalistic feeling at the expense of Islamic traditions. Among these social changes was the adoption of surnames (1935), Kemal assuming the patronymic 'Father of the Turks' (Atatürk). He died in Istanbul on 10 November 1938. His policy of wise statesmanship, steady rearmament and industrialization was continued by his successor, and former colleague in arms, INÖNÜ. Lord Kinross: *Atatürk, The Rebirth of a Nation* (1964); I. Orga: *Phoenix Ascendant, The Rise of Modern Turkey* (1958); I. and M. Orga:

Atatürk (1962); V. D. Volkan and N. Itzkowitz: *The Immortal Atatürk* (Chicago, 1984); A. Palmer: *Kemal Atatürk* (1991).

Kennedy, John Fitzgerald (1917–63), President of the United States from 1961 to 1963: born at Brookline, Massachusetts, the second son of the banker and financier, Joseph Kennedy (1888–1966), who was ambassador in London from 1938 to 1941. John Kennedy was educated at Choate School, Harvard University and the London School of Economics. During the war in the Pacific he distinguished himself as commander of a torpedo-boat (PT-109) in the Solomon Islands. He sat as a Democratic Congressman from 1947 until elected as Senator for Massachusetts in 1952. From 1957 onwards he was a prominent member of the Foreign Relations Committee in the Senate, and in January 1961 became the first Roman Catholic President in America's history; and, at 43, the youngest to take office. His thousand days of power promised more than they could fulfil: the challenge of a 'new frontier' of opportunities, aid to Latin America and to the underdeveloped nations, civil rights legislation and social reform. Some of these measures were carried through by his successor, Lyndon JOHNSON, who had served as Kennedy's Vice-President. In foreign affairs Kennedy acted with vigour, notably over the threat of Soviet missiles in Cuba in October 1962. His dynamic energy conveyed a sense of firm leadership and of mission, and this impression was emphasized by his inspiring speeches. His assassination at Dallas on 22 November 1963, apparently by Lee Harvey Oswald, shocked and dismayed the peoples of many nations and left the younger generation of politically minded Americans with a sense of frustration. A. M. Schlesinger Jnr.: *A Thousand Days* (1965); T. C. Sorensen: *Kennedy* (1965); N. Hamilton: *JFK* (1992); R. Reeves: *President Kennedy* (1993).

Kennedy, Robert Francis (1925–68), American politician: born in Brookline, Massachusetts, the third son of Joseph Kennedy and a younger brother of the later President, John KENNEDY. Robert Kennedy was primarily educated at Harvard University and the University of Virginia Law School. After serving as a naval officer from 1944 to 1946, he practised law in Massachusetts and managed the presidential campaign of his brother in 1960. From 1961 to 1964 he was US Attorney-General, winning high regard for his support of Negro civil rights legislation. He became Senator for New York State in 1965, and was leading candidate for the Democratic presidential nomination in 1968 when, on 5 June 1968, he was shot by a Jordanian refugee in Los Angeles, apparently because of his alleged support of the Zionist cause against the Arabs. He died from his wounds the following day. A. M. Schlesinger, Jnr.: *Robert Kennedy and His Times* (1978); E. O. Guthman and J. Shulman (eds): *Robert Kennedy in His Own Words* (1980); P. Collier and D. Horovitz: *The Kennedys* (1984).

Kenyatta, Jomo (c. 1897–1978), founding President of the Republic of Kenya: born at Ngenda into the Kikuyu tribe. He received his education at the Scottish mission school in Thogot from 1909 to 1914. For some years in the 1920s he worked as a clerk with the Nairobi municipal authorities, but he was deeply interested in advancing the welfare of the Kikuyu people and was their spokesman at talks in London in 1929–30. From 1931 to 1946 he lived abroad, mostly in England although he spent several months in the Soviet Union in 1932–3. His book *Facing Mount Kenya* was published in London in 1938, and in this voluntary exile he was recognized as a national leader by his people. Much of the Second World

War he spent in Sussex, near Worthing, occasionally giving lectures on African affairs. He participated in an important Pan-African Congress in Manchester in 1945, returning at last to Nairobi in September 1946. Nine months later he established the Kenya Africa Union to seek independence. On 21 October 1952 he was arrested and charged with controlling the Mau Mau society, which was responsible for numerous murders and which Kenyatta had denounced two months previously. In April 1953 he was sentenced to seven years' hard labour, and subsequently held under restraint until the government of Harold MACMILLAN changed its policy towards Kenya. Personal freedom in August 1961 was followed five months later by membership of the Legislative Council. When Kenya became independent, in June 1963, Kenyatta took office as Prime Minister, succeeding as President of the Republic, which was established in December 1964. At first he tried to check tribal divisions by centralization, collaborating with the much younger political spokesman of the Luo tribe, Tom MBOYA. When Mboya was assassinated in July 1969, Kenyatta was faced by a crisis of disintegration. To some extent he used economic 'Africanization' at the expense of Indian and white settlers as a means of countering the threat of tribal conflict. He banned the Kenya People's Union (a Communist front organization) in October 1969, not least because its leader, Oginga Odinga, was a Luo. Kenyatta was able to maintain a delicate balance of interests within the republic during his later years. He died suddenly on 22 August 1978, and was given an impressive state funeral in Nairobi nine days later. J. Kenyatta: *Facing Mount Kenya* (1937); J. Murray-Brown: *Kenyatta* (1972); E. Huxley: *Out in the Midday Sun* (1985).

Kerensky, Alexander Feodorovitch (1881–1970), Russian democratic revolutionary: born in Simbirsk, studied law at the University of St Petersburg. He was elected to the lower parliamentary chamber, the State Duma, in 1912 as a democratic socialist of the Labour Group (Trudoviki) and was, for a time, Deputy-Chairman of the Petrograd Soviet. Kerensky was never a Marxist, nor did he believe in a separate peace with Germany. On the fall of Tsar NICHOLAS II he became Minister of Justice in the Provisional Government (March 1917), taking over the War Ministry in mid-May and becoming Prime Minister on 25 July. His attempts to prosecute the war vigorously against Germany were hampered by the growing power of the Bolsheviks under LENIN and by the demoralization of the Russian people. The Bolshevik Revolution (7 November 1917) overthrew his government in Petrograd. He escaped to France, where he spent most of the years from 1919 to 1940. During the Second World War he lived in Australia, before finally settling in the United States in 1946. A. Kerensky: *The Catastrophe* (New York, 1927), *The Crucifixion of Liberty* (New York, 1934); R. P. Browder and A. Kerensky: *The Russian Provisional Government 1917* (3 vols) (Stanford, 1961); W. H. Chamberlin: *The Russian Revolution* Vol. 1 (New York, 1935); G. Katkov: *Russia 1917, The February Revolution* (1967); N. N. Sukhanov: *The Russian Revolution 1917* (1955).

Keynes, John Maynard (1883–1946), British economist: born in Cambridge, educated at Eton and King's College, Cambridge. As a civil servant before the First World War he made a specialist study of Indian financial questions. During the war he was an occasional lecturer in Cambridge and an adviser to the Treasury. His work at the Paris Peace Conference of 1919 led him to approach international economic problems in a critical frame of mind. *The Economic Consequences of the Peace*, which he wrote in 1919, was remarkable, both for its trenchant attacks on the idea of seeking reparations from the ex-enemy states and for its psychological insight into the attitudes of the principal statesmen. His chief doctrine in the inter-war period was the need to attain full employment by public investment, a cheap-money policy and the production of capital goods. His views on these matters were concentrated in his *General Theory of Employment, Interest and Money* (1936). Keynes' theories were of greater influence on the New Deal reforms of Franklin ROOSEVELT than on any British political programme, although he was himself a Liberal. He was again employed as principal wartime financial adviser from 1939 to 1945, and created a Baron in 1942. Two years later he stressed the importance of 'a Bank of Reconstruction and Development', an institution recommended at the Bretton Woods Conference of July 1944 and subsequently established as the so-called 'World Bank'. Keynes was a patron of the arts and the theatre, especially in his native Cambridge. In 1925 he married the ballerina, Lydia Lopokova (1892–1981). R. Skidelsky: *John Maynard Keynes* (2 vols to date) (1983, 1992); R. F. Harrod: *John Maynard Keynes* (1951); C. H. Hession: *John Maynard Keynes* (New York, 1984); W. Hutton: *The Revolution That Never Was; an Assessment of Keynesian Economics* (1986).

Khama Seretse (1921–80), first President of Botswana: born at Serowe, in the British protectorate of Bechuanaland. He became titular ruler of the Bamanagwato people at the age of 4, although his uncle Tshekedi Khama (1905–59) was chief Regent. Seretse Khama went to Balliol College, Oxford, subsequently reading for the bar at the Inner Temple. In February 1950, while still in London, he caused political controversy by announcing that in 1948 he had married an Englishwoman, Ruth Williams (1926–). Strong opposition to the mixed marriage came from Bechuanaland's neighbour, South Africa, on whose economy many of the Bamanagwato were dependent for work. The British authorities, bowing to South African pressure, banned Seretse Khama and his family from Bechuanaland. Almost all the Bamanagwato people remained loyal to their exiled Chief, however, and in 1956 he was allowed to return home, a year later becoming a member of the Protectorate's African Advisory Council. His wise counsel advanced Bechuanaland's constitutional transition. He formed the Bechuanaland Democratic Party in 1962, gained an electoral majority and became Prime Minister when full self-government was granted in 1965; he received a knighthood on the eve of independence. On 30 September 1966 Sir Seretse became President of the new Republic of Botswana. In his fourteen years of office he fostered communal harmony, a democratic sense of tolerance and firm opposition to the racialism in neighbouring South Africa and Rhodesia. M. Dutfield: *A Marriage of Inconvenience* (1990); E. Robins: *White Queen in Africa* (1967).

Khomeini, Ayatollah (Ruhallah Musavi Khumayni) (1902–89), spiritual leader of Iran's Islamic Revolution: born, a trader's son, near the holy city of Qum, attended a *madrasa* (Islamic college of higher education) and spent some twenty years of training in the philosophy of the Imami Shi'i sect of 'puritanical' Muslims in Iran, until he was accepted as a leader on whom the 'sign of God' (Ayatollah) was stamped. Khomeini first attracted world attention in 1963 at Qum for his forthright denunciation of the westernization policies of Shah Reza PAHLAVI. The Ayatollah was arrested in the holy city of Qum on 4 June 1963 for having preached a sermon attacking projected reforms and especially the gradual social and political emancipation of Iranian women. His arrest provoked demonstrations in Teheran and other cities. He was subsequently sent into exile, spent in Turkey, Iraq and finally near Paris. To many Iranians, he remained a persecuted puritanical and conservative religious leader, and he never abandoned his denunciation of the Shah's policy, including his failure to support the Arab cause against Israel. Mounting discontent in Iran during the closing months of 1977 and early 1978 culminated in serious riots and demonstrations in Isfahan, Teheran and Shiraz during the holy month of Ramadan (August 1978), the situation deteriorating in September, with crowds demanding the return of the exiled Ayatollah. By the beginning of December the Ayatollah was calling for the Shah's army to desert and support strikes intended to establish an Islamic Republic and end the rule of the Pähl avi dynasty. The Shah left the country on 16 January 1979, and on 1 February three million supporters of the Ayatollah gathered around Teheran and its airport to welcome their religious leader's return from his long exile. Attempts were then made to form a government of the Ayatollah's leading followers and to impose on the country his strict, Islamic code of obedience to the teachings of the Koran. For twelve months from the middle of February 1979 Khomeini was *de facto* ruler of the country. With the election on 1 February 1980 of Abolhassan Bani-Sadr (1935–) as first President of Iran, the Ayatollah reverted to the status of spiritual leader of the republic, being officially designated *vali faqih* ('moral supervisor'), giving him a position of unassailable authority which he maintained until his death on 3 June 1989. When in June 1981 Bani-Sadr's policies offended the Ayatollah, he ordered his impeachment; and it was Khomeini who decided the choice of Bani-Sadr's two successors. Among western rulers he regarded his great enemy as the US President, Jimmy CARTER; but within Islam his principal antagonist remained Iraq's Saddam HUSSEIN, with whom Iran was at war from 1980 to 1988. Khomeini claimed a moral right of judgement over all Islamic believers, wherever they lived. Thus on 14 February 1989 the Ayatollah issued a *fetwa* (edict of faith) calling on Muslims to kill the Indian-born British author Salman Rushdie (1947–) for what Khomeini maintained was blasphemy against Islam in his novel, *The Satanic Verses*. Within five weeks of the Ayatollah's death a struggle for the succession was resolved by constitutional changes which elevated the power of the President, thereby tacitly accepting the unique character of Khomeini's primacy in the Iran he had revolutionized. M. A. A. Montazzam: *The Life and Times of Ayatollah Khoumeini* (1994); M. Wright: *Iran – the Komeini Revolution* (1989); S. Bakhash: *The Reign of the Ayatollahs* (1985).

Khruschev, Nikita Sergeyevich (1894–1971), dominant personality in Soviet politics from 1955 to 1964: born in the Ukraine, at Kalinovka, the son of a miner. He, too, worked in a mine in the early 1920s while attending educational classes in his leisure hours. By 1930 he was a Communist Party official in Kiev, moving to Moscow soon afterwards and becoming secretary of the Moscow Regional Committee of the party in 1935, a post which brought him into close contact with the 'Mayor of Moscow', BULGANIN. The two men collaborated from 1936 to 1938 over construction of the Moscow Metro. In 1938 Khruschev returned to the Ukraine, remaining as an adviser to the armies in the south after the invasion of 1941 and returning with the liberating army in 1943–4, when he became chief minister of the Ukrainian Soviet Republic. From 1945 to 1947 he was concerned with the agricultural and industrial recovery in the Ukraine. His success led STALIN to give him responsibility for boosting Soviet agricultural production by drastic methods of reorganization in 1949–50, and he became a member of the inner councils of the party, the Presidium. Six months after Stalin's death Khruschev was appointed to the key post which Stalin had himself held for many years, First Secretary of the party. Khruschev thus gained control of the party machine, advancing his nominees until in February 1955 he felt strong enough to entrust the pliant Bulganin with the premiership. For three years the partnership of 'B and K' appeared to determine Soviet policy, the two men visiting London together and travelling to Belgrade for a reconciliation with Marshal TITO. In January 1956 Khruschev used the Twentieth Congress of the Soviet Communist Party as a platform in which to denounce rigid Stalinism and the 'cult of the personality'. The Congress thus unintentionally encouraged liberal tendencies in Poland (see GOMULKA) and, with tragic consequences, in Hungary (see NAGY). Yet Khruschev's hold on the party machine was sufficiently powerful for him to oust Bulganin and become Prime Minister himself on 27 March 1958. His world policy alternated between gestures of reconciliation and threats, both approaches being used during his two personal visits to the General Assembly of the United Nations in New York, 1959 and 1960. Mounting tension and personal animosity between Khruschev and MAO TSE-TUNG seemed by 1963 a greater threat to peace than the old 'cold war' confrontations, despite Soviet–American tension in October 1962 over the presence of Russian missiles in Cuba. As Khruschev gradually relaxed his hold on the party machine, so critics of his China policy edged him from office. He fell on 15 October 1964, the day preceding the news that China had exploded its first atomic bomb. KOSYGIN took over the premiership (much as Bulganin had before him) and BREZHNEV succeeded to Khruschev's posts within the party. Khruschev himself was allowed to live quietly in retirement, outside Moscow and out of touch with political affairs.

N. S. Khruschev: *Khruschev Remembers* (Boston, Mass., 1970), *The Last Testament* (Boston, Mass., 1974); G. W. Bresslauer: *Khruschev and Brezhnev as Leaders* (1982); L. B. Schapiro: *The Communist Party of the Soviet Union* (1971); M. McCauley: *Khruschev* (1991); A. Werth: *The Khruschev Phase* (1961); B. D. Wolfe: *Khruschev and Stalin's Ghost* (New York, 1957).

Kim Il Sung (1912–94), North Korean political leader: born near Pyongyang, acquired his Marxism in Soviet Russia, but returned home secretly and, from 1932, began to organize resistance to Japanese rule in Korea, building up a Korean People's Revolutionary Army. He later crossed back into the Soviet Union, arriving in Pyongyang as a Major in the Red Army when Soviet forces occupied North Korea on 8 August 1945. Kim founded and led the Korean Workers' Party (KWP) in a 'democratic patriotic front' from July 1946 and, with Soviet backing, became Prime Minister of the People's Democratic Republic of Korea when it was established on 8 September 1949. Attempts to unify North and South Korea led to war in 1949 the subsequent American-led UN invasion of North Korea prompting intervention from the Chinese. The attempt to secure unification of Korea shaped Kim's external policies for the rest of his life. He became Supereme Commander of the Armed Forces with the rank of Marshal, as well as remaining General Secretary of the KWP. After the adoption of a new constitution in December 1972 he became President. Despite changes in the Soviet Union and in China, Kim preserved a narrowly Stalinist political-economic system and basked in a personality cult which he sought to extend to his family. He also linked North Korea closely to the Soviet trading system. In Kim's last years North Korea's alleged development of nuclear weapons detracted attention from the economic turmoil caused by the collapse of the Soviet Union. He died on 8 July 1994. Within a week his son Kim Jong Il (1942–) had succeeded to all of his father's official posts. Kim Il Sung: *Collected Works* (Pyongyang, 1980–3); Dae-Sook Suh: *Kim Il Sung* (New York, 1988).

King, Ernest Joseph (1878–1956), American Admiral: born in Lorain, Ohio, and commissioned in the US navy in 1903, becoming a Rear-Admiral thirty years later. He was given the task of creating an Atlantic fleet in February 1941, but on 20 December 1941 he was appointed Commander-in-chief of the US fleet, soon afterwards also becoming Chief of Naval Operations. These posts, concentrating naval power in one man's hands, were without precedent in American history and would have been dangerous under a less naval-minded chief executive than Franklin ROOSEVELT. Admiral King, who was created a Fleet Admiral in 1944, was responsible for the strategy and naval logistics which defeated the Japanese fleet in the Pacific. As a member of the Joint Chiefs of Staff Committee, 1942–5, he was frequently at loggerheads with his British colleagues since he had a single-minded obsession with the need to defeat Japan. In this concentration on the Pacific he was also at variance with America's leaders: he argued that the European war was a matter of land and air power; the defeat of Japan seemed to him a proper task for the navies of the Allied nations. Particular difficulty arose in 1944 over his retention of landing craft for the Pacific instead of permitting them to be used for the cross-Channel invasion. His criticisms of the Royal Navy did not endear him to CHURCHILL. E. J. King and W. Whitehill: *Fleet Admiral King* (New York, 1953); S. E. Morison: *The Two-Ocean War* (Boston, Mass., 1963); R. H. Spector: *Eagle Against the Sun* (New York, 1984).

King, Martin Luther (1929–68), American civil rights leader from 1955 to his death: born in Atlanta, Georgia, graduated from Morehouse College, Atlanta, and Crozer Theological Seminary in Pennsylvania, before becoming a Doctor of Philosophy at Boston University. In the winter of 1955–6 he was serving as a Baptist pastor in Montgomery, Alabama, when he was moved to act in defence of a Negro seamstress, Rosa Parks, jailed for refusing to give up her seat on a bus to a white man. For 382 days he led a boycott of the city's buses, until the Supreme Court ordered Alabama to desegregate its transport system. Dr King's campaign, with its emphasis on non-violence and racial brotherhood, made him a national figure. In 1957 the Southern Christian Leadership Conference, of which he was founder-president, organized the first prayer pilgrimage in Washington to back civil rights demands. For three years he concentrated on 'sit-ins' at 'whites only' restaurants in the Deep South and on 'freedom rides' in districts where the buses were still segregated. The slow passage of civil rights legislation induced him to organize the Easter campaign of 1963, a prayer pilgrimage to the centre of the largest segregated city in America, Birmingham, Alabama. The response of white extremists to the originally peaceful demonstration led to five weeks of brutal repression, much of it caught on film for world television showing. The threat of intervention by the US Army forced the municipal authorities to make concessions and to release Dr King, who had been imprisoned together with some three thousand supporters. He led two major civil rights demonstrations in Washington in the summer of 1963. In 1964 he was awarded the Nobel Peace Prize. After the passage of President JOHNSON's Civil Rights Bill (July 1964), Dr King concentrated on ensuring just methods of enfranchising the Negro voters. For this purpose he led a remarkable procession of four thousand civil rights demonstrators from Selma to

Montgomery on 21 March 1965; and five months later a Voting Rights Act gave federal backing to his demands for electoral justice. His liberal Christian insistence on non-violence aroused hatred among white fanatics. In the spring of 1968 he supported a campaign by the poorly paid garbage workers of Memphis, Tennessee, for improved social status; and while visiting Memphis he was assassinated by a gunman with a long-range rifle as he stood on his hotel balcony (4 April 1968). He had brought to the civil rights movement the non-violence of a Gandhi expressed in the language and teachings of the New Testament. M. Luther King: *Strive Towards Freedom; the Montgomery Story* (1959), *The Words of Martin Luther King* (1983); C. S. King: *My Life with Martin Luther King* (1970); S. B. Oates: *Let the Trumpet Sound, a Biography of Martin Luther King* (1982); D. L. Lewis: *Martin Luther King, a Critical Biography* (1970).

King, William Lyon Mackenzie (1874–1950), Canadian Prime Minister for twenty-one years: born in Ontario in the town then known as Berlin, renamed Kitchener forty years later. He studied law at Toronto, entering the Federal Parliament as a Liberal in 1908 and remaining an MP for over forty years. After an apprenticeship as Minister of Labour he succeeded Sir Wilfred LAURIER as Liberal leader in 1919 and became Prime Minister in December 1921. His first government lasted until June 1926 and he was back again as Prime Minister in September 1926, remaining in power until August 1930. After five years of conservatism, the Canadians returned the Liberals to office again in October 1935 and Mackenzie King remained Prime Minister until November 1948. He was an astute political leader, conscious of the need to safeguard Canadian unity against separatist ideas popular in the French-speaking communities. Over foreign affairs he favoured isolation until the outbreak of the Second World War, when he acted as an intermediary between Washington and London, perhaps overplaying his role. In April 1942 he had the political courage to seek approval in a plebiscite for a major change in policy, the introduction of conscription. From 1943 onwards he supported plans for a post-war international organization, consistently seeking to counter the dominance of the Great Powers while opposing the granting of a status to the smaller powers which would be inconsistent with their size and resources. Upon his retirement in 1948 he received the Order of Merit. B. Hutchinson: *Mackenzie King, the Incredible Canadian* (1953); (J. W. Pickersill: *The Mackenzie King Record* (Chicago, 1960).

Kinnock, Neil Gordon (1942–), British Labour leader 1983–94: born, of Scottish descent, in South Wales, receiving his schooling at Pengam and his university education at Cardiff. After four years as a Workers' Educational Association tutor he was returned as Labour MP for Bedwellty in 1970 and elected to Labour's National Executive in 1978, becoming chief Opposition spokesman on education in 1979. He was returned for the new seat of Islwyn in the 1983 election. When Michael FOOT stood down as party leader, Kinnock was chosen as his successor (October 1983), even though he lacked Cabinet experience. The former Prices and Consumer Protection Minister, Roy Hattersley (1932–), a Yorkshireman, became deputy leader. Kinnock began modernizing the Party and checking the political manoeuvres of the militant Left, as well as serving in Parliament as Leader of the Opposition to the THATCHER government. Labour improved its electoral performance locally and in the General Election of 1987, but five years later the Kinnock–Hattersley combination failed to win sufficient support in south eastern England and the Midlands to defeat the Conservatives under John MAJOR in 1992. He resigned as party leader in July 1992, John Smith (1938–94) being elected his successor. Two years later Kinnock left Parliament in order to become one of the British representatives on the European Commission, from January 1995. H. Pelling: *Short History of the Labour Party* (10th edn 1993); D. E. Butler and M. Kavanagh: *The British General Election of 1992* (1992).

Kissinger, Henry Alfred (1923–), architect of American foreign policy from 1969 to 1977: born of Jewish parentage at Fürth in Bavaria, his parents subsequently settling in America to avoid Nazi persecution. He was educated at Harvard where he has held professiorial chairs, specializing in the history of international relations in the early nineteenth century. In 1968 he became a campaign adviser to NIXON and enjoyed great influence from 1969 to 1973 as Special Adviser to the President on National Security. This post gave him greater freedom than the Secretary of State in establishing contact with the Russians, Chinese and Vietnamese, as well as with the opposing sides in the Middle East. He shared the Nobel Peace Prize for 1973 because of his efforts to secure a settlement in Vietnam. Kissinger was one of the most pragmatic of American statesmen, more concerned with maintaining a balance of forces than with long-term ideals. When he was appointed US Secretary of State in September 1973 he found his peripatetic diplomatic style curbed by uncertainties at home: the Watergate scandal, culminating in Nixon's resignation eleven months later; and the lack of experience of President FORD. But Kissinger (who, because of his German birth, could not himself be a presidential candidate) was able to preserve the international standing of the United States by his skill as a negotiator, continuing his policy of Sino-American *détente*. After the inauguration of the Democrat Jimmy CARTER, Kissinger resumed his academic life. H. Kissinger: *White House Years* (1979), *Years of Upheaval* (1982); W. Isaacson: *Kissinger*, (New York, 1992); R. D. Schulzinger: *Henry Kissinger* (New York, 1990).

Kita Ikki (Kita Terujero), (1883–1937), Japanese national socialist: born at Sado, studied at Waseda University, Tokyo, publishing a book on 'nationalism and pure socialism' in 1906. He was in China from 1911 to 1913 and from 1916 to 1919, seeking to influence the revolution there and, in particular, to counter the westernizing tendencies of SUN YAT-SEN. On returning to Japan Kita became a founder-member of Yuzonsha, an extreme nationalist movement of which he was later the chief publicist, receiving financial backing from some famous business combines. In 1923 he openly advocated the setting up of a fascist regime: army leaders were to purge Japan of its parliamentary system and induce Prince Regent HIROHITO to establish a National Reorganization Council, which would place Japan's main industries under state control, confiscate excessive wealth and authorize expansionist policies to spread Yuzonsha ideals across client states in Asia. Fanatical naval officers and army cadets welcomed Kita's teachings and plunged Japan into political chaos, murdering Prime Minister Inukai in May 1932. Two former Prime Ministers and several prominent politicians were also killed during an attempted *coup* on 26 February 1936, when a thousand mutineers briefly controlled central Tokyo. After the revolt, Kita was charged with conspiracy before a military tribunal; early in 1937 he was executed by firing squad. His ideals continued to influence Japanese expansionists, notably TOJO. G. M. Wilson: *Radical Nationalist in Japan: Kita Ikki* (Cambridge, Mass., 1969);

R. Storry: *History of Modern Japan* (rev. edn 1963); D. Brown: *Nationalism in Japan* (Berkeley, Calif., 1969).

Kitchener, Horatio Herbert (1850–1916), British Field Marshal: born in County Kerry, Ireland, and educated at the Royal Military Academy in Woolwich, volunteering for service with an ambulance unit attached to the French army in the later stages of the Franco-Prussian War. In 1871 he was commissioned in the Royal Engineers, seeing service in India and the Middle East. He was appointed Commander-in-Chief of the army in Egypt in 1890. Six years later he undertook the reconquest of the Sudan, seeking to overthrow the tyranny established by the Mahdi, Mohammed Ahmed (1840–85) and perpetuated by his son and successor, the Khalifa, Abdullah el Taashi. By his victory over the Khalifa's Dervishes at Omdurman on 2 September 1898 Kitchener avenged the murder of GORDON at Khartoum. This victory alone was sufficient to make Major-General Kitchener a popular hero in Britain. It was followed later in the month by an advance to the fortified post of Fashoda on the Nile which was occupied by Kitchener in order to forestall the attempt of a French expedition, which had crossed Africa from the Congo under Colonel Marchand (1863–1934), to establish command of the upper waters of the Nile. Although the 'Fashoda crisis' brought Britain and France to the verge of war in Europe, personally good relations were maintained between Kitchener and Marchand at their point of encounter; and Kitchener, unlike many of his countrymen, showed respect for the initiative of the Frenchmen whose enterprise he frustrated. In 1899 he became Chief of Staff to Lord ROBERTS in the Boer War, taking command of the army in South Africa in 1900 and being forced to check Boer commando depredations by establishing a system of blockhouses and camps in which civilians were confined. These tactics provoked criticism in Britain and on the continent; but Kitchener (who had been made a Baron after his victory at Omdurman) was created a Viscount and appointed to command the army in India. From 1903 to 1905 he was involved in a serious dispute with the Viceroy, CURZON, over administrative details and responsibilities of the Indian army. In 1909 Kitchener received his Field Marshal's baton and in 1911 was sent to Cairo as British 'Agent', in effect ruler of the country. He returned to London on leave in July 1914, was created an Earl, and intercepted at Dover as he was about to begin his journey back to Egypt with a request that he should enter the government as Secretary of State for War. In this role he was of great value as a patriotic figurehead, giving confidence and encouraging recruitment, but he had not studied the preparations for a war in Europe and he found it difficult to collaborate with the civilian members of Asquith's Cabinet or to maintain the right relationship between a war minister and the commanders in the field. Despite his age he was prepared to travel to France, and later to Gallipoli, Alexandria and Salonika, in order to see the problems in the differing theatres of war; and in the spring of 1916 he agreed to go to Russia so as to encourage more resolute prosecution of the war on the Eastern Front. He embarked on the cruiser HMS *Hampshire* at Scapa Flow, but she struck a mine off the Orkneys soon after sailing for Archangel, and Kitchener is assumed to have drowned (5 June 1916). P. Magnus: *Kitchener* (1959); T. Royle: *The Kitchener Enigma* (1985); G. Cassar: *Kitchener, Architect of Victory* (1977).

Klerk, Frederik Willem de (1936–), South African State President: born in the Transvaal, educated at Potchefstroom University and opened a law practice at Vereeniging, the town for which he was returned to Parliament as a National

Party member in 1972, becoming party leader in the Transvaal ten years later. After holding ministerial posts in the apartheid governments of VORSTER and BOTHA, he succeeded to the State Presidency in August 1989 and, a month later, won a General Election on a programme which included gradual reform of the apartheid system so as to improve contacts abroad. With this mandate behind him, during 1990 he lifted the ban on the ANC and other African political organizations, ordering the release of MANDELA on 11 February 1990. During 1991 he secured repeal of the apartheid laws and on 20 December promoted a Convention on a Democratic South Africa, which opened with interracial talks at Johannesburg. Despite hostility from right-wing Afrikaaners and Zulu opponents of the ANC, he persevered with the talks, securing parliamentary backing for an interim multiracial constitution on 22 December 1993. The victory of the African National Congress in the multiracial election of April 1994 ended de Klerk's term as State President, but on 10 May 1994 he became Second Deputy President in the Mandela government. W. de Klerk: *F. W. de Klerk, the Man in his Time* (Johannesburg, 1991); T. H. Davenport: *South Africa, a Modern History* (1991).

Kohl, Helmut (1930–), first Chancellor of a reunified Germany: born at Ludwigshafen-am-Rhein, worked in the chemical industry before studying law at Frankfurt and Heidelberg. As early as 1956 he became Christian Democrat Chairman in the Rhineland and was party leader in the federal Parliament at Bonn, 1976–80. He headed a caretaker administration in October 1982, winning the West German elections in 1983 and again in January 1987. His strong conservatism enabled him to seek agreement with the German Democratic Republic without prejudicing his firm support of the European Community. His prospects as a unifier of the two Germanies increased after an amicable meeting with HONECKER in September 1987. When the East German economy collapsed in 1989 Kohl pressed for rapid reunification, achieved in October 1990. He led the Christian Democrats to victory on 2 December 1990 in the first democratic elections for all Germany in fifty-eight years. Rising unemployment in the eastern provinces and intensifying right-wing nationalism lowered his standing over the following four years, but the elections of 1994 hardly challenged his standing as Federal Chancellor. J. Ardagh: *Germany and the Germans* (1987).

Kolchak, Alexander Vassilevich (1874–1920), anti-Bolshevik Russian Admiral: born in the Crimea and entered the navy, rising to command the Black Sea Fleet in 1916. He was Minister of War of the 'All Russian Government' established in Siberia in the winter of 1917–18 to oppose the Bolsheviks in Petrograd. From November 1918 to December 1919 he officially called himself 'Supreme Ruler of Russia' and he enjoyed some authority over the central sector of the Trans-Siberian Railway, with his headquarters at Omsk. It was his forces which recaptured Ekaterinburg, nine days after the apparent murder there of Tsar NICHOLAS II and his family. In the hopes of unifying the 'Whites', Kolchak resigned his authority to DENIKIN in the closing weeks of 1919. Soon afterwards he was captured by the Bolsheviks and shot after a perfunctory trial at Irkutsk, February 1920. P. Fleming: *The Fate of Admiral Kolchak* (1963); R. M. Connaughton: *The Republic of Uphakovka; Admiral Kolchak and the Allied Intervention in Siberia* (1990).

Konoye, Prince Fumimaro (1891–1945), Japanese Prime Minister: born in Tokyo, a member of one of Japan's most ancient patrician families. He was educated at the Universities of Tokyo and Kyoto, attended the Paris Peace Conference of 1919–20 as a junior member of the Japanese delegation and from 1921 sat in the Japanese House of Peers, of which he became Lord Chancellor in 1933. HIROHITO appointed him Prime Minister in June 1937, regarding him as a moderate who enjoyed sufficient family prestige to stand up to the political machinations of the army leaders. But within a month of Konoye's taking office the Japanese invaded China and he proved unable to restrain the militarists. In despair, he resigned the premiership in January 1939. In July 1940 a group of five former Japanese premiers prevailed upon Konoye to form a government again, as a moderating influence on the War Minister, TOJO. His policy was, however, extremely devious: it was Konoye who on 27 September 1940 concluded the Tripartite Pact, allying Japan to Germany and Italy; and it was Konoye who declared that Japan sought a 'co-prosperity sphere' in Greater East Asia. But from December 1940 he encouraged negotiations with the USA, vainly seeking a personal meeting with ROOSEVELT in a genuine wish to prevent the spread of the war. Tojo, however, made it clear that the army would not accept leadership from a civilian Prime Minister and on 14 October 1941 Konoye stepped down in favour of his War Minister. In July 1945 Konoye was sent, unsuccessfully, on a peace mission to Moscow. After Japan's surrender he became deputy premier in the interim administration. He found, to his surprise, that he was on the Allied list of war criminals for having plotted aggression in East Asia. Rather than face trial, Konoye killed himself. R. Storry: *History of Modern Japan* (rev. edn 1963); W. L. Langer and S. Gleason: *The Undeclared War* (1953). Konoye's incomplete Memoirs appear in Part 20, *Report of Joint Committee on the Investigation of the Pearl Harbor Attack* (Washington, D.C., 1946).

Kornilov, Lavr Gheorgyevich (1870–1918), anti-Bolshevik Russian General: born at Kamenogorsk in humble conditions, distinguished himself as the officer commanding the Cossack rearguard at Mukden in the Russo-Japanese War of 1904–5 and as head of a division which penetrated deeply into Austria-Hungary in 1914. He was captured by the Austrians in Galicia in 1915 but escaped, returned to Russia, and was appointed commander of the Petrograd military district with the rank of Lieutenant-General in March 1917. He maintained discipline and was sent by the Provisional Government to command on the South Western Front, taking over as Commander-in-Chief in July 1917. Since he considered KERENSKY weak in facing the threat from the Bolshevik Soviet, he tried to carry out a *putsch* against both Kerensky and the Soviet early in September 1917. His troops fraternized with their opponents and he was put under arrest by Kerensky. After the Bolshevik Revolution, General Kornilov fought with the 'White' army in southern Russia until killed by a shell, July 1918. J. L. Munck: *The Kornilov Revolt; a Critical Examination* (Aarhus, 1987); G. Katkov: *Russia 1917, the February Revolution* (1967).

Kosygin, Alexei Nikolayevich (1904–80), long-serving Soviet Premier: born in St Petersburg and worked in textiles before becoming a Communist Party official in Leningrad in the early 1930s. He served as Mayor of Leningrad from 1938 to 1939 when he became Commissar for the Textile Industry and a member of the Central Committee of the Communist Party, in Moscow. STALIN consistently favoured Kosygin. He was Minister of Finance in 1948 and, when Stalin died in 1953, he was Minister for Light Industry. Under KHRUSCHEV he remained, as before, an inconspicuous member of the government and of the party machine. In 1956 he was given responsibility for planning the immediate economic growth. Four years later Khruschev appointed him Chairman of the State Economic Planning Commission, with the rank of first Deputy Prime Minister. He seems to have acquiesced in, rather than initiated, the overthrow of Khruschev by BREZHNEV and other close colleagues in the Politburo. Kosygin succeeded Khruschev as Prime Minister on 14 October 1964, concentrating on the domestic economy and collaborating with the more dynamic Brezhnev over foreign affairs. Although he was to become the longest-serving Soviet Premier, Kosygin never imposed any mark of personality on public affairs. Failing health forced him to resign at last on 23 October 1980. He died eight weeks later. J. W. Strong (ed.): *The Soviet Union under Brezhnev and Kosygin; the Transition Years* (New York, 1971).

Kreisky, Bruno (1911–), Austrian Socialist Chancellor: born in Vienna, of Jewish Moravian origin. He joined the socialist youth movement and was imprisoned under DOLLFUSS, but was able to emigrate to Sweden where, in 1940, he met the German socialist exile, Willy BRANDT. On returning to Austria in 1945 Kreisky became a diplomat; he was appointed State Secretary for Foreign Affairs in 1953 and helped Chancellor Julius Raab (1891–1964) to negotiate the State Treaty of 1955, which consolidated the independence and neutrality of Austria's second republic. Kreisky represented St Polten in parliament from 1956 and became Foreign Minister in Raab's 'grand coalition' in 1959, holding office until the coalition broke up in 1966. When the socialists won the 1970 elections of 1970 Kreisky became Chancellor, heading the Austrian government for thirteen years and achieving greater popularity than any previous Austrian politician. Basic social reforms raised the living standards of workers; well-balanced budgets brought prosperity; state investment developed Vienna as a centre for multinational agencies and organizations. Kreisky resigned in May 1983, partly through age but also because an upsurge of right-wing radicalism in the previous month's elections deprived the socialists of their absolute parliamentary majority and he could not face the prospect of holding together a coalition. K. L. Shell: *The Transformation of Austrian Socialism* (New York, 1962); M. A. Sully: *Political Parties and Elections in Austria* (1981); B. Jelavich: *Modern Austria, Empire and Republic* (Cambridge, 1987).

Kruger, Paulus (1825–1904), President of the Transvaal Republic: born near Colesburg in northern Cape Colony, his parents being emigrant Boer farmers of strict Calvinist beliefs. At the age of 11 he participated in the gruelling 'Great Trek' northwards, when many Boer settlers sought to establish a new home free from British rule beyond the Vaal river. His commercial and political astuteness early marked him out as a leader of his community. In 1881–2 he headed a provisional government established in the Transvaal and was recognized, by Britain and other countries, as President of the Transvaal Republic in 1883, a position confirmed by elections in 1888, 1893 and 1898. The discovery of gold and other rich mineral deposits in the Witwatersrand in 1886 suddenly changed the fortunes of his republic and threatened to overthrow its character as a predominantly farming community. Kruger sought to keep out foreign 'riff-raff' and preserve the Boer traditions. His country's new wealth enabled him to purchase arms abroad, notably from Germany, and he was encouraged to give voice to the anti-British sentiments he had imbibed as a child. In 1895 the easy defeat of the raid by Dr JAMESON increased Kruger's confidence; he believed he could count on support from Germany as well as from the Netherlands in any armed conflict with the

British. In September 1899 his forces launched a series of attacks across the borders of Cape Colony and Natal in order, as they believed, to forestall a British invasion. The early successes of the Boers were followed by a British counter-offensive early in 1900 which forced Kruger to evacuate his threatened capital, Pretoria, in May, and travel, in the following month, to Europe in the hope of securing armed mediation by Germany, perhaps even in alliance with France and Russia. Kruger found the European powers uninterested in intervention. He settled near Utrecht in the Netherlands, in poor health, and died while seeking to recuperate in Switzerland (14 July 1904). P. Kruger: *Memoirs* (1902); M. Nathan; *Paul Kruger* (rev. edn 1944); J. S. Marais: *The Fall of Kruger's Republic* (1962); S. Clete: *African Portraits* (1951).

Krupp, Alfred Felix (1907–67), German industrialist: born in the Rhineland, the son of Gustav KRUPP VON BOHLEN and great-grandson of Alfred Krupp (1812–87), who built up the family fortunes at Essen through the manufacture of arms and the control of numerous industrial enterprises in the Ruhr basin. Alfred Felix Krupp became a supporter of HITLER from 1932 onwards, and was repaid by the passage of a special 'Lex Krupp' in 1943, ensuring protection of the family's interests in the 300-year-old firm. He was arrested in 1945, and in 1947 was sentenced to twelve years' imprisonment for permitting inhumane conditions for foreign labourers forced to work in his enterprises. It was alleged he had employed concentration camp labour both at Essen and at Auschwitz. In 1951 the West German authorities released him from imprisonment. He was able to build up the Krupps industrial empire within the Common Market, thus contributing remarkably to the economic recovery of the Federal German Republic. W. L. Manchester: *The Arms of Krupp* (1968); P. Batty: *The House of Krupp* (1966).

Krupp von Bohlen, Gustav (Gustav von Bohlen und Halbach) (1869–1950), German industrialist: born at The Hague, entered the managerial side of the Krupp enterprises and in 1906 married Bertha Krupp (1886–1957), into whose hands the great Krupp industrial empire passed when her father, Friedrich Alfred Krupp, died suddenly (probably suicide) on 22 November 1902 after a smear campaign in a socialist newspaper accusing him of misconduct with Italian youths. Kaiser WILLIAM II, who refused to believe these stories, attended the marriage of Bertha and Gustav von Bohlen and authorized his change of nomenclature so as to perpetuate the name on Krupp. He had a virtual monopoly on steel for the German fleet, as well as supplying Germany and her allies with the heavy guns used during the First World War. With the return of peace he converted his factories to the manufacture of tractors, but was able to place them rapidly on a war footing after the advent of HITLER to power in 1933. Effective control of Krupps during the Nazi period was left to his son, Alfred Felix KRUPP, but Gustav was indicted as a major war criminal at Nuremberg in 1945. It was, however, ruled that he was too frail and too senile to stand trial; charges against him were dropped. Books: as previous entry.

Kubitschek de Oliveiro, Juscelino (1902–76), Brazilian President 1956–60: born in Diamantina, studied medicine at Minas Gerais University and served briefly as an army doctor before becoming a parliamentary deputy in 1934. From 1940 to 1945 he was Mayor of Brazil's third largest city, Belo Horizonte, where he encouraged municipal enterprise, particularly the building of medical clinics. After six years as Governor of Minas Gerais he became President at the head of a Social Democrat administration in 1956 and immediately began a vast public works programme, concentrating on the building of a trans-jungle highway. He is best remembered for the new inland capital, Brasilia, on which work started in May 1957; it officially became capital of the Republic on 21 April 1960, although a lakeside presidential palace was completed in the previous year. These projects were accompanied by dramatic inflation, as well as accusations of corruption and of neglecting the drought-ridden, impoverished northern regions. After the end of his four-year presidency Kubitchek retained some influence until the military *coup* of March 1964 when he went into exile for several years. He was killed in a car crash at a time when he appeared to be contemplating a return to active politics. R. Bourne: *Political Leaders of Latin America* (1969); E. B. Burns: *History of Brazil* (New York, 1980).

Kun, Béla (1886–1937), pioneer Hungarian Communist: born at Szilagycseh, Transylvania, of Jewish parentage. He was a journalist before the coming of the First World War, in which he was taken prisoner by the Russians. Early sympathies with Marxism made him welcome the Bolshevik Revolution and in May 1918 LENIN sent him to organize the first Moscow 'school' to indoctrinate foreign communists. With the collapse of Austria-Hungary Kun returned to Budapest in November 1918 as an experienced agitator, exploiting resentment over the moderate socialism of KÁROLYI and his failure to secure better terms for 'historic Hungary' from the allied military commanders. Károlyi's weakness enabled Kun to proclaim a Soviet Republic in Hungary in March 1919. But Kun had little popular support: the peasantry were alienated by his doctrinaire insistence on nationalizing land rather than sharing out the great estates, as they had hoped; and a 'red terror', instituted by his sadistic police chief Szamuelly, was long remembered for its cruelty. Kun could not prevent the Romanian army from advancing across the Hungarian plain and entering Budapest early in August 1919. He fled to Vienna, and later back to Russia, where he was executed during STALIN'S purge. R. Tókes: *Béla Kun and the Hungarian Soviet Republic* (1967); A. Palmer: *The Lands Between* (1970).

Kyprianou, Spyros (1932–), second President of Cyprus: born in Limassol where he attended the main Greek school, the Gymnasium, before coming to London, where he became a barrister in 1954. He founded the Cyprus Students' Union in England, where he also served as secretary to MAKARIOS when the Archbishop was in London. From 1961 to 1972 he was Cyprus's Foreign Minister, retiring to build up a personal following in the island as a lawyer and to found DIKO (the right-of-centre Cypriot Democratic Party) in May 1976, leading it to an electoral victory later in the year. On Makarios' death a year later he became acting President, his post confirmed by election in 1978. He worked consistently, but without success, for reunion of the island. Although he won the 1983 elections he was defeated in May 1988 by the millionaire Famagusta businessman, Georgios Vassiliou. Z. M. Necatigil: *Our Republic in Perspective* (Nicosia, 1985).

L

La Follette, Robert Marion (1855–1925), American 'Progressive' politician: born at Primrose, Wisconsin, graduating from the State University in 1879 and practising law before being elected to the House of Representatives, where he sat from 1885 to 1891 as a Republican. By the end of the century he had built up a reputation as a courageous fighter against corruption in his state and against the railway and timber interests which dominated its economy. From 1900 to 1904 he was Governor of Wisconsin, and was returned to the Senate in Washington in 1906, remaining a Senator for the rest of his life. He was a vigorous liberal reformer in domestic affairs, becoming nationally respected for his Seaman's Act in 1915, which gave the Merchant Marine a basic charter of rights for conditions of employment as well as providing a code of safety measures. Over foreign affairs La Follette was isolationist, opposing America's entry into the First World War and the League of Nations. The scandals of the Republican era under HARDING alienated La Follette from his party. In alliance with some socialist groups he founded in 1924 a Progressive Party. He stood for the presidential election, with Senator Wheeler from Montana as his running-mate, and put forward a programme of radical change, including nationalization of water resources and railways, relief to farmers, and cuts in income tax. The sitting Republican President, COOLIDGE, polled nearly sixteen million popular votes, the Democrat candidate (John W. Davis, 1873–1955, a Wilsonian lawyer) had over eight million, while La Follette gained nearly five million, but only carried his home state. He died soon afterwards, his tradition of liberal reform and strict isolationism being maintained by his son and namesake as a 'progressive Republican' Senator from 1925 to 1947. R. Hofstadter: *The Age of Reform* (New York, 1963); K. C. Mackay: *The Progressive Movement of 1924* (New York, 1947).

La Guardia, Fiorello Henry (1882–1947), Mayor of New York City: born in New York of Jewish Italian parentage, graduated from New York University in 1910, served in Italy in 1917–18 as a Major with the US Army Air Force, commanding a bomber squadron. He sat, as a Republican, in the House of Representatives after his return from Italy until 1921 and again from 1923 to 1933. He was respected as a reformer and a progressive, and in 1933 received some Democratic backing for his bid to become New York City's Mayor. La Guardia served as a colourful and energetic Mayor from 1933 to 1945: he introduced housing schemes, projects to protect work, and the first major American civil defence system against long-range bombing. He countered the external exuberance of the New Yorkers with awareness of poverty in the slum areas. He became Director of the United Nations Relief and Rehabilitation Administration (UNRRA) in 1946 – 'Ticker tape ain't spaghetti,' he reminded the UNRRA commission in New York in March 1946. His ten years of mayoralty had, however, left him exhausted, and he died suddenly on 20 September 1947. He is commemorated by the name of one of New York's airports. T. Kessner: *Fiorello* *la Guardia and the Making of Modern New York* (New York, 1989).

Lange, David Russell (1942–), New Zealand Prime Minister: born near Auckland, where he completed his university education as a lawyer, subsequently serving as a barrister for the underprivileged in the city. He was elected Labour MP for Mangere in 1977, showing such parliamentary skill that he was deputy party leader in 1979 and leader four years later. He won the General Election of July 1984 on an anti-nuclear policy over defence, subsequently strengthening contact with other Pacific nations anxious to create a nuclear-free zone in their waters. He was re-elected in 1987 but frequent bouts of ill-health forced him to resign in 1989. V. Wright: *David Lange, PM, a profile* (Wellington, 1984); G. W. Rice (ed.): *The Oxford History of New Zealand* (2nd edn Auckland, 1992).

Lansbury, George (1859–1940), British Labour leader from 1932 to 1935: born near Lowestoft in Suffolk, and active for many years in seeking improved social conditions in the East End of London. He was returned as Labour MP for Bow and Bromley in 1910, but resigned in 1912 in order to stand again on a 'votes for women' platform, though without success. His natural pacifism made him oppose the First World War. In 1919 he founded the *Daily Herald* as a democratic socialist newspaper and edited it until 1923. He returned to the Commons in 1922 and remained an MP until his death. In 1929 he attained Cabinet rank as First Commissioner of Works under MACDONALD, but he opposed the decision to form a National Government during the financial crisis of 1931. He was very popular in London, not least because of his opening up of London's parks for games and his encouragement of the plan to provide the Serpentine with a bathing station. Lansbury was the only member of the former Cabinet who remained in the Labour Party and kept his seat at the 1931 General Election, and he therefore led the party during the four following difficult years, assisted by ATTLEE. His idealistic Christian socialism pleased constituency members but puzzled many trade unionists, notably BEVIN. Lansbury resigned as leader, in favour of Attlee, after the Labour Party Conference of 1935, but he retained a personal following. His desire for a relaxation of tension led him, in April 1937, to visit HITLER in Germany, even though he loathed the basic assumptions of Nazi belief. G. Lansbury: *My Life* (1928), *My Quest for Peace* (1938); R. Postgate: *Life of George Lansbury* (1951); B. Holman: *Good Old George* (1990).

Lansdowne, Lord (Henry Charles Keith Petty-Fitzmaurice) (1845–1927), Viceroy of India and British Foreign Secretary: born in London, educated at Eton and Christ Church, Oxford, succeeding as fifth Marquess of Lansdowne at the age of 21. He held minor office in the Gladstone governments of 1868–74 and 1880–5 before serving as Governor-General of Canada from 1883 to 1888. His earlier Liberalism moved gradually towards Unionism and in 1888 he accepted the Tory Salisbury's offer of the Viceroyalty of India, where he remained until 1894. A year later he took office as Secretary of State for War in Salisbury's third ministry, but he was criticized for the initial deficiencies of the army in South Africa in 1899, and Salisbury offered him the Foreign Office in November 1900. His five years as Foreign Secretary were marked by the gradual abandonment of British isolation: alliance with Japan in 1902 was followed by the settlement of differences with France in April 1904 ('the Entente Cordiale') and by Anglo-French collaboration in the first Moroccan crisis (1905). For ten years (1905–15) Lansdowne was out of office, leading the Conservative peers in their struggle against measures passed by the Liberal majority in the Commons. This contest, famous for the rejection of the 'People's Budget' introduced by LLOYD GEORGE, led eventually to the Parliament Act of 1911 and the curbing of the Lords' legislative powers. From May 1915 to December 1916 Lansdowne was Minister Without Portfolio in Asquith's coalition, and in November 1916 he proposed, in an able memorandum, that Britain should seek a negotiated peace, a proposal rejected by his colleagues. A year later he expressed these views in a letter to the *Daily Telegraph* (the editor of *The Times* having refused to publish it), but his courageous action aroused widespread condemnation. He continued to press for a negotiated settlement in speeches in the House of Lords. His party was, however, reluctant to associate itself with him, and for the last ten years of his life he had little influence on public events. Lord Newton: *Lord Lansdowne* (1929); Z. S. Steiner: *Britain and the Origins of the First World War* (1977); G. W. Monger: *The End of Isolation* (1963).

Lansing, Robert (1864–1928), US Secretary of State from 1915 to 1920: born at Watertown, New York State, and educated at Amherst, whence he graduated in 1882. He became a lawyer, specializing in international law and acting as counsel over a succession of arbitration cases, mainly concerned with fishing rights. He succeeded BRYAN as Secretary of State in June 1915, vigorously supporting the foreign policy of Woodrow WILSON. Lansing's legalism was a natural complement to Wilson's idealism. Lansing negotiated an agreement over areas of 'special interest' with Japan at a tense moment in Japanese–American relations (1917) and, with Colonel HOUSE, helped establish the unusual wartime partnership by which the United States became an 'associated power' of Britain, France, Italy and Belgium rather than a full ally. He attended the Paris Peace Conference in 1919, where he deplored Wilson's insistence on making the basic foundation document ('Covenant') of the League of Nations an integral part of the peace treaties. After Wilson's return to Washington and physical collapse, Lansing summoned the US Cabinet for consultation over policy on several occasions, maintaining that this was a duty which devolved on the Secretary of State should the President be incapacitated. Wilson, however, maintained that he was well enough to exercise his functions as chief executive and demanded Lansing's resignation (13 February 1920). His succession as Secretary of State by the insignificant Bainbridge Colby (1869–1950) did not improve Wilson's prospects of inducing the Senate to accept the Treaty of Versailles, nor did it augur well for Democrat hopes in the 1920 presidential election. B. F. Beers: *Vain Endeavour* (Durham, N.C., 1962).

Laurier, Wilfrid (1841–1919), Canadian Prime Minister from 1896 to 1911: born into a French Canadian and Roman Catholic family at St Lin, Quebec, and educated in Montreal. He was called to the bar and entered the Federal Parliament as a Liberal in 1874, remaining a member until his death. In 1887 he became leader of the Liberals, taking office as Prime Minister nine years later. No French Canadian had reached such political eminence before Laurier, and he was the first Roman Catholic Prime Minister in any British dominion. His premiership was marked by encouragement of the idea of Canada's unity and by his championship of imperial collaboration. He was personally responsible for the decision to send Canadian regiments to serve in South Africa during the Boer War, an act of faith in the imperial connection which encouraged EDWARD VII to bestow a knighthood on him in 1902. At the same time he jealously preserved Canada's right to act independently over foreign affairs and defence. He wished to follow up his success in improving trade relations with Britain by commercial agreements with the United States. This aspect of his policy did not appeal to the Canadian electorate and he was defeated in the 1911 General Election. Sir Wilfrid remained technically leader of the Opposition for the following eight years, declining to join a coalition since he could never accept the principle of conscription. He was followed as Liberal leader by his former Minister of Labour, Mackenzie KING. J. W. Dafoe: *Laurier, a Study in Canadian Politics* (Toronto, 1922); B. Robertson: *Laurier, the Great Conciliator* (Toronto, 1978).

Laval, Pierre (1883–1945), French politician of influence from 1930 to 1936 and 1940 to 1944: born in the northern Auvergne, at Chateldon, the son of the village innkeeper. With backing from the local Mayor, Laval's family was able to send the boy to Paris for schooling at the Lycee Saint-Louis. He became a lawyer, practising in Paris from 1909 onwards, and was returned to the Chamber of Deputies in May 1914 as a Socialist, representing the working class district of Aubervilliers, in north eastern Paris. Laval was basically an 'anti-war' deputy and narrowly escaped imprisonment in 1918 for sedition. He was not re-elected in 1919, and in 1920 broke away from the Socialists and built up a following as an independent man of the Left. Good political management enabled him to become Mayor of Aubervilliers in 1923 (a post he held officially until 1944) and he again represented Aubervilliers as a deputy from 1924 to 1927. In that year he became a Senator, having earlier in his career denounced the Senate as the repository of reactionary conservatism. He was Senator for the Seine from 1927 to 1936 and for his native Puy-de-Dôme from 1936 to 1944. From 1925 he began to gain ministerial experience, notably as Minister of Justice under BRIAND in 1926. From January 1931 to February 1932 and from June 1935 to January 1936 he was Prime Minister, but he became best known for the fifteen months which he spent as Foreign Minister (1934–6). He pursued a tortuous policy, seeking reconciliation with Germany, collaboration with MUSSOLINI's Italy, and the toning down of a Franco-Soviet agreement already accepted in principle by other French ministers. He was forced into the political wilderness in January 1936 by indignation over a partition plan for Abyssinia, reached in agreement with Mussolini and with the British Foreign Secretary, Sir Samuel Hoare (1880–1959), who also resigned. In 1940 Laval re-emerged as a political leader, serving as deputy to PÉTAIN from July to December 1940 and as titular Prime Minister and Foreign Minister from April 1942 to August 1944. His adroit policy of seeking concessions from Germany by holding out a promise of military collaboration, which he had no intention of fulfilling, aroused widespread distrust both on the part of the Germans and of Frenchmen with less equivocal instincts of loyalty. Laval survived an attempt on his life at Versailles in August 1941. He was arrested by the Nazis in the summer of 1944 at a time when he was seeking an accommodation with the western Allies by attempting to summon the constitutionally recognized National Assembly as a means of preserving French political continuity. When the war ended in 1945 he escaped to Spain, but returned to Paris in order to answer charges of treason brought by the provisional government of DE GAULLE. A hurried trial began on 4 October 1945. He was given no opportunity to present a defence of his actions and was sentenced to death six days later. de Gaulle rejected pleas by his lawyers for clemency. Laval was shot at Fresnes prison on 15 October 1945, the most eminent Frenchman executed for 'collaboration'. P. Laval: *The Unpublished Diary of Pierre Laval* (1948);

G. Warner: *Pierre Laval and the Eclipse of France* (1968).

Law, Andrew Bonar (1858–1923), British Prime Minister from 1922 to 1923: born at Rexton in New Brunswick, where his father was a Presbyterian minister. From 1870 to 1909 he lived in Scotland, attending Glasgow High School and representing the Blackfriars constituency in Glasgow as a Conservative MP from 1900 to 1906. Subsequently he represented Dulwich and Bootle before being returned for another Glasgow constituency from 1918 to 1923. Law gave the impression of believing in right-wing intransigence. For this reason in 1911 he was chosen by his party as leader in succession to BALFOUR, who was considered ineffectually remote. Law showed total determination to support the Ulstermen to the point of rebellion against the Irish Home Rule proposals of ASQUITH in 1913–14. During the First World War he attained Cabinet experience for the first time as Colonial Secretary in the Asquith coalition of May 1915, subsequently sitting as Chancellor of the Exchequer in LLOYD GEORGE's War Cabinet, and as Lord Privy Seal in the coalition formed in January 1919. Ill-health forced him to retire from politics between March and December 1921, but he resumed his activities when he saw the coalition threatening to disintegrate. He formed an 'Old Tory' right-wing government in October 1922, the Conservative victory in the General Election a month later confirming him in office. But the strain of the premiership broke his health. Physical weakness and natural caution meant that, as Prime Minister, he could influence events rather than determine their precise character. In May 1923 he collapsed, and was found to be suffering from incurable cancer of the throat. He resigned on 20 May 1923, dying on 30 October. Respect for his sense of duty led to proposals that he should be buried in Westminster Abbey, an honour bestowed on no other Prime Minister since GLADSTONE. R. Blake: *The Unknown Prime Minister* (1955); H. A. Taylor: *The Strange Case of Andrew Bonar Law* (1932); A. J. P. Taylor: *Beaverbrook* (1972).

Lawrence, Thomas Edward (1888–1935), British soldier and writer, popularly known as 'Lawrence of Arabia': born at Tremadoc, went to school and university at Oxford (Jesus College), undertaking several archaeological expeditions in the Middle East on the eve of the First World War. In December 1916 he was sent on a special mission from Cairo to Jeddah in order to co-ordinate the sporadic Arab revolt against Turkish rule which had begun on a small scale six months earlier. Colonel Lawrence, in conjunction with the Emirs Faisal and Abdullah (later King FAISAL I and King ABDULLAH), led the Arabs in a series of attacks along the railway from Damascus to Medina and advanced northwards so as to establish a mobile right wing to the grand offensive of ALLENBY in Palestine in 1918. After the war Lawrence considered the British had not fulfilled their obligations to the Bedouin Arabs, largely because of commitments made to the French, who secured a mandate in Syria. Lawrence was a spokesman for the Arabs at the Paris Peace Conference of 1919 and in 1921–2 was induced by Winston CHURCHILL (then Colonial Secretary) to advise the Colonial Office on Arab affairs. In this capacity he travelled to Cairo and Palestine with Churchill on a mission which temporarily eased the friction between Jews and Arabs in the British mandated territory. Lawrence's desire for anonymity led him to enlist in the RAF under an assumed name ('Ross'). Subsequently he changed his name by deed poll to 'T.E. Shaw' and served as an aircraftman from 1923 to 1935, spending more than two years stationed in India. He was thrown from his motorbike at high speed near his home in Dorset, and died from his injuries (19 May 1935). Most of his highly literary account of the Arab Revolt, *The Seven Pillars of Wisdom*, was written while he was a Fellow of All Souls College, Oxford, in 1919–20, but it was not published until after his death. J. Wilson: *Lawrence of Arabia, the Authorised Biography* (1989); L. James: *The Golden Warrior* (1990).

Lease, Mary Elizabeth (1853–1933), intemperate American temperance agitator and Populist campaigner: born in Elk County, Pennsylvania, called to the Kansas bar in the late 1870s, became famous as an agrarian reformer and a demagogue who denounced the 'bloodhounds of money'. She was especially active between 1890 and 1918, trying to encourage political consciousness among the agrarian communities of the mid-West: 'The farmers of Kansas must raise less corn and more Hell,' she declared in a speech of 1890. Her sensationalism, which often exploited anti-Semitic and anti-British prejudices, guaranteed her a considerable following. M. Lease: *The Problem of Civilization Solved* (Chicago, 1895); R. Hofstadter: *The Age of Reform* (New York, 1963).

Lee Kuan Yew (1923–), Singapore's first Prime Minister: born into a rich Chinese Singapore family, educated at Raffles College, Fitzwilliam College in Cambridge and the Middle Temple, returning home as a barrister in 1951. He founded the People's Action Party in 1954, a progressive anti-communist organization which in 1959 won the first elections after the island gained internal self-government. For the following thirty-four years Lee dominated Singapore's politics. He took Singapore into the Malaysian federation on its formation in September 1963 but seceded in August 1965, when he believed that other members of the federation were exploiting the economic well-being of the city and port. As chief minister of the newly independent republic of Singapore, Lee imposed strict commercial guidelines and firm police controls, enabling the island city to become south east Asia's most prosperous commercial and financial centre. At the same time Lee gained respect as a moderate arbitrator in Commonwealth affairs. He retired from the premiership in 1993, but he retained great influence as 'senior minister' in the Cabinet of his successor, Goh Chock Tong; his son Lee Sien Loong (1952–) served as Goh's deputy Premier, Minister of Defence and Minister for Foreign Trade. A. Josey: *Lee Kuan Yew, the Struggle for Singapore* (1980); J. Drysdale: *Singapore, Struggle for Success* (1984).

Lee, Robert Edward (1803–70), General-in-Chief of the Confederate States of America: born in Westmoreland County, Virginia, his father having been a distinguished commander in the War of Independence. Lee graduated from the Military Academy at West Point in 1829, second in his class, was commissioned in the Engineers and severely wounded at Chapultepec, the final engagement of the Mexican War (September 1847). From 1852 to 1855 he was commandant at West Point and then served with the cavalry in Texas, although given temporary command of a force of marines which put down John Brown's rising at Harper's Ferry in 1859. Lee was a staunch Virginian, having married Mary Custis (1806–73), a member of another respected Virginian family, whose estate at Arlington on the Potomac passed into Lee's hands. In the spring of 1861 Lee was offered high command in the Union armies but loyalty to Virginia led him to resign his commission as soon as his native state seceded. He helped fortify the Southern sea coast, assisted Jefferson DAVIS as military adviser, and was finally given a vital field command, taking over the army of northern Virginia when General Joseph Johnston (1807–91) was wounded at the end of May 1862. Lee defeated MCCLELLAN in the seven-day battle (26 June to 2 July 1862), thus removing the threat to the Confederate capital, Richmond, but he failed in his strategic purpose, the total destruction of the Union army so as to force peace. In August 1862, with JACKSON, he won the second battle of Bull Run and thus threatened Washington, DC, but he struck northwards into Maryland in September and his invasion was checked at Antietam. Although Lee's audacity and strategic vision kept Confederate hopes of victory alive, the South never recovered the initiative. Lee gained another victory at Fredericksburg on 13 December 1862 when he repelled Ambrose Burnside's crossing of the Rappahanock river. At heavy cost he repulsed a second Union crossing at Chancellorsville in May 1863, but his invasion of Pennsylvania that summer was abruptly halted at Gettysburg and his army was fortunate to escape disaster. Lee's understanding of Grant's military mind enabled Lee to stave off defeat in Virginia after he became Confederate 'General-in-Chief' in February 1865. He was eventually overwhelmed by sheer weight of numbers and superiority of resources; and he surrendered to GRANT at Appomattox on 9 April 1865. Lee was treated as a paroled officer, indicted for treason but never tried. Although deprived of the Custis-Lee house at Arlington, he was allowed to accept the presidency of Washington University at Lexington, Virginia, a post he held until his death in October 1870. Lee, who had long believed that slavery was degrading and who emancipated slaves on his property as soon as he inherited it, possessed the nobility of character to become a national hero despite his loyalty to a rebel cause. D. S. Freeman: *R. E. Lee: a Biography* (4 vols) (1934–5); B. Davis: *Gray Fox: Robert E. Lee and the Civil War* (1956).

Lenin, Vladimir Ilyitch (Ulyanov) (1870–1924), leader of the Russian Bolshevik Revolution: born at Simbirsk (renamed Ulyanovsk in 1924) on the central Volga, some three hundred miles east of Moscow. Alexander Ulyanov, his elder brother, was hanged on 20 May 1887 for plotting against the Tsar, an event which threw suspicion on the future Lenin when he was seeking entry into Kazan University. He was kept under police surveillance throughout the years in which he studied law, but permitted to go to St Petersburg for the final examinations in September 1890. After some years of Social Democratic agitation, he was arrested in December 1895 and sent to exile at Shushenskoye in the Eastern Sayan mountains of Siberia. He remained at Shushenskoye from May 1897 to February 1900. In the following July he left Russia and remained abroad until 1917 except for the winter of 1905–6, when he returned to St Petersburg. Lenin was in London from April 1902 to May 1903, as well as in the spring of 1907. At other times he lived in Brussels, Paris, and Cracow but his principal home in exile was on the outskirts of Geneva. By 1903 he was accepted as leader of the revolutionary Social Democrats ('Bolsheviks'); his authority stemmed from the combination of a powerful intellect with a trenchant pen, and was expressed in numerous pamphlets and revolutionary journalism. Lenin made three major contributions to Marxist theory: his belief that imperialism was the last form of capitalism, provoking revolution in the regions where the 'chain of imperialism' was its weakest; his confidence in the necessity for building up a highly disciplined party machine as the vanguard of revolutionary activity; his development of Engels' imprecise references to a 'dictatorship of the proletariat' into a central tenet of Marxist practice. An international conference, convened at Zimmerwald in Switzerland by groups of the 'anti-war' Left during September 1915, recognized Lenin as the outstanding advocate of 'civil war, not civil peace', although his proposals for the establishment of a Third Revolutionary Socialist International were, at that time, defeated. The overthrow of Tsar NICHOLAS II in March 1917 induced Lenin to accept an offer from German agents for a journey back from Switzerland across Germany to the Baltic in a 'sealed train'. LUDENDORFF, who authorized the journey, assumed that Lenin would proceed by way of Sweden and Finland so as to undermine the morale of the Russian Army by Bolshevik propaganda. Lenin duly arrived back in Petrograd on 16 April 1917, receiving a tumultuous welcome from workers and soldiers at the Finland Station. For nine weeks he was allowed considerable freedom of movement and expression, conducting an agitation in favour of immediate peace and radical social changes, mainly expressed in speeches to the Soviet which had been established in the Tauride Palace. The threat of a seizure of power by the Soviet in mid-July provoked repressive moves by KERENSKY, inducing Lenin to seek refuge in Finland from 24 July to 23 October. But the prospect of another winter of war, together with an acute shortage of bread, enabled Lenin to return and lead a Bolshevik revolt against Kerensky's government in Petrograd (6–8 November 1917). Lenin then instituted a new system of government, 'the Council (Soviet) of Peoples' Commissars', of which he was Chairman.

Lenin attempted to carry through a maximum programme of economic revolution, including the nationalization of banks, industries, property and land. At the same time he entrusted TROTSKY with the conclusion of a peace treaty with Germany. In order to emphasize the break with Russia's past, Lenin adopted the Gregorian calendar in February 1918 and established his capital in Moscow, instead of Petrograd, on 10 March 1918. Resistance to Bolshevism by 'White' armies (see DENIKIN, KOLCHAK) hampered the development of a basically communist system and in March 1921 Lenin was forced to compromise his principles to the extent of introducing a 'New Economic Policy' (NEP), which countered famine and peasant unrest by permitting limited private commerce and the establishment of state banks. On 30 August 1918 Lenin was shot and seriously wounded by a disillusioned Socialist revolutionary, Fanya Kaplan (who was herself shot dead by a police official five days later). Lenin never completely recovered: three strokes between May 1922 and March 1923 left him unable to conduct political business for the last year of his life. By 21 January 1924, when he finally died, STALIN had succeeded in securing control of the party machine at the expense of the much more experienced Trotsky. In July 1898, while in Siberia, Lenin married Nadezhda Krupskaya (1869–1939), who was hardly separated from him for more than a few days throughout their twenty-five years of marriage. From 1918 to 1928 she was responsible for adult education within Soviet Russia, and was frequently in conflict with Stalin. V. I. Lenin: *The Essentials of Leninism* (2 vols) (1947); N. K. Krupskaya: *Memories of Lenin* (1970). L. Fisher: *The Life of Lenin* (New York, 1964); R. Payne: *The Life and Death of Lenin* (New York, 1964); B. E. Wolfe: *Three Who Made a Revolution* (New York, 1948).

Leo XIII (Vincenzo Gioacchino Pecci) (1810–1903), Pope from 1878 to 1903: born at Carpineto Romano, educated by Jesuits in Viterbo and Rome and was ordained priest in 1837. He undertook diplomatic missions to Brussels, London, Paris and Cologne before being made Bishop of Perugia at the age of 36 and created a Cardinal seven years later. He was elected Pope in succession to Pius IX on 7 February 1878 and at once began a policy of reconciliation, notably with Bismarck's Germany, and ultimately with modern systems of government which had been alienated by his predecessor's conservative intransigence. Pope Leo sent the first Apostolic Delegate to the United States (1892) and was the first pontiff since the Reformation visited by a reigning British sovereign (EDWARD VII, 1903). In a series of important encyclicals – culminating in the famous *Rerum Novarum* of May 1891 – he set out the Church's teaching over temporal authority, the claims of democracy, social justice and the relationship between workers and employers. He failed, however, to reconcile papal and temporal claims to authority within Italy; and in France his policy of encouraging royalist Catholics to accept the Republic (the so-called '*Ralliement*' of the early 1890s) was defeated in purpose by the anti-Dreyfusard activities of prominent French Catholics in 1897–9. On his death in July 1903 he was succeeded by the saintly. PIUS X. L. P. Wallace: *Leo XIII* (Durham, N.C., 1966); J. N. D. Kelly: *The Oxford Dictionary of Popes* (1986).

Leopold II (1835–1909), King of the Belgians from 1865 to 1909: born in Brussels, the son of the first King of the Belgians, Leopold I (1790–1865), and through his mother a grandson of the last King of the French, Louis Philippe. In home politics Leopold II readily accepted the responsibilities of constitutional government, keeping a balance between the Liberal and Clericalist Parties and avoiding personal involvement in the bitter disputes over the secularization of education. His private life aroused widespread criticism, although he always made generous allowances to any ex-mistresses and their children. His greatest interest was in building up a central African empire around the Congo river. He was recognized as ruler of the Congo Free State in May 1885, and it was developed as a personal possession of the sovereign rather than as a Belgian colony. In 1903–4 the revelation in England (and later in Germany and the United States) of appalling conditions of slave labour in the Congo caused widespread criticism of the King in Brussels. He authorized the despatch to the Congo of three observers in 1905; this commission of inquiry confirmed the existence of slavery and ruthless exploitation. In 1908 Leopold accordingly ceded his Congo Free State to the Belgian people, the nation being expected thereafter to develop the 'Belgian Congo' as a colonial trust. He died on 19 December 1909 and was succeeded by his nephew, the much-respected King Albert I (1875–1934). N. Ascherson: *The King Incorporated – Leopold II in the Age of Trusts* (1963); R. Slade: *King Leopold's Congo* (1962).

Lesseps, Ferdinand de (1805–94), French engineer: born at Versailles, became a diplomat in 1825, and served as Consul in Alexandria, but left the service abruptly after undertaking secret negotiations with the Italian revolutionaries in Rome in 1849. He was related to the Empress Eugènie of France and, through her intervention, was able to interest NAPOLEON III in a project for constructing a canal across the isthmus of Suez. It was this undertaking, completed in 1869, which made de Lesseps world famous. He then began to plan a canal across the isthmus of Panama, a part of the world he did not know so well as he knew Egypt. In his plans he failed to allow for the ravages of disease among his workforce, nor did he appreciate the need for locks on any canal in Panama. Most disastrously, he allowed the Panama Canal Company, although primarily a French enterprise attracting money from many thousands of small and cautious French investors, to be run by international financiers of doubtful probity. Widespread mismanagement ruined the company, which went bankrupt in February 1889. The scandal destroyed the health of de Lesseps. At the age of 87 he was sentenced to a term of imprisonment. The judgment was set aside on appeal, but he died a few months later. C. Beatty: *Ferdinand de Lesseps* (1956); A. Wilson: *The Suez Canal* (2nd edn 1939).

Lewis, John Llewellyn (1880–1969), outstanding American labour leader: born in Iowa, the son of an immigrant Welsh coal miner. He became a miner himself, seeking early in his life to develop unionism within American industry. By the age of 40 Lewis was recognized throughout America as the foremost champion of workers in the coal industry. He was President of the powerful United Mine Workers of America (UMW) from 1920 to 1960. So great was his authority that he was able to take the UMW out of the American Federation of Labor in 1935, when he disagreed with the AFL's cautious acceptance of New Deal projects without adequate collective bargaining. Lewis organized the Congress of Industrial Organizations (CIO), a body which had four million militant members by the summer of 1937. Under Lewis's presidency the CIO concentrated on the closed shop, using 'sit-in' tactics for the first time, with great effectiveness in the steel industry. Lewis gave up the presidency of the CIO in 1940 so as to concentrate once more on his miners. In 1942 he disagreed with his successor as President, Philip Murray, and withdrew the UMW from the CIO, eventually accepting membership once more of the AFL. In 1947, however, the Taft–Hartley Act, which sought to restrict union activity and banned the 'closed shop', revived Lewis's militancy. Once again the UMW seceded from the AFL because it considered its opposition to the Act lacking in vigour. Lewis personally, and his union, were fined heavily in 1948 for strike tactics, but his power was sufficient to keep his union together and win his cause. His opposition could not, however, shake the legality of the Taft–Hartley Act. When Lewis retired in 1960 the restraints on union strike militancy were as severely defined as ever. His greatest achievement was in advancing the welfare of his miners rather than in establishing a pattern of militancy for American unionism as a whole. He died at his home in Alexandria, Virginia, in July 1969. J. A. Wechsler: *Labor Baron* (New York, 1944); S. Alinsky: *John L. Lewis, an Unauthorized Biography* (New York, 1949).

Li Hung-Chang (Li Hongzhang) (1823–1901), Chinese Imperial statesman: born at Nganghui, Hopei (Hubei), entered the imperial service, with such examination success that at the age of 26 he was a Hanlin academician, the highest level of Manchu scholarship. He became a provincial judge and, in 1862, Governor of Kiangsu (Jiangsu), where he accepted help from the British gunnery officer, Captain GORDON, to put down the Taiping rebels. From being Governor-General of the provinces around Peking (Beijing) in 1864 he was confirmed as Senior Grand Secretary of the government in 1872 and remained chief minister for more than a quarter of a century. Li Hung-chang was the chief advocate of *guandu-shangban* ('state sponsorship of self management'), a system which developed Chinese armaments, merchant shipping, coal mines, mills and other industries, although westernization proceeded more slowly than in Japan. In foreign affairs Li was constantly aware of the threat from Japan; he met French colonial demands in southern China in the hopes of holding on to Korea in the north. But Li's decision in 1888 to build up a modern fleet came too late to halt the Japanese, who discredited Li's policies with their striking victories on sea and land in the short 1894 war. To save face Li set out on a diplomatic mission to the West. He visited St Petersburg in June 1896, sought advice from BISMARCK, and met SALISBURY in London. Subsequently Li was accused of accepting bribes from the Russians over railway and naval concessions. Doubts of his probity led to Li's dismissal in 1898. With the spread of the xenophobic Boxer rising in November 1900 he was reinstated as governor of the region directly subordinate to the capital; but he died a few months later. S. C. Chu and K. C. Liu: *Li Hung-chang and China's Early Modernization* (1994); M. C. Wright: *The Last Stand of Chinese Conservatism: the T'ung Chih Restoration, 1862–1874* (Boston, Mass., 1957); F. Schuurmann and O. Schell: *Imperial China* (1967); J. O. P. Bland: *Li Hung-chang* (1917). *The Memoirs of Li Hung Chang* (New York, 1913) are an American forgery.

Lie, Trygve Halvdan (1896–1968), Norwegian politician and first Secretary-General of the United Nations: born in Oslo and practised as a lawyer before entering the Storting (parliament) as a Social Democrat. He was Norwegian Minister of Justice from 1935 to 1939, Minister of Business Development 1939–40 and Foreign Minister of the Norwegian Government-in-Exile in London from 1940 to 1945. It was his experience in this capacity which fitted him for the post of founder Secretary-General to the United Nations, an office he assumed on 29 January 1946, when the first session of the General Assembly opened in Westminster. Lie's judicious chairmanship induced the members to offer him a second term of office in June 1950, which he accepted while at the same time putting forward a twenty-year peace plan. Three weeks later, however, he was forced to seek the backing of UN members for international action to assist South Korea in checking the aggression committed across her borders by North Korea. Lie's request, taken at a time when the Soviet Union was boycotting the Security Council, lost him support from the eastern European bloc of members. He offered his resignation in November 1952 and was succeeded five months later by Dag HAMMARSKJÖLD. Lie returned to Norwegian politics. He was Minister for Industry (1963–4) and Minister for Overseas Trade (1964–8). He died at Geilo, in central southern Norway, on 30 December 1968. T. Lie: *In the Cause of Peace* (1954); E. Luard: *A History of the United Nations*, Vol. 1 (1982).

Lin Piao (1908–71), Chinese Communist General: origins unknown, but it is on record that he graduated from the Whampoa Military Academy in 1926 with distinction. Unlike most other cadets, he then supported the Communists rather than Whampoa's patron, CHIANG KAI-SHEK. He commanded one of the armies during the 'Long March' of 1934–5, subsequently becoming a close associate of CHOU EN-LAI as well as of MAO TSE-TUNG. After successful campaigns on the flank of the Japanese invaders, he became commander of the Northwest People's Liberation Army in 1945, achieving his greatest successes in the Civil War against the demoralized Kuomintang troops during 1948. Lin's capture of the arsenal of Mukden on 29 October 1948 ensured Communist control over industrialized Manchuria. From 1950 to 1952 he was commander of the Chinese 'volunteer' army which supported the North Koreans. In the mid-1950s he was seriously ill with tuberculosis. He was honoured with the rank of Marshal in 1955 and became Minister of Defence in 1959. Throughout the 'cultural revolution' he collaborated closely with Mao, and the Ninth Party Congress of April 1969 confirmed his status as designated successor to Chairman Mao. Soon afterwards, however, Marshal Lin faded from the public eye. In October 1971 it was announced in Peking that Marshal Lin had been killed in the previous month: he had, it was said, attempted to seize power in the capital, and his plane had crashed in Mongolia while he was seeking to escape from China to the Soviet Union. The last days of Marshal Lin's life are hidden in as much obscurity as his first. J. Gray: *Rebellions and Revolutions* (Oxford, 1990).

Lincoln, Abraham (1809–65), President of the United States from 1861 to 1865: born near Hodgen's Mill, Kentucky, spending most of his childhood in the backwoods of southern Indiana until the family settled in Illinois. He ran a store in New Salem, educated himself by reading so as to overcome the handicaps of a frontier boyhood, and studied the law so successfully that he was admitted to the bar in 1836. For four terms he sat in the state legislature, settling in Springfield where in 1842 he married Mary Todd (1818–82) from Kentucky, three of whose brothers were to die fighting for the South in the Civil War. Lincoln sat in Congress as a Whig from 1847 to 1849 but it was the issue of slavery that fired his political zeal and in 1856 induced him to join the newly constituted Republican Party. He became a national figure through the widely reported debates which he held with his Democratic opponent, Stephen A. DOUGLAS, in the Illinois senatorial election campaign of 1858. Although defeated in his bid for the Senate, Lincoln's reputation ensured he would be chosen by the Republicans as their presidential candidate in 1860. His election platform appealed to businessmen and to small farmers as well as to abolitionist crusaders against slavery, but he gained the presidency as much through the rifts in the Democratic Party as through the appeal of his own programme. Even before Lincoln's inauguration on 4 March 1861 seven Southern slave-owning states seceded from the Union. War between North and South followed only when the new President insisted in the first week of April on provisioning the isolated garrison of Fort Sumter, a federalist island off Charleston in seceded South Carolina. Lincoln organized the Union for war, exercising greater direct executive power within the Cabinet and over the high command than any President until Franklin ROOSEVELT. He insisted that the prime reason for waging the war was to preserve the Union and it was therefore not until the Confederate armies had been effectively checked in the autumn of 1862 that he authorized the Emancipation Proclamation, freeing slaves in areas 'in rebellion against the United States'. The Gettysburg Address, delivered on 19 November 1863, brought a simple and effective high moral tone to Lincoln's cause at a time when critics accused him of seeking dictatorial rule rather than government under the Constitution. He was re-elected President in 1864, receiving 2,216,000 popular votes against 1,808,000 votes for his chief opponent, General MCCLELLAN. Lincoln's second inaugural address, on 4 March 1865, was a plea for wise reconstruction 'with malice toward none, with charity for all'. These ideals were frustrated, a week after the surrender of LEE at Appomattox, by Lincoln's assassination at Ford's Theatre in Washington by a disappointed actor, John Wilkes Booth, on Good Friday. Lincoln died early next morning (15 April 1865). J. G. Randall: *Lincoln the President* (4 vols) (Boston, 1945–55); R. H. Luthin: *The Real Abraham Lincoln* (Chicago, 1960); B. P. Thomas: *Abraham Lincoln* (New York, 1952).

Lindbergh, Charles Augustus (1902–74), American pioneer airman: born in Detroit, his father being a pacifist Republican congressman who bore the same names as his son. Lindbergh Jnr spent his boyhood in Minnesota, but learned to fly at Lincoln, Nebraska, in 1924 and joined a small airline operating from St Louis, Missouri, in the following year. After eighteen months' experience as an air-mail pilot in the mid-West, he accepted the challenge of competing for a prize of

$25,000 offered to the first airman, or air crew, to fly directly from New York to Paris. With the backing of the Ryan Airlines Company, Lindbergh supervised work on the construction of a special high-wing monoplane, *The Spirit of St Louis*, in which, on 20–1 May 1927, he made the first non-stop solo flight across the Atlantic, 3,600 miles in 33½ hours. His achievement made him a popular hero on both sides of the Atlantic and helped, as he had wished, to make the American people air-minded. In May 1929 he married Anne Morrow (1906–), the daughter of a distinguished American banker and diplomat; and together they undertook flights of aerial exploration, opening up routes across the South Atlantic and to China by way of Alaska. In March 1932 their baby son was kidnapped and later found murdered. This tragedy, which received massive Press coverage, prompted the Lindberghs to seek rest and isolation in England, but in 1936 they accepted an invitation to visit Berlin for the Olympic Games. Lindbergh was much impressed by Nazi Germany and, returning to America, spoke out against ROOSEVELT's foreign policy, in favour of Germano-American reconciliation and of isolationism. Thereafter he received adverse reporting in the American Press and, during the Second World War, he was employed purely in a civilian aeronautical advisory capacity. Subsequently he gave advice to Pan-American Airways and helped a number of good causes, notably the World Wildlife Fund. He died in Connecticut in August 1974. C. A. Lindbergh: *The Spirit of St Louis* (New York, 1953).

Litvinov, Maximilian (Meier Wallakh) 1876–1952), controller of Soviet foreign policy from 1926 to 1939: born of Jewish parentage in Bialystok, was arrested as a revolutionary in his mid-twenties, but successfully crossed the frontier in 1902 and spent most of the following sixteen years in France or Britain, marrying an Englishwoman. From November 1917 to September 1918 (when he was deported) he acted as the first Bolshevik representative in London, although all his contacts with the British government were unofficial. In 1926 he was given effective control of Russian foreign policy, although Georghy Chicherin (1872–1936) remained nominal Commissar for Foreign Affairs until 1930. Litvinov believed in bringing Soviet Russia into the European system of diplomacy. He was largely responsible for Russia's acceptance of the Kellogg Pact, for the conclusion of non-aggression pacts with her neighbours in Eastern Europe, for the Franco-Soviet alliance of 1935 and for Russia's championship of the League of Nations between 1934 and 1939. STALIN's conviction that Russia needed an accommodation with Nazi Germany, since he could not rely on support from the West after Munich, led him (in May 1939) to dismiss Litvinov in favour of MOLOTOV. After Pearl Harbor, Litvinov was sent to Washington as ambassador, remaining there until July 1943. His last years were spent in quiet retirement. His widow, Ivy Litvinov, returned to England and was the author of some collections of short stories and novels. H. D. Phillips: *Between the Revolution and the West; a Political Biography of Maxim Litvinov* (Boulder, Colo., 1992); J. Carswell: *The Exile, a Life of Ivy Litvinov* (1983); G. F. Kennan: *Soviet Foreign Policy*, 1917–1941 (Princeton, N.J., 1960).

Liu Shao-chi (1898–1974), Chinese Communist Head of State from 1959 to 1969: born into a peasant family in Hunan, studied in Moscow in 1920–21, became a Communist organizer in Shanghai and Canton and a member of the Central Committee of the Chinese Communist Party in 1927. By 1935 he was recognized as the principal Communist theoretician in China, his writings better known at that time than those of MAO TSE-TUNG. He became chief Vice-Chairman of the party when the Chinese People's Republic was established in October 1949. Ten years later he was appointed Chairman of the Republic, a post equivalent to the presidency in other states. He was, however, reckoned as second in official standing to the Chairman of the Central Committee, Mao. In 1966, during the 'cultural revolution', he was heavily criticized for supporting the primacy of the industrial workers as a proletarian force: Mao believed that the natural revolutionary body in Asia, as opposed to western Europe, was the peasantry. There was a curious meeting of the Central Committee in October 1968 which declared Liu to be a 'scab, renegade and traitor', and therefore unworthy to hold public office. Constitutionally it proved impossible to wrest the chairmanship of the Republic from him until February 1969. He appears to have remained unmolested, the Chinese Press announcing his death in November 1974. Subsequently the disgrace of one of his principal accusers, CHIANG CHIN ('Madame Mao'), partially restored his reputation as a theorist. L. Dittmer: *Liu Shao-ch'i and the Chinese Cultural Revolution* (1974).

Livingstone, David (1813–73), Scottish missionary and explorer: born at Low Blantyre in Lanarkshire, where he spent much of his boyhood and youth working in a cotton mill. At the age of 24 he enrolled as a student at Glasgow, later taking a medical degree and offering his services as a missionary in Africa. From 1841 to 1849 he worked for the London Missionary Society in Bechuanaland, subsequently crossing the Kalahari desert to explore lands to the north and so discovering Lake Ngami (1849). In June 1853 he undertook a major expedition from the Zambesi to Luanda and became the first white man to see, and name, the Victoria Falls. After eighteen months in Britain he returned to Africa and in his third expedition (1858–61) explored the tributaries of the Zambesi, discovering Lake Nyasa and gathering information for a book in which he exposed the iniquities of the Portuguese slave trade. In March 1866 he was encouraged by the Royal Geographical Society to undertake an expedition which would settle disputes about the sources of the Nile. After several years of silence the general public in Britain and America became concerned for his fate and the *New York Herald* sent Henry Morton Stanley (1841–1904) to 'find Livingstone'. This task Stanley accomplished at Ujiji on 10 November 1871. Livingstone, though in wretched health, continued to explore the area around Lake Tanganyika until he died at Ilala (now in Zambia) on 1 May 1873. He was deeply revered by Africans, by the British and by many Americans. His respect for Christian values was shown by the emphasis he gave in his medical practice to an equal standing for men and women of all races under the fatherhood of God. These beliefs brought Livingstone into conflict with the exclusive Calvinism of the Boers he had first encountered in the Transvaal soon after his arrival in Africa. D. Livingstone: *A Popular Account of Missionary Travels and Researches in Southern Africa* (1861); J. Simmonds: *Livingstone and Africa* (1955); B. Pacai (ed.): *Livingstone, Man of Africa* (1973).

Lloyd George, David (1863–1945), British Prime Minister from 1916 to 1922: born in Manchester but spent his childhood in North Wales, at Llanystumdwy near Criccieth. He entered Parliament as a radical-Liberal in 1890 and represented the same constituency (the Caernarvon Boroughs) for fifty-five years without a break. His gift of oratory soon won national recognition, but he was unpopular during the Boer War because of his opposition to Joseph CHAMBERLAIN and the imperial role in southern Africa. In December 1905 he entered the Cabinet as President of the Board of Trade, succeeding ASQUITH as Chancellor of the Exchequer in April 1908, an office he held through seven stormy years. His reputation as a social reformer rests primarily on his Old Age Pensions Act of 1908 and his support for the National Health Insurance Act of 1911, but it was his proposals for super tax and land value duties in the Budget of 1909 (later termed the 'People's Budget') that provoked the fiercest controversy. The refusal of the House of Lords to pass the Budget began a constitutional crisis which culminated in the Parliament Act of 1911, and the severe limitations imposed on the Lords' legislative powers.

Lloyd George travelled in Europe, often by car, to a greater extent than any of his colleagues in the pre-war governments and he showed interest in foreign affairs. On 21 July 1911 he gave a strong warning to Germany in a speech at the Mansion House in London during the crisis caused by the sending of a German gunboat to the Moroccan port of Agadir, a clear indication of his concern for European questions. It came only nine days after he had played a prominent part in the first investiture of a Prince of Wales (the future EDWARD VIII) at Caernarvon. His career suffered a setback in 1913, when he was alleged to have benefited from inside knowledge in order to speculate in the shares of the Marconi Company; but a Select Committee of Inquiry cleared his name and the reputations of other prominent Liberals, including the Attorney-General, Sir Rufus Isaacs (1860–1935). When Asquith formed his coalition government in May 1915 Lloyd George became Minister of Munitions (the first occasion in English constitutional practice when the word 'Minister' was used for a departmental head). Discontent with the progress of the war led Lloyd George to collaborate with leading Conservatives in securing the downfall of Asquith, and he became coalition Prime Minister on 7 December 1916. His premiership was marked by a greater concentration of power in the hands of one political leader than ever before in English history, and by the establishment for the first time of a prime ministerial secretriat, the so-called 'garden suburb'. As a war leader he showed ruthless vigour but remained on bad terms with his generals and admirals, notably HAIG and JELLICOE. On strategic questions he was not a convinced 'westerner': he backed ALLENBY in Palestine, and hoped to hasten Germany's defeat in the West by 'knocking away the props' (i.e. forcing Germany's allies to sue for peace first). In this policy he was successful. He attended the Paris Peace Conference in 1919, where he moderated some of the harsher demands proposed for the Treaty of Versailles as he was anxious to keep Germany a stable power within central Europe.

The greatest apparent success of Lloyd George's post-war coalition was the Government of Ireland Act (1920), separating the Irish Free State and Northern Ireland. In foreign affairs he strongly backed the Greece of VENIZELOS against Turkey, a miscalculation which nearly led to war between Britain and the Turkish Republic of KEMAL in September 1922. It was this 'Chanak Crisis' which induced the Conservatives to leave the coalition, forcing Lloyd George to resign (19 October 1922). From 1926 to 1931 he was leader of the Liberal Party, but he was not trusted by members loyal to the memory of Asquith. In the 1930s he led an independent faction of the Liberals. He visited HITLER in September 1936, but from 1938 onwards was highly critical of the policies of Neville CHAMBERLAIN. Old age was among the considerations which induced him to decline Winston Churchill's offer of the Washington embassy in 1940, and he was not able to attend the Commons after the first week in June 1944. He became Earl Lloyd-George of Dwyfor in the New Year Honours of 1945 but never took his seat in the Upper House, against whose powers he had fought so strongly in 1910–11. He died at his home near Criccieth on 26 March 1945 and was buried in a glade beside the stream at Llanystumdwy. J. Grigg: *The Young Lloyd George* (1973), *Lloyd George, the People's Champion, 1902–1911* (1978), *Lloyd George, from Peace to War, 1912–1916.* (1985); P. Rowland: *Lloyd George* (1975); D. R. Woodward: *Lloyd George and the Generals* (East Brunswick, 1983).

Lobengula (*c.* 1833–94), King of the Ndebele people: in 1870 he succeeded his father Mzilikazi as ruler of the Ndebele, a cattle-rearing people forced northwards from their traditional pastures some fifty years earlier by Boer incursions. The Ndebele settled in Matabeland (now in Zimbabwe) and conquered neighbouring Mashonaland early in Mzilikazi's reign. Lobengula, a physically powerful warrior much respected by his subjects, raised an army of 15,000 men and established a fortified kraal on the site of modern Bulawayo. In October 1888 he accepted a treaty with agents of RHODES by which the British South Africa Company were given exclusive rights to minerals in the Ndebele's lands in return for a subsidy. Disputes arose after December 1890 when heavily armed British settlers moved into Mashonaland, encouraged by Dr JAMESON and other agents of the company. Lobengula held back his impi warriors until October 1893 when rash raids on villages close to British settlements provoked a fierce response, Maxum guns killing the impis and allowing the company to seize Bulawayo on 4 November. Lobengula's kingdom disintegrated and he died, in hiding, two months later. He remained a legendary hero to the Ndeble during more than eighty years of 'Rhodesian' rule. S. Clete: *African Portraits* (1951); T. Pakenham: *The Scramble for Africa* (1991).

Long, Huey Pierce (1893–1935), right-wing Governor of Louisiana: born at Winnfield, Louisiana, practised as a lawyer and showed great skill and ruthlessness as a political manager. He was Governor of Louisiana from 1928 to 1930, when he was returned to the Senate, though retaining a masterly hold on the political machine in his home state. Long's demagogic gifts were harnessed during the Depression years to a 'Share the Wealth' programme, largely fascist in inspiration. He was shot dead on 10 September 1935 in the Louisiana state capital, Baton Rouge. H. P. Long: *Every Man a King; an Autobiography* (New Orleans, La., 1933); H. T. Kane: *Louisiana Hayride* (New York, 1941); V. O. Key, Jnr.: *Southern Politics* (New York, 1949).

Lubbers, Ruud (1939–), Netherlands Prime Minister: born in Rotterdam, joined the family engineering firm of Hollandia Kloos after having studied economics and remained a director from 1963 to 1977, when he entered Parliament as a Christian Democrat, taking over as party leader a year later. In November 1982 he became Prime Minister of a Centre-Right coalition and remained head of the government until May 1994, although the character of the administration was modified in 1989, when the Netherland's Labour Party replaced the People's Party in the coalition. He played a prominent part in promoting the Maastricht Treaty on European Union (1992). No previous Netherlands Prime Minister had remained in continous office for longer than nine years.

Ludendorff, Erich (1865–1937), distinguished German General in the First

World War: born at Kruszewnia, near the garrison town of Posen (now Poznan, in Poland). He was trained at the military academies of Ploen and Lichterfelde and commissioned in an infantry regiment before his eighteenth birthday. In 1906 he was posted to the General Staff with the rank of Major, and was chief of operational planning to MOLTKE from 1908 to 1912, constantly updating the famous war-plan devised by SCHLIEFFEN. It was Ludendorff's skill which captured the key Belgian citadel of Liège in the early weeks of war in 1914. At the end of August 1914 he became Chief of Staff to the newly appointed commander of the Eighth Army, HINDENBURG. The partnership of these two soldiers lasted until the final week of October 1918, beginning with the victories of Tannenberg and the Masurian Lakes and acquiring major significance when Ludendorff was appointed First Quartermaster-General on 29 August 1916. This post not only made him Deputy Supreme Commander to Hindenburg, but gave him more influence over Germany's internal and external policy than was enjoyed by the Chancellor. Ludendorff planned the great spring offensive of 1918 which brought German troops once again within sight of Paris. The counter-offensive of FOCH in August and September 1918 made Ludendorff lose his nerve. He recommended the conclusion of an armistice and fled to Sweden. Subsequently he associated himself with right-wing political groups, notably with KAPP in March 1920 and with HITLER from the autumn of 1923 onwards. From 1924 to 1928 he sat in the Reichstag as one of the few Nazi deputies, standing for election as President in 1925 but receiving only 1 per cent of the vote in a campaign won by his old commander, Hindenburg. After 1928 he came to distrust Hitler and the Nazi politicians, declining Hitler's offer of a Marshal's baton in 1935 and feeding his angry spirit by a hatred of all religions. He died in a hospital administered by a Catholic nursing order a week before Christmas in 1937. E. Ludendorff: *My War Memoirs (1914–18)* (1919); D. Goodspeed: *Ludendorff* (1966); C. Barnett: *The Swordbearers* (1963); G. Ritter: *The Sword and the Sceptre*, Vols 3–4 (1972).

Lugard, Frederick John Dealtry (1858–1945), British colonial administrator: born in Madras and educated at Rossall School. He was commissioned in the Norfolk Regiment in 1878, saw action in the Sudan and Burma and arrived in East Africa in 1888 with the rank of Captain, the Distinguished Service Order, and fame as a big-game hunter. He commanded military columns seeking to stamp out slavery around Mombasa. In 1890, while serving with the Imperial British East Africa Company, he established the first defended inland trading station in modern Kenya, at Dagoretti. He returned on leave to England and encouraged the government to pursue a forward policy in East Africa, where a British Protectorate was established in June 1895. By then Lugard was in West Africa, rapidly building up British influence in competition with French colonialists. He remained in Nigeria as a special commissioner until 1906, raising and commanding the West Africa Frontier Force in 1897, and creating a new concept of imperial authority which depended on a paternalistic relationship with the tribal chiefs. After five years as Governor of Hong Kong he returned to Lagos in 1912 as Governor of Nigeria until 1919. He then served for fourteen years on the Mandates Commission of the League of Nations, and in 1928 received a peerage. His seminal study on colonial administration, *The Dual Mandate in British Tropical Africa* (1922), expounded his belief in the mutual benefit of trust and collaboration between governors and governed in imperial dependencies. F. D. Lugard: *The Rise of*

Our East African Empire (2 vols) (1893); M. F. Perham: *Lugard* (2 vols) (1956, 1960).

Lumumba, Patrice (1925–61), first Prime Minister of the Congo Republic: born in the central Belgian Congo at Katako Kombe, becoming a postal clerk in Stanleyville (now known as Kisangani). From 1957 to 1960 he was active in the Congolese national movement (MNC), supported from 1958 by NASSER, NKRUMAH and other pan-Africans. When the Belgian authorities precipitately gave the Congo independence on 30 June 1960, they recognized Lumumba's skill and popularity as a leader, and he became Prime Minister of a unitary state which was to be governed from the old Congo capital, Léopoldville (now Kinshasa). At the same time they imposed on the radical Lumumba a more restrained head of the executive, President Kasavubu (1917–69). To some extent, Lumumba was trapped by the authority nominally entrusted to him. He was faced by mutinies in the Congolese Army and by a secessionist movement in the rich mining province of Katanga (now Shaba), which was led by Moise TSHOMBE. Lumumba was able to remain Prime Minister for only eleven weeks, when his government was overthrown by a military *coup*. He then attempted to make his way to Stanleyville, where his political strength lay, but was detained by Congolese troops who later handed him over to irregulars loyal to Tshombe. They executed Lumumba on 17 January 1961. A demand for an impartial inquiry into the circumstances of his murder made by UN authorities a month later was rejected by Tshombe. The 'Patrice Lumumba University', established in Moscow, commemorated a 'hero victim of the struggle against colonialism and the rule of mercenaries'. C. Young and D. Turner: *The Rise and Decline of the Zairian State* (Madison, Wis., 1985); C. Cruise O'Brien: *To Katanga and Back* (1962).

Luthuli, Albert John (1898–1967), African National Congress leader: born near Bulawayo (Zimbabwe), his father being a Zulu Methodist missionary. He received his basic schooling at the Edenvale Methodist Institution, Johannesburg, duly becoming a teacher and lay preacher himself and visiting the USA and India to deliver a series of missionary lectures. In 1936 he was elected tribal chief of the Abasemakholweni people, in Natal. He championed black rights under the SMUTS wartime government and in 1945 became a member of the African National Congress (ANC) executive. After MALAN's electoral victory in 1948 he intensified the (peaceful) campaign against apartheid but was deposed from his chieftainship by the government. In 1952 he was elected President General of the ANC. Four years later he was put on trial for high treason at Johannesburg, though the case fell through and all charges against him were dropped; he was banished to a remote farm under house arrest but continued to urge non-violent resistance to apartheid the segregationalism. His pleas for racial moderation won him support and sympathy worldwide; he received the Nobel Peace Prize of 1960. It was announced in September 1967 that Luthuli had died after being accidentally hit by a freight train at Stanger, Natal. A. Luthuli: *Let my People Go* (1962).

Luxemburg, Rosa (1871–1919), German socialist heroine: born at Zamosc, in Russian Poland, her father being a Jewish timber merchant whose religious faith had lapsed. Before her third birthday the family moved to Warsaw, where Rosa was educated at the High School. At the age of 15 she was appalled by the hanging of four Polish socialists in Warsaw, and she promptly joined the banned Revolutionary Proletarian Party to which they had belonged. She escaped across the frontier in 1889, fearing imminent arrest, and settled in Switzerland, studying at the University of Zurich for eight years and gaining her doctorate. In 1898 she went through a form of marriage with a German émigré and thus became a German citizen, settling in Berlin and taking part in the revolutionary activities of the extreme Left from 1899 onwards. Her pamphlets and her views were trenchant and individualistic: she much impressed both LENIN and STALIN in 1906–7, although they did not agree with her criticism of Marx's 'dictatorship of the proletariat'. From 1911 to 1914 she courageously ridiculed the prevalent militarism in German society, seeking to check the drift towards an imperialistic war. Although prosecuted, she was not imprisoned until February 1915 and, with Karl Liebknecht (1871–1919), was able to organize the Spartacist Group of socialists opposed to the war. Apart from a brief interlude in 1916, she remained in prison until November 1918 but was not badly treated. She criticized Lenin for seeking to rule by terror after the Bolshevik Revolution of 1917, but on her release in 1918 she was equally critical of the moderate German socialists for having set up a 'bourgeois republic'. She was unable to prevent her Spartacist followers from attempting a premature revolution of the Left in Berlin in January 1919. During these disturbances she was captured, along with Liebknecht, by right-wing irregular troops. Both Rosa Luxemburg and Liebknecht were murdered (15 January 1919), her body being thrown into a canal and not recovered for five months. She has remained a martyr heroine of the German Left. J. P. Nettl: *Rosa Luxemburg* (2 vols) (1966); D. W. Morgan: *The Socialist Left and the German Revolution, 1917–1922* (Ithaca, N.Y., 1975).

Lyautey, Louis Hubert (1854–1934), Marshal of France: born at Nancy, completed his military education at St Cyr and saw active service in Algeria, Madagascar and Indochina. In March 1912 he became Resident-General of the French protectorate in Morocco and, apart from a few months in Paris as Minister of War in 1916–17, he remained there until September 1925. Lyautey was a man of constant drive and personal initiative, determined to create in Morocco a model of sound administration. He authorized major public works programmes around Casablanca, introduced scientific farming to increase crop yields, and encouraged the assimilation of Islamic culture and traditions to his devout Catholicism. Lyautey received a Marshal's baton in 1921, not as a field commander, but to honour the ideal of benevolent imperial service with which he lifted the standard of administration in 'France overseas'. A. Scham: *Lyautey in Morocco* (Berkeley, Calif., 1970); W. B. Cohen: *Rulers of Empire, the French Colonial Service in Africa* (Stanford, Calif., 1971).

Lyons, Joseph Aloysius (1879–1939), Australian Prime Minister during the Great Depression: born into an Irish Roman Catholic family at Stanley, Tasmania; taught in elementary schools and was a Labour member of the Tasmanian assembly for twenty years before entering Parliament on the eve of the world recession (1929). He was more conservative than most of his Labor colleagues; with dissident National Party members he founded the United Australia Party, which won the General Election of December 1931. Lyons formed a government which successfully rode out the Great Depression, its budgetary caution helped by rising world prices for wool and gold. He early saw the danger from Japan and built up the strength of Australia's army and air force 1934–7, while pressing the government in London to complete modernization of the Singapore naval base. To the electorate Lyons was comfortably reassuring, depicted by cartoonists as the koala bear of politics. After his sudden death in April 1939 his widow Dame Enid Lyons (1897–1981) – the mother of twelve children – entered politics; in 1943 she became Australia's first woman MP. E. Lyons: *Among the Carrion Crows* (Adelaide, 1972); S. Macintyre: *The Succeeding Age* (Oxford, 1986).

M

MacArthur, Douglas (1880–1964), American General and proconsul in Japan; born in Little Rock, Arkansas, the son of a distinguished soldier. He graduated from West Point and was commissioned in the Engineers in 1903, being posted to the Philippines. He was Adjutant to his father, General Arthur MacArthur, who was sent on a special mission to Tokyo in 1905 during the Russo-Japanese War. After a series of staff appointments and a spell of active service in Mexico, MacArthur crossed to France with the first American units in 1917 and won the French *Croix de Guerre* for courageous conduct as Chief of Staff of the Forty-second Division. He became a Brigadier-General at the age of 38 and was regarded by PERSHING as the 'greatest leader of troops' in the US army. On the return of peace he was appointed Commandant of West Point and served as Chief of Staff of the US army from 1930 to 1935, gaining a reputation for right-wing repressive beliefs when he used tear gas on war veterans demonstrating in Washington during the Depression (1932). In 1935 he became military adviser to President QUEZON in the Philippines, taking EISENHOWER with him as chief assistant for five years.

On 26 July 1941 MacArthur was appointed Commander-in-Chief of all American and Filipino forces in the Far East in anticipation of war with Japan. He was, nevertheless, taken by surprise by a Japanese attacks on his principal airfield north of Manila on 7 December 1941; and, although the Bataan peninsula and the fortress island of Corregidor held out until March 1942, the Japanese met less resistance on the Philippines than MacArthur had led Washington to expect. With his wife and son he escaped by torpedo-boat to Mindanao and eventually Australia. He became Commander-in-Chief of Allied forces in the south-west Pacific and developed a strategy of defeating Japan by 'hopping' from island to island, successively throwing landing-craft against Guadalcanal, Luzon, Iwojima and Okinawa in expectation of a final invasion of the Japanese homeland. He was a good public relations man, with a gift for phrases and panache. Nevertheless he displeased General MARSHALL in Washington by his rapacious demands for men, arms and landing-craft, as well as falling foul of the Australians and of American and Allied naval commanders by his egocentricity and showmanship. MacArthur accepted the surrender of Japan aboard USS *Missouri* off Tokyo on 2 September 1945. He remained in Japan for six years as Allied Commander, autocratically imposing on Japan a modern constitution and the administrative apparatus of a westernized nation, while insisting on retaining the imperial dynasty under Emperor HIROHITO.

When war came in Korea in June 1950 he was appointed to command the UN forces, gaining remarkable success by his amphibious operation at Inchon (15 September 1950), which led to the precipitate withdrawal of North Korean forces. Two months later, however, he was confronted by the intervention of a Chinese volunteer army under LIN PIAO. As MacArthur had underrated the Japanese threat in 1941, so he minimized Chinese effectiveness in 1950. When Chinese intervention began to change the balance of forces, he wished to bomb Chinese bases in Manchuria and risk full-scale war with China, publicly airing his disagreements with President TRUMAN over strategy. Truman immediately relieved him of his command (11 April 1951) and ordered his return to Washington, where he was fêted by Congress. If he hoped for the Republican presidential nomination he was disappointed – it went to General Eisenhower, ten years his junior. MacArthur spent his last years in Manhattan, occasionally visiting West Point where his statue stands as an inspiration and example to the cadets. W. Manchester: *American Caesar, Douglas MacArthur* (1979); C. A. Willoughby and J. Chamberlain: *MacArthur 1941–1951* (1956); R. Rovere and A. M. Schlesinger, Jnr.: *The General and the President* (1951).

McCarthy, Joseph Raymond (1909–57), US Senator influential from 1950 to 1954: born at Grand Chute, Wisconsin, studied law at Marquette University in Milwaukee and was a State circuit Judge by the age of 30. After service with the Marine Air Corps he was elected a Senator for Wisconsin in 1945, insisting on taking his seat even though the Supreme Court ruled that his election was unconstitutional since he was still a serving judge. In the Senate McCarthy made his name as a 'Red-baiter', exploiting the case of Alger HISS and maintaining that President TRUMAN was 'soft on communism'. From 1950 onwards he conducted a campaign of half-truths, total smears and slanted questions so as to discredit liberal Democrats and attack intellectual 'egg-heads' in America's universities. His most famous allegation was the statement in February 1950 that he knew there were 205 communist sympathizers and fifty-seven 'card-carrying Communists' in the State Department. After the Republican electoral successes of 1952 he became Chairman of the Senate Subcommittee on investigations, extending his activities to the 'leftist' views allegedly disseminated by US Information Services abroad. When he began to attack prominent figures in the Army, he incurred the openly expressed hostility of President EISENHOWER and evidence was produced that McCarthy had sought preferential treatment for one of his aides, called up for military service. On 2 December 1954 his activities were condemned by an overwhelming vote in the Senate, and television exposed the hysteria present in McCarthy's style of campaigning. He died, still in the Senate and hoping to make a political comeback, on 2 May 1957. J. Anderson and R. W. May: *McCarthy* (New York, 1953); R. Rovere: *Senator Joe McCarthy* (New York, 1960).

McClellan, George Brinton (1826–85), American General and commander of the Federal armies in 1861–2: born in Philadelphia, the son of a surgeon, graduated from the Military Academy at West Point in 1846, seeing action in the Mexican War before becoming superintendent of engineering of the Illinois Central Railroad. LINCOLN respected his organizing abilities and, in the summer of 1861, made him responsible for building up the new army of the Union, a national force intended to supersede the ninety-day militia regiments mobilized from the individual states. McClellan possessed the energy and detailed knowledge essential for this task, and he accepted further responsibilities as commander of the army of the Potomac and, in November 1861, General-in-Chief of the Union's armies. But McClellan was tactically cautious and strategically lacking in vision; he failed in the peninsular campaign against Richmond and he permitted LEE to escape after Antietam largely through his inability to seize and exploit shifts of fortune. He was abruptly dismissed by

Lincoln on 7 November 1862 and agreed, in 1864, to stand as candidate for the Democratic Party against the sitting president. McClellan fared badly in the election. He carried only three states (Delaware, Kentucky and New Jersey) but he gained some support from regions where there had been comparatively recent immigration from continental Europe. After the Civil War he resumed his career in engineering and served as Governor of New Jersey from 1877 to 1881. W. W. Hassler: *General George B. McClellan: Shield of the Union* (1957); H. J. Eckenrode and B. Conrad: *George B. McClellan: the Man who Saved the Union* (1941).

MacDonald, James Ramsay (1866–1937), first British Labour Prime Minister: born at Lossiemouth, a small fishing harbour on the Moray Firth. He left Scotland at the age of 19, undertaking clerical work while gaining for himself a secondary education through long hours of private study. He corresponded with Keir HARDIE, joining the ILP a year after its foundation. In 1895 he married Margaret Gladstone, the daughter of a distinguished scientist and Fellow of the Royal Society, and he was able for some years to exist on her small private income, supplemented by occassional journalism. MacDonald became secretary of the Labour Representation Committee (the embyronic Labour Party) in 1900, continuing as secretary of the party itself from 1906 to 1911, when he became leader, a post he held until the outbreak of the First World War. After two unsuccessful attempts to enter Parliament he became Labour MP for Leicester in 1906, holding the seat until 1918. His pacifist principles lost him support in 1918 and he was out of Parliament until 1922 when he was returned for Aberavon, once more becoming party leader. In January 1924 he took office as Prime Minister of a minority Labour government, serving at the same time as Foreign Secretary and Leader of the Commons. The so-called ZINOVIEV Letter lost Labour the 1924 General Election and MacDonald remained leader of the Opposition until 1929, when he was able to form a second and stronger minority government. The Depression, and rising unemployment, hampered his legislative programme, and his hesitancy in dealing with the economic crisis in 1930 lost him the support of one of his ablest junior ministers, MOSLEY. The fall in the value of the pound in the summer of 1931 induced him to form a peacetime coalition – the National Government – an action condemned by the rump of the Labour Party under LANSBURY and ATTLEE. He continued to work for peace and collective security through the League of Nations, but in home affairs he was much under the influence of BALDWIN and the Conservative leadership. In 1929 he had changed constituencies and thus sat for Seaham in Durham from 1929 to 1935 when (standing as 'National Labour') he lost his seat to the Labour candidate Emmanuel Shinwell (1884–1986). MacDonald had resigned the premiership in June 1935, five months before the election. He was thereupon returned as MP for the Scottish Universities and sat as Lord President of the Council through out Baldwin's government. He died while seeking to recover his physical strength on a cruise in the south Atlantic, 9 November 1937. D. Marquand: *Ramsay MacDonald* (1977); Lord Elton: *Life of James Ramsay MacDonald* (1939); R. Skidelsky: *Politicians and the Slump; the Labour Government of 1929–31* (1967).

Maček, Vladko (1879–1974), Croatian peasant leader: born at Jastrebarsko. He was educated at the neighbouring University of Zagreb, taking a doctorate in law. Maček joined the Croatian Peasant Party in 1905 and, after the First World War, became a deputy in the *Skupstina* the Yugoslav parliament in Belgrade. He campaigned vigorously to protect

Croatian interests from Serb dominance, succeeding the murdered RADIĆ as party leader in 1928. Over the following thirteen years his popularity in Croatia made him virtually the peasants' 'uncrowned king'. Although in 1933–4 he spent twenty months in prison, Maček urged successive rulers of Yugoslavia (King ALEXANDER and Prince-Regent Paul) to adopt a federal constitution. His greatest success came in August 1939 when, by the constitutional *Sporazum* (Agreement), Croatia gained considerable autonomy and Maček joined the Serb-dominated government as Vice-Premier. But this delicate political balance was destroyed by the German invasion of April 1941 when Maček, refusing to follow the royal government into exile, retired to Zagreb, as a passive observer who would not support either PAVELIĆ or TITO; his hopes of emerging as a compromise arbitrator came to nothing. After escaping to Paris in April 1945 Maček travelled to America, where he spoke out against communism, but his following dwindled and, when he died in Washington, he was a forgotten figure. V. Maček: *In the Struggle for Freedom* (New York, 1957); J. B. Hoptner: *Yugoslavia in Crisis, 1934–41* (New York, 1962).

McKinley, William (1843–1901), President of the United States from 1897 to 1901: born at Niles in Ohio, fought with the Union army in the Civil War, reaching the rank of Major. He practised law in Ohio and was returned as a Republican congressman in 1876, sitting in the House for all except two of the following fourteen years. He became known as a protectionist, winning the backing of the able campaigner Mark HANNA, who was largely responsible for McKinley's election as Governor of Ohio from 1892 to 1896 and for his nomination as Republican candidate in the presidential election of 1896. His opponent in this campaign, BRYAN, fought as a radical agrarian Democrat, and McKinley was thus able to appeal to the urban voters as a conservative mercantilist. The Republican strength in Congress enabled McKinley to support industry with high tariffs (although in the last year of his life he was beginning to favour reciprocal trade agreements). In foreign affairs he allowed newspaper hysteria to rush his administration into the Spanish–American War of 1898, subsequently securing the Philippines for America and establishing effective control of Cuba. His imperialist beliefs induced him to support the 'Open Door' policy of his Secretary of State, HAY, in the Far East and he agreed to the annexation of Hawaii. He gained an impressive victory over Bryan in the 1900 presidential election, but on 6 September 1901, he was shot by an anarchist while attending the Pan-American Exhibition at Buffalo, New York. He died from his wounds nine days later. L. L. Gould: *The Presidency of William McKinley* (Lawrence, Kans., 1986).

Macmahon, Patrice de (1808–93), Marshal of France and French President from 1873 to 1879: born at Sully, his family being of Irish descent. He was commissioned in the army of King Charles X in 1829 and saw service under the Orleanist dynasty in Algeria but his military successes were achieved in the early years of the Second Empire and he was much favoured by NAPOLEON III. In 1855 he became a popular hero for taking and holding the Malakoff Fort in the Crimea, while his costly victory of Magenta over the Austrians in 1859 was rewarded by his Emperor with a dukedom. From 1864 to 1870 he was Governor-General of Algeria, returning to France in time to suffer defeat at the hands of the Prussians at Worth and capture at Sedan (September 1870). Upon his release he served the new French Republic despite his monarchist sympathies. With General Gallifet (1830–1909) Macmahon shared responsibility for the bloody suppression of the Commune of Paris in May 1871. His monarchism made him acceptable to the Church and to conservative politicians distrustful of the ambitions of THIERS. When Thiers resigned in May 1873 Macmahon succeeded him as President, intending to negotiate with the Pretenders to the crown a monarchical restoration. He could not, however, settle the terms with the principal claimant before a revival of republican sentiment showed itself in the elections of 1876. A year later (16 May 1877) Macmahon dismissed the Prime Minister and tried to ensure the return of royalist majorities in 'rigged' elections, but without success. He refused to stage a military *coup d'état*, as some of his supporters wished, and for two years he tried to collaborate with the republicans. Eventually he resigned on 30 January 1879 and was succeeded by the conservatively inclined republican, Jules Grèvy (1807–91). G. Chapman: *The Third Republic in France: The First Phase* (1962); D. W. Brogan: *The Development of Modern France* (1940); D. Thomson: *Democracy in France* (rev. edn. 1962).

Macmillan (Maurice) Harold (1894–1986), British Prime Minister 1957–63: born in London, the son of a much respected publisher and an American mother. He was educated at Eton and Balliol College, Oxford, served with the Grenadier Guards on the Western Front throughout the First World War and was wounded on three occasions. He represented Stockton in Parliament from 1924 to 1929 and from 1931 to 1945, when he lost the seat to Labour; but he returned to Parliament four months later at a by-election in Bromley, which he represented until 1964. As a young man he was an independently minded Conservative, deeply concerned with problems of social reform, and in the 1930s he attached himself to the Churchillian wing of the party. After more than two years of minor posts, he was sworn of the Privy Council in December 1942 and spent the remainder of the war as Minister Resident in North Africa and Italy, a special representative of the Cabinet in the Mediterranean theatre of operations.

From 1951 to 1954 he was Minister of Housing, rising rapidly in the government hierarchy as Minister of Defence (1954–5), Foreign Secretary (1955) and Chancellor of the Exchequer from December 1955 to January 1957. In each of these posts he showed distinction: completing the negotiations that restored Austria as an independent and neutral republic in 1955; and, in his one Budget (April 1956), introducing premium savings bonds. The collapse in health of EDEN after the Suez débâcle led to his appointment as Prime Minister (10 January 1957) at a time of weakness for his party, which had lost the nation's confidence. Remarkably, Macmillan succeeded in imposing his personality on the country, the Commonwealth and the western alliance so positively that the Conservatives were able by October 1959 to win a General Election with a substantially increased majority. Anglo-American relations prospered, partly because of the Prime Minister's wartime experiences in collaborating with EISENHOWER, and later because of family friendship with John KENNEDY; and at times Macmillan was able to serve as an intermediary between the American administration and the temperamentally volatile KHRUSCHEV. Macmillan's wish to see Britain as an active member of the European Community was finally frustrated by opposition from President DE GAULLE in January 1963.

In home affairs Macmillan accepted the need for life peerages to revitalize the House of Lords (1958). When the stable prices of his first years in office were replaced by uncertainty over investment and the threat of a balance of payments crisis, he encouraged the establishment of a National Economic Development Council (1961). This move, uncharacteristic of Conservative thought, was equalled by a ready willingness to accept change in Africa, notably in Kenya. His failing as Prime Minister was a tendency to become so absorbed with a world vision that he failed to notice shifts in public opinion at home. The resignation of his War Minister, John Profumo, in March 1963 after revelations of indiscreet behaviour in his private life was represented in some newspapers as, in some way, an indictment of his government's casual approach to major issues: *The Times* complained that 'Conservative rule' had 'brought the nation psychologically and spiritually to a low ebb'. Macmillan's health gave way, and he tendered his resignation from a hospital bed on 18 October 1963, after the longest unbroken spell of office of any Prime Minister since ASQUITH in 1908–16. He declined a peerage but, once his health recovered, he resumed his activities as Chancellor of Oxford University, an office to which he was elected in succession to Lord HALIFAX in 1960. The Order of Merit was conferred on him by Queen ELIZABETH in 1975. He was created Earl of Stockton in 1984 and, in his last speeches in the Lords, admonished the THATCHER administration, particularly for selling off what he regarded as national assets. H. Macmillan: *The Memoirs of Harold Macmillan* (6 vols) (1966–73); A. Horne: *Macmillan* (2 vols) (1988, 1989); A. Sampson: *Macmillan, a Study in Ambiguity* (1962).

McNamara, Robert Strange (1916–), US Secretary of Defence 1961 to 1968: born in San Francisco, served in the Army Air Force for three years and took a high administrative post with the Ford Motor Company, eventually becoming its chief executive. He agreed to take office as John KENNEDY's Secretary of Defence in January 1961, even though he had been a registered Republican for some twenty years. McNamara's term of office was unique in two respects: he assessed military needs with completely cool objectivity and detachment; and his level-headedness at moments of crisis (e.g. over Cuban missiles or the deterioration of America's position in Vietnam) enabled him to trespass into fields normally determined entirely by the President and the State Department. In 1968 he resigned office and withdrew from political life as suddenly as he had emerged into it, becoming President of the World Bank, a post he held for thirteen years. R. S. McNamara: *The Essence of Security* (1968), *The McNamara Years at the World Bank* (1981).

Madero, Francisco (1873–1913), Mexican democratic revolutionary: born into a wealthy family at San Pedro, Coahuila, educated in Paris and at Berkeley, California. He accepted basic Hindu beliefs, became a vegetarian and teetotaller, and on returning to the family estates successfully practised homoeopathy. When, in March 1908, President DIAZ, after thirty-two years of power, said that he would welcome political opposition, Madero began to compaign for a democratically elected presidency. Diaz, however, arrested Madero in June 1910, only releasing him in October, after corruptly securing re-election himself. From sanctuary in Texas Madero then drew up the Plan of San Luis Potosi, an appeal for an armed uprising to secure, not only democratic government, but the return of Amerindian peasant holdings illegally appropriated by big landowners. Although the Madero family avoided revolutionary excesses in northern Mexico, the Plan encouraged radical revolutionaries like the peasant ZAPATA in the south. To check the spread of social anarchy Diaz negotiated with Madero and fled the country (May 1911). Madero was elected President in November 1911, but his pleas to respect 'the rule of law within a broad spirit of reconciliation' provoked violence from a land-hungry Left (Zapata and Pancho VILLA) and armed uprisings from the clericalist Right, backed by some American interests. Madero became dependent on the army, whose leaders turned against him, forcing his resignation and then murdering him on 19 February 1913. There followed a succession of twelve presidents in twenty years before CARDENAS sought to carry out some of Madero's bold experiments. S. R. Ross: *Francisco Madero, Apostle of Mexican Democracy* (New York, 1955); C. C. Cumberland: *Mexican Revolution: Genesis under Madero* (Boston, Mass., 1967); A. Knight: *The Mexican Revolution*, Vol. 1 (Cambridge, 1969).

Maginot, André (1877–1932), French Minister of War: born in Paris, and for many years a popular Deputy representing one of the suburbs of the capital. He enlisted in 1914 and was gravely wounded at Verdun, while serving with the rank of Sergeant. Returning to the Chamber he led a devastating attack on the generalship of JOFFRE at a secret session (1916). He was Minister of War from 1922 to 1924 and again from 1929 to 1932. On 4 January 1930 the Senate and the Chamber of Deputies approved a law authorizing expenditure on a defence system consisting of fortifications in depth from Longwy to the Franco-Swiss Frontier. These fortifications were named the Maginot Line in honour of the ex-Sergeant who was Minister at that time. V. Rowe: *The Great Wall of France* (New York, 1959).

Mahatir-bin-Mohamad (1925–), Malaysian political leader: born at Alor Setar, Kedah, studied medicine at Singapore, and practised as a doctor from 1953 to 1964, when he was elected to the Federal Parliament as a member of United Malay's National Organisation (UMNO). He became chief spokesman for UMNO's radical youth, who favoured 'affirmative action' to raise the status of ethnic Malays and acceptance of a specifically Islamic social policy. Mahatir became Prime Minister of Malaysia in 1981, gaining the honorific title of Datuk Seri (the Malay equivalent of a knighthood). In office, he encouraged industrial development on the Japanese model. After the Kuala Lumpur Heads of Commonwealth meeting of 1987, he chaired the commission which, in 1991, presented a report on the future principles to guide the Commonwealth. Despite opposition from non-Malay ethnic groups Mahatir won general elections for UMNO in 1982, 1986 and 1990. Mahatir-bin-Mohamad: *The Malay Dilemma* (Kuala Lumpur, 1969); A. Sakaria: *Government and Politics in Malaysia* (Oxford, 1987).

Major, John (1943–), British Prime Minister: born the son of a trapeze performer, in London and educated at Rutlish School before beginning a career in banking. He gained local government experience at Lambeth as a Conservative Councillor 1968–71, unsuccessfully contesting St Pancras North in the two General Elections of 1974 but winning the Huntingdonshire seat in 1979 (the constituency becoming Huntingdon four years later). He became assistant Government Whip in 1983 and, strongly backed by Margaret THATCHER, entered her Cabinet in June 1987 as Chief Secretary to the Treasury. In July 1989 he was a surprise choice as Foreign and Commonwealth Secretary in succession to Sir Geoffrey Howe (1926–), but held the post for only ninety-one days, as, at the end of September, he was moved back to the Treasury, becoming Chancellor of the Exchequer on the sudden resignation of Nigel Lawson (1932–). When in November 1990 Thatcher resigned, she backed John Major in the party leadership contest, which he won with 185 votes, against 131 votes for Michael Heseltine (1933–) and fifty-six for Douglas Hurd (1930–). He became Prime Minister on 28 November 1990 and won the General Election of April 1992, though the Conservative overall majority was cut to twenty-one (from 101 after the 1987 election). His policies required a delicate balancing act between 'anti-Europeans' who wished to perpetuate Thatcherite government and moderate reformers. Major personally launched a 'back to basics' campaign at the Party Conference of October 1993, though doubts remained over his precise intentions. He showed more patience and determination than his predecessors in tackling the Irish Question, securing from the IRA on 31 August 1994 a 'complete cessation of military operations', not broken until February 1996. N. W. Ellis: *John Major, a Personal Biography* (1991); E. Pearce: *The Quiet Rise of John Major* (1991); B. Anderson: *John Major: the Making of a Prime Minister* (1991).

Makarios III (Mikhail Christodoulos Mouskos) (1913–77), Archbishop and President of the Republic of Cyprus from 1960 until his death: born at Ano Panayia, near Paphos, into a peasant family. He entered a monastery as a novice in 1926 and was studying theology at Athens University when the Germans occupied Greece (1941). He was ordained a priest in the Greek Orthodox Church in 1946, thereafter spending over a year in Massachusetts studying sociology as well as continuing his theological work. In 1948 he was elected Bishop of Kitium. Two years later he became head of the self-governing branch of the Orthodox Church in his native Cyprus. His predecessor as archbishop had assumed the spiritual name 'Makarios' and Bishop Mouskos followed his example. Traditionally the archbishop was also recognized as the Ethnarch, a national spokesman as well as a spiritual father for his people; and in this role Makarios III encouraged the revival of a movement for the union of Cyprus with Greece (*Enosis*). Spasmodic demonstrations in favour of *Enosis* in 1951 and 1953 were followed in the spring of 1955 by the start of a terrorist campaign by the National Organization of Cypriot Fighters (EOKA) under the leadership of Colonel GRIVAS. The British colonial Governor, Field Marshal Sir John Harding, believed that EOKA was receiving political direction from Archbishop Makarios, who in March 1956 was deported from Cyprus and detained in the Seychelles for a year. In April 1957 Makarios returned to Athens and was subsequently allowed to address the UN Assembly on the desire of his people for *Enosis*. The appointment in December 1957 of a civilian Governor, Sir Hugh Foot, gave the British government the opportunity of putting forward compromise proposals over Cyprus which were designed to safeguard the rights of the Turkish minority as well as to allow the British to retain military bases on the island. Makarios, as Ethnarch, accepted the compromise in February 1959 and was elected President of a Cypriot Republic in December 1959, taking office when the Republic was granted independence within the Commonwealth on 16 August 1960. The EOKA extremists considered themselves betrayed by Makarios's acceptance of a compromise which fell short of *Enosis*. The Archbishop survived several plots on his life and his policy was hampered by the endemic Turco-Greek conflict on the island. On 15 July 1974 an attempted EOKA *coup d'état* forced Makarios into exile and provoked a Turkish invasion, the island being effectively partitioned within a month. President Makarios returned to Nicosia at the end of the year but was unable to reach any agreement with the Turkish Cypriots, despite attempts by UN representatives to encourage inter-communal talks. The Archbishop suffered a heart attack and died suddenly on 3 August 1977, shortly after returning from the Silver Jubilee celebrations and the meeting of Commonwealth Prime Ministers in London. He was succeeded as President by a layman, Spyros KYPRIANOU. S. Mayes: *Makarios* (1981).

Malan, Daniel François (1874–1959), South African Prime Minister from 1948 to 1954: born, like SMUTS, on a farm at Riebeeck West in Cape Colony, educated at Stellenbosch and at Utrecht, remaining in the Netherlands until he was 30. From 1905 to 1915 he was a 'preacher' (*Predikant*) in the Dutch Reformed Church in South Africa. He was an austere Calvinist, sincerely believing that his Boer people were among the Elect of God, and he also encouraged the vernacular and literary use of Afrikaans, for many years editing an Afrikaans newspaper, *Die Berger*. He was elected a Nationalist MP in 1918 and took office under HERTZOG in 1924, with responsibility for education, public health, and other internal affairs. Afrikaans was recognized as an official language and the Indian minority was encouraged to seek repatriation. In 1933 the 'Malanites' broke away from Hertzog's followers to form their own 'Purified Nationalist Party' and Malan was official leader of the Opposition to Smuts throughout the Second World War. In May 1948 a distrust of Smuts' internationalism led the electorate to support Malan and his nationalists. He became Prime Minister on 3 June 1948, holding office until 2 December 1954. During the election campaign Malan had made use of the slogan 'Apartheid' ('Separation') to emphasize his wish for segregating non-whites from whites. This policy he put into force by a series of measures concerned with education, conditions of work, places of residence and so-called 'immorality' (sexual relations between whites and non-whites). Criticism was met with the Suppression of Communism Act (1950), a measure of totalitarian thoroughness, which imposed on anyone accused of holding communist beliefs the obligation of proving their innocence of such a charge. Malan's repressive policy was judged unconstitutional by the South African Supreme Court in March 1952, a decision to which Malan responded by fresh legislation which established Parliament as the highest court in South Africa. This measure guaranteed Malan a free hand to introduce any racially divisive laws which he felt ordained by God, so long as the Nationalists retained a parliamentary majority. Malan retired from active politics at the end of 1954. He outlived his successor, STRIJDOM, by a few months, dying at Stellenbosch on 7 February 1959. L. Marquand: *The Peoples, and Policies of South Africa (Oxford, 1952)*; T. Davenport: *South Africa, a Modern History* (1991).

Malcolm X (Malcolm Little) (1925–65), American Black Power leader: born in Omaha, Nebraska, the son of a Baptist minister of Caribbean origin. Malcolm Little spent his childhood and youth in Michigan and Massachusetts. During a second term of imprisonment for burglary and racketeering in 1952 he was converted to Islam, accepting the extreme radicalism of the Black Muslims, the 'Nation of Islam' separatist movement founded in the USA in 1930, with the belief that black Americans were, in origin, enslaved Muslims. On his release in 1954 Malcolm X assumed the alias by which he is generally known and used his considerable gifts of oratory to travel across America, helping to raise Black Muslim membership to over 100,000. After a pilgrimage to Mecca and the adoption of a fully Muslim name, Haji Malik El-Shadazz, he set up the Organization of Afro-American Unity (1964), an international movement which, while asserting racial solidarity, merged African socialism with Islamic beliefs. Eleven months later (February 1965) he was shot dead during a rally at Harlem, probably on the orders of an 'isolationist' faction of Black Muslims, infiltrated by CIA agents.

J. A. Geschwender: *The Black Revolt* (Englewood Cliffs, N.J., 1971); R. L. Allen: *A Guide to Black Power in America* (1970).

Malenkov, Georgy Maximilianovich (1907–88) STALIN's successor: born at Orenburg (Chkalov), becoming a member of the Communist Party in 1920. He assisted Stalin with his policy of enforced collectivization of agriculture in the early 1930s, and was promoted to the inner secretariat of the party in 1939. He was a close protégé of Stalin, serving in an advisory capacity on the State Defence Committee from 1942 to 1944, and then concentrating on reorganizing the party machine. Stalin made him Deputy Prime Minister in 1946 and showed his confidence by appointing him to give the principal speech at the Nineteenth Party Congress on 5 October 1952. When Stalin died five months later, Malenkov took over both his posts as Prime Minister and First Secretary of the party, making him at that moment the most powerful man in the world (6 March 1953). He did not possess the skills or astuteness for such responsibility. Within a fortnight he was edged out of his party position by KHRUSCHEV (whose status as First Secretary was not, however, confirmed until the following September). Malenkov's inability to deal with the problems of agriculture and industrialization led to his replacement by BULGANIN as Prime Minister in February 1955. For two-and-a-half years Malenkov served as Minister for Electrical Energy, a post better suited to his abilities, but in July 1957 both Malenkov and MOLOTOV were denounced in the Soviet Press for 'anti-party activities' and were deprived of all posts in the government and party hierarchy. Malenkov continued his descending career by becoming manager of the hydroelectric works established near his birthplace, returning to the Moscow area to pass his last twenty years of life in obscure retirement. S. Bialer: *Stalin's Successors: Leadership, Stability and Change in the Soviet Union* (Cambridge, 1980); A. Werth: *Russia, the Post-War Years* (New York, 1972).

Mandela, Nelson Rolihlahla (1918–), first African President of the South African Republic: born in the Transkei, He was allowed to study law and to practise it in Johannesburg, abandoning his career in 1952 in order to lead the African National Congress in its struggle to achieve through democratic means a free and multiracial society within southern Africa. For nine years he travelled as widely as the apartheid laws permitted, acting as a counsellor of restraint whose advice was respected even by the more extreme opponents of apartheid. In 1961 the African National Congress was declared an illegal organization. Mandela was jailed for five years in November 1962. While in prison he was charged under the Suppression of Communism Act. His trial lasted from October 1963 to June 1964, when he was sentenced to life imprisonment and incarcerated in a maximum security island prison. Worldwide protests at his long detention and concern over his health led to a relaxation of conditions in August 1988, when he was admitted to hospital suffering from tuberculosis, but it was not until 11 February 1990 that President DE KLERK ordered his release. Constitutional talks with the President and with Chief Buthelezi from January 1991 led to the signing of a National Peace Accord but violence continued in the townships intermittently over the following two years until Mandela, with extreme patience and tenacity, secured his first objective, the establishment in December 1993 of a Transitional Executive Council, which ended exclusive white rule in South Africa. He shared the Nobel Peace Prize of 1993 with de Klerk. The African National Congress's victory in the country's first multiracial general election (27–29 April 1994) enabled parliament to elect Nelson Mandela as State President and, consequently, the chief executive of the Republic. He took office on 10 May 1994 in a ceremony at Pretoria attended by royal representatives and state dignitaries from many lands. N. Mandela: *Long Walk to Freedom* (1994); M. Benson: *Nelson Mandela* (rev. edn 1994); S. Johns and R. Hunt Davis (eds): *Mandela, Tambo, and the African National Congress* (Oxford, 1991).

Mannerheim, Carl Gustaf Emil (1867–1951), Finnish Field Marshal: born at Villnaes in southern Finland, his family being of Swedish descent. He sought a military career and, since the Grand Duchy of Finland was at the time of his birth within the Russian Empire, he was commissioned in a crack cavalry regiment of the Russian Imperial Army in 1889, fighting with distinction against the Japanese in 1904–5 and attaining the rank of General in the First World War. In the spring of 1918 Finnish Communists occupied Helsinki, prompting Mannerheim to organize a 'White' army which, with German support, defeated the 'Reds' in pitched battles at Tammerfors and Vyborg (Viipuri), advancing to within twenty miles of Petrograd. From December 1918 to July 1919 he served as Finnish Head of State, with the title of Regent. He supported British and French intervention in Russia in 1919–20, continuing in arms against the Bolsheviks until 1921, when he retired from active service with the rank of Field Marshal. Between the wars he exercised great influence on Finland's development, presiding over meetings of Finland's Defence Council and suggesting the construction of a line of fortifications (similar to France's 'Maginot Line'). This 'Mannerheim Line' checked a Russian advance into Finland for thirteen weeks during the Russo-Finnish winter war of 1939–40, a campaign in which Mannerheim again served as military Commander-in-Chief. The eventual Soviet victory in this war induced Mannerheim to accept offers of assistance from Germany in 1941; and for three years he led the Finnish troops against Soviet Russia. By the summer of 1944 he realized the dangers of this policy, accepting the Finnish presidency at the request of parliament and, in September 1944, signing an armistice with Soviet representatives. In March 1945 he declared war on Germany, retaining the presidency for another twelve months until his health began to fail. He died at his home near Helsinki on 27 January 1951. C. G. Mannerheim: *The Memoirs of Marshal Mannerheim* (1954); C. Jay Smith: *Finland and the Russian Revolution, 1917–1922* (Athens, Ga., 1958); J. H. Wuorinen: *Finland in World War II* (New York, 1947).

Mao Tse-tung (Mao Zedong) (1893–1976), Chinese Communist leader: born at Chaochan in Hunan province, his family being peasant farmers. He was educated at Changsha and became a library assistant. At the age of 27 he was a founder-member of the Chinese Communist Party, joining the party's Politburo two years later (1923). For some years there was collaboration between the party and the Kuomintang (the nationalist party associated with CHIANG KAI-SHEK) and Mao even stood as a candidate for the Kuomintang's Central Committee in 1924. But by 1927 he had begun to work out his own interpretation of Marxism, the doctrine that in the East, and especially in China, the revolutionary elite is to be found among peasants in the countryside rather than in the towns, where the proletariat was socially more backward than in the West. A peasant uprising which he encouraged in 1927 was, however, soon suppressed. Mao set up a Chinese Soviet in Kiangsi province in 1931, but the military threat from Chiang's Kuomintang forced the

Communists to leave Kiangsi in 1934 and begin an eight thousand mile trek to the relative security of northern Shenshi. This famous twelve-month trial of endurance, the 'Long March', confirmed Mao's leadership of the Chinese Communists and he was accepted as Party Chairman in January 1935. From 1937 Mao collaborated with Chiang against the Japanese invaders, although keeping the Communist-controlled areas separate from Kuomintang authority and sending CHOU EN-LAI to Chiang's wartime capital, Chungking, as a virtual ambassador. Conflict with the Kuomintang was resumed in the winter of 1945–6, guerrilla operations turning to open battles in the summer of 1948, with Peking falling to Mao's troops in January 1949. When the Chinese People's Republic was proclaimed on 1 October 1949 Mao became head of the government ('Chairman of the National People's Governing Council'). He was also Chairman of the Republic (Head of State) until April 1959, when he was succeeded by LIU SHAO-CHI. Thoroughout his public life Mao retained a peasant's vivid simplicity of expression: the *Thoughts of Chairman Mao* (read widely in China and beyond from 1964 onwards) were essays or reflections on strategic and social problems written, for the most part, during the years of civil war; they lent themselves naturally to metaphor and slogan. While Mao was attempting to modernize China without destroying the concept of peasant communes, he was also engaged in disputes over the interpretation of Marxism with the post-STALIN rulers of the Soviet Union. Mao's attempt to dragoon the Chinese into increased farming production and light industry by his so-called 'Great Leap Forward' of 1958–61 was a total failure. His authority was, however, reasserted in 1965–6 by the 'cultural revolution', which favoured a traditionalist (though anarchic) Chinese peasant communal economy as opposed to the allegedly Khruschevian 'betrayals' favoured by Liu and 'his henchmen'. Yet Mao's personal victory in the 'cultural revolution' made him in his closing years a revered father-figure rather than an effective national leader: policy was shaped by Chou En-lai, by Mao's fourth wife CHIANG CHIN, and by Marshal LIN PIAO (until his elimination in 1971). It is unlikely that Mao had much influence on the party struggle for the succession (won by HUA GUA FENG) in the last months of his life. He died in Peking on 9 September 1976. S. R. Schram: *Mao Tse-tung* (1967); J. Ch'en: *Mao and the Chinese Revolution* (1965); E. Chou: *Mao Tse-tung, the Man and the Myth* (1982).

Marcos, Ferdinand Edralin (1917–89), Filipino President: born at Caviter, achieved notoriety as a 22-year-old law student for defending himself against accusations of murdering a personal enemy of his father. His exploits with the resistance against the Japanese invaders made him a war hero. From 1949 to 1959 he was a Liberal Congressman, and then a 'Nationalist' Senator for six years. Marcos won the presidential election of November 1965 with promises of industrial development and strong executive initiative and took up office on 30 December. Successes against communist insurgents maintained his popularity and he won a second term in November 1969. Under martial law Marcos imposed constitutional changes in 1973, freeing his authoritarian presidency from any fixed term of office. But the spread of his repressive system aroused resistance, and the regime was totally discredited by the murder of the Opposition leader, Benigno Aquino, at Manila airport on 21 August 1983. Popular sympathy supported and sustained the newly fired political ambitions of the widowed Cory AQUINO. Marcos's fraudulent claim to have defeated her in the presidential election of 2 February 1986 led to his final overthrow. After a switch in loyalty of senior army commanders Marcos and his wife, Imelda, flew to Hawaii on 26 February, leaving Cory Aquino as the rightful President. Charges of corruption could not be pressed home because of Marcos's failing health and, after his death in America in 1989, Imelda Marcos was left to face many of these accusations. She was able to return to the Philippines after President Aquino left office, and in 1995 won a seat in the Filipino Congress. J. Bresnan: *Crisis in the Philippines, the Marcos Era and Beyond* (Princeton, N.J., 1986).

Marcuse, Herbert (1898–1979), German-American philosopher of student revolt: born in Berlin of Jewish parentage and educated at universities there and in Frieburg, becoming a Marxist within the Social Democratic Party in the 1920s. He was associated with Max Horkheimer (1895–1973), Director of the Institute for Social Research in the University of Frankfurt from 1931. Marcuse accompanied Horkheimer and others of this 'Frankfurt School' of libertarian Marxist thought when they emigrated to America upon the advent of Nazism. He became an American citizen in 1941, the year in which his study of Hegel, *Reason and Revolution*, was published. After working for the State Department Marcuse was a professor at Brandeis University, Massachusetts, from 1953 until 1965 when he accepted a chair at the University of California, San Diego. His *Eros and Civilization* (1955) stimulated student minds already made uneasy by contradictions within a consumer society, but it was Marcuse's *One-Dimensional Man* (1964) which made him suddenly, in his late sixties, an international figure. His argument that a superfluity of material goods destroyed the workers as a revolutionary force in contemporary society in the West appealed to student protest movements in the United States and in Europe, especially in West Germany where Marcuse was lecturing at the time of the anti-Gaullist student riots in Nanterre and Paris in May 1968. By 1972 Marcuse was critical of some of his younger disciples, his *Counter-revolution and Revolt* (1972) looking coolly at the 'pubertarian struggle' which he had assessed with benevolent indulgence in *An Essay on Liberation* (1969). When he died, in America on 31 July 1979, he had already become one of yesterday's prophets. A. Macintyre: *Marcuse* (1970); M. Jay: *The Dialectical Imagination* (1973).

Margai, Milton (1896–1964), first Prime Minister of Sierra Leone: born, a member of the Mende ethnic group, at Gbangbatok and educated at a mission school and at Fourah Bay College, Freetown before going to England, studying medicine at the University of Durham. He returned to Sierra Leone as a qualified doctor and practised in the colonial medical service from 1928 to 1950. He entered politics after the Second World War in 1946, founding the Sierra Leone Organization Society (SLOS). With the granting of a constitution to Sierra Leone in 1951 the scope of the SLOS was broadened; it became the People's Party, with Milton Margai as leader. He was appointed Chief Minister in 1954 and worked harmoniously with the colonial authorities to secure independence within the Commonwealth on 27 April 1961. Sir Milton Margai – he was knighted in 1959 – served as Prime Minister for three years, seeking to develop a democratic tradition in the newly sovereign state. On his sudden death in 1964 he was succeeded by his brother, Sir Albert Margai (1910–80), a barrister and (unlike Sir Milton) a Roman Catholic. But the democratic basis of the People's Party was challenged both by the more radical All People's Congress and by impatient army leaders. Mounting unrest forced Albert Margai to settle in Britain for the last thirteen years of his life, though he died while on a visit to the

USA. A. P. Kup: *Sierra Leone* (Newton Abbot, 1975); J. R. Cartwright: *Political Leadership in Sierra Leone* (1978).

Marshall, George Catlett (1880–1959), Chief of Staff of the US army from 1939 to 1945 and Secretary of State from 1947 to 1949: born at Uniontown in Pennsylvania and passed out of the Virginia Military Institute in 1901. As a Colonel, he was operational Chief of Staff to the US First Army at the Saint-Mihiel battle in the third week of September 1918. Between the wars he saw service in China before becoming chief of the war plans division in 1938. From September 1939 to November 1945 he headed the US Army Staff and was Chairman of the Joint Chiefs of Staff from 1941. General Marshall was, above all, a supreme organizer, converting the small US army into a force of over eight million men. After retiring from the army he was sent to China on a special mission in December 1945, his task being to end the civil war between CHIANG KAI-SHEK and MAO TSE-TUNG. After twelve months of negotiation he had to report failure. He became Secretary of State on 16 January 1947, his twenty-four-month tenure of office being best remembered for the financial aid programme towards European economic recovery, the 'Marshall Plan', which he outlined in a speech at Harvard on 5 June 1947. His military knowledge – and, in particular, his grasp of logistics – was of great value during the blockade of West Berlin imposed by the Russians in the spring of 1948. He also assisted in the creation of the North Atlantic Treaty Organization, which was proposed during his term as Secretary of State. In 1950–1, during the Korean War, he served President TRUMAN as Secretary of Defence and was consulted by the President before he took the dramatic decision to dismiss MACARTHUR from his command in April 1951. The completion at the end of 1952 of the European Recovery Programme was marked by a decision to award Marshall the Nobel Peace Prize for 1953. No other senior professional soldier has received the Peace Prize. F. C. Pogue: *George C. Marshall* (3 vols) (New York, 1964, 1966, 1983); E. Larrabee: *Commander in Chief: Franklin D. Roosevelt, his Lieutenants and their War* (New York, 1983).

Marx, Karl (1818–83), theoretical founder of scientific Communism: born at Trier in the western Rhineland, the son of a Jewish lawyer who accepted nominal conversion to Christianity. He studied law at the universities of Bonn and Berlin (1835–41), where he was influenced by the metaphysical philosophy of the dialectic taught by Georg Hegel (1770–1831). Marx, however, reacted against the idealism implicit in Hegel's method and, leaving Germany, began to collaborate with the exiled German socialists in Brussels and later in Paris, where in 1844 he met his principal collaborator, Friedrich ENGELS. Marx virtually rewrote Engles' first draft of the *Communist Manifest*, which was published at the end of February 1848. The *Manifesto* sought to explain 'the history of all previous society' as 'the history of class struggle' and called on 'working men of all countries to unite' in overthrowing capitalist society. The revolutions of 1848–9, witnessed briefly by Marx in Cologne, were liberal-national in character rather than socialist (except in a few instances); and Marx spent the remaining years of his life in developing the theories of history, of economics and of revolution outlined in his earliest writings. He lived mainly in London, carrying out research in the British Museum reading room. He took little part in specifically British politics: from 1864 to 1876 he tried to coordinate the attempts of workers in Europe and America to achieve socialism, founding the International Workingmen's Association ('First International'), with its headquarters in London and later in New

York. But the International suffered from internal feuds, especially between doctrinaire socialists and anarchists, and Marx virtually despaired of the movement within eight years of setting it up. The first volume of his most famous work *Das Kapital*, was published in 1867. Since Marx hoped to analyse economic science as Charles Darwin had analysed natural morphology, he asked Darwin for permission to dedicate *Das Kapital* to him but Darwin politely declined the honour. In his other works Marx either commented on current political problems, especially in France, or engaged in criticism of his socialist rivals: he wrote with fire and invective, although hours of scholarly research trip heavily off the pages of his longer studies. Marx believed he had proved the importance of class struggles as a motive force in human history and shown the inevitability of bourgeois oppression of the workers culmlilgin a dicatatorship of the proletariat. He justified this dictatorship as a temporary revolutionary phenomenal wich would be followed by the condition of all classes and the establishment of a classes society, pure communism. *Marx, karl* at his home in Maitland park road London on 14 march 1883, and was buried in Highgate Cemetery. The second and third volumes of *Das Kapital* were edited by Engels and published posthumously in 1885 and 1894. I. Berlin: *Karl Marx* (1939); E. Wilson: *To the Finland Station* (New York, 1940); F. Mehring: *Karl Marx* (1934).

Masaryk, Jan (1886–1948): Czechoslovak Foreign Minister from 1941 to 1948: born in Prague, the son of the later President, Tomaš MASARYK. He was educated in Prague and Vienna, joined his father in exile in London in the First World War, and attended the Paris Peace Conference of 1919 as a member of the Czechoslovak delegation. From 1925 to 1938 he was Czechoslovak envoy in London, ranking in those days as a minister at the head of a legation rather than as an ambassador at the head of an embassy. Masaryk, like President BENEŠ, resigned after the apparent betrayal of Czechoslovakia by the West at the Munich Conference in 1938. He spent most of the Second World War in London, becoming well known as a broadcaster because of his fluent English. When, on 18 July 1941, Britain and the Soviet Union recognized Beneš as head of a provisional Czechoslovak government-in-exile, Masaryk accepted the post of Foreign Minister, returning to Prague with Beneš in the wake of the Soviet army in 1945. He remained Foreign Minister in the coalition headed by the Communist GOTTWALD from 1945 to 1948. When the Comniunists seized power in Prague (21–25 February 1948), Masaryk continued in office. On 10 March, however, his body was found beneath an open window of the Foreign Minustry in Prague. It is Probable he committed suicide in despair at his failure to halt the Gotteald government's policy of 'Sovletization; but he may have been murdered of Zeman: *The Masaryks, the Ministry Czechoslovakia* (1976).

Masaryk, Tomaš Garrigue (1850–1937), President of Czechoslovakia from 1918 to 1935: born, the son of a coachman, at Hodonin in southern Moravia. He was educated at Brno, Vienna and Leipzig, his doctoral thesis being concerned with dilemmas in moral philosophy raised by the problem of suicide. He married an American, Charlotte Garrigue from Boston, and from 1882 to 1914 made his home in Prague, where he was Professor of Philosophy at the Czech University. In 1891 he entered the Austrian parliament as a member of the Young Czech Party, remaining a Deputy for two years. He disagreed, however, with the traditional Czech political attitudes, helping to expose as a recent forgery some much revered 'medieval' Czech manuscripts, defending Jewish believers attacked by both German and Czech nationalists, and founding his own political movement, the 'Czech Realists', which he intended to pioneer democratic and liberal pan-Slavism within the Habsburg Monarchy. He sat in parliament again from 1907 to 1914 and became famous throughout Europe and the United States for his revelation that documents used by the Austro-Hungarian Foreign Ministry in 1909 were crude forgeries intended to discredit the spokesmen for Austria's southern Slav minority. In December 1914 Masaryk escaped to the West, settling in London as a lecturer at King's College and producing an important monthly periodical, *The New Europe* (first published in October 1916), in which he outlined plans for a post-war world based, for the most part, on liberal and national principles. As Chairman of the Czech National Council, Masaryk had contacts with the British Foreign Office. In 1917 he travelled to Russia, where he was able to form a Czech Legion, recruited from volunteers among prisoners-of-war. In the winter of 1917–18 he travelled by way of Siberia to the Pacific and to America, where his views influenced Woodrow WILSON. Support from Slovak as well as from Czech communities in America increased his international standing; and in September 1918 the State Department accorded him recognition as head of an Allied government. In December 1918 he was welcomed in Prague as President-elect. He remained at the head of the Czechoslovak Republic until December 1935, when his health deteriorated. Masaryk took little part in inter-war politics: he was respected as an elder statesman of great moral stature, the founding father of Czech and Slovak unity. He was succeeded as president by BENEŠ and died on 14 September 1937. T. G. Masaryk: *The Making of a State* (1927); O. Funda: *Thomas G. Masaryk* (1978); R. W. Seton-Watson: *Masaryk in England* (Cambridge, 1943).

Masire, Quett Ketumile Joni (1925–), second President of Botswana: born at Kanye (Bechuanaland), educated at Tiger Kloof College, South Africa, returning home to become a journalist, a member of the Bangwaketse Tribal Council and in 1961 a member of Bechuanaland's newly elective Legislative Council. In 1962 he joined Seretse KHAMA in founding the (Botswana) Democratic Party, becoming a Deputy Premier in 1965 and Vice-President when Botswana was established, with full independence, in September 1966. Masire worked closely with Seretse Khama so as to ensure that Botswana became a stable democracy, with presidential and legislative elections held every five years. On Seretse Khama s death in July 1980, Masire succeeded to the presidency, maintaining policies of racial tolerance and non-alignment, despite several border raids by South African troops pursuing alleged ANC combat units, 1985–8. J. Parsons: *Botswana, Liberal Democracy and Labour Reserve in southern Africa* (Aldershot, 1984).

Massey, William Ferguson (1856–1925), New Zealand's longest-serving Prime Minister: born in County Derry, his family being staunch Ulster Protestants who emigrated to North Island in 1870, becoming dairy farmers. In 1894 Massey entered the New Zealand parliament and was rapidly accepted as a spokesman of agrarian interests, founding the, basically conservative, Reform Party. He became Prime Minister in July 1912 at a time of fierce class division in New Zealand and achieved notoriety as a strike-breaker; he raised a special constabulary, the so-called 'Massey Cossacks', from his fellow farmers to break up strikes in the gold-fields and on the Wellington waterfront. Although an isolationist at heart he loyally supported the British Empire's war effort and won a clear majority in the New Zealand elections of December 1919, remaining Prime Minister until his death in May 1925. Massey's span of twelve years and ten months remains New Zealand's longest premiership. G. H. Scholefield: *The Rt. Hon. W. F. Massey* (Wellington, 1925); G. W. Rice (ed.): *Oxford History of New Zealand* (2nd edn Auckland, 1992).

Matteotti, Giacomo (1885–1924), Italian Socialist: born at Fratta Polesine, near Rovigo and the Po delta, where he became a comfortably rich landowner. He represented Rovigo as a Socialist in parliament in the early 1920s and, as a fearless critic of Fascism, was much respected within Italy and abroad. On 10 June 1924 he disappeared from Rome and his body was found in a shallow grave twelve miles from the capital three days later. Almost certainly, Matteotti was murdered by extreme Fascists beyond the control of MUSSOLINI. Although Mussolini was not himself responsible for the assassination, he responded to the indignation over Matteotti's fate by imposing strict censorship on newspapers and magazines and banning all Socialist meetings. In 1926 a small group of Fascists was charged with complicity in the crime: they received light sentences. Matteotti became, and long remained, the posthumous hero of the anti-Fascist resistance. D. Mack Smith: *Mussolini* (1981).

Maximilian (1832–67), Emperor of Mexico from 1864 to 1867: born in Vienna, a younger brother of Emperor FRANCIS JOSEPH. As a young man Archduke Maximilian was especially concerned with building up the Imperial Austrian Navy. He served as Governor of Lombardy-Venetia from 1857 to 1859 and, after disagreements with Francis Joseph, retired to his palace of Miramare near Trieste, where he concentrated on botanical studies. His wife, the Belgian Princess Charlotte (1840–1927), encouraged him to accept an offer of the crown of the new Mexican Empire which NAPOLEON III wished to establish by French arms. Maximilian and Charlotte arrived in Mexico in May 1864. He was able to impose orderly government around Mexico City and Vera Cruz with the help of the French, under Marshal BAZAINE, but the Mexican republican movement of JUAREZ took heart at the victory of the Union armies in the American Civil War. Pressure from the United States forced Napoleon to withdraw French troops in March 1867. Although Maximilian continued to organize resistance, he was betrayed by some of his earlier supporters and captured at Querataro, where he was executed by firing-squad on 19 June 1867. His Empress had returned to Europe, hoping to rally diplomatic support for her husband, but the strain of events overtaxed her reason. She suffered a total mental breakdown and spent sixty more years of life isolated in a moated castle in her native Belgium. J. Haslip: *Imperial Adventurer* (1971); J. Ridley: *Maximilian and Juarez* (1993).

Mboya, Tom (1930–69), leader of the Luo people in Kenya: born on a sisal plantation in the White Highlands. He showed marked ability at a Roman Catholic missionary school and completed his education at Ruskin College, Oxford. On returning to Kenya he became a trade union organizer, more in touch with a modern economy than the much-revered KENYATTA. Mboya was a consultant at the London conference on Kenya in 1960, winning the respect of the Colonial Secretary, Iain Macleod. When Kenya achieved self-government in 1963, Mboya became the first Minister of Labour, subsequently Minister of Justice and finally Minister of Economic Planning. On 5 July 1969 he was shot dead in the centre of the Kenyan capital by a member of the Kikuyu. Mboya's assassination threatened inter-tribal war between the Kikuyu and the, Luo. This danger was avoided by firm action on the part of President Kenyatta, but the assassination robbed Kenya of a gifted leader of the younger generation. D. Goldworthy: *Tom Mboya* (1982).

Meade, George Gordon (1815–72), American soldier who commanded the Army of the Potomac in 1863: born in Spain, at Cadiz, graduated from the Military Academy at West Point in 1835 and fought in the Mexican War, 1846–8. His competence in the field at the battles of First Bull Run, Antietam and Fredericksburg induced LINCOLN to give him command of the army of the Potomac in June 1863. His immediate task was to check the invasion of Maryland by LEE. This he accomplished at Gettysburg on 3 July 1863 but he was criticized for failing to pursue Lee's defeated troops during the bad weather which followed this costly victory. From March 1864 until the end of the war General Meade was subordinate to GRANT, showing himself to be a loyal, unimaginative, tough and hot-tempered lieutenant to a man of greater strategic vision. G. G. Meade: *The Life and Letters of George Gordon Meade* (2 vols) (New York, 1913); F. Cleaves: *Meade of Gettysburg* (New York, 1960).

Meany, George (1894–1980), American labour leader: born in New York, the son of a plumber, the trade he himself followed from 1910 to 1920. He was active in the American Federation of Labor (AFL) from 1915 onwards and became a union official in 1920. During the New Deal (1933–9) he helped steer beneficial legislation through the New York state legislature, achieving national stature as Secretary-General of the AFL from 1940 to 1952 when he accepted the presidency of the union. Meany was an outspoken Roman Catholic, contemptuous of Wall Street, of Moscow, and frequently of Europe's trade unionists, too. He did not always extend a fraternal hand to the other great American labour leader, John L. LEWIS; but Meany's ruthless competence, clear-headedness and positive anti-communism ensured him a loyal following. With the automobile workers' leader, Walter Reuther (1907–70), Meany established a federation of the AFL and the Congress of Industrial Organizations (CIO) in 1955. He remained President of this fifteen-million-strong federation until November 1979, only two months before his death in Washington. Meany deplored the economic restraints of the NIXON era, fulminating personally against the President after the Watergate revelations for having 'cast a shadow of shame over the spirit of the nation'. At times Meany also embarrassed the Democratic Party leaders, especially by his unremitting hostility through the years of attempted *détente* to contacts between American labour and delegations from the Soviet Union and other Comecon countries. F. Peterson: *American Labor Unions* (1963).

Meinhof, Ulrike (1934–76), West German anarchist: born in Oldenburg, studied at the University of Marburg and became a magazine columnist, also writing for radio and television. She was disillusioned both by the materialistic character of society in the Federal German Republic and by the neo-imperialism of Soviet foreign policy. The suppression of the student protest movement in France and Germany in 1968 led her, in conjunction with Andreas BAADER, to found the Rote Armee Fraktion ('Red Army Group') of anarchists. The group was held responsible for several murders, bombings and bank raids in West Germany. Meinhof herself planned an operation which rescued Baader from imprisonment in May 1970. With other terrorist leaders she was arrested in June 1972 but the process of collecting evidence and the need to build a specially protected courthouse led to a delay of three years before she was brought to trial on the major charges of murder and attempted murder. When the trial reached its eleventh month of hearing, Ulrike Meinhof was found dead in her cell at Stuttgart (9 May 1976). An inquest determined the cause of her death as suicide. Radical students questioned this verdict, staging demonstrations in which she was regarded as a left-wing martyr, much as had been Rosa LUXEMBURG to an earlier generation. J. Bicker: *Hitler's Children, the Story of the Baader-Meinhof Gang* (1977); E. Kolinsky: *Parties, Opposition and Society in West Germany* (1984).

Meir, Golda (*née* **Mabovich**) (1898–1978), Israeli Prime Minister from 1969 to 1973: born in Kiev, accompanying her parents to America when she was 8 years old and completing her schooling in Milwaukee. In 1917 she married Morris Mayerson, with whom she left America to settle in Palestine in 1921, Hebraizing their surname to Meir at the same time. They lived for several years in a kibbutz on lower Galilee, Mrs Meir becoming a member of the Mapai Labour Party when it was founded in 1930. After her husband's death she was employed on diplomatic missions by the Jewish Agency (1946–7) and became the first Israeli ambassador in Moscow through the winter of 1948–9. On her return to Israel she entered the government of BEN-GURION as Minister for Labour and Social Security, a post she held for seven years. From 1956 to 1965 she was Foreign Minister, frequently speaking out against Arab threats to Israel when she attended meetings of the United Nations. She then spent four years out of the government, occupying herself with the problems of the Mapai Party. In February 1969 she took office as Prime Minister on the sudden death of Levi Eschkol (1895–1969). She subsequently won the General Election but formed a coalition 'Government of National Unity', retaining General DAYAN as Defence Minister, even though he was out of sympathy with her socialist ideals. Mrs Meir survived in the crisis caused by the sudden Egyptian and Syrian attacks on the Day of Atonement (Yom Kippur) in October 1973. Disagreements over the Israeli attitude to UN mediation intensified divisions within her Cabinet and Israel experienced a long political crisis throughout March 1974. On 10 April, when it seemed as if Mrs Meir had successfully formed a new coalition ministry, she announced her intention of resigning the premiership, handing over to General Yitzhak RABIN at the end of the month. Mrs Meir remained a member of the Knesset (Parliament), retaining an active interest in international politics until her health gave way in the late summer of 1978. G. Meir: *My Life* (Tel Aviv, 1975); N. Sfran: *From War to War* (New York, 1969); D. Peretz: *The Government and Politics of Israel* (Boulder, Colo., 1983).

Mendès-France, Pierre (1907–82), French radical Socialist leader: born of Jewish parents in Paris. Showed brilliance as a law student and in 1932 became the youngest Deputy elected to the Assembly, serving DALADIER briefly as a junior minister in 1938. He served in the air force in the Second World War, making a courageous escape to join DE GAULLE in London in 1941 and acting as the General's chief adviser on financial matters in 1945. He spoke out against right-wing Gaullism under the Fourth Republic but in June 1954 he formed a coalition of radicals, Gaullists and socialists which checked inflation and showed initiative and far-sightedness in tackling the problems of Tunisia and in securing peace in Indo-China (Vietnam). He failed, however, to satisfy the Left over Algeria and was forced out of office after a mere 230 days of government. Although he was briefly Minister of State in 1956 he lost his parliamentary seat in 1958 for his trenchant criticism of Gaullism. He returned to the Assembly in 1967, firmly attached to a traditional radicalism but retiring from ill-health in 1975. A. Werth: *The Strange History of Mendès-France* (1957).

Menelik II (1844–1913), Emperor of Abyssinia: born in Ankober in the southern Abyssinian Kingdom of Shewa, of which he became ruler, in conflict in the 1880s with John II (ruler of Ethiopia, 1872–89). When John was killed by the Dervishes Menelik became 'king of kings' in Abyssinia, exploiting British, Italian and French missions so as to build up a well-equipped army, with which he conducted campaigns in the subsidiary kingdoms of Abyssinia (Kaffa, Jimma, Harar and the Ogaden) so as to create a unified empire. He ruled with the assistance of a council of nominated ministers from his palace in the new capital of Addis Ababa. His most remarkable achievement was the defeat of four brigades of an invading Italian army, caught in mountain passes north of Adowa (Adua) on 1 March 1896 – a victory which, at the peak of the 'scramble for Africa', safeguarded Abyssinia's independence for forty years. Menelik's health began to fail in 1909 and his daughter's son, Lij Yasu, presided over the council of ministers for the last four years of Menelik's reign. Although Lij Yasu was Menelik's designated successor, he lacked the natural authority to consolidate his position and in 1916 government effectively passed to Menelik's cousin, the future HAILE SELASSIE. A. Marcus: *The Life and Times of Menelik II* (Laurelton, N.J., 1975); R. H. Kafi Dherwah: *Shewa, Menelik and the Ethiopian Empire, 1813–1889* (1975); G. E. H. Berkeley: *The Campaign of Adowa and the Rise of Menelik* (1902).

Menem, Carlos Saul (1935–), Argentinian President: born at Anillaco in La Rioja province, studied law at the Argentinian National University in Cordoba and was a founder-member of the Peronista Youth Movement in his native province. He became well known for his defence of political prisoners after the 1955 *coup* and was leader of the, neo-Peronista, Justicalist Party in La Rioja in 1963. He was elected Provincial Governor of La Rioja in 1973, imprisoned by the ruling junta from 1976 to 1981, but re-elected Governor in 1983 and 1987. In the presidential elections of May 1989 he stood as Justicalist candidate, gaining 310 of the 600 votes in the electoral college, and was sworn in as President on 8 July 1989 for a six-year term. His administration improved relations with Great Britain and the United States. In April 1994 he convened a constituent assembly to amend provisions in the 1853 Constitution of the Republic so that an incumbent President could stand for a second term of office. L. Bethell (ed.): *Cambridge History of Latin America* Vol. 8, *1930–90* (Cambridge, 1991).

Mengistu (Mengistu Haile Miriam) (1937–), Abyssinian revolutionary Head of State for fourteen years: received military training at the Holetta Academy and was commissioned in the army of HAILE SELASSIE. As a Major he played a prominent part in the *coup* which deposed the Emperor in September 1974 and was Vice-Chairman of the Provisional Military Council led by Brigadier Teferi Benti until February 1977, when Colonel Mengistu led a second *coup* in which Benti was killed. Mengistu then became Chairman and acting Head of State, formally accepting the presidency of the newly created 'People's Democratic Republic' in September 1987. Mengistu received arms and 'volunteers' from the Soviet Union and Cuba. He imposed a harshly repressive regime and a programme of rural collectivization, disastrous in one of Africa's greatest famine areas. The activities of a National Liberation Front in Eritrea, a Western Somali Liberation Front in the Ogaden region, and a secessionist guerrilla campaign in Tigre province limited the effectiveness of Mengistu's socialist revolution. In May 1989 his regime survived an attempted *coup* while he was visiting HONECKER in East Berlin. Mounting resistance from the Democratic Front in Tigre from December 1989 reached a climax with a sustained offensive against Addis Ababa in April 1991. Mengistu's regime collapsed at the end of May; he escaped to Zimbabwe. A. Zegeye and S. Pausewang (eds): *Ethiopia in Change* (1994); E. J. Keller: *Revolutionary Ethiopia: from Empire to People's Republic* (Bloomington, Ind., 1989).

Menzies, Robert Gordon (1894–1978), Australian Prime Minister from 1939 to 1941 and from 1949 to 1966: born in Jeparit, Victoria, and educated at Melbourne University. After practising as a barrister in Victoria and taking part in state politics, he entered Parliament in Canberra in 1934 as a supporter of the former 'nationalists', the United Australia Party (UAP) headed by Joseph Aloysius LYONS, who had been Prime Minister since December 1931. He served as Attorney-General under Lyons, resigning because of differences over an insurance scheme shortly before Lyons' sudden death in April 1939. Menzies succeeded Lyons as Prime Minister and brought Australia into the Second World War in September 1939. In 1940–1 Menzies was principally concerned with the war in Europe and the Mediterranean, visiting London for consultation with Winston CHURCHILL. These signs of imperial statesmanship displeased other members of his Cabinet and aroused Press criticism in Australia. He was forced from office in August 1941 and spent the war years as leader of the Opposition. By 1945 he had broadened the basis of the UAP, converting it into a Liberal Party (with a fundamentally conservative political philosophy). With the victory of the Liberals in the election of December 1949 he became Prime Minister for a second time. In home affairs his government encouraged industrial growth, especially in Queensland and New South Wales, as well as 'white' immigration. In foreign policy he worked more closely than earlier Prime Ministers with the United States, notably through the tripartite security pact concluded with America and New Zealand on 1 September 1951 and known as the ANZUS pact. Nevertheless, in London he was recognized as one of the visionary leaders of the Commonwealth and he tried to mediate in the tension caused by Nasser's nationalization of the Suez Canal in 1956. He was knighted by Queen ELIZABETH in 1963, becoming a Knight of the Thistle in token of his Scottish descent, and in 1964 he succeeded Churchill as Lord Warden of the Cinque Ports, an honour bestowed on no other overseas statesman. At home his decision that Australian troops should support American operations in Vietnam in 1965 aroused widespread criticism and cost him much popularity. He resigned in 1966 so as to give his successor, Harold HOLT, the opportunity to prepare the Liberal Party for an election (which the Liberals won with an increased majority, despite the Vietnam agitation). Sir Robert Menzies took no further part in politics. He died on 15 May 1978; the Prince of Wales flew to Melbourne for his funeral. R. Menzies: *Afternoon Light* (1967); A. W. Martin: *Robert Menzies, a Life*, Vol. 1, *1894–1943* (Carlton, Victoria, 1993); J. Bunting: *R. G. Menzies, a Portrait* (1988); A. W. Martin and P. Hardy (eds): *Dark and Hurrying Days: Menzies's Diary for 1941* (Canberra, 1993).

Metaxas, Joannis (1871–1941), Greek dictator from 1930 until his death: born on Ithaka, commissioned in the army at the age of 19 studied military science in Germany and became Chief of General Staff in 1913. He was a supporter of King CONSTANTINE I and therefore opposed Greek involvement in the First

World War and the later republicanism of VENIZELOS. Metaxas was able to restore the monarchy, after a lapse of eleven years, in November 1935, becoming Minister of War in March 1936 and Prime Minister a few weeks later. An alleged communist threat induced him to establish a right-wing dictatorship in the first week of August 1936. His government was ruthless and efficient but, for the most part, staffed by nonentities, since Metaxas was a hard worker who distrusted initiative in any subordinate. He rejected the ultimatum delivered by the Italian ambassador in October 1940 and was pleased by the victories of the Greek army over the Italians in Albania in the ensuing winter campaign. He did not live to see the Germans invade Greece, dying suddenly on 29 January 1941, and leaving the Greek kingdom without any experienced 'strong man' to meet the challenge of war. J. O. Iatrides (ed.): *Ambassador MacVeagh Reports; Greece, 1933–1947* (Princeton, N.J., 1980); J. S. Koliopoolos: *Greece and the British Connection, 1935–1941* (Oxford, 1977); C. M. Woodhouse: *Modern Greece, a Short History* (1984).

Mihailović, Drazha (1893–1946), Yugoslav anti-Communist guerrilla leader: born at Ivanjica in southern Serbia, serving throughout the First World War in the Serbian Army. He wrote a specialist study of guerrilla operations during the 1930s and was for a time Yugoslavia's military attaché in Sofia. In 1941 Colonel Mihailović was instructed to remain in Serbia and lead a resistance movement of *chetniks*, a traditional name for Serbian guerrillas which had been used between 1804 and 1813, 1907 and 1913, and in the First World War. When *chetnik* resistance began in the forested hills of western Serbia in the autumn of 1941, he was promoted to General and made Minister of War by the exiled Yugoslav Royal government. Twelve months later the British Foreign Office received reports that Mihailović was conserving his forces in order to undertake a general uprising at a later moment. Subsequently it was suggested that he had halted all operations against the Germans and that his subordinates were collaborating with the Germans in attacks on TITO and his Communist partisans. British aid to Mihailović and the *chetniks* (never plentiful even when he was being hailed in the Allied Press as a hero of the resistance) ceased entirely in the early months of 1944. Mihailović remained in hiding in Serbia and Bosnia, hoping to stimulate resistance to communism, until he was captured by Tito's armed police in March 1946. He was charged with treason and war crimes and put on trial near Belgrade. The hearing lasted for five weeks and General Mihailović showed a fatalistic courage in marshalling the facts for his defence. He was condemned to death and executed on 17 July 1946. D. Martin: *Ally Betrayed* (New York, 1946); L. Karchmar: *Drazha Mihailović and the Rise of the Četnik Movement* (New York, 1987).

Mill, John Stuart (1806–73), British philosopher of liberalism: born in London, his father being the prominent exponent of utilitarianism, James Mill (1773–1836), who educated his son in the tradition of philosophic radicalism. Mill served in the East India Office in London from 1823 until 1856. His four most important works were *A System of Logic* (1843), *Principles of Political Economy* (1848) and his treatises on *Liberty* (1859) and on *Representative Government* (1861). Unlike his philosophic radical predecessors Mill recognized a need for the state to interfere in political and economic life so as to avoid abuse of the *laissez-faire* principle basic to English liberal thought in his generation. He insisted on the importance of respect for minority rights, and in his later years Mill championed the political emancipation of women, notably in his work *The Subjection of Women* (1869). From 1865 to 1868 Mill sat in the Commons as MP for Westminster, and in 1867 he introduced the first proposal to enfranchise women, a motion defeated by 196 votes to seventy three, most members showing no interest in the subject. Mill was secular godfather' to Bertrand RUSSELL. He died in Avignon, where he was buried. J. S. Mill: *An Autobiography* (1873); M. S. Price: *John Stuart Mill* (1954); R. P. Anschutz: *The Philosophy of J. S. Mill* (Oxford, 1954).

Milner, Alfred (1854–1925), British imperialist: born at Giessen in western Germany and educated at Tubingen before graduating with great distinction as a classicist from Balliol College, Oxford. He was both a barrister and a political journalist before penetrating to the inner core of Toryism as secretary to G. J. Goschen who became Salisbury's Chancellor of the Exchequer in 1886. Milner helped Lord CROMER stabilize Egypt's finances (1889–92), returned to London to head the Inland Revenue board for five years but was then sent by Chamberlain to South Africa as High Commissioner in 1897, at first as an intermediary between RHODES and KRUGER. His impatience with the Boers tempted Kruger to risk war in 1899 rather than wait for a build-up of British forces. When British imperial troops occupied the Transvaal and the Orange Free State Milner was made Governor, as well as remaining High Commissioner. He received a peerage in 1901 and, a year later, helped draft the Peace Treaty of Vereeniging with the Boers. For his remaining three years in Africa he pursued a policy of reconciliation with the Boers, though incurring widespread condemnation from liberals for encouraging the use of Chinese labourers in the Rand under near-slavery. He trained a group of influential young men – Milner's kindergarten – who accepted many of his preconceptions, notably his sense of imperial civilizing mission, his belief in the virtues of Empire unity and his conviction that colonies could best be prepared for self-government through education on the classical English model. Milner had a razor-sharp mind and, in his prime, showed administrative vigour. He was a member of LLOYD GEORGE'S inner War Cabinet in 1916–18 and undertook a hazardous journey to Russia in 1917 after the overthrow of the Tsar in the vain hope of persuading the Provisional Government to wage war relentlessly against Germany. Milner was War Secretary from April 1918 until January 1919 and thereafter Colonial Secretary until February 1922, helping to settle the form of constitutional monarchy in Egypt, from 1914 to 1922 a British protectorate. He remained highly critical of the peace settlement of 1919–20, mistrusting the emergence of so many small nations in Europe. T. O'Brien: *Milner* (1979); J. Marlowe: *Milner, Apostle of Empire* (1976); V. S. Halperin: *Lord Milner and the Empire* (1952).

Milosević, Slobodan (1941–), Serbian political leader: born in Pozarevač, a town in north eastern Serbia rich in traditions of insurrection against Turkish rule. He studied politics at Belgrade University and had risen to a high position in Belgrade's municipal government by the age of 25. At a meeting of the Serbian Communists' central committee in September 1987 he accused the leadership of allowing Serb minorities in the two autonomous provinces created by TITO – the Vojvodina and Kosovo-Metohija – to be exploited by the majority peoples of the region, Hungarians and Albanians respectively. This appeal to historic national sentiment, especially the anti-Albanian campaign, raised Milosević's standing in Serbia: in May 1989 he became Serbia's President – within federal Yugoslavia – and on 28 June 1989 presided over ceremonies marking the six-hundredth anniversary of the battle of Kosovo, a fateful day perpetuated in patriotic legends by Serbia's epic chroniclers. He imposed constitutional changes, which abolished the autonomous rights of both the Vojvodina and Kosovo in September 1990. By stimulating a 'Greater Serbia' patriotism he revived latent conflicts with Croatia (led by Frano TUDJMAN) and precipitated the disintegration of federal Yugoslavia in 1991. The assertion of independence by the racially mixed republic of Bosnia-Herzegovina (see IZETBEGOVIĆ and KARADZIĆ) led Milosević to support Serbian military intervention (March to May 1992); he was later accused of encouraging 'ethnic cleansing', both in eastern Slavonia and around Kosovo. He was re-elected Serbian President in December 1992, but showed increasing caution over further intervention in Bosnia in the face of growing NATO commitment. By the autumn of 1995 some Serbian officers (true to the Black Hand traditions of Apis DIMITRIEVIĆ) had become impatient with Milosevic. But he took part in the peace talks at Dayton, Ohio in November 1995; having dropped his support of Karadzić, he secured the listing of sanctions against Serbia when, a month later, he signed the Treaty of Paris, accepting a compromise settlement of the Bosnian Serb problem. M. Glenny: *The Fall of Yugoslavia* (1992); M. Robinson: *Managing Milosević's Serbia* (1995).

Mindszenty, Jozsef (Josef Pehm) (1892–1975), Hungarian Cardinal: born at Mindszent, a village some twenty miles north west of Budapest. He was ordained priest in 1915 and became a Monsignore in 1937, soon afterwards changing his surname from Pehm to the name of his native village as a gesture of anti-German Magyar pride. He was created Bishop of Veszprem in 1944 and arrested by the Germans the following winter. In October 1945 he became Primate of Hungary. He was an uncooperative with the Communist authorities as he had been with the Nazis. In 1947 he was created a Cardinal. That year he visited America, meeting the head of the Habsburg dynasty, Archduke Otto, in Chicago. On 28 December 1948 he was charged with treason and currency offences. A show trial in Budapest in February 1949 gave him the opportunity of voicing his hostility to communism forthrightly and with great courage. He was sentenced to penal servitude, which was commuted to house detention in July 1955. In October 1956 insurgent militiamen freed him during the anti-Soviet Hungarian National Rising and he broadcast to the Hungarian people from Budapest. When Soviet troops re-entered Budapest, Cardinal Mindszenty took refuge in the American Legation. He declined to leave for Rome and he refused to recognize the validity of a concordat concluded between the Vatican and the Hungarian Government of Janoš KADAR in 1964. Eventually, under strong pressure from other cardinals whom he respected, he agreed to leave the Legation for Vienna, and ultimately for Rome, in September 1971. Thereafter he travelled occasionally in the West, visiting London in 1973 and never comprömising his belief in the evil of secular Marxism. He died in Rome on 6 May 1975, but, after the downfall of communism, was in June 1991 given an impressive burial at Estzergom, the spiritual centre of Hungarian Catholicism. J. Mindszenty: *Memoirs* (1974).

Mitterrand, François Maurice Marie (1916–96), longest serving French President: born, a station-master's son, at Jarnac in the Charente departement of south western France, educated at a Catholic school in Angoulême and studied law at the University of Paris, practising as an advocate while also being a journalist. He was taken prisoner when wounded while serving with the army in 1940 but escaped from a German prisoner-of-war camp and led Resistance units before being smuggled into England in 1943 to join DE GAULLE in London and Algiers. Mitterrand's courageous war service won him the Croix de Guerre as well as the Légion d'honneur. He was a Centre-Socialist Deputy for a constituency near Dijon from 1946 to 1958 and from 1962 to 1981 and a Senator between 1959 and 1962, moving steadily towards a more radical socialism. He held ministerial office in eleven governments, most notably as Minister of the Interior under MENDÈS-FRANCE. In 1965 he was de Gaulle's principal opponent in the presidential election and, although suffering political setbacks in 1968, emerged in 1971 as first secretary of the new Socialist Party, which he used as a springboard for an anti-Gaullist 'Federation of the Left'. He was narrowly defeated by GISCARD D'ESTAING in the 1974 election but, having acquired European prestige as Vice-President of the Socialist International, he received such strong backing that in 1981 he reversed the electoral decision. He took office as fourth President of the Fifth Republic in May 1981. Programmes of nationalization and decentralized political control were checked by decisions of the constitutional council. Austerity budgets, prepared for Mitterrand by Jacques DELORS, checked inflation but caused such unpopularity that the Right triumphed in the Assembly elections of 1986; for two years Mitterrand had to accept 'political cohabitation' with the neo-Gaullist Prime Minister, CHIRAC. Mitterrand's political dexterity enabled him to defeat Chirac in the presidential election of 1988 and to secure the return of a left of centre government. In March 1993, however, the electoral victory of a right-wing alliance left Mitterrand unable to prevent measures of privatization which ran contrary to socialist principles. His health began to fail in 1993; after Chirac's presidential victory of May 1995, Mitterrand retired from public life. F. Mitterrand: *The Wheat and the Chaff: Personal Diaries, 1971–81* (1982); J. Ardagh: *The New France* (1984).

Mobutu, Sese Seko (1930–), Zaïrian President: born at Lisala and educated by Catholic missionaries who baptized him 'Joseph Desiré'. He was a Sergeant in the Belgian colonial regiment, advancing rapidly to the rank of Colonel when the Congo received independence. Mobutu ruthlessly suppressed mutinies in the newly independent state in 1960 and was largely responsible for the downfall of LUMUMBA. The backing of Belgian industrialist and of the Americans enabled General Mobutu to consolidate his position and, at the end of November 1965, he seized power and established his own brand of presidential rule, harsh and repressive but far more orderly and efficient than the Congo had known since before the departure of the Belgian colonial service. The use of African names for persons and places gave token backing to pan-African sentiment, the state being changed from the 'Democratic Republic of the Congo' to 'Zaïre' in October 1971. President Mobutu, unlike most other African leaders, had no liking for socialism and concluded profitable business agreements for the development of Zaïre's mineral resources and for harnessing the great river as a source of electrical power. He could not, however, keep a tight hold on the outlying provinces of his republic and his position was seriously endangered by two outbursts of anarchy (March 1977 and May 1978) in Shaba, the province known until 1971 as Katanga. Mounting tensions in central Zaïre forced Mobutu to promise political reforms in 1990; a constituent assembly was summoned in April 1991; three years later Mobutu promised democratic elections within fifteen months.

Moi, Daniel Arap (1924–), Kenyan President born into a family of Kalenjin ethnic origin, in a village in the Rift

Valley. He was educated at a mission school in Kabartonjo and a colonial government secondary school at Kapsabet. For eleven years he was a teacher, becoming in 1961 the first African to be appointed Minister of Education in late colonial Kenya. Moi entered politics as a supporter of more federalism than KENYATTA favoured, but he joined Kenyatta's National Union movement after independence and was successively Home Affairs Minister, 1964–67, and Vice-President until, on Kenyatta's death, he succeeded to the presidency (14 October 1978). Moi encouraged foreign investment in wide-ranging development programmes but their effectiveness was hampered by a drop in world prices for coffee and tea. He met mounting opposition from army officers, who resented secret police investigation. After thwarting a *coup* by air force officers on 1 August 1982 President Moi pursued increasingly dictatorial policies, banning all parties except KANU until December 1991 and strengthening the executive power of the presidency by imposing constitutional changes in January 1988. Criticism by church leaders and by British, American and Commonwealth critics of the narrow power base of his dictatorship led the President, in 1992, to grant political concessions. He was reelected for a fourth five-year term on 29 December 1992. But in 1995 further condemnation of the administration's repeated infringement of basic human rights led to strained relations between Nairobi and London and to increased pressure by foreign banks on Kenya's capital funds. D. G. Maillu: *Pragmatic Leadership* (Nairobi, 1988).

Molotov, Vyacheslav Mikailovich (1890–1980), Soviet statesman: born at Kukaida in the province of Vyatka. He participated as a Bolshevik in the risings of 1905, and from 1912 was engaged in revolutionary journalism. At the time he abandoned his surname Skriabin, preferring to write as 'the hammer' ('Molotov'). He played a prominent role in the revolution in Petrograd in 1917 and was admitted to the inner councils of the party, the 'Politburo', in 1921, at once throwing his support behind STALIN in all party wrangles. After helping promote the First Five Year Plan (1928) he became Chairman of the Council of Ministers (i.e. Prime Minister) in 1930. Under Stalin this post held little authority and Molotov did not achieve international stature until he succeeded LITVINOV as Foreign Minister on 4 May 1939, an office he held for ten years. He collaborated with RIBBENTROP in concluding the Nazi–Soviet Pact of Non-Aggression (23 August 1939), although he soon showed suspicion of German intentions. During the 'Great Patriotic War' of 1941–5, he cautiously worked with Soviet Russia's British and American allies. Subsequently he shaped Stalin's general world policy, expecting close collaboration with the eastern European republics, rejecting the aid programme proposed by General MARSHALL, hardening the discipline of the Communist Parties towards the independence shown by TITO, and declining any lasting settlement of German or Austrian affairs. For four years (from March 1949 until Stalin's death) he remained Deputy Prime Minister; but he served as Foreign Minister again from March 1953 until June 1956. During this period he accepted the need to negotiate a peace treaty over the status of Austria (May 1955), but strongly opposed the attempted reconciliation between Russia and Yugoslavia which KHRUSCHEV favoured. He was removed from the Foreign Ministry in June 1956 and, after an inglorious year as Minister of State Control, was expelled from the party and sent to Ulan Bator as ambassador to Mongolia (1957–60). Briefly, in 1960–1, he returned to world affairs as Soviet representative in the International Atomic Energy Agency at Vienna, living on for twenty-five years in retirement near Moscow. He was reinstated in the party three years before his death. B. Bromage: *Molotov, the Story of an Era* (1956).

Moltke, Helmuth von (1800–1891), Chief of General Staff in Berlin from 1857 to 1888: born at Parchim, spending his boyhood there during the Napoleonic Wars. He was commissioned in the Danish army in 1819 but transferred to Prussian service three years later, serving on the General Staff from 1832 to 1835, when he was granted leave to go to Constantinople and reorganize the Turkish army; the Turkish commanders ignored his advice and Moltke witnessed their defeat by the Egyptians at Nezib in June 1839. On returning to Berlin he married an Englishwoman, Mary Burt (1824–68). In 1857 Moltke became Chief of the Prussian General Staff, a post then regarded as largely administrative in character and of less importance than the responsibilities of the Minister of War (who from 1859 to 1873 was General von Roon, 1803–79). Moltke's organizational gifts, his logistical skill and phenomenal memory enabled him to build up the General Staff as the key to Prussia's success in the so-called 'Bismarck wars' – against Denmark in 1864, against Austria and her allies in 1866, and against France in 1870–1. He was created Field Marshal in 1871, spending the remaining seventeen years of his military career expanding the Great German General Staff. He died on 26 October 1891, nineteen months after the fall of BISMARCK. G. A. Craig: *The Politics of the Prussian Army, 1640–1945* (Oxford, 1955); G. Ritter: *The Sword and the Sceptre* Vol. 1 (1972).

Moltke, Helmuth Johannes Ludwig von (1848–1916), Chief of the German General Staff from 1905 to 1914: born at Gersdorff and was commissioned in the Prussian Army soon after his famous uncle, the elder MOLTKE, became Chief of General Staff. 'Moltke the Younger', though painfully conscious of his inadequacies, was induced by Kaiser WILLIAM II to become Chief of the Great German General Staff himself in succession to SCHLIEFFEN in December 1905. Although Moltke was told by his physicians that he was suffering from a disease of the heart in 1913, he remained at his post when war came a year later. He was a cultured, sensitive soldier who, in his spare time, liked to play the cello, read Goethe and Maeterlinck, and was interested in the faith-healing teachings of the Christian Scientists. The early crises of the war found him hesitant and indecisive, and he was sent on sick leave on 14 September 1914 after the failure of his troops in the first battle of the Marne. In effect the duties of Chief of General Staff were then undertaken by General von Falkenhayn (although his status was not confirmed until January 1915). Colonel-General von Moltke took part in the siege of Antwerp in October 1914 and was appointed Governor-General of Poland in August 1915. He collapsed and died in the Reichstag on 16 June 1916. A great-nephew, Count Helmuth von Moltke-Kreisau (1907–45), was a member of the anti-Hitler resistance from 1937 until his arrest in January 1944 which was followed by his execution on 23 January 1945. C. Barnett: *The Swordbearers* (1963); G. Ritter: *The Sword and the Sceptre* Vol. 2 (1972), *The Schlieffen Plan* (1958).

Mondale, Walter Frederick (1928–), US Vice-President: born at Ceylon in Minnesota, the son of a Methodist minister of Norwegian descent. He was an outstandingly gifted student at the state university and at the Minnesota Law School. After practising law in Minneapolis he became Attorney-General of Minnesota in 1960 and four years later was returned as a Democrat to the US Senate. He was chosen as running-mate with CARTER against FORD in 1976, partly because of his skills in controlling the party machine and partly to balance Carter's 'Southern' image. He served as Vice-President effectively from 1977 to 1981 but never captured the public's imagination. Rather suprisingly he was chosen as the Democratic candidate against REAGAN in the 1984 presidential election but lost disastrously and returned to private law practice. W. Mondale: *The Accountability of Power* (New York, 1982); F. Finlay: *Mondale, Portrait of an American Politician* (New York, 1984).

Monnet, Jean (1888–1979), French economist and champion of European economic collaboration: born at Cognac, becoming a civil servant attached to the Ministry of Commerce in Paris. He attended the Paris Peace Conference of 1919 as an adviser on economic questions, subsequently working for the League of Nations in Geneva. Consistently he favoured a joint approach to economic problems rather than the competition of protective tariffs. During the opening months of the Second World War he was chairman of a committee which sought closer economic union between Britain and France. For three years he assisted the British supply mission in Washington, subsequently going to Algiers as adviser to General DE GAULLE on post-war economic development. The 'Monnet Plan' of 1945–6 so benefited French reconstruction that by 1951 French industry had reached production targets higher than anything attained in pre-war years. Monnet was a special adviser to the liberal Catholic statesman, Robert SCHUMAN, and worked out the details of the 'Schuman Plan' of May 1950, which proposed the establishment of a supranational institution for Europe's production and distribution of coal and steel. When the European Coal and Steel Community began to function in 1952 Monnet served as its first Chairman, holding office for three years. He strongly disapproved of the narrowly nationalistic aspects of President de Gaulle's policy from 1961 to 1968. J. Monnet: *Memoirs* (1978); F. Duchene: *Jean Monnet; the First Statesman of Interdependence* (1994).

Montgomery, Bernard Law (1887–1976), British Field Marshal distinguished for his campaigns in North Africa and from Normandy to the Baltic between 1942 and 1945: born in London, spent much of his boyhood in Tasmania (where his father was a bishop) and was educated at St Paul's School, passing out of the Royal Military College, Sandhurst, in 1908. He served with the Royal Warwickshire Regiment in India, was wounded on the Western Front in October 1914, fought on the Somme in 1916 and later served with the occupation forces in the Rhineland and in Ireland. After a spell at the War Office, he commanded his old regiment in Palestine in the early 1930s, served once more in India, and was Major-General in command of the Third Division in the British Expeditionary Force of 1939–40, advancing into Belgium on 10 May 1940 and temporarily halting the Germans at Louvain before being forced to retreat to Dunkirk. After two years in field commands in south east England, he was appointed to the Eighth Army in Egypt in August 1942 under the overall command of ALEXANDER. Between 23 October 1942 and 23 January 1943 he led the Eighth Army from Alamein against the Afrika Korps of ROMMEL to Tripoli. He remained in the Mediterranean theatre for the capture of Tunis, the invasion of Sicily, and the advance up the Italian peninsula to the River Sangro. In Sicily and Italy Montgomery found difficulty in accommodating his ideas to American strategy and there was a major clash of personalities between the egocentric British General and the no less aggressive American, General PATTON. Subsequently Montgomery, under EISENHOWER, commanded the land forces in the invasion of France, having spent weeks boosting the morale of his forces, an aspect of generalship at which 'Monty' was superb. Although his troops became bogged down in combat with a crack Panzer Division around Caen, his basic strategy of a breakout into France by the American Twelfth Army Group was successful, Paris being liberated within twelve weeks of the Normandy landings. Montgomery's proposal of a 'pencil thrust' advance on Berlin was turned down by Eisenhower, who favoured a broad front approach. To some extent Montgomery was compensated for this personal rebuff by promotion to the rank of Field Marshal (1 September 1944), but relations remained strained between Montgomery's Twenty-first Army Group in Belgium and the Twelfth Army Group of the American, General BRADLEY, to its right. Units from Montgomery's command assisted the Americans' check of the German counter-offensive in the Ardennes in December and January. German land forces in north western Europe surrendered to Montgomery on 4 May on Lüneburg Heath. He was created a Knight of the Garter and a Viscount in 1946. From 1946 to 1948 he was Chief of the Imperial General Staff, and Deputy Commander of NATO forces in Europe from 1951 to 1958, when he finally retired from the army. He died at his home in Hampshire on 24 March 1976. F. M. Lord Montgomery: *Memoirs* (1958), *El Alamein to the River Sangro* (1948), *Normandy to the Baltic* (1947); N. Hamilton: *Monty* (1994).

Morgenthau, Henry (1891–1967), US Secretary of the Treasury from 1934 to 1945: born in New York State, a member of a much-respected Jewish family, his father and namesake (1856–1946) being a diplomat and banker, who helped finance Franklin ROOSEVELT's first presidential election campaign. Henry Morgenthau Jnr. had long been a friend of Franklin Roosevelt when, in 1933, the new President invited him to direct the Farm Credit Administration as part of the New Deal. A year later Morgenthau, a conscientious, cautious and conservative financier, was appointed Secretary of the Treasury, a post in which he desperately tried to balance the budget despite the unprecedented federal expenditure on social reform programmes. Morgenthau subsequently had to raise even higher levels of revenue in order to meet the demands of the war. In 1940–1 he supervised the sale of 'Defense Savings Bonds', subsequently known as 'War Savings Bonds', a method which provided more than $200 million for the war effort. He is best remembered for the 'Morgenthau Plan', presented to Roosevelt and Winston CHURCHILL at the Quebec Conference of September 1944, which proposed the conversion of Germany from an industrial to a pastoral nation by the removal of all surviving factories and the closing of all mines by the victorious Allies after the war. This plan, at first accepted by the Allied leaders, was much criticized by other members of the British and American governments and soon abandoned as impracticable and inequitable. News of the plan was exploited by the propaganda of GOEBBELS to strengthen Germany's will to resist the invader. Morgenthau's style never warmed the hearts of reporters; Roosevelt himself nicknamed him 'Henry the Morgue'. He was eager to resign even before Roosevelt's death, and never served under TRUMAN. H. Morgenthau III: *Mostly Morgenthaus* (New York, 1991).

Moro, Aldo (1916–78), Italian Prime Minister from 1963 to 1968 and 1974 to 1976: born at Maglie, studied law at the University of Bari and became a Christian Democrat in the Italian parliament (1948), retaining his seat for the remaining thirty years of his life. He was Foreign Minister on several occasions between 1965 and 1974 and showed a firm belief in Italy's need of the Common Market. This support for the European Community also marked his two premierships. There was a possibility of his returning as Prime Minister in 1978, but on 17 March of that year his car was ambushed in Rome and he was kidnapped by anarchists of the so-called 'Red Brigade'. The government refused the kidnapers' demand that terrorists already in custody should be set free; and on 9 May 1978 Moro's body was found in an abandoned car near the Christian Democrats' headquarters in Rome. Moderates throughout Italy were deeply shocked by the crime, and by the failure of the police to find Moro after he had been kidnapped. N. Kogan: *Political History of Italy; the Post-War Years* (New York, 1983); D. Moss: *The Politics of Left-Wing Violence in Italy, 1969–85* (1989).

Morris, William (1834–96), English socialist, poet and aesthetic craftsman: born in Walthamstow, educated at Marlborough and Exeter College, Oxford; became well-known for applying Pre-Raphaelite aesthetic standards to furniture, house decoration and wallpaper design, later pioneering clear typefaces and ornamentation in printing and publishing. Both of his principal homes – the Red House, Bexley, in Kent and Kelmscott Manor in Oxfordshire – challenged the established Victorian values which he despised. He was a poet and translator, equally inspired by Homer, Virgil, Chaucer and Icelandic epics. But he was also an idealistic socialist who believed a labourer's 'true incentive . . . must be pleasure in the work itself'. He joined the Social Democratic Federation in 1883 but his literary romanticism found the diluted Marxism of HYNDMAN 'dreary', and in 1884 he seceded and founded the Socialist League, for whom he promoted a periodical, *Commonweal*, and wrote two Utopian fantasies, *A Dream of John Bull* (1888) and *News from Nowhere* (1891). Anarchists took control of the League in 1890 and for the last six years of his life Morris propounded to the Hammersmith Socialist Society his dreams of a harmonious community for whom the state had happily withered away. Morris's unique left-wing individualism only began to be appreciated in the 1960s, largely through a massive study of his contribution to socialism by the historian, E. P. Thompson (1924–93). J. W. Mackail: *Life of William Morris* (2 vols) (1899); E. P. Thompson: *William Morris: Romantic to Revolutionary* (2nd edn 1977); J. Bruce Glasier: *William Morris and the Early Days of the Socialist Movement* (1921).

Morrison, Herbert Stanley (1888–1965), British Labour politician: born in Lambeth, the son of a policeman, passing from elementary schools to unskilled labour in south and east London, His abilities were harnessed by the embryonic Labour Party machine when he was in his early twenties, and he became General Secretary of the London Labour Party in 1915, at a time when he accepted pacifist principles. Like ATTLEE and LANSBURY, he was Mayor of an east London borough (Hackney, 1920–1) and he continued in local government rather than in national politics, although he was briefly MP for South Hackney in 1923. For eighteen years (1922–40) he was a member of the London County Council and its leader from 1934 to 1940. He was largely responsible for the creation of the London Passenger Transport Board in 1933 (he had served as Minister of Transport for six months in 1931 under MACDONALD) and for checking urban development through the creation of an outer 'green belt'. The electors of South Hackney returned him again to Westminster from 1929 to 1931 and from 1935 to 1945. He contested the election for leadership of the parliamentary Labour Party in 1935, but lost to Attlee. From May to October 1940 he was Minister of

Supply in CHURCHILL's coalition, using his dynamism to stimulate production, with the injunction 'Work at War Speed: Go to it!'. From October 1940 to May 1945 he was Home Secretary, with a seat in the War Cabinet from October 1942. Morrison established the National Fire Service and administered all matters of civil defence and internment as well as the general policy over censorship. He drafted the manifesto which Labour adopted for its victorious election campaign in 1945 and had hopes of ousting Attlee from the party leadership at that time. As Lord President of the Council from 1945 to 1951 he was, in effect, Deputy Prime Minister and a policy overlord for the new measures of nationalization and social insurance. From March to October 1951 he was Foreign Secretary, a term of office marred by hesitancy in dealing with MUSADDIQ and by uneasiness within the foreign service itself. Morrison stood once more for the party leadership in 1955 but was defeated by GAITSKELL. He remained in the Commons until 1959 as MP for East Lewisham, the constituency to which he moved from South Hackney in 1945. He was created a life peer, Baron Morrison of Lewisham, in 1959. H. Morrison: *An Autobiography* (1960); B. Donoughue and G. W. Jones: *Herbert Morrison* (1973).

Mosley, Oswald Ernald (1896–1980), British fascist leader from 1932 to 1939: educated at Winchester and Sandhurst, serving with the Sixteenth Lancers in the Ypres salient 1914–15 and later with the Royal Flying Corps. He was MP for Harrow from 1918 to 1924, originally as a Conservative but sitting as an Independent from 1922. In 1924 he joined the Labour Party and, as a socialist, was MP for Smethwick from 1926 to 1931. In 1928 he succeeded his father as a Baronet. Sir Oswald became Chancellor of the Duchy of Lancaster in MACDONALD's second Labour Government (1929). He put forward proposals for boosting the economy by direction of industry and the provision of public funds for expansion. When these proposals were rejected, Mosley resigned (21 May 1930). In February 1931 he founded an independent organization which he called, simply, the New Party. But in the 1931 General Election all thirty-one New Party candidates were defeated and in April 1932 Mosley dissolved his organization. Three months previously he had visited Rome, where he was fêted and much impressed by the apparent achievements of MUSSOLINI's fascism. He established the British Union of Fascists in October 1932, but he was soon following the example set by HITLER rather than by Mussolini. Provocative anti-Semitic marches in London's East End led to violence in the streets, and to the Public Order Act (1936) which banned paramilitary political bodies. From 1940 to 1943 Sir Oswald was interned under the wartime Defence Regulations. In 1947 he founded yet another political organization, the 'Union Movement'. He unsuccessfully contested London constituencies in 1959 and 1966. In 1958 he published *Europe: Faith and Plan*, advocating British economic leadership of a European community, for he never shared the insular 'Little Englander' views of most right-wing extremist factions. O. Mosley: *My Life* (1968); N. Mosley: *Rules of the Game; Sir Oswald and Lady Cynthia Mosley, 1896–1933* (1982), *Beyond the Pale; Sir Oswald Mosley, 1933–1980* (1983); R. Skidelsky: *Oswald Mosley* (2nd edn 1980).

Mountbatten, Lord Albert Victor Nicholas Louis Francis (1900–79). British Admiral, Supreme Allied Commander in south east Asia from 1943 to 1945, and last Viceroy of India: born in London, a great-grandson (and last godson) of

Queen VICTORIA, and a nephew of the last Tsarina. His father, Admiral Prince Louis of Battenberg (1854–1921), was First Sea Lord in 1914 and was responsible for ensuring that the British fleet reached its war stations before the start of hostilities. Subsequently Prince Louis became Marquess of Milford Haven and the family name was anglicized from Battenberg to Mountbatten in 1917. Lord Louis Mountbatten served with the battle-cruisers in the North Sea through much of the First World War. From 1939 to 1941 he commanded the fifth destroyer flotilla, his ship HMS *Kelly* being badly damaged off Norway and sunk off Crete by dive-bombers. Subsequently he became Chief of Combined Operations, planning raids on Bruneval in Normandy, on St Nazaire and on Dieppe. In October 1943 he went to Delhi as Supreme Allied Commander in south east Asia, a post full of difficult political problems as well as calling for new ideas in seeking to eject the Japanese from Burma. Fortunately he was able to rely on the brilliance in improvisation and training of General SLIM. Together they transformed the morale of the 'forgotten army' in Burma, enabling it to inflict a severe defeat on the Japanese at Imphal (March to June 1944). Seven months later Mountbatten took the vital decision to fight through the five months of monsoon, so as to recover the Irrawaddy basin and enter Rangoon on 4 May 1945. The Japanese forces in south east Asia surrendered to Mountbatten in Singapore in a formal ceremony held on the following 12 September. Seventeen months later (20 February 1947) he became Viceroy of India, accepting an earldom and taking the title Earl Mountbatten of Burma. He speeded up the transition from empire to independence and agreed to stay as the first Governor-General of India from August 1947 to June 1948. He then resumed his naval career, reverting to the rank of Rear-Admiral in command of a cruiser squadron in the Mediterranean, where he later held the highest commands.

Mountbatten was First Sea Lord from 1955 to 1959 and as Chief of the Defence Staff from 1959 to 1965 had the task of welding together the three services by sweeping reforms, an undertaking for which he was especially qualified. In 1922 he had married the Honourable Edwina Ashley (1901–60), a daughter of Lord Mount Temple. She continued her devoted work for the Red Cross and for improved social conditions, especially in India, until her sudden death while travelling on behalf of welfare organizations in south east Asia in February 1960. Earl Mountbatten's contacts with the royal family were strengthened by the marriage of his nephew, Prince Philip, to the future Queen, ELIZABETH, in November 1947. The Earl became a personal aide-de-camp to the Queen, and Governor of the Isle of Wight. On 27 August 1979 he was assassinated while taking a holiday in County Sligo, Irish terrorists having placed a bomb aboard a small boat in which he and his family were going on a fishing expedition. His elder daughter was seriously injured, and her mother-in-law was killed, as also were one of her sons and his schoolboy friend. P. Ziegler: *Mountbatten, the Official Biography* (1985); R. Hough: *Mountbatten, Hero of Our Time* (1980).

Mubarak, Mohammad Hosni (1928–), Egyptian President: born on the outskirts of Cairo, marrying an Egyptian whose mother was Welsh. Mubarak graduated from the military academy in 1950, was commissioned in the air force and received specialist training in flying duties on two prolonged visits to the USSR (1959, 1962). He then led the Egyptian fighter-bomber squadrons in the Yemen for five years, showing such undemonstrative efficiency that he rose to command the Egyptian air force from 1973 until April 1975, when SADAT secured his nomination as Vice-President. He was entrusted with shaping and controlling the official National Democratic Party when it was established in 1978. On Sadat's assassination Mubarak was the sole nominee for the presidency and duly took office on 13 October 1981. He discreetly purged the army of veteran Nasserite officers and continued Sadat's 'peace process' with Israel while slowly improving relations with his Arab neighbours. In home affairs Mubarak allowed greater political freedom than his predecessors; the 1984 and 1987 elections were contested by genuine Opposition parties. By the end of the decade an upsurge of Islamic fundamentalism made Mubarak's position look less secure and the principal Opposition groups boycotted the 1990 elections. Increased terrorism by the Egyptian Islamic Jihad movement rallied support to the President, however; in October 1993 he was again elected, unopposed, for a third six-year term of office. C. Tripp and R. Owen (eds): *Egypt under Mubarak* (1989); A. McDermot: *Egypt from Nasser to Mubarak* (1988).

Mugabe, Robert Gebriel (1924–), Zimbabwean national leader: born at Kutame, his mission school education being completed by economics degrees from Fort Hare and London universities. He taught in Rhodesia, South Africa, Zambia and Ghana 1942–58, and became Deputy Secretary-General to NKOMO on the foundation of the Zimbabwe African People's Union (ZAPU) in 1961. Mugabe was arrested by the Rhodesian white government, but escaped to Tanzania where in August 1963 he set up the Zimbabwe African National Union (ZANU), politically further to the Left than ZAPU. When Mugabe slipped back into Rhodesia he was again detained, remaining in captivity for ten years. He eventually found refuge in Mozambique, from where he directed guerrilla operations against the Rhodesian regime, 1975–9, sharing joint leadership of a Patriotic Front with Nkomo from October 1976 onwards. He was in London for the Lancaster House Conference on Rhodesia-Zimbabwe's independence in late 1979, and returned to his homeland to lead ZANU to an electoral victory which enabled him to become Zimbabwe's first Prime Minister on 4 March 1980. Cautious policies postponed direct confrontation both between ZANU and ZAPU followers and between black and white political spokesmen. But Mugabe continued to build up his power. When constitutional changes transformed the presidency into an executive post, Mugabe was duly elected; he became Zimbabwe's President on 30 December 1987. Further political moves heightened his authority in what became virtually a one-party state. But by 1992 earlier plans for socialist co-operatives seemed shelved in favour of a free market economy. D. Smith: *Mugabe* (Harare, 1981); D. Caute: *Under the Skin, the Death of White Rhodesia* (1983); P. H. Baker: *The Birth of Zimbabwe* (Washington, D.C., 1981).

Muhammad Ahmed ibn Abdallah (1848–85), 'the Mahdi': born at Dongola; served in the Egyptian civil service; became a slave-trader in the Sudan, deeply resentful of reformers in Cairo who sought to curb his commercial activities. He was also a religious fanatic, an ascetic whose intensity of passion convinced the nomadic peoples of the upper Nile that he was a Muslim Messiah, the Mahdi. Under his inspiration the Sudanese peoples rose against Egyptian rule in Kordofan province in 1881. The revolt spread rapidly after British-led troops were defeated when they attacked the Mahdi's main base, El Obeid, on 5 November 1883. The following October the Mahdists besieged Khartoum which they captured on 26 January 1885, killing

General GORDON. Five months later the Mahdi died, leaving his conquests to be organized by one of his chief lieutenants, the Khalifa Abdallah al-Taishi, whose rule in the Sudan was destroyed in 1898 after the victory of KITCHENER at Omdurman. P. M. Holt: *The Mahdist State in the Sudan* (Oxford, 1970); A. B. Theobald: *The Mahdiya* (1951).

Musaddiq, Muhammad (1881–1967), Iranian Prime Minister from 1951 to 1953: born in Teheran and held several governmental posts under the last of the Kajar dynasty Shahs of Persia (as the country was then called), including the office of Foreign Minister from 1922 to 1924. He played little part in political life under Riza Khan, Shah from 1925 to 1941, but he entered the Majlis (the Iranian Parliament) in 1942 and soon attracted a widespread nationalistic following. Musaddiq, a personally ascetic man, was a rich landowner, inclined to bursts of hysterical demagogy. Violent speeches called for the nationalization of the Iranian Oil Company on the grounds that, if foreign control were removed from the oil wells, money would become so abundant for the Iranians that all poverty would be banished from the kingdom. The Majlis nationalized the oil industry in late March 1951. Rioting in Abadan induced Shah Riza PAHLAVI to appoint Musaddiq as Prime Minister on 27 April 1951. Musaddiq sought to follow the nationalization of the industry by a social revolution, promising to break up the large estates. At first he enjoyed great popularity, not least because he appeared to have triumphed over the British. Production of oil fell, and the expected revenue was not forthcoming. In August 1952 he sought, and obtained, dictatorial powers from the Majlis which were supposed to enable him to carry through his social revolution, including redistribution of land held in great estates. Reality fell so short of promise that, on 13 August 1953, the Shah dismissed Musaddiq and appointed General Zahedi as Prime Minister. Musaddiq refused to accept dismissal and there were five days of major disturbances in Teheran before he could be arrested and the Shah's authority restored. Musaddiq was put on trial, charged with unconstitutional malpractice, and, after tearful and hysterical scenes, sentenced to three years' solitary confinement. He spent the last eleven years of his life on his estates. H. Katouzian (ed.): *Musaddiq's Memoirs* (1988); S. Zabih: *The Mussadigh Era* (Chicago, 1982); J. A. Bill and W. R. Louis (eds): *Musaddiq, Iranian Nationalism and Oil* (1988).

Mussolini, Benito (1883–1945), Italian Prime Minister from 1922 to 1943: born at Dovia di Predappio, near Forli, in the Romagna, his mother being a schoolteacher and his father a blacksmith. He settled in Switzerland in 1902, primarily to avoid military service, and while in Lausanne and Geneva became an active Socialist, not returning to Italy until the end of the year 1904. Until 1915 he remained within the Socialist Party, showing gifts as a journalist. His antimilitarism subsided in 1914 and he supported the agitation of Gabriele D'ANNUNZIO for Italy's entry into the war against Austria-Hungary. He fought on the Isonzo as a corporal in the Bersaglieri and was wounded when a mortar exploded near him in February 1917. He returned to Milan, edited the right-wing radical paper *Il Popolo d'Italia*, and in March 1919 set up a private anti-Socialist militia, the *Fascio di Combattimento*, first of the Fascist groups.

Mussolini was an impressive demagogue as well as a journalist: he demanded satisfaction of Italy's legitimate claims as a victor in the war, and firm government which would improve living standards without importing an alien Marxism. There was serious rioting between Fascist and Socialist groups in many Italian cities in 1921, notably in Milan, Florence and Bologna. Mussolini was by now accepted as 'Leader' ('*Duce*') of the Fascist groups and had developed a ready verbal contempt for the Parliament in Rome, promising to bury 'the putrefying corpse of democracy'. Fear of a Communist revolution led King VICTOR EMMANUEL III to appoint Mussolini Prime Minister on 29 October 1922. His first Cabinet, a combination of Fascists and nationalists, tolerated opposition until after the murder of MATTEOTI in 1924; and the one-party single constituency Fascist State was not set up until 1928. Among Mussolini's achievements were an impressive public works programme, the conclusion of a concordat between the kingdom of Italy and Pope PIUS XI in 1929, ending nearly sixty years of friction in Church–State relations, and economic successes in Italy's African colonies and her commercial dependencies (such as the Albania of ZOG).

Mussolini's foreign policy was aggressive and he aroused widespread hostility in the West by his invasion of Abyssinia in 1935. From 1936 onwards he collaborated closely with HITLER in what Mussolini himself described as the 'Berlin–Rome axis' (1 November 1936). He annexed Albania (April 1939), declared war on France and Britain (10 June 1940), and at the end of October 1940 launched an attack upon Greece, without prior agreement with Hitler. Defeat at the hand of the Greeks, together with the loss of most of Italy's colonies, made Mussolini dependent on German backing before the end of 1941. He was dismissed by Victor Emmanuel on 25 July 1943 and interned by his successor as Prime Minister, Marshal BADOGLIO, who sought peace with the Allies. German airborne troops under Otto Skorzeny (1908–75) rescued Mussolini from his place of detention high in the Abruzzi mountains on 12 September 1943. Hitler then established a Fascist administration under Mussolini's direction in German-occupied northern and central Italy. Mussolini was left with little authority. He sought to escape into Switzerland as the war was ending but was captured (in German uniform) by Italian partisans, one of whom on his own initiative shot both Mussolini and his mistress, Clara Petacci, who had chosen to share his fate. Their bodies were then taken from the shore of Lake Como, where they had been executed, to the Piazzale Loreto in Milan for public vilification (28 April 1945). Mussolini's widow was able to live quietly in Italy until her death in October 1979. B. Mussolini: *My Autobiography* (1928); D. Mack Smith: *Mussolini* (1981); F. W. Deakin: *The Brutal Friendship* (1962); I. Kirkpatrick: *Mussolini: the Study of a Demagogue* (1964); C. Hibbert: *Benito Mussolini* (1962).

Mutsuhito (1852–1912), Emperor of Japan from 1867 until his death: born at Kyoto, succeeded his father, Komei Tenno, in February 1867 and at once asserted the dormant sovereign powers of the Emperor to cast off the restraints imposed by the Shoguns of the Tokugawa family. This 'Meiji Restoration' of 1868 marked the beginning of the modernization of Japan through imperial decrees. Mutsuhito lifted restrictions on foreign trade, moved his court from Kyoto to Yedo (which he renamed Tokyo, or 'Eastern Capital'), set up a centralized bureaucracy, encouraged industrialization, and modelled a modern army on the pattern of Germany and a modern navy on the pattern of Britain. A reactionary rising was suppressed in 1877, and in February 1889 the Emperor promulgated a constitution prepared by Hiroboumi ITO which established a bicameral parliament. The second half of the reign was marked by Japanese penetration of Manchuria and Korea, by military defeat of China in 1894–5, and by the naval triumphs of Admiral TOGO, notably his victory over the Russians at Tsushima in

May 1905. Emperor Mutsuhito died in July 1912 and was succeeded by his eldest son Yoshihito (1879–1926), who took little part in politics, allowing his son and eventual successor, HIROHITO, to assume the powers of a Regent in 1921. G. M. Beckmann: *The Making of the Meiji Constitution* (Lawrence, Kans., 1957); H. Borton: *Japan's Modern Century* (New York, 1955); W. G. Beasley: *The Modern History of Japan* (1963).

N

Nagy, Imre (1896–1958), independently minded Hungarian Communist: born in southern Hungary at Kaposvar, taken prisoner while serving on the Eastern Front in 1915, and lived in Hungary as a Communist agitator from 1921 to 1928 when he escaped to Vienna to avoid arrest. From 1930 to 1944 he was in the Soviet Union, specializing in agricultural studies. In 1945–6 he became Hungarian Minister of Agriculture, responsible for dividing up the great estates. A brief spell as Minister of the Interior brought him into conflict with RÁKOSI and he was out of office from the spring of 1946 to July 1953 when, with the backing of MALENKOV, he replaced Rákosi as Prime Minister. Nagy was opposed to a rigidly Soviet policy in Hungary. He relaxed agricultural collectivization while allowing a freer market for farm produce and the manufacture of more consumer goods. This tentative liberalization was abruptly cut short in February 1955 when Nagy was forced to resign the premiership eleven days after Malenkov, in Russia, was replaced by BULGANIN. Nagy was even formally expelled from the Hungarian Communist Party in November 1955. Within a few months tension began to relax in Hungary with news of the speech made by KHRUSCHEV to the Twentieth Party Congress, and demands were put forward in the Hungarian Press for the reinstatement of Nagy. Anti-Stalinist demonstrations in Budapest at the beginning of the fourth week in October 1956 led to the recall of Nagy, who formed a government (24 October 1956) which included three non-Communists. He announced the withdrawal of Hungary from the Warsaw Pact and his determination to secure for Hungary the permanent neutrality already enjoyed by neighbouring Austria and by Switzerland. This policy was too radical for Bulganin and Khruschev and for the Hungarian party leaders, notably KÁDÁR. Soviet military intervention overthrew Nagy's government on 4 November 1956. For eighteen days he found diplomatic sanctuary within the Yugoslav embassy, whence he emerged believing he had a safe conduct to leave Hungary. He was, however, seized by the police and held in custody. More than eighteen months later he was tried, in secret, and sentenced to death for treason. He was executed on 17 June 1958. In 1989 his remains were re-buried in Budapest, with the honours due to a national hero. I. Nagy: *Imre Nagy on Communism; in Defence of the New Course* (New York, 1957); T. Meray: *Thirteen Days that Shook the Kremlin; Imre Nagy and the Hungarian Revolution* (1959).

Najibullah, Sayid Mohammed Ahmadzai (1947–), Communist leader in Afghanistan: born in Kabul, the son of a government official; qualified as a doctor of medicine from Kabul University; joined the underground Afghan Communist Party (PDPA) in 1965 and was twice imprisoned for seditious activity. When Soviet forces moved into Afghanistan in December 1979 Najibullah was made head of KHAD (the secret police) and given senior status in the PDPA politburo. He was soon singled out by Soviet envoys as efficient and reliable and in

May 1986 became party leader, taking over the presidency of Afghanistan from the ineffectual Barak Kemal in October. He sought reconciliation with the Islamic Mujahidin guerrillas and in April 1988 concluded an agreement with the resistance for Soviet withdrawal and for a broader based government. Najibullah brought non-PDPA members into his administration but when the last Red Army units left, in February 1989, he became politically isolated. Early in April 1992 he resigned office and went into exile; before the end of the month the Mujahidin had entered Kabul and set up the 'Islamic State of Afghanistan' in place of his 'People's Democracy'. T. T. Hammond: *Red Star over Afghanistan* (1984); A. Saikal and W. Maley: *The Soviet Withdrawal From Afghanistan* (Cambridge, 1989).

Napoleon III (1808–73), Emperor of the French from 1852 to 1870: born in Paris, a nephew of Napoleon I. His father was Louis Bonaparte (1778–1846), King of Holland from 1806–10, and his mother was Hortense Beauharnais (1783–1837), Napoleon's stepdaughter. Louis Napoleon – as Napoleon III was known until December 1852 – spent most of his boyhood and youth in exile, living in Bavaria, Italy, Switzerland, London and, briefly, New York. Abortive attempts at Bonapartist *coups d'état* in France ended in fiasco in 1836 and 1840. Until his escape in 1846 Louis Napoleon was imprisoned in the castle at Ham, on the Somme. The fall of the Orleanist monarchy in 1848 allowed him to return to Paris and he was elected to the Constituent Assembly of the Second French Republic in June 1848. That autumn he campaigned for the presidency, the Napoleonic legend carrying him to an overwhelming victory. He was sworn as 'Prince-President' on 20 December 1848. His popularity stemmed from identification of his cause with security against the 'red socialist peril' and also with national prosperity and prestige. Support for PIUS IX against GARIBALDI reconciled the French Church to Bonapartism while the army officers welcomed increasingly authoritarian rule. On 2 December 1851, with the backing of the army, the Prince-President carried through a *coup d'état* which dissolved the Assembly and gave him dictatorial powers, confirmed by a referendum, although liberal intellectuals, such as Victor Hugo, long continued to attack him as the reactionary 'Man of December'. A year later (2 December 1852) he accepted the imperial crown and his regime was recognized as the 'Second Empire'. French primacy in Europe was confirmed in 1856 when the peace congress which followed the Crimean War gathered in Paris. Napoleon III collaborated with CAVOUR in 1859 to further the unification of Italy by war against Austria: Nice and Savoy were added to France in 1860 by plebiscite as compensation for the new Italian settlement. Napoleon's marriage in January 1853 to a Spanish countess, Eugénie de Montijo (1826–1920), strengthened the influence of Catholicism at his Court and a French garrison continued to protect the Pope's temporal sovereignty in Rome until the fall of the Second Empire. In 1861–2 Napoleon allowed speculators to interest him in creating a puppet Mexican Empire as a means of curbing the anti-clerical and xenophobic radicalism of JUAREZ at a time when the United States government was too concerned with the problem of secession to enforce the Monroe Doctrine so as to exclude the spread of European colonialism on the American continent. Napoleon offered the Mexican throne to Archduke MAXIMILIAN of Austria, whose cause was upheld until 1867 by a French army under Marshal BAZAINE. This enterprise drained France's resources at a time when BISMARCK's Prussia was in the ascendancy on the European mainland. Although French commerce flourished and Paris was re-built and re-planned in spacious elegance by Baron Haussmann (1809–91), corruption and persistent political restraint weakened the Second Empire, forcing Napoleon III to adopt a conciliatory attitude to liberal demands in 1869 in the hope of recovering his lost popularity, at least in the provinces. But the creation of a parliament and a responsible ministry loosened his hold on foreign policy and in July 1870 Napoleon III was stampeded into a war against Prussia during a crisis caused by his own inept diplomacy. France was unprepared for a modern continental war: Napoleon III was defeated and captured at Sedan (3 September 1870) and, after imprisonment in Germany, spent the years 1871 to 1873 in exile in England, living mainly at Chislehurst in Kent, where he died after a series of operations to free him from stones in the kidney. He was buried eventually in a mausoleum at Farnborough in Hampshire. Napoleon III's only child, the Prince Imperial (1856–79) was killed by Zulus while serving with the British army in Africa. J. Ridley: *Napoleon III and Eugenie* (1979); J. P. T. Bury: *Napoleon III and the Second Empire* (1964); T. A. B. Corley: *Democratic Despot, a Life of Napoleon III* (1961).

Nasser, Gamal Abdel (1918–70), President of Egypt from 1954 to 1970: born near Asyut on the Nile, spent his childhood in Alexandria, where his father was a postal official. He entered the Military Academy in Cairo in 1937, becoming an instructor there in 1942, encouraging an anti-British, republican and nationalist sentiment among the cadets. He fought against Israel as a Major in 1948, later founding the Free Officers Movement, which overthrew the monarchy and brought General Neguib (1901–) to power in July 1952. When the Egyptian Republic was proclaimed in June 1953, Nasser was Neguib's deputy in the presidency as well as being Minister of the Interior. His self-confidence shaped the Egyptian national revolution, achieving major social changes by breaking up the great estates, encouraging industrialization, and making Egypt the dynamo of the pan-Arab socialist movement. He became titular Prime Minister in April 1954, adding to this post the presidency when Neguib stood down seven months later. Nasser won great popularity by his success in securing the final withdrawal of British troops from their Suez Canal bases in June 1956 in accordance with a treaty he had negotiated in October 1954. But on 26 July 1956 he announced the nationalization of the Suez Canal Company, thereby precipitating an international crisis which led to an Israeli offensive in Sinai from 29 October to 5 November 1956, followed by an Anglo-French 'police action' to recover mastery of the canal from 31 October to 7 November 1956. 'Suez', as the crisis has generally been called, resulted in United Nations and American pressure against the invaders to withdraw, and thereby boosted Nasser's prestige in the Arab world. In February 1958 he was able to secure an Egyptian-Syrian federation, the United Arab Republic, which also had links with the Yemen. He was regarded as protector of the African anti-colonialists, of the Palestinian guerrillas, and of the new republican regime in Iraq. Nasser's Egypt was not, however, rich enough to subsidize all his potential clients and he was too shrewd to remain a pliant dupe of Moscow. The secession of Syria from the UAR in September 1961 put him on the defensive. Against his better judgement he was forced to permit provocative acts against Israel by Arab guerrillas based on Cairo. In June 1967 the 'Six Day War', planned by General DAYAN inflicted a major defeat on Egypt, and Nasser resigned office, only to come back to power twenty-four hours later after demonstrations of support in all the major cities of Egypt. For the remaining three years of his life he tried to strengthen links with the United

States and to hold the Palestinians in check. He died from a heart attack on 28 September 1970 after mediating in the Jordanian Civil War. President SADAT succeeded him. G. A. Nasser: *The Philosophy of the Revolution* (1954); J. Lacoutoure: *Nasser* (1973); P. J. Vatikiotis: *Nasser and his Generation* (1978); A. Nutting: *Nasser* (1972); J. Waterbury: *The Egypt of Nasser and Sadat* (Princeton, N.J., 1983).

Nehru, Pandit Jawaharlal (1889–1964), Indian Prime Minister from 1947 to 1964: born in Allahabad, the son of a wealthy lawyer. He was educated at Harrow and Trinity College, Cambridge. In 1910 he was admitted to the Inner Temple and subsequently called to the bar, practising in India from 1912. From 1919 onwards he became active in the Indian National Congress Party, being arrested as a dangerous agitator in 1921 and imprisoned. Upon his release in 1922 he became General-Secretary of the Congress and, with the backing of Mohandas GANDHI, was elected its President in 1929. He spent much of the years 1926–7 abroad, visiting the Soviet Union and attending a congress of oppressed colonial peoples in Brussels. He was frequently under detention in India, spending, in all, some nine of the twenty-five years preceding independence in prison. In 1946 he collaborated with the Viceroy, WAVELL, in the preliminary discussions on independence, working out details in the following year with the last Viceroy, Earl MOUNTBATTEN. He became Prime Minister and, at first, Foreign Minister, in the new India. His policy was carefully neutralist and non-aligned, allowing him to mediate over such issues as Korea and Indo-China as well as to deploy Indian troops on peace-keeping missions for the United Nations in many parts of the world. Over the Kashmir problem and over the Chinese invasion of Tibet he showed more moderation than did other prominent members of the Congress Party, and in international affairs he never showed such intransigence as his daughter, Indira GANDHI. He succeeded in breaking down the Hindu reluctance to abandon social practices which, to his rational and agnostic mind, appeared archaic, and he overcame the conservatism of rural communities naturally suspicious of changes in their traditional economy. To some extent, resentment at his policies of gradual modernization showed themselves in opposition to Congress reforms after his death. So long as he lived, he was regarded as the natural father-figure of 'third world' politics. He died in Delhi on 27 May 1964. J. Nehru: *An Autobiography* (1936), *The Discovery of India* (Calcutta, 1946), *Independence and After* (1950); M. K. Akbar: *Nehru, the Making of India* (1988); S. Gopal: *Jawaharlal Nehru* (2 vols) (1975–7); M. Brecher: *Nehru, a Political Biography* (1975); B. N. Panday: *Nehru* (1976).

Ngo Dinh Diem (1901–63), South Vietnam's President, 1955–63: born at Hué, educated as a strict Roman Catholic, receiving some of his schooling in America. He was in the French colonial service in Indo-China from 1929 to 1933, and then withdrew from public life for fourteen years, spending a short period in prison under the Communists in 1945. His right-wing National Union Front of 1947 was banned by the French and he spent some years in exile in Belgium and the United States. In 1954, with American backing and French connivance, he returned to Saigon as the Vietnamese people's leader in the struggle against communism. A rigged election secured his installation as the first President of South Vietnam in October 1955. Outwardly he was successful. Vice was pushed underground in Saigon's lurid night-life while trade, especially with America, improved. But Ngo Dinh Diem did not have a party following: he advanced his family and established a harsh system of government, with his extremely unpopular brother as head of police. By 1962 the Americans recognized they had been mistaken in encouraging Ngo Dinh Diem, for his obstinate Catholicism set him at loggerheads with powerful Buddhists and thereby offended the mass of the people. Some members of the American Central Intelligence Agency encouraged a group of South Vietnamese army officers to stage a *coup d'état* on 2 November 1963, in the course of which Ngo Dinh Diem was murdered. The episode played into the hands of the Communist North Vietnamese and discredited the Americans in Saigon at a time when they were trying to build up South Vietnam as a barrier against the Marxist-Maoist tide. C. A. Bain: *Vietnam; the Roots of Conflict* (Englewood Cliffs, N.J., 1967); F. Fitzgerald: *Fire in the Lake; the Vietnamese and the Americans* (Boston, Mass., 1972); B. Fall: *The Two Vietnams* (New York, 1964).

Nicholas (1841–1921), King of Montenegro: born at Njego, the nephew of Danilo Petrović-Njegoš (1826–60), the first member of Montenegro's ruling family to proclaim himself a Prince (1852). 'Nikita', who was educated in Trieste and Paris, succeeded to the princedom on Danilo's murder at Kotor on 13 August 1860. He was a Balkan warrior and a writer of traditional epic poems but also a law-giver, ruling as an occasionally benevolent despot, who in 1905 deigned to give his 250,000 subjects a constitution. Princely schools brought basic literature to the mountain clans; roads were built; the village of Cetinje became a capital, with a royal palace. The Prince established links with other rulers, one daughter becoming Queen Elena of Italy (1873–1952), while another married the future King Peter of Serbia and was ALEXANDER of Yugoslavia's mother. Nikita played off powerful neighbours against each other, securing recognition as King in August 1910. He was a shrewd investor, who manipulated the Paris Bourse to build up a private fortune. For personal gains he precipitated the outbreak of the first Balkan War (8 October 1912). During the next six months he more than doubled the size of his mountain kingdom, although forced to forego coveted Albanian lands under threat of Austrian intervention. He fought alongside Serbia in the First World War, but had to flee to France when Montenegro was overrun by the Austrians in January 1916. Characteristically he tried to hedge his bets on the outcome of the war by settling in Paris but sending his second son to Vienna. His devious policy aroused resentment: a Montenegron popular assembly at Podgorica voted for his deposition on 26 November 1918 and the Paris Peace Conference duly recognized Montenegro's union with Serbia in Yugoslavia. Nikita ignored these developments, maintaining a government in exile until his death at Antibes in March 1921. Twenty years later his grandson, Prince Michael (1908–) rejected offers by the Axis powers to set him up as a puppet sovereign of Montenegro. B. Jelavich: *History of the Balkans* Vol. 2 (1983); J. D. Treadway: *The Falcon and the Eagle* (West Lafayette, Ind., 1982); M. Djilas: *Land without Justice* (1958).

Nicholas II (1868–1918) Tsar of Russia from 1894 to 1917: born at Tsarskoe Selo, the eldest surviving child of ALEXANDER III, whose first-born son died in infancy. His education was supervised by the reactionary POBEDONOSTSEV, who had once also served as tutor to his father. Nicholas himself narrowly escaped assassination while visiting Japan during a world tour as Tsarevich in 1891–2. His amiably weak personality was given obstinate strength by the willpower of his consort, Alexandra of Hesse, whom he married soon after his accession. In home affairs he distrusted all representative government, only agreeing to summon a parliament (duma) after European Russia was racked by revolution in 1905. Abroad he listened too readily to entrepreneurs who wished for expansion in Korea, their expanisionist policy plunging Russia into the disastrous war with Japan of 1904–5. Moreover, to the dismay of his ministers, Nicholas allowed himself to be persuaded by Kaiser WILLIAM II into signing a Russo-German secret treaty at Björköe in July 1905, the two sovereigns having met while cruising in their yachts down the Gulf of Finland. Although the politicians in Berlin and St Petersburg succeeded in scrapping the treaty, the Tsar's action was regarded as proof of his weakness of will and his desire to rule as an autocrat, free from any sense of obligation to his ministers. Increasingly the imperial family was subject to criticism for its personal conduct, the Tsarina's religious exultation inclining her too readily to believe in the mystic powers of RASPUTIN. After the first defeats of the war in 1914, the Tsar became suspicious of his leading Generals and, in September 1915, assumed the supreme command on the Eastern Front, a post for which he was ill-suited by experience or temperament: demoralization, poor administration and corruption led to the overthrow of the Tsarist monarchy in March 1917, Nicholas abdicating at Pskov on 15 March. Together with his wife, three daughters and son, Nicholas was detained for five months at Tsarskoe Selo and eight months at Tobolsk in Siberia. At the end of April 1918 the imperial family was moved, under Bolshevik guard, to Ekaterinburg (now known as Sverdlovsk). They appear all to have been killed there on 16 July 1918, at the instigation of the local Bolshevik commander who feared the imminent arrival of 'White' counter-revolutionary troops loyal to KOLCHAK. The evidence is, however, far from conclusive. R. K. Massie: *Nicholas and Alexandra* (1967); D. Lieven: *Nicholas II* (rev. edn 1994); B. Pares: *The Fall of the Russian Monarchy* (1939).

Nimeri, Gaafar Mohammad al- (1930–), Sudanese political soldier: born at Omdurman, graduated from Khartoum military college before receiving specialist training at Cairo, where he became a close associate of the Free Officers movement, inspired by NASSER. When the Sudan gained independence in January 1956 Nimeri helped suppress a succession of rebellions in the southern provinces. As a colonel he led a military *coup* in May 1969 which established a ten-man Revolutionary Council. He was elected President in October 1971; over the following fourteen years he attempted to bring order, on the Nasser-ite model, to the Sudan; a new constitution (1973) gave some legislative power to an elected assembly, while at the same time allowing limited autonomy to the southern provinces. In 1977 and 1982 he was re-elected President but his decision to impose strict Islamic laws in 1983 provoked unrest around Khartoum itself. While Nimeri was visiting the USA in April 1985 his government was overthrown by a new military council of more moderate Islamic reformers. General Nimeri went into exile in Nigeria. C. Gordon: *Sudan in Transition* (1986).

Nimitz, Chester William (1885–1966), American Admiral commanding in the Pacific from 1941 to 1945: born at Fredericksburg in Texas, passing out of the Naval Academy at Annapolis in 1905. Much of his early career was spent in the submarine service, but by 1939 he had become Director of the Bureau of Navigation, with the rank of Rear-Admiral. In 1941, ten days after Pearl Harbor, he was given command of the US Pacific Fleet, exercising effective control from land-based headquarters in Hawaii and gaining a victory over Admiral YAMAMOTO at Midway Island (4 June 1942), largely through brilliant intelligence work. He interpreted the general strategic plans of Admiral Ernest KING and was able to reconcile them easily enough with his own dispositions, as well as collaborating with General MACARTHUR in 'island hopping' towards the Japanese homeland. He was one of the signatories of the Japanese document of surrender aboard USS *Missouri*, having been promoted to Fleet Admiral in 1944. His fleet in September 1945 comprised more than 6,250 vessels, supported by some 5,000 naval aircraft (Spain's 'Great Armada' of 1588 had 130 vessels). From 1947 to 1949 he was Chief of Naval Operations in Washington, and on his retirement in 1949 he headed a commission appointed by the United Nations to seek a settlement of the dispute between India and Pakistan over Kashmir. E. B. Potter: *Nimitz* (Annapolis, Wis., 1966); S. E. Morison: *History of US Naval Operations in World War II* Vols 4 and 5 (Boston, Mass., 1949–50); W. Lord: *Incredible Victory: the Battle of Midway* (1968).

Nixon, Richard Milhous (1913–94), President of the United States 1969–1974: born in Yorba Linda, California, and lived on the small citrus farm of his parents until 1922, when the family moved into Whittier, fifteen miles nearer Los Angeles. He took a degree in law at the Law School at Duke University, North Carolina, practised as a lawyer, and was commissioned in the US Navy in 1942. From 1946 to 1950 he sat in Congress, and was a member of the House Un-American Activities Committee investigating the allegations concerning Alger HISS. From 1950 to 1952 he was in the Senate, and was selected by EISENHOWER in 1952 as his running-mate. Nixon was an active Vice-President, willing to speak out in support of the American way of life when he visited Latin America and the Soviet Union. He was chosen as Republican presidential candidate in 1960: his campaign showed he was ill-at-ease with newspaper men and television cameras; and, perhaps because of his relatively poor childhood, he was suspicious of the party machine. The election was lost to John KENNEDY, and in 1962 Nixon failed even to win the governorship of his home state. He offered no challenge for the nomination in 1964, when GOLDWATER represented a right-wing Republicanism abhorrent to Nixon. But in 1968 he won the nomination and defeated Hubert HUMPHREY, largely through the electorate's dismay at the mounting involvement in Vietnam.

Nixon's first administration was able to achieve little in domestic legislation because the Democrats continued to dominate Congress. But in foreign affairs it proved possible to relax tension with the Russians (Nixon visited Moscow in May 1972) and, as soon as a cease-fire was reached in Vietnam, with the Chinese, too – the President visiting Peking in February 1972. Much of this success sprang from the abilities of his aide, Henry KISSINGER, but it emphasized the statesmanship inherent in Nixon's ideal of the presidency, and he won forty-nine of fifty States in the presidential election of 1972. His second term was overshadowed by scandal: his Vice-President, Spiro Agnew, was forced to resign in December 1973 after a report on financial transactions when he was Governor of Maryland (1966–8); and Nixon fell foul of the Press early in April 1973 when he stopped his personal aides from giving testimony in a court action against employees of Committee to Re-elect the President (CREEP) who had broken into the Democratic Party headquarters in Watergate during the previous summer and been found there with electronic bugging devices. Increasing evidence suggesting that the President had connived at illegalities in the Watergate affair (together with evidence that he secretly taped all conversations in his White House office) rapidly lessened his standing with the American public. Threats of impeachment, first made in October 1973, were renewed the following summer. The President admitted he had attempted to cover up the original crime at Watergate. On 9 August 1974 he became the first President in American history to resign office, handing over the chief executive's responsibilities to the man whom he had nominated as Vice-President in succession to Agnew, Gerald FORD. Nixon was give a free pardon by his successor. R. M. Nixon: *The Memoirs of Richard M. Nixon* (New York, 1990); S. E. Ambrose: *Nixon* (3 vols) (New York, 1987–90); J. Aitken: *Nixon, A Life* (1993); F. Emery: *Watergate; The Corruption and Fall of Richard Nixon* (rev. edn 1995).

Nkomo, Joshua (1917–), Vice-President of Zimbabwe: born in Matopos, Matabeleland, and educated at Adam's College in Natal, receiving higher education in social work at Johannesburg. After several years as a welfare officer with the Rhodesian railways at Bulawayo, he became organizing secretary of the African railway workers' union, 1945–50, and was later an insurance agent. He worked with Nelson MANDELA in the African National Congress, becoming President in 1957. When, two years later, the Congress was banned in Rhodesia he came to London, returning home in 1960 as founder-President of the National Democratic Party. This body, too, was banned and in 1961 Nkomo accordingly set up Zimbabwe African People's Union (ZAPU), the name Zimbabwe being taken from the ruined city which had propagated an African mediaeval culture between the ninth and fourteenth centuries. ZAPU was proscribed as unlawful in 1962 and a year later Nkomo was imprisoned for six months for obstructing the police. From November 1964 to December 1974 Nkomo was detained as a political prisoner in Rhodesia. During these years he was recognized as the spokesman for Zimbabwe nationalism and was visited in detention by British government ministers seeking a Rhodesian settlement in 1968 and 1971. Upon his release from detention he became a member of the African National Council, ousting Bishop Muzorewa from its presidency and leading the ANC delegation at talks with Ian SMITH in Geneva in October 1976, the same month in which he became joint leader, with Robert MUGABE (1925–) of the Patriotic Front. Nkomo and Mugabe rejected successive compromise proposals and intensified Zimbabwe guerrilla operations against Rhodesia in 1977 and 1978. On 14 August 1978 Nkomo again met Smith, secretly, for talks in Zambia but within three weeks the Zimbabwe guerrillas shot down a Rhodesian airliner, intensifying the bitterness of civil war. Nkomo came to London in September 1979 and participated in the Lancaster House Conference, agreeing to a cease-fire after three months of talks on a future constitution of Zimbabwe-Rhodesia. He was allowed back into Rhodesia in January 1980 so as to head the ZAPU election campaign, subsequently taking office under Mugabe in the first government of Zimbabwe as Home Minister. From 1981 until 1987 he was out of office and was widely suspected of planning to overthrow Mugabe. But the two men were reconciled in December 1987, when Nkomo became one of Zimbabwe's two Vice-Presidents. J. Nkomo: *The Story of My Life* (1984); D. Caute: *Under the Skin, the Death of White Rhodesia* (1983).

Nkrumah, Kwame (1909–72), President of Ghana from 1960 to 1966: born at Nkroful in the western Gold Coast, receiving his higher education in Pennsylvania and at the London School of Economics. He founded the Convention People's Party in 1949, winning the Gold Coast

General Election of 1954. In two-and-a-half years of negotiation he obtained dominion status in March 1957 for the region which he now called Ghana. In July 1960 he became the first President of the Republic, keeping Ghana within the Commonwealth. Nkrumah was respected in Africa as a leader of independence movements who was implacably hostile to South Africa, suspicious of French-sponsored African communities, and inclined to prefer the socialism of MAO to that of Soviet leaders. In 1964 he established a one-party system and interfered seriously with the independence of the judiciary. Personal extravagance and grandiose public works schemes ruined the economy at a time when there was a sudden world slump in the price of cocoa, an important Ghanaian export. The military leaders seized the opportunity to oust him from office while he was absent from the country on a state visit to China (24 February 1966). Nkrumah died at a sanatorium in Romania in April 1972. In death he was honoured in Ghana as a founding father of the republic. H. L. Bretton: *The Rise and Fall of Kwame Nkrumah* (1966); T. Jones: *Ghana's First Republic 1960–1966* (1975).

Noriega, Manuel Antonio Morena (1940–), Panamian General: born and educated in Panama City, receiving military training in Peru. At the age of 30 he became head of intelligence in the Panamian National Guard. By 1982 he was General and Chief of Staff. This post made him *de facto* ruler of the country, independent of Presidents democratically elected in 1984 and 1989. Early links between Noriega and the CIA in Washington became embarrassing to President BUSH when Noriega was indicted by a US Grand Jury in February 1988 on drug trafficking charges. American attempts to encourage military *coups* against him failed and an invasion of Panama City was undertaken by the US on 20 December 1989 in a bid to arrest him. Though Noriega found sanctuary in the Vatican Embassy he surrendered on 3 January 1990 and was flown to the USA to stand trial. The episode lowered US prestige in central America and led to much criticism of Bush at home.

Northcliffe, Lord (Alfred Charles William Harmsworth) (1865–1922), British newspaper proprietor: the son of a Dublin barrister, left school at the age of 15 and, after eight years in journalism, brought out the first sensational weekly *Answers* (1888). In 1894 he published the *Evening News*, the first of his London ventures. The *Daily Mail* (1896) was half the price of any other daily and, with its crisper style, attracted a wider public, having twice the circulation of its nearest rival within three years. The *Daily Mirror* (1903) was the first English newspaper intended to appeal to women readers. In 1905 Alfred Harmsworth was created a Baron, taking the title Northcliffe; he became a Viscount in 1917. From 1905 to 1911 he was proprietor of the *Observer*, and from 1908 to 1922 he owned *The Times*. He continued to favour the *Daily Mail*, although he tried to bring to *The Times* some of the sensationalism which had won readers for his cheaper newspapers. In 1917 he headed a political mission to the United States on behalf of LLOYD GEORGE, and for the last year of the war was in charge of propaganda to the enemy states. For this task he relied heavily on the advice of the foreign affairs editor of *The Times*, Wickham Steed (1871–1956), who specialized in central European affairs and encouraged Northcliffe to support the demands of the subject nationalities in Austria-Hungary for independence. Towards the end of his life Northcliffe suffered from megalomania and was distrusted by leading political figures. Together with his brother Harold Harmsworth (1868–1940, created Viscount Rothermere in 1913) Northcliffe revolutionized journalism in England as had HEARST in America. The Harmsworth brothers, however, never showed the political irresponsibility of the 'Yellow Press' across the Atlantic. R. Pound and G. Harmsworth: *Northcliffe* (1959); E. Wrench: *Struggle* (1935).

Novotny, Antonin (1904–75), President of Czechoslovakia from 1957 to 1968: born near Prague, the son of a bricklayer. He worked as a boy in an arms factory and became a Communist as soon as the Czechoslovak Party was set up, in 1921. The Nazis imprisoned him for four years in a concentration camp. He served GOTTWALD as a loyal Stalinist and, when Gottwald died in March 1953, effective control passed into Novotny's hands as the new First Secretary of the Party. In November 1957 he also became President of the Republic. Novotny pressed forward the industrialization of the Czech lands, showing more concern with the pattern of economic development in the eastern socialist bloc as a whole than solely in Czechoslovakia. He became unpopular, especially in the less heavily industrialized regions of Slovakia, and from 1962 he was faced with economic discontent and clear evidence of a recession. In the autumn of 1967 he sought to win the support of the intellectuals and the students by relaxing controls. He realized that this was a disastrous step, and in January 1968 gave up the party secretaryship to DUBCEK, hoping thereby to appease the Slovaks. At the end of February he tried to encourage the Czech army to occupy Prague and enable him to recover his full authority by neo-Stalinist repression, but the army officers refused to act. President Novotny, increasingly isolated, resigned office on 22 March 1968 and withdrew from political life, although he protested when, in the following August, the 'Warsaw Pact' powers carried through the march on Prague which he had envisaged in the previous January as a purely Czechoslovak military action. E. Taborsky: *Communism in Czechoslovakia, 1948–1960* (Princeton, N.J., 1961); N. Stone and E. Strouhal (eds): *Czechoslovakia; Crossroads and Crises, 1918–88* (1989).

Nyerere, Julius Kambarage (1922–), first President of Tanzania: born, a chief's son, in a village on Lake Victoria, receiving a university education at Makerere University in Uganda and at Edinburgh. For several years he was a teacher, later maintaining his academic interest by translating two of Shakespeare's tragedies into Swahili. In 1954 he founded the Tanganyika African National Union (TANU), a non-Marxist socialist movement favouring independence within the Commonwealth. Electoral gains by TANU in 1958 were followed by even greater successes two years later. When Tanganyika was granted internal self-government on 1 May 1961 he became Prime Minister and saw his country through to independence at the end of the year. In January 1962, however, he resigned the premiership, concentrating for several months on improving the structure of his comparatively young political movement. He accepted the Presidency of Tanganyika at the end of 1962 and was elected President of the United Republic of Tanzania when Zanzibar acceded in April 1964. Re-election followed in 1970, 1975 and 1980. Nyerere's cautious response to enticements from the Marxist Left emphasized his growing skill as a Commonwealth statesman avoiding entanglement in central African affairs. In October 1985 he retired and was succeeded by President Ali-Hassan Mwingi, from Zanzibar. M. Hood (ed.): *Tanzania and Nyerere* (1988).

O

Obote, (Apollo) Milton (1924–), first President of Uganda: born in Lango Province of Uganda; completed his education at Makerere College, Kampala, and spent five years in Kenya, where he became an early member of the Kenya Africa Union. After returning to Uganda in 1955 he entered politics, joined the legislative council in 1957, founded the Uganda People's Congress in 1960 to prepare for independence, and became Uganda's first Prime Minister in October 1962. During the following five years Dr Obote worked for a unitary state, despite opposition from the province of Buganda, where a powerful movement favoured federation. He introduced a new republican constitution in May 1967, taking office as executive President. Allegations of corruption by his officials led to initial support for a military *coup* by Idi AMIN in January 1971 which deposed Obote while he was in Singapore for the Commonwealth Conference. For nine years Dr Obote remained in Tanzania but he returned to Kampala when Amin was overthrown and claimed an electoral victory in 1980, resuming his Presidency on 15 December. Although Obote personally tried to check the spread of anarchy in Uganda, many foreign observers maintain that his officials imposed a tyrannical rule barely distinguishable from the brutality of the Amin regime: inequitable distribution of the limited food resources aggravated intercommunal rivalry and violence. A second military *coup*, in July 1986, forced Obote into exile; he found refuge in Zambia. K. Ingham: *Obote, a Political Biography* (1994).

Orlando, Vittorio Emmanuele (1860–1952), Italian Prime Minister from 1917 to 1919: born at Palermo in Sicily, becoming Professor of Law before entering the Italian Parliament as a liberal and holding minor office in a succession of governments between 1903 and 1916. His apparent imperturbability as Minister of Justice in the undistinguished government of Paolo Boselli (from June 1916 to October 1917) made King VICTOR EMMANUEL III appoint him Prime Minister on 28 October 1917 after the disastrous defeat at Caporetto, in the hope that he could restore order and confidence in the country. In this, with Allied assistance, he was successful: he was Prime Minister when the Italians gained the victory of Vittorio Veneto (3 November 1918). Orlando attended the Paris Peace Conference of 1919 as one of the 'Big Four', his colleagues being CLEMENCEAU, LLOYD GEORGE and WOODROW WILSON. These three statesmen spoke from greater strength and political experience than Orlando. Wilson condemned Orlando's attempt to attain Italy's war aims as an affront to the principle of national self-determination. News of Orlando's failure to gain acceptance of the full nationalistic programme weakened his parliamentary position, and his absence from Rome left the government without any direction at a time of increasing social distress. Moreover, the strain of crises in foreign and domestic affairs was destroying his earlier reputation for political calm. On 20 June 1919, a week before the signature of the Treaty of Versailles, he was defeated in a vote in

Parliament and resigned office. He retired to private life in his native Sicily throughout MUSSOLINI's period of power. He reappeared briefly in Italian politics in 1945–6 but was too old to make any impact on events. C. Seton-Watson: *Italy from Liberalism to Fascism* (1967); R. Albrecht-Carrié: *Italy at the Paris Peace Conference* (New York, 1938).

Owen, David Anthony Llewellyn
(1938–), British politician: born at Plympton, South Devon; educated at Bradfield, Sidney Sussex College, Cambridge, and St Thomas's Hospital, London; qualified as a doctor in 1962 and specialized in neurology until elected Labour MP for a Plymouth constituency in 1966. He held several ministerial posts in the last WILSON governments and under CALLAGHAN. He was sworn a Privy Councillor in 1976, when he became Minister of State at the Foreign and Commonwealth Office. In February 1977 he was chosen to succeed C. A. R. Crosland (1918–77) as Foreign Secretary. After Labour's defeat in May 1979 Dr Owen became mistrustful of the influence of militant trade unionists within the Party; in 1981 he was one of four ex-ministers who seceded from Labour and set up the Social Democrat Party (SDP), a centre group which briefly attracted dissentients within all three main political parties. He became leader of the SDP in 1983, remaining in the House of Commons as MP for Devonport until 1992, when he accepted a life peerage. Most members of the SDP favoured a merger with the Liberal Party after electoral disappointments in 1987 and Dr Owen duly resigned the leadership. Soon afterwards, however, he persuaded a minority of members to reconstitute an independent SDP, which he led until it was formally dissolved on 3 June 1990. In August 1992 Lord Owen was appointed special EC envoy to the Yugoslav lands and for three years worked closely with the US delegate, Cyrus Vance, to seek a political solution to the conflicts in Bosnia-Herzegovina and Croatia. D. Owen: *Time to Declare* (rev. edn 1992); K. Harris: *David Owen* (1987).

P

Pahlavi, Muhammad Riza (1919–80), last Shah of Iran: born in Teheran, eldest son of Riza Pahlavi (1878–1944), a barely literate Colonel in the Cossack Brigade who, on 30 October 1925 staged the military *coup* which deposed Shah Ahmad (nominal ruler since 1909), the seventh and last sovereign of the Qajar dynasty. Riza accepted the offer from an assembly of the Crown of Darius for his family, was proclaimed Shah on 16 December 1925, and declared his eldest son Valiahd (Crown Prince) two months later. Superficial westernization of Iran continued for the next fifteen years, but intelligence reports of collaboration between Shah Riza and Nazi agents induced a joint Anglo-Soviet invasion of Iran in August 1941. The Shah then abdicated in favour of his son, Muhammad Riza Pahlavi, who was proclaimed 'Shah-in-shah of Iran' on 16 September 1941, six weeks before his twenty-second birthday. When British and Soviet troops withdrew from his empire in 1946, a bitterly xenophobic mood developed against overseas capitalists, especially the British and American managers of the oilfields along the Persian Gulf. The radical demagogue MUSADDIQ exploited this mood, which led to demands for oil nationalization and early in 1951 caused several political assassinations, the Shah himself being wounded by a revolver shot. Riza Pahlavi tolerated the radical hysteria of Musaddiq until August 1953, for a time leaving the country; but from 1953 his was the deciding voice in Iran's government. Periods of liberal experiment, notably in 1961–2, were followed by a reassertion of the Shah's autocratic authority. He encouraged welfare programmes and, in 1963, decreed the social emancipation of women, as had KEMAL in Turkey more than thirty years previously. These reforms were denounced by extreme Muslim leaders, notably by the Ayatollah KHOMEINI, who was arrested in June 1963 and sent into exile. Oil revenue made the dynasty wealthy, exciting envy from the mass of the population. Resentment at the spread of 'western degeneracy' added a puritanical Muslim opposition to student complaints that the Shah had no sympathy with the Arab cause and was a tool of western capitalism. The Shah's richly endowed political movement, 'National Resurrection Party' (founded in March 1975), gained little popular support. Rioting in the holy city of Qum in September 1978 soon spread to Teheran; demands for the return of the exiled Khomeini were coupled with threats against the Shah's life. By the end of the year he was no longer in control of events. He left Teheran 'on holiday' on 16 January 1979, settling in Morocco and later in Mexico. Two months later he was formally deposed and sentenced to death *in absentia*. In October 1979 he was admitted to hospital in New York, suffering from cancer. Iranian students stormed the American Embassy in Teheran on 4 November 1979 and seized sixty American hostages in an attempt to induce the US Government to send the Shah back to Iran. President CARTER rejected this attempt at blackmail, but the Shah subsequently left New York for the army air force hospital of Lackland in Texas. On 15 December 1979 he flew to Panama, subsequently finding refuge in Egypt, where he died seven months later. Muhammad Riza Shah Pahlavi: *Answer to History* (1980); E. Abrahamian: *Iran Between Two Revolutions* (Princeton, N.J., 1982); D. Wilber: *Riza Shah Pahlevi* (New York, 1975).

Paisley, Ian Richard Kyle (1926–), Ulster Protestant founder of a church and a political party: born in Ballymena, the son of a Baptist minister. He received theological instruction at the Reformed Presbyterian College and in March 1951 became founder-moderator of the Free Presbyterian Church in Belfast, a staunchly Protestant and rabidly 'anti-papist' denomination which, by 1991, had 14,000 members in fifty congregations across Ulster and ten overseas. Paisley first gained publicity in March 1966 when he led noisy demonstrations against a visit to Pope PAUL VI by the Archbishop of Canterbury (Michael Ramsey, 1904–88). On returning to Belfast Paisley founded a newspaper, the *Protestant Telegraph*, and called for Ulster Protestant volunteers to check the spread of Southern Irish Catholicism north of the border. In July 1966, as intersectarian violence returned to the province after twenty-seven years of relative calm, Paisley was arrested and briefly imprisoned for unlawful assembly and breach of the peace. He became Protestant Unionist MP for North Antrim at Westminster in April 1970 and founded the Democratic Unionist Party (5 October 1971). For more than twenty years he used his extraordinarily powerful voice and demagogic skills to fan protests against attempts by successive governments in London to reach accord over Ireland with Dublin. In 1979 he was elected to the European Parliament, receiving more personal votes than any other candidate in the Community; at Strasbourg, as at Westminster, he championed the narrow evangelicalism and Orangeman loyalties of uncompromising Ulster Unionism. S. Bruce: *God Save Ulster! The Religion and Politics of Paisleyism* (Oxford, 1984); R. Paisley: *Ian Paisley, my Father* (Basingstoke, 1988).

Palmerston, Lord (Henry John Temple) (1784–1865), British Foreign Secretary from 1830 to 1841 and from 1846 to 1851, Prime Minister from 1855 to 1865: born at Broadlands, near Romsey in Hampshire, and educated at Harrow and St John's College, Cambridge, succeeding to an Irish viscountcy in 1802 – a title which, since it did not confer membership of the House of Lords, enabled Lord Palmerston to sit as an elected Member of Parliament for fifty-eight years, from 1807 until his death. He first held government office as Secretary for War in 1809 but only entered the Cabinet in 1827, under Canning. His early conservatism gave way to Whig liberalism and, in his first term at the Foreign Office, he was closely identified with such 'liberal' causes as the independence of Belgium and the establishment of constitutional government in other parts of Europe. The blustering style of diplomacy associated with his name was most marked in his second term as Foreign Secretary, particularly in 1850 when he defended the action of the Royal Navy in blockading, on his orders, the Greek coast because the house in Athens of a British subject, Don Pacifico, had been attacked by a mob angered by sharp commercial practice. As Home Secretary in Lord Aberdeen's ministry (1852–5), Palmerston in Cabinet encouraged British participation in the Crimean War since he had consistently opposed Russian encroachments on the Turkish Empire. It was because public opinion regarded Palmerston as a more effective war leader than Aberdeen that he was able to form his first government in February 1855. Although popular in these later years 'Pam's' judgements were less astute than in the 1830s. He supported the Confederacy in the American Civil War, exaggerated the menace to Britain of a rearmament programme undertaken by NAPOLEON III, and he underestimated the ruthless determination of BISMARCK as chief minister in Prussia after 1862. At home Palmerston ignored the interest taken by more liberal members of his government in extending the franchise. His casual, and at times cynical, approach to public affairs exasperated Queen VICTORIA; and his firm belief in the natural superiority of 'England's' needs and 'England's' ways made him unpopular abroad. He died in office, at his wife's country home, Brocket, in Hertfordshire on 18 October 1865. J. Ridley: *Lord Palmerston* (1970); J. Bourne: *Palmerston, the Early Years* (1982).

Pankhurst, Christabel (1880–1958), British suffragette: born in Manchester, the eldest daughter of the barrister, Dr Richard Pankhurst and his wife Emmeline PANKHURST At the time of her father's death in 1898, Christabel Pankhurst was completing her education in Switzerland, but on her return home she continued the family tradition of seeking votes for women and, at the age of 23, induced her mother to form a militant body, the Women's Social and Political Union, to campaign for extension of the franchise. In January 1904 she unsuccessfully sought to be called to the bar. She was one of the first suffragettes to be imprisoned, receiving a sentence of seven days for creating a disturbance on 13 October 1905 at the Free Trade Hall in Manchester. She was again imprisoned in 1908. After a mass demonstration at the House of Commons on 18 November 1910 so many women leaders were arrested that it was decided she should seek, in future, to control the movement from abroad. When threatened with re-arrest in March 1912 she therefore crossed to Paris and set up the militant suffragettes' headquarters in the Hotel de la Cité Bergère. She returned to England when war was declared in 1914, spoke at recruiting rallies, and stood unsuccessfully as a supporter of the coalition government at the 1918 election in Smethwick. In general, she lost interest in active politics after women were enfranchised, spending her later years in Canada and the United States and becoming a vigorous propagandist for the Second Advent Christians. Her services to the political emancipation of women were recognized in 1936, when she was created DBE (Dame of the British Empire). C. Pankhurst: *Unshackled* (1959); T. Lloyd: *Suffragettes International* (1971); A. Rosen: *Rise Up Women* (1975); R. Fulford: *Votes for Women* (1957).

Pankhurst, Emmeline (*née* **Goulden**) (1858–1928), British suffragette: born in Manchester, married the barrister Dr Richard Marsden Pankhurst, who stood unsuccessfully as an Independent Labour candidate for Gorton in 1895. After his death, she was encouraged by her eldest daughter, Christabel PANKHURST, to adopt militant tactics in the search for women's political rights. The Women's Social and Political Union, which she founded in 1903, resorted to violence from 1906 onwards. Mrs Pankhurst was arrested in 1908 and 1909 and again in 1911 and 1912, being released after going on hunger strike. When the First World War began she was serving a three-year sentence in Holloway for arson but was released, with other suffragettes, under a general amnesty. She encouraged her earlier supporters to undertake war work, in the services, as nurses, or in essential industry. Women gained the vote in 1918, but she declined to stand for any socialist party, although she had belonged to the ILP since 1894. From 1919 to 1926 she lived in Canada, travelling over large areas to lecture on social welfare and hygiene. When she returned to England in 1926 she joined the Conservative Party and was adopted as parliamentary candidate for an East London constituency, but she died before there was any opportunity for her to contest an election. She was the mother of five children. As well as Christabel and Sylvia PANKHURST, a third daughter, Adela Pankhurst (1885–1961), settled in Australia where she was a socialist and pacifist in both world wars. Of Mrs Pankhurst's two sons, one died at the age of 4 and the other, Harry, died in 1910 at the age of 20. E. Pankhurst: *My Own Story* (1914); M. G. Fawcett: *The Women's Victory and After* (1920).

Pankhurst, Sylvia (1882–1960), British suffragette, socialist, and campaigner for African independence: born in Manchester, the second daughter of Mrs Emmeline PANKHURST. While supporting the efforts of her mother and elder sister, she was anxious to emphasize the appeal of the suffrage movement to the working class, fearing it might otherwise seem almost exclusively middle class. She therefore concentrated on activities in the East End of London, remaining staunchly loyal to Keir HARDIE and the Independent Labour tradition of her father, as well as supporting George LANSBURY in his attempt to become an MP committed to women's suffrage. Many terms of imprisonment broke her health, but she continued with simple charity work in the East End. During the First World War she was a pacifist, and travelled to Soviet Russia soon after the Revolution, although she showed a similar independence of spirit to that of Rosa LUXEMBURG. She was a talented artist and, unlike her elder sister, was contemptuous of social taboos in matters of sex. Hostility to fascism and hatred of war led her to ardent championship of the Abyssinians when MUSSOLINI ordered his armies to enter Abyssinia in 1935. The last twenty-five years of Sylvia Pankhurst's life were spent in supporting the Ethiopians and other African peoples seeking an end to colonialism. She finally settled on the outskirts of Addis Ababa in 1956, much respected by the Emperor HAILE SELASSIE. She was still living in Ethiopia when she died, on 27 September 1960. S. Pankhurst: *The Suffragette Movement* (1931); P. Romero: *E. Sylvia Pankhurst, Portrait of a Radical* (1987).

Papadopoulos, George (1918–), head of the ruling Greek military junta from 1967 to 1974: born near Athens, served in the Greek Army through the Second World War and the Greek Civil War, subsequently specializing in counter-intelligence against alleged Communist subversion and in political warfare. Rumours of a threatened Communist seizure of power induced Colonel Papadopoulos to collaborate with the tank commandant, Brigadier Pattakos, in bringing about a *coup d'état* in Athens on 21 April 1967. Martial law was introduced and political parties banned. A counter *coup* by King CONSTANTINE II the following December was easily frustrated, the King going into exile. Papadopoulos, promoted to General, became Prime Minister and Minister of Defence. Conservative and liberal politicians, as well as socialists, were imprisoned. All forms of entertainment and all newspapers and periodicals were censored, and attempts were made to impose a puritanical moral code; such matters fell primarily within the province of the Minister of the Interior, Pattakos. Evidence of torture and brutality in prisons and island concentration camps led 'the regime of the colonels' to be arraigned by the Dutch, Swedish and Norwegian governments and condemned by the European Commission of Human Rights. Allegations of further royalist plots led Papadopoulos to proclaim himself Regent in March 1972, establishing a republic under his own presidency on 1 June 1973. Martial law, lifted in order to encourage the formation of a so-called civilian government, was hurriedly reimposed in the following November after serious student riots in Athens and Salonika against the repressive Papadopoulos system. A desperate bid to gain popularity by securing the union of Greece and Cyprus through a military *coup* in Nicosia led to the temporary withdrawal of President MAKARIOS from Cyprus and, by provoking Turkish military intervention, completed the alienation of the majority of Greeks from the 'Colonels'. Papadopoulos relinquished authority in Athens a week later (23 July 1974), the veteran conservative Prime Minister, Constantine KARAMANLIS, returning from exile in France to preside over the reintroduction of a parliamentary system. Papadopoulos and Pattakos were later put on trial: death sentences were commuted to life imprisonment. C. M. Woodhouse: *Modern Greece, a Short History* (1984); J. A. Katris: *Eyewitness in Greece; the Colonels Come to Power* (St Louis, Miss., 1971).

Papandreou, George (1888–1968), Greek socialist leader: born in Thessaloniki (Salonika) under Turkish rule but was educated in Athens and became a lawyer, entering politics as a Republican and moderate Socialist during the 1920s, holding office in several governments before the METAXAS dictatorship was set up in 1935. He escaped from Greece after the German occupation in 1941 but returned on the liberation of Athens in 1944 and briefly headed a coalition government. The militarists who returned with the monarchy after the war found his views too far to the Left and he was in political Opposition throughout the 1950s. In 1961 he brought together the democratic socialists and the radicals in a new Centre Union Party. He was Prime Minister for eight weeks in the closing months of 1963 and his power base seemed strengthened after electoral gains in February 1964, especially in northern Greece. But his government could carry through only a few of its promised reforms. Papandreou was hampered by hostility from the army, clashes of temperament with King CONSTANTINE II and worsening relations with Turkey over the problems of Cyprus. He fell from power in July 1965. The 'Colonels'' *coup* (see *Papadopolous*) in April 1967 put an end to Centre Union hopes of a sweeping victory in new elections. Papandreou was briefly arrested but later released because of failing health: he died a year later.

His son, Andreas Papandreou (1919–), a university lecturer in economics in the USA from 1947 to 1963, continued his father's work in exile during the Colonels' regime. He built up the Pan-Hellenic Socialist Movement (PASOK) as a slightly more left-wing successor to his father's Centre Union. With the resumption of democratic rule in 1974 Andreas Papandreou led PASOK to victory in the 1981 elections, holding power until 1989, when PASOK lost its parliamentary majority. He again became Prime Minister in October 1993 but, by the summer of 1995, was in poor health and facing criticism from reformers within PASOK, who resented the influence of his young wife, a former air hostess. After many weeks in hospital, he resigned office in February 1996. C. M. Woodhouse: *Modern Greece, a Short History* (1984); J. C. Louis: *Greece under Papandreou* (1985).

Papen, Franz von (1879–1969), Chancellor of the German Republic in 1932, and diplomat: born at Werl in Westphalia, became a military cadet at the age of 12, and was commissioned in the Uhlans. He was sent as military attaché to Washington in 1913 but his activities were regarded with such suspicion that he was expelled in December 1915. He fought in the battles around Arras in 1917, and then held staff posts with the Germans attached to the Turkish army in Palestine. In 1921 he entered the Reichstag as a member of the Roman Catholic Centre Party, accepting office as successor to Chancellor BRÜNING in June 1932. His chancellorship only lasted for twenty-four weeks and was marked by the enforced removal of the Social Democratic Government of Prussia. When HITLER became Chancellor in January 1933, Papen took office as Vice-Chancellor believing that, with other non-Nazi colleagues in the Cabinet, he could keep the fanatics 'framed in'. Hitler constantly disregarded the ideas of his Vice-Chancellor: most of Papen's colleagues were killed or arrested in June 1934, and Papen was fortunate to escape with his life. He was sent as minister (ambassador) to Vienna in August 1934, maintaining delicate relations with the Austrian Government until Austria was absorbed into Greater Germany by the *Anschluss* of March 1938. In April 1939 he went to Turkey as ambassador, remaining there until the severance of Germano-Turkish relations in August 1944. His years in Ankara were marked by able intelligence work and by occasional feelers towards a negotiated peace. To Papen's surprise, he was arrested by the Americans in 1945 and put on trial at Nuremberg, charged with having conspired to wage war. In September 1946 he was acquitted. He was, however, subsequently sentenced to eight years in a labour camp by a German de-Nazification court, but was released in January 1949. Papen's reputation as a devious intriguer – a would-be German Talleyrand – was confirmed, rather than dispelled, by the memoirs which he published three years later, in order to 'correct the more outrageous misrepresentations' about his life. F. von Papen: *Memoirs* (1953).

Parnell, Charles Stewart (1846–91), leader of the Irish Home Rule movement from 1877 to 1890: born a member of the Anglo-Irish Protestant ascendancy at Avondale, County Wicklow, his maternal grandfather being a distinguished American naval commander. He was educated at Magdalene College, Cambridge, and entered Parliament in 1875 as 'Home Rule' MP for County Meath. Two years later he succeeded Isaac Butt (1813–79), the founder leader of the Home Rule movement. Parnell at once began to obstruct Commons business so as to draw attention to Ireland's grievance; and in 1878 he took up agrarian agitation, organizing defiance by the peasantry of unpopular and unscrupulous landlords by the system known as 'boycotting'. In October 1881 Parnell was arrested for incitement, but while he was in Kilmainham Jail rural anarchy became worse and the Prime Minister, GLADSTONE, ordered his release in May 1882, hoping he could curb the violence of 'moonlighting'. Parnell's influence in the House of Commons was considerable, an Irish party of eighty-six members being sufficient in February 1886 to bring down the Conservative government by voting with the Liberal Opposition. When in March 1886 Gladstone accepted the principle of giving the Irish the Home Rule they demanded, he received support from Parnell, but the defection of Joseph CHAMBERLAIN defeated their combined efforts and brought the Conservatives back, to remain in government until after Parnell's death. He won some sympathy in November 1889 by a successful libel action against *The Times*, which had published forged letters showing his alleged approval of terrorist murders. But a year later he was cited as co-respondent in a divorce case brought by an ex-Hussar officer, Captain O'Shea, against his wife, Katherine ('Kitty'), who had been Parnell's mistress since 1881 and born him three daughters. Parnell married 'Kitty' in June 1891, but the scandal ruined his political career. Before he could recover his authority within the Irish Party be contracted rheumatic fever and died at his home in Brighton on 6 October 1891. F. S. L. Lyons: *Charles Stewart Parnell* (1977); C. Cruise O'Brien: *Parnell and His Party, 1880–90* (Oxford, 1964).

Pašić, Nikola (1845–1926), predominant figure in Serbian politics from 1904 to 1926: born in the small town of Zajecar, on the Serbo-Bulgarian border. He entered political life in the late 1870s as a founder-member of the Serbian Radicals, originally a peasant party protesting at exploitation by townsfolk; and he was Serbia's Prime Minister in 1891–2. Gradually, however, he changed the nature of the Serbian Radicals, emphasizing their nationalism. In 1903 he was one of the politicians who brought back the Karadjordjević dynasty, and he served both King Peter I and his son, ALEXANDER, as chief minister, heading governments in 1904–8, 1910–18 and (as Prime Minister of Yugoslavia) 1921–6. He was also principal Yugoslav delegate to the Paris Peace Conference in 1919. Pašić never thought of himself as a Yugoslav; he believed in a Greater Serbia and distrusted the Croats and Slovenes (who were Catholics whereas the Serbs were Orthodox in religion). At the same time, he opposed the extreme militarist societies – such as the so-called 'Black Hand' of 1911–17 who, in their desire for rapid Serbian territorial expansion, were responsible for the conspiracy which led to the assassination of FRANCIS FERDINAND in 1914. C. Sforza: *Fifty Years of War and Diplomacy in the Balkans: Pashitch and the Union of the Yugoslavs* (New York, 1940); C. A. Macartney and A. Palmer: *Independent Eastern Europe* (1962).

Patton, George Smith (1885–1945), American General specializing in tank warfare: born at San Gabriel, California, passed out of West Point in 1909 and saw action in Mexico under PERSHING in 1916. While serving as a Colonel on the Western Front, he sent America's first tanks into action against the St Mihiel salient on the Meuse (12 September 1918). Inherited wealth enabled him, between the wars, to enjoy a flamboyant way of life, and his army career made little progress until General MARSHALL, who had served with him in France in 1918, secured his appointment to a newly formed tank brigade in 1940. No Allied commander in the Second World War showed such enthusiasm for tank warfare. Although occasionally in conflict with EISENHOWER for his harsh discipline, Patton was a brilliant tactician in Tunisia and Sicily. In 1944–5 his Third Army swept across France from Brittany, around Paris, up the Marne and through the countryside in which he had fought in 1918, so as to cross the Rhine into northern Bavaria and enter Czechoslovakia, being ordered to halt, for political reasons, west of Prague. He was appointed Military Governor of occupied Bavaria in May 1945, but made no attempt to disguise his feelings of sympathy for the Germans and animosity towards the Russians; and in October he reverted to a purely military command. On 10 December his jeep collided with an army lorry and he was fatally injured, dying eleven days later. G. Patton: *War as I Knew It* (Boston, Mass., 1947); M. Bluemson (ed.): *The Patton Papers* (2 vols) (Boston, Mass., 1972, 1974); H. Essame: *Patton, the Commander* (1974); L. Farrago: *Patton* (New York, 1963).

Paul VI (Giovanni Battista Montini) (1897–1978), Pope from 1963 to 1978: born at Concesio, in Lombardy, the son of a Catholic newspaper editor who was also one of the few 'Catholic Action' parliamentary deputies. Giovanni Montini was ordained priest in 1920 and, apart from a brief period as nuncio in Poland, he served continuously in the papal secretariat of state from 1924 until 1954, making an important statement on the mediatory function of papal diplomacy in 1951 and becoming pro-Secretary of State in 1952. PIUS XII appointed him Archbishop of Milan in 1954. He was elected Pope, in succession to JOHN XXIII, on 21 June 1963. His immediate task was to guide the Second Vatican Council through the remaining three of its four sessions, preventing a conservative revolt against liturgical reform. He continued Pope John's attempt to show the pontiff as a human being, deliberately simplifying all ritual of state, selling his tiara and giving the money to the poor. He travelled, not merely outside Rome, but outside Europe – to Jerusalem (January 1964), India, the UN headquarters in New York, Uganda, South America, Australia and the Far East, as well as visiting Portugal. The Pope spoke out against genocide in Nigeria, against mass bombing in Vietnam and, in old age, offered his person in place of hostages held in the hijacked aircraft by terrorists. He also received in the Vatican, not only the leaders of other churches, but political figures who had, in the past, been unsympathetic to Catholic practice, such as President TITO and the Soviet President, Nikolai Podgorny. Towards the end of his reign ill-health forced him to give less personal direction to affairs and there was some inconsistency of policy. The murder of his friend, Aldo MORO, and the spread of neo-anarchism in the Italian cities much distressed him. He died from a heart attack at Castelgandolfo on 6 August 1978. E. Noel: *The Montini Story: Portrait of Pope Paul VI* (1968); M. P. Guitton: *The Pope Speaks: Dialogues of Paul VI with J. Guitton* (1968).

Pavelić, Ante (1889–1959), Croatian Ustaše founder: a Zagreb lawyer who became bitterly opposed to Yugoslave union in the 1920s, despising the attempts of RADIĆ and MAČEK to achieve an equitable national balance in the kingdom. When King ALEXANDER set up a royal dictatorship in 1929 Pavelić secretly travelled to Italy and Hungary where he organized a terrorist organization, the *Ustaše* (insurrectionaries), seeking an independent fascist Croatian state. The movement employed a Macedonian hitman to assassinate King Alexander in Marseilles in 1934. Pavelić remained in Italy, building up the Ustaše with funds from MUSSOLINI's government, until the invasion of Yugoslavia in 1941 when he returned to Zagreb and became 'leader' (*Poglavnik*) of an independent Croatia. His Ustaše militia, modelled on Nazi SS units, waged a relentless campaign against Serbs, Jews and TITO's partisans. In 1945–6 thousands of alleged supporters of the Ustaše regime were executed in Tito's Yugoslav Federation. Pavelić escaped to Argentina; he survived an assassination attempt and encouraged a revival of Ustaše activity among exiles in Sweden and Australia. He died in Madrid. The memory of Ustaše wartime was exploited by MILOSEVIĆ's Serbs in 1989–91 to discredit TUDJMAN's independent Croatia. P. Sugar (ed.): *Native Fascism in the Successor States, 1918–45* (Santa Barbara, Calif., 1971); A. Palmer: *The Lands Between* (1970).

Pearson, Lester Bowles (1897–1972), Canadian Prime Minister and internationalist: born at Newtonbrook, Ontario, and educated at Toronto University and St John's College, Oxford. He served in the Canadian Army in the First World War and spent several years teaching at Toronto University before entering the Canadian diplomatic service in 1928. For most of the Second World War he was Canada's principal spokesman in Washington, with the rank of ambassador in 1945–6. He played a valuable role in establishing the United Nations Organization. In the closing months of 1946 he entered politics, being returned to the Canadian Parliament as a Liberal by a constituency in Ontario. He was Canada's Foreign Minister (Secretary of State for External Affairs) from 1948 to 1957, presiding over the UN General Assembly in 1952. His statesmanship in helping to reduce the successive international crises over the Middle East and Hungary was recognized by the award of the Nobel Peace Prize for 1957. From 1958 to 1963 he led the Opposition in the

Canadian Parliament to the Progressive Conservative Government of DIEFENBAKER, but when the Liberals won the General Election of April 1963, Lester Pearson was able to form his own government. His five years of office were marked by greater commitment of Canada's forces to UN peace-keeping missions and by attempts to mediate in Vietnam. Internal affairs were plagued by mounting signs of discontent from the French-speaking communities in Quebec, a problem Pearson could not resolve before his retirement from political life in April 1968. Queen Elizabeth conferred on him the Order of Merit in the year before he died, an honour bestowed on only two precious overseas Commonwealth Prime Ministers, SMUTS and Mackenzie KING. L. Pearson: *Memoirs* (3 vols) (1973–5).

Peres, Shimon (1923–), Israeli politician: born in Vilna, Poland; his family emigrated to Palestine when he was 11 and he spent many years in a kibbutz, completing his education at Harvard. When Israel was established he became director of the naval service before serving as Director-General in the Defence Ministry from 1953 to 1959, when he became a Labour deputy in the Knesset (Parliament). In 1974 he was Minister of Defence under RABIN but in 1977 became Chairman of the Labour Party. During the next seven years he led the Opposition to the right-wing Likud Party governments of BEGIN and SHAMIR. As the General Election of July 1984 was indecisive, Peres and Shamir made a political pact, establishing a Labour–Likud coalition in which Peres was Prime Minister for two years (September 1984 to October 1986), with Shamir then heading the government until the 1988 election. The November 1988 election was also indecisive and, as Peres could not gain sufficient support, the coalition pact was renewed: Peres remained deputy Premier to Shamir until March 1990, when Shamir's refusal to make concessions to the Palestinians led to the fall of the government. When the veteran Rabin formed a new government Peres again became deputy Premier; he also served as Foreign Minister, working closely with Rabin to reach compromise agreements over Palestine and the Gaza Strip both with King HUSSEIN and with ARAFAT. On Rabin's assassination in November 1995 Peres resumed the premiership. M. Golan: *Shimon Peres* (1982).

Perez De Cuellar, Javier (1920–), fifth Secretary-General of the United Nations: born and educated in Lima, joined the Peruvian Forign Ministry in 1940 and the diplomatic service in 1944; was a delegate to the first session of the UN General Assembly in 1946. He served as Peruvian ambassador in Switzerland, Venezuela and the USSR but was frequently seconded to the UN for special duties, notably in Cyprus. In 1981 he succeeded WALDHEIM as UN Secretary-General; he worked patiently to ease the problems caused by the Falklands/Malvinas dispute and to secure a ceasefire between Iraq and Iran. Although he gained considerable success in Namibia he could do little in Yugoslavia in his term of office: so much of the conflict was internecine rather than international. He retired in 1991 and was succeeded by Boutros BOUTROS-GHALI.

Peron, Eva ('Evita'), (*née* **Maria Eva Duarte**) (1919–52), the popular idol of the Argentinians from 1945 until her death: born at Los Toldos in Buenos Aires, became an actress possessed of a powerful personality. From 1943 onwards she supported General PERON in his attempts to organize the urban proletariat to back military rule. She personally gained the support of the so-called 'shirtless ones', who frustrated a clumsy American plot to overthrow Peron in October 1945; and it was after this episode that she became Peron's wife, gaining control of newspapers and considerable business interests. Her instinctive response to popular needs diminished the resentment of the Argentinian masses towards her husband's clumsily repressive dictatorship. So far as possible in such a society, she championed women's rights and promoted social welfare through the Eva Peron Foundation, which she established shortly before her premature death (26 July 1952). She remained a cult figure for many poorer Argentinians long after they were disillusioned with her husband's policies. E. Peron: *The Writings of Eva Peron* (Buenos Aires, 1950); R. Bourne: *Political Leaders of Latin America* (1969).

Peron, Juan Domingo (1895–1974), President of Argentina from 1946 to 1955 and 1973 to 1974: born at Lobos in Buenos Aires, participating as a subordinate officer in the military *coup d'état* which overthrew the corrupt regime of President Yrigoyen in 1930. Subsequently he served briefly as military attaché both in Rome and Berlin, studying fascist technique at first hand. In 1943 Colonel Peron helped organize the United Officers Group, which seized power on 4 June. As Minister of Labour and Social Security he was the strong man of the new government, introducing social reforms, and denouncing the exploitation of the Argentinian people by American 'big business'. He was supported in his demagogic campaigns by Eva DUARTE whom he married in 1945, soon after thwarting an American attempt to oust him as a discredited fascist. On 24 February 1946 he was elected President and established what was essentially a dictatorship. His re-election in November 1951 was not unexpected. Soon after Eva Peron's death he began to lose his following, partly because of conflict with the Church leaders over his plans to legalize prostitution and divorce. He was still strong enough to suppress an uprising in June 1955, but he had lost support by concessions to an American company prospecting for oil in Argentina and when, in September 1955, officers rose 'in defence of Catholic Christianity' General Peron hurriedly went into exile in FRANCO's Spain. Peronista support mounted in the comparatively free political climate of the early 1970s and the exiled General returned to Argentina on 20 June 1973, being again elected President in September. His second wife, Maria Estela, was sworn in as Vice-President. By now, however, Juan Peron was a sick man; he suffered a severe heart attack on 29 June 1974 and handed the presidency to his wife. She was confirmed in the presidency when he died two days later but, after a succession of economic crises and urban guerrilla outrages, she surrendered the presidency to the chairman of the Senate in September 1975. She was arrested and imprisoned when a military junta seized power in March 1976. L. Bethell (ed.): *Cambridge History of Latin America*, Vol. 8, *1930–90* (Cambridge, 1991); E. A Crawley: *A House Divided, Argentina 1880–1980* (1984); F. Owen: *Peron, His Rise and Fall* (1957).

Pershing, John Joseph (1860–1948), Commander of the American Expeditionary Force in Europe from 1917 to 1919: born in Linn County, Missouri, and was briefly a schoolteacher before going to West Point. He was commissioned in the cavalry in 1886, seeing immediate active service against GERONIMO and his Apache Indians. Four years later he was engaged in the Sioux Indian campaign in North Dakota. He fought in the Spanish–American war of 1898 and against the rebellion of AGUINALDO in the Philippines, as well as being an observer with the Japanese in their war against Russia (1904–5). In the spring of 1916, as a Brigadier-General, he was given command of a force of twelve thousand men sent into Mexico in revenge for a raid on an American town by the bandit, Pancho VILLA. The expedition was much publicized, even though Villa evaded capture, and Pershing became a newspaper idol, praised for his austerity, tough training routine, and determination. The imminence of war with Germany led to the recall of Pershing's force, and he told Press reporters openly that he wished to command any expedition sent abroad, his father-in-law being an influential senator. He was given command of the American Expeditionary Force on 7 May 1917 and landed in France five weeks later. In this capacity he showed remarkable skill at organization and in carrying out President WILSON's orders that American troops should remain a single US army rather than be absorbed as cannon-fodder in the Allied lines. By July 1918 he was able to put more than a quarter of a million men into the second battle of the Marne, with half a million at St Mihiel in September and considerably more than a million participating in the Meuse-Argonne offensive of the last seven weeks of war. Pershing was honoured with the conferment of the permanent rank of General of the Armies of the United States in 1919. He was Army Chief of Staff from 1921 to 1924. Thereafter he lived in retirement, speaking out resolutely in the summer of 1940 when he urged Franklin ROOSEVELT to send help to Britain 'before it is too late'. J. J. Pershing: *My Experiences in the World War* (New York, 1931).

Pétain, (Henri) Philippe (1856–1951), Marshal of France and Head of State from 1940 to 1945: born near St Omer, as a child, he heard tales of the 1812 campaign from an uncle who was a veteran of Napoleon's army. He graduated from St Cyr into the Chasseurs Alpin in 1878. In August 1914 he was promoted Brigadier and by the following spring was a Corps Commander in Artois. He was given command of the French Second Army soon after the beginning of the battle of Verdun in February 1916, succeeding in holding the city and denying the Germans victory. In 1917 he was appointed Commander-in-Chief of the French Army at a time of widespread mutinies: concern for his men and a refusal to court popularity or curry favour with politicians enabled him to keep the Army together, so as to achieve victory, under the overall command of FOCH, in 1918. Pétain was made a Marshal of France in liberated Metz on 15 December 1918. He commanded the army which defeated the Moroccan Rif rebellion of ABD-EL-KRIM in 1926, was Inspector-General of the Army in 1929 and briefly Minister of War in 1934. So great was his contempt for politicians that he refused to be a candidate for the presidency of the Republic in 1939. He was ambassador in Madrid from March 1939 until summoned back by REYNAUD to serve as deputy Prime Minister on 18 May 1940. He succeeded Reynaud as Prime Minister on 16 June, two days after the fall of Paris, and requested an armistice. Believing that France had been overwhelmed through 'moral decadence', he asked for authoritarian powers from the rump of the French National Assembly meeting at Vichy, a right conceded on 10 July 1940. He sought to preserve freedom of action in unoccupied France and maintained some contacts, through the Americans, with the natural opponents of Nazism until November 1942 when the Germans occupied the whole of France, making him virtually a puppet. He was forced to accompany the Germans across the frontier to Sigmaringen in 1944. In July 1945 he was charged with high treason and sentenced to death after a brief trial in Paris, but the sentence was commuted to life imprisonment. He was detained on the Ile d'Yeu, off the coast of the Vendée. Shortly after his ninety-fifth birthday he was technically freed, but was too frail to leave the island, dying there on 23 July

1951. R. Griffiths: *Marshal Pétain* (1970); H. Lottmann: *Pétain* (New York, 1984).

Pilsudski, Josef (1867–1935), dominant political figure in inter-war Poland: born at Zulowo, near Vilna (then part of Russia). He became a revolutionary student while studying at Kharkov and was exiled to Siberia from 1887 to 1892. His combination of intense patriotism and socialism found an outlet in the clandestine newspaper *Robotnik*, 1894–1900, edited by Pilsudski for the Polish Socialist Party (an exiled body based in Paris). After a few months in prison (1900–1) he escaped to England and France, working his way to Tokyo in 1904 to seek Japanese backing for a Polish revolt during the Russo-Japanese War. By 1910 he was tired of socialist wrangling. Soon afterwards the Austrians permitted him to begin training Polish exiles at Lemberg for operations against Russia, and he even created a small staff college in Cracow. In 1914 he led a Polish brigade, 10,000 strong, against the Tsar's troops. He became Minister of War in the Austro-German puppet administration set up in Warsaw in 1916–17. The Germans, however, distrusted him and he was interned. When Germany collapsed he made his way to Warsaw again and took command of all Polish units so as to check the spread of Bolshevism. He was accepted as provisional head of the new Polish state from November 1918 to December 1922, with the rank of Marshal. In 1920 he pursued the Red Army into the Ukraine and captured Kiev before being thrust back to the Vistula, where he saved Warsaw from the army of TUKHACHEVSKY. His success confirmed his status as the master of Poland. He remained Chief of General Staff until July 1923, when he retired to his country estate at Sulejowek, irritated by the failure of the constitution to give Poland a strong presidential executive. Angered by the instability of the parliamentary governments, he staged a military *coup* in May 1926, in which he was supported by many trade unionists. He remained a virtual dictator until his death on 12 May 1935, serving as Prime Minister in 1927–8 and in 1930, and always holding the key War Ministry. Seventy parliamentarians, from the Left and the Right, were imprisoned in the summer of 1930; and a month before he died Pilsudski harnessed Poland with a constitution providing for a strong executive: 'conducted democracy', as he called it. He was the first European statesman to seek military action against HITLER, proposing to his French ally a preventive war with Germany in the spring of 1933. When this idea was turned down, he reached a ten-year non-aggression pact with Germany as an alternative (January 1934). J. Pilsudski: *Memoirs* (1931); W. F. Reddaway: *Marshal Pilsudski* (1939); A. Polonsky: *The Politics of Independent Poland* (1972).

Pinochet Ugarte, Augusto (1915–), Chilean military dictator: graduated from the Chilean military academy in 1933 and over the following forty years rose to the rank of General. He acquired great influence over junior officers at the War Academy as an instructor from 1954 to 1964 and subsequently as deputy director. As army Commander-in-Chief in September 1973 Pinochet led the military assault on the presidential palace in Santiago in which the democratically elected left-wing president, ALLENDE, was killed. General Pinochet headed Chile's ruling junta for the following seventeen years. His government banned all political parties, brutally repressed socialists and liberals and became so alarmed over potential unrest that his police opened fire on a crowd of more than half a million who sought to attend a Mass of Reconciliation during the Pope's visit to Chile in April 1987. Despite police intimidation, in a plebiscite on 5 October 1988 56 per cent of voters opposed Pinochet's continuance in office. But the General, encouraged by his formidable and ambitious wife Lucia, followed a constitutional right to remain President for eighteen months after an electoral defeat. He retained his military command even after stepping down as President in March 1990. L. Bethell (ed.): *Cambridge History of Latin America*, Vol. 8, *1930–90* (Cambridge 1991); M. A. Garreton: *The Chilean Political Process* (1989).

Pius IX (Giovanni Mastai-Ferretti) (1792–1878). Pope from 1846 to 1878: born at Senigallia, on the Adriatic coast north of Ancona. He was ordained priest in 1819 and was sent on a special papal mission to Chile from 1823 to 1825, helping to consolidate the Church's influence in a republic which had won independence from Spain only in 1818. At the age of 33 he was consecrated Archbishop of Spoleto and was created a Cardinal in 1840. His alleged progressive beliefs led to high expectation of liberal reform when he was elected Pope in succession to the reactionary Gregory XVI on 15 June 1846. The hope that 'Pio Nono' would become presiding patron of an Italian national confederation in 1848 was dashed by his pronouncement that the papacy could not participate in any war against Catholic Austria, the dominant foreign power in the Italian peninsula. Revolutionary unrest in Rome forced Pius IX to seek refuge in Gaeta, in the kingdom of Naples, from November 1848 until April 1850, and he was thereafter protected in Rome by a French garrison until 1870. The constant threat of Italian nationalism to his temporal possessions led the Pope to concentrate on the international aspects of his authority as well as on strengthening his spiritual claims to supremacy. The restoration of Roman Catholic bishops to Britain (1850) and to Holland (1853) was accompanied by concordats with Spain (1851) and Austria (1855) which safeguarded the privileged position of the Church in those lands. His Bull of December 1854, concerning the doctrine of the 'Immaculate Conception', was the first definition of dogma since the Counter Reformation, while his 'Syllabus of Errors' in 1864 condemned trends in contemporary philosophy which seemed to him as if they challenged traditional beliefs. His temporal sovereignty was gradually eroded by CAVOUR: he lost the Romagna in 1859, Umbria and the Marches in 1860. The troops of VICTOR EMMANUEL II entered Rome in September 1870 at a time when the first Vatican Council was nearing the end of its ten-month session. The Council was responsible for publishing the Vatican Decrees, of which the most controversial was a Declaration of Papal Infallibility (18 July 1870). This new dogma was unacceptable to many believers as well as to several foreign governments and led to a long conflict with the authorities in Prussia, the so-called Kulturkampf of 1871–7, eventually settled by agreements between BISMARCK and LEO XIII. In his last years Pius IX was isolated, physically and intellectually, from the changing world around him. He died in the Vatican on 7 February 1878, his reign being considerably longer than that of any other Pope. E. E. Y. Hales: *Pio Nono* (rev. edn 1956); E. L. Woodward: *Three Studies in European Conservatism* (1929).

Pius X (Giuseppe Melchior Sarto) (1835–1914), Pope from 1903 to 1914: born in humble conditions at Riese in northern Venetia, entered a seminary at Padua when he was 15 and was ordained priest in 1858. He spent the next thirty years in Venetia and the Lombard plain, becoming Bishop of Mantua in 1884. He was made a Cardinal in 1893, becoming Patriarch of Venice in the same year. In 1903 he was elected Pope in succession to LEO XIII, making it clear in his first pronouncements that he sought to be a spiritual head of the Church rather than a political leader, like his predecessor. Pope Pius did, indeed, concern himself with spiritual matters, formally recommending the practice of daily Communion in 1905 and of Communion by the young a year later; and he was regarded by his contemporaries as someone endowed with rare qualities of holiness. He was, however, forced to take decisive action politically over attempts by the French government to perpetuate state interference in Church affairs in 1906 and by a similar programme of action in Portugal in 1911. Both in France and Italy he checked the spread of social movements which he regarded as interpreting too liberally the encyclicals of his predecessor, and he vigorously condemned modernist trends in theology. His last weeks were troubled by the mounting war crisis in Europe. He died in Rome on 20 August 1914, and there was an immediate demand for his canonization, miracles having been attributed to his intercessions even during his lifetime. He was eventually beatified in 1951 and canonized three years later. R. Merry del Val: *Memories of Pope Pius X* (1939); J. N. D. Kelly: *Oxford Dictionary of Popes* (1986).

Pius XI (Achille Ambrogio Damiano Ratti) (1857–1939), Pope from 1922 to 1939: born at Desio, near Milan, ordained priest in 1879, specialized in the care and administration of the Ambrosian Library in Milan and the Vatican Library before being sent on an important mission to the newly independent Poland in 1918. A year later he became titular Archbishop of Lepanto and was Cardinal Archbishop of Milan in 1921, at a time when the city was experiencing the full impact of Fascist and Communist violence. He was, however, only briefly in Milan, being elected Pope in succession to BENEDICT XV on 6 February 1922, eight months before MUSSOLINI became Prime Minister. In part to counter the secular appeal of Fascism and Communism, Pope Pius made the sovereignty of Christ a theme of his pontificate, instituting the Feast of Christ the King in 1925 and emphasizing the importance of divine authority in social and educational matters in his encyclical *Quadragesimo Anno* of 1931. Yet his pontificate is best remembered for the Lateran Treaties of February 1929, which recognized the independence of the Vatican City State and included a concordat confirming the unique position of the Catholic Church within the Italian state. In his final years Pope Pius XI recognized the danger from Nazi beliefs in Germany: his encyclical *Mit brennender Sorge* was read from the pulpit of every Catholic church in Germany of Palm Sunday, 1937 (21 March), and it denounced the theoretical basis of Nazi doctrines as contrary to Christian ethics. He died in February 1939. P. Hughes: *Pope Pius the Eleventh* (1937); J. D. Holmes: *The Papacy in the Modern World, 1914–78* (Tunbridge Wells, 1981); D. A. Binchy: *Church and State in Fascist Italy* (1941).

Pius XII (Eugenio Pacelli) (1876–1958), Pope from 1939 to 1958: born and educated in Rome. He was ordained priest in 1899 and two years later entered the papal diplomatic service, spending the next thirty-eight years either in the Vatican secretariat or as a nuncio, and having neither parochial nor diocesan experience. He served BENEDICT XV as Secretary for Extraordinary Ecclesiastical Affairs from 1914 to 1917, when he went to Bavaria as nuncio and was the principal intermediary between Germany and the Vatican over a possible negotiated peace, having a long conversation with Kaiser WILLIAM II in Berlin on 2 July 1917. From 1920 to 1930 he was in Germany, securing agreements over the relations of Church and state in Bavaria (1924) and Prussia (1929). He then served PIUS XI for nine years as Papal Secretary of State, reaching a new agreement with HITLER on Church–State relations in 1933 (which the Nazis repeatedly flouted). He was elected Pope on 2 March 1939. The following Christmas he appealed for world peace, but the entry of Italy into the war in June 1940 posed for him problems which had not troubled his immediate predecessors. As a Roman himself, he shared the dismay and sufferings of the Italian people caused by bombing and by German occupation; and he never took so firm a line against Nazism as had Pius XI, fearing he might provoke even worse conduct. After the war his condemnation of new communist governments in eastern Europe left no room for compromise, while in Italy he backed the Christian Democrats of Alcide DE GASPERI. He was the least neutral Pope since PIUS IX (pontiff from 1846 to 1879) and the last to insist on the full and remote majesty of papal state. In 1950 he condemned existentialist philosophy while finally defining, as a matter of belief, the Assumption of the Virgin Mary, a dogma over which popes had shown reticence in pronouncement for twelve centuries. He died on 9 October 1958 and was succeeded by Pope JOHN XXIII. J. D. Holmes: *The Papacy in the Modern World, 1914–78* (Tunbridge Wells, 1981); S. Friedlander: *Pius XII and the Third Reich* (1966); O. Chadwick: *Britain and the Vatican in the Second World War* (1987).

Pobedonostsev, Konstantin Petrovich (1827–1907), Russian lawyer and tutor to the imperial family: born in Moscow, the son of a professor, and was himself Professor of Constitutional Law at Moscow University from 1860 to 1865, being chosen by Tsar ALEXANDER II to tutor his sons, including the future ALEXANDER III. Pobedonostsev favoured modernization of the Russian state, but according to what he regarded as Russia's traditions rather than in slavish imitations of the West. From 1880 to 1905 he was Procurator of the Holy Synod, making him in effect the government minister controlling the Russian Orthodox Church: he was anti-Semitic, anti-Catholic and anti-Muslim, as well as being opposed to change in the Orthodox Church. In 1901 he signed the formal excommunication of Leo Tolstoy. Pobedonostsev's reactionary influence powerful in Alexander III's reign, continued into the early years of NICHOLAS II, since he had been Nicholas's supervisory tutor. The Tsar's hostility to representative government echoed Pobedonostsev's views: 'Parliaments are the great lie of our times,' Pobedonostsev declared two years after Nicholas's accession. He was responsible for identifying Tsarist autocracy and Orthodox religious practice so closely with each other that the nascent revolutionary movement insisted both should fall together. K. P. Pobedonostsev: *Reflections of a Russian Statesman* (1898); R. F. Byrnes: *Pobedonostsev, his Life and Thought* (Bloomington, Ind., 1968).

Poincaré, Raymond Nicolas Landry (1860–1934), French Prime Minister for seven years and President from 1913 to 1920: born at Bar-le-Duc, a cousin of the distinguished mathematical philosopher, Henri Poincaré (1854–1912). Raymond Poincaré practised law in Paris, was a moderate Republican Deputy in the Chamber from 1887 to 1903 and at 33 became Minister for Education, but only held office for fourteen months. He became a Senator in 1903 and Minister of Finance in 1906. When he formed a Republican–Radical coalition in January 1912, he showed the French people he was a strong leader concerned with problems of national defence and with electoral reform. A year later he was elected President of the Republic, at once seeking to make the presidency politically more influential than it had been for over thirty years. His state visit to St Petersburg in July 1914 was intended by him to have an international significance, affirming the identity of views between two Allied heads of state, the French

President and the Tsar. France's three principal wartime premiers, René Viviani (1863–1925), BRIAND and CLEMENCEAU, effectively prevented Poincaré from changing the role of the presidency. There were clashes between Poincaré and Clemenceau during the 1919 Paris Peace Conference, when he tried to influence the peace terms. After the expiration of his term of office in February 1920, Poincaré took the unusual decision of returning to the Senate, and less than two years later he became Prime Minister again, taking charge of the Foreign Ministry as well. This second premiership (January 1922 to June 1924) was conservative and nationalistic in character, with strong measures to secure German reparations, including the occupation of the Ruhr. A financial crisis brought him back, yet again, as 'the man to save the franc' in July 1926; and his 'government of National Union' imposed such tough economies that France was buffeted less than her neighbours by the recession which began with the Wall Street Crash of 1929. By then, however, Poincaré had retired, finally leaving office in July 1929. G. Wright: *Raymond Poincaré and the French Presidency* (Stanford, Calif., 1942).

Pol Pot (Saloth Sar) (1928–), leader of the Khmer Rouge in Cambodia (Kampuchea): born at Memot and was working on a rubber plantation in French Indo-China by 1939–40. In 1946 he supported HO CHI MINH against the restoration of French authority, becoming a communist guerrilla. From 1968 to 1975 he led the Khmer Rouge partisans against successive governments in the 'Khmer Republic' (Cambodia). In April 1975 he set up a brutal Khmer Rouge administration in Phom Penh which, over four years, caused the deaths of two-and-a-half million Cambodians, including most of the professional classes. He was ousted from power by the Vietnamese in January 1979. With some 30,000 followers he continued to resist the Vietnamese in forests and jungle, even though he formally announced his retirement from active politics in August 1985. A temporary accommodation with Pol Pot's old enemy, Prince SIHANOUK, ended in July 1994 with the setting up of a Khmer Rouge 'alternative government' along the Thai–Cambodian border, where Pol Pot's baneful influence remained menacingly strong. I. Barron and A. Paul: *Peace with Horror* (1977); K. Kiljunen (ed.): *Kampuchea: Decade of the Genocide* (1984).

Pompidou, Georges Jean Raymond (1911–74), President of France from 1969 to 1974: born in the Auvergne, at Montboudif. He was a schoolmaster in Marseilles and Paris during the 1930s, serving in the Resistance, and being recruited in 1944 to the personal staff of DE GAULLE as an adviser on education and economics. For many years he was a director of the Rothschild Bank. He was, once again, called on by de Gaulle in May 1958 to give advice on internal administrative problems. The President found him so competent and discreet that in March 1962 he entrusted him with delicate negotiations at Evian with the Algerian nationalists (notably BEN BELLA) so as to end the Algerian war. A month later Pompidou became Prime Minister. In this role he showed tact and competence, not least in handling the explosive situation caused by strikes and student demonstrations in May 1968. By then, however, he was prepared to act independently of President de Gaulle, who dismissed him in July 1968. Pompidou at once announced he would stand against de Gaulle at the next presidential election. De Gaulle, however, resigned first; and on 15 June 1969 Pompidou was elected President by the National Assembly at the second ballot (the Communists, who had opposed him at the first ballot, abstaining). President Pompidou was more willing than his predecessor to integrate France in the European Community, but ill-health cut short his activity. He died, from a rare form of cancer, on 2 April 1974, and was succeeded by his financial 'wizard', GISCARD D'ESTAING. P. M. Williams and M. Harrison: *Politics and Society in de Gaulle's Republic* (1971).

Prim, Juan (1814–70), Spanish political leader and soldier: born, a lawyer's son, at Reus and served in the volunteer militia until he was 24 when he accepted a commission in the regular army. As a Colonel he participated in the liberal military uprising in Catalonia in 1843 but he subsequently turned against the radicals in Barcelona, a change of heart which won him promotion to the rank of General. In 1847 he was appointed Military Governor of Puerto Rico and was subsequently attached to the French Army in the Crimea as an observer. He then campaigned in Morocco and was commended for courageously leading his troops at the battle of Castillejos (January 1860). A year later he showed political astuteness in command of an expedition to Mexico which protected Spain's commercial interests without provoking war with JUAREZ. Prim married a Mexican heiress and considered himself an expert on Latin American affairs. He was, above all, a political General, seeking to govern Spain as a benevolent dictator supported by the crown. An abortive insurrection in 1866 checked his plans, but he was the prime instigator of a naval and army revolt which forced Queen ISABELLA into exile in September 1868. From then until his death Prim was Minister of War and virtually Prime Minister. He failed to solve two basic problems: he could not pacify rebellious colonists in Cuba; and he could not find a king sufficiently respected in Spain to unify the nation and establish a constitutional monarchy. This search for a king inadvertently made Marshal Prim a person of major importance in Europe, for in offering the crown to a member of the Sigmaringen branch of Prussia's Hohenzollern dynasty, he alarmed the French, precipitating war in 1870 and the fall of NAPOLEON III. The Spanish crown was eventually accepted by an Italian, the Duke of Aosta, who reigned as Amadeo I from November 1870 to February 1873. Prim, however, was shot dead in a Madrid street by republican fanatics on the day Amadeo reached his kingdom (20 December 1870). The possibility of modernizing Spain through the statecraft of an army leader perished with Prim, only to reappear in a new form half a century later with General PRIMO DE RIVERA. R. Carr: *Spain, 1808–1939* (Oxford, 1966).

Primo de Rivera, Miguel (1870–1930), Spanish dictator: born near Cadiz, commissioned in the Army in 1888, and until 1898 served in the Philippines, where his father had been Spain's Governor-General. Subsequently he was mainly in Morocco, attaining the rank of Major-General in 1910. ALFONSO XIII encouraged him in September 1923 to seize power in order to check anarchism and demands for autonomy, notably from the people of Catalonia. Primo dissolved Parliament, governed by martial law and tried to emulate MUSSOLINI. Discontent mounted, showing itself in strikes, and in December 1925 he was forced to relax his dictatorship, continuing to serve Alfonso as Prime Minister until his health gave way at the end of January 1930. He died six weeks later. The basic fault of Primo's system was its artificial imposition from above. His son, José Antonio (1903–36); sought to counter this weakness by founding in 1933 a paternalistic, Catholic fascist movement rooted in popular prejudices, the Falange: he was captured and shot soon after the outbreak of the Spanish Civil War. S. Ben-Ami: *Fascism from Above; the Dictatorship of Primo de Rivera in Spain* (Oxford, 1983); S. G. Payne: *Politics and the Military in Modern Spain* (Stanford, Calif., 1967).

Prinčip, Gavrilo (1894–1918), Bosnian Serb assassin: born at Oblej, Bosnia; educated at schools in Sarajevo and Tuzla, where he became interested in the *Mlada Bosna* (Young Bosnia) anti-Austrian and pro-Serb movement. He travelled to Belgrade in May 1912 ostensibly as a student but made contact with DIMITRIEVIČ and the Black Hand organization. As he was found to be suffering from tuberculosis Prinčip did not complete his studies but spent the winter of 1913–14 in Hadzici, outside Sarajevo, only returning to Belgrade in February 1914. With six other conspirators Prinčip awaited the visit of Archduke FRANCIS FERDINAND to Sarajevo on 28 June 1914. Finding the Archduke's car less than five feet away from him he fired two shots, which killed the Archduke and his wife, thereby precipating the crisis which led to the First World War five weeks later. Prinčip and twenty-four other conspirators were put on trial in Sarajevo in October. He was found guilty of treason and murder but, as he committed the crime before his twentieth birthday, he could not – like three older conspirators – be executed. Prinčip was sentenced to twenty years' imprisonment but died from tuberculosis while incarcerated at Theresienstadt (Terezin), Bohemia, on 28 April 1918. V. Dedijer: *The Road to Sarajevo* (1960); J. Remak: *Sarajevo* (1959); L. Cassells: *The Archduke and the Assassin* (1984).

Pu-Yi, Alsin Gioro (1906–67), last Chinese Emperor of the Qing dynasty and titular Emperor of Manchukuo: acceded on 2 December 1908 at the age of 2, following the death of his uncle, Emperor Guang Xu (Zai Tian), (1871–1908). Pu-Yi was proclaimed Emperor Xuan Tong (Hsuan T'ung) but sovereignty was exercised by a Regency, headed by Zai Tian's widow until the Chinese Republic was proclaimed (1 January 1912). The boy emperor abdicated on 12 February 1912; he was allowed to live in a summer palace outside Peking (Beijing), where his education was supervised by an English tutor who called his pupil 'Henry', the first name generally accorded to Pu-Yi. On 1 July 1917 he was briefly reinstated by a monarchist warlord, Zhang Xun, but he 'reigned' for a mere eleven days before fleeing the capital and eventually finding sanctuary in the Japanese quarter of Tientsin. When the Japanese established the puppet state of Manchukuo (Manchuria) in February 1932 they invited Pu-Yi to become Chief Executive, proclaiming him hereditary Emperor of Manchukuo eleven months later: he was crowned on 1 March 1934, ruling as the Japanese puppet Emperor Kang Teng until he was captured by Soviet troops on 20 August 1945. He was imprisoned in Siberia until 1950, when he was handed over to the Chinese Communists who detained him for political re-education until 1959, when he was allowed to work in the botanical gardens of Beijing, spending his last years as an assistant with the historical archives department. H. Pu-Yi: *From Emperor to Citizen: the Autobiography of Alsin Gioro Pu-Yi* (Oxford, 1987); M. C. Wright (ed.): *China in Revolution: the First Phase, 1900–1913* (1968).

Q

Quezon, Manuel Luis (1878–1944), Filipino national leader: born near Manila, the son of Roman Catholic schoolteachers who hoped he would be a priest. He joined AGUINALDO in rebellion against the Spanish and later against the Americans. By the time he was 25 he had gained experience of running a plantation belonging to the Church, and he determined to enter the administration, in American service in the first place. He was admitted to the bar in 1903 and sat in the Philippine assembly from 1907 to 1909, when he was sent to Washington as Resident Commissioner for the Philippines, with the specific task of explaining Filipino needs to Congress. When Quezon returned to Manila in 1916 he was a national hero for having persuaded the Democratic Congress to pass legislation which allowed the Philippines a senate, with control over taxation and expenditure. Quezon was recognized as leader of the National Party and became President of the Philippine Senate. Republican Party policy towards the Philippines was, however, unsympathetic to Quezon's programme, and no progress was made until Franklin ROOSEVELT became President. In 1935 Quezon was at last elected the first President of the Philippine Commonwealth; and for the next six years he ruled the islands firmly, controlling the nominations for every appointment and beginning to improve education, food production, welfare and housing. The Philippines were easily overrun by the Japanese early in 1942 and Quezon followed MACARTHUR into exile, first in Australia and later in Washington. There he was given a seat on the Pacific War Council and recognized as head of a member government of the United Nations. He died in 1944 before his homeland was liberated; a district north east of Manila was named after him, becoming in 1949 the administrative capital of the Philippines. I. P. Caballero and M. de G. Concepcion: *Quezon* (Manila, 1935).

Quisling, Vidkun (1887–1945) puppet Prime Minister of Norway under German occupation: born the son of a Lutheran pastor at Fyredal in Telemark. So remarkable was his career at the Norwegian Military Academy that he became a General Staff officer at the age of 24, observing the Russo-Finnish conflicts of 1918–20 as a military attaché. In 1923 he retired from the army with the rank of Major and joined the Agrarian Party, entering the Norwegian Parliament (Storting) and becoming Minister of Defence in 1931. Soon after HITLER came to power in Germany, Quisling resigned from the Storting and from the Agrarians, founding in May 1933 a National Unity movement in close imitation of the Nazis. He travelled to Berlin in December 1939 and discussed a possible *putsch* in Oslo with Hitler personally. Six days before the German attack on Norway in 1940 he confided defence plans to German agents in Copenhagen. He assisted the Germans to establish their administration in Oslo and was officially recognized by the Germans and their allies as Norway's Prime Minister on 1 February 1942. When the war ended, he was charged with high treason and executed (October 1945). Even as early as the summer of 1940 British newspapers were using his surname as an eponym for a member of any enemy-sponsored puppet government, a usage that outlives its ill-advised originator.

O. K. Hoidal: *Quisling, a Study in Treason* (Oslo, 1989); P. M. Hayes: *The Career and Political Ideas of Vidkun Quisling* (Newton Abbot, 1971).

R

Rabin, Yitzhak (1922–95), Israeli soldier and Prime Minister: born in Jerusalem, the son of Russian immigrants; his mother, who died when he was 15, was an active member of Haganah, the Jewish defence movement in Palestine. Rabin studied engineering and agriculture but, in revulsion at Nazi persecution, turned to a military career and completed his training as an officer cadet in England. He fought in defence of the new Israel in 1948–9, rising to become Chief of Staff in 1964 and led the army in the brilliantly successful Six-Day War (1967). From 1968 to 1973 General Rabin was ambassador in Washington, but then entered politics; he was head of the Israeli Labour Party and Prime Minister from 1974 to 1977 and Defence Minister in the PERES coalition of 1984. He returned as Prime Minister in July 1992 and, through American mediation, patiently negotiated a preliminary settlement of the Palestine Problem with King HUSSEIN and ARAFAT, despite threats from Jewish fundamentalists. On 4 November 1995 he was fatally wounded by a student gunman belonging to one of these extremist groups as he was leaving a peace rally in Tel Aviv. Y. Rabin: *The Rabin Memoirs* (1979); D. Horowitz (ed.): *Rabin, Soldier of Peace* (1996).

Radić, Stepan (1875–1928), Croatian peasant leader: born to impoverished peasants near Zagreb, receiving his early schooling under church patronage but gaining admission to the Zagreb Gymnasium through his high intelligence. He visited and studied in Russia, France and Prague, developing ideas for reforming landownership. For participating in an anti-Magyar riot in Zagreb in 1895 he was banned from the city but had recovered his rights by 1902 when – with his brother Ante (who died young) – he founded the Croatian Peasant Party to safeguard national and sectional interests within Austria-Hungary. He supported war against the pan-Serbs of Belgrade in 1914 but from 1917 onwards accepted the need for a post-war South Slav state, provided it was a federal republic rather than an extension of Serbia. In 1919 he was arrested in Zagreb so as to prevent him from presenting a petition to the Paris Peace Conference. When elections were held for the Yugoslav parliament in 1923 the peasant party had a landslide victory within Croatia but Radić refused to participate in parliamentary affairs; he travelled through Europe, championing Croatian peasant independence and in Moscow backed the earliest of Communist 'common fronts', a Peasant International (July 1924). On his return to Zagreb in December 1924 he was imprisoned as a 'Bolshevik agent' on PAŠIĆ's orders. Seven months later he was transferred from prison to Belgrade and appointed Minister of Public Instruction in a coalition government. He resigned from this post on 1 April 1926, after a rousing speech which denounced his Cabinet colleagues as swine. For two years he encouraged his party to block parliamentary business in Belgrade until, on 20 June 1928, an exasperated Montenegrin Deputy fired his revolver at the Opposition benches, killing two Croat Deputies outright and wounding Radić, who died on 2 August. Civil war in Yugoslavia was narrowly averted: King ALEXANDER established a royal dictatorship; MAČEK, Radić's successor, led the Croatian Peasant Party with greater circumspection. J. Tomasevich: *Peasants, Politics and Economic Change in Yugoslavia* (Stanford, Calif., 1965); I. Avakumonić: *History of the Communist Party of Yugoslavia*, Vol. 1 (Aberdeen, 1964).

Rafsanjani, Hoijatolesem Ali Akbar Hasehemi (1936–), Iranian President: born at Rafsanjan, educated at Qum and from 1978 onwards was a devoted supporter of KHOMEINI in the Islamic Republican Party. He became Speaker of the Majlis (Iranian parliament) and was largely responsible for drafting successive versions of the constitution, 1980–7. Although he was nominal Commander-in-Chief of the armed forces in 1988–9 he favoured peace and cautiously sought improved relations with the West. Eight weeks after Khomeini's death he was elected President of the Islamic Republic (28 July 1989); he was re-elected in June 1993, despite losing some popular support by promoting free market economic reforms.

Rahman, Abdul, Tunku of Malaysia: see *Abdul Rahman Putra.*

Rahman, Sheikh Mujibur (1920–75), founder of Bangladesh: born at Tongipara, east Bengal, became a lawyer and in 1954 set up the Awami League to campaign for a Bangladesh state in 'East Pakistan'. He was arrested on several occasions and in August 1971 charged with high treason by the Pakistan authorities. Indian military intervention secured his release and he was welcomed in Dacca as *de facto* President of Bangladesh on 10 January 1972. He declined the presidency, preferring to be Prime Minister of his government in which he sought to give the new Bangladesh both parliamentary democracy and a socialist co-operative economic structure. To accomplish this double revolution at a time of grave famine was beyond him, however. In January 1975 he was forced to assume dictatorial powers in the hopes of imposing land reform but he aroused the hostility of landowning junior officers, who murdered him and many members of his family during a military *coup* on 15 August 1975. M. Rahman: *Bangladesh Today: an Indictment and a Lament* (1978); C. P. O'Donnell: *Bangladesh: Biography of a Muslim* Nation (Boulder, Colo., 1986).

Rákosi, Matyas (1892–1971), Hungarian Communist leader from 1945 to 1956: born in Budapest of Jewish parentage, helped to establish the short-lived Communist regime of 1919 in Hungary, escaping to the Soviet Union. In 1925 he returned to Hungary to organize Communist cells of resistance to HORTHY. He was imprisoned for eight years in 1927 and re-arrested in 1935 and sentenced to life imprisonment. In November 1940 he was one of two Communists exchanged in a deal with the Russians, the Hungarians receiving in exchange some national revolutionary flags captured by Tsarist troops in 1849. Rákosi became head of the committee of Hungarian exiles in Moscow in 1941. In 1945 he was appointed Vice-Premier in Hungary, in effect controlling Communist Party tactics, wearing down opposing factions in the progressive coalition governments, until in August 1952 he became Prime Minister himself. His rigid Stalinism and manipulation of the brutal secret police, AVO, made him both hated and feared. His policies were unacceptable to KHRUSCHEV and in the summer of 1956 he gave up all his posts in Hungary so as to take a health cure in the Soviet Union, he died where fifteen years later. H. Seton-Watson: *The East European Revolutions* (rev. edn 1956); G. Mikeš: *The Hungarian Revolution* (1957).

Rasputin, Grigori (1871–1916), Russian mystic leader; born near Tobolsk, at Pokrovskoye. By the age of 30 he was known as a 'holy man' with powers of healing. From November 1905 until his death he was frequently with the imperial Russian family because of a hypnotic healing power which he exercised over the haemophiliac heir to the throne, the Tsarevich Alexis (1904–18). From 1911 onwards it was believed in St Petersburg that Rasputin was influencing the appointment of ministers and generals. His dissolute private life, and especially his violent fits of drunkenness, were a major scandal by 1912, and he was known to be protected by NICHOLAS II and the Tsarina. Suspicion he was in German pay led in December 1916 to his murder by a group of aristocrats, headed by Prince Felix Yusupov (who was related by marriage to Tsar Nicholas). B. Pares: *The Fall of the Russian Monarchy* (1939); R. J. Minney: *Rasputin* (1972).

Rathenau, Walther (1867–1922), German industrialist and politician: born of Jewish parentage in Berlin, becoming principal director of the vast electrical trust, AEG, which his father had founded. With Kaiser WILLIAM II's support he was given control of Germany's war economy in 1916, seeking to counter the effects of manpower shortage and blockade by systematic organization of labour needs and the distribution of raw materials. On the establishment of the Weimar Republic he founded a Democratic Party, to counter the parties of the Left, the Catholic Centre, and the anti-Weimar Right. From May to December 1921 he was Minister of Reconstruction, seeking for Weimar Germany the methods of recovery employed by ADENAUER and ERHARD after the Second World War. He continued this work as Minister of Foreign Affairs in 1922 and within eleven months had gained valuable financial agreements with France and America, and established cautious co-operation between Weimar Germany and Soviet Russia (Treaty of Rapallo, 16 April 1922). His dispassionate intellectual brilliance alienated many of his countrymen, and he was assassinated in a Berlin suburb by anti-Semitic proto-Nazis of 24 June 1922. H. Kessler: *Walther Rathenau* (1929); H. Pogge von Strandmann: *Walther Rathenau, Notes and Diaries, 1907–1922* (Oxford, 1985).

Rawlings, Jerry John (1947–), Ghanaian political leader: born in Accra, the son of a Scottish father and an Ewe mother. He was educated at Achimota College and the Ghanaian Military Academy, being commissioned as a pilot officer in 1969. As a flight-lieutenant he was the principal organizer of a peaceful *coup* in June 1979 which overthrew the ruling Supreme Military Council. Six senior officers were publicly executed outside Accra before civilian rule was restored and Rawlings retired. The persistence of corruption induced Rawlings to lead a second *coup* on 31 December 1981. He then headed a Provisional National Defence Council which held supreme power until the introduction of a multiparty constitution in 1992. Rawlings duly won the subsequent presidential election. D. I. Ray: *Ghana, Politics, Economics and Society* (1986).

Rayburn, Samuel Taliaferro (1882–1961), Speaker of the US House of Representatives for seventeen years: born in Tennessee and practised law in Texas before being elected to the House of Representatives as a Democrat in 1912. He remained a member of the House until he died, a record period of service for any congressman. During the 1930s he sponsored some of the most controversial New Deal legislation, but his fame rests upon his skill as a Speaker, in managing the business of the House for more years than any predecessor. P. Brenner: *The Limits and Possibilities of Congress* (New York, 1983).

Reagan, Ronald (1911–), President of the United States from 1981 to 1989: born at Tampico, Illinois, and became a sports reporter after leaving Eureka College. He went to Hollywood in 1937: over the following twenty-seven years Reagan appeared in more than twenty films, as well as serving in the US Army Air Force from 1942 to 1946. He also played in his own television series, *Death Valley Days*, 1962–4. His best film, the melodrama *King's Row*, was released in 1942 and he used a line from it, *Where's the Rest of Me?* as the title of his (pre-political) autobiography, published in 1965, the year he turned seriously to Republican politics. He was Governor of California from 1967 to 1974. Twice he unsuccessfully sought the Republican presidential nomination (1968 and 1976). At his third attempt (the Detroit Convention of July 1980) his well-managed campaign enabled him to brush aside eleven other contenders. In the Presidential Election of November 1980 – with only 53 per cent of the electorate voting – he defeated the incumbent President, CARTER, and won forty-four states. On 30 March 1981, ten weeks after entering office, he was wounded in an assassination attempt outside a Washingtn hotel. His anti-Communism and strict monetarist policies enabled Reagan to achieve a close working partnership with the THATCHER government in Britain and in 1984 he gained even greater electoral success, at the expense of the Democrat candidate, MONDALE. His second administration (1985–9) was marred by inflation at home and tension with GADDAFI in Libya, as well as mounting involvement in Nicaragua and the Persian Gulf. He was succeeded by his Vice-President, George BUSH. R. Reagan: *An American Life* (1990); L. Cannon: *President Reagan: the Role of a Lifetime* (1991); F. I. Greenstein (ed.): *The Reagan Presidency* (Baltimore, Md., 1986).

Reynaud, Paul (1878–1966), French Prime Minister in 1940: born at Barcelonnette in the Basses-Alpes, became a barrister, gained the Croix de Guerre in the First World War and was a Deputy for his native district from 1919 to 1924, returning to the Chamber in 1928 as Deputy for a section of Paris. Politically he was slightly to the Right of centre, frequently showing an independence of party labels. Among his ministerial responsibilities were Finance (1930), the Colonies (1931–2), Justice (1938) and another important term as Minister of Finance under DALADIER from November 1938 to March 1940. Reynaud was consistently anti-Nazi, trying to alert the French to the threat from HITLER in the 1930s much as was Winston CHURCHILL in England. However, he never enjoyed Churchill's prestige nor did he command any large following: he was physically small and treated many of his political colleagues with contempt; they responded by calling him 'Micky', after Walt Disney's cartoon mouse. It was thanks largely to his formidable mistress, Comtesse Hélène de Portes, that he came to dominate the Daladier government in the winter of 1939–40, taking over the premiership on 20 March 1940. In two months he found it impossible to change the defensive mood of the French army, and he had no opportunity to inspire confidence as a war leader. He sought to strengthen his government by bringing in Marshal PÉTAIN as Deputy Prime Minister while appointing the veteran WEYGAND as Commander-in-Chief; but their insistence on seeking an armistice after the fall of Paris led to his resignation (16 June 1940). He was unable to join his former Under-Secretary, General DE GAULLE, abroad – not least because on 28 June he was hurt in a car crash (in which the Comtesse de Portes was killed). Reynaud was arrested three months later and, with other leading figures in the 1930s, was charged with failing to prepare France for war. At his trial in Riom he turned the tables on his accusers. The Germans imprisoned him, mainly in Austria, from 1943 to 1945. He re-entered politics, and was Minister of Finance again in 1948. He was invited to form a government in 1953, but failed to win support from enough groups. After the establishment of the Fifth Republic in 1958 he remained President of the Finance Committee of the National Assembly. Marriage at the age of 70 brought Reynaud happiness, and a young family. He died in Paris in September 1966, a few weeks short of his eighty-eighth birthday. P. Reynaud: *In the Thick of the Fight, 1939–45* (1955); A. Horne: *To Lose a Battle; France 1940* (1969).

Rhee, Syngman (1875–1965), first President of the Korean Republic: born near Kaesong, his family having links with Korea's ruling dynasty. He was educated at a Methodist school in Seoul and accepted Christian beliefs, rejecting the Confucianism of his childhood. In 1896 he joined the Independence Club, at a time of increasing Japanese penetration of Korea. From 1898 to 1904 he was imprisoned for campaigning in favour of democratic reform. On his release he travelled to the USA and completed his education at Harvard and Princeton, returning to Seoul in 1910 to teach for two years at a Methodist mission school. He encouraged resistance to the Japanese, who annexed Korea in 1910, and in 1919 became President of a provisional Korean government in exile. For more than twenty years he lived in the USA, where his views on Japanese affairs won him high respect: his principal book, *Japan Inside Out*, was published shortly before the attack on Pearl Harbor. Rhee returned to Korea, with American backing, in 1945 and was duly elected President of the Republic of Korea in 1948, although forced to limit his authority to the region south of the thirty-eighth parallel as the Soviet Union had installed KIM IL SUNG as head of the Democratic People's Republic in North Korea. Rhee received UN backing when the North Koreans invaded South Korea in June 1950. He remained President until April 1960, his rule marked by increasing authoritarianism and dubious electoral practices. His return for a fourth term of office on 15 March 1960 led to student protests against ballot rigging: martial law was proclaimed, the police firing on demonstrators. This slaughter of more than a hundred civil rights marchers finally deprived Rhee of American backing. On 27 April 1960 he resigned office, retiring into private life and observing the establishment of a military government under General Park Chung Hee (1917–79), who had fought in the Japanese army during the Second World War. R. T. Oliver: *Syngman Rhee* (1955); B. Cummings: *The Origins of the Korean War* (Princeton, N.J., 1981).

Rhodes, Cecil John (1853–1902), British imperialist and benefactor: born in Bishop's Stortford, Hertfordshire, the son of a vicar. The threat of tuberculosis induced him as a young man to settle in Natal, making a fortune in diamonds and founding the De Beers Consolidated Mines Company in 1888. At the same time he founded the British South Africa Company in order to develop the region later known as Rhodesia. From 1890 to 1896 he was Prime Minister of Cape Colony, being forced to resign office because of his attempts to encourage a revolt in the Transvaal through his agent, JAMESON. His ideal of a federated and white-dominated South Africa ran counter to the interests of the old Boers, such as KRUGER, although many younger Boer leaders (notably SMUTS) respected Rhodes's vision, if not his methods. During the Boer War Rhodes was besieged in Kimberley where he helped organize the defences. He died at Muizenburg on 26 March 1902, leaving his splendid house above Capetown, Groote Schuur, to 'the prime ministers of a united South Africa', an ideal not to be realized for eight years. Much of Rhodes £6 million fortune was left to Oxford University, for he had been admitted to Oriel College in 1876 (when older and wealthier than most undergraduates) and he remained well-disposed towards his university and his college. His will established scholarships at Oxford available to men (and later women) from the British overseas empire, from the United States and from Germany since (as he wrote in 1901). 'A good understanding between England, Germany and the United States of America will secure the peace of the world, and educational relations form the strongest tie.' The number of Commonwealth scholars varied from twenty in 1903 to forty in 1973, while American Rhodes scholars remained at thirty-two a year: there were five German scholars annually from 1903 to 1913, two from 1929 to 1938, and two from West Germany from 1959. Several German Rhodes scholars were in the resistance movement to HITLER. J. G. Lockhart and C. M. Woodhouse: *Rhodes* (1963); T. Pakenham: *The Scramble for Africa* (1991); H. Baker: *Cecil Rhodes* (Oxford, 1934).

Ribbentrop, Joachim von (1893–1946), German Foreign Minister from 1938 to 1945: born at Wesel in the Rhineland. He served in the cavalry in the First World War, became a wine merchant, and joined the Nazi Party in the 1920s, being admitted to HITLER's personal circle from 1932 onwards since he could boast of contacts in foreign lands. He was a Nazi Party adviser on foreign affairs from 1933 to 1936, occasionally being employed on special diplomatic missions, such as the conclusion of a naval agreement with Britain in 1935. From 1936 to 1938 he was German ambassador in London, alienating many prominent figures who were sympathetic to Germany's grievances by his arrogance. He became Foreign Minister in Berlin on 4 February 1938, holding office until the collapse of the Reich in 1945. His main achievement was the Nazi–Soviet Non-Aggression Pact, which he signed with MOLOTOV and STALIN in Moscow on 23 August 1939. He was put on trial as a war criminal at Nuremberg and was hanged on 16 October 1946, principally for 'having conspired to wage aggressive war'. J. von Ribbentrop: *The Ribbentrop Memoirs* (1954); J. Weitz: *Hitler's Diplomat* (1991).

Ridgway, Matthew Bunker (1895–1993), American General, commanding UN forces in Korea from 1950 to 1951: born at Fort Monroe, Virginia. He graduated in 1917 from West Point and between the wars followed the customary career of a US army officer, with a spell of service in the Philippines breaking a succession of regimental postings across the States. In the late 1930s he accompanied General MARSHALL on a special military mission to Brazil. After two years as a Colonel in the war plans division of the US War Department, he became Commander of the eighty-second Airborne Division for the invasion of Sicily in 1943, subsequently holding a similar posting for D-day in Normandy, 1944. From August 1944 to May 1945 he commanded an airborne corps, which helped check the German offensive in the Ardennes (January 1945). He was then given operational commands in the Philippines, as well as in Korea in 1950. On 11 April 1951 President TRUMAN appointed him to succeed to MACARTHUR as Commander-in-Chief of American and UN troops in Korea. He was responsible for checking the North Korean offensive of May 1951 and for the conduct of the difficult Panmunjom armistice talks. On 28 April 1952 he succeeded EISENHOWER as Supreme Allied Commander in Europe, a post he held until May 1953 when he became a much-respected Army Chief of Staff in Washington, retiring in 1955. M. B. Ridgway: *The Korean War* (1965); D. Rees: *Korea, the Limited War* (1964).

Roberts, Lord (Frederick Sleigh Roberts) (1832–1914), British Field Marshal: born in Cawnpore, educated at Clifton, Eton and Sandhurst, and commissioned in the Bengal artillery in 1851, taking part in the suppression of the Indian Mutiny and winning the Victoria Cross for his courage at the siege of Lucknow in 1858. His reputation for heroic leadership continued in campaigns in Abyssinia (1868) and against the Lushai (1871–2), but his fame was established in Afghanistan in 1878–80 where, after asserting British control of the country, he was called to relieve the besieged garrison at Kandahar, in August 1880. His three-week march with 10,000 men from Kabul to rout Ayub Khan outside Kandahar made him one of the most respected heroes of late Victorian England. From 1885 to 1893 he was Commander-in-Chief in India. He had been knighted in 1879, created a baronet in 1881 and was raised to the peerage in 1892, receiving his Field Marshal's baton in 1895, when he became Commander-in-Chief in Ireland. 'Bobs' was a diminutive popular idol at the turn of the century. He was sent as Commander-in-Chief in South Africa in January 1900, with KITCHENER as his Chief of Staff, sweeping victoriously through the Boer lands and occupying Johannesburg at the end of August. He returned to London early in 1901, was created Eart Roberts of Kandahar, Pretoria and Waterford, and was Commander-in-Chief of the British army until the post was abolished in 1904, when he retired. He remained an active campaigner in favour of compulsory military service. In November 1914 he crossed to France to inspect Indian troops newly arrived for service on the Western Front, but at the age of 82 the physical strain was too great for him and he died before returning across the Channel. Lord Roberts: *Forty-One Years in India* (1897); H. de Watteville: *Lord Roberts* (Glasgow, 1938).

Romero Y Galdames, Oscar Arnulfo (1917–80), Salvadorean Archbishop: born at Ciudad Barrios in eastern El Salvador. He was ordained a Roman Catholic priest in 1942, consecrated a bishop in 1970 and became Archbishop of San Salvador in 1977. Although he was by temperament a conservative traditionalist, suspicious of liberal progressives, Archbishop Romero favoured social reform and was an outspoken critic of the political violence of extremists of both Left and Right. His courageous championship of human rights won him admiration in the United States and Europe. In March 1980 he was shot down by four gunmen at the high altar of the cathedral in San Salvador; his assassins appear to have been members of a right-wing paramilitary group. The violence continued: more than twenty men and women were killed when gunmen fired into a crowd of 50,000 mourners in the piazza outside the cathedral during the Requiem Mass on 30 March. The Archbishop's assassination strengthened popular support for the Christian Democrats under DUARTE. O. A. Romero: *The Church is All of You* (1984); P. Erdozain: *Archbishop Romero: Martyr of El Salvador* (Guildford, 1981).

Rommel, Erwin (1891–1944), German soldier, best known as commander of the 'Afrika Korps' from 1941 to 1943: born at Heidenheim in Württemberg and educated at Tübingen. He was commissioned in the infantry in 1912, won the Iron Cross in France in January 1915, and showed great daring with a mountain battalion in Romania in 1916. He gained the highest German award for his courage and initiative at the battle of Caporetto in October 1917, when he cut off the Italians and took nearly 10,000 prisoners and over eighty field guns. Rommel taught at the War Academy from 1935 to 1938, and in February 1939 took command of an armoured division, even though he was basically an infantry man. On 10–11 May 1940 his Seventh Panzer Division led the initial break through the Ardennes and across the Meuse, advancing to Cambrai and Arras by 18 May. Within six weeks he had taken Le Havre, crossed the Seine to Cherbourg, and captured over 97,000 prisoners. His remarkable series of victories in the Western Desert in 1941, forcing the British back to the Alamein lines, ended with the advance of the armies of ALEXANDER and MONTGOMERY in 1942–3. From February to May 1944 he was responsible for improving defences along the Atlantic coast to check an Allied invasion of France. He commanded Army Group B defending Normandy in June 1944, but was wounded near St Lo in an air attack on his staff car (17 July 1944). Disillusionment with HITLER's regime led him to associate with some of the conspirators who tried to assassinate Hitler three days after Rommel was wounded. It is not clear how deeply Rommel was implicated, nor is his exact fate known: he was apparently either murdered by Gestapo agents or forced to commit suicide on 14 October 1944. B. Liddell Hart (ed.): *The Rommel Papers* (1953); D. Young: *Rommel. The Desert Fox* (1950); C. Douglas-Home: *Rommel* (1973); D. Fraser: *Knight's Cross* (1985).

Roosevelt, (Anna) Eleanor (1884–1962), America's 'first lady' from 1933 to 1945 and a UN executive from 1947 to 1951: born in New York, the daughter of a brother of Theodore ROOSEVELT. She was educated for three years in England, but spent much of her childhood in the very wide Roosevelt family circle. She married her distant cousin, Franklin ROOSEVELT, on 17 March 1905, being given away at the ceremony by the then President of the United States, her uncle Theodore. Although serving as a hostess for her husband both in New York state politics and at Washington, Eleanor Roosevelt was also an active campaigner herself for humanitarian causes. She expressed her views forcefully, and with much moral courage, as a newspaper columnist both during and after her husband's presidency; and she visited London during the war (October–November 1942) as his personal envoy. Her desire to protect minorities and to further international understanding made her accept President Truman's suggestion that she should be a delegate to the first assembly of the United Nations in 1946. From 1947 to 1951 she was Chairman of the UN Human Rights Commission. E. Roosevelt: *This Is My Story* (New York, 1937), *This I Remember* (New York, 1949), *On My Own* (New York, 1958); J. P. Lash: *Eleanor and Franklin* (1972); *Eleanor; the Years Alone* (1973).

Roosevelt, Franklin Delano (1882–1945), President of the United States from 1933 to 1945: born at Hyde Park in New York state, educated at Groton School, Massachusetts, at Harvard and at Columbia Law School. He practised briefly as a Wall Street lawyer before entering politics as a Democrat, and sitting as Senator in the New York state assembly at Albany from 1911 to 1913. He had already, in 1905, married his distant cousin, Eleanor ROOSEVELT, niece of the Republican President Theodore ROOSEVELT, whom they knew as 'Uncle Ted'. From 1913 to 1920 Franklin Roosevelt was Assistant Secretary to the Navy in the WILSON administration, briefly visiting Europe in July 1918 to discuss naval co-operation with the Allied leaders, including LLOYD GEORGE and CLEMENCEAU. In 1920 he was running-mate for the Democratic presidential candidate, Governor Cox, campaigning largely on the need for America to support the League of Nations: the Republican team, HARDING and COOLIDGE, won the election. After this defeat Roosevelt became a businessman in New York City but was crippled by poliomyelitis in August 1921. He recovered sufficiently to win the election for Governor of New York in 1928. He then won the Democratic nomination for the presidential election of 1932 and took forty-two states, leaving the incumbent President, HOOVER, with a mere six states.

Roosevelt's first administration was primarily concerned with combating the Depression, especially through the 'New Deal', a programme of public works, of government checks on high finance and banking, of support to agriculture, and of improved labour relations. The success of the New Deal in cutting unemployment enabled Roosevelt to achieve an even greater electoral victory in 1936. His second administration was hampered by conflict with the judiciary (caused by the President's determination to enlarge the Supreme Court, which had ruled against certain New Deal legislation). The worsening crisis in Europe caused divisions within America, where 'F. D. R.' was opposed by a strong isolationist tradition whenever he spoke out against the dictators. In 1940 he broke American constitutional convention by standing for a third term of office, defeating WENDELL WILLKIE. This fresh evidence of national support enabled Roosevelt to strengthen Anglo-American collaboration in 1940–1, supplying 'Lend-Lease' aid to any nation whose defence he considered essential to American security. The Japanese attack on Pearl Harbor (December 1941), followed by German and Italian declarations of war, enabled Roosevelt to preside over a series of conferences which aimed at greater inter-Allied unity. The effect of the President's intervention in strategic affairs was to heighten American military and naval domination of war policies, marked by the ascendancy of EISENHOWER in North Africa and Europe and of MACARTHUR in the Far East. Roosevelt conferred with Winston CHURCHILL at Casablanca, Cairo and Quebec, and both men met STALIN at Teheran (November 1943) and Yalta (February 1945). On many occasions Roosevelt used his authority to overrule decisions of the military and naval chiefs, firmly insisting that victory in Europe must have priority over the defeat of Japan. In retrospect, he appears to have overestimated his ability to 'get on with Uncle Joe' (Stalin) and to have exaggerated the power and abilities of CHIANG KAI-SHEK.

When Roosevelt was elected for a fourth term, in November 1944, his physical strength was ebbing but he wished to 'see the war through' and to help establish the United Nations Organisation as a peace-keeping institution. On 12 April 1945 he suffered a cerebral haemorrhage while resting at Warm Springs, Georgia, and died within a few hours of losing consciousness. The leadership of the United States passed to his little-known Vice-President, Harry S TRUMAN. F. Friedel: *Franklin D. Roosevelt* (3 vols) (Boston, Mass., 1952–6), *Franklin D. Roosevelt, a Rendezvous with Destiny* (Boston, Mass., 1990); A. M. Schlesinger Jnr: *The Age of Roosevelt* (2 vols) (1957, 1958); J. M. Burns: *Roosevelt: the Lion and the Fox* (New York, 1956), *Roosevelt: the Soldier of Freedom* (1971).

Roosevelt, Theodore (1858–1919), President of the United States from 1901 to 1909: born in New York City and educated at Harvard before toughening his character and physique on a ranch in Dakota. He entered Republican politics in his home state and was, for some eighteen months, Assistant Secretary to the Navy in the first MCKINLEY administration, resigning in order to organize a volunteer force, the 'Rough Riders', whom he led in Cuba in 1898 with the rank of Lieutenant-Colonel. After a brief term as Governor of New York (1899–1900), he became McKinley's running-mate for the 1900 election. When McKinley died from gunshot wounds in September 1901, Vice-President Roosevelt automatically succeeded him in the White House. 'T. R.' favoured an active presidency, denouncing monopolistic trusts in domestic affairs and pursuing a forward policy over problems of the American continent. He was prepared (1903–4) to send warships to Panama in order to obtain consent for the construction, under favourable political terms, of a Panama Canal by the Americans. His efforts at mediation in the Russo-Japanese War of 1904–5 won him a Nobel Peace Prize and also showed the emergence of the United States as a world power. He gained a sweeping electoral triumph in 1904, but believed that at the age of 50 he should stand down from politics. Most of the years 1909–10 he spent abroad. When he decided to re-enter politics in 1912, he failed to shake the hold of the incumbent President, TAFT, on the Republican party machine. He therefore stood for election as an independent progressive, a 'Bull Moose' candidate. So great was his personal following that he polled more votes than Taft, but his intervention split the Republicans and victory went to the Democratic candidate, Woodrow WILSON. Theodore Roosevelt resumed his travels, exploring a river in Brazil, named the 'Rio Teodoro' in his honour. During the First World War he criticized Wilson's stand on neutrality, urging his fifth cousin, the Democrat Franklin ROOSEVELT, to induce the President to put the US fleet on a war footing (1915). 'T. R.' welcomed the idea of a League of Nations but did not live long enough to give his backing to any campaign for its acceptance by the American people. He died on 5 January 1919. T. Roosevelt: *Autobiography* (New York, 1913); E. E. Morrison (ed.): *Letters of Theodore Roosevelt* (8 vols) (Cambridge, Mass., 1951–5); H. F. Pringle: *Theodore Roosevelt* (rev. edn New York, 1956); J. M. Blum: *The Republican Roosevelt* (Cambridge, Mass., 1954).

Root, Elihu (1845–1937), US Secretary of War and Secretary of State: born at Clinton, New York State, where he was educated at Hamilton College, later practising law in New York City and taking an interest in Republican politics, though without any narrowly partisan feelings. He was appointed Secretary of War by MCKINLEY in 1898, holding the office through the first administration of Theodore ROOSEVELT, too. He rationalized army administration and improved staff training, but he is best remembered for his formulation of the Platt Amendment (finally presented by Senator Platt of Connecticut), which introduced into the American-sponsored Cuban constitution of 1902 a requirement that Cuba would make no territorial concession to foreign powers without American approval, a stipulation that lasted until 1934. Root became Secretary of State in 1905 and in 1908 negotiated an agreement with Japan by which each country would respect the other's territorial possessions in the Pacific and the China Sea. Root left the administration at the end of Roosevelt's second term and sat as Senator from New York from 1909 to 1915. He was awarded the Nobel Peace Prize in 1912 for his advocacy of some form of international organization. R. W. Leopold: *Elihu Root and the Conservative Tradition* (Boston, Mass., 1956).

Rosebery, Lord (Archibald Philip Primrose) (1847–1929), British Prime Minister from March 1894 to June 1895: born in London, succeeding his father as Lord Dalmeny at the age of 3 and his grandfather as Earl of Rosebery in 1868. He was educated at Eton and at Christ Church, Oxford. When told by his college in 1869 that he must either sell his racehorse and concentrate on his studies or end his university career forthwith, he had no difficulty in deciding on his course of action; the horse finished last in that year's Derby. In 1878 he married the only daughter of Baron Meyer de

Rothschild. He entered politics as the manager of the Midlothian campaigns in 1879 and 1880 for GLADSTONE, who rewarded him with minor posts, bringing him into the Cabinet as Lord Privy Seal in February 1885, four months before the government fell. For six months in 1886 he was Foreign Secretary, where he had the opportunity of showing understanding of a complex Balkan problem. He remained loyal to Gladstone in the Home Rule crisis, and was one of the most popular and respected members of London society: witty, well-read, able to speak at public meetings mellifluously and with humour, and passionately addicted to horse-racing. His wide interests were reflected, too, in his acceptance of the chairmanship of the newly established London County Council in 1889. The death of his wife in 1890 left him deeply depressed, and it was only persuasion by the future EDWARD VII that induced him in 1892 to become Foreign Secretary in Gladstone's last government. There he showed his belief in Liberal imperialism, especially in Africa, a cause for which Gladstone showed no enthusiasm. In March 1894 Queen VICTORIA invited Rosebery to succeed Gladstone (whom she had not consulted over a successor when he resigned the premiership). Rosebery, however, could not hold his Cabinet together, nor would he embark on enterprises abroad, which seemed to his colleagues contrary to Liberal principles. Death duties were introduced in the Budget presented by his Chancellor, Sir William Harcourt (1827–1904), a measure resisted by the Prime Minister within the Cabinet. The public was amused when Rosebery's horses won the Derby both in 1894 and 1895; but the Queen complained that his manner lacked gravity. He left office after an adverse vote in the Commons on 21 June 1895 and never again held any ministerial appointment, resigning the Liberal leadership in October 1896. In later years he moved to the Right, particularly in opposition to LLOYD GEORGE. He was the author of several historical studies, mainly on the Napoleonic period. No other former British Prime Minister has written, as did Rosebery in 1910, 'I always detested politics.' R. Rhodes James: *Rosebery* (1963); Marquis of Crewe: *Lord Rosebery* (2 vols) (1931).

Rudolf (1858–89), Austrian Crown Prince: born at Laxenberg, the only son of FRANCIS JOSEPH and his empress, Elizabeth. Rudolf inherited his mother's individualistic temperament rather than his father's rigid sense of dynastic duty. In politics Rudolf showed liberal sympathies, favouring national minorities and deploring Viennese anti-Semitism, but it is possible that his political gestures were primarily intended to spite his father, with whom his personal relations were frequently strained. In 1881 Rudolf married Princess Stéphanie of the Belgians, second daughter of LEOPOLD II. It was not a happy marriage and he sought consolation with several mistresses. On 30 January 1889 Rudolf was found dead in the hunting lodge at Mayerling in the Wienerwald, the body of a 17-year-old girl, Mary Vetsera, beside him. It is probable that Rudolf, whose mind had seemed unbalanced for some months, killed Mary (the daughter of a minor diplomat and niece of rich Levantine bankers) in a suicide pact, then shot himself. Attempts to hush up the Mayerling tragedy inevitably encouraged the spread of rumours that the Crown Prince had been involved in a treasonable conspiracy which he feared was near exposure. Yet it is more likely to have been an episode of warped romanticism than to have possessed any direct political significance. J. Listowel: *A Habsburg Tragedy* (1978); R. Barkeley: *The Road to Mayerling* (1958); A. Palmer: *Twilight of the Habsburgs* (1994).

Rusk, (David) Dean (1909–93), US Secretary of State from 1961 to 1969:

born in rural Georgia, educated at Davidson College, North Carolina, subsequently becoming a Rhodes scholar at St John's College, Oxford. After serving in southern China under General STILWELL, he joined the US diplomatic service and eventually succeeded to the positions hurriedly vacated by Alger HISS. He gained considerable experience of Far Eastern affairs and of Korea in particular, as assistant Secretary of State from 1949 to 1951. When John KENNEDY was elected President in 1960, he appointed Rusk to the State Department. Kennedy liked to keep European affairs in his own hands and Rusk was therefore left to concentrate on the Far East. His hostility to 'Red China' became even more clearly shown during the Johnson administration and in his Press releases in the course of the Vietnam War. He was, nevertheless, widely respected for his calm refusal to be caught off balance by the professional public alarmists. After the defeat of the Democrats in 1968 he accepted the Chair of International Law in the University of Georgia. D. Rusk: *As I Saw It* (1991).

Russell, Bertrand (1872–1970), British philosopher: born near Trelleck in Monmouthshire. Much of his childhood was spent in the household of his grandfather, the first Earl Russell (1792–1878), formerly Lord John RUSSELL. Bertrand Russell graduated in mathematics and moral sciences from Trinity College, Cambridge, in 1894, and was elected a Fellow of Trinity the following year. Until the First World War he concentrated his studies and teaching on the philosophy of mathematics and on problems of logic. A study of Leibniz in 1900 was followed by his *Principles of Mathematics* in 1903. By 1912 – when he numbered the famous Austrian logician Ludwig Wittgenstein (1889–1951) among his pupils – he was primarily concerned with logical problems analysing the reality of facts, theories he developed in his *Philosophy of Logical Atomism* (1918). By 1916, however, his pacifist views had cost him his Fellowship at Cambridge, and in 1918 he was imprisoned as a conscientious objector. During the inter-war period he held a professorial chair briefly in Peking, directed a progressive and co-educational school in Hampshire, and was a lecturer at the City College of New York. His books challenged conventional beliefs of marriage and morality as well as proposing a more socially liberal approach to problems of education. In 1931 he succeeded his brother as third Earl Russell, but he declined use of the title. On the eve of the Second World War his hatred of all forms of fascism induced him to abandon his earlier pacifist principles, and he was again elected to a Trinity Fellowship in 1944, becoming more widely known than earlier great philosophers by broadcasts in which, well into his seventies, he conveyed a power of mental analysis with the stimulus of an eighteenth-century rationalist in conversation. In 1949 King GEORGE VI awarded him the Order of Merit and a year later he received the Nobel Prize for Literature. His concern with the spread of nuclear weapons, manifested first in 1949, led him seven years later to become a founder of the Campaign for Nuclear Disarmament, a cause for which he was prepared to speak and to demonstrate well into his nineties. In September 1961, at the age of 89, he was briefly imprisoned at Brixton 'for inciting members of the public to commit a breach of the peace' while demonstrating against the deployment of American nuclear weapons in Britain. A year later, during the crisis over Soviet missiles on Cuba, he corresponded personally and directly with KHRUSCHEV and with President John KENNEDY in the hope of keeping the peace. He died at his home in north Wales on 2 February 1970. B. Russell: *Autobiography* (3 vols) (1967–9); R. M.

Sainsbury: *Russell* (1979); R. W. Clark: *The Life of Bertrand Russell* (1975).

Russell, Lord John (1792–1878), British Prime Minister from 1846 to 1852 and from 1856 to 1866: born in London, the third son of the sixth Duke of Bedford. He was educated at Westminster School and Edinburgh University, entering the Commons as Whig MP for Tavistock in 1813. During his forty-eight years in the lower House he represented six different constituencies. He travelled widely in Europe as a young man, visiting Napoleon I on Elba in January 1815 and warning the British government of the exiled Emperor's boredom and discontent. In the late 1820s Russell became a strenuous campaigner for parliamentary reform and he was brought into Grey's Liberal Cabinet in June 1831 as Paymaster-General. Much of the first parliamentary reform bill was drafted by Russell and he introduced it in the Commons in 1831. As Home Secretary from 1835 to 1839 he was responsible for municipal reforms and for relaxing the severity of the penal code. He became Prime Minister on 30 June 1846, his government achieving some success with legislation over factory conditions, but the most active member of the government was the Foreign Secretary, PALMERSTON, and Russell was especially concerned with preventing the wave of revolutions in 1848–9 from spreading to Britain. He served briefly as Foreign Secretary under Lord Aberdeen in 1852–3 and held other Cabinet posts until he left office in 1855 because his relations with Palmerston were strained. He agreed, however, to return to the Foreign Office in June 1859 when Palmerston formed his second government, and Russell was the chief advocate in the Cabinet for support to CAVOUR in Italy. He went to the House of Lords as Earl Russell in 1861. When Palmerston died in October 1865, Earl Russell succeeded him as Prime Minister and at once began to prepare a second parliamentary reform bill. There were, however, such divisions within his party over the nature of the reforms that he was forced to resign (26 June 1866). He remained active in public affairs for another ten years although without holding office, and he died, at his home in Richmond Park, on 28 May 1878. Earl Russell: *Recollections and Suggestions* (1875); G. P. Gooch: *The Later Correspondence of Lord John Russell, 1840–78* (2 vols) (1925); J. Prest: *Lord John Russell* (1972).

S

Sadat, Mohammed Anwar el- (1918–81), President of Egypt 1970–81: born at Abu el-Kom in the Minufijja province, his military career closely following that of NASSER, whom he joined in the conspiracy to overthrow FAROUK in 1952. He was General Secretary of the ruling National Union from 1957 to 1961, and was Speaker of the parliamentary assembly 1960–1 and 1964. He became Vice-President of the Republic in 1969, succeeding to the presidency on Nasser's death in October 1970. At first, in order to consolidate his position in the state and his leadership of the Arab cause, President Sadat continued Nasser's policy of confrontation with Israel, permitting his army leaders to collaborate with the Syrians in launching the surprise offensive against Israel known as the 'October War', in 1973. The decisive defeat of Egypt and the appearance of an Israeli armoured column on the road from Suez to Cairo induced the President to make a drastic reassessment of his policy. Links with the Soviet Union were ended, friendlier relations established with the United States and the West, and greater attention was given to North African problems rather than the Palestinian question. Sadat was able to re-open the Suez Canal on 5 June 1975 after exactly eight years of closure. Defence expenditure, however, remained high, and beyond Egypt's resources. In November 1977 Sadat accordingly took the initiative in seeking direct talks with the Israeli Prime Minister, BEGIN, in order to hasten a Middle East settlement. Sadat's visit to Jerusalem (19–21 November 1977) was followed by long exchanges in Egypt and elsewhere, while attempts were made to establish an Egyptian–Israeli peace settlement. In September 1978 Sadat and Begin were guests of President CARTER at Camp David in Maryland, where agreement was finally reached on the principle of signing a peace treaty (which was concluded at Washington on 26 March 1979). Sadat's new course in foreign policy was bitterly denounced both by the Palestine Liberation Organization and by his western neighbour, GADDAFI of Libya. Most Egyptians welcomed the prospect of peace and the recovery of lost land in Sinai, but on 6 October 1981 Sadat was assassinated at a military parade in Cairo, the victim of a conspiracy organized by Islamic extremists within the army. He was succeeded by his Vice-President, MUBARAK. A. Sadat: *Revolt on the Nile* (1957), *In Search of Identity* (1977); J. Waterbury: *The Egypt of Nasser and Sadat* (1983); R. Israeli: *Man of Defiance* (1985).

Saddam Hussein, Sadisavan (1937–), fourth President of Iraq: born into a peasant family at Takrit. He was educated in Baghdad, under the guardianship of an uncle, an ex-officer purged from the army in 1941. Saddam joined the Ba'ath Socialist Party in 1957 and was active in the party militia. He made his career within the party, consciously modelling his progress on the technique used by STALIN to climb to power in Soviet Russia during the 1920s. Saddam was imprisoned for his conspiratorial activities in 1964 but on his release he helped plan the *coup* of July 1968 which established rule by a Revolutionary

Command Council (RRC); he served as the RRC's Deputy Chairman under President Hasan al-Bakr, whom he succeeded as head of state in July 1979. Although Saddam was not a professional soldier, he promoted himself to the highest ranks in the army and established a ruthless dictatorship. He plunged Iraq into war with Iran in September 1980, taking advantage of the instability in Teheran to seek control of the Shatt-al-Arab, the waterway formed by the confluence of the Tigris and the Euphrates at the head of the Gulf. The conflict dragged on indecisively for eight years, with heavy casualties on both sides. Saddam was widely condemned for resorting to chemical warfare in 1984 and 1986, the first use of poison gas in a campaign for half a century. He sought to stamp out all opposition within Iraq, establishing a regime of torture and brutal imprisonment. Attempts to assassinate him at Mosul in May 1987 and to shoot down his aircraft in October 1988 failed. On 2 August 1991 he sent the Iraqi army to seize Kuwait; this act of aggression was condemned by the United Nations. The USA and twenty-eight other UN members assembled a force in Saudi Arabia which ejected the Iraqis from Kuwait in a lightning campaign at the end of February 1981. Despite this military defeat, and rebellions in the Kurdish north and predominantly Shi'ite regions in the south, Saddam held on to power; UN inspectors believed he was secretly developing a nuclear weapon and there remained a constant threat of renewed war in the Middle East. A long-delayed 'election' for the presidency, held in October 1995, gave Saddam more than 90 per cent of the votes: there was no other candidate and no provision for a secret ballot. M. and P. Sluglett: *Iraq since 1958* (1987).

Saigo, Takamori (1827–77), conservative samurai reformer: born in Satsuma province (Kagoshima), the eldest of seven children in a poor samurai family. After receiving a traditionally austere military education he became a minor provincial official, moving to Edo (Tokyo) soon after Commodore Perry's US naval squadron 'opened up' Japan in 1853–4. Saigo played a prominent part in limiting the Shogunate and giving real power to Emperor MUTSUHITO in the so-called Meiji Restoration. It was Saigo who defeated the last supporters of the Shoguns in November 1867; as Commander of the imperial forces, he maintained security while a modern form of autocratic government was improvised. Until 1871 he was Mutsuhito's military adviser and chief minister but he deplored the speed with which reformers were raising a conscript army and navy from peasants who – unlike the samurai – had no military tradition to uphold. He withdrew from government, set up samurai 'schools' (Shigakko) in his home province, and urged Mutsuhito to rid himself of advisers who followed too slavishly the ways of the West. Attempts to disarm the Shigakko induced Saigo to march on Tokyo early in 1877, leading a Satsuma army pledged to purify the Meiji government. Saigo's men were, however, checked by the new conscript regulars at Kumamoto. Saigo committed suicide on 24 September 1877. Mutsuhito posthumously pardoned him in 1891. In death he became (and remains) a legendary figure, symbolizing traditional virtues menaced by alien ways. A statue by Takamura Koun honours 'Saigo the Great' in Ueno Park, Tokyo. H. Borton: *Japan's Modern Century* (New York, 1955); I. Morris: *The Nobility of Failure* (New York, 1975).

St Laurent, Louis Stephen (1882–1973), Canadian Prime Minister from 1948 to 1957: born at Compton, Quebec, and educated at Laval University, where he studied law. He was elected to the Canadian parliament as a Liberal in 1941 and, after a spell as Attorney-General, was Minister of External Affairs from 1946 to November 1948, when he succeeded

MacKenzie KING as Prime Minister. His government was responsible for some progressive social reforms, notably an Old Age Security Act, and for reaching agreement with the Americans for the eventual construction of the St Lawrence Seaway (which was opened in 1959). Although able to win the General Election of 1953, he found the Liberal hold on the electorate dwindling away, partly because of his party's monetary policy and partly because he seemed little interested in the plight of the farmers in the wheatlands, where problems were markedly different from those with which he was accustomed in the Maritime Provinces. He lost the General Election of June 1957 to DIEFENBAKER and the Progressive Conservatives. St Laurent stood down as Liberal Party leader a year later and was succeeded by Lester PEARSON. R. Bothwell, I. Drummond and J. English: *Canada since 1945; Power, Politics and Provincialism* (Toronto, 1981).

Saionji, Kimmochi (1849–1940), Japanese statesman, politically active for seventy years: born in Kyoto into the Tokudaiji family but adopted in 1851 by his influential kinsmen, the Saionjis. He became a junior government councillor in 1867, supporting the Meiji restoration under MUTSUHITO. From 1871 to 1880 he was in Europe, studying political and legal institutions in Britain and France. On his return he founded the Meiji Law School (1881); he thought the process of modernization too slow and aroused some criticism as editor-in-chief of an Opposition newspaper. He accompanied ITO to Europe in 1882, remaining until 1891, first as envoy in Vienna, later in Berlin (where he witnessed the downfall of BISMARCK). Under Ito he was Minister of Education (1892–6, 1898). He was Prime Minister 1906–8 and 1911–12, running into fierce opposition from militarists for trimming army expenditure. In 1919 he headed the Japanese delegation to the Paris Peace Conference and signed the Versailles Treaty. He was made a Prince on his return to Japan: HIROHITO respected him as the empire's elder statesman, although the army leaders tended to ignore him. Saionji constantly pressed for 'neutral' non-party governments, believing they could check the mounting influence of the militarists; he also pressed for better relations with the USA and Great Britain. In his last years Saionji's influence was weakened by an ill-disguised aristocratic contempt for army leaders who favoured collaboration with the Axis powers. P. Duus: *Party Rivalry and Political Change in Taisho Japan* (Berkeley, Calif., 1967); H. Conway, S. J. W. Day and W. Patterson: *Japan in Transition: Thought and Action in the Meiji Era, 1868–1912* (Princeton, N.J., 1984); R. A. Scalapino: *Democracy and the Party Movement in Pre-War Japan* (Berkeley, Calif., 1953).

Salazar, Antonio de Oliveira (1889–1970), dictator of Portugal from 1932 to 1968: born some forty miles north of Lisbon in the village of Vimierio, where his father kept the inn. A seminary education led him to take minor orders but he was never ordained priest. At the university of Coimbra he showed such brilliance as an economist that he was given a professorial chair before he was 30. He was co-opted as Minister of Finance in April 1928, steering Portugal through the financial crisis caused by the world recession. On 5 July 1932 he became Prime Minister. Dr Salazar was devout, ascetic and personally retiring: he had no demagogic gift, nor did he attempt to appeal to the public. He permitted only one political party, the Portuguese National Union, and he organized Portugal as a corporative state. Throughout his premiership he controlled the Ministry of Finance, serving as his own Foreign Minister from 1936 to 1947 and his own War Minister from 1936 to 1944. Living conditions were improved, major public works successfully accomplished, the basic standard of education was raised, and a uniform Catholic public morality imposed upon a country which offered little resistance to his dictatorship. In Portugal's overseas possessions Salazar's firm stand against change aroused a revolutionary spirit, and there was guerrilla warfare in Angola from 1960 and in Mozambique from 1964. Salazar was incapacitated by a stroke in the autumn of 1968. He never formally resigned office, but Professor Marcelle Caetano assumed the responsibilities of head of the government on 26 September 1968, Dr Salazar's life lingering on until the last week in July, 1970. H. Kay: *Salazar and Modern Portugal* (1970); T. Gallagher: *Portugal, a Twentieth Century Interpretation* (Manchester, 1983).

Salisbury, Lord (Robert Gascoyne-Cecil) (1830–1903), British Prime Minister from 1885 to 1886, 1886 to 1892 and 1895 to 1902: born at Hatfield House, a direct descendant of the Elizabethan statesman, Lord Burghley. He was educated at Eton and Christ Church, Oxford. He was elected to the House of Commons as Lord Robert Cecil in 1853 and remained an MP for fifteen years, succeeding his brother as Viscount Cranborne in 1865 and going to the House of Lords as third Marquess of Salisbury in 1868. In June 1866 he attained Cabinet rank as Secretary of State for India under Lord DERBY, but resigned from the government the following March because of his opposition to his party's proposed parliamentary reform bill. Salisbury was an old-fashioned Tory, who feared democracy as the embodiment of mob rule. At the same time he had a sense of the squire's duty to his tenants which, translated into national terms, made him see the Tories as 'spokesmen for the country gentlemen of England'. He was also a patrician who was prepared to take a broad interest in world affairs. DISRAELI persuaded him to return as Indian Secretary from February 1874 to April 1878 when he became Foreign Secretary, showing great mastery of detail when he attended the Congress of Berlin in 1878. Salisbury became Prime Minister in June 1885, retaining the Foreign Office for himself. At first, in his second government (August 1886 to August 1892) he followed the usual practice of separating the responsibilities of Prime Minister and Foreign Secretary, but he took over the Foreign Office as early as January 1887. He was, for a third time, Prime Minister and Foreign Secretary from June 1895 to October 1900, when he relinquished the Foreign Office although continuing to head the government until handing over to his nephew, BALFOUR, in July 1902. Salisbury accepted the partition of Africa, defending Britain's traditional interests against newer interlopers and expanding into the interior, normally through the agency of charter companies. This phase of imperialism led, against Salisbury's wishes or expectation, to the Boer War, which overshadowed the last three years of his final premiership. At a time of competing alliances within Europe, Salisbury was able to avoid commitment, collaborating at times with the Germans, Italians and Austrians (notably in the Mediterranean), but also prepared to reach settlements with France and Russia (although forward policies in the Sudan and in the Far East brought war with those two powers close in 1898). He died at Hatfield in August 1903, thirteen months after retiring from office. Lady G. Cecil: *Life of Robert, Marquis of Salisbury* (4 vols) (1921–32); A. L. Kennedy: *Salisbury, 1830–1904; Portrait of a Statesman* (1953); K. Rose: *The Later Cecils* (1975).

Sandino, Augusto Cesar (1893–1934), Nicaraguan popular hero: in his early thirties emerged as a left-wing nationalist resentful of foreign intervention and the presence in Nicaragua of US Marines. He led guerrillas who raided the American-supplied base at Las Flores on

19 September 1927 and mounted attacks on US Marine bases in January and February 1929. Further gains in April 1931 and September 1932 brought Sandino control of the Leon region when ROOSEVELT withdrew the Marines as a 'good neighbour' gesture in 1933. Effective power remained, however, with the SOMOZA family whose National Guard followers killed Sandino in an ambush at Managua's airfield on 21 February 1934. The Sandinista National Liberation Front, set up in 1962 to resist the dictatorship, revived the dead guerrilla's name. S. Ramirez and R. Conrad (eds): *Sandino, the testimony of a Nicaraguan Patriot* (Princeton, N.J., 1990); G. Selser: *Sandino* (New York, 1981); N. Macaulay: *The Sandino Affair* (Chicago, 1967).

Santer, Jacques (1937–), Luxemburger and EC politician: born at Wasserbillig, studied law and politics at the Universities of Strasbourg and Paris. Between 1966 and 1982 Santer held important posts in the Luxemburg Christian Social Party (CSV). He became a Luxemburg Deputy in 1974 and was elected to the European Parliament in 1975. From 1979 to 1994 he was Luxemburg's Finance Minister. In July 1984 he also became Prime Minister, heading a Centre-Left coalition. Ten years later he succeeded DELORS as President of the European Commission, taking up his duties in January 1995.

Sartre, Jean-Paul (1905–80), French novelist, dramatist and existentialist philosopher: born in Paris, the son of a naval officer who was a cousin of Albert Schweitzer but who died when Sartre was 2 years old. He was educated at lycées in La Rochelle and Paris, subsequently spending five years (1924–9) at the Ecole Normale in Paris. During the 1930s he taught at high schools in Le Havre, Laon and Paris, spending the critical years 1933–4 at the Institut Français in Berlin. He published an autobiographical novel and some short stories in 1938–9, before being called up for army service. From June 1940 until April 1941 he was a prisoner-of-war in Germany, returning to Paris to take up his old teaching post, to support the Resistance, and to develop the existentialist philosophy in which man is condemned to experience the limitations of his own will, outside of which there is nothing. Politically, Sartre's atheism and natural hostility to bourgeois convention made him a Communist, and he was the leader of France's intelligentsia of the Left for many years. An attempt to found a 'Democratic Revolutionary Rally' as an independent socialist movement in the Fourth Republic came to nothing, and from 1952 to 1956 he collaborated with the French communists. There remained moments after 1956 when he seemed to favour a revival of the Popular Front, in opposition to DE GAULLE, but essentially he mistrusted orthodox communism and after the Soviet occupation of Prague in 1968 he regarded himself primarily as a Maoist. He was awarded the Nobel Prize for Literature in 1964, but refused to accept it. His trilogy *Les Chemins de la Liberté* (1945–9) is a subjective study, in the form of novels, of the decline of France from 1935 to 1940, praising communism as the only effective antidote to fascism of the mind. *Les Mouches* (1943) and *Huis clos* (1944) successfully defied German censorship, championing liberty in allegory. Later plays criticized journalism (*Nekrassov*), differing standards of integrity (*Le Diable et le bon Dieu*) and Stalinist orthodoxy (*Crime passionnel*). J. P. Sartre: *Words* (autobiography translated 1964); S. de Beauvoir: *The Prime of Life* (1962); P. Thody: *Sartre* (1971); D. Caute: *Communism and the French Intellectuals* (1964).

Savage, Michael Joseph (1872–1940), New Zealand's first Socialist Prime Minister: an Australian by birth who emigrated to South Island at the age of 35 and, as a trade union official, organized the Labour movement in Auckland. He was MP for Auckland West from 1919 until 1940, becoming Labour leader in 1933 and gaining popularity by his buoyant confidence. So grave were the effects of the Depression that in the 1935 General Election he won votes from traditionally conservative farming communities. Savage was Prime Minister from 6 March 1935 until his sudden death on 27 March 1940. Among basic social reforms of the first Labour government was a marketing act which pleased the farmers and gave Savage a second electoral victory in October 1938. As well as heading the government he took ministerial charge of foreign affairs, relations with the Maori peoples and broadcasting and, from September 1939, organized the dominion's response to the coming of war in Europe. The strain proved too great for his health. He was succeeded by Peter FRASER. B. Gustafson: *From the Cradle to the Grave* (Auckland, 1986); R. S. Milne: *Political Parties in New Zealand* (Oxford, 1966).

Savimbi, Jonas (1934–), Angolan revolutionary: received a Catholic missionary education, completed at the University of Lausanne. He settled in Lusaka and from 1961 onwards supported Angola's struggle for independence from Portugal. In 1966 he broke with the People's Movement for the Liberation of Angola (MPLA), because of its socialist ideology, and formed the National Union for the Total Independence of Angola (UNITA), guerrillas who regarded foreign 'volunteers' (Cuban and Soviet) as no less enemies than the Portuguese 'imperialists'. Savimbi received support from South Africa, enabling him to establish headquarters at Jamba in southern Angola. The US anti-CASTRO lobby, angered by the Cuban presence in Angola, also backed Savimbi as a 'freedom fighter'; and in 1987 American arms, smuggled through Zaïre, enabled him to set up a northern base at Quimbele. A peace agreement was reached in May 1991. Savimbi stood unsuccessfully in the Angolan presidential election of September 1992, gaining 40 per cent of the popular vote; he complained that the final results were rigged so as to exclude him from office. Further clashes between UNITA and MPLA forces led to a resumption of Angola's civil war in January 1993, with Savimbi becoming *de facto* ruler of some two-thirds of the country in the south, west and north west. The Angolan capital, Luanda and the most populous areas remained under MPLA control.

Scargill, Arthur (1938–), British trade unionist: born at Worsborough Dale, near Barnsley, Yorkshire; educated locally. He was appalled at coal-face conditions when he became a miner (1956) and was soon active in the National Union of Mineworkers (NUM), gaining acceptance as Yorkshire area manager in 1973. He showed himself to be a skilled orator, with a vivid turn of phrase, in the tradition of earlier trade unionists. He was also politically far-sighted; as early as 1979 he rightly warned NUM members of massive pit closures if the Conservatives established a lasting hold on government. In 1981 Scargill became President of the NUM, which shortly afterwards moved its headquarters from London to Sheffield. He was soon in deep conflict with the THATCHER government. In March 1984 he led the miners into a bitter national strike against proposed closures, 140 pits answering his call for a stoppage of work. The NUM received backing from railway workers and, in the summer, from a national dock strike. Scargill's management of the strike was hampered by government use of new legislation to secure court rulings which sequestered NUM funds and by government exploitation of rifts between the miners of Yorkshire and Nottinghamshire. The discovery in late

October 1984 that the NUM had contact with GADDAFI's Libyan regime was exploited by the popular Press in a sustained bid to discredit Scargill. The miners' strike was called off in March 1985; Scargill and his union sought thereafter to safeguard miners' rights in the bleak years of closure which lay ahead. P. Routledge: *Scargill, the Unauthorized Biography* (1993); M. Adeney and J. Lloyd: *The Miners' Strike* (1986).

Schlieffen, Alfred von (1833–1913), German Field Marshal, Chief of General Staff from 1891 to 1905: born in Berlin and commissioned in the Guard Cavalry, holding staff posts in the wars of 1866 and 1870. The death in 1872 of a wife to whom he had been idyllically married for only four years left him so saddened in spirit that, for the rest of his life, he was a dedicated professional soldier whose total obsession with military science amazed even his colleagues in the Prussian officer corps. He became Chief of General Staff in February 1891, succeeding Count von Waldersee (1832–1904), who had himself taken over from the first of the great planners, the elder MOLTKE, less than three years previously. Schlieffen at once changed the fundamental assumption of Germany's strategic planning: in case of a war on two fronts, he claimed it was essential to destroy France first, rather than Russia (which, his predecessors had believed, posed a greater potential threat to Germany). Schlieffen spent more than twelve years perfecting plans for a scythe-like operation which would defeat the French within six weeks by advancing through Holland, Belgium and Luxembourg. The definitive version of this 'Schlieffen Plan' was completed in December 1905, on the eve of its author's retirement. He continued to revise it annually until Christmas 1912, dying shortly afterwards with 'Strengthen the right wing' as his last recorded words. His successor as Chief of General Staff, the younger MOLTKE, shortened the line of march by abandoning the idea of invading Holland and concentrating greater forces on the route to Paris from Luxembourg. Apologists for imperial Germany's defeat later declared that Moltke thereby ruined Schlieffen's plan for victory, but it is arguable that Schlieffen himself overrated the physical strength of Germany's infantrymen and horses, that he neglected the importance of railways and that he underestimated the resistance likely to be offered both by the Belgian army and by a British expeditionary force. G. Ritter: *The Schlieffen Plan* (1958); P. M. Kennedy (ed.): *The War Plans of the Great Powers, 1880–1914* (1979).

Schmidt, Helmut (1918–), West German Social Democrat Chancellor: born and educated in Hamburg. He was called up to serve in the German air force in the Second World War, mainly on the Eastern Front. Schmidt joined the German Social Democratic Party (SPD) in 1946, serving at first in local administration around Hamburg at a time when the city and port were seeking to recover from the bombing and holocaust of 1942. Dr Schmidt, an economist, sat in the Bundestag from 1953 to 1962 and was returned there again in 1965. From 1967 to 1969 he presided over meetings of the parliamentary group of the SPD. The party's successes in the elections of September 1969 led to the appointment of Willy BRANDT as Chancellor, and he gave Schmidt the Ministry of Defence. After the elections of 1972 Schmidt was moved to key posts responsible for finance and the economy. In May 1974 he succeeded Brandt as Chancellor and was faced by a succession of crises caused by urban guerrillas and their seizure of hostages. He accepted threats to his life with courage, and continued his predecessor's attempts to encourage *détente* and to sustain Germany's economic primacy within the EEC. He remained Chancellor until October 1982, when electoral defeat led to the establishment of a Right–Centre coalition under Helmut KOHL. J. Carr: *Helmut Schmidt, Helmsman of Germany* (1985); E. Kolinsky: *Parties, Opposition and Society in West Germany* (1985).

Schuman, Robert (1886–1963), French statesman who favoured European integration: born in Luxemburg, and was a conservatively inclined Deputy in the French Chamber from 1919 to 1940 without attaining high political office. He was deported to Germany in September 1940 but escaped a year later. Under the Fourth Republic he was a founder-member of the liberal Catholic Mouvement Républicain Populaire, and was Prime Minister for nine months in 1947–8. His fame rests on his term as Foreign Minister (July 1948 to January 1953), in which he took the first clear initiative in creating the European Community by proposing, in May 1950, the 'Schuman Plan' for pooling the coal and steel industries of France and Germany, an idea expanded through the detailed studies of Jean MONNET into the establishment of the European Coal and Steel Community. Schuman's attempts to convince his countrymen of the values of a European Defence Force led to his downfall, since he was accused (mistakenly) of encouraging Germany's military revival. In his later years he took a great interest in plans for a European currency. He was the accepted leader of the European movement from 1956 to 1962 and presided over the European Parliament from 1958 to 1960. W. Hallstein: *Europe in the Making* (1973).

Seeckt, Hans von (1866–1936), German General, responsible for circumventing the disarmament clauses of the Treaty of Versailles: born in Schleswig, commissioned in a Guards regiment in 1885 and attached to the General Staff under SCHLIEFFEN, who encouraged him to travel, not only in Europe, but even to Delhi where Lord KITCHENER took pride in displaying to him the Indian army. After serving on the Western Front in 1914, he gained a decisive victory with the Eleventh Army on the Eastern Front at Gorlice (May 1915). Later in the war he served in the Balkans, in Romania, and on the Turkish Front. In the opening months of 1919 he helped organize resistance to the Poles and to the Bolsheviks in Silesia. After visiting Paris to report on the proposed demilitarization clauses of the peace treaty, he was appointed commandant of the army in March 1920. For six years he found means of building up a force which could rapidly expand and in which a cadre of well-trained officers and specialist NCOs could form the basis of a larger conscript force at a later date. At the same time Seeckt secretly arranged for collaboration with Soviet Russia in training officers and men in the use of forbidden weapons, such as tanks. HINDENBURG, whose closely knit circle of advisers distrusted Seeckt, found an excuse to force him into early retirement in October 1926, but he remained an influential figure, sitting in the Reichstag as a member of the German People's Party from September 1930 until the establishment of HITLER's dictatorship. He twice visited CHIANG KAI SHEK in China as a military adviser, the second occasion being in 1934–5. Although in 1931–2 a supporter of Hitler, he seems to have become critical of Nazi policy before his death in December 1936; but, without his preliminary work, it would have been impossible for the German army to expand so rapidly between 1934 and 1939. H. von Seeckt: *Thoughts of a Soldier* (1930); J. W. Wheeler-Bennett: *The Nemesis of Power: the German Army in Politics* (1953).

Seward, William Henry (1801–72), American Secretary of State from 1861 to 1869: born in Florida, New York, and graduated from Union College in 1820, building up a law practice at Auburn. He was a Whig State Senator from 1830, serving as Governor of New York from 1839 to 1843. As a member of the US Senate (1849–61) he actively supported the admission of California as a free state without any compromise which might have permitted slavery in New Mexico or other developing territories. Seward joined the Republican Party in 1855, soon after its foundation, and was a candidate for presidential nomination in 1860 but he accepted the leadership of LINCOLN, who appointed him Secretary of State in March 1861. Seward, who in 1858 had described the conflict between North and South as 'irrepressible', now proposed to Lincoln that secession might be halted and the Union upheld if the nation could be united in a diversionary war against NAPOLEON III, who was intriguing in Mexico. Lincoln rejected this proposal and throughout the Civil War Seward tactfully conducted difficult negotiations with the British and the French, stopping short of armed conflict. In April 1865 Seward was attacked and wounded at his home by an accomplice of Lincoln's assassin but he recovered and supported President Andrew JOHNSON at a time when he was much criticized by Seward's fellow Republicans, an act of loyalty which virtually ended Seward's political career. He was the first American Secretary of State to take an active interest in the Pacific Ocean, seeking an open door for trade in China and the occupation of the mid-Pacific islands as coaling stations for an American fleet. In October 1867 Seward purchased Alaska from Russia, paying US$ 7,200,000 (about £1,500,000) for territory which, although twice as big as Texas, was considered an economic liability. For some thirty years Alaska was derisively known as 'Seward's folly' or 'Seward's icebox', until the Klondyke Gold Rush in 1896 indicated the region's mineral wealth. E. E. Hale Jnr: *William H. Seward* (New York, 1910); E. Conrad: *The Governor and his Lady* (New York, 1960).

Shamir, Yitzhak (1915–), right-wing Israeli political leader: born Yitzhak Jazernicki in Poland, graduating in law from Warsaw University and continuing his studies at the Hebrew University in Jerusalem, where he settled in the mid-1930s. On the eve of the Second World War he became a founder-member of the Stern Gang (Israeli freedom fighters) who carried out attacks on British bases in mandated Palestine. The British authorities arrested him in 1941 and he was deported to Eritrea, later finding sanctuary in France until the Israeli State was created, when he returned to Jerusalem. He did not enter the Israeli parliament until 1973, serving as Speaker of the Knesset from 1977 to 1980 and serving as Foreign Minister in Likud government of BEGIN (1980–3). He was briefly Prime Minister (October 1983 to July 1984) but the uncertain state of Israeli politics forced him to alternate the premiership with the Labour leader, Shimon PERES. Shamir was Prime Minister from October 1986 until March 1990, when his failure to reconcile Likud hardliners to accepting concessions to the Palestinians led to the fall of the government. Y. Bauer: *Palestine, from Diplomacy to Resistance* (Philadelphia, 1970); I. Peleg: *Begin's Foreign Policy 1977–1983* (1987); G. Aronson: *Israel, Palestinians and the Intifada* (1989).

Shastri, Lal Bahadur (1904–66), India's second Prime Minister: born at Benares, studied law, joined the Congress Party in 1920 and was imprisoned on several occasions. He became a protégé of NEHRU and between 1952 and 1963 held several ministerial posts with responsibility for railways and, finally, home affairs in general. In 1963 Nehru asked him to tidy up Congress Party administration but he was brought back hurriedly to the government early in 1964 as Nehru's chosen heir-apparent, when the Prime Minister's health began to fail. Shastri duly succeeded Nehru in June 1964. His government became entangled in the problems of Kashmir, with an open conflict between India and Pakistan breaking out in September 1965. Shastri accepted Soviet mediation and travelled to Tashkent to thrash out a compromise with Pakistan's military leader, AYUB KHAN. The search for peace overtaxed Shastri's health. He suffered a fatal heart attack on returning to India (11 January 1966). Nehru's daughter, Indira GANDHI, succeeded Shastri. A. Hall: *The Emergence of Modern India* (New York, 1981); J. Brown: *Modern India, the Origins of an Asian Democracy* (Oxford, 1987).

Shaw, George Bernard (1856–1950), Fabian socialist and dramatist: born in Dublin, where he was educated at the Wesleyan School, settling in London in 1876, writing novels and later becoming a music and drama critic. He counted himself as a Socialist from 1882 onwards, joining the Fabian Society in 1884 and writing pamphlets as well as participating in debates and discussions. He edited *Fabian Essays* (1889) and remained an active member until 1911. His enthusiasm for Ibsen is reflected in his earliest plays, notably *The Philanderer* of 1893. His first flow of plays came in the closing years of the century, from *Arms and the Man* and *Candida* in 1894 to *Captain Brassbound's Conversion* in 1899. From 1897 to 1903 he had his only experience of politics in action, sitting as a councillor for the London borough of St Pancras. His popularity as a dramatist was at its peak between 1904 and 1907 when the Court Theatre staged eleven of his plays in quick succession. *Pygmalion* and *Androcles and the Lion* (1912) marked the start of a second phase, which was cut short by criticism of his anti-war remarks in 1914. The satirical *Heartbreak House* (1917) was followed by *Back to Methuselah* (1921) and the last of his major works, *Saint Joan*, in 1924. A year later he accepted the Nobel Prize for Literature. Among the causes which he championed were vegetarianism, teetotalism and a simplified alphabet. He continued to write plays, political prefaces and provocative commentaries on economic and social problems until the Second World War. Offers of a peerage and the Order of Merit were declined. He visited Soviet Russia in 1928, and travelled round the world in 1931, finally settling at his Hertfordshire home of Ayot St Lawrence, where he died on 2 November 1950 after fracturing a leg while lopping the branches of a tree in his garden. M. MacBriar: *Fabian Socialism and British Politics, 1884–1918* (Cambridge, 1962); M. Holroyd: *G. Bernard Shaw*, Vol. 1, *The Search for Love* (1988), Vol. 2, *The Pursuit of Power* (1989).

Sheridan, Philip Henry (1831–88), American cavalry commander in the Civil War: born in Albany of Irish parentage, graduating from the military academy at West Point in 1853. As a newly promoted Brigadier he commanded a column at the battle of Perryville in October 1862 but it was in the Chattanooga campaign of September to November 1863 that he first distinguished himself as a leader of cavalry. His methodical destruction of the Shenandoah valley in September 1864 deprived the Confederacy of a vital granary, and his rallying of stragglers to mount a counter-attack at Cedar Creek on 19 October 1864 has become part of the traditional lore of the Civil War. He gained an important victory at Five Forks on 1 April 1865, hastening the end of Confederate resistance. In 1870 he accompanied the Prussians as an observer of their advance into France. For the last five years of his life he was commanding General of the US army, dying at Nonquitt, Massachusetts. P. S. Sheridan: *Personal Memoirs* (2 vols) (rev. edn New

York, 1904); R. O'Connor: *Sheridan the Inevitable* (New York, 1953).

Sherman, William Tecumseh (1820–91), Union General in the American Civil War: born at Lancaster, Ohio, graduating from the Military Academy at West Point in 1840 and seeing active service in Florida and California before resigning his commission in 1853 to enter the banking profession in San Francisco. In May 1861 he rejoined the infantry as a Colonel, fought at First Bull Run and was a divisional commander at Shiloh (6–7 April 1862) and in the protracted Vicksburg campaign of November 1862 to July 1863. At Vicksburg and later, in the final relief of Chattanooga (24–5 November 1863), Sherman collaborated closely with General GRANT, who appointed him commander in the south-west in March 1864. His invasion of Georgia that summer was followed by a decisive 300-mile 'march to the sea' which scythed destruction across the South. The last Confederate force, under General J. E. Johnston, surrendered to Sherman at Durham in North Carolina on 26 April 1865, eleven days after LINCOLN's death. Sherman, a tough and ruthless campaign commander, showed a loathing for total war in his *Memoirs*, which he wrote soon after retiring from the army as commanding General in 1884. He died in New York in 14 February 1891. His younger brother, John Sherman (1823–1900) was Secretary of the Treasury under Hayes. W. T. Sherman: *Memoirs* (original 1875 edition revised in 1877; edited by B. H. Liddell Hart, 1957); B. H. Liddell Hart: *Sherman: Soldier, Realist, American* (1929).

Shevardnadze, Eduard (1928–), Soviet Foreign Minister and Georgian national leader: born at Mamati, joined the Communist youth movement (Komsomol) in 1948, acquired a university history degree by correspondence and became an apparatchik (party official) in the Caucasus, serving as Minister of the Interior in the Georgian Soviet Republic from 1965 to 1985. By 1972 he was Communist Party boss of Georgia, controlling the local KGB and vigorously stamping out corruption, notably at party headquarters in Tbilisi. GORBACHEV, who had known Shevardnadze since his days in the Komsomol, was impressed by his effectiveness as a reformer and, in July 1985, appointed him to succeed GROMYKO as Soviet Foreign Minister, intending that he should improve relations with the West by showing more flexibility than his predecessors. His ability to work well with BUSH completed the thaw in the cold war. Shevardnadze remained, however, alarmed at the state of the Soviet economy and at the reluctance of hard-line Communists to make concessions to national majorities, especially in the Baltic states and the Caucasus. He resigned suddenly on 1 December 1990, with warnings of a Stalinist backlash and a new dictatorship. He remained in Moscow, seeking to organize a democratic political front, until the formal disintegration of the Soviet Union in December 1991. On his return to Georgia he mediated in the Civil War which convulsed the republic and in March 1992 became chairman of the state council, accepting office as President of the Supreme Soviet of Georgia in October 1992. The persistence of civil war in Georgia and the growth of a separatist movement in the northern region of Abkhazian induced Shevardnadze to bring Georgia into the Moscow-sponsored Commonwealth of Independent States (CIS) in March 1994. A year later he approved a new constitution, which offered Georgia a strong executive presidency, and announced that he would be a candidate in the presidential election of November 1995. Two months before the election he narrowly escaped death when a car-bomb exploded outside his office in Tbilisi. He gained a landslide victory in the election. E. Shevardnadze: *The Future Belongs to Freedom* (New York, 1991).

Shidehara Kijuro (1872–1951), Japanese diplomat and elder statesman: born at Osaka, graduated in law from Tokyo in 1895 and entered the diplomatic service. He gained experience in Europe and Washington before the First World War and was deputy Foreign Minister (1915–19). Shidehara admired the English-speaking nations and, as ambassador to the US, contributed considerably to the success of the Washington Conference (1921–2) on naval limitation and the relaxation of tension over China. As Foreign Minister in 1924–7 and 1929–31 he favoured Japan's fulfilment of League obligations and a 'hands-off China' policy. The growing influence of military leaders brushed aside his restraints in 1931. He resigned in dismay at the occupation of Manchuria and took no part in politics until, with the backing of MACARTHUR, he formed a government in October 1945 as nominal head of Nihon Shimpoto (Japan Progressive Party). Shidehara was a conservative reformer: his pro-western reputation made his advice readily acceptable to the American occupying authorities, particularly over HIROHITO's renunciation of his imperial divinity and the retention of an emperor as Japan's symbol of sovereign unity. Shidehara also proposed Article 9 of the constitution which outlawed war and pledged Japan never again to maintain armed forces. But he could not win popular support for Nihon Shimpoto in the first post-war election (April 1946). At the age of 77 he became Speaker of the Japanese parliament, dying two years later. A. Iriye: *After Imperialism: the Search for a New Order in the Far East, 1921–1931* (Berkeley, Calif., 1965).

Sihanouk, Norodom (1922–), Cambodian ruler: born into the royal dynasty at Phnom Penh, while Cambodia was a tributary kingdom within French Indo-China. After completing his education in Paris he was elected ruler of Cambodia in succession to King Sisowathmonivogong (ruled 1927–41). With Japanese backing, King Sihanouk formally renounced the French colonial connection on 13 March 1945. He showed great diplomatic skill in negotiating a Franco-Cambodian treaty on 7 January 1946 which recognized his authority as a constitutional monarch: in further exchanges with Paris over the following seven years he attained full independent sovereignty for Cambodia (9 November 1953). Development of the kingdom was prevented by Communist insurgency, led by POL POT and the Khmer Rouge. The King abdicated in 1955 and, after standing for election as Prince Sihanouk, served as Prime Minister for the next fifteen years, while also becoming Head of State again in 1960. He astutely kept Cambodia out of the Vietnam War but in March 1970 he was overthrown in a military *coup* engineered by the CIA. After his deposition Prince Sihanouk found refuge in China, where he collaborated with his old enemy Pol Pot until 1976. In 1982, while living in North Korea, he received international backing for a 'democratic' government-in-exile and from 1990 worked closely with UN representatives who, in May 1991, secured a cease-fire in Cambodia, pending multiparty elections. The royalist party (led by Sihanouk's son, Prince Ranariddh) won the elections in May 1993. A Council of the Throne (comprising seven religious and political elders) again elected Sihanouk as King of Cambodia on 23 September 1993: his eldest son became Prime Minister, his second son, Foreign Minster. War with the Khmer Rouge continued. M. F. Herz: *Short History of Cambodia* (New York, 1958); D. Lancaster: *The Emancipation of French Indo-China* (Oxford, 1974); (1984). M. Vickery: *Cambodia, 1975–82* (1984).

Sikorski, Wladyslaw (1881–1943), Polish military leader: born at Tuszow in

Austrian Galicia and served under PILSUDSKI in the First World War, rising to the rank of General in the war against the Bolsheviks (1919–20). His success in helping defend Warsaw led to his appointment as a non-party Prime Minister in December 1922, when he established some degree of collaboration with the Democrats and the peasant parties. Thereafter Pilsudski regarded him with suspicion, helping to bring down his government in May 1923 and placing him on the retired list at the age of 45. He was shunned by the Polish authorities from 1926 onwards, his offer to take command again in 1939 being turned down out of hand. After escaping to the West, he established a Polish army in France early in 1940, bringing his men to England and setting up a government-in-exile, recognized by the British authorities and by the Soviet Union in 1941. Sikorski's leadership enabled the formation of an army of over 100,000 men, most of whom served in the Mediterranean theatre of operations. Friction developed between Sikorski and the Soviet Union in 1942, the Poles maintaining that the Russians were not liberating Polish prisoners taken in 1939. German propaganda assertions that thousands of Poles had been massacred by the Russians in the Katyn Forest were believed by Sikorski to be basically substantiated by other reports. His relations with the Soviet Government were therefore severed in April 1943, Winston CHURCHILL complaining that such disputes should be left for investigation until after the defeat of HITLER. Ten weeks later (4 July 1943) an aircraft in which General Sikorski was flying to inspect Polish units crashed on take-off from Gibraltar, and he was killed. The allegation that Churchill personally engineered Sikorski's death was given publicity by Rolf Hockhuth in his verse tragedy drama, *Soldaten* (1967): the canard is without foundation. J. Garlinski: *Poland in the Second World War* (1985); K. Sword (ed.): *The Formation of the Polish Community in Britain, 1939–50* (1989); S. Mikolajczyk: *The Pattern of Soviet Domination* (1948).

Slim, William Joseph (1891–1970), British commander of the Fourteenth Army in Burma: born in Birmingham and educated there, at King Edward VI School. He enlisted in the Royal Warwickshire Regiment in 1914 and was wounded at Gallipoli, later serving with distinction in Mesopotamia as well as on the Western Front. Between the wars he served with the Gurkhas as an officer in the Indian army. During the Second World War he never fought in Europe, but he showed brilliant powers of improvisation in Eritrea in 1940–1, later commanding operations in Syria and Iraq. Early in 1942 he was sent to Burma, where he had the difficult task of keeping the army's morale and discipline together during the retreat through the jungle in April and May 1942, a withdrawal of 1,000 miles from Rangoon to Imphal. Slim's unique achievement in the following fifteen months was to accustom an army trained for European warfare to the techniques of fighting in the jungle and using it to advantage. In November 1943 he was appointed to the Fourteenth Army, under the supreme command of MOUNTBATTEN. Even though his troops were called 'the forgotten army' (because directives and supplies too often failed to reach them from England), Slim's foresight and training methods enabled him to lead the army back through Burma and liberate both Rangoon and Mandalay, inflicting on the Japanese the greatest defeat on land in their national history. He was knighted in September 1944 and given the task of reopening the Imperial Defence College in 1946. From 1948 to 1952 he was Chief of the Imperial General Staff, with the rank of Field Marshal from January 1949. He served as Governor-General of Australia from May 1953 to January 1960, when he was created Viscount. He died in December 1970. W. Slim: *Defeat into Victory* (1956); R. Lewin: *Slim, the Standard-bearer* (1976).

Smith, Alfred Emanuel (1873–1944), Governor of New York and prominent Democratic politician: born of Irish Catholic parentage in the East Side of New York City. He found employment with the powerful Democratic Party organization, Tammany Hall, holding local political offices and sitting in the state legislature from 1903 to 1915. He ran for State Governor in 1918, serving until 1929 and becoming popular through his social welfare laws, his rejection of excessively conservative legislative proposals for civil rights and his openly expressed contempt for Prohibition. Smith's personal fortunes blossomed and he became controlling chairman of the corporation which built the Empire State Building on New York's Fifth Avenue. He was nominated by the Democratic Convention in 1928 but had four disadvantages: his Catholicism; his Eastern seaboard urbanism; his unfortunately abrasive manner when broadcasting on what he termed 'the raddio'; and his support for 'legalized liquor'. In the South and the Midwest Al Smith could not hope to pull votes away from his Republican opponent, HOOVER. After his defeat he virtually retired from politics until stirred into action as a critic of his former ally, Franklin ROOSEVELT. From 1934 to 1940 Smith led the right-wing Democratic opponents of the 'socialistic' New Deal, organizing party opposition in the much-publicized, but largely ineffectual, 'American Liberty League'. A. E. Smith: *Up to Now* (New York, 1929); R. V. Peel and T. C. Donnelly: *The 1928 Campaign* (New York, 1931).

Smith, Ian Douglas (1919–), Rhodesian Prime Minister from 1964 to 1978: born in Selukwe, graduating from Rhodes University, Grahamstown, before becoming a farmer and enlisting in the Royal Air Force as a fighter pilot. He was severely injured when his plane crashed in north Africa in 1941, and baled out over northern Italy in June 1944, but was able to return to his squadron with aid from the Italian resistance movement. He entered politics in 1948, sitting for five years in the Southern Rhodesian legislature and for nine years in the Federal Rhodesian Parliament, opposing the much-disputed ideas of Sir Roy WELENSKY. Smith founded the Rhodesia Front Party in 1962, becoming Prime Minister of Southern Rhodesia in April 1964 but showing total opposition to British proposals for majority rule, which, he held, would hand over the country to 'the blacks'. On 11 November 1965 he defied the British Labour government by making a unilateral declaration of independence. Abortive talks with the British Prime Minister, Harold WILSON, aboard the cruiser *Tiger* in December 1966 and the assault vessel *Fearless* in October 1968, were followed in March 1970 by the establishment of a Rhodesian republic. Attempts to secure agreement through the good offices of other British, American and UN intermediaries failed, the United Nations supporting an oil embargo established by the British against Smith's Rhodesia, which was also threatened by guerilla action from the Patriotic Front movement led by Joshua NKOMO. In October 1976 Smith flew to Geneva for conversations with black nationalist groups, under British and UN auspices. After the conference he found it possible to achieve some form of collaboration with the moderate nationalists, led by Bishop Muzorewa, Chief Chirau and the Reverend Ndabaningi Sithole. The four men agreed in March 1978 to form an Executive Council which would prepare the way for Rhodesian independence under majority rule. Ian Smith announced on 26 May 1978 that he would retire from politics at the end of the year, but, although he handed over the premiership to Bishop Muzorewa, he remained a prominent member of the government and came to London in September 1979 for the Lancaster House Conference which led to independence for Zimbabwe in April 1980. Smith sat in Zimbabwe's first parliament. D. Caute: *Under the Skin, the Death of White Rhodesia* (1983).

Smuts, Jan Christian (1870–1950), Boer General and South African statesman: born on a farm near Riebeeck West, south western Cape Colony, learning no English until he was 12. He completed his education at Victoria College, Stellenbosch, before reading law at Christ's College, Cambridge, where he gained a double first. He was called to the bar at the Middle Temple, serving as State Attorney to KRUGER in the Transvaal and drafting the ultimatum to Britain which began the Boer War in 1899. In 1901 and 1902 he held the rank of General, commanding a Boer force which raided deep into Cape Colony. After three years as a lawyer in Pretoria, he held high office in the Transvaal colonial administration and was a delegate to the National Convention of 1909–10, which established the Union of South Africa. Most of the constitution of the Union was drafted by Smuts and he sat in the parliaments of the Union for the remainder of his life (forty years). As Minister of Defence from 1910 to 1924 be built up the army which, as a Major-General, he led into German South-West Africa in 1915. He was Commander-in-Chief of Allied forces in German East Africa in 1916–17 and a member of the War Cabinet in London from June 1917 to 14 December 1918. He carried out a special mission in Switzerland with Austrian representatives hoping to make a separate peace (December 1917) and played a prominent part in the Paris Peace Conference of 1919 and in establishing the League of Nations. In August 1919 he succeeded BOTHA as Prime Minister. Unrest in the mines led to serious disturbances in the Rand in March 1922 and Smuts' South African Party was defeated in the elections of June 1924 by a coalition of Labour with the Nationalists. For nine years Smuts remained leader of the Opposition, using his leisure hours for botanical studies and for perfecting the philosophy which he called 'holism', a theory that the fundamental principle of existence is the attainment of 'Wholes', self-contained systems which possess characteristics not identifiable in their constituent parts. He was Deputy Prime Minister and Minister of Justice in the coalition headed by General HERTZOG from 1933 to 1939. Hertzog's reluctance to enter the Second World War split the coalition and enabled Smuts to return as Prime Minister in September 1939. He remained Prime Minister, as well as Minister of Defence and Minister for External Affairs, until 1948. From 1940 to 1945 he was Commander-in-Chief of the armed forces of South Africa and Rhodesia, being created Field Marshal by King GEORGE VI in May 1949. Winston CHURCHILL respected Smuts as the senior statesman of the Empire, and he came to London four times during the war. At the San Francisco Conference of 1945 he sought to improve the UN Charter, which he thought 'a far from perfect document'. Much of the preamble was drafted by Smuts. The South African electorate lacked his sense of world statesmanship and in May 1948 gave a majority to the Nationalists of Dr MALAN. Smuts remained leader of the Opposition for another two years. Outside South Africa he had been honoured by many universities and was Chancellor of the University of Cambridge from January 1948 until his death. King George VI awarded him the Order of Merit in 1947. He died on the Doornkloof farm at Irene in the Transvaal on 11 September 1950. J. C. Smuts, Jnr.: *Jan Christian Smuts* (1952); K. Ingham: *Jan*

Christian Smuts (1986); B. Williams: *Botha, Smuts and South Africa* (1946); S. G. Millin: *General Smuts* (1936).

Soares, Mario Alberto Nobre Lopez (1924–), Portuguese Socialist and President: born and educated in Lisbon before studying law at the Sorbonne, Paris. On his return to Lisbon he was forbidden to practice as an attorney because of his socialist sympathies and received twelve prison sentences over the following twenty years before being exiled to a penal settlement on the island of Sao Tome (1968–70). After SALAZAR's death he settled in Paris where, in 1973, he set up the Partido Socialista (PS), the first Portuguese socialist party since its 50-year-old predecessor was outlawed in 1928. Soares was Foreign Minister in the first multiparty government (1974–5). When full constitutional government returned to Portugal in 1976, he became Prime Minister, presiding over a moderate coalition of the Left for two years. In his second term of office (June 1983 to June 1985) he completed preparations for Portugal to join the EEC in January 1986. Soares was elected President in February 1986 and re-elected for a second five-year term in January 1991. T. Gallagher: *Portugal, a Twentieth Century Interpretation* (Manchester, 1983); R. Harvey: *Portugal, Birth of a Democracy* (1978).

Somoza Garcia, Anastasio (1900–56), Nicaraguan dictator: patriarch of a wealthy landowning family from the traditionally conservative region of the republic around Granada. When, in November 1932, US marines were preparing to end their twenty-year protection of Nicaragua they gave General Anastasio Somoza supreme command of the National Guard, a force raised by the Americans in 1927 to combat attacks from SANDINO's left-wing guerrillas. On Somoza's orders National Guard sharpshooters assassinated Sandino in February 1934. The Guard became Somoza's personal militia; their methods of intimidation enabled him to become President on 8 December 1936, establishing a family hold on political power which lasted for forty-three years. For most of this period US administrations backed the Somozas, who were implacable anticommunists. When President Somoza was shot and fatally injured while visiting Panama (22 September 1956) he was replaced as Head of State by his eldest son Luis, who in turn was succeeded in February 1967 by his brother, General Anastasio Somoza Debayle (1926–80), the most notorious member of the family. Revelation in the mid-1970s of his blatant violation of human rights led the CARTER administration to discourage US investment, thus fatally weakening the regime. In a last display of terror Somoza ordered the bombardment of Nicaragua's capital before fleeing the country (20 July 1979) and finding sanctuary in Paraguay. On 17 September 1980 unknown gunmen used a bazooka to kill him in his car in the Paraguayan capital, Asuncion. J. A. Booth: *The End of the Beginning, the Nicaraguan Revolution* (Boulder, Colo., 1984); B. Diederich: *Somoza and the Legacy of US Involvement in Central America* (1982).

Soong, Tse Ven (Song Ziwen) (1894–1971), Chinese Nationalist politician: born in Shanghai, eldest son of the wealthy merchant and eminent Methodist missionary, C. J. Soong (*c*.1860–1927), whose eldest daughter, Ching Ling (Song Qingling 1890–1981) married SUN YAT-SEN, and whose youngest daughter, Mailing (Song Meiling, 1901–) married CHIANG KAI-SHEK. T. V. Soong was educated at St John's College, Shanghai, and at Harvard. At the age of 23 he was chief administrator of a coal and steel complex in Manchuria but was soon appointed Minister of Finance by his brother-in-law Sun Yat-sen, introducing a westernized banking system to China which he perfected while serving as Finance Minister for his other brother-in-law, Chiang, at Nanking between 1928 and 1933. Soong founded the Bank of China in 1936. From 1942 to 1945 he was China's Foreign Minister, in close touch with ROOSEVELT. He settled in the USA in 1949. L. Eastman: *The Abortive Revolution, China under Nationalist Rule, 1927–1937* (New York, 1974); A. N. Young: *China's Nation Building Effort, 1927–1937: the Financial and Economic Effort* (Chicago, 1992).

Spaak, Paul-Henri (1899–1972), Belgian Prime Minister and internationalist: born at Schaerbeek, practised law in Brussels from 1922 to 1932, though hampered by his total ignorance of Flemish. He was elected to parliament as a socialist for a working-class district of Brussels in 1932, becoming Belgium's first socialist Prime Minister in May 1938, although forced from office in April 1939. He escaped to England in 1940 and was Foreign Minister of the government-in-exile until 1945, helping to improve relations with the Netherlands and Luxembourg and thereby establishing the principles of 'Benelux' collaboration. After presiding over the first meeting of the UN General Assembly, he served as Belgium's Prime Minister from March 1937 to June 1949. By then, however, he was especially interested in the idea of European unity, and he presided over the consultative assembly of the Council of Europe from 1949 to 1951. He was not, however, a starry-eyed idealist: his realism made him accept the need for the North Atlantic Treaty Organization, helping build up the organization when he served as NATO's Secretary-General from 1957 to 1961. As Foreign Minister of Belgium, from 1954 to 1957 and from 1961 until his retirement in 1966, he was a firm champion of the European Community.

Spencer, Herbert (1820–1903), British philosopher and sociologist: born at Derby and educated for the most part by his uncle, an Anglican vicar with a parish near Bath. For some eight years Spencer was a railway engineer, but in 1846 he became a journalist and was appointed deputy editor of *The Economist* at the age of 28. His reaction to the revolutions of 1848–9 was to begin to study social behaviour in depth, his *Social Statics* of 1850 being followed by *The Principles of Psychology* (1855) in which he outlined a pre-Darwinian theory of evolution. Subsequently he tried to apply Darwinism to society, which he claimed was an organism as subject to evolutionary change as mankind. These ideas he sought to analyse in his *Principles of Sociology* (1877). From 1879 to 1893 he developed *Principles of Ethics* which attempted to reconcile utilitarianism and evolution with social behaviour. The historian Thomas Carlyle thought Spencer 'the most immeasurable ass in Christendom': Darwin, more charitably, confessed he could not follow the logic of Spencer's philosophy. Nevertheless Spencer had considerable influence in late Victorian England as the last defender of *laissez-faire* economics, a man who denounced Gladstonian liberal concern with public welfare in his *Man Versus the State* (1884) and who was prepared to claim that taxation imposed by the state for public education was 'tyrannical'. H. Spencer: *An Autobiography* (1903); L. A. Coser: *Masters of Sociological Thought* (New York, 1971).

Stalin, Josef Vissarionovich (Djugashvili) (1879–1953), Soviet dictator: born at Didi-lilo, a village near Tiflis in the Caucasian mountains, Georgia. By the age of 20 he was known to hold revolutionary views and was exiled to Siberia in 1903, escaping a few months later. He attended the Russian Social Democratic Congress in London in May 1907 and, on his return to the Caucasus (Baku), was twice arrested, escaping each time. From 1913 to 1916 he was exiled to the Siberian

Arctic but succeeded in making his way to Petrograd early in 1917, arriving there three weeks ahead of LENIN and seven weeks ahead of TROTSKY. He assisted in preparations for the October Revolution and was appointed Commissar for Nationalities. From July to October 1918 he was engaged in conflict with the 'Whites' on the Volga around Tsaritsyn, which was renamed Stalingrad seven years later in honour of these events. In the winter of 1922–3 he was in Moscow, becoming General-Secretary of the Central Committee and building up his position in the party. Lenin's ill-health and Trotsky's preoccupation with other matters helped Stalin to dominate the Twelfth Party Congress in April 1923. Political dexterity enabled him to outmanoeuvre Trotsky, who was expelled from the Politburo in 1926 and forced to leave the Soviet Union in 1929.

Stalin's attempt to make his 'Socialism in One Country' work began in earnest in 1928 with the First Five Year Plan, which developed heavy industry and enforced collectivization on the peasants, liquidating the '*kulak*' class (created by the reforms of STOLYPIN). Although more consumer goods were produced under the Second Five Year Plan, beginning in 1933, opposition to Stalin's methods and his use of the secret police (NKVD) made him strike at the Old Bolsheviks and at the army leaders in show trials and courts-martial (1936–8) (see YEZHOV, TUKHACHEVSKY, ZINOVIEV). For nineteen years he was content with his position as General-Secretary, but in May 1941, while not relinquishing his party post, he succeeded MOLOTOV as head of the government, taking over as Commissar of Defence after Germany's attack on the Soviet Union a month later. He conferred with Winston CHURCHILL and the US president in the wartime conferences at Teheran, Yalta and Potsdam. It is not clear how far he intervened in military matters, though he became a Marshal of the Soviet Union on 6 March 1943 and his services were recognized by conferment of the unique title of 'Generalissimo of the Soviet Union' seven weeks after the final victory in Europe. The Red Army's successes left him as master of Eastern Europe and pliant 'Stalinists', such as GOTTWALD, RÁKOSI and ULBRICHT, emulated his example in Czechoslovakia, Hungary and East Germany: only Marshal TITO in Yugoslavia successfully defied him.

Towards the end of his life Stalin became paranoiac, suspecting plots by his doctors and giving free rein to an anti-Semitism which may, in earlier years, have influenced his attitude to Trotsky and the Old Bolsheviks. He continued in his last years to rely on Molotov and on his new discoveries, MALENKOV and BERIA, but he despised his eventual successor, the Ukrainian KHRUSCHEV. Stalin made his last speech – a call for 'death to the warmongers' – at the Nineteenth Party Congress in Moscow on 14 October 1952. His own death was announced on 9 March 1953. He was buried beside Lenin in the Mausoleum in Red Square until October 1961, when Soviet reassessment of his role in history downgraded him to a plain grave beside the wall of the Kremlin. A. Bullock: *Hitler and Stalin, Parallel Lives* (1991); I. Deutscher: *Stalin* (rev. edn Oxford, 1961); R. McNeal: *Stalin, Man and Ruler* (1988); D. Vologonov: *Stalin, Triumph and Tragedy* (1991); R. Medvedev: *On Stalin and Stalinism* (Oxford, 1979).

Stamboliisky, Alexander (1879–1923), political leader of Bulgarian peasantry: born near Radomir, studied agriculture in Germany. He entered politics in 1907 as an agitator for land reform, soon becoming a radical demagogue. From 1915 to 1918 he was imprisoned as a critic of King FERDINAND's war policy. Briefly he was provisional President of a Bulgarian Republic in late 1918 but he accepted the accession of King BORIS, who in October 1919 appointed him Prime

Minister. The Stamboliisky government was unique: a Peasant Party dictatorship, hostile to both Communism and to urban capitalism. Heavy taxes were imposed on town-dwellers while the peasantry was left almost tax-free. In June 1923 Stamboliisky was murdered by right-wing nationalists who resented not so much his agrarian dictatorship as his willingness to accept existing frontiers in Macedonia and to co-operate with Bulgaria's old Balkan enemy, Serbia. G. C. Logio: *Bulgaria, Past and Present* (Manchester, 1936); J. Swire: *Bulgarian Conspiracy* (1937); J. Rothschild: *The Communist Party of Bulgaria, Origins and Development 1883–1936* (1959).

Stambulov, Stefan (1854–95), Bulgarian national leader: born in Trnovo, educated at an Odessa seminary from which he ran away at the age of 17, fearing exile to Siberia. After spending some months in Romania he returned to Trnovo and became a teacher, soon gaining a reputation as an outstanding orator, encouraging hopes for a unified, independent Bulgaria. When ALEXANDER of Battenberg abdicated in September 1886 the Great Powers recognized Stambulov as Regent of Bulgaria. He surrendered his powers to the country's newly elected prince, FERDINAND of Saxe-Coburg, in July 1887; but he remained head of the government, seeking reconciliation with Turkey and pursuing a fiercely anti-Russian policy. Stambulov's ruthlessness made him many political enemies and in January 1894 Ferdinand dismissed him from office. In July 1895 Stambulov was hacked to death by assassins in a Sofia street, in a plot of which Ferdinand was not entirely ignorant. R. Crampton: *History of Bulgaria, 1878–1918* (New York, 1983); H. Nicolson: *Lord Carnock* (1930).

Stevenson, Adlai Ewing (1900–65), American Democratic politician: born in Los Angeles, although the family had political roots in Illinois. His grandfather – Adlai E. Stevenson (1835–1914) – was Vice-President throughout the second administration of Grover CLEVELAND. After graduating from Princeton, Adlai, jnr. spent two years editing an Illinois newspaper and then practised law in Chicago. He held New Deal posts under Franklin ROOSEVELT, was assistant in the Navy Department from 1943 to 1945 and was assigned much of the preliminary work for the San Francisco Conference on the foundation of the United Nations Organisation. He served on several American delegations to the UN under TRUMAN, and he won the governorship of Illinois in 1949, capturing the vote in several traditionally Republican areas. His governorship was marked by efficiency, and an anti-corruption drive, and by a courageous liberalism, especially when liberal causes were denounced as 'Red' by Senator MCCARTHY and his followers. He was nominated as presidential candidate by the Democratic Conventions in 1952 and 1956, but on both occasions his Republican opponent was the highly popular EISENHOWER. Stevenson's urbane style, his obvious integrity of character and his wit made him the natural choice of America's intellectuals; but his fluency of spoken English, his genuine humility, and, what the New York *Daily News* called his 'typical Harvard lace-cuff liberalism' alienated the ordinary, folksy American voter. In 1961 John KENNEDY brought him into his Cabinet while giving him the post of Special Ambassador to the United Nations. Possibly Adlai Stevenson was too traditionally British in style for American political life. It is not inappropriate he should have died suddenly in a London street, on 14 July 1965. A. E. Stevenson: *Call to Greatness* (1954), *What I Think* (1956); N. F. Busch: *Adlai E. Stevenson* (1976); A. Cooke: *Six Men* (1977).

Stilwell, Joseph (1883–1946), American General specializing in Chinese affairs:

born in Florida, passed out of West Point in 1904 and served in the First World War, with the rank of Colonel. He then learned Chinese and studied China's history and culture, being appointed military attaché in China in 1932, remaining there through seven years and coming to know personally the strengths and weaknesses of CHIANG KAI-SHEK and other Chinese leaders. In 1939 he returned to California as commanding General of the Third Corps. He was hurriedly flown back to Chungking in January 1942 with responsibility for all American troops in the Chinese theatre of operations and with orders to keep open, if possible, the Burma Road. He found 'Peanut' (as he unaffectionately called Chiang in his diaries) unco-operative and thought little of the will to fight of the Chinese troops in northern Burma. 'Vinegar Joe', as Stilwell was nicknamed, was a difficult colleague; he collaborated easily enough with SLIM, but MOUNTBATTEN found him insubordinate. An attempt in July 1944 to allow Stilwell to secure overall command of China's armies led to strained relations with Chiang, and Stilwell was recalled to Washington in November 1944. He commanded the Tenth Army in Okinawa during the last two months of the war against Japan. T. H. White (ed.): *The Stilwell Papers* (New York, 1948); B. Tuchman: *Sand Against the Wind; Stilwell and the American Experience in China, 1911–45* (New York, 1970).

Stimson, Henry Lewis (1867–1950), American statesman: born in New York, educated at Yale, becoming a legal partner with Elihu ROOT. His energetic political campaigning for the Republicans in New York state was rewarded by service in President TAFT's Cabinet from 1911 to 1913 as Secretary of War. From 1927 to 1929 he was Governor-General of the Philippines, showing great tact in overcoming Filipino suspicion of the slow progress being made towards independence. In 1929 he returned to Washington as Secretary of State under HOOVER. By now he was convinced, from personal observation, that Japanese imperialism threatened America's interests in the Pacific and in China. His active policy as Secretary of State offended the isolationist wing of the Republicans, but the President supported his statement of 7 January 1932 – the so-called 'Stimson Doctrine – that the United States would never recognize any treaty which impaired the integrity of the Chinese Republic. Stimson finally rejected Republican isolationism in 1939, when he supported Franklin ROOSEVELT's efforts at giving the British every aid short of formal co-belligerency; and for this stand Stimson was expelled from the Republican Party. He joined Roosevelt's Cabinet as Secretary of War in 1940, holding the post continuously until after the surrender of Japan. His long experience helped him reconcile opposing views both within the Cabinet and among the army commanders. Despite his old concern with the Far East, he supported the need to defeat Germany before dealing with the Japanese, but he clashed with Winston CHURCHILL over the timing of the Allied invasion of Europe, believing it should be attempted in 1943 and failing to understand why the British wished to wait until the Allies had developed overwhelming strength and resources. He was the departmental politician responsible for all development of the atomic bomb, and accompanied TRUMAN to the Potsdam Conference in 1945. No other politician has served in the Cabinets of two Republican and two Democratic presidents. H. L. Stimson and M. Bundy: *On Active Service in Peace and War* (New York, 1949); G. Hodgson: *The Colonel* (New York, 1990).

Stolypin, Peter (1862–1911), Russian Prime Minister from 1906 to 1911: born on family estates on the lower Volga, spending the first forty years of his life, like most big landowners in the Tsar's Empire, completely outside politics. In 1904–5 he was Governor of Saratov province where his energy in suppressing agrarian unrest attracted court attention in St Petersburg. NICHOLAS II appointed him Minister of the Interior in May 1906 and he became Prime Minister two months later. He ordered summary trial by courts-martial of all captured terrorists in an effort to check the spread of anarchy; and in the first eight months of his premiership there were over a thousand official executions carried out. This harshness was accompanied by anti-Semitic mob violence, which Stolypin did nothing to curb. On the other hand, his political actions in the capital were far-sighted and might, had they been adopted earlier, have saved the Tsarist state. He encouraged governmental aid to hard-working and ambitious peasants, creating for the first time in Russia a class of medium farmers, the '*kulaks*'. Improved educational schemes, expansion of the local government system, and the first attempt in Russia to provide state social insurance were accompanied by a restriction in the franchise, the right to elect to the Duma being now limited to those with a property qualification. By 1911 Stolypin's drastic measures were beginning to improve the stability of the Russian government, but he fell into disfavour with the Tsar by seeking to oust RASPUTIN from the court. On 14 September 1911 he was assassinated by a police agent (who was Jewish) while attending, with the Tsar, a gala performance in the Kiev Opera House. He was the last strong man of Tsardom. M. P. von Bock: *Reminiscences of My Father, Peter A. Stolypin* (Metuchen, N.J., 1970); V. I. Gurko: *Features and Figures of the Past* (Palo Alto, Calif., 1939); H. Seton-Watson: *The Decline of Imperial Russia* (1952).

Stresemann, Gustav (1878–1929), German Chancellor in 1923 and Foreign Minister 1923 to 1929: born in Berlin, sat as a National Liberal in the Reichstag 1906 to 1918, leading the party in the last year of the German Empire, and became well known for ardently nationalistic speeches. With the establishment of the Weimar Republic he dissolved the old political organization, substituting for it a 'People's Party', which he dominated until his death. Stresemann sought to gain the confidence of the British, French and Americans by a policy of 'Fulfilment' rather than indignant rejection of the peace terms. Although only Chancellor from August to November in 1923, he determined the form of German foreign policy for most of the 1920s. The Locarno Pact of December 1925, guaranteeing Germany's frontier in the west, marked the success of his statesmanship. His apparent moderation secured not only a reduction in the sum of reparations, but admission of Germany to the League of Nations in 1926, with a permanent seat on the League Council. He collaborated closely with the Frenchman, BRIAND, the two men sharing the Nobel Peace Prize for 1926. He died suddenly, still in office, on 3 October 1929, his last triumph being agreement on the withdrawal of Allied occupation troops from the Rhineland. H. A. Turner: *Stresemann and the Politics of the Weimar Republic* (Princeton, N.J., 1963); M. L. Edwards: *Stresemann and the Greater Germany, 1914–1918* (New York, 1963).

Strijdom, Johannes Gerhardus (1883–1958), South African Prime Minister from 1954 to 1958: born at Willowmore in Cape Province and practised law in the Transvaal before entering parliament as a Nationalist in 1929. Five years later he was recognized as the most extreme of the Afrikaaner parliamentarians. He succeeded MALAN as Prime Minister on 2 December 1954. Legislation introduced during his premiership disfranchised Cape coloured voters, rigidly segregated South Africa's older university institutions, and tightened the restrictions on movement introduced by Malan's apartheid laws. Strijdom, who was openly contemptuous of liberal opinion outside South Africa, was also responsible in December 1956 for the initial proceedings of the great Treason Trial, in which 156 supporters of the 'Freedom Charter' were charged with conspiracy against the established structure of the state. He died on 3 September 1958 and was succeeded by VERWOERD. T. Davenport: *South Africa, a Modern History* (rev. edn 1991).

Stroessner, Alfredo (1912–), Paraguayan military dictator for thirty-five years: born into a German immigrant family at Encarnacion. He became a military cadet in 1928, was commissioned in 1932 in time to fight with distinction in the three-year war against Bolivia for control of the Chaco plain, which ended in a costly Paraguayan victory in June 1935. By 1950 he was a full General; a year later he became Commander-in-Chief and, through the right-wing Partido Colorado, built up a political influence which enabled him to seize power on 11 July 1954. His despotic government ensured that he was re-elected on seven occasions until deposed by General Andres Rodriguez on 3 February 1989. No earlier Paraguayan President held office for so long. Stroessner introduced a series of major public works programmes, especially hydro-electric projects, but his long dictatorship became notorious for its denial of civil rights. R. Bourne: *Political Leaders of Latin America* (1968); P. H. Lewis: *Paraguay under Stroessner* (Chapel Hill, N.C., 1980); L. Bethell (ed.): *Cambridge History of Latin America*, Vol. 8, *1930–89* (Cambridge, 1991).

Suharto, Thojib (1980–), Indonesian General and second President: born on Java at Kemuju, Jogjakarta. He received a military training in the Royal Netherlands Indies Army but, under Japanese patronage, in 1943 accepted command of Pembela Tanah Air, an auxiliary military force from which the Indonesian army evolved at the end of the Second World War. Technically he did not become Chief of Staff until 1965 but he was, in effect, Indonesia's military strong man throughout the SUKARNO years. He narrowly escaped death during the attempted left wing revolt of 30 September 1965 but rallied anti-Communists to 'restore peace'. Several hundred thousand Indonesians were executed. Further unrest early in 1966 led Suharto to take over executive power from President Sukarno, who resigned as Head of State in Suharno's favour on 22 February 1967. A year later General Suharno's authority was confirmed by the vote of a People's Consultative Assembly. He was re-elected in 1973, 1978, 1983, 1988 and 1993. Criticism of the government was forbidden: although the elections were contested by as many as ten different 'partis', President Suharno ensured that political power remained in the hands of his military organization, Golkar. H. McDonald: *Suharto's Indonesia* (Hawaii, 1981); H. Thoolen: *Indonesia and the Rule of Law* (1987); H. Benda: *The Crescent and the Rising Sun, Indonesian Islam and the Japanese Occupation* (The Hague, 1958).

Sukarno, Achmed (1901–70), founding President of Indonesia from 1945 to 1968: born in eastern Java at Blita, and was well educated in Dutch schools, becoming a qualified engineer. The inspiration of Mohandas GANDHI led him in 1927 to establish a movement which sought recognition from the Dutch colonial authorities of the rights of the Indonesian people, urging his followers to adopt tactics of civil disobedience rather than of violence. He was arrested in 1929, only enjoying personal freedom in Java for two of the following thirteen years. With other members of his Indonesian Nationalist Party (PNI), he collaborated with the Japanese when they occupied the Dutch East Indies in March 1942. The surrender of the Japanese at the end of the Second World War left a power vacuum which the PNI filled: an Indonesian Republic was proclaimed in Batavia (Jakarta) on 17 August 1945, with Sukarno describing himself as President three months later. This title, and the existence of the Indonesian state, was disputed by the Dutch when they reasserted colonial rule, and a bitter civil war flared up, Dutch 'police actions' in 1946, July 1947 and the closing months of 1948 winning much world sympathy for Sukarno. The Netherlands government formally recognized Sukarno as President of a unified Indonesia in August 1950. For seventeen years Sukarno governed the Indonesian islands with great personal authority, commanding respect from the Indonesian peoples if not affection. He was recognized as a leader of the 'uncommitted world' and, in April 1955, was host to the first political conference of the Asian and African nations, in Bandung. From 1963 to 1966 there was intermittent fighting between Sukarno's troops and British and Gurkha forces helping to defend Malaysia, since Sukarno laid claim to the whole of Borneo. This aggressive foreign policy, called 'confrontation' by Sukarno, was a costly strain on Indonesia's economy, and the President was conscious that alleged Javanese domination was much resented in Sumatra (where there had been a serious revolt in 1956). Unrest in 1965 and 1966 emphasized that grandiose public works programmes announced by Sukarno remained mere blueprints. The Defence Minister, General SUHARTO, assumed executive power in March 1967, fearing a breakdown of order as well as of the economy. He permitted Sukarno to remain titular President until 28 March 1968. Sukarno died on 21 June 1970. J. Legge: *Sukarno, a Political Biography* (1972); C. L. M. Penders: *Life and Times of Sukarno* (1974).

Sun Yat-sen (1867–1925), Chinese revolutionary: born at Tsuiheng, south of Canton, educated in Honolulu by a wealthy elder brother, graduating as a doctor of medicine from Hong Kong University in 1892 and establishing a 'New China Party' among exiles in Britain, Japan and America. The imperial Chinese authorities rated him so serious a threat that they kidnapped him in London in 1896, holding him in the Legation until ordered to set him free by the intervention of Lord SALISBURY. Sun Yat-sen believed in three principles – 'Nationalism, Democracy, Socialism' – and these principles formed the basis for his political movements from 1898 onwards, including the Chinese National Party (Kuomintang), which he set up in 1905. Sun's propaganda led to the overthrow of the Manchu Emperors in 1911 and the proclamation of a republic. Although recognized as first President of the republic, his authority was challenged by the ambitious warlord Yuan Shih-kai (1859–1916), in whose favour Sun stood down in 1913, only to find himself forced to resort to arms in order to prevent President Yuan from setting himself up as Emperor of a new dynasty. Sun was once again accepted as President in Canton in 1923. At that time he held conversations with the Communists to see if they could collaborate with him behind his 'three principles'. However, his most influential supporter, General CHIANG KAI-SHEK, urged him to abandon the third of his principles ('socialism') in favour of the less doctrinaire concept, 'livelihood'. These differing strands of political development troubled Sun's later years and came at a time when he was already suffering from cancer. He died, while seeking to reconcile the opposing factions, at a conference in Peking (12 March 1925). His widow, Ching Ling (Song Quinling, 1890–1981), supported MAO against her brother-in-law, Chiang Kai-shek, whom she accused of distorting the teachings handed down by her husband to the Kuomintang. Communists and non-Communists recognize Sun Yat-sen as the founding father of the Chinese Republic. H. Z. Schiffran: *Sun Yatsen, Reluctant Revolutionary* (New York, 1980), *Sun Yatsen, the Origins of the Chinese Revolution* (1968); A. Lineberger: *The Political Doctrines of Sun Yatsen* (1937).

T

Taft, Robert (1889–1953), American Republican Senator: born at Cincinnati, Ohio, eldest son of William TAFT. Robert Taft studied law at both Yale and Harvard, working for a time on food administration in Europe after the First World War before practising law in his home state. He was returned to the Senate in 1938 and at once showed himself a vigorous opponent of Franklin ROOSEVELT's domestic and foreign policy and an extreme isolationist. He was outmanoeuvred in seeking the Republican nomination in 1940, even though a stronger contender than the eventual choice, WILLKIE. In 1947 Robert Taft was the main sponsor of the Labour Management Act, better known as the Taft–Hartley Act, which restricted union power and outlawed the closed shop. Despite the publicity which followed this measure he failed to secure nomination yet again in 1948. In 1950 he became the strongest Republican critic of involvement in Korea. His old-fashioned isolationism seemed, at first, to appeal to the Chicago Party Convention of 1952, but the potential vote-winning of EISENHOWER's candidacy robbed him of selection for a third time. He died of cancer a few months later, his brand of conservatism passing to the newly elected Senator from Arizona, Barry GOLDWATER. J. Gunther: *Inside USA* (1949).

Taft, William Howard (1857–1930), President of the United States from 1909 to 1913: born at Cincinnati, his father being active in Republican politics and serving in the Cabinet of President GRANT in 1876–7. William Taft was educated at Yale and Cincinnati Law School. He practised law in Ohio, becoming Solicitor-General under President HARRISON in 1890, and was the first of the civilian governors in the Philippines from 1901 to 1904, when he entered the Cabinet of Theodore ROOSEVELT as Secretary of War. In 1909 he defeated BRYAN to become President. His years at the White House were infelicitous, for he could not handle Congress while his natural conservatism drove many liberal Republicans out of the party. In the unusual 1912 election he gained fewer votes than either the Democrat Woodrow WILSON or his predecessor, Roosevelt, now standing as an independent progressive. After nine years as a professor at Yale, Taft was appointed Chief Justice of the US Supreme Court in 1921, an office he held with distinguished detachment for the remainder of his life. H. E. Pringle: *Life and Times of William Howard Taft* (2 vols) (New York, 1939); P. E. Coletta: *W. H. Taft* (Lawrence, Kans., 1984).

Talaat, Mehmed (1874–1921), Young Turk leader: born into a peasant family at Edirne, became a telegraph clerk to the Turkish postal service at Salonika where, in September 1906, he secretly founded the Ottoman Freedom Society. With support from officers in the Salonika garrison the society merged with other reform groups to create the Young Turk movement which secured a pledge of constitutional parliamentary government in July 1908 and forced Sultan ABDUL HAMID to abdicate nine months later. Talaat, a man of considerable intelligence and political dexterity, was Minister of the Interior from May 1909 to July 1912 and from January 1913 to February 1917; he then became Grand Vizier, the head of the Ottoman government, a post he held until 8 October 1918. Progress was made in centralizing and streamlining the cumbersome Ottoman administrative system but Talaat's genuine desire for reform was hampered by the succession of crises in foreign affairs which culminated in Turkey's alliance with Germany in the First World War. Talaat never shared the pro-German sympathies of his colleague ENVER and, before Turkey entered the war, even visited Tsar NICHOLAS II in the Crimea in the vain hope of gaining territorial concessions in return for a pledge of neutrality. During the war Talaat put out peace feelers as early as March 1915 and appointed a liberal Minister of the Interior in July 1918. He could not, however, save the Young Turk regime. F. Ahmad: *The Young Turks* (Oxford, 1969); A. Palmer: *The Decline and Fall of the Ottoman Empire* (1992).

Teresa, Mother (Agnes Goxha Bedjanxhiu) (1910–), humanitarian and founder of the Missionaries of Charity: born, of Albanian parentage, in Skopje, which was then in Turkish Macedonia and later in Yugoslavia. She was educated by Roman Catholics, became a nun in the Irish Order of the Sisters of Loreto at Dublin in 1928 and was sent to Calcutta in 1929, where she taught at a high school until 1948. Concern for the poor in the Calcutta slums induced her to seek permission to leave her religious order, and in 1948 she undertook intensive training as a nurse from American missionaries in Patna. She became an Indian citizen at the same time and set up a school in one of the slum areas, Moti Jheel, as well as taking food and medical succour to the destitutes of Calcutta. In October 1950 her new order, the Missionaries of Charity, was founded in Calcutta, spreading throughout India by 1961, with centres later established in Ceylon, Tanzania, Ethiopia, among the aborigines of Australia, in Peru, New Guinea, Mexico, and in many other lands. Under Mother Teresa's direction the Missionaries of Charity set up homes for abandoned children, alcoholics, the chronically sick, lepers, drug addicts, and destitutes. Her work received world recognition in the 1970s, culminating in the Nobel Peace Prize for 1979. Changing attitudes a decade later led critics who were unable to comprehend the nature of her vocation to complain of the specifically Catholic Christian motivation of the Missionaries of Charity. D. Doig: *Mother Teresa, her People and her Work* (1976); D. Porter: *Mother Teresa, the Early Years* (1986).

Thant, Sithu U (1909–74), Secretary-General of the United Nations from 1962 to 1971: born at Pantanaw, becoming a schoolmaster, entering Burmese government service at the end of the Second World War. He was Minister of Information from 1948 to 1959, when he led Burma's delegationto the UN Assembly in New York. His calm objectivity impressed delegates from both East and West and he was accepted as acting Secretary-General upon the death of HAMMARSKJÖLD in September 1961. His successful mediation between the authorities in the Congo and in Katanga, together with his handling of the Soviet–American confrontation over missiles in Cuba in October 1962, facilitated his formal election as Secretary-General on 30 November 1962. His main achievements were a gradual acceptance of the Communist Chinese as spokesmen for their peoples at the United Nations, the stationing of UN peace-keeping forces in Cyprus from 1964 onwards, and the conclusion of a cease-fire under UN auspices after the Six Day War of 1967. He retired on 31 December 1971, settling in the town of Harrison in New York State, and he died in New York on 15 November 1974. U. Thant: *Towards World Peace* (New York, 1964); E. Osmanczyk: *Encyclopaedia of the United Nations* (1985).

Thatcher, Margaret Hilda (*née* **Roberts**) (1925–), Britain's first woman Prime Minister: born at Grantham, educated locally and at Somerville College, Oxford. After working for some years as a research chemist she married Denis Thatcher in 1951, studied law, and was called to the bar at Lincoln's Inn (1953). She was elected Conservative MP for Finchley in 1959, holding junior government office from 1961 to 1964. HEATH raised her to Cabinet rank as Minister of Education and Science (1970–4); on 11 February 1975 she defeated him in a contest for the Conservative leadership. The General Election of May 1979 gave the Conservatives an overall majority of forty-three and she formed a government more markedly right-wing than any in Britain for forty years. She believed strongly in monetarism and 'rolling back the state' by privatization of nationalized industries. Her attitude to foreign affairs was robustly nationalistic, uncompromisingly hostile to communism, highly critical of the EEC, opposed to sanctions against South Africa, and sympathetic to the right-wing policies of REAGAN. Her hectoring style of speech and advocacy of the 'politics of conviction' inclined her to look for scapegoats, notably in home affairs the miners and their union leader, Arthur SCARGILL; legislation drastically curbed trade union opportunities to strike. Although taken by surprise when GALTIERI seized the Falkland Islands in 1982 she responded to the challenge with Churchillian defiance, always refusing to compromise over sovereignty. Encouragement of home ownership and the purchase of shares in denationalized industries broadened the class of small property owners, traditional Conservatives. Unprecedently she won two further General Elections, increasing her majority to 144 in June 1983 and holding it at 101 in June 1987. In January 1988 Mrs Thatcher became the longest-serving Prime Minister since Lord Liverpool in 1812–27, before the reform acts made Britain a parliamentary democracy. By 1989 her popularity was in decline, except in those areas of southern England which enjoyed a surface prosperity: the community charge, levied in Scotland earlier than in England, was derided as a 'poll tax'; cuts in the National Health Service and in education aroused resentment. Her autocratic style of Cabinet government left her isolated from senior colleagues over taxation, European issues and general economic policy. A clash of personalities led to the resignation of the deputy Prime Minister, Sir Geoffrey Howe (1926–) on 1 November 1990. Her party leadership was then challenged by her former Defence Secretary, Michael Heseltine (1933–). Although 204 Conservative MPs continued to support Thatcher and only 152 backed Heseltine, she decided that the size of the revolt indicated she should resign. After a further leadership election (in which Mrs Thatcher did not stand) she was succeeded on 28 November 1990 by John MAJOR. Margaret Thatcher received the Order of Merit, a life peerage (Baroness Thatcher of Kesteven, 1992) and was made a Knight of the Garter in 1995. M. Thatcher: *The Downing Street Years* (1993), *The Path to Power* (1995); H. Young: *One of Us* (1989).

Thérèse of Lisieux (**Marie Françoise-Thérèse Martin**) (1873–97), Carmelite nun and Saint: born at Alençon in Normandy, a watchmaker's daughter. Her mother died when she was 4 and the family moved to Lisieux, some fifty-five miles to the north. Thérèse Martin early showed remarkable awareness of spiritual experience, notably during a visit to Italy, where she received a personal blessing from Pope LEO XIII (1887). Soon afterwards (9 April 1888) she entered the

Carmelite convent at Lisieux, as had two of her sisters before her. She was professed as a nun in 1890 and was preparing to join the Carmelites in Hanoi when her health gave way in the first week of April 1896. For the last eighteen months of her life she suffered from tuberculosis, dying in the infirmary of her convent on 30 September 1897. Her natural holiness – a conscious attempt to reach the ideals of saintliness – impressed the religious at Lisieux. Her prioress asked her to write a spiritual autobiography which was circulated soon after her death; miracles of healing were reported and the first steps to secure her beatification were taken within thirteen years of her death. She was beatified in April 1923 and canonized by PIUS XI on 17 May 1925, five years after the canonization of Joan of Arc. She became the centre of a popular cult, probably because she symbolized sanctity through the renunciation of everyday temptations. A huge basilica was erected at Lisieux, and in 1947 she was formally linked with St Joan as patroness of France. T. N. Taylor (ed.): *The Autobiography of St. Theresa of Lisieux* (1925); H. Gheon: *St Theresa of Lisieux* (1935); A. Dansette: *Religious History of Modern France* (2 vols), abridged in translation (Edinburgh, 1961).

Thiers, Adolphe (1797–1877), French historian and President from 1871 to 1873: born at Marseilles, studied law, practising intermittently in Paris while compiling a ten-volume history of the French Revolution which was published between 1823 and 1827. He helped establish the Orleanist constitutional monarchy of King Louis Philippe in 1830, was Minister of the Interior in 1834 and briefly Prime Minister in 1836 and 1840, vainly striving to prevent the King from going into exile when the first revolutionary disturbances shook Paris in February 1848. At first Thiers supported NAPOLEON III but he was arrested and briefly exiled in 1851 and for some years he concentrated on completing his twenty-volume history of the Consulate and Empire before returning to active politics as a liberal monarchist in 1863. He denounced the folly of Napoleon III's foreign policy in the Assembly, especially opposing the Chamber's bellicose attitude to Prussia in 1870. In February 1871 the National Assembly, meeting at Bordeaux, elected Thiers 'Chief of the Executive Power' of the Republic and he travelled to occupied Versailles for six days of talks with BISMARCK on peace terms. The radicals in Paris refused to acknowledge Thiers' authority, and on 21 May 1871 he sent a French army into the capital to suppress the Paris Commune in a week of bloody street-fighting. Yet, though the urban working class hated Thiers, he was respected by foreign bankers and won the confidence of the French peasantry. He successfully floated two government loans which paid off the war indemnity imposed by the victorious Germans in the Treaty of Frankfurt; and he thus secured the final evacuation of France by the German army in September 1873, earlier than anticipated. When in August 1871 Thiers was formally accorded the title of President he began to shed his inherent royalism. The political mood of the Assembly remained predominantly sympathetic to a restoration, and in May 1873 Thiers was forced to resign in favour of Marshal MACMAHON, whom it was wrongly assumed would bring back the monarchy. Thiers won a seat in the Chamber of Deputies in 1876 and was campaigning for the Republicans on the eve of further elections when he died from apoplexy at St Germain-en-Laye (3 September 1877). D. W. Brogan: *The Development of Modern France* (1940); A. Horne: *The Fall of Paris, the Siege and the Commune* (1965); J. M. Allison: *Thiers and the French Monarchy* (Boston, Mass., 1926).

Tilden, Samuel Jones (1814–86), American Democratic politician in the 1870s:

born, a farmer's son, at New Lebanon, New York. He became an eminent lawyer, specializing in railway legislation, and he served as Chairman of the Democratic Party in New York during the period from 1866 to 1871, the years in which the pernicious influence of 'Boss' TWEED was destroyed. As Governor of New York State in 1875–6 Tilden won a reputation as a reformer. The Democratic Party chose him to oppose Rutherford HAYES in the presidential campaign of 1876. Popular votes in the election gave Tilden a majority of a quarter of a million, but the Republicans disputed the electoral college returns from three southern states (Florida, Louisiana and South Carolina) as well as from Oregon. The dispute was referred to an electoral commission of seven Democrats and seven Republicans which was completed by the addition of the allegedly impartial Justice Bradley, a former member of the Republican Party who had been appointed to the Supreme Court by the outgoing President, GRANT. The Commission decided, by Bradley's casting vote, that Hayes defeated Tilden by 185 electoral votes to 184. Although public feeling was bitterly indignant at this ruling, Tilden accepted the Commission's interpretation of the 'will of the people' and retired from politics. Upon his death ten years later he left a considerable sum of money to endow a free public library in New York City. A. C. Flick: *Samuel Jones Tilden, a Study in Political Sagacity* (New York, 1939).

Tirpitz, Alfred von (1849–1930), German Admiral and Minister of Marine from 1897 to 1916: born at Küstrin, and was a cadet in the Prussian navy at the age of 15. He became a torpedo specialist in the late 1880s, attracting the attention of Kaiser WILLIAM II by his proposals for constructing a large battle-fleet in 1895. After serving in the Far East, Admiral Tirpitz was appointed Minister of Marine in June 1897 with authority to create a 'high seas fleet' sufficiently powerful to deter a greater naval power from risking the losses which would follow from an attack upon it. The German 'Navy Laws' of 1898 and 1900 heralded a new arms race between Britain and Germany which was intensified by the rival construction of all-big-gun battleships ('dreadnoughts') from 1906 and which reached an expensive and dangerous climax in the period from 1909 to 1912. Tirpitz gained financial backing for his projects as a result of the mass propaganda for a large fleet undertaken, on his instructions, by the German Navy League. After the outbreak of the First World War Tirpitz found that the Kaiser would not permit his surface warships to undertake any offensive sweep in European waters, nor would he authorize unrestricted submarine warfare. Grand-Admiral Tirpitz was so angered by the Kaiser's veto that he resigned office in March 1916. He sat as a Nationalist member of the Reichstag from 1924 to 1928, dying on 6 March 1930, a fortnight before his eighty-first birthday. H. H. Herwig: *'Luxury' Fleet. The Imperial German Navy 1888–1918* (1980); V. R. Berghahn: *Germany and the Approach of War in 1914* (1973).

Tito, Josip (Broz) (1892–1980), Yugoslav Marshal and President: born at Kumrovec in Croatia, serving with the Austrian Army in the First World War. He was taken prisoner by the Russians in April 1915, escaping from a prisoner-of-war camp in 1917 and helping the Red Army against the 'Whites' of KOLCHAK at Omsk in 1918. By September 1920 he was back in Croatia, working as an engineer and building up the banned Yugoslav Communist Party. He was arrested and imprisoned from 1928 to 1934, subsequently making several visits to Moscow. In 1937 he became General-Secretary of the Yugoslav Communist Party, being by then known under the code name of 'Tito'. After the Germans occupied Yugoslavia in 1941, he organized resistance among the 'Partisans' of southern Serbia, Bosnia-Herzegovina and Montenegro. By November 1943 he controlled sufficient territory to convene a congress of the National Liberation Committee in the Bosnian town of Jajce, which bestowed on him the title 'Marshal of Yugoslavia'. Assistance from a British mission marked his attainment of international recognition: he was fortunate to escape death or capture during a surprise German airborne attack on his headquarters at Drvar at the end of May 1944. When Yugoslavia became a republic in November 1945, Marshal Tito was effective head of the government. For two years he collaborated closely with the Russians, rounding up resolute anti-Communists (notably the *chetnik* leader MIHAILOVIĆ), and exerting pressure on the Italian frontier, especially around Trieste. Tito also sought an independent Balkan policy, at first in collaboration with DIMITROV of Bulgaria. His unwillingness to accept Moscow's general ruling on policy prompted a verbal attack from STALIN in the spring of 1948, followed by expulsion 'from the family of fraternal Communist Parties' (28 June 1948). Tito successfully defied Stalin, experimenting with systems of workers' self-government and calling on other socialist states to follow his lead in pursuing a non-aligned policy, an attitude which won him much prestige in Africa and Asia. He was elected President in January 1953 and President-for-life in May 1974. In a visit to Belgrade by KHRUSCHEV and BULGANIN (May 1955) efforts were made to tempt Tito back into the Soviet camp, but he remained critical of Soviet policy on several occasions, notably after Russian intervention against NAGY in Hungary (1956) and against DUBCEK in Czechoslovakia (1968). His own position suffered from a revival of nationalist feeling, especially in Croatia, and from the outspoken criticism of his former friend and colleague, DJILAS. Despite the weakness of Yugoslavia's economy, his international stature remained high. He died at Ljubljana on 4 May 1980 after four months of illness. Later events in Yugoslavia have raised doubts over the wisdom of his statecraft. J. Ridley: *Tito* (1994); F. Maclean: *Disputed Barricade* (1957); S. Pavlowitch: *Yugoslavia's Great Dictator, Tito – a Reassessment* (1992).

Togo, Heihachiro (1847–1934), Japanese Admiral, victorious against Russia in 1904–5: born at Kagoshima and commissioned in his new navy by the Emperor MUTSUHITO soon after his accession. Togo was one of several Japanese naval officers sent to England for training at Greenwich. In 1894–5 he had the opportunity of using his fleet in a brief war with China. He was Commander-in-Chief of the Japanese fleet which bombarded the Russian naval base and warships at Port Arthur in a surprise attack (February 1904). His greatest success was the interception of the Russian Baltic Fleet in the Straits of Tsushima (which separate Korea from Japan) on 27 May 1905. The Russian fleet, which had been despatched from Kronstadt seven months previously in the hopes of restoring Russian naval strength after the attack on Port Arthur, was virtually destroyed, thus inducing the government in St Petersburg to seek peace. Togo's vessels suffered little damage in the largest naval battle fought since Trafalgar, a hundred years previously. Togo remained an Anglophile, successfully urging the despatch of a Japanese squadron for service with the Allies in the Mediterranean in 1916. N. Ogasawara: *A Life of Admiral Togo* (Tokyo, 1934); R. Storry: *A History of Modern Japan* (rev. edn 1963).

Tojo, Hideki (1884–1948), Japanese General and Prime Minister from 1941 to 1944: born in Tokyo, showed brilliance as a cadet at the War Academy and was sent to Germany as a military attaché in the early 1920s. From 1931 he was principal spokesman for the expansionist Military Party in Japan, as well as serving in Manchuria and Kwantung. He was appointed War Minister in July 1940 in the government of Prince Konoye (1891–1945), and it was Tojo's influence that led to signature of the German–Italian–Japanese Tripartite Pact of 27 September 1940, the basic form of collaboration between those who sought a 'new order' in Europe and in Asia. Tojo succeeded Konoye as Prime Minister on 14 October 1941, authorizing final preparations for the surprise attack on the American fleet at Pearl Harbor seven weeks later and the general Japanese advances in south east Asia and the Pacific. Tojo was, in effect, a military dictator until the summer of 1944 when Japan came within range of American bombers on recaptured islands in the Pacific. It was argued in Tokyo that he was too concerned with attack and unable to think defensively; and he was induced to offer his resignation to Emperor HIROHITO on 9 July 1944. Subsequently he was tried as a major war criminal and hanged on 23 December 1948. E. L. I. Butow: *Tojo and the Coming of the War* (Princeton, N.J. 1961); Y. C. Maxon: *Control of Japanese Foreign Policy – Civil-Military Rivalry 1930–1945* (Westport, Conn., 1975).

Trotsky, Lev Davidovich (Bronstein) (1879–1940), Russian revolutionary: born of Jewish parentage at Ianovka in the Ukraine. He was arrested as a revolutionary in 1897 and eventually sent to Siberia. In October 1902 he was able to join LENIN in London. He was never content to obey, preferring even as early as 1904 to develop his own theories of revolution. By 1905 he was back in St Petersburg, organizing the first Soviet. After another term of imprisonment in Siberia he succeeded in making his way to Vienna and later to America, whence he returned to Petrograd in May 1917, having acted totally independently of Lenin (who had his own group of close followers in Geneva). Trotsky helped organize the Bolshevik seizure of power in Petrograd, subsequently debating peace-terms with the Germans and Austrians at Brest-Litovsk and showing ingenuity in delaying signature in the hope that revolution would spread to Germany and Austria-Hungary. He became Commissar for War in 1918 and was responsible for building up the Red Army. These tasks prevented him from securing a hold on the party machine, which was controlled either by Lenin's Genevan associates or by revolutionaries who had remained in Russia, notably STALIN. Trotsky argued in favour of 'Permanent Revolution' after Lenin's death: Stalin favoured 'Socialism in One Country', a pragmatic approach at variance with Trotsky's internationalism. By 1925 Stalin had politically isolated Trotsky, who was unable to build up any following on the Central Committee. He was expelled from the Communist Party in 1927 and deported in January 1929. At first he settled in Turkey, later living in France, and finally in a heavily-defended villa in Mexico. There he was murdered by his secretary, a Spaniard who was a Soviet secret police agent, on 20 August 1940. L. Trotsky: *History of the Russian Revolution* (1934); I. Deutscher: *The Prophet Armed, 1879–1921* (1954), *The Prophet Unarmed, 1921–1929* (1959), *The Prophet Outcast, 1929–1940* (1963).

Trudeau, Pierre Elliott (1919–), Canadian Prime Minister from 1968 to 1979: born in Montreal, of wealthy parents, educated by Jesuits, at the Universities of Montreal and Harvard, and at the London School of Economics, practising law in Quebec before entering the Federal Parliament in 1965 as a Liberal. Under Lester PEARSON in 1967–8 he was Minister of Justice and Attorney-General, succeeding to the party leadership and the premiership in April 1968. While believing in social and political reforms and rejecting old-fashioned clerical teachings, he was firmly opposed to separatist tendencies, especially among the French Canadians in his native province. Ten weeks after taking office he won a General Election, with a boosted majority, partly because his 'contemporary' style of life appealed to the younger generation. The threat of separatism cost his party many seats in the election of October 1972, and he held power precariously as head of a minority government for twenty-one months, until he was able to recover some lost ground in the General Election of July 1974. Criticism of his backing for the costly 1976 Olympiad and for other projects put him on the defensive by 1978. He failed to hold the electorate in May 1979, the Liberals passing into opposition for only the third time this century, but he speedily won back support and gained a decisive victory in the General Election of February 1980. He remained Prime Minister until June 1984. The main achievement of this second term of office was constitutional reform, completing Canada's assertion of independence of Great Britain. R. Bothwell, I. Drummond and J. English: *Canada since 1945; Power, Politics and Provincialism* (Toronto 1981).

Trujillo (y Molina) Rafael (1891–1961), Dominican politician and archetypal President of a 'banana republic': born at San Cristobal, fighting his way successfully through the gangster politics of the Dominican Republic until he was accepted as President in February 1930. Corrupt rule, maintained through secret police and murder squads, was accompanied by an impressive public works programme which benefited members of his family. Technically he was President for eighteen years, 1930–8 and 1942–52, but in fact he held authority as a dictator from 1930 until his death. He encouraged the massacre of several thousand Haitian settlers in 1937, established a form of rule by terror and tried to foment right-wing revolutions in the smaller central American republics and even in Venezuela. On 30 May 1961 he died when his car was ambushed on a remote road not far from 'Trujillo City', as he had renamed the capital, Santo Domingo. The political influence of his family ended with him. H. Wiarda and M. Kryzanek: *The Dominican Republic* (Boulder, Colo., 1982).

Truman, Harry S (1894–1972), President of the United States from 1945 to 1953: born at Lamar in Missouri, fought in France as an artillery Captain in 1918. After running a haberdashery business in Missouri he studied law in Kansas City, joined the Democrats and was an elected county judge for eight years. In 1934 he was returned to the US Senate where, in 1942, he became head of a committee to keep check on wartime expenditure. Although little known nationally or internationally, he became Vice-President in January 1945, automatically succeeding to the presidency on the death of Franklin ROOSEVELT eleven weeks later. He met STALIN, Winston CHURCHILL and ATTLEE for the Potsdam Conference in July 1945 and gave final orders for dropping the atomic bombs on Japan. His presidency was marked by a willingness to accept world responsibilities for the United States: the plan associated with General MARSHALL helped European recovery; the so-called 'Truman Doctrine' of March 1947 pledged American support for peoples threatened with communist subversion; the Berlin airlift and the North Atlantic Treaty showed his belief that the United States should maintain the *status quo* in Europe; while his energetic backing for the South Koreans when they were invaded by Communist North Korea in 1950 indicated America's willingness to use the United Nations as a shield against aggression. At home his administration saw a gradual increase in recognition of the civil rights of the black population together with the growth of an 'anti-Red' hysteria, best remembered through the accusations of Senator MCCARTHY. Truman unexpectedly won the 1948 campaign against Thomas DEWEY. His courage in dismissing General MACARTHUR in April 1951, because the General publicly criticized the administration's attitude to the Korean War, showed Truman's resolute exercise of a chief executive's prerogatives. He declined to stand again in 1952, retiring into private life in Independence, Missouri, from where he occasionally issued astringent criticisms of the Eisenhower–Nixon administration which succeeded him. He died at Independence in 1972. H. S Truman: *Memoirs* (2 vols) (1956); D. McCulloch: *Truman* (New York, 1992); R. J. Donovan: *Conflict and Crisis, the Presidency of Harry S Truman 1945–1948* (New York, 1977).

Tshombe, Moise (1919–69), Congolese politician of great influence between 1960 and 1965: born at Mushoshi in the interior of the Belgian Congo, near the present border with Zambia. His family owned a chain of stores in the mining province of Katanga and he had close commercial links with the European mining companies. From 1960 to 1962, with the backing of whites and mercenaries, he maintained an independent Katangan state, opposed to LUMUMBA and the official centralized Congo which was recognized by the United Nations. In January 1963 UN forces overthrew his regime and forced him into exile. He returned in July 1964 and became President of the Congo Republic. His repressive policies and reliance on white mercenaries, made him especially hated by pan-Africans. The magnitude of corruption in the republic under Tshombe forced General MOBUTU to seize power in November 1965. Tshombe found sanctuary in Spain, but in July 1967 he was kidnapped aboard a private aircraft which was flown to Algeria, where he was kept under arrest. The Algerians announced he had died from a heart attack on 29 June 1969. C. Young: *Politics in the Congo; Decolonization and Independence* (Oxford, 1965); J. McHaffey: *Entrepreneurs and Parasites, the Struggle for Indigenous Capitalism in Zaire* (Cambridge, 1988).

Tubman, William (1895–1971), Liberian President: born in Monrovia; entered politics as an active and reforming member of the True Whig Party, which came to power in Liberia in 1870 and provided successive executive presidents until 1980. Tubman, as incumbent Vice-President, succeeded President Edwin Barclay in 1943 and was re-elected regularly every eight years until his death. His powerful personality ensured large-scale foreign investment, especially American; economic development maintained Liberia's long record of political stability until 1966, when smouldering conflict between workers from the coast and from the interior prompted him to take authoritarian emergency powers for twelve months. Tubman's experience gave him great prestige in black Africa and in 1961 he was host to the Monrovia Conference of African leaders. But his close links with American capitalism aroused mistrust among the socialist politicians in the emerging black republics. He was succeeded as Head of State by Vice-President Tolbert, who in 1980 was to fall a victim to the sudden eruption of radical unrest aroused by DOE's 'Progressives'. C. M. Wilson: *Liberia, Black Africa in Microcosm* (New York, 1991).

Tudjman, Franjo (1922–), first President of an independent Croatian republic: born in Zagorje, his father being an ardent supporter of MACEK and the Croatian Peasant party. Tudjman joined TITO's partisans in 1941, became a convinced Communist and remained in the Yugoslav army after the end of the Second World War, serving both at the military academy and in the Defence Ministry in Belgrade. He retired from the army as a Major-General in 1961 and became director of the Historijski Institut in Zagreb, undertaking academic research in recent history. He decided that the Titoist establishment had exaggerated the extent of Ustaše atrocities at the Jasnovac concentration camp; he also complained of Serb attempts to stifle Croatian literary expression. These assertions of Croatian national patriotism led to Tudjman's dismissal in 1967 and the ultimate Communist disgrace of expulsion from the party. In 1972 allegations of anti-Yugoslav activities led to his imprisonment for two years and in 1981 (soon after Tito's death) he was again arrested and given three years' hard labour. These sentences atracted attention abroad and made him for many Croatians a martyr-hero in the RADIĆ tradition. His influence increased rapidly when Communist uniformity began to crumble in the late 1980s. In June 1989 he founded the HDZ (Croatian Democratic Union) in support of home rule: in April 1990 the HDZ won two-thirds of the seats in free elections to a Croatian assembly (Sabor) in Zagreb. Tudjman was elected President of Croatia by the Sabor deputies in May 1990, preparing the way for Croatia's secession from Yugoslavia in June 1991. The newly devised Croatian constitution alienated the Serb minority who set up a separate administration in the Krajina, a region covering 28 per cent of Croatian territory, along the historic 'military frontier' between Catholic Europe and Islam. Further elections in August 1992 confirmed Tudjman's presidency; he was accepted as Commander-in-Chief of the army. In carefully planned lightning campaigns his army recovered western Slavonia in May 1995 and crushed Krajina in August 1995. Tudjman was re-elected President at the end of October 1995 but the HDZ failed to gain sufficient support for him to change the constitution and become, as his domestic enemies feared, a virtual dictator. M. Glenny: *The Fall of Yugoslavia* (1992); L. Silber and A. Little: *The Death of Yugoslavia* (1995).

Tukhachevsky, Mikhail Nicolayevich (1893–1937), Soviet Marshal: born in St Petersburg, his family being members of the lesser nobility. He was admitted to the Corps of Pages at NICHOLAS II's court, a guarantee of privileged education since membership of the Corps was restricted to four hundred boys whose fathers or grandfathers had held the rank of Lieutenant-General in the Tsar's Army. He was commissioned in the crack Semyonovsky Regiment on the eve of the First World War but taken prisoner by the Germans in 1915, escaping from Ingolstadt prison camp in the autumn of 1917 and offering his services to TROTSKY in raising and training the new Red Army. He was given command of the northern sector of the Red Army's front in the Ukraine in mid-May 1920, launching a remarkable counter-attack against the Poles which recaptured Kiev and brought the Russians to the outskirts of Warsaw by the second week of August. His strategic planning was brilliant but he was forced to retreat, largely through the incompetence of the commanders to the south of him. He held other important military commands against the remaining 'White' armies and was made Chief of Staff of the Soviet armies in 1926, becoming Deputy Commisar of Defence in 1931. In September 1935 he was one of five civil war commanders promoted to the new rank of Marshal of the Soviet Union; and in January 1936 he came to London to attend the funeral of GEORGE V, passing on to Paris where he met the top French military leaders. Reports subsequently reached STALIN suggesting that Marshal Tukhachevsky – whom newspapers in the West had dubbed 'the Red Bonaparte' – was planning a military *coup d'état*. Although no evidence supports this rumour, Stalin ordered his arrest in the third week of May 1937. He was tried in secret and executed in the first week of June, allegedly for a treasonable conspiracy with the Germans. At least twelve high-ranking officers were shot with him. J. Erickson: *The Soviet High Command, 1918–1941* (1962); D. Fedotoff-White: *The Growth of the Red Army* (Princeton, N.J., 1944); R. Conquest: *The Great Terror* (rev. edn 1971).

Tutu, Desmond Mpilo (1931–), Archbishop of Cape Town: born in Klerksdorf, Transvaal and educated at the Johannesburg Bantu High School. He was a teacher from 1952 to 1958, when he began training for the Anglican priesthood. He was ordained deacon in 1961 and, after serving a curacy in Johannesburg, came to London for advanced study. He was appointed Dean of Johannesburg in 1975, though he insisted on living in Soweto township rather than the city deanery which his white predecessors had made their home. He constantly warned the South African government of the mounting danger of unrest if the apartheid laws were maintained, although he favoured non-violent passive resistance. He was consecrated Bishop of Lesotho in 1976 although from 1978 he was also General Secretary of the South African Council of Churches and led the civil disobedience campaign which sought to achieve multiracial democracy in South Africa. He was awarded the Nobel Peace Prize in October 1984, only a few weeks before he was enthroned as Johannesburg's first non-white Bishop. Tutu's prestige, sincerity and studied moderation ensured that he was accepted abroad as an ambassador of goodwill for South Africa's civil rights movement. He addressed the UN General Assembly in October 1985. When he became Archbishop of Cape Town and Primate of South Africa in September 1986 his authority helped promote the reconciliation between DE KLERK and MANDELA; his influence with Zulu spokesmen also lessened the communal violence which accompanied South Africa's final abandonment of apartheid in 1991–2. D. Tutu (ed. J. Allen): *The Rainbow People of God, South Africa's Victory over Apartheid* (1994); S. du Boulay: *Tutu, Voice of the Voiceless* (1989); A. Sparks: *The Mind of South Africa* (1991).

Tweed, William Marcy (1823–78), American party 'boss': born in New York and was a chairmaker by trade, securing control of the Tammany Society (the most powerful section of the Democratic Party in New York City) by 1855. In collaboration with Mayor Oakley Hall, 'Boss' Tweed became wealthy on bribes, extortion and the corrupt sale of city contracts. The operations of the 'Tweed Ring' were exposed by the reforming Democrat, TILDEN, in 1871. Tweed was arrested and served a year in prison before escaping to Cuba and so to Spain. From Spain he was extradited in New York in 1876, but he died awaiting trial for further frauds totalling some six million dollars. D. T. Lynch: *Boss Tweed* (New York, 1927).

Tzu Hsi (Yehenala) (*c.* 1834–1908), Dowager Empress of China and effective ruler from 1862–1908: probably born in, or near, Peking. She assumed the title by which she is generally known when she became a concubine of the Emperor Hsien Feng, who was ruler from 1851 to 1861, a reign marked by disorders and rebellion, centred on Nanking. In 1856 she gave birth to a son who came to the throne as the Emperor Tung Chih at the age of 5. She acted as Regent for twelve years. Soon after Tung Chih asserted his right to rule, he died in circumstances which cast grave suspicion on his mother. He was succeeded by a 4-year-old cousin who took the title Kuang Hsu and who nominally ruled China from 1875 to 1908. In reality the Dowager Empress remained Regent at least until 1889. Her authority sprang from her ruthlessness, her willingness to grant favours in response to generous bribes and from the terrifying impact of her personality. From 1889 to 1898 her power seemed on the wane, and the Emperor even announced a programme of drastic reforms, aimed at modernization of his empire, on 11 June 1898. Fearing for her life, the Dowager Empress carried through a palace revolution on 22 September 1898, imprisoning Kuang Hsu and encouraging xenophobic hostility as a means of discrediting the 'western ideas' which seemed to be tempting the young Emperor to accept reforms. This hostility to foreigners exploded in the Boxer Rising of 1900, an outbreak of violence which led to intervention by an international expedition, the Dowager Empress (and her imperial prisoner) fleeing to distant Sian (15 August 1900). They returned to Peking by rail in January 1902, outwardly accepting the need for political and economic reforms. Both Tzu Hsi and the Emperor died mysteriously within twenty-four hours of each other on 14–15 November 1908, their deaths emphasizing the need for a revolutionary movement which would cast out the antiquated Manchu system. The long dominance of Tzu Hsi helped to perpetuate the backwardness of China at a time when Japan was responding to European and American influence. Three years after her death SUN YAT-SEN emerged as the first westernized Chinese leader. M. Warner: *The Dragon Empress, the Life and Times of Tzu'hsi* (1971); V. Purcell: *The Boxer Uprising* (1963).

U

Ulbricht, Walther (1893–1973), East German Communist leader from 1946 to 1971: born in Leipzig, and was originally a Social Democrat and trade unionist. He was a founder-member of the German Communist movement in 1919, sat as a Communist in the Reichstag from 1928 to 1933, but found refuge in the Soviet Union throughout the HITLER period. He returned to Berlin in the spring of 1945, and a year later founded the 'Socialist Unity Party', of which he remained General-Secretary for twenty-five years. The proclamation of the Democratic German Republic in October 1949 gave Ulbricht's party the opportunity of imposing regimented 'socialist construction' on eastern Germany. Ulbricht was an out-and-out Stalinist, ready to call in Soviet tanks in June 1953 when discontent with enforced agricultural collectivization led to strikes and rioting in East Berlin. By ordering the erection of the Berlin Wall in 1961 he checked the flood of refugees to the West, although recognizing a semi-permanent division of Germany which he had long been at pains to deny. In September 1960 Ulbricht became Chairman of the Council of State, virtually Head of State. In May 1971 he handed over his party posts to Erich HONECKER, who was able to ease relations with West Germany during the chancellorship of Willy BRANDT. On Ulbricht's death, Honecker also succeeded him as Chairman. D. H. Childs: *East Germany* (1969), *The GDR, Moscow's German Ally* (1983); M. McCauley: *The German Democratic Republic since 1945* (1983).

V

Vargas, Getulio Dornelles (1883–1954), Brazilian President for eighteen years: born into a wealthy rancher family at Sao Boria in Rio Grande del Sul province. He was federal deputy for Rio Grande, 1923–6, and then became a dynamic, reforming and popular provincial governor, 1928–30. He stood for election as President in March 1930 but was defeated in a highly dubious contest during which his running-mate was assassinated. A military *coup* on 3 November 1930 reversed the electoral decision. Vargas headed a 'provisional government' which eased the burden of the world depression by a public works programme, by forcing up the price of coffee on the world market and giving Brazilian labourers a forty-eight-hour week and a minimum wage. This socioeconomic revolution was completed by the adoption of a new constitution in July 1934 which gave women the vote and confirmed the establishment of a corporate state (*Estadi Novo*), which owed more to SALAZAR's Portugal than to Italian fascism. Brazil's communists suffered harsh repression (1936–7) and there was strict censorship of books and the Press, but a combination of paternalistic reforms and a state capitalism which boosted exports checked the spread of sustained opposition. A shrewd assessment of world affairs induced Vargas to declare war on Germany and Italy on 22 August 1942; an expeditionary force of 25,000 crack Brazilian troops served in Italy. Vargas stepped down as President in 1945, promising free elections; he remained in politics as Senator for Rio Grande del Sul, stood again for the presidency in 1950 and gained a landslide victory. He lacked, however, the dynamic energy of his first term of office: corruption spread, and he was to some extent a prisoner of conservative army leaders. When, in his fourth year of office, he sought to assert himself, he was falsely accused of ordering the murder of a newspaper editor. On 24 August 1954 Vargas killed himself rather than bow to demands from the military that he resign. K. Lowenstein: *Brazil under Vargas* (New York, 1942); T. L. Smith: *Brazil, People and Institutions* (Baton Rouge, La., 1954); L. Bethell (ed.): *Cambridge History of Latin America*, vol. 8, *1930–1990* (Cambridge, 1991).

Venizelos, Eleutherios (1864–1936), Greek national leader: born at Canea in western Crete, being active in the Cretan struggle for independence from Turkey from 1895 to 1909, when he entered the politics of mainland Greece. He was Prime Minister during the Balkan Wars of 1912–13 which enabled Greece to acquire Macedonia. Venizelos believed in a Hellenic State which would cover, not only present-day Greece, but areas within Turkey where there were sizeable Greek settlements. He hoped Constantinople and the coast of Asia Minor would pass into Greek hands. This policy prompted him to seek Greek entry into the First World War on the side of the Allies and against Turkey and Germany. King CONSTANTINE I, a brother-in-law of Kaiser WILLIAM II, opposed Venizelos, who in September 1916 set up a pro-Allied government in Crete (later moving to Salonika) which entered the war and secured Constantine's abdication. Venizelos played a prominent part in the Paris Peace Conference of 1919 but gained neither Constantinople nor Anatolia, and he was forced out of office by an electoral defeat in November 1920. He was Prime Minister again for three weeks in 1924 and from 1928 to 1932, when he achieved some improvement of Greece's position within Europe, as he still enjoyed much prestige abroad; but he could not give Greece a stable government. In March 1935 he attempted a *coup d'état* against the mounting influence of right-wing royalist generals, but the uprising was badly planned and, after ten days of civil war, he was forced to flee to Paris, where he died a year later. D. Alastos: *Venizelos* (1942); J. K. Campbell and P. Sherrard: *Modern Greece* (1968).

Verwoerd, Hendrick Frensch (1901–66), South African Prime Minister from 1958 until his death: born in Amsterdam but settled in South Africa as a child. He was educated at Stellenbosch University and in Germany, teaching for some years in Berlin. From 1927 to 1937 he was Professor of Sociology at Stellenbosch. He showed sympathy with German Nazism, opposing offers of sanctuary to Jewish victims of Nazi oppression and South African participation in the Second World War. He became a Nationalist Senator in 1948, and as Minister of Native Affairs from 1950 to 1958 was responsible for detailed enforcement of the apartheid laws. He succeeded STRIJDOM as Prime Minister in September 1958. His premiership saw the withdrawal of South Africa from the Commonwealth and its establishment as an independent republic on 31 May 1961. This decision was taken, in part, because of the general criticism of Verwoerd's policy after the Sharpeville shootings of 21 March 1960, in which sixty-seven Africans were killed and almost two hundred wounded during a demonstration against the apartheid pass laws. Three weeks after the Sharpeville shootings a European farmer unsuccessfully tried to assassinate Verwoerd at Johannesburg. On 6 September 1966 Dr Verwoerd was killed in the Parliament buildings by a mentally unstable Portuguese East African of Greek origin. Dr VORSTER became Prime Minister in succession to the murdered Verwoerd seven days later. T. R. H. Davenport: *South Africa, a Modern History* (rev. edn 1991); L. Thompson: *A History of South Africa* (New Haven, Conn., 1990).

Victor Emmanuel II (1820–78), King of Sardinia-Piedmont from 1849 and of Italy from 1861 until his death: born in Turin, the son of King Charles Albert (1798–1849). He succeeded to the throne on his father's abdication after Sardinia-Piedmont's defeat by the Austrians in the battle of Novara (23 March 1849). Victor Emmanuel insisted on retaining the liberal constitution which his father had granted in 1848 and he loyally supported CAVOUR in the policies which secured the unification of Italy in 1859–60, even though the King did not always agree with Cavour's realistic opportunism. Victor Emmanuel received from GARIBALDI the conquests of the Thousand in Sicily and Naples when King and General met on the battlefield of the Volturno (26 October 1860). He was proclaimed King of a united Italy on 14 March 1861 although he had to wait until 1866 for the incorporation of Venetia and did not enter Rome until September 1870. Victor Emmanuel scrupulously observed the constitution and was popular with most of his subjects although frowned upon by the Church. His queen, Maria Adelaide of Habsburg-Lorraine, whom he married in 1842, died in 1855, and for the last nine years of his life he was morganatically married to the Contessa di Mirafiori. His private affairs scandalized other European courts although the Italians remembered him indulgently as '*Il Re Galantuomo*' (The Cavalier King). Books: see following entry.

Victor Emmanuel III (1869–1947), King of Italy from 1900 to 1946: born in Naples, becoming the third king of a united Italy on 29 July 1900 when his father, Umberto I, (1844–1900), was assassinated at Monza. He first intervened decisively in 1915 when he brought Italy into the First World War on the side of the Allies. After the war, fascism seemed to him the least dangerous of the new threats to the old, ordered society and he was responsible for appointing MUSSOLINI Prime Minister in 1922. There remained an uneasy alliance between fascism and monarchy for twenty years. Victor Emmanuel accepted the titles of Emperor of Abyssinia (1936) and King of Albania (1939) bestowed upon him through the successes of Mussolini's forward policy, but he never visited either realm. In July 1943 he collaborated with BADOGLIO in overthrowing Mussolini and securing an armistice with the British and Americans. He escaped from Rome to Brindisi, giving formal approval to Italy's declaration of war against Germany in October 1943. This changing of sides failed to reconcile anti-fascist Italians to the monarchy. Victor Emmanuel abdicated on 9 May 1946, hoping that a referendum would accept the continuance of the monarchy under his son, Umberto II (1904–83); but three weeks later the Italian people voted for a republic by 12½ million votes to 10½ million. Victor Emmanuel died in Egypt a year later. D. Mack Smith: *Italy and the Monarchy* (1989).

Victoria (1819–1901), Queen of Great Britain and Ireland, etc., from 1837, and Empress of India from 1877: born at Kensington Palace, only child of George III's fourth son, the Duke of Kent (1767–1820) and Princess Victoria of Saxe-Coburg (1766–1861). She succeeded her uncle, King William IV, in 1837 and married her first cousin, Albert of Saxe-Coburg-Gotha (1819–61) in February 1840. The Queen accepted the constitutional convention of being outside politics, but she expressed herself strongly on both national and international issues and never disguised her preferences: she had little liking for PALMERSTON, GLADSTONE or Randolph CHURCHILL among her politicians, while she exaggerated the qualities of DISRAELI and ROSEBERY. As a recluse she lost popularity with her subjects in the late 1860s and 1870s, only recovering it as the matriarch of Empire during the last ten years of her reign. As mother of four sons and five daughters she established dynastic links throughout non-Catholic Europe, enabling her to exert a limited influence as a peacemaker in world affairs. She delighted in 'the Empire' (especially India), although she never set foot in any overseas possessions, apart from Ireland. Her liking for Scotland induced her to spend several months each year at Balmoral, the Deeside castle which Prince Albert designed for her in the early 1850s; and she died on 22 January 1901 at another of his residences, Osborne House, in the Isle of Wight. E. Longford: *Victoria RI* (1964); F. Hardie: *The Political Influence of Queen Victoria* (Oxford, 1938).

Villa, Pancho (1877–1923), Mexican revolutionary: born in northern Mexico and was the son of a farm worker. He acquired the skilled horsemanship of a cowboy, mingled with the ruthlessness of a robber baron who (unexpectedly) was also a total abstainer from alcohol. In 1909 Villa sided with MADERO in the first stages of the Mexican Revolution, later raising a private army which by October 1913 numbered more than 10,000 men who he claimed to be defending the rights of the people of northern Mexico against wealthy dictators from the cities 'who have always slept on pillows'. In April 1914 he won a bloody battle at

Torreeon, with arms purchased from the Americans in return for selling 'confiscated' cattle. Though he briefly worked in partnership with ZAPATA, Villa lacked the southerner's commitment to a peasant revolution. At heart Villa remained a bandit chief who dabbled in political anarchy. He lost support from his earlier US patrons by allowing his men to execute sixteen American mineworkers taken from an ambushed train in January 1916; Villa's army then crossed the border into New Mexico and sacked the town of Columbus. This affront brought General PERSHING into Mexico with a punitive expedition which, at the end of March 1916, virtually destroyed Villa's army. He took to the mountains as a fugitive for four years, was pardoned by the Mexican authorities in July 1920 and granted a life pension in return for a pledge to spend his remaining days as a peaceful rancher. He was assassinated three years later. A. Knight: *The Mexican Revolution*, Vol. 2 (Cambridge, 1986); H. F. Chine: *The United States and Mexico* (Cambridge, Mass., 1953).

Vorster, Balthazar Johannes (1915–83), South African Prime Minister, 1966–78 and briefly President: born at Jamestown in the north of Cape Province and educated at Stellenbosch. He was interned as a member of an extreme right-wing Afrikaaner movement in 1942 and did not enter the South African Parliament as a member of the Nationalist Party until 1953, after the beginning of the apartheid policy under Dr MALAN. In 1961 he became Minister of Justice and was best known for his security measures against 'subversion'. He succeeded the assassinated Dr VERWOERD as Prime Minister on 13 September 1966 and held office until 20 September 1978. His repressive policy and strict insistence on rigid apartheid aroused repeated protests outside South Africa but was approved by the white electorate within the republic. After resigning because of ill-health, he took office as State President but was forced to step down a few months later when the so-called 'Muldergate Scandal' discredited, in retrospect, his premiership by suggesting he misused funds for propaganda purposes. T. R. H. Davenport: *South Africa, a Modern History* (rev. edn 1991); L. Thompson: *A History of South Africa* (New Haven, Conn., 1990).

Vyshinsky, Andrei Yanuaryevich (1883–1954), Soviet Public Prosecutor and Foreign Minister: born in Odessa, studied law at Moscow University before the Revolution, and served in the Red Army from 1918 to 1921, becoming Professor of Criminal Law at Moscow in the late 1920s. He was Public Prosecutor in all the state trials of the period 1936–8, but from 1940 onwards assisted MOLOTOV conduct foreign affairs. In 1943 he became Soviet representative on the Allied commission for the Mediterranean. He attended the Potsdam Conference (1945) and was chief Soviet delegate to the United Nations from 1945 to 1949. In March 1949 he became Soviet Foreign Minister, holding the post until March 1953, when he reverted to his earlier duties as a delegate to the United Nations. Over legal affairs he was notorious for his contention that confession of a crime adequately proved guilt; and as a diplomat he was no less notorious for his coldly negative response to any initiatives from other powers. A. Vyshinsky: *The Law of the Soviet State* (New York, 1948); R. Conquest: *The Great Terror* (rev. edn 1971); J. Mackintosh: *The Strategy and Tactics of Soviet Foreign Policy* (New York, 1962); A. Dallin: *The Soviet Union at the United Nations* (New York, 1962).

W

Waldheim, Kurt (1918–), fourth Secretary-General of the UN and Austrian President from 1986 to 1992: born on the outskirts of Vienna, served in the German army in the Balkans and Russia, joined the Austrian foreign service in 1945 and was Foreign Minister from 1968 to 1970. After a narrow defeat in Austria's 1971 presidential election he succeeded U THANT as UN Secretary-General in January 1972 and held office until December 1981. Success in negotiations over Cyprus was offset by disappointments in the Middle East, and over South Africa; an initiative to secure the release of US hostages in Teheran also failed. Waldheim returned to Vienna in January 1982 and stood for president again in June 1986 as a People's Party candidate. Although he gained 54 per cent of the votes, the campaign was embittered by assertions that, as a wartime intelligence officer in the Balkans, he had known of atrocities committed against Jews and prisoners-of-war and that he had accepted a high decoration from the Croatian Ustaše fascist government. As a result of these revelations several foreign governments ostracized Waldheim during the six years he was Austrian President. K. Waldheim: *In the Eye of the Storm* (1985); R. Bassett: *Waldheim and Austria* (1988); R. E. Herzsteim: *Waldheim, the Missing Years* (1988).

Walesa, Lech (1943–), Polish trade unionist and President: born near Mochowo on the Vistula, trained as an electrical engineer but began work in the Gdynia shipyards in 1967, serving as a trade union organizer from 1970 until 1976, when he was sacked for criticizing mismanagement. Rising food prices prompted him to co-ordinate trade union activity. His 'Inter-institutional Strike Committee' was an embryonic independent national trade union from which, in August 1980, the Solidarity movement developed. With backing from the Church, Solidarity organized a wave of strikes to seek economic reforms and civil rights throughout Poland in 1980–1. When General JARUZELSKI imposed martial law in December 1981 Walesa was interned and Solidarity declared illegal (a ban not lifted until 1983). Pressure from abroad led to Walesa's release in November 1982; he used the prestige he had accumulated so as to prevent armed clashes in the workers' struggle for civil rights. He was awarded the Nobel Peace Prize in 1983 and allowed to visit Pope JOHN PAUL II in Rome. When Poland moved towards democratic government, Walesa became the chief spokesman for the Catholic workers. He was elected President of Poland in December 1990; four months later he became the first Polish Head of State to make an official visit to London. But by November 1995, when he ran again for the presidency, he faced increasing opposition from Poland's new Left, disappointed by the fruits of economic liberalization, and was defeated by the former Communist, Alexander Kwasniewski (1954–), who succeeded Walesa as President on 22 December 1995. M. Craig: *The Crystal Spirit, Lech Walesa and his Poland* (1986); N. Ascherson: *The Struggles for Poland* (1987).

Wallace, Henry Agard (1888–1965), Vice-President of the United States: born in Adair County, Iowa, the son and grandson of prominent American agriculturalists. His grandfather, Henry Wallace (1836–1916), was founder of the influential periodical *Wallace's Farmer* which the grandson edited from 1924 to 1929, developing several new strains of hybrid corn. Franklin ROOSEVELT brought so enterprising a farmer into his Cabinet as Secretary of Agriculture in 1933, even though he came from a staunchly Republican background, and he administered the important agricultural agencies set up as part of the New Deal. He was Vice-President from 1941 to 1945, deeply angering Roosevelt by an ill-considered speech on 29 June 1943, in which he openly attacked his Cabinet colleague, Jesse Jones, the Secretary of Commerce. Wallace's intemperate conduct made Roosevelt switch support to TRUMAN when looking for a running-mate in 1944. Truman appointed Wallace Secretary of Commerce in April 1945, but dismissed him in September 1946 as his public utterances showed him critical of American foreign policy. In the 1948 election Wallace stood as an independent 'Progressive', but he polled only 2 per cent of the popular votes and carried the electoral votes of no state. H. Wallace: *New Frontiers* (New York, 1936); R. Lord: *The Wallaces of Iowa* (Des Moines, 1943).

Wang Ching-Wei (Wang Jingwei), (1883–1944), Chinese political defector: born in Canton, became an early supporter of SUN YAT-SEN and, after Sun's death, was regarded as a spokesman of the 'Left' in the Kuomintang, highly critical of CHIANG KAI-SHEK and the 'Right'. Briefly, from May to December 1931, he led an alternative government at Canton in defiance of Chiang's authority. An uneasy coalition survived for four years, until Wang was seriously wounded in an assassination bid on 1 November 1935. His suspicions of Chiang intensified Wang's provincialism. When the Japanese invaders thrust deeply into southern China and occupied Canton (21 October 1938) they induced Wang to defect (18 December 1938), hoping that, through his mediation, they could impose peace on 'Greater East Asia'; he did not, however, carry as much political authority as they assumed. In March 1940 the Japanese acknowledged Wang as President of a 'reformed Chinese government' in Nanking, to which they gave full diplomatic status the following November, though ensuring that Wang was dependent on 'advisers' appointed in Tokyo. He annexed the former international zones in Shanghai in June 1943 and raised a Chinese army of half a million men which policed rural areas of occupied China so as to free Japanese troops for service elsewhere. In November 1944, however, he died from the long-term effects of the bullet which had wounded him nine years previously. G. Bunker: *The Peace Conspiracy, Wang Ching-wei and the China War* (Cambridge, Mass., 1972).

Warren, Earl (1891–1978), Chief Justice of the US Supreme Court: born in California. He was for thirteen years a district attorney in his home state, serving as California's Attorney-General from 1939 to 1942, when he was elected Governor, a post he held until 1953. Governor DEWEY chose him as his vice-presidential running-mate for the Republicans in the election of 1948, largely because of Earl Warren's reputation as a liberal upholder of civil rights in California. EISENHOWER appointed him Chief Justice in September 1953, and he won high regard eight months later by securing a unanimous ruling in the famous case of Brown *v.* Board of Education of Topeka that racial segregation in schools was contrary to the Fourteenth

Amendment of the Constitution. The 'Warren Years' saw the court consistently giving a liberal interpretation to claims by individuals against restrictive procedures in several states. Earl Warren also headed the Commission of Inquiry into the assassination of President John KENNEDY, deciding that responsibility for the killing rested with Lee Harvey Oswald and that there was no conspiracy by plotters of the Right or of the Left. Critics have claimed that the Warren Commission did not go fully into all the evidence, an accusation frequently levelled at inquiries which refute sensational stories. Earl Warren retired in June 1969. J. D. Weaver: *Warren – the Man, the Court, the Era* (1968).

Wavell, Archibald Percival (1883–1950), British Commander-in-Chief in the Middle East from 1939 to 1941 and Viceroy of India from 1943 to 1947: born at Winchester, where he was educated, and commissioned in the Black Watch in 1901, almost immediately seeing service in South Africa. During the First World War he fought at Ypres (where he lost the sight of an eye) and was on the staff of ALLENBY in Palestine. Much of the inter-war period was spent in the Middle East and in July 1939 he was given responsibility for building up a new command in Egypt, which had to face the prospect of war on several geographically widely dispersed fronts, from the Balkans through to Abyssinia. Troops responsible to Wavell inflicted major defeats on the Italians in the first desert campaigns, in Abyssinia and in Somalia. In the spring of 1941 he was required to spare some of his best units for service in Greece and later Crete, as well as intervening in Syria and Iraq. In July 1941 he was sent to India and, as war threatened with Japan, given the task of co-ordinating Allied resistance over the South China Sea and the Indian Ocean. Once again, he was asked to defend too many fronts with too little material; and he could not stop the Japanese advance. He was Viceroy of India from June 1943 to February 1947, still concerned in part with matters of defence but also with the relief of famine in Bengal and with the problems posed by Mohandas GANDHI, NEHRU and JINNAH, as the sub-continent advanced towards political independence. Wavell was created a Viscount and a Field Marshal in 1943, becoming an Earl at the end of his viceroyalty. A. P. Wavell: *Generals and Generalship* (1941); P. Moon (ed.): *The Viceroy's Journal* (1973); R. Lewin: *The Chief* (1980).

Weizmann, Chaim (1874–1952), Zionist leader from 1921 to 1946 and President of Israel from 1948 to 1952: born in Russian Poland, at Motyli near Pinsk, founding in 1901 the Democratic Zionist Movement in support of HERZ. In 1906 he was appointed Reader in Biochemistry at the University of Manchester and was naturalized in 1910. He continued to campaign in favour of a national home for the Jewish people in Palestine and was largely responsible for obtaining from BALFOUR the famous declaration in favour of a Jewish national home (2 November 1917). Weizmann was director of the Admiralty scientific laboratories from 1916 to 1919. Throughout the inter-war period he presided over the World Zionist Organization (apart from an interlude between 1932 and 1934) taking the chair at Zionist congresses in Karlsbad (1923), Vienna (1925 and 1935), Basle (1927 and 1931), Zurich (1929 and 1937) and Geneva (1939). He was also Chairman of the Jewish Agency, the representative body for Jews in mandated Palestine. During the Second World War he became chemical adviser to the British Ministry of Supply but spent some twelve months in the United States (1942–3), where he had opportunities of winning support for an Israeli state from members of the administration. He had several meetings with Winston

CHURCHILL and ATTLEE in 1941, 1943 and 1944. His diplomacy was hampered by the activities of Zionist terrorists who, on 5 November 1944, murdered the British Minister Resident in Cairo, Lord Moyne (1880–1944, previously Walter Guinness, MP), for many years a personal friend of Churchill. Weizmann himself was disappointed at British treatment of the Jewish cause in 1946–7, seeing Ernest BEVIN as blatantly anti-Zionist. Nevertheless he accepted office as the first President of Israel in 1948. His health, however, was by now giving way, and he died at Rehovot in Israel on 9 November 1952. V. Weizmann: *The Impossible Takes Longer* (1967); B. Litvinoff: *The Essential Chaim Weizmann* (1982); B. Halpern: *The Idea of the Jewish State* (Cambridge, Mass., 1969).

Weizsacker, Richard von (1920–), German President: born in Stuttgart, the son of Baron Ernst von Weizsacker (1882–1951), chief secretary of the German Foreign Office under RIBBENTROP. Richard von Weizsacker studied law and history at the Universities of Berlin, Oxford and Grenoble, fought on the Eastern Front and became a lawyer after the war. He was an active Lutheran layman, for six years presiding over the German Protestant Congress, but he was also a strong supporter of ADENAUER's Christian Democrat Union. He was returned to the Bundestag as a deputy in 1969, accepting office as Mayor of West Berlin twelve years later. In May 1984 he was elected federal President, a post which he held with skilled detachment from party rancours for ten years, thus becoming in September 1990 the first President of a unified Federal Republic. R. von Weizsacker: *A Voice from Germany* (1986).

Welensky, Roy (1907–89), Rhodesian Prime Minister from 1956 to 1963: born in Salisbury, Rhodesia, his family being Lithuanian and Jewish in origin. He was a railwayman and trade union official in Northern Rhodesia (now Zambia), becoming founder-Chairman of the Northern Rhodesian Labour Party in 1938. During the Second World War he controlled the direction of manpower in Northern Rhodesia, an experience which confirmed his earlier belief in the need for a central African federation of the two Rhodesias and Nyasaland. He was largely responsible for the establishment of the Federation of Rhodesia and Nyasaland in 1953, his work being recognized by conferment of a knighthood. Sir Roy was Federal Minister for Transport and Communications until November 1956 when he became Prime Minister. His premiership suffered from mounting suspicion among the Africans that the Federation was perpetuating white domination, and there was disquiet over constitutional changes which in 1959 reduced African representation in Parliament. Recognition by the Colonial Office in London in October 1960 that any of the three colonies in the Federation had a right of secession doomed the experiment. Sir Roy attended a constitutional conference in London in 1961, which showed the totally different political objectives of Rhodesia and of the future Malawi and Zambia. The Federation was accordingly dissolved in December 1963. Since Sir Roy did not approve of the unilateral independence movement of Ian SMITH, he then withdrew from active politics. He remains the only Commonwealth Prime Minister to have been, in his youth, an amateur heavyweight boxing champion. R. Welensky: *Welensky's 4000 Days* (1964); G. Allighan: *Welensky's Story* (1962).

Weygand, Maxime (1867–1965), French General: birth registered in Brussels but his parentage is unknown. His mother was probably the Empress Charlotte of Mexico, sister of King LEOPOLD II of Belgium. Weygand was educated in France, passing out of St Cyr in 1889 as a cavalry officer noted for his horsemanship. For almost all of the First World War he was Chief of Staff to Marshal FOCH, and was much respected, especially by the British. His admiration for Foch may have made him, in later years, see events too much in terms of the past, asking 'What would Foch have done?' rather than assessing problems in the context of their time and place. He headed a military mission to Poland in 1920, assisting PILSUDSKI defend Warsaw. Between the wars he was successively French Commander in the Levant, head of the staff college, and Commander-in-Chief of the French army from 1931 until January 1935 when he reached retirement age. In August 1939 he was recalled to service as commanding general in Syria but was summoned back by REYNAUD to take command in northern France in May 1940 after the Germans had already broken through the French defences and reached the lower Somme. His attempt to mount an effective counter-offensive was frustrated by the pace of events. He advised Marshal PÉTAIN to seek an armistice after the fall of Paris. Weygand was critical of moves to encourage Franco-German collaboration in 1940–1 and remained in secret contact with Franklin ROOSEVELT and Winston CHURCHILL. The Germans arrested him in November 1942 and he was imprisoned for more than two years in Austria. On his release by the Americans in 1945 he was detained by the French authorities, but an attempt to put him on trial for treason was soon abandoned. He remained an outspoken critic of any proposals to allow the French colonies in Africa independence or self-determination and he was never reconciled to the government of General DE GAULLE. He died in Paris on 29 January 1965, a week after his ninety-eighth birthday. M. Weygand: *Recalled to Service* (1952); J. Weygand: *The Role of General Weygand* (1948); P. C. F. Bankwitz: *Maxime Weygand and Civil–Military Relations in Modern France* (Cambridge, Mass., 1967).

Whitlam, Edward Gough (1916–), Austrialian Prime Minister from 1972 to 1975: born at Kew, Victoria, the son of a lawyer. He went to school in Sydney and Canberra and graduated in law from Sydney University in 1946 after serving five years with the RAAF. From 1952 to 1978 he was a Labor Member of Parliament in Canberra, becoming Labor leader and also leader of the Opposition in 1967. He formed a government on 2 December 1972 which carried through a series of long-promised Labor reforms, including the abandonment of conscription, the introduction of the Medibank national health service and the abolition of university fees. His government also brought home Australian servicemen from Vietnam and gave diplomatic recognition to communist China. A constitutional crisis arose when the Senate (in which there was no Labor majority) refused to pass a budget agreed by the House of Representatives unless Parliament was dissolved and an election called. When Whitlam refused to ask Governor-General Sir John Kerr for a dissolution, Kerr withdrew Whitlam's commission as Prime Minister and invited the Opposition leader, Malcolm FRASER, to form a government; Fraser then asked for the General Election which Whitlam had refused to call. Kerr's constitutional move was controversial: for Labor supporters it discredited the office of Governor-General and, indirectly, the sovereign whom he represented. Whitlam left active politics when Labor lost the General Election. He accepted a professorial chair at Canberra and concentrated on academic studies, publishing *The Italian Inspiration in English Literature* in 1980. Later he served as a special envoy in the Australian diplomatic service. E. Gough Whitlam: *The Truth of the Matter* (1979), *The Whitlam Government* (1985); C. Johnson: *The*

Labor Legacy; Curtin, Chifley, Whitlam, Hawke (1989).

William I (1797–1888), King of Prussia from 1861 to 1888, German Emperor from 1871: born in Berlin, the second son of King Frederick William III (1770–1840) and the heroic Queen Louise (1776–1810). He fought in the final campaign against Napoleon Bonaparte in 1814, accompanying his father and Tsar Alexander I on a triumphal entry into Paris. He remained a professional soldier, his attitude towards the liberals in 1848 making him so unpopular that he went into exile in London for two months. The mental deterioration of his elder brother, Frederick William IV (1795–1861), made it essential for him to become Regent in 1858, and he made plans to strengthen the army. These army reforms were opposed by Parliament and it was in order to carry them through, despite parliamentary opposition, that he chose BISMARCK as his chief minister in September 1862, retaining him in office for the rest of his reign. There was occasional friction between the two men, notably during the wars of 1866 and 1870. William agreed reluctantly to a change in status in 1871, his son FREDERICK and Bismarck inducing him to accept the creation of a German Empire. At a ceremony in the Hall of Mirrors at Versailles (where the Prussians had established military headquarters during the siege of Paris) he was proclaimed 'German Emperor' (18 January 1871), but he disliked the title, and would have preferred 'Emperor of Germany'. William narrowly escaped assassination twice in 1878 and again in 1883. He distrusted the apparent liberalism of his son, encouraging the martial tastes of his eldest grandson, WILLIAM II. He died in Berlin on 9 March 1888. G. A. Craig: *Germany 1866–1945* (Oxford, 1978); T. Aronson: *The Kaisers* (1971).

William II (1859–1941), German Emperor and King of Prussia from 1888 to 1918: born in Berlin, the son of FREDERICK III and, through his mother, the first-born grandson of Queen VICTORIA. He suffered from a withered arm and other disabilities which, together with a Spartan education, made him exaggerate soldierly characteristics. As he identified himself with the younger generation he had no use for the restraints exercised in home and foreign policy by Chancellor BISMARCK, whom he dismissed in March 1890. 'The Kaiser' encouraged German expansion overseas and consistently favoured the growth of a large navy, especially after appointing TIRPITZ as Minister of Marine in 1897. His unfortunate gift for arrogant phrases and his excessive trust in the longest-serving of his Chancellors, the egregious BÜLOW, created an impression of bellicosity which successive attempts to improve Anglo-German and Russo-German relations could not dispel. An ostentatious visit to Jerusalem and the Holy Land in 1898 marked a change in German policy, the Kaiser favouring friendship with Turkey and economic penetration of the Middle East. From 1908, when he suffered a mild nervous breakdown, he had little direct control of affairs. By 1914 he had convinced himself that Germany was threatened with encirclement which she could only overcome by winning a short, preventive war, aimed primarily against France and Russia. He did not anticipate a long war, nor one fought on such a large scale and with so many million casualties. From 1916 his leadership of Germany was largely nominal, all important decisions being taken by HINDENBURG and LUDENDORFF. It was on their advice that he escaped to Holland in 1918. The victorious powers subsequently requested the Netherlands government to hand over 'the ex-Kaiser' so that he could be arraigned for war crimes, but the Dutch refused. He lived for twenty years at Doorn, near Utrecht. In 1940 Winston CHURCHILL offered him sanctuary in England, but he declined to leave Holland. He similarly rejected an offer by HITLER that he should return to Germany as an ordinary citizen and live on one of the Prussian royal estates. The Kaiser remained a staunch Lutheran who regarded the teachings and practice of Nazism as evil. He died at Doorn on 4 June 1941, and was interred there in a specially constructed mausoleum. M. Balfour: *The Kaiser and His Times* (rev. edn 1975); A. Palmer: *The Kaiser, Warlord of the Second Reich* (1978); L. Cecil: *Wilhelm II, Prince and Emperor, 1859–1900* (1989).

Willkie, Wendell Lewis (1892–1944), American Republican internationalist: born at Elwood in Indiana, graduating from Indiana State University in 1913. He was a lawyer before becoming chief executive of a Wall Street financial corporation. Democratic Party affiliations were cast aside in opposition to the New Deal and in 1940 he won the Republican Party nomination for the Presidency even though he had no political experience. Unlike the other contenders for the nomination – DEWEY, TAFT and Vandenberg – Willkie deplored isolationism. His progressively conservative idealism won him wide support. Although unable to defeat Franklin ROOSEVELT, he gained a larger popular vote than any previous Republican candidate, not exceeded until Eisenhower's victory of 1952. After the election, Willkie broadcast an appeal to Republicans to 'constitute a vigorous, loyal and public-spirited opposition party', and in 1941–2 he visited Britain, Russia and China as a personal emissary of President Roosevelt. He died suddenly on 8 October 1944. J. Barnes: *Willkie* (New York, 1952).

Wilson (James) Harold (1916–95): British Prime Minister from 1964 to 1970 and 1974 to 1976: born in Huddersfield and educated at Wirral Grammar School and Jesus College, Oxford. He was a Fellow of University College, Oxford, and a tutor in economics from 1938 to 1943, subsequently working for the Ministry of Fuel and Power. In 1945 he was elected Labour MP for Ormskirk, but changed to the constituency of Huyton in 1950. He entered the Cabinet as President of the Board of Trade in 1947, resigning on principle when GAITSKELL, as Chancellor of the Exchequer, introduced a cut in the social services to pay for a rearmament programme (1951). He continued to oppose Gaitskell, whom he believed would have changed the character of the socialist movement by abandoning commitments to common ownership. In February 1963, one month after Gaitskell's death, Wilson was elected party leader. He won the General Election of October 1964 by a small majority which he increased considerably in the election of April 1966. In his first government, Wilson raised the world prestige of the British Prime Minister, nearly ending the Vietnam War through his contacts with KOSYGIN early in 1967, and he showed much interest in the development of 'technology'. In 1970, choosing to fight the election in the summer, he was defeated by the Conservatives under HEATH. When he returned as Prime Minister in March 1974 he inherited a grave balance-of-payments crisis and a major dispute with the miners. His 'social compact' with the trade unions, which lasted from 1974 to 1976, was based on the idea that his government's policies would meet the desires of the trade union movement which, for its part, would moderate wage demands, so as to reduce inflation. This bargain enabled Wilson to win the October 1974 General Election with an overall majority of five, making him the first Prime Minister since GLADSTONE to have won four general elections. Soon after his sixtieth birthday he announced his retirement from the premiership, although remaining in the Commons. He resigned, in favour of

CALLAGHAN, on 5 April 1976. Seventeen days later he was created a Knight of the Garter. He became a life peer, Baron Wilson of Rievaulx, in 1983. H. Wilson: *The Labour Government 1964–70* (1971), *Final Term, the Labour Government 1974–76 (1979)*, B. Pimlott: *Harold Wilson* (1993); P. Ziegler: *Wilson, the Official Biography* (1992).

Wilson, (Thomas) Woodrow (1856–1924), President of the United States from 1913 to 1921: born at Staunton in Virginia, where his father was a Presbyterian minister. Most of his childhood was spent, in strictly Calvinist family surroundings, in Georgia and North Carolina when both states were seeking to recover from the Civil War. He graduated from Princeton at the age of 23, practised law briefly in Atlanta, completed a doctorate on congressional government at Johns Hopkins University in Baltimore (1885), and held a professional chair at Princeton from 1890 to 1902, when he became the first layman president of the university. His reforming zeal at Princeton alienated conservative academics who forced him to resign in 1910, but the publicity he received induced the Democratic party machine in New Jersey to run him that year for Governor, an office he held when he was chosen as presidential candidate by the Democratic Convention at Baltimore in 1912, at the forty-sixth ballot. The rift between TAFT and Theodore ROOSEVELT enabled the Democrats to win the 1912 campaign, and Wilson's idealistic inaugural in March 1913 emphasized to the American people that for the first time in eighty years a 'college professor' was in the White House.

Wilson's intellectual reserve, his feeling for humanity in the abstract rather than for people, won him respect but not affection. His domestic programme reformed the federal banking system and introduced some anti-trust laws. When war came to Europe he observed strict neutrality, although reacting indignantly to the torpedoing by a German U-boat of the British liner *Lusitania* in May 1915, with the loss of 128 American lives. He authorized the punitive expedition of General PERSHING into Mexico in 1916, but won the presidential campaign of that year on his record of being 'too proud to fight'. The resumption by Germany of unrestricted submarine warfare in 1917 and the revelation by the intercepted Zimmerman telegram of anti-American intrigues by Germany in Mexico induced Wilson to seek from Congress a declaration of war on Germany on 6 April 1917.

At home Wilson's second administration saw passage of the Eighteenth Amendment, which introduced Prohibition (1919) and the Nineteenth Amendment which gave women the vote (1920). The President put forward a series of high-sounding war aims in his Fourteen Points speech of 8 January 1918, and he broke precedent in leaving America to come personally to Paris for the Peace Conference of 1919, hoping that he could achieve a settlement based on the principle of self-determination. He was a champion of the League of Nations, believing it would right the wrongs of treaties more influenced by national greed than he would wish. Obstinacy blinded Wilson to shifts of American public opinion back towards isolationism: in Paris he declined to listen to Colonel HOUSE, his political adviser since the Baltimore Convention; and on his return to Washington he found the US Senate unwilling to accept the Treaty of Versailles and thereby to back American membership of the League. For three weeks Wilson campaigned in America for support of his internationalism, but his health gave way on 26 September 1919. He was able to do little during the last eighteen months of his presidency, and he had the bitterness of seeing the Democratic candidates, Governor Cox and Franklin

ROOSEVELT, overwhelmed by the isolationaist Republicans, HARDING and COOLIDGE, in the election of 1920. Wilson died on 3 February 1924. A. Heckscher: *Woodrow Wilson* (New York, 1991); R. S. Baker: *Woodrow Wilson, Life and Letters* (8 vols) (New York, 1925–7); A. S. Link: *Woodrow Wilson and the Progressive Era* (New York, 1954), *The Road to the White House* (Princeton, N.J., 1947), *The New Freedom* (Princeton, N.J., 1956).

Wingate, Orde Charles (1903–44), British Major-General: born in India but educated at Charterhouse, being commissioned in the Royal Artillery in 1922. He served for many years in the Sudan, Transjordan and Palestine, where he became interested in the problems of the Jewish community. His guerrilla unit, known as 'Gideon's Force', which operated on the borders of Italian-occupied Abyssinia in 1940–1, took hundreds of prisoners and destroyed several forts in daring raids. Thereafter he suffered a physical and nervous breakdown. By May 1942 he had sufficiently recovered his strength to accept the invitation of WAVELL to come to India and organize long-range guerrilla forces which would penetrate deeply behind the Japanese lines in Burma. Wingate led the first of these 'Chindit' groups from February to June 1943: they were supplied by air, keeping in touch with headquarters by radio; and they inflicted much damage on Japanese supply routes along the Irrawaddy. A second wave of Chindits, despatched in February 1944, caused chaos among the Japanese as they were mounting the offensive which culminated in their defeat by the Fourteenth Army under SLIM at Imphal. Wingate was killed when his aircraft crashed in Assam on 24 March 1944. T. Royle: *Wingate, Imaginative Soldier* (1993); C. Sykes: *Orde Wingate* (1959); D. Tulloch: *Wingate in Peace and War* (1972).

Witte, Serge (1849–1915), Russian Prime Minister from 1905 to 1906: born in Tiflis, his family being landowners from the Baltic littoral, of German origin. He was educated at Odessa, becoming a civil servant with responsibility for the administration of railways. His efficiency and energy led to a succession of important administrative posts from 1892 onwards; he served at various times as Minister of Commerce, of Finance and of Communications. Tsar NICHOLAS II warmly supported Witte's proposals for the construction of the railways which would link Moscow, Vladivostok and Peking, thus enabling Russia to dominate mainland China, Manchuria and Korea both commercially and strategically. Witte's policy of penetration by the Trans-Siberian and Chinese Eastern Railways ran counter to the militaristic schemes of a group of adventurers in St Petersburg, whose folly plunged Russia into the disastrous war with Japan of 1904–5. Nicholas II called on Witte to negotiate peace with Japanese envoys at Portsmouth, New Hampshire, in September 1905, a task achieved by Witte with remarkable diplomatic skill. Upon his return home he took office as Russia's first Prime Minister (16 November 1905). Foreign opinion was so impressed by Witte's abilities that he succeeded, largely through his own prestige, in floating loans from Britain and France to aid Russia's recovery from defeat and revolution. By now, however, the Tsar disliked Witte personally: he thought him arrogant and overbearing, too inclined to write bulky memoranda. Within a fortnight of securing the French loan, Witte was abruptly dismissed by Nicholas II from the premiership (5 May 1906). Despite his abilities he was never again asked to serve the government, gloomily predicting the revolution which overthrew Tsarism within two years of his death. S. Witte: *Memoirs* (New York, 1921); T. H. Von Laue: *Sergei Witte and the Industrialization of Russia* (New York, 1963);

H. D. Mehlinger and J. Thompson: *Count Witte and the Tsarist Government in the 1905 Revolution* (Bloomington, Ind., 1972).

Wolseley, Garnet Joseph (1833–1913), British Field Marshal: born in County Dublin, served in Burma 1852–3, was badly wounded in the Crimea, saw further service in India during the Mutiny and in China in 1860. He helped put down the Red River rebellion in Canada in 1870 without losing a man. Most of his active service was in Africa; he became one of the great Victorian imperialist heroes through campaigns in the Ashanti War (1873–4), in Natal and the Transvaal (1879) and by his remarkably successful occupation of Egypt (1882). Wolseley sought to rescue GORDON from Khartoum in 1884, but he was despatched too late. From 1890 to 1895 he was Commander-in-Chief of the British army. He also wrote a largely forgotten novel, *Marley Castle* (1877). Viscount Wolseley: *Story of a Soldier's Life* (2 vols) (1903, 1904); C. Barnett: *Britain and her Army* (1970).

Y

Yamagata, Aritomo (1838–1922), Japanese Field Marshal and conservative reformer: born into the lower samurai class at Hagi in Chosu. He served in the Kiheitai militia of Chonshu in backing MUTSUHITO in the Meiji Restoration of 1868. He was sent to Europe to study the principal continental armies in 1869 but returned to Tokyo as assistant vice-minister of military affairs in 1870 and was largely responsible for Japan's adoption of conscription in 1873 and for the Prussianized army organization instituted in 1878 with the creation of a Japanese General Staff. Indirectly he was also responsible for the defeat of Takamori SAIGO in 1877. Yamagata was himself Chief of General Staff from 1879 to 1882, building up a military system independent of outside political interference. At the same time he gave great personal attention to civil administration: he was, in effect, Minister of the Interior for twelve years, creating both a police force and a local government system; and he was Prime Minister from December 1889 to May 1891 and again from November 1898 to October 1900. His first government saw the passage of major educational reforms and his second government codified public order and police laws. Yamagata remained an army officer: he became a full General in 1890 and a Field Marshal in 1898. He saw active service against China as commander of the First Army in 1894–5 and he again became Chief of General Staff during the Russo-Japanese War of 1904–5, retiring in 1907 as a Prince. He remained, however, Japan's most respected and influential elder statesman for the last fifteen years of his life. A. Craig: *Chōsū in the Meiji Restoration* (Cambridge, Mass., 1961); W. G. Beasley: *The Modern History of Japan* (1963); E. H. Norman: *Japan's Emergence as a Modern State* (New York, 1940).

Yamamoto, Isoruku (1884–1943), Japanese naval Commander-in-Chief from 1939 to 1943: born at Nagaoka, near Niigata, educated in Tokyo and briefly at Harvard. He joined the navy where his talents led to rapid promotion, becoming an Admiral in 1927, after serving for a few months as naval attaché in Washington. He was deputy to the minister responsible for naval affairs in 1937. Yamamoto was the first Japanese strategist to see the importance of air-power. On 30 August 1939 he was appointed Commander-in-Chief, but opposed war with Britain and America, arguing that Japan could not survive in any long war against two such enemies. Nevertheless, he accepted the need to prepare plans for a conflict, seeking such rapid victories that he hoped peace could be negotiated within six months. His strategic genius worked out the details of the devastating attack on Pearl Harbor, and his ability to co-ordinate naval and air operations gained him victories in the Java Sea which made him the most popular national hero in Japan since Admiral TOGO. He failed, however, at the battle of Midway Island in June 1942, partly because of good intelligence by Admiral NIMITZ and his staff, and partly because Yamamoto was uncertain of his own objectives. American cryptologists discovered from Japanese signals that

Yamamoto was flying, with his staff, on a tour of inspection in the south west Pacific on 17 April 1943. His plane was duly intercepted over the Solomon Islands and shot down, the Admiral dying in the wreckage. H. Agawa: *The Reluctant Admiral: Yamamoto and the Imperial Navy* (New York, 1979); M. Carver (ed.): *The War Lords (1976).*

Yamashita, Tomoyuki (1885–1946), Japanese General, the captor of Singapore: born near Tokyo, graduating from the Military College at Hiroshima in 1908 and becoming a junior staff officer in 1916. He served as military attaché in Switzerland and in Berlin during the 1920s and appears to have had contacts with the German right-wing politicians. In 1936 he was in disgrace for countenancing the activities of a fascist movement, which threatened a *coup d'état* in Tokyo, and was posted to serve in Korea. Four years later he headed a military mission to Rome and Berlin. He was given command of the Twenty-fifth Army in November 1941, completing plans for landings in Malaya and a southward advance through the jungle to the Johore Strait. His capture of Singapore on 15 February 1942 inflicted the worst defeat sustained by British forces in 160 years. He was Commander-in-Chief defending the Philippines in 1944–5, refusing to acknowledge the formal ending of hostilities on 14 August 1945, and only surrendering when surrounded in the mountains of northern Luzon on 1 September. He was put on trial for failing to prevent his troops committing brutal atrocities and was hanged on 23 February 1946. A. Barker: *Yamashita* (1973); J. Potter: *A Soldier Must Hang* (1963).

Yeltsin, Boris (1912–), post-Soviet Russian President: born in Sverdlovsk, worked as a construction engineer from 1955 to 1968 when he became a Communist Party official. Eight years later he was a member of the Supreme Soviet and began to build up for himself a powerful following in Moscow, where in 1985 he became head of the party organization in the city. By 1987 he stood out as a populist speaker, courageously seeking democratic reforms and complaining that GORBACHEV'S perestroika proposals did not go far enough in dismantling the centralized state. He resigned from the party in June 1990 and put forward an ambitious, demagogic programme for giving Russia 'a full, free market economy within 500 days'. He was accepted as the leader of liberal-radical opposition and on 12 June 1991 he was elected President of the Russian Republic, at that time still within the Soviet Union. In the third week of August 1991 he stubbornly resisted attempts by Communist hardliners to overthrow Gorbachev and suppress all liberal opposition. Yeltsin's defiance made him the effective ruler of Russia when the USSR ceased to exist at the end of the year. His administration was faced by threats of secession, notably in the Chechen region of the northern Caucasus, and by the hostility of many members of the Congress of People's Deputies. By 20 March 1993 he had to impose 'special rule' on Russia, establishing an emergency dictatorship which received electoral support after a referendum in April 1993. The conflict between traditional Soviet parliamentarians and the Yeltsin reformers culminated in several days of street fighting in Moscow (2–4 October 1993), in which nearly 200 people were killed. Two months later elections to a new Duma showed considerable support for anti-reform groups of Left and Right. Yeltsin's socioeconomic revolution remained stopped halfway: the President's health declined: he recovered from a heart attack in June 1995 but was incapacitated by a second heart attack in late October when he returned to Moscow from the fiftieth anniversary meeting of the UN in New York.

B. Yeltsin: *Against the Grain* (New York, 1990); D. Remnick: *Lenin's Tomb* (1993).

Yezhov, Nikolai Ivanovich (1894–?1939), Soviet secret police chief from 1936 to 1938: born at Rostov-on-Don, where he was a factory worker until moving into the Communist Party bureaucracy when he was in his mid-twenties. His ruthless efficiency appealed to STALIN during the course of 1935, bringing him into the Central Committee of the party and giving him posts previously held by Old Bolsheviks. On 26 September 1936 Yezhov was made 'People's Commissar for Internal Affairs', with absolute control of the secret police (NKVD) and with orders from Stalin to unmask the followers of TROTSKY and ZINOVIEV. There followed two years of terror, known in Russian as the *Yezhovschina* ('the Yezhov Era'), in which as many as seven million people were arrested throughout the Soviet Union, the majority of whom were executed or died in forced-labour camps. Public attention was centred on the show trials of some of LENIN's closest associates in Moscow in January 1937 and March 1938, and on the secret court-martial and execution of Marshal TUKHACHEVSKY and other Red Army leaders in the summer of 1937. Soviet revelations during the KHRUSCHEV years show that Yezhov's terror penetrated far more deeply into the party, removing any figure of strong personality who was opposed – or was likely to oppose – Stalin. It is possible that Yezhov overreached himself. He was downgraded in November 1938, when he became Commissar of Water Transport, and was never heard of again. It is likely he was liquidated by his successor as secret-police chief, Lavrenti BERIA. R. Conquest: *The Great Terror* (rev. edn 1971); M. Fainsod: *How Russia is Ruled* (Cambridge, Mass., 1953).

Yoshida, Shigeru (1878–1967), Japanese diplomat and Prime Minister: born in Yokohama, probably the illegitimate son of a minor politician. He was brought up by Yoshida Kenzo, a wealthy merchant, and graduated in law from Tokyo University in 1906, serving in a succession of foreign diplomatic postings, becoming ambassador in Rome in 1930. He spent two years as ambassador in London (1936–8) before retiring to an estate in Oisu. He emerged in October 1945 to become Foreign Minister, becoming first chairman of Japan's Liberal Party and was Prime Minister of five governments between May 1946 and December 1954. In many respects Yoshida was to Japan what ADENAUER became in West Germany: a reforming conservative who helped keep Japan a political entity during the transition from Allied military control to post-war sovereignty. The Yoshida era exploited America for Japanese backing against communism in east Asia. Yoshida vigorously countered earlier proposals for local autonomy which would have destroyed centralized government from Tokyo. Although he accepted a 'mutual defence pact' with the USA in March 1954, his hopes of inducing the Americans to co-operate in a 'Marshall Plan for Asia' were never realized. This failure left him politically isolated; in the first week of December 1954, he was manoeuvred from office by younger conservatives. K. Yoshida (ed.): *The Yoshida Memoirs* (New York, 1962); J. W. Dower: *Empire and Aftermath, Yoshida Shigeru and the Japanese Experience, 1878–1954* (New York, 1979).

Yrigoyen, Hipolito (1850–1933), Argentine's first radical President: born at Buenos Aires, became leader of a Radical Civic Union Party (1896), campaigning vigorously for electoral reform. Free presidential elections brought him to power on 12 October 1916 and he introduced some basic liberal reforms during his term of office. With scrupulous observance of the constitution he stepped down on 12 October 1922, stood again for President six years later, and began a second term on 12 October 1928. By now, however, he had shed earlier radical sympathies. Brutal repression of a strike movement at the start of the world slump enabled the military to win enough support to depose him in a *coup* early in September 1930. Y. F. Rennie: *The Argentine Republic* (New York, 1945); D. Rock: *Argentina, 1516–1982* (1986).

Z

Zapata, Emiliano (1879–1919), peasant radical Mexican revolutionary: came, of richer peasant stock, from Morelos, south of Mexico City. He was an early supporter of MADERO in the revolution against DIAZ but was always a more radical land reformer. When he thought the Madero's revolt too bourgeois in appeal, he published the 'Plan of Ayala' proposing a mass distribution of land to the peasantry, a programme which attracted many recruits to his army (December 1911). Zapata was more politically committed than his occasional ally, VILLA, and as his army threatened the capital geographically he frequently held a balance of power during the revolution. He failed to win support from any of the interim government regimes and, after seven years of resistance, became in effect a bandit leader. In April 1919 he was ambushed by government troops and killed. A. Knight: *The Mexican Revolution*, Vol. 2 (Cambridge, 1986).

Zeppelin, Ferdinand von (1838–1917), German soldier and inventor of a rigid airship: born at Lake Constance, educated in Stuttgart and commissioned in a Württemberger regiment in 1858. He then travelled to America in 1860 and subsequently served for a time in the Union Army, fighting under General Hooker in the Antietam campaign of the Civil War. When he returned to Europe, Count Zeppelin fought for Württemberg against Prussia in the brief war of 1866. By 1870 Württemberg was allied with Prussia and the North German Confederation against France, and Count Zeppelin distinguished himself as a cavalry officer in the first days of the Franco-Prussian War by leading a patrol on a daring raid eight miles into Alsace. He was a Colonel of Uhlans in the 1880s serving as the King of Württemberg's envoy in Berlin from 1887 to 1889, when he was promoted General on retiring from the army. In 1890 he founded a company for the making of airships, having been impressed by the use made of balloons both in America and in the siege of Paris. Experimental flights with a twin-engined ship 420 feet long began at Friedrichshafen on Lake Constance in 1898, achieving considerable success by 1900. Zeppelin became well known when a twelve-hour flight over Switzerland and Bavaria was commended by Kaiser WILLIAM II (who in November 1908 described the Count 'as the greatest German of the twentieth century'). In the four years preceding the First World War the Zeppelin Company carried passengers over some 100,000 miles without any loss of life. During the war the rigid airships – known everywhere as 'Zeppelins' – made bombing raids on Antwerp, Liège, Warsaw, Paris, London, Naples, Humberside, East Anglia, Tyneside and other towns, as well as providing naval reconnaissance. Count Zeppelin died in March 1917, but his company maintained a commercial service between the wars.

Zhukov, George Konstantinovich (1896–1976), outstanding Soviet Marshal of the Second World War: born near Kaluga, a peasant's son. He fought in the ranks in the First World War, joining the Red Army in 1918 as a Captain. In 1921–2 he was trained in tank warfare by a German military mission at Kazan. Sporadic fighting against the Japanese along the Mongolian frontier in the summer of 1939 showed his strategic vision. He was summoned from the Far East in 1941 to check the advance on Leningrad, and then surprised the Germans on the central sector of the front by launching a winter counter-offensive around Moscow (6 December 1941). He was responsible for the relief of Stalingrad in 1942, for the massive tank battle near Kursk in July 1943, and for the final advance from the River Oder to capture Berlin (April–May 1945). Marshal Zhukov remained in command of the Soviet army of occupation in East Germany and was appointed Minister of Defence by KHRUSCHEV in 1955. At the end of October 1957 he was relieved of all his duties, official statements accusing him of failing to perceive the importance of Communist Party education within the army and of encouraging the cult of personality in his own interests. The remaining nineteen years of his life were passed in obscure retirement. G. K. Zhukov: *Memoirs* (1971); O. P. Chaney: *Zhukov* (Norman, Okla., 1971); W. J. Spahr: *Zhukov, the Rise and Fall of a Great Captain* (Novajo, Calif., 1993).

Zia Ul-Haq, Mohammed (1924–88), Pakistani military leader: born at Jalandhar, commissioned from the Indian Military Academy at Dehra Dun and fought in Burma and Malaya during the Second World War before joining the Pakistani army on independence. He received staff training at Fort Leavensworth in America and moved rapidly through the echelons of command in Pakistan to become a full General in 1976. He led a military *coup* against Zulfiqar Ali BHUTTO in July 1977, became martial law administrator and from September 1978 until his death was President of Pakistan, ruling dictatorially and long maintaining martial law. Zia encouraged the spread of a free market economy but also imposed strict Islamization on the country. Martial law was at last lifted, under foreign pressure, in December 1985, but opposition intensified. He perished on 17 August 1988 when his aircraft mysteriously crashed in south eastern Punjab. A. Hyam (ed.): *Pakistan: Zia and After* (1989); N. Waseem: *Pakistan under Martial Law, 1977–85* (Lahore, 1987).

Zinoviev, Grigori Evseyevich (Apfelbaum) (1882–1936), Russian revolutionary: born at Elizavetgrad (now Kirovograd) in the Ukraine, becoming a Marxist before the Revolution of 1905, passing into exile and participating in the important London Conference of exiled Russian socialists in 1907, which confirmed the leadership of LENIN. Zinoviev was one of Lenin's closest associates both in exile and in Petrograd, where he became Chairman of the Soviet in 1917. Subsequently he was organizing President of the Third International (Comintern). In this capacity he is alleged to have sent a letter to the British Communist Party in 1924, urging its members to indulge more vigorously in subversive activities. Publication of the letter in the *Daily Mail* (25 October) on the eve of the General Election may have induced some British voters to feel safer with BALDWIN and the Conservatives than with Labour. Zinoviev lost his main posts in the party in 1926, for STALIN regarded him as a personal enemy. In August 1936 he was one of the Old Bolsheviks charged with plotting against the state and, after a hurried trial, was shot in the Lubyanka Prison in Moscow.

Zog (Ahmed Bey Zogu) (1895–1961), King of Albania from 1928 to 1939: born at Burgayet in the Mati region of central Albania, where his father, Djemal Pasha, was a powerful chieftain. He sent his son to be educated in Constantinople. During the First World War Ahmed Zogu held an Austrian commission. In the highly confused conditions under which Albania acquired independence after the war, Zogu emerged as a strong man: he was Minister of the Interior in 1921 and Prime Minister from December 1922 to June 1924. In January 1925 he proclaimed Albania a republic with himself as President, and he reached agreements with Italy for the commercial development of his country, the headquarters of the Albanian National Bank being in Rome. On 1 September 1928 he was proclaimed 'King Zog I of the Albanians', and over the next ten years he began to modernize the Durazzo and Tirana regions of his kingdom, nine-tenths of which remained inaccessible. Zog's personal fortunes flourished. In 1938 he married the Hungarian aristocrat, Geraldine Apponyi, to whom a son was born in March 1939. A few weeks later MUSSOLINI's desire for a strategic foothold in the Balkans led Italy to invade Albania on Good Friday (7 April 1939). King Zog, his four sisters, Queen Geraldine and her infant son escaped across the mountains and out of Albanian politics. He lived in Buckinghamshire throughout the Second World War, later settling at Cannes and dying in hospital in Paris on the twenty-second anniversary of his flight from his kingdom. B. J. Fischer: *King Zog and the Struggle for Stability in Albania* (Boulder, Colo., 1984); S. Pollo and P. Arben: *History of Albania* (1981).

Printed in the United States
by Baker & Taylor Publisher Services